Second Edition
CRIMINAL JUSTICE

Second Edition
CRIMINAL JUSTICE

JAMES A. INCIARDI
University of Delaware

Harcourt Brace Jovanovich, Publishers

San Diego   New York   Chicago   Austin
London   Sydney   Tokyo   Toronto

For Carolyn

ISBN: 0-15-516102-4
Library of Congress Catalog Card Number: 85-82634
Printed in the United States of America

Cover photo © Bruce Wald
Endpapers: *Front*, San Diego Historical Society. *Back*, courtesy of James A. Inciardi.

Copyrights and Acknowledgments and Illustration Credits on pages 741–43, which constitute a continuation of the copyright page.

Preface

As an independent academic activity, the study of criminal justice is comparatively new in the United States. The first degree-granting program appeared less than half a century ago, and as recently as the 1950s fewer than five thousand college students were focusing primarily on the study of crime and justice. During the past two decades, however, this situation has changed dramatically. Interest in criminal justice education was spurred by the "war on crime" during the middle and late 1960s and the resulting massive federal funding for the upgrading of criminal justice personnel, agencies, technology, and programming. Current enrollments in criminal justice courses well exceed 200,000 annually, and the upward trend is expected to continue.

Criminal justice refers to the structure, functions, and decision processes of agencies that deal with the management and control of crime and criminal offenders—the police, courts, and corrections departments. It is often confused with the academic disciplines of criminology and police science. Criminology focuses on the role of crime in organized society, the nature and causes of crime and criminal behavior, and the relationships between crime and social behavior. Police science concentrates on the pragmatic aspects of law enforcement operations—the prevention and detection of crime, the apprehension of criminal offenders, the location and preservation of evidence, the questioning of suspects, the application of police resources, and the development of police–community relations.

Although criminal justice may be relatively new as a separate curriculum, much of its subject matter has been apparent for centuries. It is indeed an interdisciplinary branch of knowledge. From the perspective of legal studies, it examines aspects of criminal law and procedure; from political science it takes elements of constitutional law and appellate court practice; from the viewpoint of sociology it examines the structure of certain social institutions and how they affect the administration of justice. Criminal justice also uses ongoing research from psychology, history, public administration, anthropology, economics, and many other disciplines.

New to This Edition

Along with the growth in criminal justice education has come vigorous research into justice processes. This has resulted in a dramatic proliferation in criminal justice literature as scholars, researchers, and administrators seek to disseminate their work. So great has been the demand for classroom materials that during the past decade publishers have responded with thousands of new texts, supplementary readings, manuals, anthologies, monographs, and reports. Several dozen new introductory texts and revised editions of older texts appear every year.

It was in this context of rapid change that the first edition of *Criminal Justice* was published; and when a field changes rapidly, so must the classroom material—especially for introductory courses. For the Second Edition, therefore, new statistics, research findings, and significant court decisions were plentiful. Further, the major issues in criminal justice were changing with the times as policies, procedures, and viewpoints evolved. Moreover, the interests and concerns of instructors using the first edition have also grown. For the Second Edition we sought to address these new demands by appealing first to its intended users. Questionnaires were sent to a stratified random sample of instructors at small and large colleges and universities who had adopted the first edition. All were asked about the nature and extent of the changes and additions they felt were necessary. A cross-section of students from several two-year and four-year colleges who had used the book also contributed their comments.

In response to these recommendations and in addition to the necessary updating of facts, court decisions, and research throughout, the material on criminal statistics in Chapter 4 has been reduced somewhat and an entire chapter on juvenile justice (Chapter 18) has been added. Many new boxed exhibits on a wide range of subjects have been added. Both the Student Study Guide and the Instructor's Resource Guide have been expanded.

The Second Edition has been designed to achieve a number of goals for introductory criminal justice courses. First, it offers basic knowledge of the nature of crime and the processes of justice. Second, in theme and perspective it provides an analysis of the administration of justice in its contemporary forms and historical roots. In addition, it attempts to reveal some of the myth, folklore, and stereotypic images that pervade students' thinking about crime and justice in the United States. Third, it has been conceived and written to interest a range of students. Intended for those at both the community college and four-year college levels, the data and subject matter in the Second Edition have been drawn from the professional and popular media as well as from the fields of law, sociology, political science, history, popular culture, anthropology, and oral tradition. In addition, to better explain certain phenomena and to maintain readers' interest, a portion of the more than 200 photographs and cartoons—some comical, many serious, and all informative—emphasize the fads and foibles that have characterized the administration of justice in the United States. Fourth, and most important, the Second Edition presents the many facets of justice administration in the context of the changing political, social, cultural, and economic events that have shaped the evolution and implementation of criminal justice in this century.

Each chapter contains a Summary, Key Terms, Questions for Discussion, and Suggested Readings. The Second Edition contains an expanded glossary of major and minor terms and more than one hundred boxed exhibits, which focus on important aspects of criminal justice processing, the history of criminal justice, and court cases mentioned in the text. More marginal glosses have been added, and tailored for use as a guide to the topics covered. Finally, this edition contains three comprehensive indexes, of cases, names, and subjects.

The Student Study Guide to the Second Edition includes summaries, key terms, chapter objectives, sample examination questions, supplementary readings, and tear-out homework exercises for each text chapter. The Study Guide also contains two unique features: a section entitled "Understanding Supreme Court Opinions" and an essay on careers in the field of criminal justice. The Instructor's Resource Guide presents chapter summaries, topic outlines, a review of the major objectives and key terms, and comments and answers for many of the discussion questions in the text. In addition, it offers extensive and useful supplementary lecture materials, as well as discussion topics and class projects. The Test Book, available in both printed and computer format, contains more than 1800 multiple choice, true-false, fill-in, and essay questions with answers. Sixty transparency masters are also available.

Acknowledgments

The number of debts one accumulates in writing a book is surprisingly large. As such, gratitude first must go to my wife, Carolyn J. Inciardi, for her continuous support and editorial assistance; to Susan E. Loring and Warren Abraham, former editors with Academic Press, whose input during the revision process was invaluable; to the team at Harcourt Brace Jovanovich—Marcus Boggs, Johanna Schmid, Jack Thomas, Craig Avery, Chris Nelson, Susan Holtz, Cheryl Solheid, Diane Pella, Schamber Richardson, and Avery Hallowell—who were responsible for creating the Second Edition; to the many students and instructors who used the first edition and made recommendations for the second; to Gennaro Vito and Kenneth C. Haas for their critical, yet needed, comments on some of the new material in the text; to David B. Gulick, J. Robert Lilly, J. Michael Hunter, and Richard A. Ball for their contributions to some of the exhibits; and to Nancy Quillen for her assistance in the preparation of a clean manuscript. Finally, I wish to express my special debt to a wide selection of persons who must remain anonymous, yet without whom portions of this book could not have been written.

James A. Inciardi

Contents

Part 2
The Police / 153

Part 5
Juvenile Justice / 673

Second Edition

CRIMINAL JUSTICE

1

The Rediscovery of Criminal Justice in America

Justice is too good for some people and not good enough for the rest.
— Norman Douglas

More than two decades ago, the noted scholar and columnist Max Lerner offered a rather curious description of criminal justice in America:

> The administration of American criminal justice has been often scored as inefficient, corrupt, and archaic, and all three charges are probably true, but again probably no truer than of past eras and other societies. The supervision of criminal justice is mainly in the hands of the local authorities; the Federal courts handle crimes under Federal jurisdiction but try to minimize the appeals from local and state jurisdictions. A lawbreaker is tracked down by local police, prosecuted by a local district attorney and defended by a local lawyer, tried in a local court house in a trial reported predominantly in the local press, convicted or cleared by a local jury, sentenced by a local judge, and shut up in a local or state prison. At every point there is a good deal of bungling, prejudice, poor judgement, or corruption. Yet on the whole there is a widespread feeling that the results are tolerably good and that the frailties of the whole process are a reflection of the frailties of the society in which it takes place.[1]

Lerner's comment, written in his widely acclaimed and sweeping reappraisal of American life, *America as a Civilization,* may appear to be somewhat cynical in its suggestion that the processes of justice are both lame and corrupt. Yet a glance over the twentieth century prior to his reflections offers considerable support. The literature on American law, crime, and justice clearly shows an overwhelming concern with inefficiency and corruption in the machinery of justice and crime control — problems emanating chiefly from the chaos that existed in urban areas throughout most of the nineteenth century. From the middle through late 1800s, criminal districts, street gangs, and political corruption were visible characteristics of major American cities. Initially, areas of vice and crime had appeared in which were concentrated houses of prostitution, dance halls, concert saloons, and gambling casinos. To these were added scores of organized street gangs, whose members stole and killed, as well as waged street battles against rival gangs. And finally, during the post–Civil War era, political corruption became commonplace, aiding and even helping shape the commercialization and organization of both vice and crime. The pleasure districts and urban guerrillas were able to operate openly because regular protection payments were made to corrupt police and political overlords.[2] The relentless muckraking of city presses and the resultant public outcry, however, started a reform movement at the turn of the century aimed at establishing political responsibility in public office.[3] But the reform movement was short-lived, and by 1910 the problem of crime in

Gamblers caught by police are taken away in a paddy wagon.

American cities was greater than ever before. The evils of the earlier decades seemed to have reemerged on an even larger scale, and the machinery available for social control was clearly ill-equipped to deal with the magnitude of the problem. As a consequence, a series of crime surveys was made during the 1920s in various parts of the country, and for the first time in the national experience, the actual operations of the criminal justice process in urban America were closely and extensively examined.

The 1920s: Attempts at Reform

The first of the crime surveys was made in Cleveland, Ohio, and began in 1920 on the assumption that criminal justice in what was then the country's fifth largest city was the least efficient function of government. The investigators set out to determine the system's defects and to trace them to their sources.[4] The effort in Cleveland was followed in 1925 by the *Missouri Crime Survey*, which examined state-level processes of law enforcement, judicial procedure, and correctional practice.[5] And finally, in 1926, the *Illinois Crime Survey* extensively investigated crime and justice in Cook County, Illinois, as well as completed a landmark study of organized crime in Chicago.[6] Collectively, the surveys resulted in a series of documents that clearly demonstrated the suspected faults with urban police and court systems and problems in local and state prison organization. Furthermore, combined with the unquestionable failure of the Prohibition Amendment and the rise of organized crime from the East to the Midwest, the findings resulted in a sweeping investigation by the National Commission on Law Observance and Enforcement. Known as the **Wickersham Commission** (its chairman was the former U.S. attorney general George W. Wickersham), it explored numerous aspects of crime and justice across America. Its conclusions were so damaging to the credibility of criminal justice administration that they resulted in public debate that would last for some time to come.[7]

The Wickersham Commission

Crime and Justice: The 1930s Through the 1950s

By the 1930s it was well established that justice in America was outmoded, inept, and marked by venality. The level of lawlessness in law enforcement, combined with the jaded quality of due process in the court system, was unprecedented. Yet few changes emerged from the decade of crime surveys, for the country suddenly had a host of new and more pressing concerns. In mid-October of 1929, America was a land of plenty, and average middle-class citizens saw a seemingly unlimited prosperity ahead. Newly inaugurated president Herbert Hoover announced that the conquest of poverty was no longer just a mirage, and economist Irving Fisher assured the people that the nation's economy was on a permanently high plateau. But by 1931, when the Wickersham Commission reports appeared in print, the national income had been cut in half. By 1932, unemployment had hit an all-time high, banks had begun to fail, and the shantytowns that sprang up on the outskirts of every city had become known as Hoovervilles.[8] This was the age of the Great Depression.

The Great Depression

In the grimness of the national economic crisis, public interest was drawn to the great wave of crime that continued throughout the decade. The Depression years were the era of John Dillinger, Charles "Pretty Boy" Floyd, George "Baby Face" Nelson, and Bonnie Parker and Clyde Barrow.[9] Armed with machine guns and fast cars, the new breed of bandits recreated a frontier pattern of rapid assault followed by immediate and elusive retreat. Bank robbery was one of their usual crimes, and the masses of unemployed, absorbed in the exploits of this army of "public enemies" that was assaulting the very banking system they blamed for the loss of prosperity, had little reason to press for criminal justice reform. Later, as the thirties drew to a close and the nation began to pull out of the Depression, world events intervened, and again reform was pushed to the background. On December 7, 1941, the Japanese

Shantytowns called Hoovervilles sprang up at the edges of American cities during the Great Depression. This one sits grimly in New York's Central Park.

attacked the Pacific Fleet in Pearl Harbor, causing the deaths of more than three thousand American servicemen, and the greatest humiliation in American military history. The nation's energy was consumed by the urgency of World War II.

World War II

The United States emerged from the war as the most powerful nation in the history of the world, not only in terms of its military capability, but in its technological and economic posture as well. The war ended the Great Depression and led to postwar prosperity. By 1947, the United States was producing 43 percent of the world's electricity, 57 percent of its steel, and 62 percent of its oil. Americans owned three-fourths of the automobiles in the world, and their average income was many times greater than that in other countries. By the close of the decade, unemployment had stabilized at about three million persons, roughly 5 percent of the labor force, and Americans, at least those in the white middle class, enjoyed an unprecedented state of economic privilege. In this opulent postwar society, which flowed with a superabundance of resources, the question of justice was of low priority, superseded by images of white houses with front lawns and all-electric kitchens.[10]

The prosperity of the late forties continued into what the nostalgia craze has called the "Fabulous Fifties." The 1950s has been romanticized as a golden age of simplicity and innocence, a thrilling time of bobby sox and soda fountains, Elvis Presley and James Dean, hot rods and "American Bandstand." There were no wars, no riots, and no protests. But the fifties was hardly a time of enthusiasm and contentment. To social critic Michael Harrington the period "was a moral disaster, an amusing waste of life," and author Norman Mailer pointedly described the fifties as "one of the worst decades in the history of man."[11] True, it *was* a time of leisure and cultural pursuit. In record numbers people traveled, listened to music, pulled weeds in their backyards, read *Reader's Digest* condensed books, and bought mink-trimmed clothespins and hula hoops. But it was also a time of fear and suspicion. The cold war with the Soviet Union, the perceived threat of communist

The "Fabulous Fifties"?

Senator Joseph McCarthy testifies during the McCarthy–Army hearings on the organization of the Communist Party in the United States, in June 1954.

infiltration, and the development of the hydrogen bomb were among the debilitating realities, crystallized by accusations, loyalty oaths, and the anti-communist witch hunts of Senator Joseph McCarthy. The fifties was also a time of conservatism. Life was bland, moral, and patriotic; people became suburbanized, domesticated, and buttoned-down. And the problems of poverty, sexual and racial discrimination, militarism, and ecology were ignored.[12]

In the area of crime and justice, American interest was focused on organized crime. From May 10, 1950, to May 1, 1951, the **Special Committee to Investigate Crime in Interstate Commerce** (the **Kefauver Committee**), chaired by Estes Kefauver, the U.S. senator from Tennessee, held hearings that were televised as a public service, but that rapidly became a media event. Although there were only 7,000 television sets in the country in 1946, the figure had increased to tens of millions by 1950, and many Americans were spending more hours watching their sets than they were spending at work. When the independent New York City station WPIX set up its cameras in Manhattan's Foley Square Courthouse where the Kefauver Committee was meeting, and began feeding the video to stations across the country, the potency of the hearings was felt almost immediately. Underworld figures like Frank Costello, Joe Adonis, Charlie Fischetti, and Ben Siegal became instant visitors to American living rooms. An estimated 30 million people watched Costello's courtroom antics as network stations began carrying the full hearings, and the nation became totally absorbed:

> Merchants complained to the Committee that their businesses were paralyzed. Movie houses became ghost halls during the hours of the proceedings. . . . Housewives did their ironing and fed the baby in front of the set. In many big cities business and home life were noticeably affected. One Chicago department store manager took a look at the number of customers in his aisles and ran an ad: "Ten Percent Off During Kefauver Hours." [13]

Although most Americans were well aware that criminals existed at all levels of the social order, the impact of the Kefauver telecasts was staggering. People learned directly of the sordid intertwining of crime and politics and of the extent of dishonor in public life. Many questioned what could be done about these problems, but issues that were more pressing pushed such concerns about crime, once again, into the background.

The issues that claimed the country's attention this time included the "menace of domestic communists," as the late FBI director, J. Edgar Hoover, put it,[14] the cold war with the Soviet Union, and the growing hot war in Korea. There was also "the bomb" and nuclear war, for China had fallen to the communists and the Soviets possessed the plans for the atomic bomb. Then, on March 1, 1954, American scientists set off the first explosion of an H-bomb, and with that came a reshaping of the public mind. Overnight, private and public bomb shelters became necessities, and bombing and survival drills became common in schools and places of business.[15]

The specter of the bomb hovered over America throughout the fifties, but the early hysteria eventually waned. Also, the communist threat grew less impressive, and the Korean conflict came to an end. In addition, the fear of domestic espionage lessened, and Senator Joseph McCarthy fell from power.

This was the setting within which Max Lerner made his comments about criminal justice in *America as a Civilization*. It was within this context that he claimed that in spite of its bungling, prejudice, and corruption, people felt that the justice system was tolerably good. Perhaps Lerner's observations were not so cynical after all! The country was aware that there were difficulties with the justice system, but they had forgotten just how bad the problems actually were. Furthermore, during this same time, justice was swift and certain for those perceived as the most visible and wanton offenders. During the fifties, for example, more than 1,400 persons were legally executed for serious crimes. But the complacency that Lerner wrote about was to be short-lived, for the problems of organized crime, juvenile gangsterism, racism, and disenfranchised youth, combined with a nation guided by the hypocrisy of many of its political leaders, changed national priorities and ideologies for the coming decades.

In 1957, the year the Soviet sputniks were placed into orbit, Jimmy Hoffa, already exposed as a labor racketeer by Arkansas Senator John L. McClellan, was named president of the Teamsters—the nation's largest union.[16] Many Americans then began questioning the democratic system's basic conceptions of justice and morality.[17] In November of that year, the country was again taken by surprise when at least seventy-five of the nation's alleged crime leaders were inadvertently discovered at a meeting in the home of Joseph Barbara in Apalachin, New York. They had come from all parts of the country: at least twenty-three from New York City or New Jersey, nineteen from upstate New York, eight from the Midwest, three from the West, two from the South, as well as two delegates from Cuba and one from Italy.[18] The reasons for the meeting were never uncovered, but its discovery strengthened the notion that organized crime was a nationwide and international alliance with monopolistic controls over numerous businesses, industries, and branches of government.

The Apalachin Convention

In addition to the rediscovery of syndicate crime, there was a growing awareness of corruption in law enforcement. The fifties were marked by a series of random exposures of police crime. In New Orleans, the superintendent of police and the chief of detectives were indicted for malfeasance in their inept handling of a case involving two officers accused of burglarizing a drug store. In addition, more than a dozen other officers in that city were investigated regarding their unexplained "outside income." In Detroit, eighteen patrolmen were indicted for bribery. In Chicago, the chief of police was suspended when the *Sun-Times* published his "little red book," a list of taverns and bars making weekly protection payments. In Birmingham, Alabama, a series of thefts organized by a ring of police officers was discovered. In Brooklyn, bookmaker Harry Gross was found to be paying $1 million in protection money to police, and it was estimated that throughout New York City some 18,000 officers were receiving payoff money.[19]

To these issues were added the growing problems of juvenile delinquency and an apparent increase in street crime. But the most difficult problems—ones that had been festering since World War II—would not reach their fullest intensity until the decade of the sixties.

The Sixties: A Decade of Rebellion

The fifties had been a decade of waste. In the belief that the good life had arrived, Americans rushed to the suburbs to escape urban congestion. Throughout the country, tract-built developments appeared, as landscapes were bulldozed flat. Between 1950 and 1960 the number of U.S. homeowners increased by 9 million to a total of almost 33 million.[20] This mass migration to the suburbs left the cities to deteriorate. In addition, Americans opted for the family automobile as never before, resulting in the construction of a 40,000-mile interstate highway system and an increase of more than 21 million in the number of cars registered. This reliance on the automobile, in turn, resulted in a breakdown in mass transportation, and in pollution, congestion, and a rapid depletion of fossil fuels. These problems were most deeply felt in the central cities, where the poor had been left behind.

The racism of the fifties also had consequences for the sixties. In that decade of growing prosperity, blacks continued to face the legacy of Jim Crow. Early in the fifties, for example, black war veteran Harvey Clark attempted to move his family into an apartment that he had leased in Cicero, Illinois. Police stopped Clark's van and the chief of police struck him, suggesting that he leave town or be shot. Upon Clark's second attempt to move into the apartment, the premises were besieged by a mob of 4,000 whites who, for four days, plundered the building and stole and destroyed Clark's belongings while the police stood idle. The mob was eventually dispersed and the case investigated, but those indicted were an NAACP attorney, the owner of the apartment building, her lawyer, and her rental agent. They were charged with conspiracy to injure property by causing "depreciation in the market selling price."[21]

In the South, blacks were repeatedly the victims of mob murders, lynchings, and all forms of disfranchisement. On August 28, 1955, Emmett Till, a 14-year-old black, was kidnapped from his Mississippi home after having allegedly whistled at a white woman. Four days later his body was recovered from the Tallahatchie River, and an all-white jury later acquitted the two white men accused of Till's murder. Racism was apparent, furthermore, not only for the poor or southern blacks, but for those in the northern middle class as well. In 1957, for example, William and Daisy Myers moved with their three children to Levittown, Pennsylvania, and immediately became the targets of stoning, burning crosses, and obscene phone calls. In addition, the house immediately behind theirs became the center for segregationist forces, who played "Old Man River" through loudspeakers around the clock.[22]

To add to these problems, the country's youth faced the enforcement of conformity, a transparency of sexual morals, and a set of cultural regulations and prohibitions that stressed achievement, prejudice, waste, compliance, and consensus, yet failed to explain or recognize the confusion and absurdity of it all. As a result of such contradictions, a teenage ethic emerged that made serious negative value judgments about the nature and meaning of life. As Kenneth Rexroth warned in an early issue of *Evergreen Review:*

> Listen you—do you *really* think your kids are like bobby soxers in those wholesome Coca-Cola ads? Don't you know that across the table from you at dinner sits somebody who looks on you as an enemy who is planning to kill him in the immediate future? Don't you know that if you were to say to your English class, "It is raining," they would take it for granted that you were a liar? Don't you know they never tell you nothing? that they can't? that . . . they simply can't get through, can't, and won't even try anymore to communicate. Don't you know this, really? If you don't, you're heading for a terrible awakening.[23]

The late social critic Paul Goodman tended to disagree with the conception that there had been a communication failure between youth and adult; he felt, on the contrary, that social messages had been communicated very

Jim Crow laws. Beginning in the 1880s, a number of ordinances were passed in southern states and municipalities legalizing segregation of blacks and whites. The term *Jim Crow* is believed to have derived from a character in a minstrel song. The Supreme Court ruling in *Plessey* v. *Ferguson* (1896) held that separate facilities for blacks and whites were constitutional. The decision in *Plessey* was ultimately overturned by *Brown* v. *Board of Education* in 1954.

The Rebellion of youth

clearly and that the young had found them totally unacceptable.[24] Whatever the reason, however, disaffection and rebellion were in the wings.

A recognition of the pressures on youth began to surface by the middle of the decade in the popular culture media. In 1954 Marlon Brando played in Columbia Pictures' *The Wild One* as a tough motorcycle leader whose gang rampages beyond his control and who is then unjustly attacked by adult mobs. The youth of the day recognized that adults distrusted their behavior somewhat, and they readily empathized with the brutality and perceived heroism of the young Brando character. The following year MGM's *Blackboard Jungle* examined another aspect of the youth problem, focusing on central city juvenile delinquency. Also appearing in 1955 was Warner Brothers' potent film *Rebel Without a Cause*, which targeted the disaffection of middle-class youth. In bringing delinquency from the slums to the suburbs, the film hinted that the social ills at the base of youthful rebellion were widespread.

Marlon Brando in The Wild One, *a film that reflected the growing pressures on youth in the 1950s*

All three of the stars of Rebel Without a Cause *suffered premature violent deaths — James Dean at age 24, in 1955, in an automobile crash; Natalie Wood at age 43, in 1981, in a drowning accident; and Sal Mineo at age 37, in 1976, in a street mugging.*

In the sixties, the problems of enforced conformity, increasing rate of delinquency and youth rebellion, racism, crime and corruption, cultural values that canonized both consumption and waste, and other problems that had been growing through the late forties and fifties came to a head, together with the problems in the criminal justice system that had been ignored since the 1920s. These problems and contradictions resulted in perhaps the most violent era of the twentieth century.[25]

The Freedom Riders

The turbulent events of the 1960s began in the South in early 1961, when civil rights workers sought to win enforcement of a 1958 Supreme Court ruling ordering the desegregation of bus line stations and waiting rooms. Led by James Farmer and the Congress of Racial Equality, two buses carrying thirteen Freedom Riders — six whites and seven blacks — left Washington, D.C., on May 4 for New Orleans. When they reached Alabama, one bus was firebombed and the demonstrators were beaten. The following year when James Meredith, a black student, attempted to enroll in the University of Mississippi at Oxford, the ensuing clash between thousands of southern whites and a small force of federal marshals lasted for more than fifteen hours and resulted in more than seventy casualties.* And while southern opposition to racial equality was generally expressed through violent mass protests, it

---

* An earlier attempt to desegregate an all-white southern college had been unsuccessful. In 1956, University of Alabama officials had expelled their first black student, Autherine Lucy, on the grounds that her presence was a threat to public order.

The March on Washington for Jobs and Freedom took place on August 28, 1963.

also emerged through individual political murders. The list of civil rights workers, both black and white, who were martyred in the early 1960s is a lengthy one. It includes some well-known names: Medgar Evers, the NAACP field secretary; white civil rights volunteer Viola Liuzzo, a Detroit housewife and mother who was shot by nightriders while ferrying marchers between Selma and Montgomery, Alabama; and James Chaney, Andrew Goodman, and Michael Schwerner, three young civil rights workers murdered by members of the Ku Klux Klan in Mississippi, with the connivance of local law enforcement officers.

Also of national concern were the ghetto riots, brought on by racism, poverty, and the deterioration of central city slums. The first occurred in the early sixties in New York City's Brownsville, Bedford-Stuyvesant, and Harlem areas; they were followed in August 1965 by a riot in the Watts section of Los Angeles that began with an incident of alleged police brutality and ended with 34 persons killed and 1,032 injured, $40 million in property destroyed, 600 buildings damaged or demolished, and 4,000 persons arrested. By 1967 ghetto uprisings had erupted across the country. During the first nine months of that year there were some 164 disorders and 83 deaths, capped by major outbreaks in Newark, New Jersey, and Detroit, Michigan.

But the violence associated with the civil rights movement and oppression in the ghettos was only the beginning, for the decade was marked by considerable bloodshed of a highly political character. On November 22, 1963, John Fitzgerald Kennedy—the symbol of an era that, in hindsight, many believe to have been the beginning of an American Camelot—became the fourth U.S. president to be assassinated. His alleged assassin, Lee Harvey Oswald, was shot to death within thirty-six hours. Less than thirteen months later, Black Muslim leader Malcolm X was killed in a Harlem auditorium in New York City, thus becoming a cultural hero for a new and activist generation of black Americans. In 1967 George Lincoln Rockwell, leader of the American Nazi party—the extremist right-wing group dedicated to "saving" the United States from communists, blacks, and Jews—was murdered by one of his followers. And in 1968, civil rights leader Dr. Martin Luther King, Jr., and Senator Robert F. Kennedy were assassinated. In addition, there were battles at Kent State, Ole Miss, Jackson State, and numerous other college campuses when students protesting the Vietnam War were fired upon by police and National Guardsmen.

The incidents at Kent State and at other colleges and universities illustrate how the 1960s protest over the Vietnam War led to polarization and violence. U.S. involvement in Vietnam actually began during the 1950s. In part, the war was a legacy of France's colonial administration of Indochina, which effectively ended with the Geneva Accords of 1954. Indochina was then provisionally divided into the Democratic Republic of Vietnam (North Vietnam) and the Republic of Vietnam (South Vietnam). This was followed by refugee movements between the two new states and reprisals by each regime against suspected enemies. Elections scheduled for 1956, which would have reunified Vietnam, were cancelled by South Vietnamese President Ngo Dink Diem. This angered the Communist government of North Vietnam, since they expected to benefit from the considerable popular support they had in the south. Increasing opposition came from the South Vietnamese guerrilla insurgents known as the Viet Cong, who were backed by the North Vietnam Communists.

In 1954 the United States recognized the government of South Vietnam. In 1961 a military and economic aid treaty was signed, which led to the

George Lincoln Rockwell, leader of the American Nazi party, was murdered by one of his followers in 1967.

The Vietnam War

arrival of the first U.S. support troops, and the formation of the United States Military Assistance Command in 1962.[26] By 1963 there were over 23,000 American troops in South Vietnam. By mid-1968, there were over half a million.

When President John F. Kennedy assumed office in 1961 there were said to be only 900 Americans in Vietnam. Within a year the number had risen to 3,200, and at the time of Kennedy's assassination in late 1963 American troop levels in South Vietnam had increased to 23,300.

A turning point in the American involvement in Vietnam came in August 1964, when the USS *Maddox,* a destroyer assigned to intelligence operations in the Gulf of Tonkin, was allegedly attacked by North Vietnamese PT boats while it was reported to be in international waters. An outraged Congress made the overhasty decision to give President Lyndon Johnson advance approval to "take all necessary steps, including the use of armed force" to assist the South Vietnamese government. What followed was a major commitment to the conflict. By the end of 1965 troop levels reached 184,300 and in mid-1968 they exceeded one-half million.

As the war escalated, television coverage brought the Vietnam War into American living rooms. Americans became divided over U.S. involvement in Vietnam — over a war that had seemingly few, if any, implications for the safety of American democracy. Furthermore, it appeared to be a conflict that could not be won, and yet a conflict in which tens of thousands of American soldiers were losing their lives. As the number of casualties mounted, so did the numbers opposed to the war. There were antiwar groups, speeches, and an organized march on the nation's capital.

Chicago, August 1968

Then in August 1968, a protest rally was held at the Democratic National Convention in Chicago. Anger over the war in Vietnam had led numerous antiwar groups, radicals, Yippies (an organization of primarily young political activists), members of the SDS (Students for a Democratic Society), supporters of Senator Eugene McCarthy, and thousands of others to Chicago to denounce the war, President Lyndon Johnson, the Democratic party, and Vice President Hubert H. Humphrey. Mayor Richard Daley's decision not to

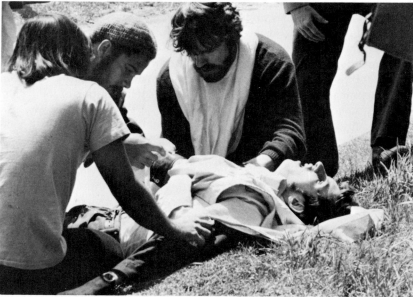

Students attend to one of their fellow demonstrators, shot by National Guardsmen on the campus of Kent State University on May 4, 1970.

allow peace marches was backed by a force of 6,000 police officers, 6,000 Illinois National Guardsmen, and 6,000 regular army troops armed with rifles, flamethrowers, and bazookas. The final conflict, referred to by many as a "police riot,"[27] resulted in tear gas attacks and the clubbing of hundreds of protesters, journalists, news photographers, and bystanders.[28] Both ironically and curiously, during the very moments of that conflict in Chicago on August 28, 1968, Philip M. Hauser, in his presidential address to the membership of the American Sociological Association in Boston, made the following observations on the means for resolving conflicts of interests:

> No matter how laudable the goals, when force is employed by labor and management, by students, by advocates of peace, by minority groups, or in most extreme form by nations of war, it is a mechanism incompatible with the continued viability of contemporary society.[29]

Street crime also increased during the sixties. In 1960, for example, there were almost 300,000 known violent crimes. By the close of the decade the number of murders had increased by 76 percent, serious assaults by 117 percent, forcible rapes by 121 percent and robbery by 224 percent. Furthermore, the number of burglaries had increased by 142 percent, larcenies by 245 percent, and the overall crime rate by 144 percent.[30]

But the final horror of the sixties came in August 1969, with antecedents in the **counterculture,** which had first become visible a few years earlier. The counterculture, as many have described it, was a whole complex of new behavior patterns and beliefs.[31] It was a revolution against the Protestant ethic and the bourgeois American concept of life that emphasized work, duty, morality, maturity, and success. Members of the counterculture rejected the traditionally accepted values of American culture; many lived in communes and used drugs; they wrote poetry, listened to acid rock music, embraced the teachings of mystical religions, and read *I Ching* or the *Tibetan Book of the Dead.* They were called "dropouts," "freaks," or, to use the term coined by a reporter from the *San Francisco Chronicle* during the summer of 1965, "hippies."

Then in 1967 came the "Summer of Love" and the "flower children." It all began on March 26 of that year when 10,000 youths congregated in New York City's Central Park to honor love. They joined hands in "love circles," flew kites, sang, and took drugs. On the West Coast that Easter Sunday, another 15,000 youths met in San Francisco and participated in a similar happening. The crossroads of the Summer of Love was the Haight-Ashbury section of San Francisco, where the natives were known as flower children. One participant described that historic summer scene:

> As we were traveling across, Scott McKenzie was singing on the radio, "If you're going to San Francisco, put flowers in your hair." Sure enough if we didn't arrive with flowers in our hair. We went into that town and I couldn't believe it. It was a carnival. That one big street, Haight Street . . . was just packed with every kind of freak you could imagine. Guys with Mohawk hair cuts, people walking around in commodore uniforms, you know, the hat with the fuzz all over it. Everything! You couldn't believe it. It was an incredible street scene.[32]

But as Ed Sanders described it in his book *The Family,* the Haight-Ashbury district of the flower children was "a valley of plump rabbits surrounded

By 1970 Haight-Ashbury had lost its innocence.

The "Summer of Love"

A hippie "crash pad" of the 1960s

by wounded coyotes." [33] During the spring and summer of 1967, the word had gone out across the country to come to San Francisco for love and flowers. Yet other things also waited in "the Haight." There were vicious criminals who grew long hair, bikers who tried to take over the drug market with sadistic tactics, "speed freaks" going through aggressive paranoid delusions, and satanist-rapist death freaks. Among these last was a bearded little psychotic who haunted the Grateful Dead concerts at the Avalon Ballroom, curling into a fetal position on the dance floor. As William Manchester put it in *The Glory and the Dream,* "he would be well remembered in Hashbury." [34] And indeed he would — his name was Charles Manson.

The so-called Summer of Love ended on October 8, 1967, with the murder of Linda Rae Fitzpatrick in New York.[35] She had been raped four times, her face smashed, and her naked corpse found in the boiler room of a Lower East Side tenement. She had been a flower child, one of many who had met violent death. Later that week in San Francisco's Golden Gate Park other flower children burned a gray coffin marked "Summer of Love." That summer had been crippled by violence and came to an end, but the specter of the Haight's death freaks was soon to reemerge.

The Manson Family

Charles Manson was not typical of the disaffected middle-class youth who made up the flower children. Born in Cincinnati, Ohio, in 1934, Manson was a wandering vagrant who was in trouble most of his life, spending much of his time in jails and reformatories throughout the country. At age 35, he was the organizer of a commune located on the edge of Death Valley that practiced free love and pseudoreligious ceremonies centering around his role as a Christ-like leader. On August 8, 1969, Manson directed five of his followers to the Los Angeles mansion of film director Roman Polansky. Spouting Manson's doctrines of "peace, love, and death," the group proceeded to brutally murder the five persons there. The victims were shot and stabbed to death, and various slogans were written on the walls of the house with the blood of those slain. Among the victims was Polansky's wife, actress Sharon Tate. A few hours later, Manson's protégés — one man and three women — invaded the home of two additional victims, leaving their bodies mutilated and arranged in grotesque positions.[36] (See Exhibit 1.1 for more on Manson and his "family.")

The decade of the sixties was marked by crime, violence, rebellion, and a discontentment with the processes of justice. Even before it ended, however, people began responding to the growing disorder and the criminal justice system's inability to manage it.

The Issue of Law and Order and the War on Crime

Emotionally charged appeals for **law and order** were heard well before the 1960s had reached their midpoint. The cries were, in part, a reflection of the temperament of grass-roots America, which was seeking a return to the morality of previous decades. But they came also from citizens who not only despised crime in general, but waste, anarchy, and government control over individual destinies as well. At the extreme right of this growing consciousness were organizations such as the John Birch Society and the Minutemen. The most visible was the John Birch Society, an ultraconservative, anticommunist organization founded in 1958 by manufacturer Robert Welch and named after Captain John Birch, a U.S. intelligence officer killed by communists in China in 1945. Although the original goal of the society was to fight subversive communism in the United States, it was also solidly opposed to integration and the New Left student movements.[37]

Also visible at this time was a trend toward the "nationalization" of the Bill of Rights. The writers of the Bill of Rights had intended that it apply on the national level — that is, the level of the federal government — and not the state level. Thus, defendants in state criminal trials were not accorded many of the constitutional protections that were routinely given to those tried in federal courts. But in the 1930s the U.S. Supreme Court began extending these rights to state defendants. It was not until the 1960s, however, that significant gains were made. By 1969, nearly all the provisions of the Bill of Rights relating to criminal violations were binding on the states, including the prohibitions against compulsory self-incrimination, illegal search and seizure, and cruel and unusual punishment, as well as the rights to counsel, speedy trial, and confrontation of hostile witnesses.[38] Several of these decisions came early in the 1960s, and they were interpreted by many as Supreme Court attempts to "handcuff police" and "coddle criminals."

Law and order emerged as a political issue during the Johnson/Goldwater presidential campaign of 1964. Barry Goldwater, the senior senator from Arizona and the choice of the Republican party, was an extreme conservative. The GOP believed that throughout the nation there was a hidden conservative majority — a *silent majority* — that would swarm to the polls to

Law and order

The John Birch Society

Nationalization of the Bill of Rights

The law-and-order issue in the Johnson/Goldwater campaign of 1964

EXHIBIT 1.1

Whatever Happened to . . .

The Manson Family

Reports of the number of people who lived with Charles Manson at his commune on the edge of Death Valley varied — anywhere from twenty to forty at any given time. The bona fide members of Manson's "family," however, were relatively few, and included Susan Atkins, Patricia Krenwinkel, Leslie Van Houten, Charles Watson, Lynette Fromme, and Sandra Good.

It was Atkins, Krenwinkel, Van Houten, and Watson who actually carried out the Tate–LaBianca murders, under Manson's direction. All five were convicted in the slayings and were sentenced to death. In 1972, however, the death penalty was declared unconstitutional in California and their sentences were commuted to life. They became eligible for parole in 1978, but their releases were denied. Subsequent parole hearings had the same outcome.

Although behind bars, Manson has remained a visible personality, appearing in numerous magazine and television interviews over the years. In 1984 he was set afire by a fellow inmate at the California Medical Facility — a state prison for psychiatric cases — but recovered quickly. As for his co-defendants in the Tate–LaBianca murders, they maintain their innocence in the case, claiming that they had been seduced into committing the crimes and were under Manson's spell at the time. They describe their former leader as a charismatic sociopath for whom death was a blessing and murder a sacrament.

The other two members of Manson's group, Lynette Fromme

and Sandra Good, also made their way into correctional institutions. On the morning of September 5, 1975, Fromme attempted to assassinate President Gerald R. Ford. Her purpose was to call attention to the fact that the world was being contaminated by pollutants. She felt that saving the world could be accomplished by killing those in high power who permitted such destruction. At her trial, against the advice of the court, she acted as her own attorney. For her efforts, she was convicted and sentenced to natural life.

Sandra Good, a close friend of Fromme and equally anxious to save the world from pollution, also found her way to prison in 1975. She had written such virulent letters to chemical industry executives and their wives and made so many verbal threats that she was convicted and sentenced to fifteen years. In 1985, after serving two-thirds of her term, she was eligible for release on the condition

that she not associate with any members of the Manson family. At first she refused, stating, ". . . I want to be where my family is, and my family is in prison." By the close of the year, however, she exchanged her prison environment for supervised parole in Vermont.

In retrospect, there is an interesting curiosity about the Manson case and the Tate–LaBianca murders. Charles Manson has become a household word that denotes bizarre criminality and he is cited as the worst example whenever mass murders are reported in the media. Yet, while Manson ordered the Tate–LaBianca killings, he did not participate in them, and there are likely few people who even remember the names of the four actual killers — Susan Atkins, Patricia Krenwinkel, Leslie Van Houten, and Charles Watson. Furthermore, there have been homicides far more bizarre than those committed by the Manson family. Not many people remember

John Wayne Gacy, the owner of a Chicago construction firm, who committed more murders than any other person in United States history. From 1972 to 1977, Gacy killed no fewer than thirty-three young men and boys that he had lured to his home for sex. And not many people have even heard of Albert Fish, one of America's few known cannibals, who abducted 12-year-old Grace Budd in 1928, butchered her alive, and ate her. Perhaps it is because of the media attention given the case since the gruesome killings involved a well-known actress. Perhaps it is because there was always something mystical about Manson — a long-haired Svengali described by his followers as a Christ-like leader who could mesmerize young women into submission with seductive rhetoric. Whatever the reasons, in the minds of many Americans Charles Manson remains as the ultimate personification of evil.

SOURCES: Clara Livsey, *The Manson Women: A "Family" Portrait* (New York: Richard Marek, 1980); *People*, September 13, 1982, p. 80; *New York Times*, June 14, 1981, p. 35; *USA Today*, September 26, 1984, p. 2A; *Time*, October 8, 1984, p. 74; *New York Times*, March 19, 1985, p. A16; *New York Times*, December 8, 1985, p. 30.

Above: Charles Manson. Manson's "family," below, actually carried out the Tate–LaBianca slayings. From left: Linda Kasabian, Tex Watson, Susan Atkins, Patricia *Krenwinkel, and Leslie Van Houten. Kasabian was a key witness for the prosecution in the conviction of Manson and the other four.*

elect a "real American," and Goldwater seemed to have the appropriate image. As William Manchester once described the candidate:

> Barry Goldwater was fifty-five years old, a man of absolute integrity, and one of the most charming politicians ever to run for the Presidency. Handsome, leonine, silver-haired, with the black horn-rimmed spectacles which were his trademark, he had become one of the most celebrated public men in the nation and certainly the best-known conservative. Goldwater represented a love for the best of the past and defiance toward the worst of the present. In his crisp low southwestern drawl he reminded the country of American maxims and ethical certitudes which had lost their validity but not their fascination. It was his special talent that he could make them seem both plausible and relevant.[39]

Goldwater's campaign issues included opposition to the absolute centralization of government, to the creation of a welfare state, and to accommodation to communism abroad. Also, he had voted against the 1964 Civil Rights Act, and he favored the replacement of U.S. Supreme Court justices whose decisions were allegedly handcuffing the police. As a mark of his general opposition to the growing permissiveness in the country, as well as to the government's failure to take a strong stand against communism, Goldwater billboards, pins, and bumper stickers read "In Your Heart You Know He's Right."[40]

Because of his attack on numerous sacred cows in the federal bureaucracy, many Americans came to believe in their hearts that Goldwater *was* right. But his comments were often rather bizarre. He offered to sell the Tennessee Valley Authority for $1, and he said that he wished it were possible to saw off the eastern seaboard and let it float out to sea. On these issues,

This television commercial from the Democratic party was in response to Senator Barry Goldwater's suggestion that NATO be authorized to use nuclear weapons.

"Ten, nine, eight, seven . . .

six, five, four, three . . .

two, one . . .

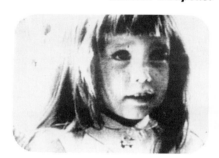

These are the stakes. To make a world in which all of God's children can live . . .

or to go into the dark. We must either love each other or we must die . . .

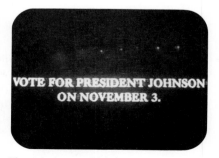

The stakes are too high for you to stay home."

Americans knew in their hearts that he was wrong, or "too far right." Then Goldwater brought the hydrogen bomb into the campaign, suggesting that NATO commanders be authorized to use tactical nuclear weapons; in one speech he suggested "lobbing one into the men's room in the Kremlin." In response, the Democrats came up with the slogan "In Your Heart You Know He Might!" Finally, Goldwater's law-and-order slogan got mixed up with civil rights. Because "law and order" was also the slogan of white segregationists, and because Goldwater had voted against civil rights, he became, like George Wallace, a segregationist hero. The end result was Goldwater's overwhelming defeat in the presidential election. He received only 38.5 percent of the national vote, and carried, in addition to his home state of Arizona, only the hardened segregationist states of Alabama, Georgia, Louisiana, Mississippi, and South Carolina.

Goldwater's defeat, however, did not mean the death of the law-and-order issue. Fear of crime in America was growing, as was discontent with the existing processes for crime control and prevention. "Law and order" became a shorthand term for the general fear not only of street crime but also of the violence and demonstrations surrounding the civil rights and antiwar movements. In response to the public's uneasiness, President Johnson launched his so-called **war on crime** only two months after his inauguration. In a message to the 89th Congress on March 8, 1965, Johnson commented that "crime had become a malignant enemy in America's midst." His strategy for the effort to combat crime involved federal intervention in the processes of criminal justice:

The war on crime

- increased federal law enforcement efforts
- assistance to local law enforcement efforts
- a comprehensive, penetrating analysis of the origins and nature of crime in modern America[41]

This growing fear of crime was further reflected in the May 1965 Gallup poll, which reported for the first time that crime was viewed by Americans as the most important problem facing the nation.[42] On July 25, 1965, the Johnson administration's "war on crime" was formally launched with the establishment of the **President's Commission on Law Enforcement and Administration of Justice**. And unknown to Americans, and even to Johnson himself, the President's Commission was to initiate a new era for criminal justice in the United States.

The President's Commission on Law Enforcement and Administration of Justice

The President's Crime Commission

The President's Commission on Law Enforcement and Administration of Justice, more commonly referred to as the President's Crime Commission, appointed several task forces to study the crime problem and the structure of criminal justice administration, and to make recommendations for action. The commission, made up of 19 commissioners, 63 staff members, 175 consultants, and hundreds of advisors, studied most aspects of the crime problem and the machinery of criminal justice. Even before its findings appeared, however, President Johnson announced to the nation that new approaches to old problems must be sought:

> The problems of crime bring us together. Even as we join in common action, we know that there can be no instant victory. Ancient evils do

not yield to easy conquest. We cannot limit our efforts to enemies we can see. We must, with equal resolve, seek out new knowledge, new techniques, and new understanding.[43]

After hundreds of meetings, tens of thousands of interviews, and numerous national surveys, the President's Crime Commission released a series of task force reports on the police, courts, corrections, juvenile delinquency, organized crime, science and technology, drunkenness, narcotics and drugs, and the assessment of crime, all of which were summarized in its general report, *The Challenge of Crime in a Free Society.*[44] This summary report targeted seven specific objectives, which in many ways would shape the direction of criminal justice for the years to come:

First, society must seek to prevent crime before it happens by assuring all Americans a stake in the benefits and responsibilities of American life, by strengthening law enforcement, and by reducing criminal opportunities.

Second, society's aim of reducing crime would be better served if the system of criminal justice developed a far broader range of techniques with which to deal with individual offenders.

Third, the system of criminal justice must eliminate existing injustices if it is to achieve its ideals and win the respect and cooperation of all citizens.

Fourth, the system of criminal justice must attract more people and better people — police, prosecutors, judges, defense attorneys, probation and parole officers, and corrections officials with more knowledge, expertise, initiative, and integrity.

Fifth, there must be much more operational and basic research into the problems of crime and criminal administration by those within and without the system of criminal justice.

Sixth, the police, courts, and correctional agencies must be given substantially greater amounts of money if they are to improve their ability to control crime.

Seventh, individual citizens, civic and business organizations, religious institutions, and all levels of government must take responsibility for planning and implementing the changes that must be made in the criminal justice system if crime is to be reduced.[45]

Besides these seven major objectives, the reports of the commission also made more than 200 specific recommendations.

The objectives and recommendations were, however, generally disappointing. The conclusions, for example, were very similar to those the Wickersham Commission had offered forty years earlier. In addition, the reasoning of the President's Crime Commission that by simply spending enough energy and money crime could be abolished was naive. But, although they were disappointing, the results were not, in retrospect, too surprising, since the commission's work was also part of the Johnson administration's Great Society effort — an ill-fated series of programs conceived in a utopian ethos for the purpose of upgrading the quality of American life. A Johnson biographer later described its agenda:

The Great Society

> The Great Society would offer something to almost everyone: Medicare for the old, educational assistance for the young, tax rebates for business, a higher minimum wage for labor, subsidies for farmers, vocational training for the unskilled, food for the hungry, housing for the homeless, poverty grants for the poor, clean highways for commuters, legal protection for blacks, improved schooling for the Indians, rehabilitation for the lame, higher benefits for the unemployed, reduced

quotas for the immigrants, auto safety for drivers, pensions for the retired, fair labeling for consumers, conservation for hikers and campers, and more and more and more.[46]

The commission, as well as the President himself, was naive to suggest, for example, that "warring on poverty, inadequate housing, and unemployment is warring on crime"; that "a civil rights law is a law against crime"; that "money for schools is money against crime." The relationship between crime and poverty had been studied at length for many generations, and the inescapable conclusion had been reached that the root causes of crime could not be found in any simplistic equation involving only the disadvantaged segments of society.

The war on poverty

Poverty and segregation may clearly serve to perpetuate crime, the noted criminologist Edwin H. Sutherland, among others, argued, but "poverty as such is not an important cause of crime."[47] Also, the peculiarity of the poverty–crime nexus was well targeted by Harvard University professor James Q. Wilson in his phrase "crime amidst plenty: the paradox of the sixties."[48] Wilson was referring to the fact that at the beginning of the 1960s, this country began the longest sustained period of prosperity since World War II. During this time the economy as a whole was strengthened, many of the financially disadvantaged improved their income positions, and the educational attainments of the young rose sharply. Yet, at the same time, crime increased at an alarming rate, along with youthful unemployment, drug abuse, and welfare. For the President's Commission to suggest, then, that the major weapon in the war on crime was to be simply money caused acute disappointment among those who had spent their lives studying the problem.

In contrast, the commission's analyses of the processes of criminal justice were to have a great impact. They awakened a consciousness of criminal justice as an integrated procedure, as a "system" — an orderly flow of managerial decision making that begins with the investigation of a criminal offense and ends with the offender's reintegration into the free community:

Criminal justice as a "system"

> The criminal justice system has three separately organized parts — the police, the courts, and corrections — and each has distinct tasks. However, these parts are by no means independent of each other. What each one does and how it does it has a direct effect on the work of the others. The courts must deal, and can only deal, with those whom the police arrest; the business of corrections is with those delivered to it by the courts. How successfully corrections reforms convicts determines whether they will once again become police business and influences the sentences the judges pass; police activities are subject to court scrutiny and are often determined by court decisions.[49]

According to the guidelines of the President's Crime Commission, **criminal justice** refers to the structure, functions, and decision processes of those agencies that deal with the management of crime — the police, the courts, and corrections. However, the concept of criminal justice, as described by the commission, is only an ideal. The notion of criminal justice operating as a system was at that time, and still is, somewhat of a myth. The unity of purpose and organized interrelationships among police, the courts, and corrections are beset with inefficiency, fallout, and failure. In most jurisdictions, the courts are a dumping ground for arrested offenders; correctional systems serve as holding pens for convicted offenders; and the free community — under the protection and patrol of law enforcement — is the reentry point for

Criminal justice: the structure, functions, and decision processes of those agencies that deal with the management of crime — the police, the courts, and corrections.

those released from corrections. Rarely does each segment of the criminal justice system operate with a full awareness of the long-term cyclical implications of its activities. For this lack of coordination and failure of purpose, the American Bar Association has referred to criminal justice in America as a "nonsystem."[50]

The criminal justice "nonsystem"

The President's Crime Commission, however, was not altogether unaware of the shortcomings of what it called the "system" of criminal justice, and it called for extensive research and an upgrading of criminal justice personnel. In these areas, the commission had its most visible impact on criminal justice in America.

The Omnibus Crime Control and Safe Streets Act of 1968

The year 1968 occupies a unique summit in our ragged images of crime in America. It was a year of riots, protests, and assassinations. It was also a year of increasingly visible street crime. Among the 4.5 million known major crimes that occurred that year, there were almost 13,000 homicides, 31,000 rapes, 262,000 robberies, 283,000 serious assaults, 778,000 auto thefts, 1.3 million larcenies, and 1.8 million burglaries. Furthermore, at least 1 out of every 45 Americans was the victim of a serious crime.[51]

Crime in the streets

The drug revolution

In addition, 1968 marked the beginning of a new epoch in the **drug revolution** among American youth. Changes in drug technology that had begun almost two decades earlier were perfected, allowing a wide array of substances to be offered to an eager, drug-taking, disaffected youth.[52] Primary among these were newer varieties of amphetamine stimulants, sedatives, and hallucinogens, some of which could be produced in high school chemistry labs and fraternity house bathtubs. They were called "speed," "goofballs," "reds," "yellows," "blues," "black beauties," and other more colorful names. However, few drugs captured the attention and concern of the public as did marijuana and LSD.

Marijuana was not a new drug; it is a mild hallucinogenic substance derived from the crushed leaves and stems of the hemp plant and has been used for thousands of years. Before the late 1920s, few in the United States had heard of the drug, but by the close of the thirties it was being called the "weed of madness," "killer weed," a "sex-crazed drug menace," and "the burning weed of hell." Across the country, news stories detailed the insanity and violence resulting from marijuana use. The hysteria over the drug was provoked by a federal propaganda effort to outlaw its use, but the misinformation distributed about the drug served to type it as an "evil monster of destruction."[53] Even lawmakers of the day, who were creating legal controls on marijuana, were ignorant of its pharmacology and effects, as illustrated, for example, by the following comment from the January 29, 1929, issue of the *Montana Standard*:

> There was fun in the House Health Committee during the week when the Marihuana bill came up for consideration. Marihuana is Mexican opium, a plant used by Mexicans and cultivated for sale by Indians. "When some beet field peon takes a few rares of this stuff," explained Dr. Fred Fulsher of Mineral County, "he thinks he has just been elected president of Mexico so he starts out to execute all his political enemies. I understand that over in Butte where the Mexicans often go for the winter they stage imaginary bullfights . . . after a few whiffs of Marihuana. . . ." Everybody laughed and the bill was recommended for passage.[54]

An antimarijuana message in Omaha, Nebraska, in 1938 reflects misconceptions about the drug common until the 1960s.

Marijuana is not Mexican opium, and it does not have the properties of a narcotic drug. Furthermore, its use does not precipitate the execution of one's enemies — political or otherwise. Nevertheless, the concept of marijuana as a "weed of madness" that leads its user "along a path of destruction and death" persisted into the 1960s.

LSD (D-lysergic acid diethylamide), however, is another story. This drug was first isolated in 1938 by Dr. Albert Hoffman of Sandoz Research Laboratories, but its hallucinogenic properties were not discovered until years later. In the early 1960s, when it was still relatively unknown, two Harvard University psychologists, Timothy Leary and Richard Alpert, began experimenting with the drug on themselves and their colleagues, as well as on artists, writers, students, prison inmates, and others, to determine its effects. Although the two professors were eventually dismissed from Harvard, LSD had already gained a reputation. "Taking a trip" or "turning on" became a status symbol on college campuses. By the late sixties, LSD had become a household word, and chilling stories were told to scare potential users away from the drug.[55] The 1967 so-called "Summer of Love," however, further escalated the popularity of hallucinogenic drugs, and not only LSD, but mescaline, peyote, and marijuana were sold openly. By 1968, marijuana and LSD use were believed to have reached epidemic proportions, and even the parents of young children became frightened when their sons and daughters returned home from their grade schools chanting, to the tune of "Frère Jacques":

The psychedelic revolution

Mar — i — jua — na, mar — i — jua — na L — S — D, L — S — D,

Coll-ege kids are mak-ing it, sch-ool kids are tak-ing it, Why can't we? Why can't we?

Heroin use had also reached significant proportions by 1968, having expanded from the ghettos to suburbia during the early part of the decade.[56] Usually associated with heroin use was street crime — burglaries, robberies, and muggings.

Fear of crime

It was in this setting of street crime, drug abuse, political protest, and violence that *fear of crime* emerged as an even more important concern than it had been when the President's Crime Commission was established. Noting this growing fear, the commission wrote that the purpose of its report was to reduce the fear of crime through its recommendations for a broad and comprehensive attack on the "root causes" of crime. Or as journalist Richard Harris described it:

> Like other crime studies, this one showed "that most crimes, wherever they are committed, are committed in cities." The facts were not particularly surprising, but to many readers the Commission's conclusions were. While it recommended immediate steps to upgrade the quality of the police and their methods, to revise outdated court systems, and to improve correctional techniques, it repeatedly stated that a lasting solution would require widespread recognition of basic matters that had long been overlooked or ignored and the development of a comprehensive program that would take as much money and understanding as the nation could muster.[57]

However, the recommendations of the commission did not and could not culminate in the type of war on crime that was envisioned. To launch a comprehensive attack on the "root causes" of crime was unrealistic, for the causes per se have never been fully known. The search for the causes of crime has been going on for generations with only minimal results. In fact, numerous researchers have concluded that a search for causes is a "lost cause" in criminology.[58]

The Omnibus Crime Control and Safe Streets Act

President Johnson's proposals for the war on crime resulted in the passage of the **Omnibus Crime Control and Safe Streets Act** of 1968, a piece of legislation that generated heated controversy in government, legal, and civil rights sectors across the nation. The act was not directly designed to bring about major reforms in the criminal justice system. Rather, it appeared to be more of a political maneuver aimed at allaying current fears about crime, and calming agitation over ghetto riots and anger over Supreme Court decisions that allegedly tied the hands of the police. One provision of the act (Title II) attempted to overturn numerous Supreme Court decisions by stating that all voluntary confessions and eyewitness identifications — regardless of whether a defendant had been informed of his or her rights of counsel — could be admitted in federal trials.[59] Title III of the act empowered state and local law enforcement agencies to tap telephones and engage in other forms of eavesdropping — for brief periods even without a court order. Primarily because of these two provisions, the Omnibus Crime Control and Safe Streets Act was looked upon as a bad law, one that constituted a significant move toward the establishment of an American police state. This concern was forcefully voiced by segments of liberal-minded America.

The Law Enforcement Assistance Administration

The Law Enforcement Assistance Administration (LEAA)

The primary provision of the Omnibus Crime Control and Safe Streets Act was Title I, which created the **Law Enforcement Assistance Administration (LEAA)**. Three years earlier, in 1965, the Office of Law Enforcement Assistance (OLEA) had been set up within the U.S. Department of Justice to make funds available to states, localities, and private organizations to improve methods of law enforcement, court administration, and prison operations. The legislation that created this agency was the first federal law to provide local government with funds for criminal justice; yet for all practical purposes, funding was severely limited. Under Title I of the new crime bill, OLEA was replaced by the new superagency, LEAA, which was an embodiment of more pervasive plans for federal involvement in law enforcement and crime control. LEAA was organized to function in five ways:

1. by supporting statewide planning in the field of criminal justice through the creation of state planning agencies (SPA's);
2. by supplying states and localities with block grants of federal funds to improve their criminal justice systems;
3. by making discretionary grants to special programs in the field of criminal justice;
4. by developing new devices, techniques, and approaches in law enforcement through the National Institute of Law Enforcement and Criminal Justice, the research arm of LEAA; and,
5. by supplying money for the training and education of criminal justice personnel.[60]

Reproduced courtesy Penthouse Magazine

During the early years of LEAA, the agency received considerable criticism for overemphasizing the funding of a "technological" war on crime and for providing grants for purposes beyond its original mission. One critic, in reviewing LEAA-funded projects from 1969 through 1972, noted the following expenditures:

- $750,000 to the cities of Miami and San Diego for the development of defenses against potential demonstrations at political conventions
- $16,464 to the Louisiana State Police for the purchase of a "command and control vehicle" — an armored tank used to storm a New Orleans Black Panther headquarters
- $150,000 to Tampa, Florida, for a grocery store and shopping center parking lot surveillance system
- $288,405 to the Mississippi State Commission for "developing plans and procedures for coping with civil disorders (riot control and natural disaster) and organized crime," and which was used for arresting more than one-third of the students enrolled at the all-black Mississippi Valley State College — thereby breaking a peaceful campus-wide strike[61]

However, not all LEAA funds were misdirected or misused, nor were all funds channeled for the development of technological tools for a war on crime. A significant portion of LEAA expenditures were also targeted for social programming and research, court reform, and correctional programs. Furthermore, throughout the 1970s LEAA provided more than $40 million per year for the education of some 100,000 persons employed in or preparing for a career in criminal justice. Known as the Law Enforcement Education Program, the report of the Twentieth Century Fund Task Force, which examined the operations of LEAA, maintained that the education program was among the agency's most constructive and successful efforts. Nevertheless,

Criminal justice education

and in spite of the many billions of dollars it spent, LEAA was deemed a failure. According to the Twentieth Century Fund:

> Since LEAA's establishment, crime rates—especially for violent crime—have continued to soar (except for a brief and unexplained respite in 1972). Last year alone, reported crimes went up 18 percent, the largest increase since the Federal Bureau of Investigation began collecting statistics almost 50 years ago. Meanwhile, all the manifest ills of the criminal justice system persist. State and local criminal justice systems remain as fragmented as ever. The courts are still overloaded; jails are still crowded; prosecutorial offices are generally underfunded; and sentencing and parole procedures and decisions remain arbitrary and uncoordinated. Nor do we know any more about the causes of crime than we did before LEAA came into being.[62]

The Nixon–Mitchell Years

The Johnson administration's war on crime continued into the early 1970s under President Richard M. Nixon and his attorney general, John Mitchell. It became muddled, however, by what is considered by many to be the major political scandal of the twentieth century.

The post–World War II era had witnessed the structuring of the Central Intelligence Agency (CIA) as an international secret police and as a mechanism of domestic social coercion that not only spied on Americans, but engaged in break-ins, burglaries, wiretapping, mail opening, and other forms of lawbreaking in an effort to control the government's political enemies — all in the name of national security.[63] During the same period, the Federal Bureau of Investigation (FBI) moved from pursuing "public enemies" into accumulating secret files on hundreds of thousands of Americans, including some high up in government. Under the directorship of J. Edgar Hoover, the FBI grew into a national police force, spying on selected groups in American society that did not agree with Hoover's own political philosophies.[64]

When the offices of the Democratic National Committee, located in the Watergate Hotel and office buildings in Washington, D.C., were broken into in June 1972, knowledge of the secret and illegal operations being pursued by the government slowly came to light. The actual Watergate burglary and wiretapping had been undertaken by a White House special investigations unit known as the "Plumbers," organized by White House assistant John Ehrlichman to plug White House "leaks." Their assignments included inquiries — accomplished through *any* necessary means — into the personal habits of President Nixon's political enemies. **Watergate**, and its subsequent "cover-up," were performed with the complicity of Nixon and Mitchell. These Watergate disclosures, combined with those concerning illegal CIA, FBI, and Internal Revenue Service (IRS) activities, not only helped discredit the Nixon administration, but deeply shook the public's confidence in American concepts of law and order as well.[65]

The Watergate cover-up

Also, the Nixon administration was prone to exaggerate about the crime problem in America. Law and order and the war on crime remained political issues, and by 1972 the fear of crime had climbed to new heights. According to a national Gallup poll of that year, almost half of those surveyed were afraid to walk in their neighborhoods at night, and drug addiction was cited among the major reasons for the high crime rate.[66] By January 1973, crime was ranked highest among the nation's urban problems, with drug use ranking third.[67]

Nixon responded almost immediately, with a statement on March 14, 1973, reemphasizing the war on drugs:

> No single law enforcement problem has occupied more time, effort and money in the past four years than that of drug abuse and drug addiction. We have regarded drugs as "public enemy number one," destroying the most precious resource we have—our young people—and breeding lawlessness, violence and death.[68]

In one sense, Nixon was not exaggerating. Estimated federal expenditures for drug abuse prevention and law enforcement programs were indeed staggering—increasing from $150.2 million in 1971 to $654.8 million in 1973.[69] But his descriptions of the drug problem and its relation to crime often went beyond the parameters of reasonable estimate. He referred to the heroin problem as a plague that threatened every man, woman, and child in the nation with "the hell of addiction." Nixon based his statements on published data which noted that the number of addict-users had increased from 68,000 in 1969 to 550,000 in 1971. What he did not point out, however, was that these figures did not necessarily represent a real increase in the number of heroin users, but rather a change in the methods for counting them. The earlier estimate had been based solely on the number of users coming to the attention of federal authorities through arrest or placement in U.S. Public Health Service treatment facilities. By 1971, however, estimates were being made based on the results of systematic surveys of the population as a whole. Even more outrageous was the estimate the Nixon administration made of the amount of drug-related crime. White House officials indicated that addict crime—largely crime on the streets—cost the country roughly $18 billion. Yet, the $18 billion worth of crime the government claimed addicts were committing to buy their supply of heroin was actually over 25 times greater than the value of all property reported stolen and unrecovered throughout the United States in 1971.[70]

The so-called war on heroin

Investigative reporter Edward Jay Epstein has maintained that the Nixon administration, in making statements like these, was using the so-called **war on heroin** to increase the power of the White House bureaucracy:

> Under the aegis of a "war on heroin," a series of new offices were set up, by executive order, such as Office of Drug Abuse Law Enforcement and the Office of National Narcotics Intelligence, which, it was hoped, would provide the president with investigative agencies having the potential and the wherewithal and personnel to assume the functions of "the Plumbers" on a far grander scale. According to the White House scenario, these new investigative functions would be legitimized by the need to eradicate the evil of drug addiction.[71]

Whether the White House accomplished this goal, or whether it even *was* a goal of the Nixon administration, is not known and perhaps never will be. It is significant, however, that the momentum generated by the Johnson administration toward criminal justice reform, no matter how misconceived it may have been, was never supported through any direct action by the Nixon–Mitchell war on crime.[72]

The National Strategy to Reduce Crime

LEAA believed that change in the criminal justice process would be unlikely without specific standards and goals for police, courts, corrections, and crime prevention. Thus, on October 20, 1971, it appointed the National Advisory Commission on Criminal Justice Standards and Goals to formulate these specifics. After two years of study, this commission offered a national strategy to reduce crime, with the particular goal of reducing what it called "high fear" crime by 50 percent within ten years. It believed that by 1983 homicide could be cut by at least 25 percent, forcible rape by 15 percent, serious assault by 25 percent, robbery by 50 percent, and burglary by 50 percent.

Unlike previous crime panels, however, no actual predictions were made. The commission felt that, by suggesting more than 400 standards and recommendations, it was offering not a solution, but a mechanism for a solution. Some attempts were made to implement the standards at the state and local levels, but on the whole they had little impact. By 1983, high-fear crime had not been cut in half. In fact, over the ten-year period from 1974 through 1983, the volume of serious crime in the United States had increased by almost 20 percent.[73]

As the 1970s came to an end and the new decade began, the interest in criminal justice continued. But, as will be seen in later chapters, reform took on many new meanings. During the first half of the 1980s there *was* a slight decline in the overall crime rate. Nevertheless, there were public demands for a renewed war on crime and legislation that would restrict the rights of the accused and establish more severe punishments for criminal offenders.

Summary

There were a variety of social, cultural, and political events that influenced the course of criminal justice in America during the twentieth century. The problems of crime and justice administration had been left untended during most of the first six decades of the century. Although there was dissatisfaction with the justice system of that era, other, more pressing concerns, such as the Great Depression and World War II, captured the nation's attention. With the onset of the 1960s a variety of events served to stimulate interest in criminal justice reform. For the first time in U.S. history, the federal government took an active role in the enhancement of state and local criminal processing. During that decade in the years that followed, however, neither the problems nor many of the inconsistencies in the administration of justice were solved. Nevertheless, the era did witness a rediscovery of the workings of the justice process in America, combined with a new interest in the upgrading of the quality of criminal justice policy and procedure.

Key Terms

counterculture **(15)**
criminal justice **(23)**
drug revolution **(24)**
law and order **(17)**
Law Enforcement Assistance
    Administration (LEAA) **(26)**
Omnibus Crime Control and Safe
    Streets Act **(26)**

President's Commission on Law
    Enforcement and
    Administration of Justice **(21)**
Special Committee to Investigate
    Crime in Interstate Commerce
    (Kefauver Committee) **(8)**
war on crime **(21)**
war on heroin **(30)**

Watergate **(28)**
Wickersham Commission **(5)**

Questions for Discussion

1. Why can it be said that criminal justice was rediscovered during the late 1960s and early 1970s?

2. Why has the "war on crime" been considered a failure?

For Further Reading

Harris, Richard. *The Fear of Crime*. New York: Praeger, 1968.
Hofstadter, Richard. *The Age of Reform*. New York: Random House, 1955.

Viorst, Milton. *Fire in the Streets: America in the 1960s*. New York: Simon and Schuster, 1979.
Wilson, James Q. *Thinking About Crime*. New York: Vintage, 1983.

Notes

1. Max Lerner, *America as a Civilization: Life and Thought in the United States Today* (New York: Simon and Schuster, 1957), p. 433.
2. For a discussion of and bibliography on this period, see James A. Inciardi, *Reflections on Crime* (New York: Holt, Rinehart and Winston, 1978), pp. 32–45.
3. See, for example, Richard Hofstadter, *The Age of Reform* (New York: Random House, 1955); Walter C. Reckless, *Vice in Chicago* (Chicago: University of Chicago Press, 1933).
4. The Cleveland Foundation Survey of the Administration of Justice in Cleveland, Ohio, *Criminal Justice in Cleveland* (Cleveland: Cleveland Foundation, 1922).
5. The Missouri Association for Criminal Justice, *The Missouri Crime Survey* (New York: Macmillan, 1926).

6. Illinois Association for Criminal Justice, *The Illinois Crime Survey* (Chicago: Illinois Association for Criminal Justice, 1929).
7. National Commission on Law Observance and Enforcement, *Wickersham Commission Reports*. 14 volumes (Washington, D.C.: U.S. Government Printing Office, 1931).
8. See Dixon Wecter, *The Age of the Great Depression* (New York: Macmillan, 1948).
9. See L. L. Edge, *Run the Cat Roads* (New York: Dembner, 1981).
10. Godfrey Hodgson, *America in Our Time* (New York: Random House, 1976), pp.19–20. See also Eric F. Goldman, *The Crucial Decade—And After: America, 1945–1960* (New York: Random House, 1960): Frederick Lewis Allen, *The Big Change: America Transforms Itself, 1900–1950* (New York: Harper & Brothers, 1952).

11. Cited by Douglas T. Miller and Marion Nowak, *The Fifties: The Way We Really Were* (Garden City, N.Y.: Doubleday, 1977), p. 6.

12. For commentaries on social and political life in the 1950s, see Miller and Nowak, *The Fifties;* David Caute, *The Great Fear: The Anti-Communist Purge under Truman and Eisenhower* (New York: Simon and Schuster, 1978); Daniel Bell, *The End of Ideology: On the Exhaustion of Political Ideas in the Fifties* (New York: Free Press, 1960).

13. Goldman, *The Crucial Decade*, p. 195. For a fuller discussion of the Kefauver hearings, see Estes Kefauver, *Crime in America* (New York: Greenwood Press, 1968).

14. J. Edgar Hoover, *Masters of Deceit: The Story of Communism in America and How to Fight It* (New York: Henry Holt, 1958), p. 4.

15. For a discussion of the political and social context within which the "bomb culture" emerged, see Theodore H. White, *In Search of History* (New York: Harper & Row, 1978), pp. 383–436.

16. See Walter Sheridan, *The Rise and Fall of Jimmy Hoffa* (New York: Saturday Review Press, 1972); John L. McClellan, *Crime Without Punishment* (New York: Duell, Sloan and Pearce, 1962).

17. See Frederic Sondern, *Brotherhood of Evil* (New York: Farrar, Straus, and Cudahy, 1959).

18. Donald R. Cressey, *Theft of the Nation: The Structure and Operations of Organized Crime in America* (New York: Harper & Row, 1969), p. 57.

19. Bell, *The End of Ideology*, pp. 162–163.

20. Miller and Nowak, *The Fifties*, pp. 7–8.

21. Fletcher Martin, "We Don't Want Your Kind," *Atlantic*, October 1958, p. 55; "Convictions in Cicero," *Newsweek*, June 16, 1952, pp. 34–35.

22. David B. Bittan, "Ordeal in Levittown," *Look*, August 19, 1958, pp. 84–85.

23. Kenneth Rexroth, "San Francisco Letter," *Evergreen Review*, Spring 1957, p. 11.

24. Paul Goodman, *Growing Up Absurd* (New York: Vintage, 1956).

25. For discussions of the social values and dissent of the 1960s, see Peter Joseph, *Good Times: An Oral History of America in the Nineteen Sixties* (New York: William Morrow, 1974); Roderick Aya and Norman Miller, eds., *The New American Revolution* (New York: Free press, 1971); Hodgson, *America in Our Time*. Many of the violent episodes of the 1960s are described at length in H. D. Graham and T. R. Gurr, eds., *Violence in America: Historical and Contemporary Perspectives* (New York: Bantam, 1970); Richard Hofstadter and Michael Wallace, eds., *American Violence: A Documentary History* (New York: Random House, 1970).

26. See Lawrence M. Baskir and William A. Strauss, *Chance and Circumstance: The Draft, the War and the Vietnam Generation* (New York: Vintage, 1978).

27. Hofstadter and Wallace, *American Violence*, p. 379.

28. The events of the Chicago confrontation are discussed in Mike Royko, *Boss: Richard J. Daley of Chicago* (New York: E. P. Dutton, 1971).

29. Philip M. Hauser, "The Chaotic Society: Product of the Social Morphological Revolution" (Presidential address delivered before the 63rd annual meeting of the American Sociological Association, Boston, August 28, 1968); *American Sociological Review* 34 (February 1969): 1–19.

30. J. Edgar Hoover, *Crime in the United States: Uniform Crime Reports*—1970 (Washington, D.C.: U.S. Government Printing Office, 1971), p. 65.

31. See, for example, Theodore Roszak, *The Making of a Counter Culture* (Garden City, N.Y.: Doubleday, 1969).

32. Joseph, *Good Times*, p. 133.

33. Ed Sanders, *The Family* (New York: Avon, 1972), pp. 39–40.

34. William Manchester, *The Glory and the Dream* (Boston: Little, Brown, 1974), p. 1368.

35. Manchester, *The Glory and the Dream*, pp. 1368–1370.

36. For an account of the Tate–LaBianca murders and the activities of the Manson clan, see Sanders, *The Family*, and Vincent Bugliosi and Curt Gentry, *Helter Skelter* (New York: W. W. Norton, 1974).

37. See J. Allen Broyles, *The John Birch Society: Anatomy of a Protest* (Boston: Beacon, 1964).

38. Henry J. Abraham, *Freedom and the Court: Civil Rights and Liberties in the United States* (New York: Oxford, 1977), pp. 33–105.

39. Manchester, *The Glory and the Dream*, p. 1257.

40. See Theodore H. White, *The Making of a President 1964* (New York: New American Library, 1965).

41. "Crime, Its Prevalence, and Measures of Prevention," Message from the President of the United States, House of Representatives, 89th Congress, March 8, 1965, Document No. 103.

42. James Q. Wilson, *Thinking About Crime* (New York: Basic Books, 1975), p. 65.

43. Lyndon B. Johnson, "Message to the Congress," March 9, 1966.

44. President's Commission on Law Enforcement and Administration of Justice, *The Challenge of Crime in a Free Society* (Washington, D.C.: U.S. Government Printing Office, 1967).

45. President's Commission, *The Challenge of Crime*, p. vi.

46. Doris Kearns, *Lyndon Johnson and the American Dream* (New York: Harper & Row, 1976), p. 216.

47. Edwin H. Sutherland and Donald R. Cressey, *Principles of Criminology* (Philadelphia: J. B. Lippincott, 1966), pp. 95, 241, 265.

48. Wilson, *Thinking About Crime*, p. 3.

49. President's Commission, *The Challenge of Crime*, p. 7.

50. American Bar Association, *New Perspectives on Urban Crime* (Washington, D.C.: ABA Special Committee on Crime Prevention and Control, 1972), p. 1.

51. J. Edgar Hoover, *Crime in the United States: Uniform Crime Reports*—1968 (Washington, D.C.: U.S. Government Printing Office, 1969).

52. James A. Inciardi, "Drugs, Drug-Taking and Drug-Seeking: Notations on the Dynamics of Myth, Change, and Reality," in *Drugs and the Criminal Justice System*, ed. James A. Inciardi and Carl D. Chambers (Beverly Hills: Sage, 1974), pp. 203–220.

53. For a discussion of marijuana use and the movement to criminalize it, see L. Sloman, *Reefer Madness: The History of Marijuana in America* (Indianapolis: Bobbs-Merrill, 1979).

54. Richard J. Bonnie and Charles H. Whitebread II, *The Marihuana Conviction: A History of Marihuana Prohibition in the United States* (Charlottesville: University of Virginia Press, 1974), p. 40.

55. The LSD phenomenon is described in David Solomon, ed., *LSD: The Consciousness-Expanding Drug* (New York: G. P. Putnam, 1964); Andrew I. Malcolm, *The Pursuit of Intoxication* (New York: Washington Square Press, 1972); Bernard Aaronson and Humphrey Osmond, eds., *Psychedelics: The Uses and Implications of Hallucinogenic Drugs* (Garden City, N.Y.: Doubleday, 1970).

56. See Leon Gibson Hunt and Carl D. Chambers, *The Heroin Epidemics* (New York: Spectrum Publications, 1976).

57. Richard Harris, *The Fear of Crime* (New York: Praeger, 1968), pp. 15–16.

58. Nigel D. Walker, "Lost Causes in Criminology," in *Crime, Criminology, and Public Policy*, ed. Roger Hood (New York: Free Press, 1974), pp. 47–62.

59. The Omnibus Crime Control and Safe Streets Act of 1968, Public Law 90-351, 90th Congress, June 1968, 18 U.S.C., Sec. 2518.

60. Twentieth Century Fund Task Force on the Law Enforcement Assistance Administration, *Law Enforcement: The Federal Role* (New York: McGraw-Hill, 1976), p. 4.

61. Jeff Gerth, "The Americanization of 1984," *Sundance Magazine* 1, April/May 1972, pp. 58–65.

62. Twentieth Century Fund Task Force, *Law Enforcement*, pp. 4–5.

63. See William R. Corson, *The Armies of Ignorance: The Rise of the American Intelligence Empire* (New York: Dial Press, 1977); Morton H. Halperin and Daniel Hoffman, *Freedom vs. National Security: Secrecy and Surveillance* (New York: Chelsea House, 1977).

64. See Pat Watters and Stephens Gillers, eds., *Investigating the FBI* (Garden City, N.Y.: Doubleday, 1973); David Wise, *The American Police State* (New York: Random House, 1977).

65. For intensive analyses of Watergate and its aftermath, see Carl Bernstein and Bob Woodward, *All the President's Men* (New York: Simon and Schuster, 1974); John Dean, *Blind Ambition: The White House Years* (New York: Simon and Schuster, 1976); Donald W. Harward, ed., *Crisis in Confidence: The Impact of Watergate* (Boston: Little, Brown, 1974).

66. *New York Times*, April 23, 1972, p. 23.

67. *Washington Post*, January 16, 1973, p. A3.

68. Cited by Carl D. Chambers and James A. Inciardi, "Forecasts for the Future: Where We Are and Where We Are Going," in *Drugs and the Criminal Justice System*, ed. Inciardi and Chambers, p. 221.

69. Chambers and Inciardi, "Forecasts for the Future," p. 222.

70. Edward Jay Epstein, *Agency of Fear* (New York: G. P. Putnam, 1977), pp. 174–179.

71. Epstein, *Agency of Fear*, p. 8.

72. For a discussion of the contrasts between the "mission of justice" under Johnson versus under Nixon, *see* Richard Harris, *Justice: The Crisis of Law, Order, and Freedom in America* (New York: E. P. Dutton, 1970).

73. Federal Bureau of Investigation, *Crime in the Unted States—1983* (Washington, D.C.: U.S. Government Printing Office, 1984), p. 43.

The Foundations of Crime and Justice

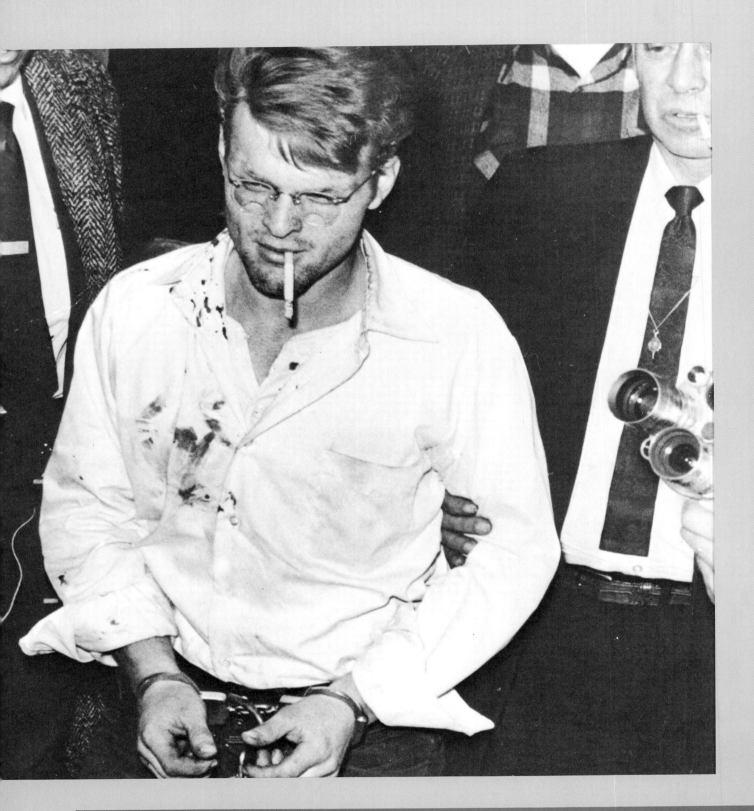

2

Crime and the Nature of Law

Morality cannot be legislated but behavior can be regulated.

—Martin Luther King, Jr.

Charles Starkweather

O
n January 21, 1958, Charles Raymond Starkweather set out on a murderous rampage across the American plains states, epitomizing the 1950s specter of teenage violence. His mass slaughter lasted only eight days, but it claimed the lives of ten people. Three of the victims were the parents and baby sister of Charlie's 14-year-old girlfriend, Caril Ann Fugate, who accompanied him on his trail of morbid violence. Yet curiously, while the nation was shocked by the murders, Charlie and Caril quickly became a macabre adornment of twentieth-century American folklore. People were fascinated with the seemingly matter-of-fact way in which much of the killing had been done. After shooting and stabbing three members of Caril's family, for example, the teenage couple ate sandwiches and watched television only a few yards from where their victims' bodies lay hidden.

But more importantly, Charlie Starkweather was a symbol. At age 19, he was a caricature of the then-popular James Dean image. Dean was the brilliant and eccentric star of *Rebel Without a Cause, Giant,* and *East of Eden* who, after his death in an automobile crash in 1955 at age 24, became a symbol of the moral young outsider too sensitive to survive in a conformist adult society. For the many who had revered Dean in his films and who would continue to send him fan mail more than twenty years after his death, and to the rebellious youth of the decade for whom individuality and status meant confrontation by brute force, Charlie Starkweather was a hero. Like Robin Hood, Jesse James, and Billy the Kid, he had defied the established order, and had done so in a most visible and savage way. And like Dean, he too would become a martyr. When Starkweather was finally executed in the Nebraska State Penitentiary electric chair on June 24, 1959, his death was mourned by his followers — those across the country and those outside the prison walls who wanted to be with him to the very end.[1]

The public's conception of crime

The episode of Charlie Starkweather is recalled here because it vividly illustrates the American fascination with **crime.** Stories of brutal violence and clever theft are continually offered to the public imagination, and the virtues and vices of such personages as Charles Manson, Al Capone, and Lee Harvey Oswald, to name only a few, have become well known. Murderers, rapists, and sinister sneak thieves are given prominent attention by the news media; violent crime is traditionally the major pursuit of the villains and scoundrels who appear in popular mystery and detective literature; and homicide, robbery, and assault are the common themes in both television and Hollywood portrayals of crime. In consequence, many Americans have developed rather distorted and one-sided conceptions of crime. Most of us feel that we have a reasonably good understanding of what crime is all about. We have learned, for example, to think of crime as something that is intrinsically evil, as something that threatens individual rights, civil liberties, and perhaps the very foundations of society. We are conscious of the presence of crime and respond to it by protecting ourselves — we lock our doors and windows to secure our property; we spend billions of dollars yearly to insure our valuables and precious possessions; we cautiously orient our activities away from dangerous places and situations to safeguard our lives. And we think of crime as something alien, something that exists outside of organized society. Our conceptions of crime lead directly to such common phrases as "organized crime," "crime in the streets," "gang delinquency," and "the underworld." However, even when we think about these common references to crime, we have only a minimal comprehension of what they really mean.

"Organized crime" conjures up images of Eliot Ness and his "Untouchables," firing machine guns through the open windows of a speeding 1925 Packard; of Mario Puzo's *The Godfather,* or of speakeasies, Al Capone, and the St. Valentine's Day massacre. Yet we have little idea of how organized crime actually affects our daily lives through its close associations with business, industry, and government. Also, the phrase "crime in the streets" is used by everyone, but actually has no precise meaning (see Exhibit 2.1).

Crime, in contrast, goes well beyond the undefined parameters of street crime and the limited catalog of violence and theft we find in the popular media. Furthermore, the volume and rates of crime vary considerably from what conventional knowledge might arbitrarily suggest.

Although violence and the most commonly discussed categories of theft may appear to be the most typical forms of lawbreaking, crime includes literally thousands of offenses. And the majority of these rarely come to our attention. White-collar crime, for example, is associated with the illegal activities of businesspeople that take place alongside the legitimate day-to-day activities of their business or profession. It involves billions of dollars annually in price fixing, embezzlement, restraint of trade, stock manipulation, misrepresentation, bribery, false advertising, and consumer fraud. The economic toll to the average citizen from white-collar crime well exceeds the dollar losses from all known robberies, burglaries, and other thefts — yet it is rarely considered. Also, the criminalization of conduct once deemed immoral — gambling, prostitution, alcohol and drug abuse — reflects an attitude that has resulted in the arrest and conviction of more persons than have the more serious offenses of larceny and assault. Violations in the areas of traffic control, building codes, fire ordinances, standards of quality, and safety precautions result in more deaths each year than criminal homicide. Corruption in public office and private business in the form of bribes, payoffs, fixes, and conflicts of interest occur in every branch of government and every kind of business, and at every level. And there is police crime, juvenile crime, and a range of property offenses that receive only minimal attention in the popular media.

At the same time, there are varieties of crime that the public associates only with the past, but that nevertheless continue to exist. When we think of pirates and buccaneers on the high seas, for example, we generally think of such colorful predators as Blackbeard, Henry Morgan, and Captain Kidd, who raised the Jolly Roger in the Caribbean and in the waters around India and Africa during the eighteenth century.[2] Yet piracy still lives and the Jolly Roger still flies — in the Caribbean, as part of the smuggling and trafficking of illegal drugs, and in the sea lanes of Southeast Asia, where fishing fleets and coastal freighters are hijacked.[3] Also common, but rarely presented by the media, is

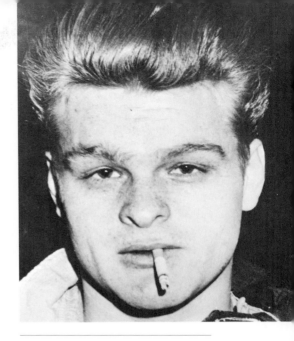

Striking a James Dean pose, Charles Starkweather pleaded innocent to murder at his arraignment for one of eleven slayings.

The real James Dean, later to be caricatured by multiple murderer Charles Starkweather, in Rebel Without a Cause

EXHIBIT 2.1

"Crime in the Streets"

What is "crime in the streets" or, more popularly, "street crime"? Does it include such happenings as murder, rape, and robbery? Or is it limited only to those crimes that occur on a city street? Almost a decade after street crime first became a popular topic in both political and public discussions, members of the House Select Committee on Crime, in the midst of hearings on the subject during the week of April 9–13, 1973, suddenly discovered that they had been focusing their efforts and resources on a totally undefined term:

Street crime has no generally accepted definition, and the label itself is somewhat misleading in that burglaries and indoor robberies (about half of all robberies, and about one-fourth of all urban robberies) are frequently categorized as "street crime" though they occur off the street. Street crime is generally not organized criminal activity, although there is increasing evidence of "organization" in burglary and auto theft rings. Street crime could be defined as those crimes of robbery, rape, assault, and the like committed by strangers; [but] this definition would exclude four-fifths of all reported murders, non-negligent manslaughters, and aggravated assaults, and almost two-thirds of all reported rapes.

Their discussions went on for five days. Despite the uncertainty, the discussions culminated in a report of some 266 pages that offered recommendations on ways to reduce this phenomenon, whose content and boundaries they had never even properly explained or defined.

SOURCE: House Select Committee on Crime, *Street Crime: Reduction Through Positive Criminal Justice Responses* (Washington, D.C.: U.S. Government Printing Office, 1973).

Man has excelled at everything, except crime. —**Goldfinger**

When the President does it, that means it is not illegal. —**Richard M. Nixon**

the crime of poaching. In Zimbabwe, lured by the international demand for rhinoceros horns, poachers have pushed one of Africa's oldest and rarest creatures to the edge of extinction.[4] And poaching is not an offense confined to exotic and faraway lands. In the United States, the commercial poaching of everything from desert Gila monsters to bighorn sheep has become a $500-million-a-year industry.[5]

Finally, there are literally hundreds of activities that are considered crimes in some jurisdictions but not in others. There are events that were crimes at one time and are no longer considered as such. Additionally, there are behaviors people engage in daily that are viewed by many in society as normal and common but that, under the law, are defined as criminal.

Crime, then, is a term that is subject to both variable and uncritical usage, and conceptions of crime are often distorted and narrow, textured by misplaced emphasis on the more violent and lurid. The task of this discussion is to develop a fuller understanding of the meaning of crime, and to do so through an analysis of crime and its relation to law.

Crime

Crime is a logical extension of the sort of behavior that is often considered perfectly respectable in legitimate business. — Robert Rice, 1956

Crime is an aspect of human experience that brings to mind images of evil and lawbreaking, and that has been subject to a variety of definitions and interpretations. For the classical and literary scholar, crime can be drama, a presentation of conflict between elements of the good and the profane as typified so eloquently in the Greek tragedies, Shakespeare's *Macbeth,* and Dostoyevsky's *Crime and Punishment.* To the moralist and reformer, crime is a manifestation of spiritual depravity; it is that festering evil and disease of the soul that must be eradicated both fully and immediately by the powers of restraint and virtue. Crime has also been equated with sin — with violations of a natural law, the Ten Commandments, or the proscriptions embodied in the Bible, the Talmud, and the Koran. For others, crime has different meanings: to the reporter it is news, to the detective it means work, to the thief it is business, and to the victim it suggests fear and loss. But to most individuals, crime is no more than the violation of a generally accepted set of rules that are backed by the power and authority of the state. Yet, while these and many other conceptions of crime may be important to a particular perspective, they are of little help in arriving at an explicit definition of crime. Nevertheless, the notion of crime as sin suggests a starting point, for the evolution of criminal definitions is intricately linked to historical images of right and wrong and the concept of natural law.

Crime as drama

Crime as sin

Natural Law

Natural law, a concept that has run through human affairs for more than twenty centuries, focuses on perhaps the earliest understanding of crime. Natural law refers to a body of principles and rules, imposed upon individuals by some power higher than man-made law, that are considered to be uniquely fitting for and binding on any community of rational beings. It consists of a set of standards, ideals, and limitations imposed upon individuals by some higher power. As such, natural law is synonymous with "higher law" and is believed binding even in the absence of man-made law. As stated by Hugo Grotius, the Dutch jurist and statesman whose *De Jure Belli ac Pacis,* published in 1625, is regarded as the first work on international law:

Natural law generally refers to principles that determine what is right and wrong according to some higher power.

> The law of nature is a dictate of right reason which points out that an act, according as it is or is not in conformity with rational nature, has in it a quality of moral baseness or moral necessity; and that, in consequence, such an act is either forbidden or enjoined by the author of nature, God.[6]

Since natural law has generally referred to that which determines what is right and wrong and whose power is made valid by nature, it follows that its precepts should be eternal, universal, and unchangeable. But an examination of natural law from the time of the ancient Greeks to the present suggests that there is no single and unchanging view of the concept.[7] To Roman jurists, for example, *jus naturale,* or natural law, meant a body of ideal principles that people could understand rationally and that included the perfect standards of right conduct and justice. Throughout the Middle Ages the law of nature was

One of 21 victims of the mass murder at a McDonald's restaurant in San Ysidro, California, on a hot July afternoon in 1984. Nineteen others were injured as well by the gunman, James Huberty, before he was dropped by a SWAT team marksman 75 minutes after the shooting started.

Incest — a natural crime?

identified with the Bible, with the laws and traditions of the Catholic church, and with the teachings of the church fathers.[8]

The cogency of natural law would suggest the existence of *natural crimes*—"thou shalt not kill," "thou shalt not steal"—acts considered criminal by rational persons everywhere. However, research has failed to yield examples of activities that have been universally prohibited. Incest, for example, is believed by some to be a universal crime or taboo, for there are rules forbidding such behavior in one form or another in every known society.[9] However, there is considerable variation among societies and cultures as to what exactly constitutes incest. While it refers in virtually all settings to sexual relations between parents and children and between any sibling pair, it has been extended in others to include many categories of kin whose relationship may not be necessarily biological. Furthermore, in certain contexts — as in some royal marriages and sacred rituals — the incest taboo has been lifted.[10] As another example, even the act of murder is not universally viewed as criminal. In Comanche society, for example, for a husband to kill his wife — with or without good cause — was not murder. It was an absolute privilege and right that not even the family of the victim would move to challenge. In fact, the only crime in the Comanche legal system was excessive sorcery, for it was considered a threat to the tribe as a whole.[11]

Criminologist Hermann Mannheim has made a thorough and complex examination of the evolution of natural law throughout Western history, concluding that even the concept of natural law has been subject to widely varying interpretations:

> There is no single and unchanging concept of natural law. While its underlying idea is the longing of mankind for an absolute yardstick to measure the goodness or badness of human actions and the law of the State and to define their relations to religion and morality, the final lesson is that no such yardstick can be found.[12]

In sum, there has been a persistent conviction throughout history that there exist superior principles of right, some higher law, the violation of which constitutes crime. But the differing conceptions of natural law have served to discredit its importance in the understanding and definition of crime, which has led legal scholars and social scientists to other areas in their search for the meaning and parameters of crime.

Natural law is significant, however, in both the evolution of criminal laws and modern conceptions of natural crimes. Elements of the natural law concept were incorporated into the Code of Hammurabi, the first known written legal document, which dates back to about 1900 B.C. Natural law also played a key role in the formulation of Greco-Roman law, and it is a cornerstone of a portion of contemporary Anglo-American law.

Crime as a Social Construction

The ideas of natural law and natural crime assume the existence of universal standards as to what constitutes sin or immoral behavior, but a definition of crime framed in these terms lacks both clarity and precision. Furthermore, conceptions of crime as amoral behavior become even more confused when one considers that there is no moral code to which all persons, even in a single society or community, subscribe. A number of social scientists, therefore, have examined crime as a human construction. They suggest that the definition of behavior as "deviant" or "criminal" comes from individuals and social groups, and involves a complex social and political process that extends over a period of time. As such, they suggest, persons and social groups create crime by making rules whose infraction constitutes crime.

This more sociological view of deviance and crime rejects the notion that the rightness or wrongness of actions is of divine origin, and begins with an examination of how behaviors become deviant and criminal within societies. Known as the "sociology of deviance" or the "labeling perspective," this point of view focuses specifically on **deviance** — a concept considerably broader than that of crime. This position rests on the idea that rules that might be violated are not created spontaneously but, rather, come about only in response to behavior perceived to be harmful to a group. Thus, as sociologist Kai T. Erikson has suggested, "The term *deviance* refers to conduct which the people of a group consider so dangerous or embarrassing or irritating that they bring special sanctions to bear against the persons who exhibit it."[13] More specifically, and in contrast to the natural law concept,

Deviance: Conduct which the people of a group consider so dangerous, embarrassing, or irritating that they bring special sanctions to bear against the persons who exhibit it.

> deviance is *not* a quality of an act the person commits, but rather a consequence of the application by others of rules and sanctions to an "offender." The deviant is one to whom that label has successfully been applied; deviant behavior is behavior that people so label.[14]

The mechanisms through which behavior becomes viewed as deviant were described by Howard S. Becker as a process of discovery undertaken by "crusading reformers," "rule creators," and "moral entrepreneurs."[15] The reformer or crusader views certain elements in society as truly, totally, and unconditionally evil, and feels that nothing can be right in the society until rules are made to correct and remove the wickedness he or she has perceived. The crusader's mission becomes a holy war, for the wrongs that have been observed are a breach in the stability of the social order, and only their eradication can ensure a better way of life for all. The crusader's role, then, involves bringing the evil to the attention of the public at large, to the society's opinion makers, and ultimately to the designated rule creators and rule enforcers.

An illustration of this process was the antiliquor crusade that resulted in the ratification in 1919 of the Eighteenth Amendment to the United States Constitution, which prohibited the manufacture, sale, and distribution of

It ain't no sin if you crack a few laws now and then, just so long as you don't break any.
—**Mae West**

intoxicating liquors. The prohibition "movement" asserted the rural Protestant ethic, which was in contrast to the urban culture that was emerging at the close of the nineteenth century. The earliest colonial settlers designated country and village life as good, and deemed only the farmer and his agrarian way of life to be pure and wholesome; life in the city was seen as wicked. The farmer was viewed as the solid man of the earth, the backbone of American democracy; living in communion with nature, he had an integrity that could never be attained by those surrounded with the evil and depravity of the city. This agrarian myth so permeated the ideals and thinking of the frontier people and their descendants that it tended to shape their perception of reality and overt behavior. Their anticity bias extended to drinking and the liquor trade, which they saw as symbols of urban morality — or immorality — and of urbanism in general. They viewed urbanism as diametrically opposed to the rural creeds of the Methodists, Baptists, Presbyterians, and Congregationalists, with their emphasis on individual human toil and a profound faith in the Bible. And to them, the commercialism of the cities was destroying the self-sufficiency of the farm and village, creating a situation of unwanted dependence. Urbanism, therefore, was the real sin in society, and the reform movement was simply an organization of rural interests striving against the wicked city and its impending dominance.

The crusading reformers included many members of the middle and upper classes who felt that prohibition would bring salvation to the cities and to the less privileged members of society. The best known of the reformers was Carry Nation, the uncrowned queen of the temperance movement, who often referred to liquor sellers as "booze-sodden, soul-killing, filth-smeared spawn of the Devil," or words to that effect.[16]

Note that although the deviance perspective can suggest how some deviance and crime can come into being, it fails to account for all definitions of crime. That is, some crimes may come into being by moral enterprise, and some behavior may become criminal when that label is applied to acts previously regarded as noncriminal; but this does not explain how or why many long-standing definitions regarding crimes against person and property came into being. Murder, for example, appears as a proscription in both the Old and New Testaments, and its designation as a capital offense appears in an early chapter of the Book of Genesis.

Is all crime deviant behavior, and is all deviant behavior crime?

Furthermore, not all deviant behavior is criminal behavior, and conversely, not all criminal behavior is deviant behavior. Numerous kinds of activities receive social disapproval and may even be deemed as blatantly antisocial, but they are not necessarily crimes. While picking one's nose in public, espousing the doctrines of communism or nazism, or being an alcoholic are considered deviant by most Americans, the activities themselves are not criminal and they are not treated as such. Social disapproval might even be strong, with the deviants being subject to severe ostracism by their peers, but criminal sanctions would not be brought to bear against them.

By contrast, numerous other behaviors are indeed criminal, but the actors are not even called deviant. The Saturday night poker game for modest stakes may be a violation of the criminal law in some jurisdictions, yet to the society at large the occasional poker player is hardly a deviant. Similarly, many of the intimate sexual practices that occur between adults in contemporary society may violate state and local criminal laws, but within the context of a consenting adult relationship the activities are considered normal.

The streets are safe in Philadelphia, it's only the people who make them unsafe.
—**Frank Rizzo**

And finally, although the labeling perspective fails to offer a basis for a working definition of crime, it does point out how some crime comes into

"Someday you'll look back at this and laugh."

being and, in that sense, how crime can be a social construction. More importantly, however, it provides a useful perspective for understanding how persons come to be labeled as deviant or criminal, how society may react to them, and how the process of labeling them as outsiders can affect their behavior. Society may react to disapproved behavior in a variety of ways — with disgust, anger, hate, gossip, isolation, physical punishment, incarceration, or even execution. Societal reaction is strong or weak depending upon the degree of antisocial behavior involved, how socially visible the behavior is, and the general norms and rules of the society regarding the particular behavior. The process of labeling individuals as deviants, delinquents, or criminals may result not only in rejection or punishment, but also in alteration of the intended behavior of both deviants and others. The anticipated effects of labeling, for example, may deter some persons from engaging in deviant or criminal acts. Furthermore, for those who already are considered deviants, delinquents, criminals, or outsiders, such labels may foster further unacceptable behavior. That is, the labels may lead them to view themselves as offenders who have only limited opportunities for socially approved pursuits.

Societal reaction to crime

Crime as a Legal Definition

If definitions of crime as violations of natural law or as antisocial behavior or deviance lack precision and are ambiguous, then we may need to look directly at law for a formal definition of crime. This need was best stated almost half a century ago by Jerome Michael and Mortimer J. Adler during their attempt to unravel the nature of crime:

> The most precise and least ambiguous definition of crime is that which defines it as behavior which is prohibited by the criminal code. The criminal law describes many kinds of behavior, gives them names such as murder and arson and rape and burglary, and proscribes them. If crime is defined in legal terms, the only source of confusion is such ambiguity as may inhere in the legal definitions of specific crimes. It is sometimes difficult to tell whether specific conduct falls within the legal definition, whether, for example, a specific homicide is murder or what degree of murder, as that offense is defined by law. But even so, the *legal rules are infinitely more precise than moral judgments or judgments with regard to the antisocial character of conduct* [emphasis added]. Moreover, there is no surer way of ascertaining what kinds of behavior are generally regarded as immoral or antisocial by the people of a community than by reference to their criminal code, for in theory, at least, the criminal code embodies social judgments with respect to behavior and, perhaps, more often than not, fact conforms to theory.[17]

It's strange that men should take up crime when there are so many legal ways to be dishonest. — Al Capone

The word *crime* has its roots in the Latin *crimen,* meaning judgment, accusation, and offense, and its origins are clearly legalistic. Numerous social scientists and legal scholars have offered definitions of crime within this legal perspective. The late Edwin H. Sutherland, perhaps the most renowned American criminologist of the mid-twentieth century, suggested that "the essential characteristic of crime is that it is behavior which is prohibited by the State and against which the State may react."[18] *Black's Law Dictionary* defines crime as "a positive or negative act in violation of the penal law; an offense against the state."[19] In the field of criminal justice it is defined simply as "a violation of the criminal law."[20] Yet these definitions, while correct in focusing on the law to delineate the limits of crime, fail to offer the kind of precision necessary for a full understanding of the term. We cannot simply call crime a violation of the law, for there are numerous circumstances under which identical behaviors would not be classified as criminal.

However, lawyer and sociologist Paul W. Tappan has offered a definition that does mark the major boundaries of this phenomenon:

> Crime is an intentional act or omission in violation of criminal law (statutory and case law), committed without defense or justification, and sanctioned by the state as a felony or misdemeanor.[21]

Tappan's definition will be accepted as the meaning of the term crime throughout this text. It is analyzed in detail in the following sections.

Crime Is an Intentional Act or Omission

Central to the American system of law is the philosophy that a person cannot be punished for his or her thoughts. Thus, for there to be a crime, an act or the omission of an act that is legally required must be present. A person may wish to commit a crime, or think of committing a crime, but the crime does not occur until the action takes place. If one were to consider murdering a relative, there would be no crime until the killing, or its attempt, had actually occurred. Furthermore, one could conceivably *plan* for a long while to commit a crime,

Since crime is an intentional act or omission, persons cannot be punished for their thoughts.

but again, the crime would not necessarily come into being until the action took place. In this respect, consider the case of Jack Gilbert Graham, who hoped to gain access to his mother's large estate by killing her. Graham went through some elaborate preparations to construct a bomb that he would place in her luggage, set to detonate ten minutes after her plane departed from Denver's Stapleton Airport bound for Seattle. In spite of his planning and his intent, had he dismantled the bomb and not placed it in his mother's suitcase, there would have been no crime. However, Graham did put his plan into action, and in the early evening of November 1, 1955, United Airlines flight 629 was blown apart over a beet farm near Longmont, Colorado, killing all 44 passengers and crew members aboard.[22]

Contrast the case of Jack Gilbert Graham, who acted alone, with the well-known Leopold and Loeb killing of 14-year-old Robert Franks. Nathan F. Leopold, Jr., was a graduate of the University of Chicago and the son of a multimillionaire shipping magnate; Richard A. Loeb was a University of Michigan graduate and the son of Sears, Roebuck and Company's vice president, Albert A. Loeb. Leopold and Loeb had structured what they felt would be the perfect crime — the kidnapping, ransoming, and killing of some innocent youth. Their planning extended over many weeks, and involved renting a car; opening a bank account for the ransom money; riding trains to the tentative ransom site; purchasing rope, a chisel, and hydrochloric acid with which they would garrote, stab, and mutilate their victim; gathering rags with which they would bind and gag the victim; selecting wading boots to be worn in the swamp where they would leave the victim's body; preparing a ransom note; and discussing potential victims. Unlike Graham, who had acted alone and who would have been innocent of any crime had he not planted the bomb in his mother's belongings, Leopold and Loeb were already guilty of **conspiracy** to commit crime (see Exhibit 2.2). Their very agreement to murder, combined with their extensive preparations, constituted a crime. When Leopold and

Conspiracy: Concert in criminal purpose.

Nathan F. Leopold, Jr., and Richard A. Loeb

Conspiracy to Commit Crime

Conspiracy means *concert in criminal purpose.* It refers to the combining of two or more persons to accomplish either an unlawful purpose or a lawful purpose by some unlawful means. Under federal statutes, four elements must be present for the crime of conspiracy to exist:

1. An act of agreement between two or more persons
2. An "object," or intention to do some unlawful act
3. A plan or scheme for accomplishing the object crime
4. An overt act implementing the agreement and intent

Thus, under federal law (18 U.S.C. 371),

if two or more persons conspire either to commit any offense against the United States, or any agency thereof in any manner or for any purpose, and one or more of such persons shall do any act to effect the object of the conspiracy, each shall be fined not more than $10,000 or imprisoned not more than five years, or both.

Many state conspiracy laws are similar to those at the federal level, but in some jurisdictions conspiracy becomes an offense as soon as the agreement to commit crime takes place. In most instances, however, some overt act that furthers the conspired crime must be apparent. This does not necessarily mean, though, that the intended crime must take place or even be attempted. And the overt act of implementation could be some minor noncriminal activity that sets the conspired plan into motion.

Legislatures have made conspiracy a separate offense because they perceive collective criminal activity to be a greater risk than individual actions.

Loeb selected Robert Franks as their victim, and then abducted and murdered him, their crimes advanced from the conspiracy stage to include kidnapping and homicide.[23]

Failure to act in a particular case can also be a crime if there is some legal duty to do so. Consider, for example, the case of *People* v. *Beardsley,*[24] which involved a man who spent a weekend with his mistress. After a serious argument, the woman took an overdose of morphine tablets and the man made no attempt to obtain medical help to save her life. His failure to assist her did *not* constitute a crime. Although he may have had a moral obligation to help her, he had *no legal duty* to do so. There was no contractual relationship as might exist between parents and a day care center or between a patient and a hospital; there was no status relationship that imposed a legal duty such as that between husband and wife; and there was no legal statute imposing a legal duty on the man.

Misprision of felony is the concealment of a felony committed by another.

Less complex instances of failures to act that constitute crime can be found under the misprision of felony statutes. **Misprision of felony** refers to the offense of concealing a felony committed by another, even if the party to the concealment had not been part of the planning or execution of the felony.[25] Thus, if two individuals should overhear a group discussing their participation in a recent bank robbery, that couple would be guilty of misprision of felony if they failed to report the conversation to the authorities.

Criminal Intent

For an act or omission to be a crime, the law further requires criminal intent, or *mens rea* — from the Latin meaning "guilty mind." The concept of *mens rea* is based on the assumption that people have the capacity to control their behavior and to choose between alternative courses of conduct. Thus, the notion of criminal intent suggests the actor's awareness of what is right and wrong under the law with an intention to violate the law, as contrasted with the retarded, the insane, or the young, who may not have their full use of reason.

Most legal commentaries divide *mens rea* into two basic types of intent: specific and general. *Specific intent* is present when one can gather from the circumstances of the crime that the offender must have consciously and subjectively desired the prohibited result. In the Leopold and Loeb case mentioned earlier, specific criminal intent was present. From the facts surrounding the case, it is clear that the murder of the victim was specifically intended. Similarly, the crime of burglary reflects the notion of specific intent. Burglary involves two broad elements: entry into the dwelling of another and the intention to commit a crime (usually a theft) therein. The burglar manifests specific intent because he or she consciously desires the prohibited result — theft.

By contrast, consider the case of a man outraged by his neighbor's barking dog. He expresses his disfavor by warning that if the dog is not quieted, he will shoot the animal. When the threat is ignored and the dog continues to bark, the angered man fires three shots through his neighbor's window intending to kill the dog. Instead, one of the bullets kills his neighbor. Although specific intent is not present in this case, general intent is. As such, *general intent* refers to a matter of conscious wrongdoing from which a prohibited result follows, without a subjective desire for the accomplishment of that result. Or more specifically, general criminal intent involves the conscious and intentional commission of a crime when the specific result of that crime was not necessarily intended.

Although criminal intent, whether specific or general, is necessary for an act to be a crime, there are some exceptions to this rule of law. Under the doctrine of **respondeat superior**, liability can be imposed on an employer for certain illegal acts of his employees committed during the course and scope of their employment. This doctrine is generally directed at the protection of the public, as is indicated in the two following examples. In one case, the president of a pharmaceutical company was charged and convicted of a violation of the Pure Food and Drug Act of 1906. One provision of the act had required proper labeling of drugs, and unknown to him, his product had been mislabeled by his employees.[26] In another case, the defendant owned a tavern and his bartender had served minors in violation of the Pennsylvania Liquor Code. The tavern owner was neither aware that minors were served alcoholic beverages, nor was he present when the event occurred. Nevertheless, under the doctrine of *respondeat superior* he was convicted. On appeal, the Pennsylvania Supreme Court upheld the conviction with the following statement:

> While an employer in almost all cases is not criminally responsible for the unlawful acts of his employees, unless he consents to, approves, or participates in such acts, courts all over the nation have struggled for years in applying this rule within the framework of "controlling the sale of intoxicating liquor." We find that the intent of the legislature in enacting this Code was not only to eliminate the common law requirement of a *mens rea*, but also to place a very high degree of responsibility upon the holder of a liquor license to make certain that neither he nor anyone in his employ commit any of the prohibited acts upon the

Mens rea (criminal intent): A person's awareness of what is right and wrong under the law with an intention to violate the law.

Specific intent

General intent

Respondeat superior: The doctrine under which liability is imposed upon an employer for the acts of employees that are committed in the course and scope of their employment.

licensed premises. Such a burden of care is imposed upon the licensee in order to protect the public from the potentially noxious effects of an inherently dangerous business.[27]

Violation of Criminal Law

Criminal law: The branch of jurisprudence that deals with offenses committed against the safety and order of the state.

For an act, or its omission to be a crime, not only must there be criminal intent, but the behavior must be in violation of the criminal law. **Criminal law,** as opposed to noncriminal law or civil law, is that branch of jurisprudence that deals with offenses committed against the safety and order of the state. As such, criminal law relates to actions that are considered so dangerous, or potentially so, that they threaten the welfare of the society as a whole. And it is for this reason that in criminal cases the government brings the action against the accused. **Civil law,** by contrast, is the body of principles that determines private rights and liabilities. In these cases, one individual brings an action against another individual—a *plaintiff* versus a *defendant*—as opposed to the state versus an accused, as in criminal cases. More specifically, civil law is structured to regulate the rights between individuals or organizations; it involves such areas as divorce, child support, contracts, and property rights. Civil law also includes *torts,* civil wrongs for which the law gives redress.

Civil law

A plaintiff is the party complaining in an action or proceeding. A defendant is the person against whom an action or proceeding is brought.

Statutory law

Case law

Criminal law includes a variety of types: statutory law, case law, and common law. **Statutory law** is law passed from the legislatures, which create it by statute. Each state has a statutory criminal code, as does the federal government. The laws that define the boundaries of such commonly known offenses as homicide, rape, burglary, robbery, and larceny are generally of a statutory nature. By contrast, **case law** is law that results from court interpretations of statutory law or from court decisions where rules have not been fully codified or have been found to be vague or in error.

A classic example of case law is the Supreme Court decision involving ***Robinson* v. *California,***[28] which resulted from Robinson's appeal of his conviction as a narcotic addict under a section of the California Health and Safety Code, which read:

***Robinson* v. *California:* In a new approach to the Eighth Amendment's ban on "cruel and unusual punishments," the United States Supreme Court declared in 1962 that sickness may not be made a crime, nor may sick people be punished for being sick. The Court viewed narcotic addiction to be a "sickness," and held that a state cannot make it a punishable offense any more than it could put a person in jail "for the 'crime' of having a common cold."**

> No person shall use, or be under the influence, or be addicted to the use of narcotics, excepting when administered by or under the direction of a person licensed by the State to prescribe and administer narcotics. It shall be the burden of the defense to show that it comes within the exception. Any person convicted of violating any provision of this section is guilty of a misdemeanor and shall be sentenced to serve a term of not less than 90 days nor more than one year in the county jail.

Robinson had been convicted after a jury trial in the Municipal Court of Los Angeles. In terms of evidence, the arresting officer testified that he had observed scar tissue, discoloration, and what appeared to be needle marks on the inside of the defendant's left arm, and that the defendant had admitted to the occasional use of narcotics. Under the California law, the use of narcotics was considered a status or condition—not an act; it was a continuing offense that could subject the offender to arrest at any time before he or she "reformed." Robinson was convicted of the offense charged. He then took his case to the Appellate Department of the Los Angeles County Superior Court, where the original judgment of conviction was affirmed. Upon appeal to the United States Supreme Court, the decision was reversed on the grounds that status offenses such as "being addicted to the use of narcotics" were unconstitutional, and that imprisonment for such an offense was cruel and unusual punishment in violation of the Eighth Amendment to the Constitution. Thus, the *Robinson* v. *California* case, after the lower courts' decisions were reversed, represented case law in that it defined narcotic addiction as a status that was no longer punishable under the law.

Common law refers to those customs, traditions, judicial decisions, and other materials that guide courts in decision making but that have not been enacted by the legislatures into statutes or embodied in the Constitution. Among the better-known aspects of common law are the rights set forth in the Declaration of Independence, and other doctrines protecting life, liberty, and property.

Common law

Defense or Justification

For an act (or the omission thereof) to be a crime, it must not only be intentional and in violation of the criminal law, but it must also be committed without defense or justification. *Defense* is a broad term that can refer to any number of causes and rights of action that would serve to mitigate or excuse an individual's guilt in a criminal offense. Defenses that have been raised include insanity, mistake of fact, mistake of law, duress and consent, consent of the victim, entrapment, and justification.

Insanity is any unsoundness of mind, madness, mental alienation, or want of reason, memory, and intelligence that prevents an individual from comprehending the nature and consequences of his or her acts or from distinguishing between right and wrong conduct. Insanity is a legal concept rather than a medical one. Furthermore, it is a complex legal issue. A few jurisdictions recognize that some defendants can be partially insane in respect to the circumstances surrounding the commission of a crime, but sane as to other matters. The cornerstone of the insanity defense emerged from the case of Daniel M'Naghten in 1843. M'Naghten killed the secretary to England's Sir Robert Peel. At his trial he claimed that at the time he committed the act he had not been of a sound state of mind. From this came the **M'Naghten Rule** — the "right-or-wrong" test of criminal responsibility — which states:

Insanity

The M'Naghten Rule

> If the accused was possessed of sufficient understanding when he committed the criminal act to know what he was doing and to know that it was wrong, he is responsible therefor, but if he did not know the nature and quality of the act or did know what he was doing but did not know that it was wrong, he is not responsible.[29]

The M'Naghten test has been severely criticized on the grounds that it is arbitrary and applies to only a small percentage of people who are actually mentally ill. In 1954 the U.S. court of appeals for the District of Columbia broadened the M'Naghten test in favor of what has become known as the Durham Rule. In *Durham* v. *United States*[30] it was held that an accused is not criminally responsible if he or she suffers from a diseased or defective mental condition at the time the unlawful act is committed. This rule has also been criticized, but on opposite grounds from M'Naghten. Critics claim that it is far too broad and places too much power in the hands of psychiatrists and juries for determining the legal issue of insanity (see Exhibit 2.3).

Mistake of fact is any erroneous conviction of fact or circumstance resulting in some act that would not otherwise have been undertaken. Mistake of fact becomes a defense when an individual commits a prohibited act in good

Mistake of fact

faith and with a reasonable belief that certain facts are correct, which, if they were indeed accurate, would have made the act innocent. Further, the mistake must be an honest one and not the result of negligence or poor deliberation.

For example, if Smith walks away with Jones's suitcase thinking that it is his own, Smith's defense would be that he was operating under a mistake of fact since both parties had identical luggage. Such a mistake precludes Smith from having criminal intent and, as a result, he has a defense against a conviction for larceny. Mistake of fact has been used as a defense in cases of statutory rape. Statutory rape refers to sexual intercourse with a female under a certain age (usually 16 or 18) despite her consent. Although a defendant may claim that his underage female partner looked older than her actual age, or even misrepresented her age, the courts are decidedly mixed in their acceptance of the defense. In 1984, for example, the Utah Supreme Court accepted the defense of reasonable mistake of age on the grounds that "a person cannot be found guilty of a criminal offense unless he harbors a requisite criminal state of mind."[31] During the same year, however, the Michigan Supreme Court refused to recognize the defense, holding that the statutory-rape laws impose criminal liability without requiring proof of specific criminal intent.[32]

EXHIBIT 2.3

The Insanity Plea on Trial

The defense of "not guilty by reason of insanity" has been debated for generations. Critics of the defense argue that defendants acquitted on insanity pleas spend less time in mental institutions than do those sent to prison for similar crimes. Supporters of the insanity defense claim that it would be morally unjust to convict and punish an individual who acted under the condition of an unsound mind. As Harvard University law professor Alan M. Dershowitz once put it, "Would anyone seriously think of convicting someone for murder who thought he was shooting a robot or squeezing a melon?"

John W. Hinckley, Jr., was tried in the shooting of President Ronald Reagan in 1981. His acquittal on insanity grounds by a Washington, D.C., jury in 1982 fully rekindled the controversy over the insanity defense.

Confidence was lost in the criminal justice system because in this case it was unable to punish a man who admitted trying to assassinate the president of the United States. There were calls for reform, even abolition of the insanity defense entirely. An ABC News poll found that the majority of American people opposed laws allowing defendants to plead not guilty by reason of insanity, while an Associated Press/NBC survey revealed that almost 90 percent of the public believed too many murderers were using the insanity plea to avoid incarceration.

In the aftermath of the Hinckley verdict, Montana and Idaho barred the insanity defense except in extreme cases. Several other states adopted a procedure that permits juries to find defendants "guilty but mentally ill." The aim of such a finding is to guarantee psychiatric treatment to

an offender while insuring that he or she will serve as much prison time as another convicted person. Moreover, the U.S. Supreme Court's decision in 1983 in *Jones* v. *U.S.* (US SupCt [1983] 33 CrL 3233) held that persons found not guilty of crimes by reason of insanity may be confined to mental hospitals for a longer time than they would have spent in prison if convicted—a ruling that applied to John W. Hinckley, Jr.

Yet despite the new state statutes and the ruling in *Jones,* in the insanity defense has actually been expanded in this post-Hinckley era of the 1980s. A number of Vietnam veterans suffering from the disorientation and flashbacks associated with P-TSD (post-traumatic stress disorder) have successfully argued that the intense reliving of their war experiences destroyed their ability to distinguish between right

Mistake of law is any want of knowledge or acquaintance with the laws of the land insofar as they apply to the act, relation, duty, or matter under consideration. There is a well-worn cliché that "ignorance of the law is no excuse," which suggests that the notion of mistake of law offers no release from prosecution of such a crime. Indeed, simple ignorance of forbidden behavior is not usually an acceptable defense against crime; all persons are assumed to have knowledge of the law. This is true for both citizens and aliens alike. If an Englishman, for example, were to take a motor tour of the United States and unknowingly drive on the left side of the road as is the law in his native land, his ignorance would be no defense against a U.S. traffic violation. Similarly, in many jurisdictions it is a crime to fail to come to the aid of a police officer when so ordered and if the request is not hazardous to the citizen. This law is not well known to most citizens. Nevertheless, should an individual fail to comply with such an order on the basis of ignorance, his or her lack of knowledge of the law would not be an adequate defense against the crime. In contrast, however, as the Supreme Court ruled in *Lambert* **v.** *California*,[33] ignorance of the law may be a defense against crime if the law has not been made reasonably well known (see Exhibit 2.4).

> **Mistake of law is no release from prosecution.**

> *Lambert v. California*

and wrong. The P-TSD–insanity defense has been used to acquit veterans accused of homicide, armed robberies, and drug law violations.

The problem with the insanity defense is that *insanity* is a legal, not a medical, term. Furthermore, there is little agreement on the actual meaning of the word. On the other hand, and in contrast to conventional wisdom, few serious offenders use the insanity plea to avoid incarceration. Studies demonstrate that the plea is used in less than one percent of serious criminal cases, is rarely successful, and when it is defendants generally spend more time in mental institutions than they would have spent in prison had they been convicted.

Sources: *National Law Journal*, May 3, 1982, pp. 1, 11–13; Valerie P. Hans and Dan Slater, "John Hinckley, Jr., and the Insanity Defense: The Public's Verdict," *Public Opinion Quarterly* 47 (1983): 202–212; *Psychology Today*, August 1984, pp. 30–38; *U.S. News & World Report*, June 27, 1983, pp. 52–55; *Time*, July 5, 1982, pp. 22, 25–27; *Newsweek*, May 24, 1982, pp. 56–61.

John W. Hinckley, Jr., who attempted to assassinate President Ronald Reagan in 1981, holds a pistol to his head in this self-portrait.

Duress and consent

> **Duress and consent** is any unlawful constraints exercised upon an individual forcing him or her to do some act that would not have been done otherwise. Duress implies that one is not acting of his or her own free will, and the American system of law emphasizes both criminal intent and responsibility. A typical example of duress and consent has been seen often in television and movie themes. The local bank official is forced to aid the thieves in a bank robbery while his wife and children are held captive by a second group of bandits. If the banker fails to cooperate, his family will be harmed. In this case duress and consent is a legal defense against crime, since there is no criminal intent and since the rule includes injuries, threats, and restraints exercised not only against the individual, but on his or her parent, child, or spouse as well. However, such threats or restraints must be against the person (as opposed to property), and they must be immediate (not future). Had the bank official been threatened with the slaying of his family at some future date, there would be no immediate and imposing threat. Similarly, if the threat was to destroy his house, again the notion of duress would be a poor defense.

Consent of the victim

> **Consent of the victim** is any voluntary yielding of the will of the victim, accompanied by his or her deliberation, agreeing to the act of the offending party. The victim's consent to a crime can be a defense recognized by the law, but there are several elements to a defense of consent. First, the victim must be capable of giving consent, and this rule excludes any consent offered by the insane, the retarded, or those below the age of reason. Second, the offense must be a "consentable" crime. Murder is considered to be a nonconsentable crime, as is statutory rape. Furthermore, there are offenses such as disorderly conduct for which no consent can generally be given. Third, the consent cannot be obtained by fraud. For example, should an auto mechanic suggest to a customer that her transmission must be fully replaced when indeed only a

In *Lambert,* the petitioner was found guilty of failing to register, fined $250, and placed on probation for three years. On appeal to the United States Supreme Court, the conviction was reversed. The Court recognized the importance of the rule that ignorance of the law is not an excuse. However, as Justice William O. Douglas commented:

Due process places some limits on its exercise. Engrained in our concept of due process is the requirement of notice. Notice is sometimes essential so that the citizen has the chance to defend charges. . . . Notice is required in a myriad of situations where a penalty or forfeiture might be suffered for mere failure to act.

That is, where a person did not know of the duty to register and where there was no proof of the probability of such knowledge, he or she may not be convicted with due process. Were it otherwise, the evil would be as great as when the law is written in print too fine to read or in a language foreign to the community.

small bolt requires tightening, the victim's consent to have it replaced is not a legal defense. Fourth, the person giving consent must have the authority to do so. Although one party may have the right to give consent to have his or her property taken, such authority cannot be given to the property of another party.

Entrapment is the inducement of an individual to commit a crime not contemplated by him or her, undertaken for the sole purpose of instituting a criminal prosecution against the offender. Cases of entrapment occur when law enforcement officers, or civilians acting at their behest, induce a person to commit a crime that he or she would not have otherwise undertaken. *Inducement* is the key word in the entrapment defense and refers to the fact that the accused had no intention of committing the crime until persuaded to do so by the law officer. Should police officer Jones approach Smith and convince him to rob Brown, and then place Smith under arrest after the crime is committed, the defense of police entrapment would be available. Similarly, in some jurisdictions, if a vice squad officer in plain clothes approaches a prostitute and offers her a sum of money for sexual favors, and then arrests her after their encounter, entrapment might be an available defense. Even though the accused is by profession a prostitute, the case could nevertheless be one of entrapment since the particular offense for which she was arrested had occurred only because of police inducement.

In recent years, the strength of the entrapment defense has been weakened by court decisions that have considered the offender's "predisposition" to committing a crime. In the 1976 case of *Hampton* v. *United States,*[34] the Supreme Court ruled that it was not entrapment for an undercover agent to supply illicit drugs to a suspected dealer and then for another agent to act as a buyer, when there was reason to believe that the suspect was inclined, or

Entrapment

"predisposed," to commit the crime anyway. What makes this case different from that of the prostitute is the legality of the primary behavior in question. Sexual intercourse, whether the female partner is or is not a prostitute, is generally legal behavior. What constituted the crime was her acceptance of money for the sexual act, and what constituted entrapment was the plain-clothes officer's inducement of money. In contrast, Hampton's dealing in illicit drugs was illegal behavior, and it was not the undercover agent's inducement that made the primary act illegal. Furthermore, as opposed to the case of Officer Jones convincing Smith to rob Brown, Hampton was reputedly a drug dealer while Smith was not by trade a robber.

Justification

Justification is any just cause or excuse for the commission of an act that would otherwise be a crime. The notion of justification as a defense against crime typically involves the use of force or violence in the protection of one's person or property, the lives and property of others, the prevention of crime, and the apprehension of offenders. *Justifiable homicide* includes those instances of death that result from legal demands — the execution of a duly condemned prisoner, the killing of a fleeing inmate by a prison guard, or the shooting of an armed robber by a police officer. *Excusable homicide* includes deaths from accidents or misfortunes that may occur during some lawful act. Self-defense or the defense of some other individual can be viewed as either a justifiable or excusable act depending on the circumstances surrounding the particular case.

Beyond these general areas, some jurisdictions have particular statutes that may extend the boundaries of justifiable cause or excuse. Until 1974, for example, a Texas law defined as justifiable homicide a husband's shooting and killing his wife's lover if he found them in the very midst of the act of adultery. The law specified, however, that the actual shooting had to occur before the couple separated and that the husband must not have been a party to, or approved of, the adulterous connection. (Interestingly, this Texas statute did not extend to women who found their husbands engaging in adultery.)

Finally, there are many issues raised as defenses against crime that in most instances are not allowed by the courts. Although the First Amendment to the Constitution guarantees religious freedom, *religious practice* that violates criminal law can generally not be used to justify or excuse criminal conduct. Similarly, if it is *custom* that a given law is typically not enforced, such a tradition does not justify the violation of that law. Finally, many have attempted to use *intoxication* as a defense against crime, claiming that while under the influence of alcohol or drugs they were not in control of their behavior and therefore not criminally responsible. However, most jurisdictions make a distinction between voluntary and involuntary intoxication. Voluntary intoxication is not a defense under most circumstances. In cases of involuntary intoxication, however, where liquor or drugs are forced upon an individual, a reasonable defense can be mounted depending on the defendant's "degree of intoxication" at the time of the criminal act.

The necessity defense

On the other hand, there have been a number of unusual defenses that the courts have periodically accepted. In 1984, a New Jersey appeals court ruled that medical *necessity* was a legitimate defense for a man charged with possession of marijuana. The decision involved a quadriplegic who argued that he smoked marijuana to relieve his chronic pain, and that the marijuana had fewer side effects than prescription drugs.[35] Similarly, in *People* v. *Lovercamp*[36] in 1975 and *Jorgensen* v. *State*[37] in 1984, courts have accepted the necessity defense for inmates charged with escaping prison custody. In both cases, the prisoners were faced with threats of forcible sexual attack or death (see Chapter 16). And finally, in a 1985 Alaska trial there was the *traditional-conduct* defense. Jack Jones, an Eskimo, had been charged with several counts of child sexual abuse as the result of swatting at the crotch areas of his son and grandson and pulling down their pants. In a traditional-conduct defense, it was argued that Jones was partaking in a long-standing tradition of teasing behavior meant to teach young boys to laugh off adversity, protect themselves from attack, and respond quickly.[38]

The traditional-conduct defense

Law Sanctioned by the State

Under the American system of law the maxim *nullum crimen sine poena* (no crime without punishment) dictates that a law must be written, that persons cannot be tried for acts that are not crimes in law, and that persons cannot be punished for acts for which the state provides no penalty. In the absence of such doctrines a social order would quickly fall into a state of *anomie.* If a legal system had no written law, *any* act could potentially be construed as a crime at the pleasure of the court or state, resulting in a situation of ironbound tyranny. Furthermore, if certain types of behavior were defined as crimes but no penalties were embodied in the law for their commission, then again a hopeless level of confusion and disregard for law would likely ensue. In contrast, American law consists of written codes describing the various prohibited forms of behavior and the range of punishments that would occur for their commission.

Anomie: A condition within a society or group in which there exists a weakened respect or lack of adherence to some or most of the norms.

The law must be specific, however, for there are many acts that, depending upon the attendant circumstances, may or may not be crimes. The physical act of sexual intercourse, for example, describes any number of situations, including adultery, fornication, forcible and statutory rape, seduction, and incest. And, in addition to these six different crimes, it is also a normal, lawful act between mates. However, as a lawful act even between married couples, the act might be called obscenity, pornography, indecent exposure, or disorderly conduct, depending on the place it occurs. Further, at one time the ethnicity of each partner might have been considered, and it could have been called *miscegenation* (marriage involving people of different races), which was a crime. Thus, the law must be specific as to what sex acts are prohibited and among whom and where and under what circumstances they may and may not occur.

Also significant in American criminal law is the doctrine that only the offender can be punished. This posture has its roots in the Old Testament, that "every man shall be put to death for his own sin," and has endured in current legal doctrine. However, there are a variety of situations in which this may not necessarily be the case. Recall, for example, the doctrine of *respondeat superior,* which says an employer can be held responsible for certain crimes of his employees.

Felonies and Misdemeanors

Crimes have been classified in many ways, among which are *mala in se* and *mala prohibita* offenses. Acts are considered to be *mala in se* when they are inherently and essentially evil — immoral in their nature and injurious in their consequences — such as murder, rape, and theft. *Mala prohibita* crimes are those that may not necessarily be wrong in themselves, but that are wrong simply because they have been prohibited by statute. Moral turpitude, that is, depravity or baseness of conduct, is the basis of distinction between these two types of crime, but since attitudes regarding moral turpitude tend to vary from one jurisdiction to the next, the distinction that is almost universally used instead is that between felonies and misdemeanors.

Felonies

Misdemeanors

Historically, under common law felonies were crimes punishable by death or forfeiture of property, and included such offenses as murder, rape, theft, arson, and robbery. Misdemeanors were considered lesser offenses that lacked the moral reprehensibility of felonies. The current distinction between the two is similar. In most jurisdictions, **felonies** are serious crimes punishable by death or by imprisonment in a federal or state penitentiary. **Misdemeanors** are minor offenses generally punishable by no more than a $1,000 fine and/or one year of imprisonment, typically in a local institution. The felony – misdemeanor classification goes beyond the *mala in se – mala prohibita* distinction, since a number of felonies fail to reflect moral turpitude. For example, the crimes of prison escape, wiretapping, carrying a concealed deadly weapon, or possession of forgery instruments are felonies in some jurisdictions in spite of the perpetrator's lack of moral turpitude.

In the legal codes of most jurisdictions, felonies and misdemeanors encompass the boundaries of what is defined as crime. In a few states, however, there is a third generic category. This category has resulted from the

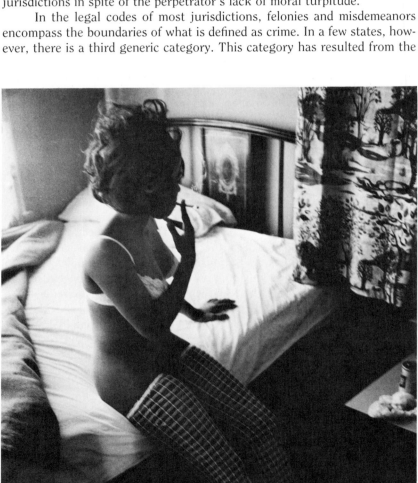

Prostitution—mala in se, or a consequence of the legislation of morality?

redefinition of certain offenses as less serious than misdemeanors; such offenses are generally referred to as *violations*. In the New York Penal Law, for example:

> "Violation" means an offense for which a sentence to a term of imprisonment in excess of fifteen days cannot be imposed.[39]

Included in this category of violations are such minor offenses as disorderly conduct, loitering, public intoxication, and patronizing a prostitute.

Criminal Law

Law is experience developed by reason and applied continually to further experience. —Roscoe Pound

---

Law is a statement of the circumstances in which the public force will be brought to bear upon man through the courts. —Justice Oliver Wendell Holmes, Jr.

Legal scholars Sir Frederick Pollock and F. W. Maitland have commented that "law may be taken for every purpose, save that of strictly philosophical inquiry, to be the sum of the rules administered by the courts of justice."[40] To legal scholar Sir James Fitzjames Stephen, law is "a system of commands addressed by the sovereign of the state to his subjects, imposing duties and enforced by punishments."[41] There have been numerous attempts to frame more philosophical definitions of law, but few have been widely accepted. Even more numerous have been definitions that are more pragmatic. These have all generally signified that law is a body of rules of human conduct that the courts recognize and enforce.

The origins of law are buried in antiquity, for they likely date before the beginning of recorded history. It would be safe to assume, however, that even the crudest forms of primitive social organization needed some regulation, and law quickly evolved to fill that need.

Since the beginnings of civilization a number of distinct legal systems have emerged, including the Egyptian, Mesopotamian, Chinese, Hindu, Hebrew, Greek, Roman, Celtic, Germanic, Catholic church (canon), Japanese, Islamic, Slavic, Romanesque, and Anglican.[42] The earliest of these was the Egyptian, dating to perhaps 4000 B.C., followed by the Mesopotamian in 3500 B.C., and the Chinese in 3000 B.C. United States law is comparatively recent; it draws from Greek, Roman, and Catholic church law, but has its major roots in the Anglican or English common law. Other sources of U.S. law include the state and federal constitutions, statutory law, and the regulations of administrative agencies.

Common Law

The history of common law can be traced to eleventh-century England, when the existing collection of rules, customs, and traditions were declared the law of the land by King Edward the Confessor. Much of it was unwritten, "preserved mainly in the breasts and closets of the clergy, who, as a rule, were the only persons educated in the law; in the knowledge and recollection of the thanes [barons] and the land owners whose lands and whose persons were governed by it; and in the traditions handed down from fathers to sons."[43] During the years after the Norman Conquest in 1066 when William the Conqueror seized the English throne, he found a system of law that was not based on statute, but on the customs of the people as reflected in the decisions of judges:

> Common law was judge-made law—molded, refined, examined, and changed in the crucible of actual decision, and handed down from generation to generation in the form of reported cases. In theory, the judges drew their decisions from existing principles of law; ultimately these principles reflected the living values, attitudes, and ethical ideas of the English people. In practice, the judges relied on their own past actions, which they modified under the pressure of changing times and changing patterns of litigation.[44]

As time passed, a process emerged whereby this largely unwritten customary law of the land was translated into specific rules. As judges reached their decisions in judicial proceedings, a body of maxims and principles developed that was derived, in theory, from customs. The result was a set of legal rules in the form of judicial decisions, rather than legislative statutes, that provided precedents for the resolution of future disputes. It is this body of decisions that became what is referred to as common law. Thus, common law was case law as opposed to law created by statute. Much of common law, furthermore, reflected natural law ideas of right and wrong, as well as direct statements from the Holy Scriptures.

The early criminal laws of the American colonies developed within the tradition and structure of English common law and the English charters for the founding of settlements in the New World. As the colonies became more mature, they developed their own legal systems, but in substance these varied little from English common law. The *Original Criminal Code of 1676,* for example, handed down by the Duke of York and applied to the residents of the Pennsylvania colony, was among the early bodies of law in the New World. Much of it was based on common law, combined with a series of rules structured for maintaining British dominance over colonial interests. The influence of biblical proscriptions was also apparent in this code, as evidenced by its statement of capital offenses:

1. If any person within this Government shall by direct, express, impious or presumptuous ways, deny the true God and His attributes, he shall be put to death.
2. If any person shall commit any wilful and premeditated murder he shall be put to death.
3. If any person slayeth another with a sword or dagger who hath no weapon to defend himself, he shall be put to death.
4. If any man shall slay, or cause another to be slain by lying in wait privily for him or by poisoning or any other such wicked conspiracy, he shall be put to death. . . .
5. If any man or woman shall lie with any beast or brute creature by carnal copulation they shall be put to death, and the beast shall be burned.
6. If any man lieth with mankind as he lieth with a woman, they shall be put to death, unless the one party were forced or be under fourteen years of age, in which case he shall be punished at the discretion of the Court of Assizes.

7. If any person forcibly stealeth or carrieth away any mankind, he shall be put to death.

8. If any man bear false witness maliciously and on purpose to take away a man's life, he shall be put to death.

9. If any man traitorously deny his Majesty's right and titles to his Crowns and Dominions, or shall raise armies to resist his authority, he shall be put to death.

10. If any man shall treacherously conspire or publickly attempt to invade or surprise any town or towns, fort or forts, within this Government, he shall be put to death.

11. If any child or children, above sixteen years of age, and of sufficient understanding, shall smite their natural father or mother, unless thereunto provoked and forced for their self-protection from death or maiming, at the complaint of said father and mother, and not otherwise, there being sufficient witnesses thereof, that child or those children so offending shall be put to death.[45]

Other Sources of Criminal Law: Constitutional Law, Statutory Law, and Administrative Law

Although English common law rests at the foundation of American criminal law, contemporary criminal codes also reflect the content of constitutional law, administrative law, and federal and state statutory laws. At the apex of American legal system is **constitutional law,** or law set forth in the Constitution of the United States and in the constitutions of the various states. Constitutional law is the supreme law of the land. As such, it presents the legal rules and principles that define the nature and limits of governmental power as well as the rights and duties of individuals in relation to the state and its governing organs, and that are interpreted and extended by courts exercising the power of judicial review.

The U.S. Constitution, which embodies the fundamental principles upon which the affairs of the United States are conducted, was drawn up at the Federal Constitutional Convention in Philadelphia in 1787. The Constitution was signed on September 17, 1787, was ratified by nine states by June 21, 1788, and superseded the Articles of Confederation — the original charter of the United States — which had been in force since 1781. It is brief and concise, and includes a preamble, seven articles, and twenty-six amendments. Although not all of the Constitution relates to criminal law, Supreme Court and lower court interpretations of its articles and amendments have had a direct impact on criminal law and criminal procedure, as will be seen throughout this text.

Next in order of authority to constitutional law are the federal statutes, enacted by Congress, and state statutes, ordained by state legislatures. Federal statutes must conform to the prescriptions and proscriptions of the Constitution, and state statutes must conform to the Constitution as well as to that of the jurisdiction in which they are enacted.

With fifty separate state legislatures creating laws, and an even greater number of separate court systems interpreting them, the application of statutory laws becomes exceedingly complex. Furthermore, statutory laws are far from uniform. For this reason criminal laws established by statute tend to vary from one jurisdiction to another, and what may be a violation of the criminal law in one state may not necessarily be so in another.

Constitutional law: The legal rules and principles that define the nature and limits of governmental power, and the duties and rights of individuals in relation to the state.

Administrative law: A branch of
public law that deals with the
powers and duties of government
agencies.

Finally, criminal law can descend from **administrative law,** a branch of public law that deals with the powers and duties of government agencies. More specifically, administrative law refers to the rules and regulations of administrative agencies; the thousands of decisions made by them; their orders, directives, and awards; and the court opinions dealing with appeals from the decisions and with petitions by the agencies to the courts for the enforcement of their orders and directives. Much of the content of administrative law is not concerned directly with criminal behavior. Nevertheless, the rules of certain agencies bear directly on violations of behavior that would be dealt with by the criminal courts. The scheduling of drugs by the Drug Enforcement Administration, for example, is an administrative regulation that has been translated into criminal statutes in the federal as well as many state jurisdictions.

Summary

The concept of crime is only minimally understood by most people. It goes well beyond the rather imprecise boundaries of "street crime" or the limited issues of violence and theft that are focused upon by mass-media news and entertainment. Drawing upon standards of what constitutes "sin" or immoral behavior, people have often defined crime as violations of natural law. Many social scientists have focused on the processes through which crime comes into being and have suggested that crime is a social construction. The only precise definition of crime, however, comes from a more legalistic posture. As such, crime is an intentional act or omission in violation of criminal law (statutory and case law), committed without defense or justification, and sanctioned by the state as a felony or misdemeanor.

Key Terms

administrative law **(62)**
case law **(50)**
civil law **(50)**
common law **(51)**
conspiracy **(47)**
constitutional law **(61)**
crime **(46)**

criminal law **(50)**
deviance **(43)**
felony **(58)**
Lambert v. *California* **(53)**
mens rea **(48)**
misdemeanor **(58)**
misprision of felony **(48)**

M'Naghten Rule **(51)**
natural law **(41)**
respondeat superior **(49)**
Robinson v. *California* **(50)**
statutory law **(50)**

Questions for Discussion

1. How do natural law conceptions of "sin," sociological considerations of deviance, and legalistic definitions of crime differ?
2. In the Leopold and Loeb case, when did the conspiracy actually begin? What elements were present?

3. Under what kinds of circumstances would the consent of the victim be an acceptable defense against crime? What are some examples?
4. What should be done about the insanity plea? Why?

For Further Reading

Erikson, Kai T. *Wayward Puritans: A Study in the Sociology of Deviance.* New York: Wiley, 1966.
Friedman, Lawrence M. *A History of American Law.* New York: Simon and Schuster, 1973.

Morris, Norval. *Madness and the Criminal Law.* Chicago: University of Chicago Press, 1982.

Notes

1. See James M. Reinhardt, *The Murderous Trail of Charles Starkweather* (Springfield, Ill.: Charles C. Thomas, 1960); William Allen, *Starkweather: The Story of a Mass Murderer* (Boston: Houghton Mifflin, 1976).

2. See Hugh F. Rankin, *The Golden Age of Piracy* (New York: Holt, Rinehart and Winston, 1969).

3. See G. O. W. Mueller and Freda Adler, *Outlaws of the Ocean* (New York: Hearst Marine Books, 1985).

4. *Manchester Guardian Weekly*, July 14, 1985, p. 18.

5. *USA Today*, April 23, 1985, p. 3A.

6. Hugo Grotius, *De Jure Belli ac Pacis*, cited by Cornelia Geer Le Boutillier, *American Democracy and Natural Law* (New York: Columbia University Press, 1950), p. 57.

7. See Leo Strauss, *Natural Right and History* (Chicago: University of Chicago Press, 1953).

8. See Charles Grover Haines, *The Revival of Natural Law Concepts* (Cambridge: Harvard University Press, 1930), pp. 6–11; Benjamin Fletcher Wright, *American Interpretations of Natural Law* (Cambridge: Harvard University Press, 1931), p. 6.

9. See Fernando Henriques, *Love in Action* (New York: Dutton, 1960), pp. 200–201.

10. Margaret Mead, "Incest," in *International Encyclopedia of the Social Sciences*, ed. David L. Sills (New York: Macmillan, 1968), vol. 7, pp. 115–122.

11. E. Adamson Hoebel, *The Law of Primitive Man: A Study in Comparative Legal Dynamics* (Cambridge: Harvard University Press, 1954), pp. 127–142.

12. Hermann Mannheim, *Comparative Criminology* (Boston: Houghton Mifflin, 1967), p. 47.

13. Kai T. Erikson, *Wayward Puritans: A Study in the Sociology of Deviance* (New York: Wiley, 1966), p. 6.

14. Howard S. Becker, *Outsiders: Studies in the Sociology of Deviance* (New York: Free Press, 1963), p. 9.

15. Becker, *Outsiders*, pp. 147–163.

16. See J. C. Furnas, *The Life and Times of the Late Demon Rum* (New York: Capricorn, 1973).

17. Jerome Michael and Mortimer J. Adler, *Crime, Law and Social Science* (New York: Harcourt, Brace, 1933), p. 2.

18. Edwin H. Sutherland, *White Collar Crime* (New York: Dryden, 1949), p. 31.

19. Henry Campbell Black, *Black's Law Dictionary*, 4th ed. (St. Paul, Minn.: West, 1968), p. 444.

20. George B. Rush, *Dictionary of Criminal Justice* (Boston: Holbrook, 1977), p. 92.

21. Paul W. Tappan, *Crime, Justice, and Correction* (New York: McGraw-Hill, 1960), p. 10.

22. "Case of 44 Mid-Air Murders," *Life*, November 28, 1955.

23. For the story of the Leopold and Loeb case, see Nathan F. Leopold, *Life Plus Ninety-Nine Years* (New York: Doubleday, 1958).

24. People v. Beardsley, 113 N. W. 1128 (1907).

25. United States v. Perlstein, C.C.A.N.J., 126 F. 2d 789, 798.

26. United States v. Dotterweich, 320 U.S. 277 (1943).

27. Commonwealth v. Koczwara, 155 A. 2d 825 (1959, Penna.).

28. Robinson v. California, 370 U.S. 660 (1962).

29. Black, *Black's Law Dictionary*, p. 1101.

30. Durham v. United States, C.A.D.C., 214 F. 2d 862 (1954).

31. State v. Elton, Utah SupCt (35 CrL 2071).

32. People v. Cash, Mich SupCt (35 CrL 2345).

33. Lambert v. California, 355 U.S. 225 (1957).

34. Hampton v. United States, 425 U.S. 484 (1976).

35. *New York Times*, December 9, 1984, p. 78.

36. People v. Lovercamp, 118 Cal Rptr 110 (1975).

37. Jorgensen v. State, Nev SupCt (1984) 36 CrL 2093.

38. State v. Jones, 4 FAS84-2933 (Alaska); *National Law Journal*, February 4, 1985, p. 6.

39. State of New York, *Penal Law*, 10.00 (3).

40. Sir Frederick Pollock and F. W. Maitland, *The History of English Law Before the Time of Edward I* (Cambridge: University Press, 1911), p. xxv.

41. Sir James Fitzjames Stephen, *History of the Criminal Law of England*, vol. 2 (New York: Macmillan, 1883), p. 75.

42. John H. Wigmore, *A Panorama of the World's Legal Systems* (Washington, D.C.: Washington Law Book Co., 1936), p. 4.

43. F. A. Inderwick, *The King's Peace* (London: Swan Sonnenschein, 1895), p. 3.

44. Lawrence M. Friedman, *A History of American Law* (New York: Simon and Schuster, 1973), p. 17.

45. In Harry Elmer Barnes, *The Repression of Crime: Studies in Historical Penology* (New York: George H. Doran, 1926), pp. 44–45.

3

Legal and Behavioral Aspects of Crime

Crime, like virtue, has its degrees.

— Jean Racine

EXHIBIT 3.2

Grand versus Petty Larceny by Value of Property Stolen

Alabama	$ 25	Montana	$ 150
Alaska	100	Nebraska	100
Arizona	50	Nevada	100
Arkansas	35	New Hampshire	100
California	200	New Jersey	500
Colorado	100	New Mexico	100
Connecticut	50	New York	250
Delaware	100	North Carolina	—
Florida	100	North Dakota	100
Georgia	100	Ohio	150
Hawaii	200	Oklahoma	20
Idaho	150	Oregon	200
Illinois	150	Pennsylvania	2,000
Indiana	100	Rhode Island	500
Iowa	20	South Carolina	20
Kansas	50	South Dakota	50
Kentucky	100	Tennessee	100
Louisiana	100	Texas	200
Maine	500	Utah	250
Maryland	100	Vermont	100
Massachusetts	100	Virginia	100
Michigan	100	Washington	200
Minnesota	100	West Virginia	50
Mississippi	100	Wisconsin	100
Missouri	50	Wyoming	100

SOURCE: Kenneth M. Wells and Paul B. Weston, *Criminal Law* (Santa Monica: Goodyear, 1978), p. 241. (Reprinted by permission of Random House, Inc.)

Sex Offenses

The scope of illegal sexual activity is quite broad in American society. This is due in part to the legacy of the early Puritan codes and the Holy Scriptures; to attempts to maintain standards of public decency through the legislation of morality; to requirements of community consensus as to an individual's right to sexual self-determination; and to an effort to protect those who are too young or otherwise unable to make decisions as to their own sexual conduct. Although in recent years the codes regulating many sexual activities, such as abortion, contraception, and miscegenation, have been eliminated or severely limited, the list is still long and includes the following:

Forcible rape Having sexual intercourse with a female against her will and through the use of threat of force or fear.

Statutory rape Having sexual intercourse with a female under a stated age (usually 16 or 18, but sometimes 14), with or without her consent.

Seduction The act of enticing or luring a woman of chaste character to engage in sexual intercourse by fraudulently promising to marry her or by some other false promise.

Fornication Sexual intercourse between unmarried persons.

Adultery Sexual intercourse between a man and woman, at least one of whom is married to someone else.

Incest Sexual intercourse between parent and child, any sibling pair, or between close blood relatives.

Sodomy Certain acts of sexual relationship including *fellatio* (oral intercourse with the male sex organ), *cunnilingus* (oral intercourse with the female sex organ), *buggery* (penetration of the anus), *homosexuality* (sexual relations between members of the same sex), *bestiality* (sexual intercourse with an animal), *pederasty* (unnatural intercourse between a man and a boy), and *necrophilia* (sexual intercourse with a corpse).

Indecent exposure (exhibitionism) Exposure of the sexual organs in a public place.

Lewdness Degenerate conduct in sexual behavior that is so well known that it may result in the corruption of public decency.

Obscenity That which is offensive to morality or chastity and is calculated to corrupt the mind and morals of those exposed to it.

Pornography Literature, art, film, pictures, or other articles of a sexual nature that are considered obscene by a community's moral standards.

Bigamy The act of marrying while a former marriage is still legally in force.

Polygamy The practice of having several spouses.

Prostitution The offering of sexual relations for monetary or other gain.

Child molesting The handling, fondling, or other contact of a sexual nature with a child.

Sexual assault Any sexual contact with another person (other than a spouse) that occurs without the consent of the victim or is offensive to the victim.

Voyeurism (peeping) The surreptitious observance of an exposed body or sexual act.

In 1981, the California statutory rape law was challenged before the U.S. Supreme Court on the ground that it discriminated on the basis of gender — men alone were criminally liable under the statute. The Court upheld the power of the states to enact such statutes since they were intended to prevent teenage pregnancies. (Michael M. v. Superior Court of Sonoma County, 458 U.S. 747 [1981])

Although the offenses of forcible rape, incest, and child molesting appear in all jurisdictions throughout the United States in one form or another, not all of the sexual behaviors listed are universally prohibited. Adultery, fornication, seduction, and pornography are disappearing from the penal codes of many state and local areas; indecent exposure, in the form of topless dancing and live sex shows, have been decriminalized in several jurisdictions; and prostitution is legal in one jurisdiction — in Las Vegas County, Nevada, outside the city limits of Las Vegas. However, American sodomy statutes, although neither uniform nor universal, and in most instances unenforced, continue to persist in modern criminal codes. The great majority of sodomy arrests that occur in the United States involve male homosexuals caught in the act of fellatio in public restrooms, parks, and other public places. Other sodomous acts, however, can be and are prosecuted. Even acts of fellatio and cunnilingus between husband and wife have resulted in criminal processing.[25] Furthermore, violation of the sodomy statutes is a felony in North Carolina, and sentences of up to ten years for such crimes have been upheld as recently as 1975.[26] Recently, however, the federal courts have begun to reevaluate state sodomy statutes in light of their infringements on the right to privacy. In a 1985 Georgia case, for example, the U.S. court of appeals held that the state's sodomy law infringed upon the constitutionally protected right of privacy insofar as it forbade the private homosexual acts of consenting adults.[27]

Without doubt, forcible rape is the one sex offense about which there is the most concern, and it is a crime whose statutes are often quite peculiar. In most jurisdictions, **rape** is defined as the unlawful carnal knowledge of a female without her consent and against her will. This suggests that the law of rape defines men as the only possible offenders and women as the only possible victims. However, one cannot discount the many instances of homosexual assault that occur in American prisons and jails,[28] or the cases of forced oral-genital and other body contacts attempting to simulate heterosexual intercourse that have been manifest in women's institutions.[29] Furthermore, this raises the question as to whether a man can be raped by a woman. Authors Neil C. Chamelin and Kenneth R. Evans have suggested that a female *cannot* actually rape a male.[30] But, although it is unlikely that any man raped by a woman would bring the crime to the attention of the authorities for fear of ridicule, this does not mean it cannot happen. Numerous such cases have been documented, and studies by sex therapists Philip M. Sarrel and William H. Masters have indicated that male victims of sexual assault by women suffer aftereffects similar to those seen in women who have been raped.[31]

Rape is considered the most serious of the sex offenses, but prostitution seems to be the most visibly common. **Prostitution** is sex for hire, implying some gain, typically money. It includes not only sexual intercourse, but also any other form of sexual conduct with another person for a fee. Where prostitution is illegal, it is typically a misdemeanor or some lesser offense.

Related to prostitution is procuring, also referred to as pandering or "pimping." **Procuring** involves promoting prostitution through the operation of a house of prostitution or by managing the activities and contacts of one or more prostitutes for a percentage of their earnings. Procuring is most often a felony at the state level, and in some circumstances can be prosecuted under federal law. For example, the White Slave Traffic Act of 1910, more commonly known as the *Mann Act,* prescribes a heavy fine and imprisonment for the transportation of a woman in foreign or interstate commerce for immoral purposes. The act was intended to intervene in the practice of white slavery, which was allegedly common at the turn of the twentieth century, and which involved the large-scale transportation of women and young girls and their detention in vice resorts for the purpose of forced prostitution. The

Rape

Carnal knowledge: The act of having sexual bodily connection. Under many statutes, there is carnal knowledge if there is the slightest penetration of the sexual organ of the female by the sexual organ of the male; it is not necessary that the vaginal canal be entered. Sexual contact without any penetration is generally referred to as carnal abuse.

Prostitution

The White Slave Traffic Act (Mann Act)

(f) Not being a peace officer, displays a deadly weapon in a public place in a manner calculated to alarm.[33]

In recent years, the constitutionality of many criminal codes designed for the preservation of public order and safety has been challenged. Numerous cases of disorderly conduct, breach of the peace, and vagrancy have come before the Supreme Court on the grounds that they violate First Amendment protections of free speech and assembly or because they are too vague. Furthermore, the use of such statutes as mechanisms for penalizing those who are viewed in some communities as political and social undesirables has been questioned as a violation of rights of due process. Nevertheless, these statutes remain in force in the criminal codes of most American jurisdictions, and arrests for vagrancy and disorderly conduct alone approach half a million annually.

Behavior Systems in Crime

The preceding discussion provides a basis for understanding the legal definitions and boundaries of the major categories of crime. However, in their descriptions of prohibited acts and their delineations of penalties, what the criminal codes cannot do is offer some insight and explanation of the social and behavioral contexts in which certain crimes tend to occur, the lifestyles associated with particular offenses, and the relationship of certain criminal acts to the wider social order. Further, the criminal law tells us nothing of the differences in styles and patterns of crime, of the various types of offenders, of victim–offender relationships, of varying techniques for committing crimes, and of how all of these affect the criminal justice management of crime. In short, each variety of crime has two important aspects — its legal description as stated in the law, and the behavior system that brings it into being. Consider, for example, the crime of shoplifting, which penal codes define as the theft of money, goods, or other merchandise from a store or shop. As such, the law is quite clear as to what may constitute shoplifting. But the law cannot help us understand the numerous behavior patterns associated with shoplifting. For example, there are many housewives, students, and others for whom an instance of shoplifting may be a first or only offense, committed perhaps out of desperation or for the sake of excitement. There are also numerous department store employees who pilfer merchandise in an attempt to supplement their legal incomes in a potentially safe manner. There are street hustlers in the central cities for whom shoplifting is but one of many petty crimes undertaken on a sporadic basis for the sake of economic gain. And finally, there are professional *boosters,* a small fraternity of skilled thieves who have elevated their techniques to an art form and carry them out regularly as a full-time business and vocation. The skills and techniques of the four types vary considerably, as do the frequency of their thefts and their methods for the disposal of the stolen goods. Furthermore, the first two varieties of shoplifters rarely view themselves as criminals, while the others are often proud of the labels of "hustler" and "professional thief."

Within this context, then, we can examine six behavior systems in crime: (1) violent personal crime, (2) occasional property crime, (3) organized robbery and gang theft, (4) white-collar and corporate crime, (5) organized crime, and (6) professional theft. Before proceeding with this analysis, however, two points must be emphasized. First, while this list of six behavior

Six behavior systems in crime

systems includes a wide variety of criminal activities and offense categories, it clearly does not include all prohibited acts. Any attempt to construct a schema that includes all types of behavior designated by the law as criminal would be pointless, primarily because the resulting classification would be so long and complex that it would be of minimal value for the purposes intended here. However, what is included reflects the vast majority of serious criminal activities. Second, a given criminal offense can fall within one or more behavior systems. For example, shoplifting can be carried out in different ways, under different circumstances, with different levels of skill, and with different relationships to the offender's social, economic, and criminal careers.

Violent Personal Crime

Violent personal crime

Violent personal crime consists of criminal acts resulting from differences in personal relations in which death or physical injury is inflicted. Thus, violent personal crime is a reflection of individual and personal violence, and includes specific forms of criminal homicide, assault, forcible rape, and child abuse.

The boundaries of violent personal crime are somewhat limited. First, studies of murder, assault, rape, and child abuse have suggested that in many cases (particularly in crimes of passion), the offenders had limited, if any, prior involvement in crime. Second, murderers, assaulters, and rapists generally do not view themselves as criminals, and their crimes are not always a predominant part of their life organization. Finally, most instances of personal violence are not a reflection of some group activity — rather, the violence is directed by the offender against a specific victim.[34]

A further aspect of personal violence is the victim–offender relationship, a factor that suggests that a large portion of such behavior is well beyond the control of law enforcement. In the case of murder, for example, the majority of offenses occur among persons who know one another. In 1984, for example, of the 16,689 murders reported during that year, 8.4 percent of the victims were spouses, 9.1 percent involved other family members, and 39.0 percent included neighbors or other close acquaintances. In the remaining cases, the homicide was of the "stranger-to-stranger" type, or the relationship could not be established. Interestingly, as these figures indicate, the majority of these killings involved circumstances of "romantic triangles," quarrels over money or property, or other arguments (see Exhibit 3.4).

Although official statistics on assaults are not as complete as those on criminal homicide, similar patterns of personal violence are apparent. Street muggings do indeed occur, but it is also relatively clear that nearly two-thirds of all known aggravated assaults result from domestic quarrels, altercations, jealousies, and arguments over money and property. Further, victim–offender relationships are typically intimate, close, and frequent, primarily involving family members and close acquaintances.[35]

Child abuse, which is a particular variety of homicide or assault directed against children, is a form of personal violence that has received attention only during recent years. Known in medical terminology as the "battered child syndrome," it is but one of the many forms of family violence (see Exhibit 3.5). Studies suggest that the offenders are typically parents or guardians; that they do not view themselves as criminals; and that although the abuse of their children may be an enduring pattern of behavior, they rarely have generalized criminal careers. Rather, they are individuals who are provoked by the forms of aggravation that can be typical of children — persistent crying, failure to

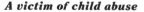
A victim of child abuse

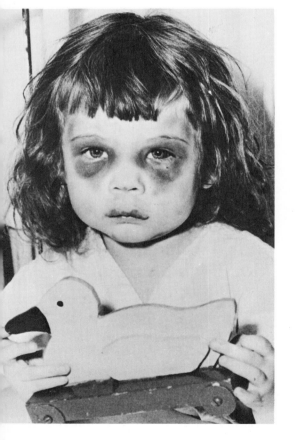

EXHIBIT 3.4

Percentage Distribution of Criminal Homicides by Relationship and Circumstance, 1984

Victim	Total	Felony Type	Suspected Felony Type	Romantic Triangle	Argument over Money or Property	Other Arguments	Miscellaneous Nonfelony Type	Unable to Determine
Total* (n = 16,689)	100.0	100.0	100.0	100.0	100.0	100.0	100.0	100.0
Husband	3.2	.4	—	3.9	1.3	6.9	3.1	.5
Wife	5.2	.8	—	7.4	2.4	9.0	7.4	1.8
Mother	.8	.3	—	—	.7	.9	1.8	.4
Father	1.2	.3	.2	—	1.1	2.3	1.4	.2
Daughter	1.3	1.0	—	—	.4	.5	4.3	.8
Son	1.6	1.2	.2	—	.7	1.3	4.7	.5
Brother	1.3	.1	—	.2	2.4	2.5	1.7	.2
Sister	.3	.2	—	.5	.4	.5	.5	.1
Other family	2.6	1.2	.2	.2	4.6	4.3	3.3	1.1
Acquaintances	29.8	23.8	9.3	57.6	56.9	39.3	37.8	9.7
Friend	3.9	1.7	.9	4.4	12.8	6.1	4.6	1.2
Boyfriend	1.6	.2	—	3.7	1.3	3.3	1.2	.4
Girlfriend	2.4	.5	—	7.4	1.3	4.7	2.0	.7
Neighbor	1.3	1.2	—	1.0	1.8	1.9	1.3	.5
Stranger	17.6	40.5	66.4	11.3	8.8	11.3	13.9	7.5
Unknown relationship	25.8	26.7	22.8	2.5	2.9	5.3	11.1	74.5

* Because of rounding, percentages may not total 100.

SOURCE: *Uniform Crime Reports — 1984*, p. 11.

use the toilet, aggression toward siblings, breaking toys or household items, or disobedience — and who respond by anger that strikes out in full force.

Not all forms of personal violence are clear-cut instances of differences of opinion in personal relations as are most homicides and assaults. Rape, for example, is not generally a crime that evolves from an intimate personal relationship, although in many cases the victim and offender are known to one

EXHIBIT 3.5

Violence in the Family

Each year in the United States more than 8 million men, women, and children are the victims of severe physical attacks at the hands of their spouses or parents. Even more astonishing are the number of murders that take place involving family members. Over 3,000 persons are intentionally killed each year by a family member—spouses kill one another, parents kill their children, children kill their parents, and brothers and sisters kill each other. Most often, it is wives who are killed by their husbands, but an almost equal number of husbands are murdered by their wives. It would appear, then, that physical violence is not uncommon in American families, and that the family is not necessarily a haven from aggression.

Marital Violence

Spouse abuse is not new. Although it has received considerable attention in the media in recent years, there is no reason to believe that it was any different in previous generations. Spouses likely have always been pushed, shoved, slapped, bitten, spanked, punched, kicked, knocked down, struck with an object, chocked, stabbed, and, since the invention of firearms, shot. Studies suggest that 16 percent of all couples come to blows with each other annually, and more than a third of these violent confrontations are severe. Moreover, over the course of a marriage the chances are greater than one in four (28 percent) that a couple will have an interspousal assault.[a]

When thinking of marital violence, what almost immediately comes to mind is the "battered wife syndrome." Conventional mythology does not seem to allow for battered husbands. But studies and court records demonstrate that both partners can be violent. In one survey of physical violence in the American family, 4.9 percent of the men said that they were the victims of abuse and 4.2 percent of the women admitted to abusing their husbands. Also, 4 percent of the women reported being abused by their husbands and 3.4 percent of the men acknowledged assaults on their wives.[b] Yet in spite of the reported greater frequency of abuse by wives, it was the women who were seriously hurt more often than the men. Moreover, some two million wives are abused each year by their husbands, and one in four of these victims were abused while pregnant.[c]

A recent topic in the discussions of wife abuse is *marital rape*. According to the laws of most states, there is no such thing as marital rape. As Sir Matthew Hale, the English jurist and Member of Parliament, explained to his peers in the seventeenth century:

A husband cannot be guilty of rape upon his wife for by their mutual matrimonial consent and contract the wife hath given up herself in this kind to her husband, which she cannot retract.[d]

This attitude is clearly reflected in the statutes of a number of state jurisdictions, including the *West Virginia Criminal Code*:

A person is guilty of sexual assault in the first degree [rape] when he engages in sexual intercourse with another person by forcible compulsion. . . . "Sexual intercourse" in this article means any act between persons not married to each other involving penetration of the female sex organ by the male sex organ. . . .[e]

Legally, then, it would seem that in many places a husband can do anything he wants to his wife sexually, as long as he does not leave evidence of other physical abuse, such as broken bones, whip marks, or a broken jaw. The laws of some states have changed on this point, and in 1979 an Oregon woman became the first to charge her husband with rape. (The husband was found not guilty; the couple reconciled their differences but later separated.)

What explains such widespread marital violence? This question can only be answered in terms of the reasons for violence in general. Marital violence seems to be an accepted, pervasive attribute of American life. Whatever the reasons, prevailing attitudes add to the problem. Not long ago, the National Commission on the Causes and Prevention of Violence estimated that between one-fourth and one-fifth of all adult Americans held that it was acceptable for spouses to strike one another under certain circumstances.[f]

Child Abuse

Most people may find it shocking to know that small children are far more likely to be injured by their parents than by anyone else. It is not that uncommon for physicians to find themselves treating children with unexplained fractures, severe bruises, or multiple abrasions. It is difficult to estimate the number of children who are the objects of physical violence at the hands of their parents, but studies suggest that roughly 2 million children are beaten up by their parents in any given year, more than 2,000 of these die as a result of the attacks, and at least 1 million are threatened with a gun or knife.[g] Many parents hit their children when they will not behave, and they have a legal right to do so. But a spanking for the sake of eliciting compliance with some parental rule is not child abuse. Studies indicate that parental violence against children goes well beyond ordinary physical punishment and is not only extensive but also a patterned phenomenon in parent–child relations. Mothers are the more typical users of violence, and sons and young children are the more common victims. Moreover, it appears that abusive parents re-create the conditions under which they were raised. That is, child abusers were themselves abused as children.

Although no single instance of a child being abused by his or her parent can be considered routine, child abuse does manifest itself in a number of typical forms — hitting, punching, repeated punching, and throwing something at the child. The use of a knife or gun are less common. However, more bizarre episodes arise now and then. In 1983, for example, a prominent Miami attorney and former chief counsel for the U.S. Environmental Protection Agency beat his son with a baseball bat in a school playground because the boy had failed to "hustle" during a local league game.[h] And in 1984, a Camden, New Jersey, woman murdered her four children by placing them in a rain-swollen river while they slept.[i]

There are other forms of child abuse by parents that have been construed as being in the realm of family violence — parent–child incest, rape, and other sexual abuses; the use of children in pornographic films; and the promotion of child prostitution.[j] Perhaps the most extreme case came to the attention of the U.S. attorney general's Task Force on Family Violence in 1983 when a woman from Media, Pennsylvania, testified that from ages 2 through 16, she was repeatedly raped and sexually assaulted by her brother, father, and grandfather.[k]

Other Forms of Family Violence

Family violence is not limited to spouse and child abuse. Children commit acts of violence against one another and against their parents. The assault of a parent by a child is often in defense of, or retaliation for, the parent's violent behavior. Such was the case in a Cheyenne, Wyoming, homicide in 1982, when a brother and sister, ages 16 and 17, ambushed their father with a 12-gauge shotgun and a .30-caliber semiautomatic carbine as a result of the many severe beatings they had received for what had been only minor infractions.[l]

Many incidents of family violence evolve from the combination of arguments and bad tempers that erupt into assault or homicide. One need only remember the 1984 killing of singer Marvin Gaye, who was shot twice by his father during an argument over insurance money.

Reverend Marvin Gaye, Sr., was arrested for the murder of his son, singer Marvin Gaye, in the former's home on April 1, 1984.

c. *Justice Assistance News,* February/March 1984, p. 2; Richard J. Gelles, *The Violent Home: A Study of Physical Aggression Between Husbands and Wives* (Beverly Hills: Sage, 1974).
d. Cited by Susan Brownmiller, *Against Our Will: Men, Women, and Rape* (New York: Simon and Schuster, 1975), p. 380.
e. *West Virginia Code,* 61-8B-3.
f. Gerald R. Leslie, *The Family in Social Context* (New York: Oxford, 1982), p. 442.
g. Richard J. Gelles, Murray A. Straus, and Suzanne K. Steinmetz, *Violence in the American Family* (Garden City, N.Y.: Doubleday, 1978); *Justice Assistance News,* February/March 1984, p. 2.
h. The Miami Herald, April 25, 1983, p. 3B; April 30, 1983, p. 2B.
i. Wilmington (Delaware) *News-Journal,* February 22, 1984, p. B5.
j. Robert L. Geiser, *Hidden Victims: The Sexual Abuse of Children* (Boston: Beacon, 1979).
k. Wilmington (Delaware) *News-Journal,* December 4, 1983, p. B3.
l. *Time,* December 13, 1982, p. 34.

SOURCES:
a. Murray A. Strauss, Richard J. Gelles, and Suzanne K. Steinmetz, *Behind Closed Doors* (New York: Doubleday, 1980).
b. Richard J. Gelles, *Family Violence* (Beverly Hills: Sage, 1979), p. 140.

another, and in some instances forced intercourse results from an anticipated sexual encounter. Recent studies have documented an increased number of stranger-to-stranger rapes, and available data suggest that forcible rape is but one of many crimes in the offenders' criminal careers.[36] Similarly, child molestation does not follow the general pattern of personal violence. In fact, much of what is called child molesting is not violence in the strict sense of the word. It may include instances of forcible rape, but its most frequent manifestations involve parent–child incest, the sexual fondling of a child, or the persuasion or coercion to engage in or submit to oral-genital contacts or to masturbate the adult.[37] Few cases have been reported where direct physical assault was associated with such "carnal abuse" of children. Nevertheless, child molesting is generally viewed as a variety of personal violence since it involves a sexual attack on persons who are not fully capable of making decisions as to their own sexual conduct.

However, what does combine most homicides, assaults, rapes, and incidents of child abuse and molesting into a single behavior system in crime is that they are all invasions of the rights of the victim's person. Whether the crime be direct assault or indecent liberties, the violence is of a personal nature. Furthermore, it is "individual violence," with the aggression directed typically by a single offender.

Occasional Property Crime

Occasional property crime

Occasional property crime refers to those types and instances of burglary, larceny, forgery, and other thefts undertaken infrequently or irregularly, and often quite crudely. Offenders who engage in this level of property crime do not pursue it as a career. They include amateur thieves for whom crime is incidental to their way of life, as well as the rank and file of urban street criminals or youthful groups who partake in sprees of burglaries, auto thefts, shoplifting, and vandalism as part of peer-group activities or for economic gain.

Offenders of this type generally have a petty or noncriminal orientation. They are often first or infrequent offenders who do not view themselves as criminals. They are unacquainted with criminal subcultures; their techniques for committing crimes are unskilled and undeveloped; they have little or no access to structured mechanisms for the disposal of stolen property. Rather, they generally steal for their own immediate purposes and little planning is apparent. Young vandals and burglars see themselves more often as "pranksters" than as thieves. Nonprofessional forgers, shoplifters, and pilferers are typically victims of temporary or desperate financial situations, or they engage in an occasional theft for the sake of adventure and excitement.

I'm convinced that every boy, in his heart, would rather steal second base than an automobile.
— Supreme Court Justice Tom Clark

The "naive check forger"

Edwin M. Lemert's study of "naive check forgers," undertaken many decades ago, clearly illustrates the factors associated with one common form of occasional property crime as a behavior system. Lemert found that many arrested forgers included professional, clerical, skilled, and craft workers who were, for the most part, respectable members of their communities. Many had no prior criminal records, and those who did had been involved in only minor offenses on an infrequent basis. The situations that led them into forgery included such contingencies as business failure, unemployment, gambling losses, alcoholic sprees, family or marital conflict, and separation and divorce. Elaborate planning of the forgery was quite untypical of this group of offenders, and the forgeries were extremely simple — the forgers wrote fictitious checks, passed falsified checks, and issued personal checks without sufficient funds. And finally, Lemert's "naive" check forgers were easily identified and apprehended, and readily admitted their guilt.[38]

Shoplifting

Shoplifting has persisted as the most common form of occasional property crime throughout the twentieth century. Patterns of shoplifting have been studied at length, and although professional boosters appear in every location, most thieves are of the occasional type and include amateur pilferers and store employees who steal for their own use. The value of goods taken from retailers annually during the 1950s and 1960s by shoplifters was estimated to be as high as $3 billion, not including losses of some $5 million per day from employee pilferage.[39] The pressures of inflation and recession in the late 1970s and early 1980s initiated an even higher level of amateur shoplifting. Most of the offenders were generally law-abiding types who would slip a few articles into their pockets, purses, and shopping bags, generally restricting their thefts to expensive pieces of clothing, electronic gadgets, jewelry, leather goods, and small appliances — all for personal consumption.

Finally, not all instances of occasional property crime are totally nonviolent. In many robberies and armed holdups the predators are amateur, first-offender types, and the patterns and contingencies are the same as those apparent among naive check forgers and shoplifters. Consider, for example, the case of a 19-year-old Wilmington, Delaware, youth who had an urgent need for cash to cover the impending cost of extensive car repairs. His crime was the armed robbery of a local liquor retailer. The event was his first criminal offense and his lack of aptitude was apparent from the very beginning. With little planning, the youth parked his car directly in front of the establishment he had targeted for the crime. In the presence of at least five witnesses, he emerged from his vehicle with his gun already drawn and entered the store. By the time he had completed the robbery, his license plate had been recorded and the police had been contacted. And if this identification had not been sufficient, the youth left his jacket, containing his wallet, driver's license, name, address, and phone number, behind at the scene of the crime.

D. B. Cooper

Perhaps the most spectacular and well-known of the occasional offender types was D. B. Cooper, the man who boarded a Northwest Orient Airlines jet on November 24, 1971, and then hijacked it. After receiving the $200,000 ransom and parachute he had demanded from airline officials, Cooper jumped from the jetliner over a rural area of Washington State. Cooper was not a known criminal, and all indications suggested that his ransom of the jetliner had been undertaken with little planning and expertise.[40] (For more about Cooper, see Exhibit 3.6.)

Organized Robbery and Gang Theft

Organized robbery and gang theft, or "heavy" crime, involves skilled criminals.

Organized robbery and gang theft, often called professional "heavy" crime, involves highly skilled criminal activities using or threatening to use force, violence, coercion, and property damage, and accomplished by planning, surprise, and speed in order to diminish the risks of apprehension.

"Heavy" criminals of this type pursue crime as a career for financial gain; they generally work in teams and are heavily armed; their planning is careful and their timing precise; and their pursuits include armed robbery, hijacking, kidnapping, and large-scale industrial theft. Although there is some variation from group to group, most organized robberies and gang thefts follow a planned pattern: (1) there is a definite target, ensuring a profitable outcome; (2) the target is fully studied (*cased*) in advance; (3) mock

It is a rather pleasant experience to be alone in a bank at night. —Willie Sutton

or practice trials are made; (4) timetables are established and escape routes are charted; (5) there is a getaway vehicle with a special driver; (6) there is a lookout person and a gunman with an accomplice for inside operations; and (7) there is a planned time, place, and method for the division of the plunder.

With organized armed robberies and hijacks, although they are generally planned in advance, the skill levels can vary. For example, as Werner J. Einstadter has pointed out, robbery tactics can emerge at any of three basic levels:

Three levels of skill in robbery tactics

1. *The ambush* Little planning; participants attack an establishment in guerrilla fashion; random selection of the victim; high incidence of violence
2. *The selective raid* Some planning; limited analysis of site conditions; tentative plan of approach and escape
3. *The planned operation* Well planned and well structured in every aspect; risks held to a minimum[41]

Individuals who engage in organized robbery and gang theft are usually long-term criminals who move from petty offenses to auto theft, burglary, and robbery. Their repeated experiences as young adults with police, courts, and reformatories add to their sophistication in criminality and to criminal self-conceptions. They live on the fringes of organized society, and they view the "heavy" rackets as a way to "get rich quick," to become socially mobile, or to start anew, rather than as a vocation or occupational career.

Willie Sutton, the best known "heavy" offender

Perhaps the best known of the "heavy" offenders was Willie Sutton, America's most famous bank robber. During his half-century career, Sutton plundered almost one hundred banks using a variety of ruses, disguises, pioneering safecracking techniques, and the timing of an athlete. (See Exhibit 3.6.) As for his general preparations for robbing a bank, Sutton once commented:

> I studied the habits of the employees and the guards and the cops on the beat. I learned the complete layout of the bank, and drew a plan. . . . I learned the location of every burglar alarm and safeguard. . . . I rehearsed my men thoroughly in their parts.[42]

The most recent forms of organized robbery and gang theft to come to the attention of law enforcement agencies occur within the industrial sector, with losses accumulating to billions of dollars annually. Armed robbers, thieves, hijackers, and river pirates of the 1980s now focus on farm and construction equipment, loaded gasoline trucks, and energy pipelines. Raids occur at railroad yards, construction sites, and plants and wholesaling locales where goods are stored or shipped.

White-collar and Corporate Crime

White-collar crime

White-collar crime and corporate crime refer to those offenses committed by persons acting in their legitimate occupational roles. The offenders include businesspeople, members of the professions and government, and other varieties of workers who, in the course of their everyday occupational activities, violate the basic trust placed in them or act in unethical ways. Crime is neither the way of life nor the chosen career of white-collar or corporate offenders, but rather something that occurs in conjunction with their more legitimate work activities. For example:

- In the business sector — financial manipulations, unfair labor practices, rebates, misrepresentation of goods and consumer deception by false labeling, fencing of stolen goods, shortchanging, overcharging, black-marketeering
- In the labor sector — misuse of union funds, failing to enforce laws affecting unions, entering into collusion with employers to the disadvantage of union members, illegal mechanisms for controlling members
- In the corporate sector — restraint of trade, infringement of patents, monopolistic practices, environmental contamination, misuse of trademarks, manufacture of unsafe goods, false advertising, disposal of toxic wastes
- In the financial sector — embezzlement, violation of currency control measures, stock manipulation
- In the medical sector — illegal prescription practices, fee-splitting, illegal abortions, fraudulent reports to insurance companies
- In the legal sector — misappropriation of funds in trusts and receiverships, securing prejudiced testimony, bribery, instituting fraudulent damage claims
- In the criminal justice sector — accepting bribes, illegal arrest and detention practices, illegal correctional practices
- In the civil sector — illegal commissions, issuance of fraudulent licenses and certificates, illegal tax evaluations, misuse of campaign funds, illegal campaign practices

At all levels of white-collar criminality, the offenders have no criminal self-concept. Rather, they rationalize their behavior as sharp business practice, taking advantage of an "easy rip-off," or maintaining that certain laws are unfair or that whatever they gained "was coming to them."

Currently, losses through white-collar and corporate crime are estimated to be as high as $200 billion annually.[43] Such an estimate might be quite conservative, however, since crimes of this type pervade all levels of the economic spectrum. Many white-collar thefts are small, but even these can accumulate to extensive capital losses. Consider for example, the proprietor of a small grocery store in Brooklyn, New York, known to the author during the mid-1960s. This shopkeeper kept a small $2.98 broom at the end of his checkout counter, which he would routinely ring up as part of the purchases of transient customers. The broom would never be packed with the customers' goods, and if a buyer later returned to complain about the questionable $2.98 charge on the register receipt, the grocer would simply say "Sir," or "Madam, you forgot your broom!" That same broom, or some similarly priced item, was sold at least ten times each day, and over one year's time the fraud would accumulate to thousands of dollars. Or consider the ploy of a bartender-cashier when a customer presented an American Express card to pay for his three drinks. The cashier cheerfully accepted the card and got away with billing his customer for $1,655.70.[44] In the area of medical abuse, clinical laboratories in many areas routinely charge their Medicaid patients up to $42 for tests that cost others only $5.[45] And then there was Raymond A. Galati, former fire chief of New Britain, Connecticut, who pleaded guilty to

Any company executive who overcharges the government $5 million will be fined $50 or have to go to traffic school three nights a week. —Art Buchwald

EXHIBIT 3.6

Whatever Happened to . . .

Ronald O'Bryan

Candy Man Ronald O'Bryan

It did not take Pasadena, Texas, police long to solve the 1974 "trick-or-treat" murder. O'Bryan had made inquiries about how much cyanide it would take to kill a person, and he had been seen purchasing the poison not long before his 8-year-old son died from the lethal dose he had given him. Moreover, he had been seen giving cyanide-laced candy to his son and several other children.

On June 3, 1975, after a two-week trial in which O'Bryan claimed his innocence, it took the jury only 45 minutes of deliberation to convict him. The following day he was sentenced to die in the electric chair. Then the appeals process began, and continued for eight years, nine months, and five days. In the meantime, Texas changed its method of execution from electrocution to lethal injection.

O'Bryan never received a new trial, and on March 30, 1984, any further stays of execution were denied. At 12:04 A.M. the following day, O'Bryan was strapped to the hospital gurney in the execution room at the Texas State Penitentiary in Huntsville. At 12:27, a needle was inserted into his arm and saline solution began flowing into his vein. At 12:40, the lethal injection began. Thirty seconds later he was dead.

Skyjacker D. B. Cooper

After receiving the $200,000 ransom he had demanded from Northwest Orient Airlines officials, Cooper parachuted from the plane over Ariel, Washington. The FBI launched a massive manhunt, but Cooper was never found. However, almost immediately he became a modern-day folk hero—a twentieth-century Robin Hood. Popular mythology holds that he got away, that he beat the system. Every year on the Saturday after Thanksgiving in Ariel, the festivities of D. B. Cooper Day are held. Hundreds of people, some from as far away as England, clog the little town's only street to pay tribute to the perpetrator of America's only unsolved skyjacking. It is an article of faith among them that somehow, somewhere, Cooper is managing to live a discreetly decadent life on his marked money. But what the cultists do not understand, or refuse to believe, is that when Cooper jumped from the plane at an altitude of 10,000 feet into 200 mile-per-hour air and freezing rain, dressed only in a light business suit and raincoat, it is likely that his body was thrown into immediate shock and that he did not stay conscious long enough to even open his parachute.

Bank Robber Willie Sutton

Willie Sutton's career in crime was a long one, providing him with an

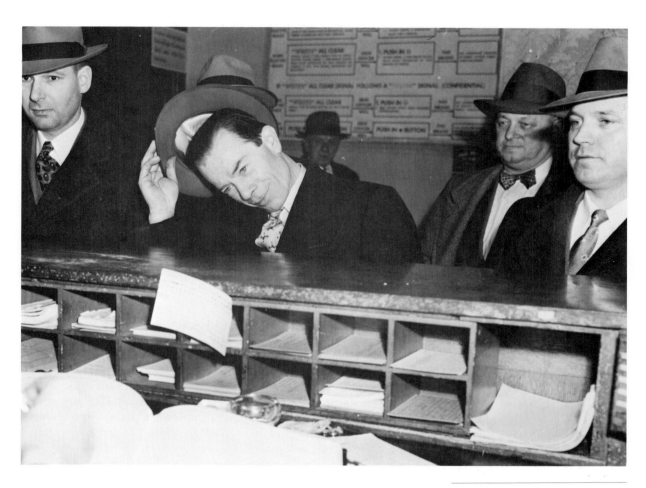

estimated $2 million over a period of 35 years. Moreover, his techniques earned him many names. For his use of ingenious disguises he became known as Willie "the Actor." Because he went over the wall of New York's Sing Sing Prison on more than one occasion, he was called Willie "the Escape Artist." And because he dug under the wall of Pennsylvania's "escape-proof"

Holmesburg Prison, he was dubbed Willie "the Mole." Sutton died of a stroke on November 2, 1980, at the age of 79. In an epitaph, columnist Pete Axthelm suggested that Sutton should more properly be called Willie "the Loser." Sutton had spent almost half his life in jails and penitentiaries, and died without a nickel of the $2 million he claimed to have heisted.

"Kickbacks, embezzlement, price fixing, bribery . . . this is an extremely high-crime area."

white-collar crimes including bribery and extortion. Galati was involved in selling jobs and promotions, with firm price tags on every forthcoming civil service examination in his department — $1,000 for the answers to the lieutenant exam and $3,000 for the assistant chief exam.[46]

At the other end of the spectrum, E. F. Hutton, Wall Street's fifth largest brokerage firm, was found guilty in 1985 of more than 2,000 separate charges of mail and wire fraud. Hutton executives had engaged in a sophisticated form of *check kiting* to avoid high interest rates. They deposited funds in local banks and then wrote checks for sums greater than the amounts in the accounts. Those checks were then covered a few days later by checks from other Hutton branches. The practice provided E. F. Hutton with interest-free loans of as much as $250 million a day.[47] Another case involved Exxon, the nation's largest oil company. In 1985, the firm was found to have overcharged its customers $2 billion from 1975 through 1979 and was ordered to repay the amount. During the same year, General Electric was found guilty of defrauding the United States Air Force of $800,000.[48]

For years it has been argued that white-collar criminals are rarely punished, and that if and when penalties are imposed, corporate officers generally escape criminal sanctions. This certainly has been the case in the past, but there are indications that the trend may be reversing. In 1985, for example, Paul Thayer, the chairman of LTV Corporation and President Reagan's former deputy secretary of defense, was given a $5,000 fine and a four-year prison term for stock manipulation.[49] In another case, a Chicago judge decided that under certain conditions an industrial death could be defined as murder. The case involved the cyanide poisoning death of a worker in an Illinois silver recovery plant. On the basis of their total disregard for

Al Capone taking it easy waterside at Miami's Biscayne Bay

safety regulations, the three officers in charge of the plant were found guilty of murder and sentenced to 25-year prison terms.[50]

Organized Crime

Organized crime designates business activities directed toward economic gain through unlawful means. Organized crime provides illegal goods and services through activities that include gambling, loan-sharking, commercialized vice, bootlegging, trafficking in narcotics and other drugs, disposing of stolen merchandise, and infiltrating legitimate businesses.

At the heart of what is often meant by organized crime are the types of enterprises just noted that sell illegal goods and services to customers. Such activities, however, are not always highly organized. Instead, they range on a continuum from free-lance prostitutes and neighborhood bookies, on the one hand, to regionally organized gambling or drug syndicates, on the other.

Organized crime, as a behavior system, is typically pursued as an occupational career. In its most organized aspects, there is a hierarchical structure that includes leaders (or "godfathers," as mass media and popular culture would insist) at the uppermost levels, followed by a middle echelon of gangsters and "lieutenants" who carry out the orders of their "bosses." And at the bottom of the structure are people only marginally associated with the "organization" — prostitutes, "enforcers," drug sellers, bookies — who may sometimes operate independently of the power structure and who typically deal directly with the public.

People who pursue organized crime as an occupational career most often focus on this type of criminality as a mechanism of upward mobility and

Organized crime

I know what the Mafia can do to a man who has crossed them. One day you wake up with your head in one room and your legs in another.
—**Vincent "Big Vinnie" Teresa**

are recruited on the basis of kinship, friendship, or contacts within lower-class environments, where such activities are sought out as means for economic respectability. Whether individual criminals are within a highly structured "syndicate" or are low-level independent prostitutes or bookies, their commitment to the career is long-term and their whole social organization and lifestyle revolve around crime.[51]

Professional Theft

Professional theft

Professional theft refers to nonviolent forms of criminal occupation pursued with a high degree of skill to maximize financial gain and minimize the risks of apprehension. The more typical forms of professional theft include pickpocketing, shoplifting, safe and house burglary, forgery, counterfeiting, sneak-thieving, and confidence swindling.

What separates professional thieves from other criminals who engage in the same types of offense behavior are the social organization and occupational structure that circumscribe their criminal activities. Professional thieves make a regular business of stealing; it is their occupation and means of livelihood, and they devote their entire working time and energy to stealing. Professional thieves also operate with proficiency. Like members of legitimate professions, they have an organized body of knowledge and skills that they utilize in the planning and execution of their activities, and they are graduates of a developmental process that includes the acquisition of specialized attitudes, knowledge, skills, and experience. Moreover, in identifying themselves with the world of crime, they are members of an exclusive fraternity that extends friendship, understanding, sympathy, congeniality, security, recognition, and respect. As residents of this remote corner of the underworld, they also have access to specialized patterns of communication, a complex system of argot, and a network of contacts within the legal profession and criminal justice system that enable them to steal for long periods of time without going to prison.

The first intensive examination of professional theft as a behavior system appeared more than four decades ago in Edwin H. Sutherland's *The Professional Thief.*[52] The work of Sutherland and later researchers documented the fact that professional theft was an outgrowth of the disintegration of the feudal order in Europe during the years 1350–1550, and that it remained relatively unchanged for centuries. The types of crime, techniques, skills, attitudes, patterns of recruitment and training, interactional setting, style of life, and to some extent the argot of twentieth-century professional thieves were characteristically like those of previous periods. This system of criminal behavior seemed to persist in its unchanged and unmolested state in spite of social and technological changes and the repressive efforts of the criminal justice system, due to a highly functional structure of low visibility built around its subculture.

Professional thieves, for example, maintained a low profile in the nexus of victim–offender relationships due to the nature of the crimes and victims that were targeted. Confidence games and extortion presented little risk since the victims themselves were violators of the law and were acting in collusion with the thieves. Shoplifting offered only a limited danger since businesspeople were reluctant to accuse those persons of theft who often appeared to be legitimate customers. In other instances, such as pickpocketing, the thief's manipulative abilities often allowed him to arrange payments of restitution in lieu of complaint and prosecution. Immunity was furthered by the thief's many contacts, who could fix many of the criminal cases that did come to the attention of the criminal justice system.

Although this criminal behavior system sustained itself for many centuries, historical study indicates that it began to decline shortly after World War I and all but perished by the 1970s. The development of private police systems and police technology and communications, the bureaucratization of the criminal justice system, the enactment of federal laws aimed at interstate flight, and the shrinkage of vice areas all served to erode the foundations of the professional criminal underworld. Over time, thieves were more often identified, apprehended, prosecuted, convicted, and sentenced. The result of these efforts was to make the enterprise unprofitable, severely curtailing the number of new recruits to the profession.[53]

Nevertheless, professional theft in this classic form continues to persist at some levels. Specifically, recent research has documented that the social organization and occupational structure of professional pickpockets or "class cannons" endures in the style of nineteenth- and early twentieth-century professional thieves.[54] And too, there is evidence that highly skilled thieves of the professional caliber continue to operate in very lucrative enterprises. In March 1980, for example, Miami's Trendline Jewelry, a large wholesaler of precious metals, was the victim of still unknown and highly sophisticated groups. The thieves thwarted complex alarm systems that used sonar equipment and electric eyes, and then proceeded to carry off thousands of 14-karat bracelets and ring mountings plus over 800 pounds of gold and 3,000 pounds of silver.[55]

As a final note, it must be emphasized again that these six behavior types — violent personal crime, occasional property crime, organized robbery and gang theft, white-collar and corporate crime, organized crime, and professional theft — do not represent the full spectrum of criminal behavior systems. There remains, for example, **political crime**, which includes treason, sedition, espionage, sabotage, war collaboration, and radicalism and protest, in which offenders violate the law when they feel that such illegal activity is essential and appropriate in achieving necessary changes in society. There is also public order or "victimless" crime, which reflects a major segment of police arrest activity and includes many public safety and minor sex offenses, drug violations, and nuisance offenses. In such crimes, no real injury to another person is involved, nor is the theft of goods and services involved. Rather, the morals, safety, and tranquility of the community is placed at risk, and typically the offenders are not viewed by others or even themselves as criminals per se, but rather as drunks, hookers, perverts, and junkies.

Political crime

Summary

There are thousands of acts that are prohibited by law and designated as felonies or misdemeanors in federal, state, and local criminal codes across the United States. Such crime categories as homicide, assault, robbery, arson, burglary, sex offenses, drug law violations, and offenses against the public order and safety are by no means all that appear in criminal statutes and codes, but they account for some 90 percent of the criminal law violations that are processed by U.S. courts. However, although crime may be conduct prohibited by criminal law, its dynamics include certain patterns and systems of behavior. It is important for any student of crime and criminal justice to understand not only the content of criminal codes, but the behavior systems that surround the prohibited acts as well.

Key Terms

arson (75)
assault and battery (73)
breaking and entering (75)
burglary (75)
Carrier's Case (78)
Controlled Substances Act (84)
deliberation (68)
disorderly conduct (86)
felony-murder doctrine (70)

homicide (68)
larceny (78)
malice aforethought (68)
manslaughter (70)
murder (68)
occasional property crime (92)
organized crime (99)
political crime (101)
premeditation (69)

professional theft (100)
public order crime (85)
rape (82)
robbery (73)
theft (77)
violent personal crime (88)
white-collar crime (94)

Questions for Discussion

1. In cases where the felony-murder doctrine has been invoked, the intent to commit murder has often been absent. In such circumstances, is conviction of murder in the first degree a just disposition? Why or why not?
2. Which sex offenses, if any, should be abolished from contemporary criminal codes? Why?
3. Are there any types of property offenses other than those listed in this chapter?
4. Should penalties for white-collar crimes be equal to those for street crimes when victims' losses are similar? Why or why not?

For Further Reading

Geiser, Robert L. *Hidden Victims: The Sexual Abuse of Children.* Boston: Beacon Press, 1979.
Meier, Robert F., ed. *Major Forms of Crime.* Beverly Hills: Sage, 1984.

Sutherland, Edwin H. *The Professional Thief.* Chicago: University of Chicago Press, 1937.

Notes

1. James A. Inciardi, "In Search of the Class Cannon: A Field Study of Professional Pickpockets," in *Street Ethnography: Selected Studies of Crime and Drug Use in Natural Settings*, ed. Robert S. Weppner (Beverly Hills: Sage, 1977), pp. 55–77.
2. This incident in the life of Thomas Bartholomew Moran was reported to the author by Hester Marc, an old-line professional pickpocket who had worked on and off with Moran for more than thirty years. Corroborating evidence of the presence of career thieves on the *Titanic* and other Atlantic liners during the early part of this century appears in the unpublished working papers of the late Edwin H. Sutherland. For a discussion of the era of the luxury liners and the sinking of the *Titanic*, see Walter Lord, *A Night to Remember* (New York: Holt, Rinehart and Winston, 1955).
3. John Janus Powell was an alias used by a heroin addict personally known to the author.
4. John Godwin, *Murder U.S.A.: The Ways We Kill Each Other* (New York: Ballantine, 1978), pp. 29–31.
5. Paul B. Weston and Kenneth M. Wells, *Criminal Law* (Santa Monica: Goodyear, 1978), pp. 184–185.
6. Jerome Hall, "Analytic Philosophy and Jurisprudence," *Ethics* 77 (October 1966): 14–28.
7. *USA Today*, January 25, 1985, p. 3A.
8. *Delaware Code*, Title 11, Section 632.
9. *Delaware Code*, Section 601.
10. *Penal Code of California*, Section 203.
11. David M. Maurer, *Whiz Mob* (New Haven: College and University Press, 1964), p. 68.
12. This comment was made to the author by a Miami Beach pickpocket in early 1976. Additional comments on this topic can be found in James A. Inciardi, "The Pickpocket and His Victim," *Victimology: An International Journal* 1 (Fall 1976): 446–453.
13. People v. Rosen, 11 Cal. 2d 147 (1938).
14. People v. Lavender, 31 P.2d 439 (1934).
15. John F. Boudreau, Quon Y. Kwan, William E. Faragher, and Genevieve C. Denault, *Arson and Arson Investigation: Survey and Assessment* (Washington, D.C.: U.S. Government Printing Office, 1977), p. 1.
16. James A. Inciardi, "The Adult Firesetter: A Typology," *Criminology: An Interdisciplinary Journal* 8 (August 1970): 145–155; James A. Inciardi, *Reflections on Crime* (New York: Holt, Rinehart and Winston, 1978), pp. 127–128.
17. See, for example, *Delaware Code*, Title 11, Sections 824, 825, 826.
18. 58 *Delaware Laws*, c. 497, Section 1.

19. *Louisiana Criminal Code*, Section 67.

20. *Delaware Code*, Title 11, Section 840.

21. *Ohio Code*, 2913.02.

22. Carrier's Case, Yearbook, 13 Edward IV, 9, pl. 5 (1473).

23. Pear's Case, 1 Leach 212, 168 Eng. Rep. 208 (1779).

24. United States v. Sheffield, 161 F. Supp. 387 (1958, Md.).

25. Mahone v. State, 44 Ala. 372, 209 So. 2d 435 (1968).

26. *General Statutes of North Carolina*, Sections 14–177; State v. Enslin, 25 N.C. App. 662, 214 S.E. 2d 318 (1975).

27. Hardwick v. Bowers, CA 11 (37 CrL 2196).

28. See, for example, David M. Petersen and Marcello Truzzi, eds., *Criminal Life: Views from the Inside* (Englewood Cliffs, N.J.: Prentice-Hall, 1972), p. 165; Haywood Patterson and Earl Conrad, *Scottsboro Boy* (Garden City, N.Y.: Doubleday, 1950).

29. David A. Ward and Gene G. Kassebaum, *Women's Prison: Sex and Social Structure* (Chicago: Aldine, 1965); Rose Giallombardo, *Society of Women: A Study of a Women's Prison* (New York: Wiley, 1966); Dorothy West, "I Was Afraid to Shut My Eyes," *The Saturday Evening Post* (July 13, 1968), p. 23.

30. Neil C. Chamelin and Kenneth R. Evans, *Criminal Law for Policemen* (Englewood Cliffs, N.J.: Prentice-Hall, 1976), p. 109.

31. *Miami Herald*, September 17, 1982, p. 1B; *Psychology Today*, September 1983, pp. 74–75.

32. See David F. Musto, *The American Disease: Origins of Narcotic Control* (New Haven: Yale University Press, 1973).

33. *Colorado Penal Code*, 18-9-106.

34. See Marvin Wolfgang, *Patterns in Criminal Homicide* (Philadelphia: University of Pennsylvania Press, 1958); David J. Pittman and William Handy, "Patterns in Criminal Aggravated Assault," *Journal of Criminal Law, Criminology and Police Science* 55 (December 1964): 462–470; Marshall B. Clinard and Richard Quinney, *Criminal Behavior Systems: Typology* (New York: Holt, Rinehart and Winston, 1967), pp. 20–33.

35. President's Commission on Law Enforcement and Administration of Justice, *The Challenge of Crime in a Free Society* (Washington, D.C.: U.S. Government Printing Office, 1967), p. 18.

36. See Duncan Chappell, Robley Geis, and Gilbert Geis, eds., *Forcible Rape: The Crime, the Victim, and the Offender* (New York: Columbia University Press, 1977); D. J. West, C. Roy, and F. L. Nichols, *Understanding Sexual Attacks* (London: Heinemann, 1978).

37. Charles H. McCaghy, "Child Molesters: A Study of Their Careers as Deviants," in *Criminal Behavior Systems*, ed. Clinard and Quinney, pp. 75–88; Vincent De Frances, "Protecting the Child Victim of Sex Crimes Committed by Adults," *Federal Probation* 35 (September 1971): 15–20; Robert L. Geiser, *Hidden Victims: The Sexual Abuse of Children* (Boston: Beacon Press, 1979).

38. Edwin M. Lemert, "An Isolation and Closure Theory of Naive Check Forgery," *Journal of Criminal Law, Criminology, and Police Science* 44 (1953): 296–307.

39. Mary Owen Cameron, *The Booster and the Snitch* (New York: Free Press of Glencoe, 1964); Loren E. Edwards, *Shoplifting and Shrinkage Protection for Stores* (Springfield, Ill.: Charles C. Thomas, 1958).

40. Robert J. Trotter, "Psyching the Skyjacker," *Science News* 101 (February 12, 1972): 108–110; Sam A. Angeloff, "The FBI Agent Who Has Tracked D. B. Cooper for Nine Years Retires, but the Frustrating Search Goes On," *People*, March 3, 1980, pp. 45–46; *New York Times*, November 25, 1979, p. 45.

41. Werner J. Einstadter, "The Social Organization of Armed Robbery," *Social Problems* 17 (Summer 1969): 64–83.

42. Quentin Reynolds, *I, Willie Sutton* (New York: Farrar, Straus & Young, 1953), p. 19; see also Willie Sutton with Edward Linn, *Where the Money Was* (New York: Viking Press, 1976).

43. *U.S. News & World Report*, May 20, 1985, p. 83.

44. *Miami Herald*, February 24, 1980, p. 2G.

45. *U.S. News & World Report*, June 4, 1979, p.. 43.

46. *New York Times*, March 30, 1980, p. E5.

47. *Time*, May 13, 1985, p. 51.

48. *Time*, June 10, 1985, p. 56.

49. *Newsweek*, May 20, 1985, p. 54.

50. *Newsweek*, July 8, 1985, p. 58.

51. For a discussion of organized crime, see Joseph L. Albini, *The American Mafia: Genesis of a Legend* (New York: Appleton-Century-Crofts, 1971); Daniel Bell, *The End of Ideology: On The Exhaustion of Political Ideas in the Fifties* (New York: Free Press, 1962), pp. 127–150; Norval Morris and Gordon Hawkins, *The Honest Politician's Guide to Crime Control* (Chicago: University of Chicago Press, 1970), pp. 202–235; James A. Inciardi, *Careers in Crime* (Chicago: Rand McNally, 1975), pp. 109–121.

52. Edwin H. Sutherland, *The Professional Thief* (Chicago: University of Chicago Press, 1937).

53. Inciardi, *Careers in Crime*, pp. 5–82.

54. Inciardi, "In Search of the Class Cannon," pp. 55–77.

55. *Time*, March 24, 1980, p. 28.

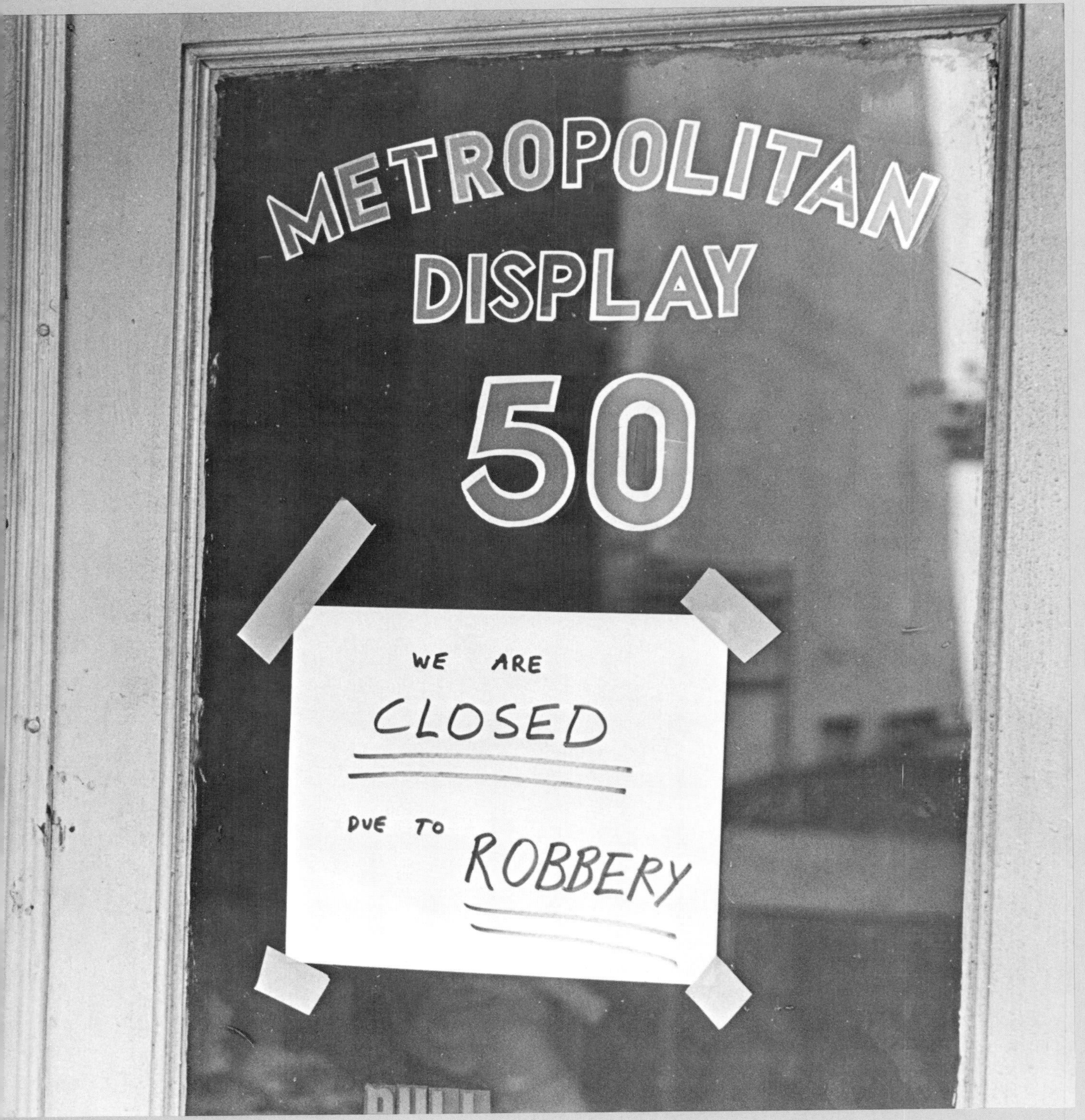
METROPOLITAN
DISPLAY
50
WE ARE
CLOSED
DUE TO
ROBBERY

4

Criminal Statistics and the Extent of Crime

Every now and then there occurs the phenomenon called a crime wave. New York has such waves periodically; other cities have them; and they sweep over the public and nearly drown the lawyers, judges, preachers, and other leading citizens who feel that they must explain and cure these extraordinary outbreaks of lawlessness. Their diagnosis and their remedies are always the same: the disease is lawlessness; the cure is more law, more arrests, swifter trials, and harsher penalties. The sociologists and other scientists go deeper into the wave; the trouble with them is they do not come up.

—Lincoln Steffens[1]

These curious and rather cynical comments, written over half a century ago by journalist Lincoln Steffens, are resurrected here because they relate to a series of events that remain pertinent to discussions of and reflections on the extent and measurement of crime. In 1891, Steffens inaugurated the era of journalistic "muckraking" — so-called by Theodore Roosevelt — by publishing a series of exposés of corruption in business and city government. Throughout most of the 1890s Steffens was a police reporter for the New York *Evening Post*, and much of his leisure time was spent in the basement of police headquarters trading stories of the underworld with detectives, prisoners, and other reporters. It was on one of these occasions that he, with the help of rival reporter, and later philanthropist, Jacob Riis, actually started what appeared to be a crime wave in New York City.

One evening at police headquarters, Steffens was told the story of how an old professional thief, with the aid and protection of the police, had burglarized the Madison Avenue home of a popular Wall Street broker. Steffens put together the facts of the crime and reported them in the *Post* the following day. Jacob Riis, who was the police reporter for the New York *Evening Sun* at that time, was immediately called down by his city editor and criticized for not having the story of such a sensational crime. That afternoon Riis "scooped" a new burglary, reported it in his column, and the competition had begun in earnest. What followed over the succeeding weeks was a growing series of crime stories in the *Post*, the *Sun*, and the other New York dailies, written in a manner that suggested that there was indeed a crime wave on the streets of the city. As Steffens himself described it:

> I called on my assistant, Robert, and told him we must get some crimes. We spent the day buttonholing detectives; I sat an hour asleep in the basement in vain. Nothing but old stories. Robert saved the day. He learned, and I wrote, of the robbery of a Fifth Avenue club. That was a beat, but Riis had two robberies that were beats on me. By that time the other evening papers were having some thefts of their own. The poker club reporters were loafers only by choice. They could get the news when they had to, and being awakened by the scrap between Riis and me, they broke up their game and went to work, a combine, and they were soon beating me, as Riis was. I was sorry I had started it. Robert or I had to sleep in turns in the basement, and we picked up some crimes, but Riis had two or three a day, and the combine had at least one a day. The morning newspapers not only rewrote ours; they had crimes of their own, which they grouped to show that there was a crime wave.[2]

Because of the sudden and persistent "outbreak of crime," explanations were demanded from the police for the increased lawlessness and their inability to deal with New York's criminal element. Ultimately, Theodore Roosevelt, who was then president of New York City's Board of Police Commissioners, ordered Steffens and Riis to discontinue their lurid reporting of robberies and thefts, and the period of sudden lawlessness quickly abated.

In retrospect, Lincoln Steffens and Jacob Riis had generated what appeared to be a crime wave by taking reports of robberies and run-of-the-mill burglaries and thefts from police blotters and featuring them in black headlines. Yet there had not been a crime wave in New York during that period, but rather a "crime-reporting wave," spirited by overzealous police reporters and competition among the daily presses. This pattern, initiated by Steffens and Riis, continues in many communities, Radio, television, and newspaper accounts of lawbreaking and scandal, combined with word-of-mouth reports by victims and their families, are the main sources of the public's knowledge and images of crime. Crime stories do have some impact on newspaper circulation and local television news ratings. Furthermore, even when crime is not overplayed in the media, the very mechanisms through which information on crime is collected and compiled are beset with so many difficulties that even honest attempts to report on the magnitude and rates of crime are distorted. In short, although there are likely more data on crime than on any other social phenomenon, there are also so many problems associated with using crime statistics that we must be aware of their limitations if we are to understand them and use them properly.

This chapter describes the major sources of information on the magnitude and trends of crime. It explains how the information is compiled, what it includes, how it might be best interpreted, and how it has been misused. The shortcomings and the usefulness of official crime statistics are also discussed. The final section looks at alternate and supplementary sources of crime data.

The Uniform Crime Reports

The uniform collection of crime statistics on a national basis in this country began only about half a century ago. At the 1927 annual meeting of the International Association of Chiefs of Police, the Committee on Uniform Crime Reports was appointed to respond to a demand for national crime data. It was commissioned to prepare a manual on standardized crime reporting for use by local police agencies. Based on the efforts of this committee, Congress, on June 11, 1930, authorized the Federal Bureau of Investigation (FBI) to collect and compile nationwide data on crime.[3] Pursuant to the congressional order, the FBI assumed responsibility for directing the voluntary recording of data by police departments on standardized forms provided by the FBI and for compiling and publishing the data received. Known as the *Uniform Crime Reports* (*UCR*), they were issued monthly at first, quarterly until 1941, semiannually through 1957, and annually since 1958.

The *Uniform Crime Reports*

As early as 1932, FBI director J. Edgar Hoover was boasting in his congressional testimony about the value and usefulness of the *UCR*. The purpose, Hoover maintained, was "to determine whether there is or is not a crime wave and whether crime is on the increase or decrease."[4] From that time on, crime often reflected a statistical increase, and the FBI charted the degree and nature of that increase, any geographical variations, and other trends that were deemed significant.

The main publication of the *UCR* is an annual booklet, *Crime in the United States,* which has helped to establish the FBI's image as the nation's

leading authority on crime trends. This annual periodical is the only source of information on the magnitude and trends of crime in the United States. It is relied upon heavily by administrators, politicians, policy and opinion makers, the press, criminal justice agencies, and the public at large. Yet the FBI reports have their problems. They are incomplete and structurally biased, resulting in the creation and persistence of many myths about crime in the United States. Furthermore, they have been misused and misinterpreted. In consequence, inaccurate and distorted representations of crime are continually being offered to both professional and lay audiences, and public pronouncements about "the crime problem" often have only limited basis in fact. The following commentary includes an explanation of official criminal statistics, an examination of their reliability, and a discussion of how these and other sources of information can be used to understand the nature and extent of crime in America.

Structure and Content

The FBI's *Uniform Crime Reports* presents us with a nationwide view of crime based on statistics submitted by city, county, and state law enforcement agencies throughout the country. As of 1984, more than 16,000 law enforcement agencies were contributing crime data to this reporting program, representing coverage for more than 98 percent of the national population.[5]

The crime clock   The *UCR* begins with a rather alarming **crime clock.** The one in Exhibit 4.1 suggests that in 1984 there was one murder every 28 minutes, one

EXHIBIT 4.1

The Crime Clock for 1984

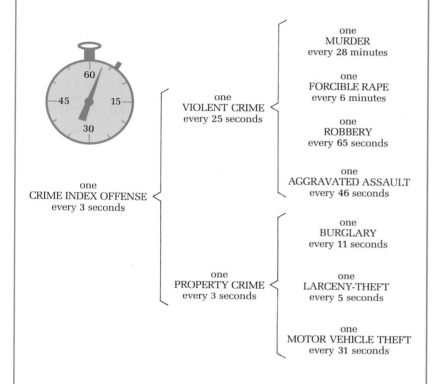

one
CRIME INDEX OFFENSE
every 3 seconds

one
VIOLENT CRIME
every 25 seconds

one
MURDER
every 28 minutes

one
FORCIBLE RAPE
every 6 minutes

one
ROBBERY
every 65 seconds

one
AGGRAVATED ASSAULT
every 46 seconds

one
PROPERTY CRIME
every 3 seconds

one
BURGLARY
every 11 seconds

one
LARCENY-THEFT
every 5 seconds

one
MOTOR VEHICLE THEFT
every 31 seconds

Note: The crime clock should be viewed with care. The most aggregate representation of *UCR* data, it is designed to convey the annual reported crime experience by showing the relative frequency of occurrence of Crime Index offenses. This mode of display does not imply a regularity in the commission of the offenses; rather, it represents the annual ratio of crime to fixed time intervals.

SOURCE: *Uniform Crime Reports — 1984,* p. 5.

forcible rape every 6 minutes, one robbery every 65 seconds, a property crime every 3 seconds, as well as other crimes in similarly frequent intervals. The reader is quickly cautioned in the FBI report that the crime clock display should not be interpreted to imply some regularity in the commission of crimes; it simply represents the annual ratio of crime to fixed time intervals. Unfortunately this cautionary comment is easily overlooked, and invariably, mass-media commentary on crime in the United States makes frequent reference to the literal meaning of the crime clock.

The *UCR* places its compilations into two categories: **"crimes known to the police"** and **arrests.** "Crimes known to the police" include all events

"Crimes known to the police" and arrests are the two categories of crimes compiled in the *UCR*.

either reported to or observed by the police in those categories of crime that the FBI designates as **Part I offenses:**

1. Criminal Homicide   a. Murder and nonnegligent manslaughter: the willful [nonnegligent] killing of one human being by another. Deaths caused by negligence, attempts to kill, assaults to kill, suicides, accidental deaths, and justifiable homicides are excluded. Justifiable homicides are limited to: (1) the killing of a felon by a law enforcement officer in the line of duty; and (2) the killing of a felon by a private citizen. b. Manslaughter by negligence: the killing of another person through gross negligence. Excludes traffic fatalities. While manslaughter by negligence is a Part I crime, it is not included in the Crime Index.

2. Forcible rape   The carnal knowledge of a female forcibly and against her will. Included are rapes by force and attempts or assaults to rape. Statutory offenses (no force used — victim under age of consent) are excluded.

3. Robbery   The taking or attempting to take anything of value from the care, custody, or control of a person or persons by force or threat of force or violence and/or by putting the victim in fear.

4. Aggravated assault   An unlawful attack by one person upon another for the purpose of inflicting severe or aggravated bodily injury. This type of assault usually is accompanied by the use of a weapon or by means likely to produce death or great bodily harm. Simple assaults are excluded.

5. Burglary–breaking or entering   The unlawful entry of a structure to commit a felony or a theft. Attempted forcible entry is included.

6. Larceny-theft (except motor vehicle theft)   The unlawful taking, carrying, leading, or riding away of property from the possession or constructive possession of another. Examples are thefts of bicycles or automobile accessories, shoplifting, pocket-picking, or the stealing of any property or article which is not taken by force and violence or by fraud. Attempted larcenies are included. Embezzlement, "con" games, forgery, worthless checks, etc., are excluded.

7. Motor vehicle theft   The theft or attempted theft of a motor vehicle. A motor vehicle is self-propelled and runs on the surface and not on rails. Specifically excluded from this category are motorboats, construction equipment, airplanes, and farming equipment.

8. Arson   Any willful or malicious burning or attempt to burn, with or without intent to defraud, a dwelling house, public building, motor vehicle or aircraft, personal property of another, etc.

Arrests include compilations of arrest reports for all the Part I offenses *combined with* those of twenty-one additional categories, which the FBI designates as **Part II offenses:**

9. Other assaults (simple)   Assaults and attempted assaults where no weapon was used and which did not result in serious or aggravated injury to the victim.

10. Forgery and counterfeiting   Making, altering, uttering, or possessing, with intent to defraud, anything false which is made to appear true. Attempts are included.

11. Fraud   Fraudulent conversion and obtaining money or property by false pretenses. Included are larceny by bailee and bad checks, except forgeries and counterfeiting.

12. Embezzlement   Misappropriation or misapplication of money or property entrusted to one's care, custody, or control.

13. Stolen property; buying, receiving, possessing   Buying, receiving, and possessing stolen property, including attempts.

14. Vandalism   Willful or malicious destruction, injury, disfigurement, or defacement of any public or private property, real or personal, without consent of the owner or person having custody or control.

15. Weapons; carrying, possessing, etc.   All violations of regulations or statutes controlling the carrying, using, possessing, furnishing, and manufacturing of deadly weapons or silencers. Included are attempts.

16. Prostitution and commercialized vice   Sex offenses of a commercialized nature, such as prostitution, keeping a bawdy house, procuring, or transporting women for immoral purposes. Attempts are included.

17. Sex offenses (except forcible rape, prostitution, and commercialized vice)   Statutory rape and offenses against chastity, common decency, morals, and the like. Attempts are included.

18. Drug abuse violations   State and local offenses relating to narcotic drugs, such as unlawful possession, sale, use, growing, and manufacturing of narcotic drugs.

19. Gambling   Promoting, permitting, or engaging in illegal gambling.

20. Offenses against the family and children   Nonsupport, neglect, desertion, or abuse of family and children.

21. Driving under the influence   Driving or operating any vehicle or common carrier while drunk or under the influence of liquor or narcotics.

22. Liquor laws   State or local liquor law violations, except "drunkenness" (offense 23) and "driving under the influence" (offense 21). Federal violations are excluded.

23. Drunkenness   Drunkenness or intoxication. Excluded is "driving under the influence" (offense 21).

24. Disorderly conduct.   Breach of the peace.

25. Vagrancy   Vagabondage, begging, loitering, etc.

26. All other offenses   All violations of state or local laws, except offenses 1–25 and traffic offenses.

27. Suspicion   No specific offense; suspect released without formal charges being placed.

28. Curfew and loitering laws   Offenses relating to violation of local curfew or loitering ordinances where such laws exist.

29. Runaways   Limited to juveniles taken into protective custody under provisions of local statutes.

Note that these definitions of offense categories vary somewhat from the strict legal definitions discussed in Chapter 3. These more simplified and

less technical definitions are given in a uniform crime reporting handbook provided by the FBI to law enforcement agencies as a guide for the compiling and reporting of local data.

Information on Part I offenses, which are the most widely quoted and often misinterpreted, are grouped by city, metropolitan area, state, region, and the nation as a whole to reflect an "Index of Crime" for the given year, and it is these **Crime Index** data that are relied upon for estimating the magnitude and rates of crime. A sample of the *UCR* data appears in Exhibit 4.2, which contains ten classifications of crime, their absolute numbers, rates, and percent changes between 1975 and 1984. Some of the terms and variables in the table are important for reading and interpreting any crime statistics:

The Crime Index

Total Crime Index   The sum of all Part I offenses reported to or observed by the police (that is, "crimes known to the police") during a given period of time in a particular place (in this example, during 1984 for the total United States).

Violent Crime   The sum of all Part I violent offenses (homicide, forcible rape, robbery, and aggravated assault).

Property Crime   The sum of all Part I property offenses (burglary, larceny-theft, motor vehicle theft, and arson).

Computing the crime rate

Rate per 100,000 inhabitants   The **crime rate,** or the number of offenses that occurred in a given area for every 100,000 persons living in that area, calculated as follows:

$$\frac{\text{Total Crime Index}}{\text{Population}} \times 100{,}000 = \text{Rate}$$

In Exhibit 4.2, the crime rate in the United States for the 1984 was 5,031.3 per 100,000 inhabitants. That is, 5,031.3 Part I offenses were "known to the police" for every 100,000 persons in the nation. As such:

$$\frac{\text{1984 Total Crime Index}}{\text{1984 Population}} \times 100{,}000 = \text{Rate}$$

$$\frac{11{,}881{,}800}{236{,}158{,}000} \times 100{,}000 = 5{,}031.3$$

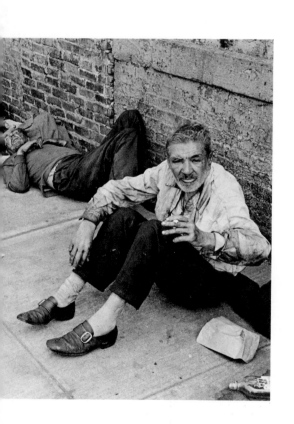

Percent change   The percentage of increase or decrease (+ or −) in the crime index or crime rate over some prior year, calculated as follows:

$$\frac{\text{Current Total Crime Index} - \text{Previous Total Crime Index}}{\text{Previous Total Crime Index}}$$
$$= \text{Percent change}$$

The Total Crime Index was 11,292,400 in 1975. The Total Crime Index increased by 5.2 percent from 1975 to 1984. This percentage is calculated as follows:

$$\frac{\text{1984 Total Crime Index} - \text{1975 Total Crime Index}}{\text{1975 Total Crime Index}}$$

$$= \text{Percent change}$$

$$\frac{11,881,800 - 11,292,400}{11,292,400} = \text{Percent change}$$

$$\frac{589,400}{11,292,400} = 0.052 = 5.2\%$$

While most *UCR* data present Part I offense information for thousands of cities and towns throughout the nation (some 150 pages of tables in 1984), other material also appears. For example arrest data are broken down for each offense by the age, sex, and race of those arrested, and by population area, for both Part I and Part II offenses. In addition, the *UCR* provides totals of the number of law enforcement personnel in the communities that contribute to the reporting system, as well as extensive information on the number of law enforcement officers assaulted or killed during the given year.

The Extent of Crime

The data presented in Exhibit 4.2 provide some preliminary indicators of the extent of crime in the United States, at least in terms of those Index crimes that become known to the police. There were almost 12 million Part I crimes reported during 1984, including 18,690 murders; 84,230 rapes; 485,010 robberies, 685,350 serious assaults; 2,984,400 burglaries; 6,591,900 larcenies; and 1,032,200 motor vehicle thefts.

It was noted earlier that Part II offenses are reported in the *UCR* only in terms of arrests. Therefore, there is no measure of even the relative incidence and prevalence of these crimes throughout the nation. As indicated in Exhibit 4.3, however, there were approximately 11,564,000 arrests during 1984, of which over 9 million involved Part II–type crimes.

Reliability of Estimates

It must be emphasized at the outset that with the exception of the data on homicide, *UCR* estimates of the volume and rates of crime are considerably lower than the actual frequency of such occurrences. Homicide figures tend to be nearly complete, since most deaths and missing persons are investigated in one way or another. Furthermore, comparisons of homicide rates compiled by the FBI and by the Office of Vital Statistics reflect similar figures.[6] But in all other crime categories *UCR* estimates are severely deficient.

Crime, by its very nature, is not easily measurable. It is subject to both concealment and nonreporting — concealment by victims and offenders, and nonreporting by authorities — with the result that official crime statistics fall significantly short of the full volume and range of offenses. There are, for example, wide areas of criminal behavior that rarely find their way into official compilations. When sex, family, and other human relationships are involved, criminal codes are often in sharp conflict with emotions and social norms,

EXHIBIT 4.2

Index of Crime for the United States, 1975–1984

	Total U.S. Population	Total Crime Index*	Violent Crime	Property Crime	Murder
1984	236,158,000	11,881,800	1,273,280	10,608,500	18,690
Rate per 100,000 inhabitants	—	5,031.3	539.2	4,492.1	7.9
1975	213,124,000	11,292,400	1,039,710	10,252,700	20,510
Rate per 100,000 inhabitants	—	5,298.5	487.8	4,810.7	9.6
Percent change, 1975–1984: by crimes	—	+5.2%	+22.5%	+3.5%	−8.9%
by rate	—	−5.0%	+10.5%	−6.6%	−17.7%

* Arson is not included due to incomplete reporting.

SOURCE: *Uniform Crime Reports — 1984*, p. 41.

resulting in the concealment of homosexual relations, statutory rape, adultery, sodomy, illegal abortion, desertion, and nonsupport. In the legal and health professions there are unreported white-collar crimes by both practitioners and clients, primarily in the areas of illegal child adoption practices, fee-splitting, illegal prescription and drug dispensing practices, falsification of claims, perjury, bribery, and conflicts of interest. Within the business sector there are instances of consumer fraud, purchase and sale of stolen merchandise, shortchanging, price-fixing, and concealment of income. As noted in Chapter 3, employees are responsible for countless cases of embezzlement and pilferage, while customers engage in shoplifting, tag-switching, and petty check forgery. Within the public sector there is untold bribery and corruption, and to these offenses can be added "victimless crimes" and syndicate rackets involving prostitution, procuring, commercialized vice, drugs, gambling, and liquor violations, which involve another group of nonreporting clientele. Finally, to these might be added the perhaps millions of victims of Part I and Part II offenses who fail to report crimes to the police out of fear of publicity and reprisal, a lack of confidence in law enforcement or other criminal justice authorities, or a desire not to want to get involved with crime reporting and control.[7]

The killing of Kitty Genovese

A classic case of people not wishing "to get involved" with the reporting of crime occurred during the killing of Kitty Genovese — although in this instance the nonreporting was by witnesses rather than victims. On March 14,

Forcible Rape	Robbery	Aggravated Assault	Burglary	Larceny, Theft	Motor Vehicle Theft
84,230	485,010	685,350	2,984,400	6,591,900	1,032,200
35.7	205.4	290.2	1,263.7	2,791.3	437.1
56,090	470,500	492,620	3,265,300	5,977,700	1,009,600
26.3	220.8	231.1	1,532.1	2,804.8	473.7
+50.2%	+3.1%	+39.1%	−8.6%	+10.3%	+2.2%
+35.7%	−7.0%	+25.6%	−17.5%	−.5%	−7.7%

1964, at 3:20 A.M., 28-year-old Kitty Genovese returned home from work and parked her car only 150 feet from her apartment at 82-70 Austin Street in Queens County, New York, a residential borough of New York City. Ms. Genovese had walked only a few feet when a man came out of the shadows, stabbed her, and began to sexually assault her. She began to scream and lights blinked on in the apartment houses along Austin Street. For the next 25 minutes the attacker stalked, assaulted, and stabbed Ms. Genovese until she eventually died just before 3:50 A.M. Although 37 witnesses heard the woman's cries for help and watched the assault, the first call to the police did not occur until some minutes after her death — almost half an hour after the attack began. Days later, while the nation was still shocked over the witnesses' behavior during the crime, the *New York Times* published the following editorial comment:

> Seldom has the *Times* published a more horrifying story than its account of how thirty-seven respectable, law-abiding middle-class Queens citizens watched a killer stalk his young woman victim in a parking lot in Kew Gardens over a half-hour period, without one of them making a call to the police department that would have saved her life. They would not have been exposed to any danger themselves: a simple telephone call in the privacy of their own homes was all that was needed. How incredible it is that such motives as "I didn't want to get

involved" deterred them from this act of simple humanity. Does residence in a great city destroy all sense of personal responsibility for one's neighbors? Who can explain such shocking indifference on the part of a cross section of our fellow New Yorkers?[8]

There are many specific reasons for not wishing to become involved with the police, including one that came from a liquor shop owner in New York City whose place of business was held up at gunpoint on three separate occasions during 1975. His combined losses were more than $10,000 in money and goods, which could have been reimbursed by his insurance coverage had he reported the robberies to the authorities. He did not, however, for he was

---

EXHIBIT 4.3

Total Estimated Arrests for the United States in 1984

Crime		Number of Arrests	Crime		Number of Arrests
Total		11,564,000	Drug abuse violations		708,400
Murder and nonnegligent			Opium or cocaine and		
manslaughter		17,770	their derivatives	181,800	
Forcible rape		36,700	Marijuana	419,400	
Robbery		138,630	Synthetic or manufactured		
Aggravated assault		300,860	drugs	19,000	
Burglary		433,600	Other — dangerous non-		
Larceny-theft		1,291,700	narcotic drugs	88,300	
Motor vehicle theft		121,200	Gambling		34,700
Arson		19,000	Bookmaking	3,200	
Violent crime	493,960		Numbers and lottery	8,800	
Property crime[a]	1,865,600		All other gambling	22,700	
Crime Index total[a]	2,359,500		Offenses against family and children		44,300
			Driving under the influence		1,779,400
			Liquor laws		505,500
Other assaults		527,000	Drunkenness		1,152,300
Forgery and counterfeiting		82,400	Disorderly conduct		665,900
Fraud		270,700	Vagrancy		29,100
Embezzlement		8,100	All other offenses (except traffic)		2,406,900
Stolen property; buying, receiving,			Suspicion (not included in total)		21,300
possessing		123,100	Curfew and loitering law violations		86,600
Vandalism		245,900	Runaways		147,000
Weapons; carrying, possessing, etc.		177,500			
Prostitution and commercialized vice		112,200			
Sex offenses (except forcible rape					
and prostitution)		97,800			

Note: Arrest totals are based on all reporting agencies and estimates for unreported areas. Because of rounding, items may not add to totals.

[a] These categories include arson, a newly established Crime Index offense in 1979.

SOURCE: *Uniform Crime Reports — 1984*, p. 163.

---

hoping to sell his business and felt that if word got out that his establishment was a "target," its potential market value would have diminished significantly.

At the same time, crime statistics are also subject to concealment, nonreporting, overreporting, and other manipulations by criminal justice authorities, either for political and public relations purposes or for reasons of personnel shortage. Law enforcement agencies wishing to secure more equipment and staff, for example, typically report (on some occasions overreport) all officially known complaints. However, if such equipment or personnel has already been obtained, the agencies may report fewer crimes, in order to suggest an efficient use of prior funding.[9]

Also, methods of recording crimes at the local level can have an impact on the reliability of statistics. Studies by the National Opinion Research Center (NORC) at the University of Chicago suggest that police may report only three-fourths of the complaints received for certain crimes.[10] Other studies have documented that as many as 20 percent of citizen complaints may not be recorded in police figures, depending on the presence or absence of a suspect; the victim–offender relationship; and the victim's age, ethnicity, and methods of interacting with law officers (see Exhibit 4.4).[11]

Clearly, procedures such as these can have serious effects on the compilation of crime statistics. In 1984, for example, in a study sponsored by the Justice Department it was found that the FBI was not informed of about one in every five crimes reported by the public.[12]

In addition to these problems of concealment and nonreporting, which occur at the victim and agency levels, there are other contaminations of the statistics that result from the *UCR* process itself.

One reason many people do not want to become involved in reporting a crime, or even in coming to the aid of the victim, may be the number of other people around. The more crowded the city street, as in this scene, the fewer may be willing to help.

As noted earlier, the FBI's *Uniform Crime Reporting Handbook* provides specific definitions of the 29 crime categories in the *UCR;* the FBI also provides standardized reporting forms to police agencies across the country for compiling their data. However, not all law enforcement bureaucracies follow directions and instructions to the letter, resulting in many contaminated categories. In 1985, for example, the FBI estimated that some 7,000 inaccurate reports were being received daily in the area of stolen vehicles alone.[13]

The *UCR* in Retrospect

How useful, then are the *Uniform Crime Reports?* Are they reliable enough to provide the researcher, administrator, and observer with baseline data on the phenomenon of crime? As has been pointed out, the *UCR* data do have limitations, including incompleteness and bias, and they fall considerably short in reporting the full extent of crime in the United States.

By examining *UCR* figures within the perspective of rates and proportions, as opposed to absolute numbers, a degree of bias is eliminated. Such analyses can help determine the overall growth, decline, or persistence of

---

EXHIBIT 4.4

The Strange Career of "Detective Can"

Throughout the 1960s, in one of the most active police precincts in New York City, it was observed by the author that on busy nights less than half of the "in person" complaints to the desk officer were either acted upon or recorded. If the victim was intoxicated, an adolescent, or black and the crime was a purse snatching, simple assault, or burglary, the complainant was told to go home and return some other time. If the victims insisted on making a complaint, many were harassed and threatened with arrest for interfering with police officers in the performance of their duties. Those who did manage to have their case put on paper were unaware that as soon as they left the squad room the matter was thrown in the wastebasket.

This practice was not at all new in New York City. A decade earlier, substantial increases had suddenly become apparent in all of the Part I offense categories listed in the *Uniform Crime Reports*. In its investigation into these drastic changes, the New York City Institute of Public Administration found that the problem stemmed from the new police commissioner's demand that more honest and complete records be maintained. In other words, as in the "crime wave" started by Lincoln Steffens and Jacob Riis during the 1890s, New York was simply experiencing a "crime-reporting wave." The final report on the matter pointed out that

in most cases arising prior to October 1950, the information furnished by a complaint quickly found its way to a wastebasket. This practice was referred to cynically as "canning" a complaint or referring the matter to "Detective Can."

During the early 1980s, "Detective Can" reappeared in Chicago, but this time as a police captain. Television station WBBM charged that for decades police officers in that city had been burying many of their cases in order to keep crime statistics down. City officials ultimately admitted that the exposé was correct, that detectives had been routinely transferring victims' files to "Captain Can," chief of the "circular precinct." Procedures were changed, and during the months that followed, crime statistics jumped by 25 percent, a clear example of a "paper crime wave."

SOURCE: Institute of Public Administration, *Crime Records in Police Management* (New York: Institute of Public Administration, 1952); *Newsweek*, May 16, 1983, p. 63.

Purse-snatching is the type of crime that is not always reported to police.

particular offense behavior; they can be a mechanism for determining the extent to which the phenomenon is or is not being brought under control; they can suggest the parameters of the population cohort or cohorts most responsible for a particular form of criminality; and they can indicate the changing social and economic severity of a given offense.

Second, the most effective use of rate and proportion analysis occurs at the local level. Combining existing *UCR* data with statistical compilations available from local, county, and state criminal justice agencies provides planners, administrators, and observers with the specific information necessary for isolating community crime trends.

Victim Survey Research

In 1965, in an effort to determine the parameters of crime that did not appear in official criminal statistics, the President's Commission on Law Enforcement and Administration of Justice initiated the first national survey of crime victimization ever conducted. During that year, the National Opinion Research Center surveyed 10,000 households, asking whether the person questioned, or any member of his or her household, had been a victim of crime during the preceding year, whether the crime had been reported to the police, and if not, the reasons for not reporting.[14] The households were selected so that they would be representative of the nation as a whole, and as is the case with political polling and election forecasting, the results were considered to be accurate within a small degree of error. More detailed surveys were undertaken in medium- and high-crime areas in Washington, D.C., Boston, and Chicago by the Bureau of Social Science Research, located in Washington, and the Survey Research Center of the University of Michigan.

These **victimization surveys** quickly demonstrated that the actual amount of crime in the United States at that time was likely to be several times

Victimization surveys

Is this a mugging, or are they break-dancing? It may be difficult for a bystander to tell.

that reported in the *UCR*. As indicated in Exhibit 4.5, the NORC survey suggested that during 1965, forcible rapes were almost four times the reported rate, larcenies were almost double, and burglaries and robberies were 50 percent greater than the reported rate. Vehicle theft was lower, but by a smaller amount than the differences between other categories of crime, and the homicide figure from the NORC survey was considered too small for an accurate statistical projection. As high as the NORC rates were for violent and property crimes, they were still considered, to have understated the actual amounts of crime to some degree, since the victimization rates for every member of the surveyed household were based on the responses of only one family member interviewed. There are many circumstances and situations in which the crimes of one family member may not be known to another.

The National Crime Survey

The interest and knowledge generated by the initial victim survey research stimulated the Law Enforcement Assistance Administration (LEAA) to continue the effort with surveys of its own. Its first survey, conducted by the U.S. Bureau of Census in 1972, further documented the disparities between unreported crime and "crimes known to the police." In some cities the ratio of the two was greater than 5 to 1.[15]

Since this 1972 effort, victimization research has continued under the title of the National Crime Survey (NCS). NCS data reflect the nature and extent of criminal victimization, the characteristics of the victim, victim–

EXHIBIT 4.5

Comparison of Crime Rates from the NORC Survey and the *UCR*

Crime	NORC Survey	*UCR*
Homicide	3.0	5.1
Forcible rape	42.5	11.6
Robbery	94.0	61.4
Aggravated assault	218.3	106.6
Burglary	949.1	605.3
Larceny	606.5	393.3
Motor vehicle theft	206.2	251.0
Total violent crimes	357.8	184.7
Total property crimes	1,761.8	1,249.6

SOURCE: President's Commission on Law Enforcement and Administration of Justice, *Crime and Its Impact—An Assessment* (Washington, D.C.: U.S. Government Printing Office, 1967), p. 17.

offender relationships, the times and places of the crimes, the degree of weapon use, extent of personal injury, extent of victim self-protection, amount of economic and worktime loss due to victimization, the degree to which crimes are reported to police, and the reasons for nonreporting.[16] For example, 1977 survey findings were based on interviews with 128,000 occupants in 60,000 housing units and projected to the population of the nation as a whole. Although NCS and *UCR* data are not fully comparable (this is discussed in the next section), Exhibit 4.6 suggests that the 2,970,000 violent crimes projected by the NCS go well beyond what appeared in *UCR* data for the same year.

The major reason for these large discrepancies is that significant numbers of these crimes were not reported to the police by victims. The NCS chart in Exhibit 4.7 suggests that the reporting rate for violent crimes was about half; for larcenies, less than a third. The major reason for this high level of nonreporting was the victims' beliefs that there was nothing the police could do about the crimes or their beliefs that the victimizations were simply not important enough to report. Less frequently mentioned were such reasons as fear of reprisal, reporting was too inconvenient or time-consuming, the police would not want to be bothered, or the crime was a private and personal matter.

Although *UCR* and NCS data have been often compared, the two are still not fully comparable. First, the *UCR* bases its crime rates on the total U.S. population, while the NCS victimization data relate only to those persons who are ages 12 years and older. Second, the NCS measures crime by the *victimization* rather than by the incident, and for crimes against persons the number

Reasons for nonreporting of crimes

EXHIBIT 4.6

Crimes of Violence: National Crime Survey and *Uniform Crime Reports,* 1984

Crime	National Crime Survey		Uniform Crime Reports	
	Number	Rate	Number	Rate
Total	2,970,000	1,550	1,254,590	531
Forcible rape	180,000	90	84,230	36
Robbery	117,000	580	485,010	205
Aggravated assault	1,673,000	880	685,350	290

Note: The National Crime Survey rate per 100,000 persons is based on a survey population of all persons ages 12 years and over. The *Uniform Crime Reports* rate per 100,000 is based on the total U.S. population.

SOURCES: *Criminal Victimization 1984,* Bureau of Justice Statistics Bulletin, October 1985; *Uniform Crime Reports—1984.*

of victimizations is normally greater than the number of incidents, since more than one person can be involved in any given incident. Third, NCS and *UCR* crime classifications are not always uniform. While purse snatching is included with robbery according to *UCR* definitions, it appears as theft in NCS data. Fourth, NCS data on homicide are considered to be unreliable because violence of that type is relatively rare, and the few unreported instances that do emerge during a survey of a population cross-section are too small in numbers to project accurately for the nation as a whole.

Comparisons between NCS and *UCR* crime figures and rates must be viewed with caution. Neither reporting mechanism alone can offer a fully accurate picture of the extent of specific crimes. Nevertheless, comparisons do indicate some general weaknesses of the *Uniform Crime Reports* and suggest the relative amounts of crime that go unreported to the police.

Victimization Survey Applications and Limitations

The rediscovery of the victim as a more complete source of information on instances of criminal activity has been the chief contribution of victim survey research. The material derived from crime victim surveys helps determine to a

The uses of victimization surveys

great degree the extent and distribution of crime in a community. In addition, the surveys target not only victimizations but also public conceptions of the fear of crime, characteristics of the victim and offender, conceptions of police effectiveness, as well as other data. Therefore victim-focused studies such as these can also be used to do the following:

1. Describe the characteristics of victims and high crime areas
2. Evaluate the effectiveness of specific police programs
3. Develop better insights into certain violent crimes through the analysis of victim–offender relationships
4. Structure programs for increased victim reporting of crimes to the police
5. Sensitize the criminal justice system to the needs of the victim
6. Develop training programs that stress police–victim and police–community relations
7. Structure and implement meaningful public information and crime prevention programs

Nevertheless, victimization studies do have limitations. A number of weaknesses affect their accuracy. The researchers who conduct these surveys find that those interviewed tend to incorrectly remember exactly when a crime occurred; in property offenses, they forget how much the losses were. Furthermore, the same respondents are used from one year to the next. As a result, respondents may be prone to "panel bias," the tendency of some of those who are continually selected to become less willing to cooperate in the long and complex interviewing process.[17] But by far the major problem associated with the victimization survey technique is its cost. The greatest advantages come from surveys at the local level that focus on what can be done to upgrade neighborhood crime prevention and police effectiveness programs. One such community-based study occurred during 1974 in Pueblo, Colorado, a small city of some 100,000 persons at that time.[18] The cost of the Pueblo study exceeded $50,000. The cost of conducting similar studies on an annual basis in most communities would be staggering, and most communities would simply not be able to afford them.[19]

The limitations of victimization data

Self-reported Criminal Behavior

Since the 1930s, when the FBI began publishing the *Uniform Crime Reports,* criminological research has produced studies confirming the limitations of official crime statistics. Among the earliest of these research efforts was a rudimentary victimization survey in 1933, which found that of some 5,314 instances of shoplifting that occurred in three Philadelphia department stores, less than 5 percent were ever reported to the police.[20]

Another primary mechanism for determining the nature and extent of this "dark figure," or *unknown* crime, has been the study of self-reported offense behavior, or **self-reported crime.** The first major study of self-reported crime came in 1947, when two researchers obtained completed questionnaires from 1,020 men and 678 women of diverse ages and with a wide range of conventional occupations regarding their involvement in 49 different offenses. Ninety-nine percent of the respondents admitted committing one or

The "dark figure" of unknown crime includes self-reported crime

more of the offenses listed. The percentages of both men and women who had engaged in many types of crime were significant:[21]

Crime	Percent	
	Men	Women
Petty theft	89	83
Disorderly conduct	85	76
Malicious mischief	84	81
Assault	49	5
Tax evasion	57	40
Robbery	11	1
Fraud	46	34
Criminal libel	36	29
Concealed weapons	35	3
Auto theft	26	8
Other grand theft	13	11
Burglary	17	4

The uses and advantages of self-report studies

This pioneer effort demonstrated that criminal activity was considerably more widespread than police files even began to suggest. Since then, studies of self-reported criminal involvement have become more common. In addition to their use as a check on the limitations of standard crime-reporting mechanisms, they can also be used to determine

1. the extent of crime commission within the "normal" (typically noncriminal) population
2. what kinds of crime typically remain unknown
3. how the official system of crime control selects its cases
4. whether certain categories of offenders are over- and under-selected by official control mechanisms
5. whether explanations and theories of crime developed for officially known offenders apply to nonregistered offenders as well[22]

The limitations of self-reports

Validity

Reliability

Studies of self-reported crime have provided numerous insights into these issues, but such research has not been without limitations and problems. First, there are methodological questions of validity and reliability. **Validity** refers to how good an answer the study yields. When the respondents admit to criminal behavior, are their answers true? Do they underreport or exaggerate their offense behavior? Are the respondents' estimates of the frequency of their crimes accurate? **Reliability** refers to the precision or accuracy of the instruments used to record and measure self-reported behavior. In other words, does the interview measure what it is intended to measure? Does the respondent interpret the meaning of words such as *burglary, robbery,* or some other offense the same way the researcher does? Besides these

EXHIBIT 4.7

Percent of Victimizations Reported to the Police, 1984

Personal crimes

Crime	Percent
Rape	56%
Robbery	55%
Assault	44%
Personal larceny	26%

Household crimes

Crime	Percent
Burglary	49%
Household larceny	27%
Motor vehicle theft	69%

Percent reported

0 10 20 30 40 50 60 70 80 90 100

SOURCE: Adapted from *Criminal Victimization 1984,* Bureau of Justice Statistics Bulletin, October 1985.

potential methodological problems there are other possible sources of error, such as the following:

- Those who agree to answer questions may be markedly different from those who refuse, which leaves in doubt the representativeness of any sample of persons interviewed.
- Those who respond to such inquiries may be truthful in their answers but may elect to conceal large segments of their criminal backgrounds.
- Most studies have focused on groups of students and other juveniles, stressing the incidence of unrecorded *delinquency,* while few efforts have targeted populations of adult offenders.

One of the more recent studies that did examine the extent of unknown crime within an adult population involved the collection of extensive self-reported data on drug use and criminality in Miami, Florida, between 1978 and 1981.[23] The sample included 573 male and female narcotics users, the majority of whom were actively using drugs and committing crimes in the community at the time of the interview. All subjects were interviewed at length about the number of their crimes and arrests during the previous 12 months. According to the study's findings, the incidence of crime was strikingly high while the rate of arrest was almost insignificant (see Exhibit 4.8). There were a total of 215,105 offenses; *less than 1 percent resulted in arrest.* Although more than half of these offenses were the "victimless" crimes of procuring, drug sales, prostitution, and gambling, the number of Index crimes was significant — almost 6,000 robberies and assaults and almost 50,000 larcenies of one type or another.

In general, despite sample biases and other methodological limitations, the studies of self-reported crime that have been made over the past four decades are important to criminological research. First, there are the advantages mentioned earlier. In addition, studies that focus on particular populations (such as narcotics users) can tell us more about the patterns and styles of criminal careers than any other form of data.

Other Sources of Data on Crime and Justice

Throughout the history of crime statistics in the United States, writers in this field have recognized the gaps and abuses in crime data and have stressed the need for a comprehensive statistics program that would give an accurate picture of crime in the United States. One of the earliest suggestions for achieving this appeared in Louis Newton Robinson's *History and Organization of Criminal Statistics in the United States* in 1911. Robinson proposed to use a model designed by the Bureau of the Census for collecting mortality statistics, with the responsibility for compilation resting with individual states and cities.[24] In 1931, the National Commission on Law Observance and Enforcement (the Wickersham Commission) recommended the development of a comprehensive plan for a complete body of statistics covering crime, criminals, criminal justice, and correctional treatment of federal, state, and local levels, with the responsibility of the program entrusted to a single federal agency.[25] More than 30 years later, in 1967, the President's Commission on Law Enforcement and Administration of Justice again called for a national crime statistics program.[26] In 1973, the same plea was made by the National Advisory Commission on Criminal Justice Standards and Goals.[27] As recently as 1984, the Justice Department made a similar recommendation.[28]

To date, the long-awaited national statistics program has yet to emerge. The *Uniform Crime Reports* still continues as the primary data source on crime, supplemented to some extent by victimization surveys, and to a lesser degree by a scattering of self-report studies. However, these are not the only sources of data on crime, criminals, and criminal justice processing. Many state and federal agencies compile data on their own particular areas of interest, which are available to students and researchers in crime and justice. Until 1973, however, such data could be found only within the individual reports of particular agencies and were rather difficult to retrieve. In that year, the Law Enforcement Assistance Administration began sponsoring an ongo-

EXHIBIT 4.8

Criminal Activity During the One-Year Period Prior to Interview of 573 Narcotics Users in Miami, Florida

Crime	Total Offenses	Percentage of Total Offenses	Percentage of Sample Involved	Percentage of Offenses Resulting in Arrest
Robbery	5,300	2.5%	37.7%	0.8% (n = 44)
Assault	636	0.3%	20.9%	5.5% (n = 35)
Burglary	6,669	3.1%	52.7%	0.8% (n = 52)
Vehicle theft	841	0.4%	19.4%	0.8% (n = 7)
Theft from vehicle	3,708	1.7%	28.1%	0.4% (n = 15)
Shoplifting	25,045	11.6%	62.1%	0.4% (n = 104)
Pickpocketing	2,445	1.1%	4.5%	<0.1% (n = 2)
Prostitute theft	4,093	1.9%	15.9%	<0.1% (n = 4)
Other theft	6,668	3.1%	31.1%	0.6% (n = 39)
Forgery/counterfeiting	7,504	3.5%	37.5%	0.8% (n = 59)
Con games	3,162	1.5%	23.9%	<0.1% (n = 1)
Stolen goods	17,240	8.0%	53.4%	0.1% (n = 22)
Prostitution	26,045	12.1%	22.2%	0.3% (n = 89)
Procuring	7,107	3.3%	24.1%	<0.1% (n = 3)
Drug sales	82,449	38.3%	83.9%	0.1% (n = 86)
Arson	17	<0.1%	1.7%	0.0% (n = 0)
Vandalism	322	0.1%	7.2%	0.9% (n = 3)
Fraud	1,165	0.5%	10.5%	0.5% (n = 6)
Gambling	12,939	6.0%	36.1%	<0.1% (n = 4)
Extortion	240	0.1%	7.5%	0.0% (n = 0)
Loan sharking	795	0.4%	7.0%	0.0% (n = 0)
Alcohol offenses	296	0.1%	6.6%	7.1% (n = 21)
All other	419	0.2%	2.3%	3.1% (n = 13)
TOTAL	215,105	100.0%		0.3% (n = 609)

Note: n refers to the actual arrests the percentage reflects.

SOURCE: James A. Inciardi, *The War on Drugs: Heroin, Cocaine, Crime, and Public Policy* (Palo Alto, California: Mayfield, 1986), p. 127.

ing project, the outgrowth of which has been the annual *Sourcebook of Criminal Justice Statistics,* which has broad coverage and includes information about most aspects of crime and justice.

Summary

Most of the data on the nature, extent, and trends of crime in the United States comes from official crime statistics. Official statistics are collected and compiled by the FBI and published annually as the *Uniform Crime Reports* (*UCR*). The *UCR* includes "crimes known to the police" and arrests. Data are broken down into Part I and Part II offenses, and arrests are subdivided by age, race, and sex. The *UCR* also includes rates of crime, percent changes from year to year, and breakdowns by region, state, and metropolitan area.

Although official statistics are the primary source of crime data, they have numerous shortcomings. Most criminal acts are not reported to the police, and statistical data are subject to concealment, overreporting, nonreporting, and other manipulations. On the other hand, despite these difficulties, *UCR* data are useful for gaining insight into the relative amount of crime and for analyzing crime and arrest trends.

In an effort to determine the parameters of crime that did not appear in official statistics, in 1965 the President's Commission initiated the first national survey of crime victimization ever conducted. Similar surveys have been undertaken since then. These surveys demonstrate that the actual amount of crime is probably several times greater than that estimated in the *UCR*. Victimization and *UCR* data, however, are not fully comparable. The bases of their rates are different, the yardsticks of measurement are different, and crime classifications are not uniform.

Victimization data have numerous useful applications for understanding the characteristics of victims, evaluating the effectiveness of police programs, developing insights into victim–offender relationships, sensitizing the criminal justice system to the needs of the victim, and structuring more focused crime prevention programs. On the other hand, victimization surveys have their shortcomings. They are expensive and they raise a number of basic methodological issues.

Self-reported data on offenses represent a third source of information on crime. This data reflects the so-called "dark figure" or unknown crime. The findings of these studies suggest the extent of crime in "normal" populations, what kinds of crimes are committed that typically remain unknown, and how the official system of crime control may select its cases. Self-report studies, however, have problems of validity and reliability.

Key Terms

arrests (109)
crime clock (108)
Crime Index (112)
crime rate (112)

"crimes known to the police" (109)
Part I offenses (110)
Part II offenses (110)
reliability (124)

self-reported crime (123)
Uniform Crime Reports (107)
validity (124)
victimization surveys (119)

David Burnett/Woodfin Camp

An Overview of the Criminal Justice Process

EXHIBIT 5.F

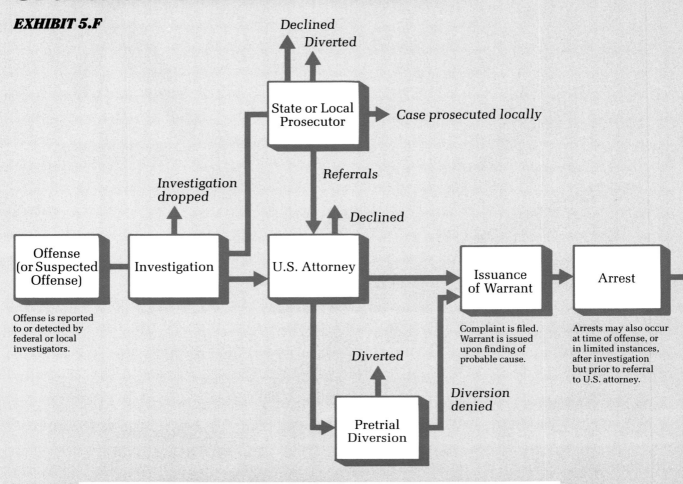

Declined
Diverted

State or Local Prosecutor → Case prosecuted locally

Referrals

Investigation dropped

Declined

Offense (or Suspected Offense) → **Investigation** → **U.S. Attorney** → **Issuance of Warrant** → **Arrest**

Offense is reported to or detected by federal or local investigators.

Diverted

Diversion denied

Pretrial Diversion

Complaint is filed. Warrant is issued upon finding of probable cause.

Arrests may also occur at time of offense, or in limited instances, after investigation but prior to referral to U.S. attorney.

Theo Westenberger/Sygma

Martin J. Dain/Magnum

© Paul Conklin

Questions for Discussion

1. What issues of validity and reliability are most apparent with regard to official criminal statistics?
2. Can the *UCR* be improved? How?
3. How might official statistics, victimization data, and self-reported crime data be collected and combined to provide a more accurate picture of crime in the United States?

For Further Reading

Black, D. I. "Production of Crime Rates," *American Sociological Review* 35 (1970): 735–739.

Inciardi, James A. "Heroin Use and Street Crime," *Crime and Delinquency* 25 (July 1979): 335–346.

O'Brian, Robert M., *Crime and Victimization Data.* Beverly Hills: Sage, 1985.

Notes

1. Lincoln Steffens, *The Autobiography of Lincoln Steffens* (New York: Harcourt, Brace, 1931), p. 285.

2. Steffens, *Autobiography,* pp. 287–288.

3. Albert Morris, *What Are the Sources of Knowledge About Crime in the U.S.A.?* United Prison Association of Massachusetts, Bulletin No. 15, November 1965.

4. Sanford J. Ungar, *FBI* (Boston: Little, Brown, 1976), p. 387.

5. Federal Bureau of Investigation, *Crime in the United States — 1984* (Washington, D.C.: U.S. Government Printing Office, 1985), p. 1. Throughout this text, these FBI crime reports will be referenced simply as *Uniform Crime Reports,* followed by a designation of the year to which they refer.

6. Daniel Glaser, "National Goals and Indicators for the Reduction of Crime and Delinquency," *The Annals* 371 (May 1967): 104–126.

7. See Harry Manuel Shulman, "The Measurement of Crime in the United States," *Journal of Criminal Law, Criminology and Police Science* 57 (1966): 483–492; Donald R. Cressey, "The State of Criminal Statistics in the United States — 1960," *Journal of Criminal Law, Criminology and Police Science* 51 (1960): 49–65.

8. Cited by Jonathan Craig and Richard Posner, *The New York Crime Book* (New York: Pyramid, 1972), p. 176.

9. See D. Seidman and M. Couzens, "Getting the Crime Rate Down: Political Pressure and Crime Reporting," *Law and Society Review* 8 (1974): 457–493; C. C. Van Vechten, "Differential Case Mortality in Select Jurisdictions," *American Sociological Review* 7 (1942): 833–839.

10. President's Commission on Law Enforcement and Administration of Justice, *Crime and Its Impact: An Assessment* (Washington, D.C.: U.S. Government Printing Office, 1967).

11. D. I. Black, "Production of Crime Rates," *American Sociological Review* 35 (1970): 735–739.

12. *New York Times,* November 19, 1984, p. B11.

13. *Christian Science Monitor,* August 28, 1985, p. 15.

14. President's Commission on Law Enforcement and Administration of Justice, *Crime And Its Impact — An Assessment* (Washington, D.C.: U.S. Government Printing Office, 1967), p. 17.

15. Law Enforcement Assistance Administration, *Criminal Victimization in the United States — 1977* (Washington, D.C.: U.S. Government Printing Office, 1979).

16. LEAA, *Criminal Victimization — 1977.*

17. See James Garofolo, *An Introduction to the National Crime Survey* (Washington, D.C.: U.S. Government Printing Office, 1977), p. 5.

18. E. L.Willoughby and James A. Inciardi, "Estimating the Incidence of Crime: A Survey of Crime Victimization in Pueblo, Colorado," *Police Chief* (August 1975): 69–70.

19. For a more detailed discussion of the victim survey research technique, see Richard F. Sparks, Hazel G. Genn, and David J. Dodd, *Surveying Victims: A Study of the Measurement of Criminal Victimization* (New York: Wiley, 1977).

20. Thorsten Sellin, *Research Memorandum on Crime in the Depression* (New York: Social Science Research Council, 1937).

21. James S. Wallerstein and Clement J. Wyle, "Our Law-Abiding Law-Breakers," *Probation* 35 (April 1947): 107–118.

22. J. Andenaes, N. Christie, and S. Skirbekk, "A Study in Self-reported Crime," in *Scandinavian Studies in Criminology,* Scandinavian Research Council on Criminology (Oslo: Universitelsforloget, 1965), pp. 87–88.

23. See James A. Inciardi, *The War on Drugs: Heroin, Cocaine, Crime, and Public Policy* (Palo Alto, Calif.: Mayfield, 1986).

24. Louis Newton Robinson, *History and Organization of Criminal Statistics in the United States* (New York: Hart, Schaffner & Marx, 1911).

25. U.S. National Commission of Law Observance and Enforcement, *Report on Criminal Statistics* (Washington, D.C.: U.S. Government Printing Office, 1931).

26. President's Commission on Law Enforcement and Administration of Justice, *The Challenge of Crime in a Free Society* (Washington, D.C.: U.S. Government Printing Office, 1967), pp. 123–137.

27. National Advisory Commission on Criminal Justice Standards and Goals, *A National Strategy to Reduce Crime* (Washington, D.C.: U.S. Government Printing Office, 1973). The most recent volume in the series is: Bureau of Justice Statistics, *Sourcebook of Criminal Justice Statistics — 1980* (Washington, D.C.: U.S. Government Printing Office, 1981).

28. *New York Times,* November 19, 1984, p. B11.

5

The Process of Justice: An Overview

The general law of the land is in favour of the wager of battle, and it is our duty to pronounce the law as it is, and not as we may wish it to be. Whatever prejudices therefore may justly exist against this mode of trial, still as it is the law of the land, we must pronounce judgment for it.

— The Lord Chief Justice Edward Law, Earl of Ellenborough, 1818

The Constitution of the United States speaks of liberty and prohibits the deprivation of liberty without due process of law.

— Chief Justice Charles Evans Hughes,
Supreme Court of the United States, 1935

Part 2

The Police

6

Law Enforcement in the United States: History and Structure

Every policeman knows that, though governments may change, the police remain.

— Leon Trotsky, 1932

I don't wear silk T-shirts, I don't have a pet alligator or an Italian sports car, and I hardly look like Sonny Crockett or Rico Tubbs.

— A Miami vice officer, 1986

*T*he police are the largest and most visible segment of the criminal justice process. As organized agents of law enforcement, police officers are charged with the prevention and detection of crime, the apprehension of criminal offenders, the defense of constitutional guarantees, the resolution of community conflicts, the protection of society, and the promotion and preservation of civil order. They represent that "thin blue line" between order and anarchy.

The starting points for an analysis of police in the United States are history and structure, both of which reflect a number of curiosities. Policing is a relatively modern phenomenon, having emerged as a formally organized institution less than a century and a half ago. At the same time, however, the origins of policing go back many hundreds of years, and to numerous European cultures. Structurally, law enforcement in the United States has the characteristic of decentralization. That is, there is no national police force per se. Rather, there are literally tens of thousands of independent police agencies throughout the country that developed separately and operate under a policy of local autonomy. In spite of this diversity, though, the organization of these enforcement units is remarkably similar.

The Emergence of Modern Police

Modern policing can be traced to the latter part of the ninth century when England's Alfred the Great was structuring the defenses of his kingdom against an impending Danish invasion. Part of Alfred's strategy depended on internal stability. To gain this, he instituted a system of **mutual pledge,** which organized the country at several levels. At the lowest level were *tithings,* ten families grouped together who each assumed responsibility for the acts of their members. At the next level, ten tithings, or 100 families, were grouped together into a *hundred;* the hundred was under the charge of a **constable.** Hundreds within a specific geographic area were combined to form *shires*—administrative units (now called counties) under royal authority that were governed by a *shire-reeve,* or **sheriff.**[1] In thirteenth-century England, the **night watch** appeared in urban areas to protect late-night city streets; the watch represented the most rudimentary form of metropolitan policing.[2] Modern police forces did not emerge, however, until centuries later, due to the efforts of Henry and John Fielding, Patrick Colquhoun, and Sir Robert Peel.

Alfred the Great's system of mutual pledge

The constable

The sheriff
The night watch

Magistrates, Constables, Beadles, and Thief-takers

At least metaphorically, every citizen in seventeenth-century England was a policeman, and every policeman was a citizen. That is, law enforcement was the duty of all the people. In practice, however, this system was ineffectual, even including the few officials whose duties included enforcing the law and keeping the peace. There were *magistrates,* for example, who not only presided in courts, but ordered arrests, called witnesses, and examined prisoners. There were *parish constables,* carryovers from the days of Alfred the Great, who had limited powers of arrest and whose authority was confined to relatively small districts. And there were *beadles,* constables' assistants, who were paid £20 a year and who did little more than clear vagrants from the city streets. But the impact of magistrates and constables was minimal, for most were corrupt and justice rarely prevailed.

To these could be added the **thief-takers** — private detectives of a sort who were paid by the Crown on a piecework basis.[3] They had no official status as police and no more authority than the private citizen, yet anyone could be a thief-taker. Like the bounty hunters of the American West, thief-takers received a reward in return for the apprehension of a criminal.

Thief-takers, a response to highway robbers

Thief-takers emerged in England in response to the troublesome nature of highway robbery, which had been flourishing since the early years of such legendary outlaws as Robin Hood and Little John. By the seventeenth century, although romanticized in literature, highway robbery in the grand manner of Jack Sheppard, Dick Turpin, Claude Duval, and Captain Lightfoot made traveling through the English countryside so perilous that no coach or traveler was safe. As a result, in 1693 an Act of Parliament established a reward of £40 for the capture of any highwayman or road agent.[4] The reward was payable upon conviction, and to the thief-taker also went the highwayman's horse, arms, money, and property, unless these were proven to have been stolen.

This system was extended during the reigns of Anne and George I to cover offenses other than highway robbery, and soon a sliding scale of parliamentary rewards came into existence. Burglars, housebreakers, and footpads (street robbers), for example, were worth the same as the highwayman, but the sheep stealer brought only £10, and the army deserter only £1. In some communities, homeowners joined together and offered supplementary rewards, typically £20, for the apprehension of any highwayman or footpad within their district. When there were especially serious crime waves, Parliament provided special rewards of £100 for particular felons.

As the system expanded, a class of professional thief-takers sprang up. Not unexpectedly, many thief-takers were themselves criminals, since the offer of a pardon was an additional incentive. But thief-taking also had its drawbacks. Arresting desperate criminals was dangerous, rewards were not paid if the criminal was acquitted, and thief-takers always had to fear the private revenge of their victims' friends and associates.

Thief-makers

The result was that thief-takers often became *thief-makers.* Many would seduce youngsters into committing crimes, then have another thief-taker arrest the youth in the midst of the offense. Others framed innocent parties by planting stolen goods on their persons or in their homes. Although some real criminals were apprehended by the professional thief-takers, the system generally created more crime than it suppressed.[5]

Henry Fielding, the "Blind Beak," and the Bow Street Runners

Henry Fielding laid the foundation for modern policing.

Although probably best known as the eighteenth-century novelist who wrote *Tom Jones*, **Henry Fielding** might also be credited with laying the foundation for the first modern police force. In 1748, during the age of English highwaymen, Fielding was appointed magistrate in Westminster, a city adjacent to central London. He located himself in a house on Bow Street that became both his home and his office, and it was there that the first English police force began to form.

It was a time when burglaries, street and highway robberies, and other thefts had reached new heights, and it was Fielding's aim to reduce the profitability of such criminal activities. First he established relationships with local pawnbrokers, provided them with lists and decriptions of recently stolen property, and urged them to notify him should the contraband come to their attention. He then inserted the following notice into the London and Westminster newspapers:

> All persons who shall for the future suffer by robbers, burglars, etc., are desired immediately to bring or send the best description they can of such robbers, etc., with the time and place and circumstances of the fact, to Henry Fielding Esq., at his house in Bow Street.[6]

What Fielding suggested was original for his time, for few people had ever before reported thefts to the authorities. Although Fielding could accomplish little singlehandedly, within a year he had obtained the cooperation of Saunders Welch, the High Constable of Holborn, and several other public-spirited constables. Together they formed a small but unofficial investigative division that was the first organized force ever used in England against criminals. Fielding's constables — the **Bow Street Runners** — were not paid as police officers, but they were nevertheless entitled to the standard thief-takers' rewards.

The Bow Street Runners

In time, Henry Fielding's efforts were noticed by the government, and some £200 was periodically provided to support the activities of his Bow Street Runners. Only four years after his appointment as magistrate, however, Fielding's health began to deteriorate, forcing him into a wheelchair. He then persuaded the authorities to appoint his half-brother, John Fielding, to share his magistracy. John soon took over the operations of the unofficial Bow Street Police, and was quickly dubbed the "Blind Beak." This name derived from the facts that John was blind, and that in English cant — the slang of the London underworld — "beak" was a term referring to any judge or magistrate.[7]

The Horse Patrol, England's first uniformed police

The Bow Street Runners endured, but only on a small scale. Then in 1763, Fielding was allotted £600 to set up a civilian Horse Patrol of eight men for the direct curtailment of robbers and footpads on the London streets. The patrol seemed to be a success, but after only nine months it was disbanded due to a lack of support by the English government. During the next decade, however, a permanent Foot Patrol was established, and in 1804, some 22 years after John Fielding's retirement, a new Horse Patrol was set up. It included 2 inspectors and 52 men, outfitted in red vests and blue jackets and trousers. This was England's first uniformed police.[8]

Patrick Colquhoun and Sir Robert Peel

The Bow Street Runners had been born and nurtured in secrecy, for had it been known that even an unofficial band of organized police was in operation, it would have been denounced as an instrument of oppression and tyranny. Even John Fielding's Horse Patrol, as effective as it had been, was disbanded for this very reason. The English people were emphatic that they did not want a professional police force because of their love of freedom, their faith in private enterprise, their respect for tradition, and their dislike for spending public money. In spite of these feelings, which were deeply rooted in English culture, when Glasgow businessman Patrick Colquhoun was appointed as a London magistrate he soon crystallized the idea of a "new science of preventive police."[9] His suggestions for a large, organized police force for greater London were quickly rejected, but in 1789 he did form a special river police patterned after Fielding's Bow Street model. Although successful, Colquhoun's efforts met with little support, for throughout that century and decades thereafter the English continued to harbor mistrust for enforcement authority.

Sir Robert Peel

Although popular belief has credited Sir Robert Peel with the establishment of a professional police force of the modern variety,[10] it is clear that others came before him. Nevertheless, Peel was a significant figure in this evolutionary process, for it was he who, basing his thoughts on the ideas of Colquhoun, in 1828 drew up the first police bill that was ultimately passed by Parliament. London's new Metropolitan Police, established in 1829, was a centralized agency with the responsibilities of both the prevention of crime and the apprehension of offenders. Simultaneously, the "blood money" paid to thief-takers was abolished, and the modern police force came into being.

Law and Order in Colonial America

From the time the first were founded, the villages and towns in the New World were constantly threatened — on land by Indians and from the sea by pirates and foreign enemies. These problems of defense were dealt with by the military. The towns had no protection, however, against their own disorderly, lawbreaking inhabitants. Then in the seventeenth century, village authorities began selecting men to serve as guardians of the peace. The titles and functions of these first police officers were similar to those of the English constable, and the range of their duties can be seen from a typical Massachusetts law of 1646, reprinted here in the style of its colonial authors:

Colonial constables and watches

> Evry cunstable . . . hath, by virtue of his office, full powr to make, signe, & put forth pursuits, or hues & cries, after murthrers, manslayrs, peace breakrs, theeves, robers, burglarers, where no ma[gis]trate is at hand; also to apphend without warrant such as are our taken with drinke, swearing, breaking ye Saboth, lying, vagrant psons, night walkers, or any other yt shall break o[u]r laws; . . . also to make search for all such psons . . . in all houses licensed to sell either beare or wine, or in any othr suspected or disordered places, & those to apphend, & keepe in safe custody.[11]

*Jailer, San Angelo (Texas)
County Jail, 1915*

**The duties of sheriffs in
the trans-Mississippi West**

Constables, or *schouts* in the Dutch settlements, appeared in all the colonies as soon as local governments were organized. They were paid for their services through fines. Nighttime security was provided by "military watches," "rattle watches" composed of paid volunteers, "bellmen," and other forms of the night watch. By the eighteenth century, the daytime peacekeeping of the constables and the nighttime protection of the watches was common everywhere. Unlike England, where the notion of a paid police force was despised, most colonial peacekeeping activities were supported by municipal authority.

As the colonial towns grew, the number of street riots, drunken brawls, and other types of violent behavior increased considerably. Those charged with keeping the peace were not only incapable of enforcing all of the laws, but often they were lax in their duties, as was noted in Massachusetts's *Bristol Journal* on March 16, 1760:

> *The watch burn Tobacco while Houses are burning,*
> *And the* Glass, *not the* Watch, *goes its rounds,*
> *A burning shame this and sad subject of mourning,*
> *That our Guard's such a mute Pack of Hounds.*[12]

Despite these difficulties, however, the constable and the watch were maintained throughout the 1700s and into the early part of the next century as the only sources of urban law enforcement. Some cities did expand the numbers of these paid officers, but to little avail. And growing levels of lawlessness combined with corruption within the ranks of the watch ultimately led to the organization of formal police forces by mid-century.

The Trans-Mississippi West

As settlers moved west, they reached the frontier well before peace officers and courts of law. Violence and crime were inevitable in these sparsely populated regions. Frontiersmen, who used firearms for hunting and self-defense, turned easily to fists, knives, and pistols to settle disputes. Indian tribes, often with cultures that glorified war and acts of revenge, naturally resisted white encroachment. Whites themselves, with European traditions of feuding and revenge, applied these practices to both their neighbors and the Indians. In the absence of any formal mechanisms of frontier justice, the West also served as a sanctuary for a lawless minority of outlaw and criminal migrants.

The *sheriff,* the first of the formal law enforcement agents to appear in the vast territories beyond the Mississippi River, was closely modeled after the British counterpart. But while the powers of the English sheriff had diminished over time, those of the American sheriff expanded to include not only the apprehension of criminals, but also the conduction of elections, the collection of taxes, and the custody of public funds. Furthermore, the sheriffs of the new republic were eventually chosen by popular election.

As the West became more populated, and more lawless, the sheriff evolved into an active agent of law enforcement. Duties as fiscal administrator and executive arm of the courts were quickly subordinated to the more colorful activities of rounding up cattle thieves, highwaymen, and other bandits, and engaging in gun play with serious outlaws. Typically, the local sheriff's office did not include a paid staff of trained deputies that could, for example, be called upon to track fleeing outlaws. Thus, use of the posse became crucial in frontier law enforcement. (For weaknesses of the sheriff system, see pages 172-173.)

During the time of Alfred the Great, when mutual pledges bound together the members of a tithing, one of the peacekeeping instruments was the **posse comitatus,** Latin for "the power of the county," which consisted of all the able-bodied men in a county. This group was at the absolute disposal of a sheriff, and members were required to respond when called to do so. The institution of posse comitatus was transferred intact to American soil.[13] Here, it became an important component of criminal justice machinery as the frontier moved westward, for it could place the entire power of a community under the leadership of the sheriff (see Exhibit 6.1).

The posse comitatus

Also among the lawmen of the West were territorial police agencies. The **Texas Rangers,** known well in both history and legend, was the first of these. Equipped by Stephen Austin in 1823 to help protect settlers against the Indians, the Rangers were organized as a corps of irregular fighters at the outbreak of the Texas revolution against Mexico in 1835. After 1870, the Rangers evolved into an effective law enforcement agency.[14] Following the lead of the Texas Rangers, the Arizona Rangers was established in 1901 and the New Mexico Mounted Police in 1905, but these were primarily border patrol forces and were abandoned within a few years after their inception.[15]

The Texas Rangers

Federal marshals were also a part of law enforcement in the American West. When the United States came into being with the ratification of the Constitution, the dual sovereignty of state and republic required the designation of special officers to represent the authority of the federal courts. In 1789, Congress established appointive positions of federal marshals, but they did not come into particular prominence until after the Civil War. The popular

Company D of the Texas Rangers in 1893

EXHIBIT 6.1

Posse Comitatus, "Fat Albert," and the War on Drugs

Traditionally in the Old West, a posse consisted of the entire population of a county above age 15 that could be summoned to assist the local sheriff. During the post–Civil War years, U.S. marshals in occupied southern states often called upon federal troops to form a posse for purposes of enforcing local laws. Once southern states regained representation in Congress, it became a unanimous goal of southern congressmen to prevent such practices in the future. The result was the **Posse Comitatus Act,** passed by the 45th Congress on June 18, 1878. The law prohibited the army, and eventually other branches of the military, from enforcing federal, state, and local civilian law, and from supplementing the efforts of civilian law enforcement agencies.

But the Posse Comitatus Act was never a constitutionally mandated statute. In fact, its very wording permitted the assistance of the military if specifically authorized by an act of Congress. Over the years, Congress has approved the use of military forces for the control of civil disorder, and it was for this reason that Chicago's Mayor Richard Daley was able to call in the Illinois National Guard and regular army troops at the Democratic National Convention in 1968. Moreover, the act did not prevent the United States Coast Guard from intercepting and seizing vessels at sea that were transporting contraband to American ports.

When President Ronald Reagan signed the Department of Defense Authorization Act of 1982 into law, it included several amendments to the century-old Posse Comitatus Act. Although military personnel were still prohibited from physically intercepting suspected drug vessels and aircraft, conducting searches and seizures, and making arrests, the entire war chest of the U.S. military became available to law enforcement for training, intelligence gathering, and detection. Moreover, members of the Army, Navy, Air Force, and Marines could operate military equipment for civilian agencies charged with the enforcement of drug laws.

Beginning in 1982, the "war on drugs" had a new look. Put into force was the Bell 209 assault helicopter, more popularly known as the Cobra. No helicopter in the military arsenal was faster, and in its gunship mode it could destroy a tank. There was the Navy's EC-2, an aircraft equipped with a radar disc capable of detecting other aircraft from as far as 300 miles away. There was "Fat Albert" and his pals—surveillance balloons 175 feet in length equipped with sophisticated radar and listening devices. Albert could not only pick up communications from Cuba and Soviet satellites, but could also detect traffic in "Smugglers' Alley," a wide band of Caribbean sky that is virtually invisible to land-based radar systems. And

image of federal marshals and their deputies maintaining law and order along the trail and in the violent mining communities, however, has little foundation in fact. Most of their working time was spent on routine functions related to civil and criminal court activity. Criminal investigation and the apprehension of outlaws did occur on occasion, but these constituted only a fraction of the duties performed.[16]

Finally, it should be noted that not all marshals were federal marshals. There were also city and town marshals appointed by a mayor or city council. These were community lawmen who served purely as local police. "Wild Bill" Hickok, for example, was a local marshal in the towns of Hays City and Abilene, Kansas, as was Wyatt Earp in Dodge City, Kansas.

Policing the Great Metropolis

In 1845, New York City established the first organized metropolitan police force in the United States. But this occurred only because the fear of crime and

there were NASA satellites to spy on drug operations as far apart as California and Colombia, airborne infrared sensing and imaging equipment that could detect human body heat in the thickest underbrush of Florida's Everglades, plus a host of other high technology devices.

Although the infusion of military resources has had some success in the war on drugs, civil libertarians were opposed to this militarization from the very beginning. They feared that the use of the military in civilian law enforcement would lead to an erosion of private rights and a broadening of military power in civilian life. To date, civil liberties have not been compromised by the military, and Fat Albert continues to roam Smugglers' Alley.

SOURCES: James A. Inciardi, *The War on Drugs: Heroin, Cocaine, Crime, and Public Policy* (Palo Alto: Mayfield, 1986); *Aviation Week & Space Technology*, February 16, 1981, p. 24; *New York Times*, June 28, 1981, p. 21; *Drug Enforcement*, Summer 1982, p. 17.

The Bell 209 Cobra assault helicopter was put into operation in the South Florida "war on drugs."

ensuing social disintegration were stronger than cultural opposition to a standing army.

At the beginning of the nineteenth century, New York was no longer the homogeneous community with a common culture and a shared system of values and moral standards that it had been in colonial times. During the five and a half decades before the establishment of the new police force, the population of the city had increased by more than 1,000 percent — from 33,131 in 1790 to 371,223 by 1845.[17] With a significant proportion of the new immigrants being of foreign birth, the city had become a mosaic of subcommunities, separated from one another by barriers of class, culture, language, attitudes, and behavior derived from vastly different traditions.

The increased population combined with growing levels of poverty served to increase the crime rate. The rise in the population brought with it greater conflicts associated with class and cultural differences. A highly visible and mobile wealth attracted criminal predators, both foreign and domestic, resulting in sharp increases in crime and vice. In 1840, New York's

Commercial Advisor commented on how the city's streets had become pathways of danger:

> Destructive rascality stalks at large in our streets and public places, at all times of day and night, with none to make it afraid; mobs assemble deliberately . . . in a word, lawless violence and fury have full dominion over us. . . . [18]

And in 1842, a special citizens' committee made melodramatic reference to the constant increase in crime and the inability of the police to deal with it:

> The property of the citizen is pilfered, almost before his eyes. Dwellings and warehouses are entered with an ease and apparent coolness and carelessness of detection which shows that none are safe. Thronged as our city is, men are robbed in the street. Thousands that are arrested go unpunished, and the defenseless and the beautiful are ravished and murdered in the daytime, and no trace of the criminals is found.[19]

During this period the city was patrolled by a few hundred marshals, constables, and watchmen who were unsalaried, but received fees for their services. As with the British experience, this system resulted in numerous instances of graft, corruption, laxity, and misdirected effort. Officers concen-

EXHIBIT 6.2

Some Memorable Passages from the Annals of American Policing

"Who knows what evil lurks in the hearts of men?"
— The Shadow, 1939

"Criminals are a superstitious, cowardly lot, so my disguise must be able to strike terror into their hearts . . . black, terrible . . . a bat."
— Batman, 1940

"There's still a little law and order left in this country."
— Sheriff Buford Pusser, 1967

"The hell with the law!"
— Detective "Dirty Harry" Callahan, 1974

"My hatred for punks and crime is absolute."
— Lt. Theo Kojak, 1975

"I've come to fight for truth, justice, and the American way."
— Superman, 1980

"Go ahead, make my day."
— Detective "Dirty Harry" Callahan, 1984

trated on duties that would earn them money rather than on bringing criminals to justice. Since the recovery of stolen property brought a greater fee than the apprehension of an offender, for example, few thieves were deliberately sought out. This situation also led to arrangements between police and criminals before some robberies and burglaries actually took place—an officer would know of a crime in advance, would recover the stolen property, and would forward a share of the reward to the thief.[20]

From 1841 to 1844, several plans for the organization of a London-style police force were introduced in the city, but none could command enough support for adoption. In 1844, however, the New York state legislature authorized communities to organize police forces and appropriated special funds to be given to cities to provide 24-hour police protection. When the Democrats won the city's mayoral election of 1845, Mayor William F. Havermeyer called for the adoption of the new state statute. The bill was signed into law on May 23, 1845, and a police force akin to London's was finally created. By the outbreak of the Civil War, Chicago, New Orleans, Cincinnati, Baltimore, Newark, and a number of other large cities had followed New York's lead. The foundation of today's municipal police departments had been established.

Police Systems in the United States

With a population well in excess of 240 million people, all of whom are under the authority of competing political jurisdictions at federal, state, county, and local levels, law enforcement in the United States today reflects a structure more complex than in any other country. There are more than 40,000 professional police agencies in the public sector alone—each representing the enforcement arm of a specific judicial body. To these can be added numerous others in the private sphere. The duties and authority of each are generally quite clear, but in many respects they can also be rather vague and overlapping. Although enforcing the law and keeping the peace may be the responsibilities of a *municipal* police agency within a small suburban village, for example, also active in that same community may be the officers from a county sheriff's department, a state police bureaucracy, and numerous federal enforcement bodies. This level of complexity can be further complicated by possible jurisdictional disputes, agency rivalries, lack of coordination and communication, and failure to share intelligence and other resources.

Consider, for instance, the jurisdictional and administrative complexities that exist in Dade County, Florida. Located at the southeastern tip of the state of Florida, Dade County has a population of more than 1.8 million, and occupies some 2,109 square miles — a land area larger than the entire state of Delaware or Rhode Island. In addition to the city of Miami Beach, the county includes 21 other incorporated municipalities.* Each of these is an independent political jurisdiction with its own municipal police force. Also included in this essentially urban-suburban county is the Dade County Public Safety Department — whose jurisdiction is countywide — as well as the Florida State Police and the Florida Marine Patrol. At the federal level, the following agencies also have jurisdiction: the Federal Bureau of Investigation, the Immigration and Naturalization Service, the Drug Enforcement Administration, the Internal Revenue Service, the Customs Service, the United States Coast Guard, and a number of others. Within the private sphere, detective agencies control all security operations at the Miami International Airport and other locations; the railroad industry has its own police force; and hundreds of other businesses and industries use private police agencies.

New York City reflects an even more complex situation. In addition to the New York City Police Department, whose jurisdiction covers the five boroughs that make up the city as a whole, both the transit system and the public housing authority have their own public police forces, each of which is larger than some state police agencies. There are also the state police, private police, federal enforcement bodies, and an interstate agency — the New York/New Jersey Port Authority Police, whose jurisdiction and authority cross both state and county lines.

Because of such complexities, jurisdictional issues in law enforcement are often ignored in studies of police. The rest of this chapter attempts to differentiate among these various levels of authority.

Federal Law Enforcement Agencies

Federal law enforcement agencies have two features that make them unique within the spectrum of police activity. First, since they were structured to enforce specific statutes — those contained in the U.S. Criminal Code — their units are highly specialized, often with specialized resources and training. Second, since they are the enforcement arms of the federal courts, their jurisdictional boundaries, at least in theory, have been limited by congressional authority. The major agencies include the Federal Bureau of Investigation (FBI); the Drug Enforcement Administration (DEA); the Immigration and Nat-

---

* The political jurisdictions in Dade County, Florida, include Bal Harbour, Bay Harbor Islands, Biscayne Park, Coral Gables, Florida City, Golden Beach, Hialeah, Hialeah Gardens, Homestead, Miami, Miami Beach, Miami Shores, Miami Springs, North Bay Village, North Miami, North Miami Beach, Opa Locka, South Miami, Surfside, Sweetwater, and West Miami.

A border patrolman follows a group of illegal aliens captured near San Diego, California.

uralization Service (INS); the U.S. Marshal Service; the Organized Crime and Racketeering Section (OCR) of the U.S. Department of Justice; the Intelligence Division of the Internal Revenue Service (IRS); the Secret Service; the Bureau of Alcohol, Tobacco, and Firearms (ATF); the Customs Service; the Postal Inspection Service; and the U.S. Coast Guard (see Exhibits 6.3 and 6.4).

In addition to these, there are a variety of other federal agencies with enforcement functions. For example, the Departments of Labor, Agriculture, Defense, Interior, and others have developed enforcement or quasi-enforcement units to deal with operations of a criminal or regulatory nature. Independent regulatory bodies such as the Interstate Commerce Commission (ICC), the Securities and Exchange Commission (SEC), and the Federal Trade Commission (FTC) require enforcement powers to ensure compliance. During peacetime, the Department of Transportation has administrative authority over the Coast Guard, whose enforcement powers overlap with those of the Customs Service, FBI, DEA, and INS. Special investigative and enforcement bodies appear from time to time, descending directly from the executive branch of the government. During 1972, for example, the Office of National Narcotics Intelligence (ONNI) and the Office of Drug Abuse Law Enforcement (ODALE) were created by President Richard M. Nixon as part of his "war on heroin." In 1973, however, these agencies were essentially abolished by the creation of the Drug Enforcement Administration, which represented a consolidation of the activities of ONNI, ODALE, and the old Bureau of Narcotics and Dangerous Drugs (BNDD).

Interpol and the U.S. intelligence community also play a role in the federal law enforcement bureaucracy. **Interpol,** the International Criminal Police Organization, headquartered in St. Cloud, France, is an international organization of 120 member countries that serves as a clearinghouse and depository of intelligence information on wanted criminals. For example, it keeps data on criminal identification and circulates wanted notices. It is

Interpol

EXHIBIT 6.3

The Federal Law Enforcement Agencies

Department of Justice

Federal Bureau of Investigation (FBI)

The chief investigative body of the Justice Department, with legal jurisdiction extending to all federal crimes that are not the specific responsibility of some other federal enforcement agency. The more significant crimes that fall into FBI jurisdiction are kidnapping, crimes against banks, aircraft piracy, violations of the Civil Rights Act, interstate gambling, organized crime, and interstate flight to avoid prosecution, custody, or confinement.

Drug Enforcement Administration (DEA)

The DEA was formed in 1973 as a consolidation of other drug enforcement agencies. Its major responsibility is control of the use and distribution of narcotics and other dangerous drugs. During the latter part of 1981, the DEA merged with the FBI, becoming a semiautonomous subsidiary of the FBI.

Immigration and Naturalization Service (INS)

Created in 1891, it is responsible for administering the laws that regulate the admission, exclusion, naturalization, and deportation of aliens. Its **Border Patrol** is charged with preventing the illegal entry of aliens and the smuggling of illegal goods.

U.S. Marshal Service

Under the direct authority of the U.S. Attorney General's Office, it has the power to enforce all federal laws that are not the specific responsibility of some other federal agency, although its major activities involve administering proceedings at the federal courts. U.S. marshals also protect relocated witnesses.

Organized Crime and Racketeering Section (OCR)

It was created in 1954 to coordinate investigations of organized crime with responsibilities in the areas of intelligence gathering, investigation, and prosecution.

Treasury Department

Internal Revenue Service (IRS)

As the federal agency responsible for the administration and enforcement of the federal tax

neither an investigative nor an enforcement agency. The Treasury Department is the United States's representative to this international group, and its American liaison office is staffed by federal law enforcement personnel.[21] As for the U.S. intelligence community, the relationship is less clear. Intelligence operations focus primarily on issues of national security, but the activities of the FBI, the Drug Enforcement Administration, and the Treasury Department

laws, its major enforcement activities in the criminal area fall within the Intelligence Division, which investigates possible criminal violations of the tax law.

Secret Service

Known primarily for its role in protecting the president of the United States, his family, and other government officials, its investigative units focus on the forgery and counterfeiting of U.S. currency, checks, bonds, and federal food stamps.

Bureau of Alcohol, Tobacco and Firearms (ATF)

Originally organized to enforce Prohibition, ATF has responsibility for enforcing the tax laws that relate to the manufacture of alcohol and tobacco, and for enforcement of the Gun Control Act of 1972. As of early 1986, the future of this agency was uncertain. Late in 1981 its dissolution was recommended by President Reagan, with many of its functions to be transferred to the Justice Department.

Customs Service

The Customs Service has both inspectors and investigators, whose responsibilities include the administration of laws related to the importation of foreign goods; the collection of duties, penalties, and other fees; and the prevention of smuggling.

United States Postal Service

Postal Inspection Service

As the law enforcement and audit arm of the Postal Service, it has jurisdiction in all criminal matters infringing on the integrity and security of the mail, and the safety of all postal valuables, property, and personnel.

Department of Transportation

Coast Guard

A special naval force with responsibilities for suppressing contraband trade and aiding vessels in distress. It was formed in 1915 when an act of Congress combined the Revenue Cutter Service (established in 1790 to prevent smuggling) and the Life Saving Service.

can also be of an intelligence-gathering nature quite unrelated to law enforcement issues. In contrast, disclosures during the 1970s indicated that the FBI, IRS, and DEA, along with the Central Intelligence Agency (CIA) and the National Security Agency (NSA) have conducted investigations in cooperation with one another that had both enforcement and national security objectives.[22]

EXHIBIT 6.4

The FBI: In Search of Public Enemies

Although almost all police work is undertaken by county and municipal law enforcement agencies, the **Federal Bureau of Investigation** also does its share. Somewhat controversial at times, the FBI is considered to be the nation's elite law enforcement body, and it is among the most famous police agencies in the world.

The beginnings of the FBI can be traced to President Theodore Roosevelt's "trust-busting" and his war with the "malefactors of great wealth" and their kept men in Congress. Roosevelt was handicapped in these efforts against industrial combines and graft because, when the need to gather evidence arose, the Department of Justice's lack of an investigative arm forced the president to borrow detectives from other federal agencies. As a result of this problem, Roosevelt's attorney general, Charles J. Bonaparte (who was also the grandnephew of Emperor Napoleon I), appealed to Congress in 1907 and 1908 to create a permanent detective force in Justice. Bonaparte's requests were denied. The major reason was the Congress's expressed fear that a "secret police" would be created—a force so powerful that it might escape all control and turn its investigative energies against even Congress itself.

Congressional response to Bonaparte's appeal went even beyond denial, however. On May 30, 1908, Congress passed a law that specifically forbade the Justice Department from borrowing any investigative agents from other federal organizations.

Nevertheless, on July 1, 1908, some 30 days after Congress had adjourned, Bonaparte went ahead and quietly established in the Justice Department the very investigative force that the Congress had refused to authorize. He called it the Bureau of Investigation.

During its earliest years, the Bureau occupied itself with small investigations—antitrust prosecutions, bankruptcy and fraud cases, crimes committed on government reservations, and interstate commerce violations. But with the passage of the Mann Act in 1910, sponsored by Congressman James Robert Mann, the Bureau of Investigation stepped into a more national posture.

It was a time when prostitution and commercialized vice had become big business, and there was growing worry over the number of women and young girls who were being imported into the United States "for immoral purposes." Proponents of Victorian morality led an outcry for stern law enforcement action. Under the Mann Act, officially known as the White Slave Traffic Act, it was forbidden to transport women for immoral purposes in interstate or foreign commerce, to assist in procuring transportation for immoral purposes, or to persuade or induce any female to cross state lines for such purposes.

Stanley W. Finch, appointed the first director of the Bureau by Charles J. Bonaparte, saw the Mann Act as an opportunity to secure funds for the expansion of his agency. He portrayed white

slavery as a national menace, suggesting that only his Bureau could save the American people from such a festering horror. He offered grim descriptions of white slave traffic:

Unless a girl was actually confined in a room and guarded, there was no girl, regardless of her station in life who was altogether safe. . . . There was need that everyone be on his guard, because no one could tell when his daughter or his wife or his mother would be selected as a victim.

Not unexpectedly, with the virtue of every wife, mother, and daughter in the nation at stake, the Bureau got its funding and the full support of Congress. Bureau agents proceeded with zeal, and by 1916 some 2,414 cases had been prosecuted.

During the years that followed, the Bureau began investigating a new "menace" to American society—the radical alien. Among the more onerous statutes passed by Congress during World War I was the Alien Act of 1918, a law designed to exclude and expel from the United States any aliens who were considered to be anarchists. In 1919, as the result of numerous postwar bombings attributed to subversive organizations, William J. Flynn, former head of the Secret Service, was named the new Bureau director and given the mission of a holy war against radicals and dissidents. The General Intelligence Division was organized to concentrate on the alleged alien menace, and the first assistant in charge of the new GID was a 24-year-old up-and-coming

Justice Department lawyer named John Edgar Hoover.

In 1922, congressional investigations into rumors of graft and corruption within the Harding administration left the image of the Bureau somewhat tarnished. The secretary of the interior was found to have accepted a bribe and leased naval oil reserves at Teapot Dome, Wyoming, to a private oil company; the attorney general was found to have taken money in lieu of prosecuting Prohibition law violators; and the head of the Veterans' Bureau was convicted of fraud, bribery, and conspiracy. Where, asked congressional critics, had been the watchdog of Justice while the naval oil reserves were being looted? Had it been sleeping, or had it simply closed its eyes?

In the aftermath of the implied involvement of the Bureau in the Teapot Dome scandal, President Calvin Coolidge appointed Harlen Fiske Stone as his new attorney general. Stone was ordered to find a new director of the Bureau of Investigation. On May 10, 1924, the position was offered to young J. Edgar Hoover. Hoover set out to clean house and build a new image for his national police force. He established new qualifications for his agents, preferring those with legal or accounting backgrounds; he improved existing training standards; and he created a career service in which the salaries and retirement benefits would be better than in any comparable agency in the federal government or elsewhere. And Hoover did more.

By 1935, when the name of his agency had been changed to the Federal Bureau of Investigation, he had established a vast fingerprint file, a crime laboratory, the Uniform Crime Reporting system, and a training academy. During the same decade, he mounted a campaign to offset the glamorous publicity that was given John Dillinger, Alvin Karpis, Bonnie Parker and Clyde Barrow, and other criminals. For a time his "G-men" were included among the top heroes of American culture. The Bureau's list of "ten most wanted criminals" and "public enemies" provided a continuing scoreboard of Hoover's successes against bank robbers, kidnappers, gangsters, and other lawbreakers, and the entire agency reveled in its image of fearless law enforcement — an image that endured for many decades.

By 1960, Hoover's FBI was considered to be the finest law enforcement agency in the world. It had the respect of the American people. Its 6,000 agents were deployed in a manner that would enable the Bureau to place one of them at the scene of a federal crime anywhere in the nation within an average of one hour or less.

With the revolution in values that occurred in the United States during the 1960s, however, FBI activities became better known, and the image of both Hoover and his empire began to pale. The Bureau had grown into an enormous bureaucracy, with far-reaching power over the life of the nation. It led an autonomous existence and its director had lasted through eight presidencies. Information began to leak out as to the number of files the Bureau had developed on tens of thousands of noncriminals, including presidents and members of the Senate and House.

Disclosures revealed the FBI to have engaged in illegal wiretapping, a mail-opening program aimed at American citizens, the discrediting of its political enemies by attempting to destroy their jobs and credit ratings, accepting kickbacks and bribes, systematically stealing government property, and inciting radicals to commit illegal acts.

Amidst the turmoil surrounding his years as director, J. Edgar Hoover died on March 2, 1972, at the age of 77. After a succession of directors who did little to improve the image of the agency, President Jimmy Carter decided in 1977 that the FBI needed a new director — someone free of any connection with former FBI scandals. On February 15, 1978, Carter appointed Federal Judge William H. Webster, and the FBI has since assumed a new image. Agents are chasing fewer bank robbers and car thieves, focusing more on organized and white-collar crime, public corruption, espionage, terrorism, and drug trafficking.

SOURCES: Fred J. Cook, *The FBI Nobody Knows* (New York: Macmillan, 1964); Don Whitehead, *The FBI Story* (New York: Random House, 1956); Sanford J. Unger, *FBI* (Boston: Little, Brown, 1976); Nelson Blackstock, *COINTELPRO: The FBI's Secret War on Political Freedom* (New York: Vintage, 1976); John Dean, *Blind Ambition* (New York: Simon and Schuster, 1976); *Time,* May 1, 1978, p. 18; *U.S. News & World Report,* February 18, 1980, pp. 23–26; *National Law Journal,* June 6, 1983, pp. 1, 8, 25.

J. Edgar Hoover

State Police Agencies

The Texas Rangers, as noted earlier, was the earliest form of a state police body to appear on American soil. It was established during the earliest days of the Texas Republic, largely for military service along the Mexican border, and even today it retains some of its original frontier flavor. In other locales, state police forces emerged through a slow process of evolution. In 1865, for example, the governor of Massachusetts appointed a small force of "state constables," primarily for the suppression of commercialized vice. In 1879, the group was reorganized into the Massachusetts District Police and was granted more general police powers.[23] In 1920 it was absorbed into a new department of public safety and designated as the Massachusetts State Police.

During this period other states began experimenting with similar forces, all because of the basic deficiencies in existing rural police administration and practices. In the decades that followed the Civil War and Reconstruction, population growth and demographic shifts, changing economic conditions, and the numerous complexities characteristic of any pluralistic society resulted in numerous increases in crime. The office of the sheriff, the only form of law enforcement that existed in many communities, manifested a variety of **Weaknesses of the sheriff system** weaknesses that limited its effectiveness in the prevention and control of

crime. Most sheriffs were elected by popular vote for terms of only two years, a practice that inhibited freedom from political and local influence and limited the possibility of securing sheriffs with professional qualifications and experience. Statutes in many states prohibited incumbents of the office from succeeding themselves, and in many instances deputies could not even succeed their sheriffs. Furthermore, sheriffs were responsible for the execution of civil processes, for the administration of the county jail, and in some cases for the collection of taxes as well. Also, the fee system under which they received compensation made civil duties more attractive, resulting in an unwillingness to exercise their law enforcement powers. These difficulties also existed in communities where civil and police duties were in the hands of local constables.[24]

If the unwillingness and inability of sheriffs and constables to combat rural crime were not enough, there was an additional problem that affected both rural and urban areas. Crime had become more global in nature and was less often localized in a particular community. Improvements in transportation and communication had opened new vistas for criminals, providing them with convenient access to numerous geographical areas and ready means of escape to others. Yet there was no effective communication or cooperation between the police of one municipality and those of other cities and towns. The emergence of state police agencies was in direct response to these issues. The agencies were a mechanism of law enforcement that was geographically unconfined, with organization, administration, resources, training, and means of communication adaptable to an entire state.

The beginning of modern state police administration dates to 1905, with the creation of the Pennyslvania State Constabulary. It was the first professional statewide force whose superintendent had extensive administra-

Modern state police administration began in 1905.

Allan Pinkerton immigrant **Allan Pinkerton.** "The Pinkertons," as they were called, initially gained notoriety just before the Civil War through their thwarting of the alleged "Baltimore Plot" to assassinate president-elect Abraham Lincoln. During the decades that followed, Pinkerton agents played major roles in numerous industrial clashes between workers and management. The best known of these were the one involving the Molly Maguires in 1874–1875 and the Homestead strike in Pittsburgh in 1892. Hired to protect the railroads during the era of America's outlaw West, they were responsible for the arrests of John and Simeon Reno, who were credited with having organized the nation's first band of professional bank robbers. They were persistent adversaries of Jesse James, Cole Younger, and other members of the James–Younger gang. In Texas, they were retained by railroad executives to hunt down the legendary Sam Bass, and have been credited with the deaths of Jim and Rube Burrows — well known in the 1880s as proficient robbers of both trains and express offices. And they appear in the annals of Western Americana as the group who rid Montana and Wyoming of Robert Leroy Parker (Butch Cassidy), Harry Longbaugh (the Sundance Kid), Blackjack Ketchum, Etta Place, and other members of the now romanticized Wild Bunch from Robbers Roost. Allan Pinkerton himself, with his insistence on detailed descriptions of known criminals — including physical characteristics, back-

---

EXHIBIT 6.5

The Pinkerton Rogues' Gallery

The Pinkerton rogues' gallery was the forerunner of today's police "mug books." Allan Pinkerton insisted on having detailed descriptions of known criminals, including their physical characteristics, backgrounds, companions, and hideouts. His organization never closed a rogues' gallery case until the individual was officially declared dead.

Here are four typical criminals from the Pinkerton rogues' gallery:

- Maximilian Shinburn, 1839–1919. Known as the "King of Bank Burglars."
- Charles Bullard. Accomplished burglar and pianist. Distinguishing features: speaks fluent French.
- Sophie Lyons, 1850–1924. Occupation: criminal tendencies since early childhood. Criminal occupations: pickpocket, shoplifter, blackmailer, stall for bank sneaks.
- Frederick J. Wittrock, 1858–1921. Occupation: store proprietor. Criminal occupation: express robbery. Distinguishing features: reads dime novels voraciously.

MAX SHINBURN
alias "Max Shinborn"

Bank burglar

---

munities trim the size of their police forces, the number of private police agents continues to expand. Many middle- and upper-income groups with the resources to hire private police for protection are doing so — and withdrawing their support for municipal law enforcement agencies. The result is diminished police services in poor neighborhoods where protection is needed the most.[34]

Volunteer Police and the American Vigilante Tradition

The vigilante tradition, in its most classic sense, refers to the organized and extralegal movements of individuals who take the law into their own hands. From the 1760s through the beginning of the twentieth century, vigilante activity was an almost constant factor in American life. It appeared in numerous forms, ranging from unorganized mobs to quasi-military groups that banded together to establish "law and order" and administer **vigilante justice** in areas where courts and law officers were nonexistent, corrupt, unwilling, or incapable of dealing with the problems at hand. Unlike the frontier lynch mobs, the better-known vigilante groups, such as the South Carolina Moderators (1767), the East Texas Regulators (1840–1844), and the California Vigilance Committees (1850–1856), were highly structured and served in all phases of their own criminal justice proceedings. As University of Oregon history professor Richard Maxwell Brown described their vigilante operations:

> The characteristic vigilante movement was organized in command or military fashion and usually had a constitution, articles, or a manifesto to which the members would subscribe. Outlaws or other malefactors taken up by vigilantes were given formal (albeit illegal) trials, in which the accused had counsel or an opportunity to defend himself. An example of a vigilante trial is found in the northern Illinois regulator movement of 1841. Two accused horse thieves and murderers were tried by 120 regulators in the presence of a crowd of 500 or more. A leading regulator served as judge. The defendants were given a chance to challenge objectionable men among the regulators, and, as a result, the number of regulators taking part in the trial was cut by nine men. Two lawyers were provided — one to represent the accused and one to represent the "people." Witnesses were sworn, an arraignment was made, and the trial proceeded. In summation, the prosecuting attorney urged immediate execution of the prisoners. The crowd voted unanimously for the fatal sentence, and, after an hour allotted to the two men for prayer, they were put to death. The accused were almost never acquitted, but the vigilantes' attention to the spirit of law and order caused them to provide, by their lights, a fair but speedy trial.[35]

Not all vigilante and regulator groups were this well organized, and not all followed rules of criminal procedure. Like the posse comitatus, in taking the law into their own hands they often seized innocent persons, and they were guilty of depriving all persons — innocent and guilty — of justice and constitutional rights.

There was a noticeable decline in the incidence of vigilantism by the close of the nineteenth century, but it never fully disappeared. During periods of stress, fear, and intergroup tension, it periodically reemerged in rural areas. In the more turbulent and crime-ridden years of the 1960s, 1970s, and early

George Witherell was lynched on December 4, 1888, for an alleged multiple murder.

EXHIBIT 6.6

Urban Vigilantism

Crime and the fear of crime have combined in the 1980s to add a new chapter to the history of American vigilantism. Groups have organized to protect city neighborhoods where police patrols appear insufficient, and some individuals even carry out their own varieties of "street justice." The first such group to come along in this new wave of urban vigilantism was the well-known Guardian Angels.

The Guardian Angels were founded by Brooklyn-born Curtis Sliwa, whose job had him riding New York City's No. 4 subway, known as the "muggers' express." To protect the riders on the No. 4, arch-Angel Sliwa organized a group of his friends as "The Magnificent Thirteen," and on

February 13, 1979, they went on their first subway patrol. They quickly expanded into the Guardian Angels, a group of unarmed but streetwise youths, self-appointed peacekeepers who patrol the city's buses, subways, and streets. Dressed in white T-shirts and red berets, the 700-person force has had a reassuring effect on many New Yorkers. Because they have broken up numerous fights and made hundreds of civilian arrests, New York City police authorities consider their presence to be significant in the prevention of crime.

The popularity of the Guardian Angels enabled the group to expand to some forty cities by 1985, but they have also been

controversial. Some city officials consider them untrained and unregulated meddlers out to make police look bad. A Chicago police administrator branded them a "goon squad"; to others, they are no more than urban vigilantes who take the law into their own hands for the sake of some perverted ego fulfillment.

Their less-than-cordial acceptance in some locales has been based on the beliefs that the roles of enforcing the law and keeping the peace should be filled

The Guardian Angels: "In T-shirts and red berets, they stand where civilization ends and the jungle begins." —New York Daily News, 1982

only by well-trained police officers, that the Angels' presence in some situations might provoke trouble, and that they themselves run the risk of serious harm. Yet despite the mixed reactions, the Guardian Angels have endured and continue to expand, not only in cities but in suburban areas as well.[a]

More troublesome groups have emulated the Guardian Angels. A case in point was the Young Dillingers, for a time the most violent street gang in the nation's capital. In 1980 they decided to fight crime instead, pledging to wage a war against local drug dealers. They were encouraged at first, even by Nancy Reagan. But their techniques were unorthodox and exactly which side of the law they were on was never fully clear. Their impromptu beatings of drug dealers quickly led to the violent deaths of several of their members. Moreover, by 1985 all of the Young Dillingers were facing new criminal charges, including their cofounder, Robert Merritt, who was found guilty of a fraud involving $163,000.[b]

On December 22, 1984, urban vigilantism took on an altogether new look when Bernhard Hugo Goetz, a 37-year-old self-employed electrical engineer, gunned down four youths who demanded $5 from him on a New York City subway car. The youths had criminal records, and for urban dwellers who were fed up with crime in the streets, Goetz was an immediate hero. Subsequent evidence suggested that Goetz's actions may have been unprovoked, but when one of his victims was

Bernhard Goetz

arrested six months later on rape and robbery charges, New York's "subway vigilante" received new support. In a national poll conducted by the Roper organization during September 1985, Goetz ranked sixth (following Lee Iacocca, Dan Rather, Peter Jennings, Mike Wallace, and Tom Brokaw) among the most admired personalities in the nation.[c]

The apparent success of the Guardian Angels and the 1984 shooting by Bernhard Goetz have had an aftermath. New groups of citizens have armed themselves and some have even carried out summary street justice. Moreover, a Gallup Poll in 1985 found that almost three out of four Americans agreed that occasionally "taking

the law into one's own hands" is justified. Criminal justice and political officials have come to fear that the United States could evolve into a nation of vigilantes.[d]

SOURCES:
a. New York *Daily News*, January 17, 1982, pp. 5, 61; *New York Times*, February 15, 1981, p. 46; *USA Today*, January 3, 1985, p. 2A; *Newsweek*, July 1, 1985, p. 45.
b. *Newsweek*, July 1, 1985, p. 45.
c. *Newsweek*, January 7, 1985, pp. 10–11; *Time*, January 14, 1985, p. 22; *New York Times*, January 6, 1985, pp. 1, 22; *National Law Journal*, May 13, 1985, pp. 1, 40–43; *New York Times*, June 29, 1985, p. 30; *USA Today*, September 9, 1985, p. 1A.
d. *Time*, August 15, 1983, p. 15; Wilmington (Delaware) *News-Journal*, May 25, 1985, p. A5; *Newsweek*, April 8, 1985, p. 27; *U.S. News & World Report*, April 15, 1985, pp. 42–47.

1980s, a number of sectors of the American public became vigilante-prone. The Deacons for Defense and Justice were typical of the many black quasi-vigilante groups in the North and South whose members felt a need to protect themselves from white harassment during the middle 1960s. Conversely, the North Ward Citizens' Committee of Newark, New Jersey, was founded in 1967 predominantly by Italian-Americans who felt threatened by a possible incursion of black rioters and looters. Finally, the Maccabees of Crown Heights, Brooklyn, composed mainly of white Hasidic Jews, was formed in reaction to what was believed to be black street crime.[36]

The Maccabees and similar groups continue to exist, but they are only quasi-vigilante in nature. Characteristically, they cooperate to some extent with the police, and their main activity is patrolling in radio-equipped vehicles for the purposes of spotting, reporting, and discouraging criminal acts against the residents of their communities. On the other hand, newer types of urban vigilantes have emerged in recent years that have generated great concern among both law enforcement groups and political officials (see Exhibit 6.6).

In contrast to vigilantes, auxiliary police groups consist of volunteer civilians working *with* local police. They come under the direct supervision of police, are trained and uniformed, and serve as the "eyes and ears" of law enforcement. Auxiliary police reserves, however, do not have formal enforcement powers, and they are not armed. In addition, they have no more authority than ordinary citizens, and they typically do not take direct action against suspects.

Auxiliary police currently exist in most major cities. In New York, for example, each police precinct has a volunteer auxiliary police unit. Members do not receive compensation, but they are supplied with uniforms and some

A citizen patrol in the East Midwood section of Brooklyn

equipment. Volunteers may not issue summonses and are not allowed to carry firearms, but they do have the power of arrest and may use physical force when necessary. Applicants must meet certain minimum requirements and, once accepted, are required to attend a ten-week lecture course. Each member of this auxiliary reserve usually patrols three nights a week and must put in at least eight hours per month to remain active. At last count, the New York Auxiliary Police had about 3,200 volunteers, with an additional 1,100 in training.[37]

In contrast are volunteer police reserves — armed and uniformed groups with powers similar to those of full-time officers. The reserve units emerged during the early 1940s when many police officers were drafted for the war effort. Today they are popular in many large cities — including Los Angeles, Washington, D.C., Dallas, and Miami — that do not have the fiscal means to hire additional full-time officers. The Los Angeles County Sheriff's Department currently has the largest and perhaps the most structured national police reserve corps. There are some 1,200 reserve police, the majority of whom are uniformed officers with 24-hour-a-day police authority. But to qualify they must pass a physical and psychological screening and take 600 hours of classroom and field training over a six-month period, a course with a nearly 50 percent dropout rate. They have to work at least two eight-hour tours a month to stay accredited. The program has been deemed a success, and shoulders almost 10 percent of the sheriff's department workload.[38]

Police reserves

Summary

The police represent the largest and most visible segment of the criminal justice system. Charged with enforcing the law and keeping the peace, they represent that "thin blue line" between order and anarchy.

Modern policing can be traced back to the latter part of the ninth century and the mutual pledge system of England's Alfred the Great. By the seventeenth century, thief-takers were being used by the Crown as private detectives paid on a piecework basis. The foundations for the first modern police were put into place by Henry Fielding in 1748. His Bow Street Runners were an organized investigative division that earned the standard thief-takers' rewards. The later efforts of Patrick Colquhoun and Sir Robert Peel led to the establishment of the first modern police force.

In the United States, constable and night watch systems were common in most colonial communities. As settlers moved west, sheriffs emerged as active agents of law enforcement. They were assisted by the posse comitatus, which consisted of all the able-bodied men in a county. Nineteenth-century America also saw the establishment of state police agencies and federal marshals. In addition, cities set up metropolitan police forces after the London model.

Today there are more than 40,000 public police agencies across the United States at the federal, state, and local levels. Federal law enforcement agencies enforce specific statutes as contained in the U.S. Criminal Code, and their units are highly specialized. State police agencies generally fulfill a number of the regulatory and investigative roles of the federal enforcement groups as well as a portion of the uniformed patrol duties of local police. The majority of modern policing, however, is provided by county and municipal authority.

Police in the private sector became well known in this country during the last century with the efforts of the Pinkerton National Detective Agency. Private police today include a variety of organizations and individuals who provide guard, patrol, detection, and alarm services, armored-car transportation, crowd control, insurance investigation, and retail and industrial security. Nonpublic police also include civilian police auxiliaries and neighborhood watch groups.

Key Terms

Allan Pinkerton (176)
Border Patrol (168)
Bow Street Runners (158)
constable (156)
Federal Bureau of
   Investigation (170)

Henry Fielding (158)
Interpol (167)
mutual pledge (156)
night watch (156)
posse comitatus (161)
Posse Comitatus Act (162)

sheriff (156)
Texas Rangers (161)
thief-takers (157)
vigilante justice (179)

Questions for Discussion

1. What has been the role of the sheriff down through the ages?
2. To what extent do the functions of federal, state, and local police vary and overlap?

3. Do private police agencies create more problems than their protection is worth? Why or why not?

For Further Reading

Pringle, Patrick. *Hue and Cry: The Story of Henry and John Fielding and Their Bow Street Runners.* New York: William Morrow, 1965.

Reppetto, Thomas A. *The Blue Parade.* New York: Free Press, 1978.
Unger, Sanford J. *FBI.* Boston: Little, Brown, 1976.

Notes

1. Luke Owen Pike, *A History of Crime in England,* vol. 2 (London: Smith, Elder, 1873–76), pp. 457–462.
2. Pike, *Crime in England,* vol. 1, p. 218.
3. See Patrick Pringle, *Hue and Cry: The Story of Henry and John Fielding and Their Bow Street Runners* (New York: William Morrow, 1965), pp. 29–58.
4. Arthur L. Hayward, *Lives of the Most Remarkable Criminals* (New York: Dodd, Mead, 1927), p. 234.
5. See Patrick Pringle, *The Thief-Takers* (London: Museum Press, 1958).
6. Pringle, *Hue and Cry,* p. 81.
7. For the derivation of the term "beak" and a discussion of underworld cant, see James A. Inciardi, *Careers in Crime* (Chicago: Rand McNally, 1975), pp. 136–139.
8. The complete story of the Bow Street Runners can be found in the works of Patrick Pringle, *Hue and Cry,* as well as in his *Highwaymen* (New York: Roy, 1963).
9. Patrick Colquhoun, *A Treatise on the Police of the Metropolis* (London: J. Mawman, 1806).
10. Thomas A. Reppetto, *The Blue Parade* (New York: Free Press, 1978), p. 14.
11. Cited by Carl Bridenbaugh, *Cities in the Wilderness: Urban Life in America, 1625–1742* (New York: Capricorn, 1964), pp. 63–64.
12. Cited by Carl Bridenbaugh, *Cities in Revolt: Urban Life in America, 1743–1776* (New York: Knopf, 1965), p. 107.
13. Bruce Smith, *Rural Crime Control* (New York: Columbia University Institute of Public Administration, 1933), pp. 61–63.
14. Walter Prescott Webb, *The Texas Rangers: A Century of Frontier Defense* (Boston: Houghton Mifflin, 1935).
15. Bruce Smith, *Police Systems in the United States* (New York: Harper & Brothers, 1949), p. 168.
16. Frank R. Prassel, *The Western Peace Officer: A Legacy of Law and Order* (Norman: University of Oklahoma Press, 1972).
17. Ira Rosenwaike, *Population History of New York City* (Syracuse, N.Y.: Syracuse University Press, 1972), pp. 18–36.
18. *Commercial Advisor,* August 20, 1840, cited by James F. Richardson, *The New York Police: Colonial Times to 1901* (New York: Oxford University Press, 1970), p. 26.
19. Cited by Richardson, *New York Police.*
20. Richardson, *New York Police,* p. 31.

21. See David R. MacDonald, ''Treasury Department Assistance Programs to State and Local Law Enforcement Agencies,'' *Police Chief* 42 (July 1975): 30; Michael Fooner, *Interpol* (Chicago: Henry Regnery, 1973).

22. See David Wise, *The American Police State* (New York: Random House, 1976); Edward Jay Epstein, *Agency of Fear* (New York: G. P. Putnam's Sons, 1977); William R. Corson, *The Armies of Ignorance* (New York: Dial Press, 1977).

23. R. H. Whitten, *Public Administration in Massachusetts* (New York: Columbia University Studies, 1898).

24. Bruce Smith, *The State Police: Organization and Administration* (New York: Columbia University Institute of Public Administration, 1925), pp. 1–40.

25. Katherine Mayo, *Justice To All: The Story of the Pennsylvania State Police* (New York: Putnam, 1917).

26. See Advisory Commission on Intergovernmental Relations, *State-Local Relations in the Criminal Justice System* (Washington, D.C.: U.S. Government Printing Office, 1971).

27. James D. Horan and Howard Swiggett, *The Pinkerton Story* (New York: G. P. Putnam's Sons, 1951); James D. Horan, *The Pinkertons: The Detective Dynasty That Made History* (New York: Crown, 1967).

28. D. J. Cook, *Hands Up* (Denver: Republican, 1882).

29. Eugene B. Block, *Great Train Robberies of the West* (New York: Avon, 1959); Stuart H. Holbrook, *The Story of American Railroads* (New York: Bonanza, 1962); Freeman H. Hubbard, *Railroad Avenue* (New York: McGraw-Hill, 1945).

30. See Edward Hungerford, *Wells Fargo: Advancing the American Frontier* (New York: Bonanzá, 1949); Carolyn Lake, *Undercover for Wells Fargo* (Boston: Houghton Mifflin, 1969).

31. Law Enforcement Assistance Administration, *Private Police in the United States* (Washington, D.C.: U.S. Government Printing Office, 1971), pp. 10–12.

32. *U. S. News & World Report,* March 12, 1979, p. 54.

33. James S. Kakalik and Sorrel Wildhorn, *The Private Police: Security and Danger* (New York: Crane, Russak, 1977).

34. *New York Times,* January 29, 1984, p. 33.

35. Richard Maxwell Brown, ''The American Vigilante Tradition,'' in *Violence in America: Historical and Comparative Perspectives,* ed. Hugh Davis Graham and Ted Robert Gurr (Beverly Hills: Sage, 1979), p. 162.

36. *New York Times,* May 27, 1964, pp. 1, 25; May 28, 1964, pp. 1, 30; May 15, 1965, p. 33; October 31, 1971, p. 9.

37. National Advisory Commission on Criminal Justice Standards and Goals, *Community Crime Prevention* (Washington, D.C.: U.S. Government Printing Office, 1973), p. 318.

38. *Wall Street Journal,* December 21, 1983, pp. 1, 12.

7

Enforcing the Law and Keeping the Peace: The Nature and Scope of Police Work

There is a sleeping cop in all of us. He must be killed.

—French graffiti, 1968

The policeman is the little boy who grew up to be what he said he was going to be.

—Raymond Burr, 1968

You can't measure what a patrolman standing on a corner has prevented. There is no product at the end of a policeman's day.

—Charles E. McCarthy, 1968

Cops and taxis have one thing in common . . . they're never around when you need them most.

—A New York shopkeeper, 1979

Cocaine trafficking through Miami and snowstorms in Alaska have at least one thing in common: you can't stop either.

—A U.S. customs officer, 1986

W hether they emerge from the antiestablishment graffiti of a European student movement, the script of a prime-time television series, a police inspector's comments in a newspaper interview, or the discontented grumblings of a restless urban dweller, attitudes about police and policing in modern society reflect a broad range of opinion. Michael Harrington, a leading exponent of democratic socialist philosophy in the United States, commented in his well-known book *The Other American* that "for the middle class, police recover stolen property, give directions, and help old ladies," but "for the urban poor, police are those who arrest you." And for others, police are simply "coppers," or perhaps "pigs" and "fascists," as they were often called during the turbulent decade of the 1960s.

Such a range of opinion is likely to endure for as long as the police establishment continues as the visible machinery of law and order. Also, the more emotional and compelling opinions about police will remain negative. This kind of criticism and hostility is, to some extent, a function of the role law enforcement officers must play in maintaining social order; but to suggest that antipolice sentiment is justified is another matter entirely.

Police abuse of authority has been well documented, and, as we will discuss in Chapter 9, incidents of corruption, brutality, and the unwarranted use of force and power, particularly against minority groups, are not uncommon. Furthermore, it is these abuses that we are likely to remember when we think about police. In general, however, people's ambivalence toward the police and their negative opinions of police work and behavior come mainly from a lack of understanding of the nature of police work and of the social, organizational, and legalistic constraints that shape its course. This ambivalence is further fueled by scandals and individual events of great importance. Karl Menninger, perhaps the most admired and widely acclaimed American psychiatrist of this century, summed it up quite accurately when he commented:

> There is no question that the police are misunderstood, looked down upon, unfairly treated, ridiculed, criticized, underestimated, and generally given a bad go of it in America.[1]

This chapter examines the character and structure of police work and offers some perspectives on the complexities and frustrations of attempting to enforce the law and maintain order in a democratic society. The following analysis seeks to answer such questions as these: What do police do? What do citizens ask them to do? What do they decide to do upon their own initiative? And what influences their decisions to do what they do?

There's only one Dick Tracy and he's in the funny papers.
—Chicago police official

The Functions of Police

Police work suggests dramatic confrontations between police and law-breakers, with victory going to those with the greater strength, power, and resources. It suggests initiation of the process of justice, an enterprise bounded by the dusting for fingerprints and the search for elusive clues, the investigation and chase, and the ultimate apprehension and arrest of the suspected offender. It might also suggest that the functions of law enforcement are only the control of crime and the protection of society. But police work — the **police role** — goes well beyond these tasks.

The police role

The Police Role

Although police work does entail the dangerous and competitive enterprise of apprehending criminals, officers assigned to patrol duties, even in large cities, are typically confronted with few, if any, serious crimes during the course of a single assignment. In smaller cities and towns such crimes occur with even less frequency, and in some rural jurisdictions they may be extremely rare. Most police work is a **peacekeeping** operation. In this capacity it can include intervening in situations that may represent only potential threats to the public order — sidewalk agitators exercising their rights of free speech amidst

The peacekeeping operations of the police are primarily of a nature not involving criminal activities.

Issuing parking citations in New York City

hostile crowds, street-corner gatherings whose intentions seem questionable, belligerent drinkers who annoy or intimidate passersby. It can include the enforcement of civil ordinances whose violation can in no way be construed as criminal activity, but that is illegal nevertheless — for example, issuing citations for parking and minor traffic offenses, vending merchandise without a license, obstructing sidewalks, failing to post certain certificates of authority to conduct business, or perhaps even littering. Peacekeeping can also include more general areas of public service that are in no way related to the violation of law: directing traffic, settling disputes, locating missing children, returning lost pets, offering counsel to runaways, providing directions to confused pedestrians, and delivering babies.

Police patrol

Police work encompasses preventive and protective roles as well, for peacekeeping also includes *patrol*, which lessens opportunities to commit crimes. In addition, prevention and protection can involve initiating programs to reduce racial tensions, promote safe driving, reduce opportunities for crime victimization, and educate the public about home security measures.

Finally, police work involves many tasks that occur well beyond public notice and that are often time-consuming, overly routine, and excessively burdensome. Such activities include maintaining extended surveillances, transporting suspects, protecting witnesses, writing arrest and other reports, and testifying in court.[2] In short, peacekeeping operations generally do not involve criminal activities, and often are not even in the area of law enforcement.

Police themselves have done little to describe the full range and importance of their activities, and the better studies and descriptions have been compiled by persons outside police agencies. James Q. Wilson, for example, conducted studies of calls to the police in Syracuse, New York, during the period June 3–9, 1966. He found that only one-tenth of the calls afforded the police an opportunity to exercise their enforcement functions.[3] Sociologist Albert J. Reiss, Jr., monitored all calls during a one-day period in 1966 to the Central Communications Center of the Chicago Police Department.[4] He reported that of the 6,172 calls received, 58 percent were requests concerning criminal or potentially criminal matters, broken down as follows: breaches of the peace, 26 percent; offenses against property, 16 percent; offenses against persons, 6 percent; auto violations, 5 percent; suspicious persons, 3 percent; and other, 2 percent. Thirty percent of the calls were requests for assistance. Reiss further noted that the Chicago police themselves categorized as noncriminal some 83 percent of the incidents handled in a 28-day period.

More recently, Richard J. Lundman of Ohio State University reported on the findings of a comparative study of police patrol work in five different jurisdictions.[5] "Law enforcement" ranged from a high of 33 percent of all activities in the urban police department to a low of only 13 percent in one of the suburban departments. Most of the patrol time seemed to be occupied by traffic, service calls, and maintaining order (see Exhibit 7.1).

Even in the law enforcement aspects of police work, a significant proportion of activity does not involve "dangerous crime." One perspective on

*An assault on police
in Los Angeles*

EXHIBIT 7.1

Percent of Police Patrol Activities, by Type of Department

Activity	Type of Department					
	Midwest City, Urban Department	Smithville, Suburban Department	Pinewood, Suburban Department	East Coast, State Police Station	Township Department	Total
Information gathering[a]	8	6	5	19	12	9
Service[b]	13	23	10	12	5	13
Order maintenance[c]	24	29	16	13	26	24
Law enforcement[d]	33	19	13	19	27	30
Traffic[e]	18	21	52	29	30	21
Other[f]	3	3	4	8	0	3
Total percent	99	101	100	100	100	100
Total number	(2,835)	(264)	(214)	(150)	(168)	(3,631)

[a] Includes calls to take a report of a criminal incident, calls about missing persons and collection of property, and calls to "see the person."

[b] Includes calls about vehicular and nonvehicular accidents, lockouts, and assists of elderly persons.

[c] Includes calls about barking dogs, loud parties, televisions, or radios; domestic disturbances, juvenile disturbances; landlord–tenant, customer–proprietor, or neighbor disputes; and public drunkenness.

[d] Includes assaults, robberies, burglaries, auto thefts, larceny, homicides, rape, and certain less serious crimes.

[e] Includes both parking and moving violations.

[f] Includes a variety of infrequent calls and tasks, such as transporting witnesses to court.

SOURCE: Richard J. Lundman, "Police Patrol Work: A Comparative Perspective," in *Police Behavior: A Sociological Perspective*, ed. Richard J. Lundman (New York: Oxford University Press, 1980), p. 56.

Police arrest activity

this issue emerges through an examination of police *arrest activity*. Exhibit 7.2 gives arrest statistics for the nation as a whole during 1984 as compiled by the FBI. Of the 11,564,000 arrests, only 20.4 percent involved the more serious Index crimes of homicide, forcible rape, robbery, aggravated assault, burglary, larceny, vehicle theft, and arson. In contrast, almost 40 percent of the arrests were for such lesser crimes as gambling, driving while intoxicated, liquor law violations, disorderly conduct, prostitution, vagrancy, and drunkenness.

These data should not be interpreted as suggesting that arrest activity in areas other than Index crime is either unimportant or not dangerous. On the contrary, of the tens of thousands of assaults on police officers that occur in the United States each year, one-third result from the follow-up of "disturbance" calls. Less than a fourth result from responding to robbery and burglary calls and attempting other arrests.

EXHIBIT 7.2

Total Estimated Arrests in the United States for 1984

Crime	Number of Arrests		Percent	
Total*		11,564,000		100.0
Murder and nonnegligent manslaughter		17,770		0.2
Forcible rape		36,700		0.3
Robbery		138,630		1.2
Aggravated assault		300,860		2.6
Burglary		433,600		3.7
Larceny-theft		1,291,700		11.2
Motor vehicle theft		121,200		1.0
Arson		19,000		0.2
Violent crime	493,960		4.3	
Property crime	1,865,600		16.1	
Crime Index total	2,359,500		20.4	
Other assaults		527,000		4.6
Forgery and counterfeiting		82,400		0.7
Fraud		270,700		2.3
Embezzlement		8,100		0.1
Stolen property; buying, receiving, possessing		123,100		1.1
Vandalism		245,900		2.1
Weapons; carrying, possessing, etc.		177,500		1.5
Prostitution and commercialized vice		112,200		1.0
Sex offenses (except forcible rape and prostitution)		97,800		0.8
Drug abuse violations		708,400		6.1
Opium or cocaine and their derivatives	181,800		1.6	
Marijuana	419,400		3.6	
Synthetic or manufactured drugs	19,000		0.2	
Other — dangerous nonnarcotic drugs	88,300		0.8	
Gambling		34,700		0.3
Bookmaking	3,200		<0.1	
Numbers and lottery	8,800		0.1	
All other gambling	22,700		0.2	
Offenses against family and children		44,300		0.4
Driving under the influence		1,779,400		15.4
Liquor laws		505,500		4.4
Drunkenness		1,152,300		10.0
Disorderly conduct		665,900		5.6
Vagrancy		29,100		0.3
All other offenses (except traffic)		2,406,900		20.8
Suspicion (not included in total)		21,300		—
Curfew and loitering law violations		86,600		0.7
Runaways		147,000		1.3

Note: Arrest totals based on all reporting agencies and estimates for unreported areas.

* Because of rounding, items do not add to totals.

SOURCE: *Uniform Crime Reports — 1984*, p. 163.

The data from these and other studies of the police testify to the fact that police work involves keeping the peace more so than enforcing the law. And the value of police peacekeeping activities should not be underestimated. A large proportion of the annual homicide and assault rates is an outgrowth of various kinds of disputes, and responding to such disputes takes up a considerable amount of police time. If police no longer intervened in these disputes, we could expect a considerable increase in assaults.

The Right to Use Force

The use of force

The peacekeeping role is what mainly separates the functions of police from those of private citizens. This role involves the legitimate right to **use force** in situations whose urgency requires it. One police observer described it this way:

> My neighbor is sick and tired of apples from my tree falling into his yard. He yells to me that he's fed up with my stinking apples and threatens to cut the tree down unless I do. "No way," I say. He revs up his chain saw. Modern democratic society offers me two options in such circumstances. One, I can drive to court and file a civil suit against my

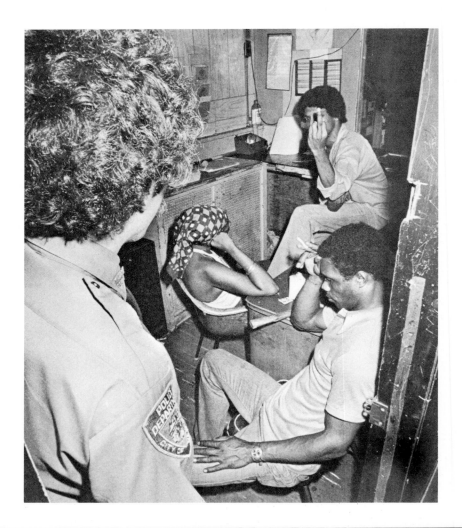

neighbor and, years hence, recover damages from him. The problem with this remedy is that I love my apple tree and don't want it cut down even if at some time in the future I am rewarded handsomely for its loss. Hence, modern democratic society gives me another option: call the cops and get them to stop my chain-saw-wielding neighbor before the chain bites bark. What the cops have which suits them to this task is a monopoly on the legitimate right to use force. That is, they can tell my neighbor to stop, and if he doesn't, they can use whatever force is necessary to stop him. This is not true of me, of course. Modern democratic society would look very dimly on me if I appeared on the scene with a gun and blasted my neighbor and his revving chain saw to the great orchard in the sky.[6]

The point is simply that modern democratic society severely restricts the right of private citizens to use force and urges them to use legal channels to work out their disputes. This restriction extends to virtually all cases except self-defense; and even there one must show that all reasonable means of retreat were exhausted. The law does recognize, however, that there are occasions in which something has to be done immediately — occasions in which resort to the courts or other mechanisms of dispute settlement would simply take too long and the damage would already be done. It is for handling such occasions that there are police — an idea based on the notion that it is better to have a small group of people (police) with a monopoly on the legitimate right to use force than to allow anyone with a club, gun, knife, or chain saw to use force in such immediately demanding situations. That right to use force in situations that demand it is held by the police in modern democratic society and justifies their role in crime control, peacekeeping, traffic, and everything else they do.

The police can't use clubs or gas or dogs. I suppose they will have to use poison ivy.
—**William F. Buckley, Jr.**

The Police Bureaucracy

Policemen are soldiers who act alone; soldiers are policemen who act in unison.
— Herbert Spencer, 1851

The analogy between police and soldiers given by English philosopher Herbert Spencer more than a century ago remains appropriate today, for virtually every police organization throughout the Western world is structured around a military model. Furthermore, combined with their paramilitary character and with modifications related to size, police departments are bureaucratically structured. Thus, there are clearly defined roles and responsibilities. Activities are guided by rules and regulations, and there is both a chain of command, and an administrative staff charged with maintaining and increasing organizational efficiency. Both the military and bureaucratic characteristics of police organizations are best illustrated by a description of the organizations' division of labor, chain and units of command, and rules, regulations, and discipline.

The military model of police organization

Division of Labor

All large police organizations and many smaller ones have a relatively fixed and clearly defined division of labor. As in Exhibit 7.3, a diagram of the organization of the Chicago Police Department, each separate responsibility falls within a specific unit, and the designated tasks of one division or unit are

EXHIBIT 7.3

Organization of the Chicago Police Department

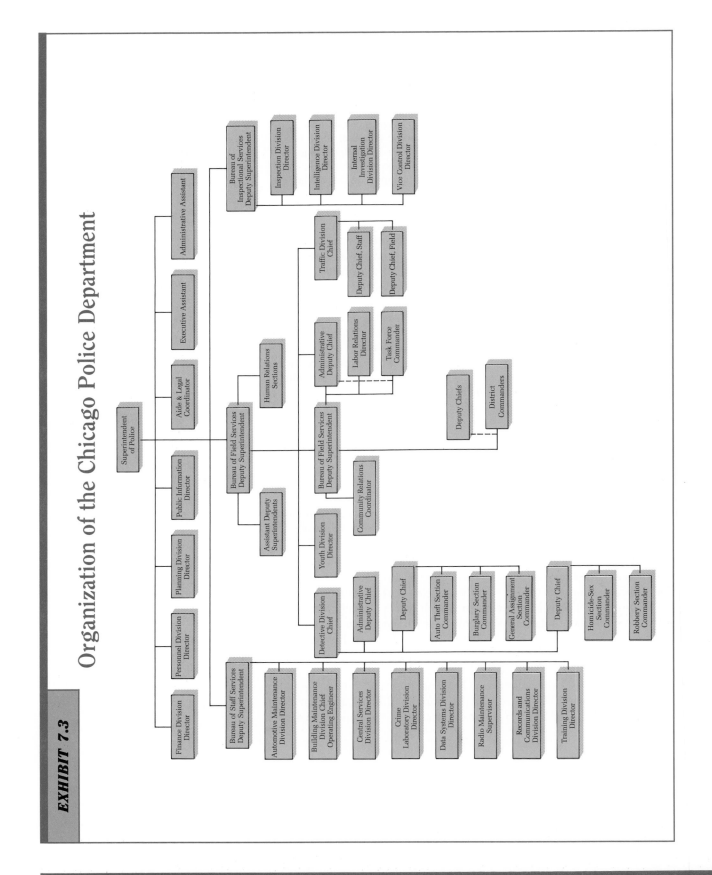

precluded from being carried out in others. Intelligence, internal investigation, inspection, vice control, and criminal investigation (detective division), for example, clearly fall within the authority of separate divisions, and only under extraordinary circumstances would the personnel assigned to one division work in the area of another. Furthermore, within the detective division, robbery, burglary, homicide, and auto theft fall into separate subunits. The organizational arrangements of smaller police agencies are similar, although scaled down in proportion to their size and work load.

Chain and Units of Command

In theory at least, individual orders, requests, or any other types of information should flow up or down through each level in the organizational hierarchy, and no level of supervision or command should be bypassed. In Exhibit 7.3, should a detective in the robbery division, for example, have a request that must be acted upon by the superintendent of police, the communication would go up through the chain of command—from the detective, to the commander of the robbery division, to the deputy chief of the detective division, to the chief of the detective division, to the deputy superintendent of field services (and perhaps even an assistant deputy superintendent prior to that), and finally, to the superintendent of police.

Within this structure, each employee of a police agency has but one immediate superior to whom he or she must answer. In addition, the bureaucratic principle of delegation of responsibility is quite refined. Supervisors in the chain of command have complete and full authority over their subordinates, and the subordinates, in turn, are fully responsible to their immediate superiors.

Although no uniform terminology has been adopted in American police service for ranks, grades of authority, functional units, territorial units, and time units, those most commonly used are military-style designations. Ranks and titles include *officers, commanders, sergeants, lieutenants, captains, majors, chiefs,* and sometimes even *colonels.* Functional units include *bureaus,* which are composed of *divisions,* and these, in turn, can include *sections, forces,* or *squads.* Territorial units may be called *posts* (fixed locations to which officers are assigned for duty), *routes* or *beats* (small areas assigned for patrol purposes), *sectors* (areas containing two or more posts, routes, or beats), and *districts* and *areas* (large geographic subdivisions). Finally, time units include *watches* and *shifts,* and those assigned to a particular watch or shift are members of a *platoon* or *company.*[7]

Rules, Regulations, and Discipline

Most police organizations have a complex system of rules and regulations designed to control and guide the actions of officers. Operations manuals and handbooks are generally lengthy, containing regulations and procedures to guide conduct in most situations (although, unlike the military, there are no rule books suggesting "proper" conduct for officers' spouses). In New York City, the current police rule book is almost one foot thick.[8] Officers are instructed as to when they can legitimately fire weapons (clear and present danger of injury to an officer or citizen, no warning shots, and never from a moving car). If any shots are indeed fired, there are detailed rules and procedures for "sweeping the street" (locating spent bullets and determining if any injury or property damage occurred at the base of the trajectory of a bullet

that missed its target). Reports of such matters must follow certain guidelines and their preparation must be done in a specific manner (in black ink with no erasures). Elaborate regulations also exist dealing with such varied phases of a police agency's internal operations as the receipt of complaints from citizens, the keeping of records, the transportation of nonpolice personnel in official vehicles, and the care and replacement of uniforms, ammunition, and other equipment. And there are policies and rules to guide the manner in which an officer makes an arrest, deals with medical emergencies, inspects the residence of a vacationing citizen, or takes a stray dog into custody. There are even rules governing procedures for mundane activities:

> *Even going to the toilet* . . . the rules dictate the formula by which . . . [an officer] . . . must request permission from a superior officer to leave post for "personal necessity."[9]

While the existence of so many rules may seem absurd at first glance, most were established with good reason. In organizations with such crucial responsibilities, particularly one that can use deadly force, rules must be carefully spelled out. Even the procedure for taking care of "personal necessity" is not without importance, for it involves an officer leaving his or her assigned post. Over time, as circumstances change or become more complex, the number of rules tends to grow.

Most observers of police activity agree, however, that many police rules and regulations are essentially useless and for the most part unenforceable. The police process demands compliance with departmental regulations as well as vigorously productive law enforcement. These demands sometimes conflict, and when they do, proper conduct must often take a back seat to the desirability of "good 'collars' [arrests]." Furthermore, although in theory some procedures seem explicit and comprehensive, in practice they are no more than vague sermonizing as to what should be done. For example, in the area of police intervention in domestic disputes, no single rule can cover the possible number of contingencies. Officers are told to deal politely, impartially, and uniformly with citizens, but in a domestic quarrel one or more persons may express aggression, fear, or anger. One might be ill, the other might be drunk and abusive, and there could be children or other parties involved. What the officer must do depends more often on the nuances of the situation than on any regulation or published procedure.

There are other areas as well—because of the very nature of police work—where rules can be unenforceable. Since most officers are assigned to some type of patrol work on the street or in cars, they are unsupervised and their superiors have no way of determining what they actually are or are not doing.[10] Patrick V. Murphy, president of the Police Foundation and former police chief in the cities of New York, Detroit, and Washington, D.C., recalled a situation regarding the regulations that existed in his day as a rookie cop during World War II:

> Take the police signal box system. Its official purpose was to maintain a management check on the movement of officers out on patrol. Each precinct had a large number of call boxes that were laid out in the pattern of an electronic grid, more or less in a logical schematic pattern across the territory of the precinct. However, there was a hitch in the scheme's logic which required all officers to phone the precinct switchboard once an hour, the line on which the call was received identifying the caller's location.
>
> The hitch was that there might be two to four boxes on the same line. One learned this beat-the-system fact on the first day. "Kid," one veteran explained, "you can call in on any one of these three boxes, and for all they know at the switchboard, you could be at any one of the three locations. They're all on the same line. You can call up and say, 'This is Murphy on Box Four,' and since Four is connected to Six and Eight, be at either place." What the experienced hand was saying was that Murphy could be playing poker in a "coop"* near Box Four, but could call in and give the impression that he was blocks away. An hour later, to give the impression that he was on the move, he could call back from the same box and give a different location entirely. Yet the system was designed, and publicized, as a management control measure to insure constant movement; this was the great police omnipresence.[11]

Because many rules are unenforceable, police management must practice strategic leniency. Administrators routinely ignore the minor violations of departmental regulations in exchange for adherence to a few important rules and a modicum of organizational loyalty. Historian Jonathan Rubinstein offers the following illustration:

> Although nobody questions a supervisor's right to punish his men . . . he will exhaust every available alternative before exercising his formal authority. For example, the operations room occasionally

If you aren't in complete control of a situation, anything you do will make it worse. —Howard Leary, former commissioner, New York City Police Department

---

* A sleeping or loafing location kept by officers.

fills up with men who come in to drop off their reports and hang around to drink a cup of coffee. . . . The supervisors, even when they are annoyed, rarely tell the men in a direct fashion to get back on the street. . . . One day a captain from outside the district was about to enter the operations room when he noticed how many policemen were standing inside. He quickly turned away and walked over to the drinking fountain, where he took a long drink. Their sergeant, who had been urging the men to move . . . said only, "I think he wants to come in here, but he does not want to embarrass anyone so he is waiting for you to leave."[12]

The Organization of Policing

Line services

Administrative services

Auxiliary services

Line services are the primary aspect of policing.

As bureaucratic organizations, most police agencies are broken down into a variety of administrative components — all of which focus either directly or indirectly on the basic police mission. **Line services** include such activities as patrol, criminal investigation, and traffic control. Depending on the size of the agency, line services might also have specific divisions or units that focus on vice, organized crime, intelligence, and juvenile crime. There are also a variety of **administrative services,** which are structured to back up the efforts of the line staff and include such activities as training, personnel issues, planning and research, legal matters, community relations, and internal investigation. **Auxiliary services** assist the line staff in carrying out the basic police function, with specialized units assigned to communications, record keeping, data processing, temporary detention, laboratory studies, and supply and maintenance.

A number of the staff and auxiliary services, such as internal investigations, are discussed elsewhere in this book. However, we examine the basic activities of the line services in greater detail in the following sections since they reflect the primary and most visible aspects of policing.

Patrol

Patrol

The functions of police patrol

For generations, the "cop on the beat" has been considered the mainstay of policing. In fact, to most people, the omnipresent force of officers dispersed throughout a community, in uniform, armed, and on call twenty-four hours a day, *is* policing. Whether officers are on foot or in cars, **patrol** remains basic to police work in both concept and technique.

Policing city streets entails a variety of tasks. Some of these are mundane, others are somewhat routine and boring, and a few can be dangerous. Patrol work includes such a wide spectrum of activities that it defies any specific description. It could involve dog-catching, administering first aid, breaking up family fights, pursuing a fleeing felon, directing traffic, investigating a crime scene, calming a lost child, or writing a parking ticket. Whatever the tasks might include, the patrol force is the foundation of the police department and its largest operating unit. In both cities and towns, along highways and in rural areas, uniformed patrol personnel directly perform all the major functions of modern law enforcement.

More specifically, police patrols have five distinct functions: to protect public safety, to enforce the law, to control traffic, to conduct criminal investigations, and to interpret the law.[13] In their role as *protectors*, patrols promote and preserve the public order, resolve conflicts, and respond to requests for defensive service. Patrol enforcement duties include both the preservation of constitutional guarantees and the enforcement of legal statutes. The *traffic control functions* of patrol involve enforcing the motor vehicle and traffic laws, and handling accidents and disasters. As *investigators*, police officers on patrol conduct preliminary examinations of complaints of criminal acts, gather physical evidence and interview witnesses. During such investigations they may also uncover evidence, identify and apprehend suspects, and recover stolen property. Finally, patrol officers have *quasi-judicial functions*: they make the first interpretation of whether a law has been violated, it is here that the discretionary aspects of policing begin to surface. In such circumstances police may choose to take no action or to arrest, or they may only advise, instruct, or warn.

Traditionally, the prevention and suppression of crime was regarded as the mission of police patrols. For decades, if not a century or more, this interpretation of duties was accepted by the police, public officials, and the general public. As an historical outgrowth of the early watch system, the first formal police patrols were on foot, and the cop on the beat became the symbol and very essence of policing in America. But even as early as the 1930s, well before the automobile had fully become part of the American way of life, foot patrols were beginning to vanish.[14] By the 1960s, their efficiency was being more seriously called into question. Foot patrols were deemed geographically restrictive and wasteful of personnel. Close supervision of officers had proven difficult, and without immediate transportation, foot patrols could not be deployed quickly to locations where their services might be needed. In 1968, the District of Columbia Crime Commission stated:

> The department's continued reliance on foot patrol is an inefficient and outdated utilization of manpower resources. . . . Leading police authorities are in general agreement that, with few exceptions, foot patrol is not the most efficient method of patrol. . . . Of course, officers should be assigned walking beats in particular commercial and high-crime areas where the need can be demonstrated. As long as the Department uses foot patrol as the primary method of patrol, however, available economics will not be realized and the city will not be provided the best possible police service.[15]

This was at a time when Kansas City, Dallas, Phoenix, Omaha, Oklahoma City, Birmingham, and other large cities had shifted almost totally away from foot patrols, replacing them with more deployable two-person motorized patrols. However, as a report of the Kansas City, Missouri, police department pointed out, in 1966 the number of foot patrol beats per shift in Boston, Baltimore, Pittsburgh, and other major urban centers still remained in the hundreds.[16]

At almost the same time the reports from Kansas City and the District of Columbia came out, the International Association of Chiefs of Police took the matter one step further, strongly advocating the idea of a conspicuous patrol that conveyed a sense of police omnipresence. The association felt that this could be best achieved using a highly mobile force of one-person cars:

> The more men and more cars that are visible on the streets, the greater is the potential for preventing a crime. A heavy blanket of conspicuous patrol at all times and in all parts of the city tends to suppress violations of the law. *The most economical manner of providing this heavy blanket of patrol is by using one-man cars when and where they are feasible.*[17] [emphasis added]

A beat cop in New York City

I'd love to be a policeman here, but I'm not brave enough.
—British constable, training in New York City

Motorized patrols

The reappearance of foot patrols in major cities

The Kansas City experiment

With the start of the 1970s, police officers on foot patrol were seen less often, and one-person motor patrols became more common. Today, one- and two-person foot patrols still exist, but primarily in densely populated areas of a city and in central business districts. Similarly, two-person cars are generally assigned to areas where the likelihood of assaults on police officers is high, and where there are too many incidents in a short period of time for one person to handle. However, because of the general lack of police – citizen contact that has resulted from motorized patrols, there are indications that current trends are turning once again in favor of putting the cop back on the beat. By 1985, foot patrols had reappeared in Oakland, Los Angeles, Newark, Detroit, New York, Houston, Boston, Minneapolis, and Cincinnati, and the trend is spreading to other cities as well (see Exhibit 7.4).

Whether police are deployed singularly or in teams, in vehicles or on foot, however, the essential value of police patrol in the prevention and suppression of crime has been called into question. In a study conducted by the Police Foundation in 1972 and 1973, three different levels of preventive patrol in Kansas City were closely compared. The setting was fifteen police beats, which were divided into five groups of similarly matched beats. One beat in each of the five groups was randomly selected for each of the three levels of patrol: normal, proactive, and reactive. *Normal* patrol involved a single car cruising the streets when not responding to calls; the *proactive* patrol strategy involved increasing the level of preventive patrol and police visibility by doubling or tripling the number of cruising cars; *reactive* patrol was characterized by the virtual elimination of cruising cars, with police entering the designated areas only in response to specific requests. At the

Taking care of the "crazies"

EXHIBIT 7.4

Foot Patrol:
The Flint Experiment

The police officers of Flint, Michigan, serve as the basis for the comparisons made in this research report. The Flint police department operated solely with motorized or preventive patrols until January 1979, when the Charles Stewart Mott Foundation provided funding for experimental community-based foot patrols.

Flint's Neighborhood Foot Patrol Program was unique in a variety of ways. It emerged from an initiative that integrated citizens into the planning and implementation process through citywide neighborhood meetings in 1977 and 1978. It attempted to ameliorate three distinct problems: (1) the absence of comprehensive neighborhood organizations and services; (2) the lack of citizen involvement in crime prevention; and (3) the depersonalization of interactions between officers and residents. The program began in 1979 with 22 foot patrol officers assigned to 14 experimental areas which included about 20 percent of the city's population.

The Flint program's salient features were a radical departure from both preventive patrol and traditional foot patrol models. Flint's foot patrol officers did not limit their activities to downtown or business areas. They were based in and accessible to all types of socioeconomic neighborhoods. Their crime prevention efforts went beyond organizing neighborhood watches. They attempted to serve as catalysts in the formation of neighborhood associations which articulated community expectations of the police and established foot patrol priorities and community programs. Foot patrol officers also worked in partnership with community organizations and individual citizens to deliver a comprehensive set of services through referrals, interventions, and links to governmental social agencies. The foot patrol officers reconciled their role with the reality of policing. They not only provided full law enforcement services, as did their motorized counterparts, but they made a conscious effort to focus on the social service aspects of their job. They were unusual in that they mobilized citizens to provide a matrix within which communities could deal with many of their own problems, including — but not exclusively — crime. Since they patrolled and interacted in the same areas day after day, week after week, they developed a degree of intimacy with residents which translated into an effective cooperative relationship.

The Neighborhood Foot Patrol Program reduced crime rates by 8.7 percent. More dramatic were the reductions of service calls, which decreased by 42 percent over the period 1979–1982. Citizens began handling minor problems themselves or the foot officer acted as mediator on an informal basis, negating the need for a formal complaint. Although the impact on service calls alone was significant, additional evidence indicated that citizens were satisfied that the program, had reduced the crime rates, made them safer, and improved relations between the police and the community by allowing much closer interaction between foot officers and citizens. Over 33 percent of neighborhood residents knew their foot patrol officers by name and 50 percent of the rest could provide accurate descriptions of foot officers. Citizens also felt that foot officers were more effective than motor officers in encouraging crime reporting, involving citizens in neighborhood crime prevention efforts, working with juveniles, encouraging citizen self-protection, and following up on complaints. The foot patrol experiment was so successful that the citizens of Flint passed a tax increase in August 1982 which extended the program to the entire city. There are presently 64 foot beats in Flint.

SOURCE: Robert C. Trojanowicz and Dennis W. Banas, *Perceptions of Safety: A Comparison of Foot Patrol Versus Motor Patrol Officers* (East Lansing: National Neighborhood Foot Patrol Center, School of Criminal Justice, Michigan State University, 1985), pp. 4–5. Reprinted by permission of the authors.

conclusion of the study, no significant differences were found in any of the areas — regardless of the level of patrol — in the amount of crime officially reported to the police or according to victim surveys, observed criminal activity, citizen fear of crime, or the degree of citizen satisfaction with police.[18] In effect, the Kansas City experiment suggested that police patrol was not deterring crime.

Detective Work

Detective work

Although patrol units conduct preliminary investigations of criminal acts, most sustained investigations are assigned to a police department's detective force, which specializes in the apprehension of offenders. Detective-level policing, specifically **detective work**, includes a variety of responsibilities, all of which fall into the area of criminal investigation: (1) the identification, location, and apprehension of criminal offenders; (2) the collection and preservation of physical evidence; (3) the location and interviewing of witnesses; and (4) the recovery and return of stolen property. In addition, detective duties may involve some of the law enforcement functions of patrol units, such as responding to the dispatch of a ''burglary in progress,'' but these would generally be exceptions rather than general practice.

In small police departments, detective functions are often carried out by members of the patrol force, or there may be a single detective generalist who handles all or most of the criminal investigations. In the larger departments, however, there are not only detective squads, but special investigative units that focus only on homicides, robberies, burglaries, or rape. Typically, a detective unit will handle the investigation of all crimes that occur in its geographically assigned area; not all homicides or robberies or burglaries would necessarily be assigned to detectives from one of the specialized units. However, should the nature and method of the offense suggest a link to similar crimes in other areas, or if it is determined that the crime might have political repercussions, then the specialized unit would become involved in the case.

Special detective units

In metropolitan areas where crime rates are high, there may also be several rather exotic detective units whose concerns are very narrowly focused. Historically, for example, the New York City police department has been well known for its Auto Squad, Missing Persons Unit, Pickpocket and Confidence Squad, Wall Street Unit, Bureau of Special Services, and its Safe, Loft, and Truck Squad.[19] Similarly, Detroit has a special homicide squad called Squad Six that handles only drug-related homicides. Special detective squads may also be organized for specific instances of crime or investigation.

Media portrayals of detectives suggest that they spend much of their time in the pursuit of criminal offenders and that their efforts at detection are quite successful. But in reality this is simply not the case. Former police administrator Herman Goldstein has pointed this out in his *Policing a Free Society:*

> Part of the mystique of detective operations is the impression that a detective has difficult-to-come-by qualifications and skills; that investigating crime is a real science; that a detective does much more important work than other police officers; that all detective work is exciting; that a good detective can solve any crime. It borders on heresy to point out that, in fact, much of what detectives do consists of very routine and rather elementary chores, including much paper processing; that a good deal of their work is not only not exciting, it is down-

right boring; that the situations they confront are often less challenging and less demanding than those handled by patrolling police officers; that it is arguable whether special skills and knowledge are required for detective work; that a considerable amount of detective work is actually undertaken on a hit-or-miss basis; and that the capacity of detectives to solve crimes is greatly exaggerated.[20]

Police work is often routine and boring.

In fact, detectives are responsible for proportionately few arrests. They generally receive their cases in the form of reports of criminal incidents written by patrol officers. Although practically all serious offenses are investigated by detectives in one way or another, such crimes are extremely difficult (and often impossible) to solve. In most robberies, burglaries, and thefts — which account for the majority of the FBI Index offenses — physical evidence that can be subjected to any kind of serious analysis is rarely found, Furthermore, if witnesses to a crime are available, many are unwilling to cooperate or their descriptions of the offender are so vague that they are of little value to an investigator. Even victims themselves are typically uncertain about the facts of the case. Only in those few instances where positive information can be found at the scene of a crime, or when victims or witnesses can provide substantial information to an investigating detective, are crimes likely to be solved. As a result, detectives engage in a selecting-out process when making decisions as to which crimes to investigate.[21] Detectives are evaluated on the basis of the number of felony arrests they make during the course of a year, and on the "clearance rate" for specific crimes. A crime is "cleared" when the offender has been taken into custody, and the **clearance rate** refers to the proportion of crimes that result in arrest. Thus, detectives generally choose to investigate seriously and intensively only those crimes that are most likely to be cleared. It is for this reason that clearance rates for homicide, aggravated

All but about 5 percent of serious crimes that are solved by detectives are solved because a witness tells the detective whodunit, or by thoroughly routine clerical procedures.
—Carl B. Klockars

A crime is "cleared" when the offender has been taken into custody.

assault, and forcible rape are relatively high. A large proportion of these offenses occur as the result of differences of opinion in personal relations, and the victims and offenders are often at least minimally acquainted. Thus, in many cases victims or members of their families can provide detectives with the identity of the offender or with leads and clues that can result in a possible identification. In contrast, clearance rates for robbery and burglary are quite low. In fact, a two-year study conducted in Atlanta, Georgia; St. Petersburg, Florida; and Wichita, Kansas, by the Police Executive Research Forum during the 1980s found only an 8 percent clearance rate for burglaries. Moreover, 75 percent of all robbery and burglary cases were dropped within a day after being reported.[22]

The multiple-clearance method

Since detective bureaus are under organizational, administrative, and political pressure to solve crimes, they also use a variety of mechanisms, sometimes illegitimate, to increase local clearance rates. Through the *multiple-clearance method,* one single arrest may ultimately clear numerous unsolved crimes. In the Son of Sam case, for example, the arrest of David Berkowitz resulted in the clearing of six homicides and almost a dozen felony assaults.[23] Similarly, if an individual is arrested for purse-snatching, detec-

---

EXHIBIT 7.5

"Cops" and "Coppers"
Some Etymological Considerations

American slang has a long and curious history, and much of it is traceable to the underworlds of vice and crime of past centuries. Such currently popular slang terms as "beef" (to complain), "fence" (a receiver of stolen goods), "hick" (a farmer), "hump" and "screw" (sexual intercourse), "lush" (a drunk), "snitch" (to inform on someone), and "tail" (a woman's buttocks or sexual intercourse) have their origins in the cant, or slang, of the sixteenth-century Elizabethan professional thief. Other slang usages date back to seventeenth-century England.

"Cop" and "copper," both meaning a policeman, also have their origins in the underworld.

Etymological investigation suggests that *cop* is associated with the root of the Latin *cap-ere*

(to seize or snatch) or the Gypsy *kap* and *cop* (to take). In the nineteenth-century cant of both English and American thieves, "to cop" came to mean to snatch, grab, or arrest; hence, the "cop" or "copper" was the policeman who grabbed a thief or made an arrest. And from the same root came such slang terms as "copped" (arrested), "cop a plea" (accept a plea of guilty to a lesser crime), "cop a feel" (to surreptitiously touch or grab a woman's breasts), and "cop out" (to offer a plea or excuse). Some obsolete terms of this genre include "copper house" (a police station), and "copper-hearted" (at heart a policeman).

The following excerpt, taken from George W. Matsell's *The Rogue's Lexicon,* published in 1859, illustrates some of these

usages in nineteenth-century American underworld slang:

The knuck was copped to rights, a skin full of honey was found in his kick's poke by the copper when he frisked him.

That is, the pickpocket was arrested, and a purse full of money was found in his pants pocket by the policeman when he searched him.

SOURCES: Godfrey Irwin, ed., *American Tramp and Underworld Slang* (New York: Sears, 1931); George W. Matsell, *Vocabulum; or, The Rogue's Lexicon* (New York: Matsell & Co., 1859); J. S. Farmer and W. E. Henley, *Slang and Its Analogues* (1890–1904, 7 vols.; reprint ed., New York: Arno Press, 1970); Eric Partridge, *Dictionary of Slang and Unconventional English* (New York: Bonanza Books, 1961); James A. Inciardi, *Careers in Crime* (Chicago: Rand McNally, 1975).

---

tives may contact recent purse-snatch victims to see if they can identify the suspect in an effort to clear previous, unsolved cases. But the multiple-clearance method can also be abused. One Miami Beach detective told the author this story several years ago:

> It was a damn good *collar* [arrest]. The officer catches him climbing ass first out of a kitchen window with a TV set under his arm. . . . He *bags* [arrests] him, and finds a *piece* [gun] in his back pocket, burglar's tools in his raincoat, and three bags of heroin in his sock. . . . Now we know that this junkie burglar has been doing his thing up and down the coast all year, so we offer him a deal: "You help us and we'll help you." . . . In the end, he *cops* [admits] to twenty-odd burglaries so we can get them off the books, and we drop the gun charge and tell the prosecutor that he's just some poor junkie stiff that cooperated and just needs a little help with his drug problem.

Unfounding and reclassification are also reliable, although sometimes illegitimate, methods of increasing clearance rates and getting the crime rate down.[24] *Unfounding* is a formal declaration that certain crimes previously thought to have occurred never actually happened. *Reclassification* is the reduction of certain crimes from felonies to misdemeanors. There are also "exceptional clearances," when some element beyond police control precludes taking the offender into custody, such as the death of a known but unapprehended criminal, a deathbed confession, or the refusal of a victim to prosecute after the perpetrator is identified. **Other clearance methods**

All of this should not suggest that clearance rates are always manipulated. Furthermore, since the number of arrests made by detectives represents only a small part of police business, one should not become cynical about the actual value of detective work. The perseverance of many detectives can be impressive. And routine follow-up investigations often produce new information that can lead to the identity of a perpetrator. In addition, the public relations value of detective work is immeasurable. Victims treated sympathetically offer greater assistance to the police in the future, and detective advice to victims plays an important role in crime prevention.

Specialized Police Units

In addition to the patrol and investigative aspects of police work, there are numerous specialized approaches to crime and control that occur within the context of highly focused bureaus and squads. For example, many large urban police departments have juvenile or *youth bureaus,* which employ proactive strategies to prevent and deter delinquent behavior. These large departments also have specialized units for enforcing vice laws or gathering intelligence concerning organized crime. **Youth bureaus**

Of a less conventional nature is the use of police decoys and "blending" — essentially, two related types of undercover work. In *decoy* operations, nonuniformed officers pose as potential high-risk victims — drunks, tourists, young women, the elderly, and the disabled — in high-crime areas in order to attract and apprehend street criminals. *Blending* involves the use of police officers posing as ordinary citizens, who are strategically placed in high-risk locations to observe and intervene should a crime occur. Among the more effective decoy and blending operations was New York City's Taxi-Truck Surveillance Unit, launched in 1970 to combat the growing number of night assaults on truck and cab drivers. From 1970 to 1975, specially equipped **Police decoys** **Blending**

Sting operations

The policeman on post is in all truth the court of first instance; he is a de facto judge just as truly as any ermined magistrate, and a wise patrolman can be guide, philosopher and friend as he carries on his daily, hourly court. —Arthur Woods, former commissioner, New York City Police Department

officers from both patrol and detective bureaus were selected to play the roles of cabbies and truckers; this undercover approach ultimately reduced the assaults and robberies by almost 50 percent.[25]

The most controversial of the special approaches to crime control are the elite police teams that use aggressive military procedures in exceptionally dangerous or potentially explosive situations. The forerunner of these groups was perhaps New York City's Tactical Patrol Force, a fast-moving battalion of shock troops trained in mob control and culled from the very best of police academy recruits. During the 1960s and early 1970s, the TPFs, as they are still known, viewed their 1,000-member force as the elite of incorruptible law enforcement. In addition to mob and riot control, the TPFs swept into high-crime areas to hunt down muggers and robbers, often using a variety of decoy units that readily blended into the life on the street.[26] Even more visible and controversial are the newer commando-style police units known as SWAT teams, which are carefully chosen and trained in the use of weapons and strategic invasion tactics and are typically used in situations involving hostages, airplane hijackings, and prison riots. The first of these police "guerrilla" units was the Philadelphia Police Department's 100-man Special Weapons and Tactics (SWAT) squad, which was organized in 1964 in response to the growing number of bank robberies throughout the city.[27] SWAT teams were also created in other cities during the 1960s, generally in response to riots and similar disturbances, that erupted. This type of army-style warfare in big-city police work was dramatically brought to the attention of a national audience with the television series "S.W.A.T." in 1975. The protagonists were Vietnam veterans dressed in semimilitary attire and organized like a front-line patrol. By the mid-seventies, SWAT teams had become popular among police agencies throughout the nation, with squads ranging in size from small two-person teams in suburban and rural areas to large 160-member teams in densely populated metropolitan regions.[28]

Sting operations have also become a part of urban law enforcement in recent years. The typical sting involves using various undercover methods to control large-scale theft. Police officers pose as purchasers of stolen goods ("fences"), setting up contact points and storefronts wired for sound and videotape. Perhaps the best known of these was the Washington, D.C., sting operation in 1975, in which local police officers joined agents from the FBI and the Treasury Department in posing as members of the New York mafia. During a five-month period, they purchased some $2.4 million in stolen property (for $67,000) and arrested a total of 180 "customers."[29]

Police Discretion and Selective Law Enforcement

Among the major roles of police peacekeeping operations is the enforcement of laws that protect people and property. In carrying out this directive, police have the power to make arrests—official accusations of law violation. Thus, police officers stand on the front lines of the criminal justice process and must serve as chief interpreters of the law. Based on their knowledge of criminal codes, they must make immediate judgments as to whether a law has been violated, whether to invoke the powers of arrest, and whether to exercise the use of force when invoking that power. This situation tends to be exceedingly complex, especially since laws are not and cannot be written to take into account the specific circumstances surrounding every police confrontation.

Moreover, all laws cannot be fully enforced, and most police officers, having only minimal if any legal training, are not equipped to deal with the intricacies of law. Therefore, police must exercise a great deal of discretion in deciding what constitutes a violation of the law, which laws to enforce, and how and when to enforce them.

To define **police discretion** in a single phrase or sentence would be difficult, for the term has come to mean different things to different people. In the broadest sense, discretion exists whenever a police officer or agency is free to choose among various alternatives — to enforce the law and to do so selectively, to use force, to deal with some citizens differently than with others, to provide or not provide certain services, to train recruits in certain ways, to discipline officers differently, and to organize and deploy resources in a variety of forms and levels. Most discussions of police discretion seem to focus on a narrower area, examining decisions regarding only when and how to enforce the law, and hence, invoke the criminal justice process.

Police discretion

By and large, police discretion is paradoxical since it appears to flout legal demands. In most jurisdictions the police officer is charged with the enforcement of laws — *all* laws! Yet discretion in terms of selective enforcement is necessary because of limited police resources, the ambiguity and breadth of criminal statutes, the informal expectations of legislatures, and the often conflicting demands of the public. The potential for discretion exists whenever an officer is free to choose from two or more task-relevant, alternative interpretations of the events reported, inferred, or otherwise observed in any police – civilian encounter.

Studies of actual police practices demonstrate that discretion is not only widespread, but also that it occurs in many different kinds of situations. Based on extensive field observations of police practices, sociologist Wayne R. LaFave identified many of the reasons for this exercise of discretion.

The reasons for police discretion

A. Circumstances in which the conduct in question is clearly unlawful, but where police believe that the legislature may not have intended full enforcement. This would involve decisions not to arrest when:
   (1) the law is ambiguous (e.g., complaints regarding obscene materials);
   (2) the statutes are vague and may appear to have been designed as devices to deal with nuisance behavior rather than to call for full criminal processing (e.g., vagrancy and loitering);
   (3) the statutes were written ever so broadly for the purpose of simply foreclosing any "loophole" opportunities for criminal entrepreneurs (e.g., laws which not only prohibit large-scale organized gambling, but friendly poker games as well);
   (4) the intent of the law was seemingly to express a moral standard without an expectation of its full enforcement (e.g., the sodomy statutes which prohibit certain sexual acts among consenting adults);
   (5) the legislation is apparently out of date (e.g., the age-old "blue laws" which regulate the sale and/or consumption of alcoholic beverages).
B. Circumstances in which police action would place constraints on a law enforcement agency's time, personnel, and financial resources. This would include decisions not to arrest when:
   (1) the offenses are trivial (e.g., smoking in an elevator);
   (2) the conduct is considered common, even accepted, among a particular group even though generally prohibited by statute (e.g., barroom fights or family assaults within certain ethnic, national, or socioeconomic groups);

(3) the victim refuses to bring a complaint or testify at a trial (e.g., rape victims who do not wish the additional humiliation associated with trial proceedings);

(4) the victim is a party to the offense (e.g., the client of a massage parlor who complains of being "rolled" by a prostitute).

C. Circumstances in which an arrest would have been technically correct and where legislative intent or limited resources are not at issue. This would include decisions not to arrest when:

(1) arrests would be inappropriate or ineffective (e.g., arrests of skid row drunks);

(2) arrests would cause loss of public support (e.g., sudden crackdowns on gambling);

(3) arrests that would endanger long-range enforcement goals (e.g., arrests of police informants or states' witnesses);

(4) arrests that would cause undue harm to the offender (e.g., young first offenders or persons with good reputations whose offenses were only minor).[30]

Selective law enforcement is inescapable, for full enforcement of the law is both impossible and impractical.

The issue of police discretionary power is a problematic one, for the need for selective law enforcement is inescapable. **Full enforcement** of the law would involve an investigation of every disturbing event and every complaint, and the tenacious enforcement of each and every statute on the books — from homicide, robbery, and assault, to spitting on the sidewalk or littering the street. Full enforcement would mean arresting the little old lady down the street for gambling at an illegal bingo game, arresting your neighbor for not having his dog licensed, or perhaps even arresting your spouse for initiating oral sexual contacts on your wedding night.

The problems of selective law enforcement

Full enforcement, of course, is impossible and undesirable. It establishes mandates that exceed the capabilities and resources of police agencies and the criminal justice system as a whole. It places demands on police officers that exceed their conceptions of justice and fairness. And it transcends the public's conception of the judicious use of police power. Thus, police departments and officers are forced to select the options of underenforcement of some laws and nonenforcement of others, according to the dictates of any given situation. However, there are few clear-cut policies available to police describing when to invoke powers of arrest, and therein lies the problem. The very nature of police discretion creates situations in which good judgment suggests that enforcement should be initiated, *but it is not,* and others in which police power ought not be invoked, *but it is.*

Studies of police discretionary power have demonstrated that the most significant factor in the decision to arrest is the seriousness of the offense committed. This is supplemented by other information such as the offender's current mental state, past criminal record (when known to the arresting officer), whether weapons were involved, the availability of the complainant, and the relative danger to the officer involved.[31] In addition to these seemingly objective criteria, other factors come into play as well. What many police view as "safe" arrests often involve individuals without the power, resources, or social position to "cause trouble" for the officer. The social position of the complainant is also a matter of concern. In addition, a variety of studies have documented that police use their discretionary power of arrest more often when "disrespect" is shown them. Irving Piliavin and Scott Briar's well-known study, "Police Encounters with Juveniles," gives a particularly useful perspective on these aspects of discretion and differential law enforcement.[32] Their research demonstrated that, with the exception of offenders who had committed serious crimes or who were already wanted by the authorities, the disposition of juvenile cases depended largely on how a youth's character was evaluated by an officer. Such evaluations and decisions were typically limited to the information gathered by police during their actual encounters with juveniles. Piliavin and Briar found that this had serious implications for both the accused and the system of justice as a whole. When police officers believed that a youth's demeanor, race, or style of dress were good indicators of future behavior or criminality, arrests became totally discriminatory — the youths who were arrested were those who typically did not fit the officer's idea of normalcy.

The more problematic aspects of police discretion have become manifest in numerous other ways. Consider, for example, the following conversation between a complainant and a dispatcher reported in a recent study:

> "Hello, is this the police?"
> "Yes, Madame, what is the problem?"
> "He is coming up to get me."
> "Where are you, Madame?"
> "At home."
> "Where?"
> "230 Sutton Avenue."
> "Who's coming to get you?"
> "George."
> "How do you know?"
> "He just telephoned and said he would take the kid."
> "Is it his child, Madame?"
> "Yes."
> "Is he living with you?"
> "Yes."
> "When is he coming?"
> "Now."
> "Why would he want to kill you?"
> "I don't know."
> "Does he have a weapon?"
> "I don't know."
> Pause by dispatcher. "Madame, if George arrives and causes any trouble, you call the station and we will send a car."
> Dispatcher hangs up.[33]

In this instance, the police may have been able to prevent a crime, for the caller was subsequently assaulted by George. In another instance, a New York City detective related the following incident to the author:

> So there I am sitting in the car waiting for my partner to come out of this saloon. All of a sudden this clown comes running out with a fist full of money and a gun in his hand. . . . I know my partner wasn't interested in stopping him — he had only three more months to retirement and he'd been avoiding trouble for years. . . . And me, I was headed for the mountains the next day and I had no intention of spending my vacation sitting in court with some goon. So we looked the other way and let him go.

A different level of police discretion involves decisions made by police command staff regarding departmental objectives, enforcement policies, the deployment of personnel and resources, budget expenditures, and the organizational structure of police units. Known as *command discretion*, it is implicit in the very structure and organization of a police force. It tends to be less

Command discretion

The police subculture and the working personality

problematic than other types of discretion since it provides at least some uniform guidelines for street-level decision making.[34] Examples of command discretion might involve orders to "clear the streets of all prostitutes," or conversely, "look the other way" when observing the smoking of marijuana at rock concerts. A curious example of this level of discretion occurred during February 1981, when the police chief of a small town in New Jersey made it departmental policy that there would be a moratorium on the issuance of citations for parking and minor traffic violations. The police department had run low on its stock of summonses, and new supplies would not be readily forthcoming.[35]

Exactly how police discretion can be effectively controlled poses a complex dilemma, for it must be done in a manner that does not destroy the polar objectives of law enforcement — effective crime control and the protection of the rights of citizens. On this point, Professor Herman Goldstein commented:

> As a minimum it would seem desirable that discretion be narrowed to the point that all officers in the same agency are operating on the same wavelength. The limits on discretion should embody and convey the objectives, priorities, and operating philosophy of the agency. They should be sufficiently specific to enable an officer to make judgments in a wide variety of unpredictable circumstances in a manner that will win the approval of top administrators, that will be free of personal prejudices and biases, and that will achieve a reasonable degree of uniformity in handling similar incidents in the community.[36]

The Police Subculture

A *subculture* is the normative system of a particular group that is smaller than and essentially different from the dominant culture. It includes learned behavior common to the group and characterizes ways of acting and thinking that, together, constitute a relatively cohesive cultural system. The police are members of a subculture. Their system of shared norms, values, goals, career patterns, style of life, and occupational structure, and thus their social organization, is essentially different from those of the wider society within which they function and are charged to protect. Entry into the **police subculture** begins with a process of socialization whereby police recruits learn the values and behavior patterns characteristic of experienced officers. Ultimately, many develop an occupational or **working personality,** characterized by authoritarianism, suspicion, racism, hostility, insecurity, conservatism, and cynicism.

The Police Personality

They're all alike. There's gotta be something really weird about the kind who want to become cops.   — a Philadelphia shopkeeper, 1980

For generations, the notion that policing attracts persons predisposed toward authoritarianism and cynicism has been shared by many. There is even a body of research that supports this point of view.[37] Yet, the overwhelming majority of studies over the past two decades have consistently indicated that policing does *not* attract a distinctive personality type, but rather, that the nature of police socialization practices create a working personality among many patrol officers.[38]

Perhaps the most definitive statement on the development of the police personality comes from Jerome H. Skolnick, who summarized the process as follows:

> The policeman's role contains two principal variables, danger and authority, which should be interpreted in the light of a "constant" pressure to appear efficient. The element of danger seems to make the policeman especially attentive to signs indicating a potential for violence and lawbreaking. As a result, the policeman is generally a "suspicious" person. Furthermore, the character of the policeman's work makes him less desirable as a friend, since norms of friendship implicate others in his work. Accordingly, the element of danger isolates the policeman socially from that segment of the citizenry which he regards as symbolically dangerous and also from the conventional citizenry with whom he identifies.[39]

Skolnick further suggests that the element of authority reinforces the element of danger in isolating the policeman. That is, police are required to enforce laws that often reflect a puritanical morality, such as those prohibiting gambling and drunkenness — although in their personal lives they are not known to uphold the values that they are called upon to enforce. Police are also charged with enforcing the traffic laws and other codes that regulate the flow of public activity. In these situations, where police direct the citizenry and enforce unpopular laws that come from some idealized middle-class morality, they become viewed as adversaries. The public denies any recognition of police authority, while stressing the police obligation to respond to danger.

Skolnick and others have elaborated on other elements that contribute to the development and crystallization of the police personality. All officers, for example, enter the police profession through the same mechanism: academy training followed by the constabulary role of the "cop on the beat." Because of this, officers share early experiences in a paramilitary organization that places a high value on similarity, routine, and predictability. Furthermore, as functionaries charged with enforcing the law and keeping the peace, police are required to respond to all assaults against persons and property. Thus, in an occupation characterized by an ever-present potential for violence, many police develop a perceptual shorthand to identify certain kinds of people as "symbolic assailants."[40] As a consequence, police develop conceptions that are shaped by persistent suspicion. In fact, police are specifically *trained* to be suspicious.

In sum, the police personality emerges as a result of the very nature of police work and of the kindred socialization processes in which most police officers seem to partake. To combat the social isolation that descends from the authoritarian role of the police, they develop resources within their own world — other police officers — to combat social rejection. In the end, most police become part of a closely knit subculture that is protective and supportive of its members, and that shares similar attitudes, values, understandings, and views of the world. This sense of isolation and the solidarity that grows out of it is typified by the following comment made to the author by a Delaware state trooper in late 1977:

Police solidarity

> After only three months on the job I sensed that things were changing. I heard less and less from my high school buddies, old friends didn't call me over to play some poker or have a beer, even my own brother got a little distant. . . . My wife and I didn't get invited to

parties any more—maybe they thought I'd arrest them if they pulled out a joint. . . . Enough was enough. We started sticking with the people from Troop 6 . . . and it was better, they were police people.

Police cynicism

Finally, an integral part of the police personality is **cynicism**—the notion that all people are motivated by evil and selfishness. Police cynicism develops among many officers through their contact with the police subculture and by the very nature of police work. Police officers are set apart from the rest of society because they have the power to regulate the lives of others, a role symbolized by their distinctive uniform and weapons. Moreover, their constant dealing with crime and the more troublesome aspects of social life

---

EXHIBIT 7.6

Police Cynicism

"I look back over almost thirty-five years in the police service, thirty-five years of dealing with the worst that humanity has to offer. I meet the failures of humanity daily, and I meet them in the worst possible context. It is hard to keep an objective viewpoint."[a]

"The policeman's world is spawned of degradation, corruption, and insecurity. He sees men as ill-willed, exploitative, mean and dirty; himself a victim of injustice, misunderstood and defiled."[b]

"The whole damn area is made up of junkies and thieves—every last one of them. There's only one way to clean it up. Round them all up and put them on an island in the Pacific. Then give each of them $100, a bag of heroin, and a knife. They'll end up killing each other off."[c]

"What the hell do you expect from an animal like that. In fact they're *all* animals!"[d]

"I am convinced that we are turning into a nation of thieves. I have sadly concluded that nine out of ten persons are dishonest."[e]

"It's the *ass-hole* of the city. All you have to do is rub your fingers on any wall and ten thieves jump out."[f]

"I hate citizens."[g]

SOURCES:
a. *The Police: An Interview by Donald McDonald with William H. Parker, Chief of Police of Los Angeles* (Santa Barbara: Center for the Study of Democratic Institutions, 1962), p. 25.
b. William A. Westley, "The Police: A Sociological Study of Law, Custom, and Morality." (Ph.D. dissertation, University of Chicago, 1951), p. ii.
c. Personal communication from a New York City detective, February 7, 1981.
d. Personal communication from a New York City Transit Authority police officer, June 18, 1980.
e. Dorothy Crowe, "Thieves I Have Known," *Saturday Evening Post*, February 4, 1961, p. 78.
f. Statement by a police officer patrolling New York's Times Square, cited in James A. Inciardi, *Careers in Crime* (Chicago: Rand McNally, 1975), p. 52.
g. Elaine Cumming, Ian Cumming, and Laura Edell, "Policeman as Philosopher, Guide, and Friend," *Social Problems* 12 (Winter 1965): 285.

serve to diminish their faith in humanity. (See Exhibit 7.6.) As the late Arthur Niederhoffer put it:

> Cynicism is an emotional plank deeply entrenched in the ethos of the police world, and it serves equally well for attack or defense. For many reasons police are particularly vulnerable to cynicism. When they succumb, they lose faith in people, society, and eventually in themselves. In their Hobbesian view, the world becomes a jungle in which crime, corruption, and brutality are normal features of the terrain.[41]

Police Operational Styles

Without question, not all police officers manifest the level of cynicism expressed here, and there are others who possess little, if any, cynicism at all. Furthermore, the degree to which police officers develop the outstanding characteristics of the working personality also varies widely. In addition, approaches to police work reflect considerable variation. Research on police behavior suggests that most police adopt an operational style, a general role to which they tend to conform that embodies an abstract perception of law enforcement and their responsibilities to the community they are pledged to serve. The primary roles played by individual police officers are those of the enforcer, the idealist, the realist, and the optimist. No officer conforms solely to one of these roles in his or her behavior to the exclusion of the others — they are not specific personality types or pure categories of policing — but rather manifests the general attitude associated with one of these ideal types.[42]

Enforcers

Enforcers include police officers who place high merit on maintaining order and "keeping society safe," and a relatively low value on individual rights and constitutional due process. Since removing dangerous criminals from the streets is their main preoccupation, enforcers are generally critical of the Supreme Court and its decisions, which serve to "handcuff the police," and of police administrators, politicians, and others "who think that they know more about the law than the policeman does."

In general, enforcers express considerable dissatisfaction with their jobs. Even though they may arrest murderers and thieves, they see the same criminals being released and begin to wonder if their time has been well spent. They adapt by becoming resentful, cynical, and distrustful, and tend to stereotype people in various ways. Furthermore, as guardians of the public safety they see less serious crimes as being of little importance. They view intervening in domestic disputes or enforcing the traffic laws as a poor use of their time. On the other hand, although they are unhappy with police work, enforcers are committed to upholding "the law." They wish to return to "the good old days" when there was respect for the law and the cop on the beat.

Idealists

Idealists share many of the characteristics of enforcers, but in other ways they are very different. While placing a high value on maintaining order and protecting society, they also take seriously such notions as individual rights and due process of law. At the same time, while emphasizing the need to deal with dangerous criminals, idealists accept the notion that police officers should be involved in a wide variety of activities, even those not necessarily related to law enforcement.

The dissatisfactions and occupational frustrations known among enforcers are also manifest among idealists. Although concerned with rights and due process, they do see inequities within the courts. Furthermore, they view their jobs as difficult and feel rejection when understanding and respect for their contributions is not forthcoming. Although more flexible than enforcers, idealists too tend to become cynical.

Realists

Realists share many of the same resentments and dissatisfactions with the court system and other social institutions as do other types of officers, but they are less frustrated with their roles in life. Since they place relatively low emphasis on both maintaining order and individual rights, they more easily find ways to cope with their jobs.

Realists see due process of law as an obstacle to effective enforcement and simply conclude that keeping society safe is impossible. What remains for these officers, then, is the "police group" — the group loyalty, mutual support, and the special ethos of being a police officer. Realists do not try to change the world, offenders, or even the police department, and cynicism becomes a very real part of their thinking. They internalize the idea that if you

can't succeed because of the courts, or because of the politicians and public who do not understand the difficulties of police work, "then the hell with it—just don't let it get to you."

Optimists

Optimists are the most people-oriented members of the police force. They place a high value on individual rights and are less likely to define their jobs as keeping society safe. Optimists see law enforcement as providing opportunities to help people in trouble. Since much of police work involves activities other than crime fighting, optimists find much of their job rewarding. Although they are indeed full-fledged members of the police subculture, they tend to manifest little frustration, dissatisfaction, or cynicism.

There are many police officers who could be readily described as enforcers, idealists, realists, or optimists. However, there are numerous others who manifest characteristics of several of these types, and still more who reflect totally different operational styles. James Q. Wilson has identified an alternative type, for example—the *watchman*—who reflects a number of the attitudes of both the enforcer and the idealist. The watchman style of policing involves keeping a low profile, and intervening only when there is a clear indication of public danger and disorder. These types of officers realize the importance of enforcing the law, but they tend to do so only when the public safety appears threatened.[43]

Summary

Police have many functions. In a democratic society like the United States they serve as enforcers, protectors, investigators, and traffic controllers, and they act in many other roles as well. Yet, contrary to popular notions, their chief function is not enforcing the law but keeping the peace. This peacekeeping role is the key factor that separates the police from private citizens. Peacekeeping involves the mobilization of the legitimate right to use force in situations where urgency requires it.

Police departments are bureaucratically structured on a military model. All large police orangizations and many smaller ones have a fixed division of labor, chains and units of command, and rules, regulations, and discipline.

Patrol is the most basic concept and technique of police work. It is by means of patrol that police protect public safety, enforce the law, control traffic, conduct criminal investigations, and interpret the law. In years past, foot patrols were considered the mainstay of policing. They have been replaced almost universally by motor patrols, but currently there is a trend favoring "putting the cop back on the beat" to increase contact between police and citizens.

A police department's detective force specializes in the apprehension of offenders. Detective work includes the identification and arrest of criminal offenders, the collection and preservation of physical evidence, the locating and interviewing of witnesses, and the recovery and return of stolen property. In spite of this concentrated activity, however, for their numbers detectives make proportionately few arrests.

Police officers, whether detectives or those in uniform, are called on to judge immediately whether a law has been violated, whether to invoke the powers of arrest, and whether to use force in invoking that power. Considerable discretion must be used in making these judgments. This discretionary power can lead to selective law enforcement.

Finally, there is a police subculture — a system of shared norms, values, goals, and style of life that is essentially different from that of the wider society within which officers function and which they are charged to protect. Within this subculture there are numerous styles of policing, including those of enforcer, idealist, realist, optimist, and watchman.

Key Terms

administrative services **(200)**

auxiliary services **(200)**

clearance rate **(205)**

cynicism **(214)**

detective work **(204)**

full enforcement **(210)**

line services **(200)**

patrol **(200)**

peacekeeping **(189)**

police bureaucracy **(195)**

police discretion **(209)**

police role **(189)**

police subculture **(212)**

use of force **(194)**

working personality **(212)**

Questions for Discussion

1. What is the relative importance of patrol units, detective forces, and specialized squads to big-city policing?
2. In what ways are police agencies similar to military organizations? If you could imagine a police department *not* organized along military lines, what would it be like?
3. Do the advantages of police discretion outweigh the disadvantages?
4. What might be the most effective combination of foot patrols, motor patrols, and one-person patrols versus team patrols?

For Further Reading

Bristow, Allen P. *Rural Law Enforcement.* Boston: Allyn and Bacon, 1982.

Goldstein, Herman. *Policing a Free Society.* Cambridge, Mass.: Ballinger, 1977.

Klockars, Carl B. *Thinking About Police.* New York: McGraw-Hill, 1983.

Rubinstein, Jonathan. *City Police.* New York: Farrar, Straus and Giroux, 1973.

Notes

1. Karl Menninger, *A Psychiatrist's World: Selected Papers* (New York: Viking Press, 1959).
2. For a more detailed discussion of police tasks, see Egon Bittner, *The Functions of Police in Modern Society* (New York: Jason Aronson, 1975); Jonathan Rubinstein, *City Police* (New York: Farrar, Straus and Giroux, 1973); Herman Goldstein, *Policing a Free Society* (Cambridge, Mass.: Ballinger, 1977).
3. James Q. Wilson, *Varieties of Police Behavior: The Management of Law and Order in Eight Communities* (Cambridge, Mass.: Harvard University Press, 1968).
4. Albert J. Reiss, Jr., *The Police and the Public* (New Haven, Conn.: Yale University Press, 1971).
5. Richard J. Lundman, "Police Patrol Work: A Comparative Perspective," in *Police Behavior: A Sociological Perspective*, ed. Richard J. Lundman (New York: Oxford University Press, 1980), pp. 52–65.
6. Personal communication from Carl B. Klockars, April 1982.
7. O. W. Wilson and Ray C. McLaren, *Police Organization* (New York: McGraw-Hill, 1977), pp. 70–73.
8. Lawrence W. Sherman, *Scandal and Reform: Controlling Police Corruption* (Berkeley: University of California Press, 1978), p. 128.
9. Arthur Niederhoffer, *Behind the Shield* (Garden City, N.Y.: Doubleday, 1967), pp. 41–42.
10. Richard J. Lundman, *Police and Policing* (New York: Holt, Rinehart and Winston, 1980), p. 53; Bittner, *Functions of Police in Modern Society*, p. 56; President's Commission on Law Enforcement and Administration of Justice, *Task Force Report: The Police* (Washington, D.C.: U.S. Government Printing Office, 1967), p. 17.
11. Patrick V. Murphy and Thomas Plate, *Commissioner: A View from the Top of American Law Enforcement* (New York: Simon and Schuster, 1977), pp. 32–33.
12. Rubinstein, *City Police*, pp. 41–42.

13. National Advisory Commission on Criminal Justice Standards and Goals, *Police* (Washington, D.C.: U.S. Government Printing Office, 1973), p. 192.

14. Bruce Smith, *Police Systems in the United States* (New York: Harper & Brothers, 1949), p. 14.

15. President's Commission on Crime in the District of Columbia, *A Report on the President's Commission on Crime in the District of Columbia* (Washington, D.C.: U.S. Government Printing Office, 1966), p. 53.

16. Police Department of Kansas City, *1966 Survey of Municipal Police Departments* (Kansas City, Mo.: Police Department, 1966), p. 53.

17. International Association of Chiefs of Police, *A Survey of the Police Department of Youngstown, Ohio* (Washington, D.C.: International Association of Chiefs of Police, 1964), p. 89.

18. George L. Kelling, *The Kansas City Preventive Patrol Experiment: A Summary Report* (Washington, D.C.: Police Foundation, 1974).

19. Robert Daley, *Target Blue: An Insider's View of the N.Y.P.D.* (New York: Delacorte Press, 1973), p. 225.

20. Goldstein, *Policing a Free Society,* pp. 55–56.

21. See, for example, Donald J. Black, "The Social Organization of Arrest," *Stanford Law Review* 23 (June 1971): 1087–1111.

22. *USA Today,* May 16, 1983, p. 1A.

23. See Lawrence D. Klausner, *Son of Sam* (New York: McGraw-Hill, 1981).

24. Lundman, "Police Patrol Work," pp. 64–65.

25. Patrick J. McGovern and Charles P. Connolly, "Decoys, Disguises, Danger — New York City's Nonuniform Street Patrol," *Law Enforcement Bulletin* (October 1976): 16–26.

26. Charles Whited, *The Decoy Man* (New York: Playboy Press, 1973), p. 12.

27. *Philadelphia Bulletin,* March 28, 1976, section 3, p. 1.

28. See William L. Tafoya, "Special Weapons and Tactics," *Police Chief* (July 1975): 70–74; "The SWAT Squads," *Newsweek,* June 23, 1975, p. 95.

29. Ron Shaffer, Kevin Klose, and Alfred E. Lewis, *Surprise! Surprise!* (New York: Viking, 1979).

30. Wayne R. LaFave, *Arrest: The Decision to Take a Person into Custody* (Boston: Little, Brown, 1965).

31. Larry J. Siegel, Dennis Sullivan, and Jack R. Greene, "Decision Games Applied to Police Decision Making," *Journal of Criminal Justice* (Summer 1974): 131–142; Kenneth Culp Davis, *Police Discretion* (St. Paul, Minn.: West, 1975).

32. Irving Piliavin and Scott Briar, "Police Encounters with Juveniles," *American Journal of Sociology* 70 (September 1964): 206–214.

33. Brian A. Grossman, "The Discretionary Enforcement of Law," in *Politics and Crime,* ed. Sawyer F. Sylvester and Edward Sagarin (New York: Praeger, 1974), p. 67.

34. Paul M. Whisenand and R. Fred Ferguson, *The Managing of Police Organizations* (Englewood Cliffs, N.J.: Prentice-Hall, 1973), pp. 199–201.

35. WCAU-TV News, Philadelphia, February 16, 1981.

36. Goldstein, *Policing a Free Society,* p. 112.

37. For example, see Richard Bennett and Theodore Greenstein, "The Police Personality: A Test of the Predispositional Model," *Journal of Police Science and Administration* 3 (1975): 439–445.

38. The most significant studies of this viewpoint include Niederhoffer, *Behind the Shield;* Jerome H. Skolnick, *Justice Without Trial: Law Enforcement in Democratic Society* (New York: Wiley, 1966).

39. Skolnick, *Justice Without Trial,* p. 44.

40. Skolnick, *Justice Without Trial,* pp. 45–46.

41. Niederhoffer, *Behind the Shield,* p. 9.

42. This discussion is based on the typology found in John J. Broderick, *Police in a Time of Change* (Morristown, N.J.: General Learning Press, 1977).

43. Wilson, *Varieties of Police Behavior,* pp. 140–141.

8

The Law of Arrest, Search, and Seizure: Police and the Constitution

The Constitution of the United States was made not merely for the generation that then existed, but for posterity.

—Henry Clay (1777–1852)

Policing constantly places its practitioners in situations in which good ends can be achieved by dirty means.

—Carl B. Klockars, 1980

I'd like to tell the Supreme Court where it can put its search and seizure rules.

—A former Key West police official, 1985

Los Angeles police using a shark net to capture a suspect considered too dangerous to approach

LAWS

U. S. Marshal's Office,
Western District of Arkansas,
Fort Smith, Arkansas.

GOVERNING U.S. MARSHAL

...... AND ......

His Deputies.

U. S. Deputy Marshals for the Western District of Arkansas
may make arrests for

MURDER, MANSLAUGHTER,
ASSAULT, WITH INTENT TO KILL OR TO MAIM,
ATTEMPTS TO MURDER,
ARSON, ROBBERY, RAPE, BURGLARY,
LARCENY, INCEST, ADULTERY,
WILFULLY AND MALICIOUSLY PLACING OBSTRUCTIONS
ON A RAILROAD TRACK.

These arrests may be made with or without warrant first issued and in the hands of the Deputy or the Chief Marshal. It is always better for the Deputy to have a warrant before making an arrest, yet if he knows of any one of the above crimes having been committed and has good reason to believe a particular party guilty of the crime, his duty is to make the arrest.

For violations of the revenue law and for introducing ardent spirits into the Indian Country, the Deputy can not make an arrest without warrant, unless the offender is caught in the act, when he can arrest for these offenses without a warrant. The Deputy can arrest for violations of the revenue law, the intercourse law and the laws of the United States against counterfeiting, and for violations of the postal laws, or for larceny of the property of the United States, when any of these offenses are committed by an Indian. Also when an assault with intent to kill or maim, a murder, or manslaughter has been committed by an Indian upon an Indian Agent, Indian Policeman, Indian United States Deputy Marshal or guard or any person at any time while in the discharge of duty or at any time

Police powers are numerous, and can be broadly divided into two general areas: investigative powers and arrest powers.[1] Police **investigative powers** include, but are not necessarily limited to:

- the power to stop
- the power to frisk
- the power to order someone out of a car
- the power to question
- the power to detain

Police **arrest powers** include:

- the power to use force
- the power to search
- the power to exercise seizure and restraint

Because the Constitution of the United States was designed to protect each citizen's rights, it placed certain restrictions on the exercise of these powers. This chapter discusses the legal constraints on police powers and traces their evolution through Supreme Court decisions, focusing on the Court's impact on law enforcement practice.

Search Warrants

The right of the people to be secure in their persons, houses, papers, and effects, against unreasonable searches and seizures, shall not be violated, and no warrants shall issue, but upon probable cause, supported by oath or affirmation, and particularly describing the place to be searched, and the persons or things to be seized.
— Fourth Amendment, Constitution of the United States

The law enforcement functions of the police are accomplished through the investigation of crimes and the apprehension of offenders. Each of these functions becomes manifest by means of a complex and interrelated series of specific activities. The first objective of investigation is to determine if a crime has been committed (although not all crimes require investigation) and, if so, what type of crime it was. Police generally analyze the available information to learn if the elements are present that constitute violation of criminal codes.

The next objective is to identify the offender through further gathering of intelligence. When the investigation has been fruitful, an arrest is made; that is, a suspect is taken into custody. Beyond the investigation and apprehension aspects of law enforcement, police also have responsibility for gathering additional evidence if necessary, and for preserving it so that the prosecution phase of the criminal justice process can be effective. Yet each and every action in police investigation and apprehension is circumscribed by procedural issues that are governed by law and constitutional rights, and it is when these procedures and issues are called into question that law enforcement practice becomes a matter for judicial review.

At the outset, evidence gathering typically depends on *search*—the examination or inspection of premises or person with a view to discovering stolen or illicit property or evidence of guilt to be used in the prosecution of a criminal action. Associated with search is *seizure*—the taking of a person or property into the custody of the law in consequence of a violation of public law. **Search and seizure**, then, involves means for the detection and accusation of crime: the search for and taking of persons and property as evidence of crime.

Search and seizure

The very language of the **Fourth Amendment**, however, prohibits "unreasonable searches and seizures." Unreasonableness, in the constitutional sense, is an elastic term with an ambiguous definition that may vary depending on the particular considerations and circumstances of a given situation. In general, however, it refers to that which is extreme, arbitrary, and capricious, and which is not justified by the apparent facts and circumstances.

The Fourth Amendment

Search warrants obviate much of the problematic nature of search and seizure, for they reflect the formal authority of the law in their sanctioning of the use of police search powers. A **search warrant** is a written order, issued by a magistrate and directed to a law enforcement officer, commanding search of a specified premises for stolen or unlawful goods, or for suspects or fugitives, and the bringing of these, if found, before the magistrate.

Search warrant: A written order, issued by a magistrate and directed to a law enforcement officer, commanding a search of a specified premises.

Probable Cause

Warrants authorizing a search must pass the constitutional test of reasonableness. In the language of the Fourth Amendment, "no warrants shall issue, but upon probable cause." **Probable cause**, in the constitutional sense, refers to facts or apparent facts that are reliable and generate a reasonable belief that a crime has been committed. In the absence of such "facts," the probable cause element has not been met, and the validity of the warrant can be questioned. And while probable cause "means less than evidence which would justify condemnation,"[2] it does require "belief that the law was being violated on the premises to be searched; and the facts are such that a reasonably discreet and prudent man would be led to believe that there was a commission of the offense charged."[3]

Probable cause: Facts or apparent facts that are reliable and generate a reasonable belief that a crime has been committed.

Establishing probable cause for the issuance of a search warrant is a matter that the Supreme Court has addressed at length in recent years. As a result of *Aguilar* v. *Texas* in 1964 and *Spinelli* v. *United States* in 1969,[4] the general rule for many years was that probable cause for search could not be based solely on hearsay information received by the police. Rather, a valid warrant had to contain a statement that there was a reasonable cause to believe that property of a certain kind might be found "in or upon a designated or described place, vehicle, or person," combined with "allegations of fact"

Illinois v. Gates

supporting such a statement. The High Court's ruling in ***Illinois v. Gates*** in 1983,[5] however, eliminated the *Aguilar-Spinelli* test, replacing it with a "totality of circumstances analysis." *Gates* required magistrates to simply make a practical, commonsense decision whether, given all the circumstances set forth in the affidavit, there was a fair probability that contraband would be found in a particular place (see Exhibit 8.1).

Warrantless Search

A civilized system of law is as much concerned with the means employed to bring people to justice as it is with the ends themselves. A first principle of jurisprudence is that the ends do not justify the means. — Justice William O. Douglas, 1956

Although the general rule regarding the application of the Fourth Amendment is that any search or seizure undertaken without a valid search warrant is unlawful, there are exceptions, provided that the arrest, search, and seizure are not unreasonable. Such exceptions include:

- a search incident to a lawful arrest
- stop and frisk procedures
- probable cause and inventory searches of automobiles
- fresh pursuit
- consent searches

Search Incident to Arrest

Traditionally, a search without a warrant is allowable if it is made incident to a lawful arrest. The Supreme Court explained why in 1973:

> It is the fact of the lawful arrest which establishes the authority to search, and we hold that in the case of a lawful custodial arrest a full search of the person is not only an exception to the warrant requirement of the Fourth Amendment, but is also a "reasonable" search under that Amendment.[6]

But given the language expressed by the Court, what would constitute a lawful arrest?

Until recently, it was generally assumed that the Fourth Amendment did not require the issuance of a warrant for an arrest to be lawful. Moreover, in 1976, the Supreme Court ruled that a police officer could make an arrest in a public place without a warrant even if he had enough time to obtain one.[7] However, in 1980 the Court ruled that in the absence of exigent circumstances the home of an accused could not be entered to make an arrest without a warrant.[8]

The foregoing at least suggests that arrests made *with* warrants are lawful, assuming, of course, that the arrest warrants themselves are procedurally correct. Furthermore, as indicated in the language of *Gates*, the provisions that determine the validity and legality of search warrants also apply to arrest warrants.

In the absence of a warrant, the legality of an arrest can be somewhat more problematic. As a general rule of common law, an arrest could not be

EXHIBIT 8.1

Illinois v. *Gates:* From the Supreme Court's Opinion

On May 3, 1978, the police department of Bloomingdale, Illinois, received an anonymous letter which included statements that Mr. and Mrs. Gates were engaged in selling drugs; that the wife would drive their car to Florida on May 3 to be loaded with drugs, and the husband would fly down in a few days to drive the car back; that the car's trunk would be loaded with drugs; and that Mr. and Mrs. Gates presently had over $100,000 worth of drugs in their basement. Acting on the tip, a police officer determined the Gates's address and learned that the husband had made a reservation on a May 5 flight to Florida. Arrangements for surveillance of the flight were made with an agent of the Drug Enforcement Administration (DEA). The surveillance disclosed that Mr. Gates took the flight, stayed overnight in a motel room registered in his wife's name, and left the following morning with a woman in a car bearing an Illinois license plate issued to Mr. Gates, heading north on an interstate highway used by travelers to the Bloomingdale area. A search warrant for the defendants' residence and automobile was then obtained from an Illinois state court judge, based on the Bloomingdale police officer's affidavit setting forth the foregoing facts and a copy of the anonymous letter. When Mr. and Mrs. Gates arrived at their home, the police were waiting and discovered marijuana and other contraband in the defendants' car trunk and home. Prior to their trial on charges of violating state drug laws, the court ordered suppression of all the items seized, and the Illinois Appellate Court affirmed. The Illinois Supreme Court also affirmed, holding that the letter and affidavit were inadequate to sustain a determination of probable cause for issuance of the search warrant under *Aguilar* v. *Texas*, and *Spinelli* v. *United States*, because they failed to satisfy the "two-pronged test" of (1) revealing the informant's "basis of knowledge" and (2) providing sufficient facts to establish either the informant's "veracity" or the "reliability" of the informant's report. The Court held the following:

1. The question—which this Court requested the parties to address—whether the rule requiring the exclusion at a criminal trial of evidence obtained in violation of the Fourth Amendment should be modified so as, for example, not to require exclusion of evidence obtained in the reasonable belief that the search and seizure at issue was consistent with the Fourth Amendment will not be decided in this case, since it was not presented to or decided by the Illinois courts. . . . Nor does the State's repeated opposition to respondents' substantive Fourth Amendment claims suffice to have raised the separate question whether the exclusionary rule should be modified. The extent of the continued vitality of the rule is an issue of unusual significance, and adhering scrupulously to the customary limitations on this Court's discretion promotes respect for its adjudicatory process and the stability of its decisions. . . .

2. The rigid "two-pronged test" under *Aguilar* and *Spinelli* for determining whether an informant's tip established probable cause for issuance of a warrant is abandoned, and the "totality of the circumstances" approach that traditionally has informed probable-cause determinations is substituted in its place. The elements under the "two-pronged test" concerning the informant's "veracity," "reliability," and "basis of knowledge" should be understood simply as closely intertwined issues that may usefully illuminate the common-sense, practical question whether there is "probable cause" to believe that contraband or evidence is located in a particular place. The task of the issuing magistrate is simply to make a practical, common-sense decision whether, given all the circumstances set forth in the affidavit before him, there is a fair probability that contraband or evidence of a crime will be found in a particular place. And the duty of a reviewing court is simply to ensure that the magistrate had a substantial basis for concluding that probable cause existed. This flexible, easily applied standard will better achieve the accommodation of public and private interests that the Fourth Amendment requires than does the approach that has developed from *Aguilar* and *Spinelli*.

3. The judge issuing the warrant had a substantial basis for concluding that probable cause to search respondents' home and car existed. Under the "totality of the circumstances" analysis, corroboration of details of an informant's tip by independent police work is of significant value. Here, even standing alone, the facts obtained through the independent investigation of the Bloomingdale police officer and the DEA at least suggested that respondents were involved in drug trafficking. In addition, the judge could rely on the anonymous letter, which had been corroborated in major part by the police officer's efforts.

SOURCE: Illinois v. Gates, 462 U.S. 213 (1983).

made without a warrant, but if the felony or breach of the peace that was threatened or committed occurred within the view of an officer who was authorized to make an arrest, it was that officer's duty to arrest without warrant. If a felony had been committed and there was probable cause to believe that the particular person was the offender, then he or she could be arrested without a warrant. This common law rule of arrest, which is not at odds with constitutional guarantees, tends nevertheless to be vague, leaving much to the interpretation of the individual police officer. Even in the more definitive statements of this rule as they appear in the criminal procedure codes of most jurisdictions, it is the officer's responsibility to fully determine the probable cause for, and hence the potential legality of, an arrest. For example, Section 1b-10-3 of the code of criminal procedure of the state of Alabama states:

> An officer may arrest any person without a warrant, on any day and at any time, for:
>
> 1. Any public offense committed or a breach of the peace threatened in his presence;
> 2. When a felony has been committed, though not in his presence, by the person arrested;
> 3. When a felony has been committed and he has reasonable cause to believe that the person arrested committed it;
> 4. When he has reasonable cause to believe that the person arrested has committed a felony, although it may afterwards appear that a felony had not in fact been committed; or
> 5. On a charge made, upon reasonable cause, that the person arrested has committed a felony.
>
> In most warrantless arrest situations, when one of these conditions prevails, the arrest is lawful and the search incident to the arrest is also lawful.

The consequences of "unlawful" arrest

There can be several consequences of "unlawful" or "false" arrest. First, evidence seized as an outgrowth of an unlawful arrest is inadmissible. Similarly, any conviction resulting from an illegal arrest may be overturned. Typically, however, if it is clear in the early stages of the criminal justice process that the arrest in question was indeed unlawful, it is likely that the charges against the suspect will be dropped before adversary proceedings follow their full course. Second, in most jurisdictions a citizen wrongly taken into custody can institute a civil suit against the officer and the police department that initiated or authorized the arrest (although these suits are seldom won).

However, a number of other issues associated with wrongful arrest vary greatly from state to state. Under Tennessee law, for example, as early as 1860 and as recently as the 1970s, numerous court decisions have declared that if "the officer acts at his peril, if he has no right to make an arrest without a warrant, or if his warrant is not valid, he is a trespasser."[9] Under such circumstances, the police officer is liable for money damages. However, where the arrest "would have been proper without a warrant, it is immaterial whether or not the warrant was good or bad."[10]

In Tennessee, Alabama, and numerous other jurisdictions, case law has dictated that every person has a right to resist an unlawful arrest, and "in preventing such illegal restraint of his liberty he may use such force as may be necessary."[11] In Idaho, by contrast, the suspect has no such right.[12] Further, in those jurisdictions where resistance to wrongful arrest is lawful, the means or amount of resistance cannot be disproportionate to the effort of the police officer to execute the arrest.

Finally, virtually all states place no liability for wrongful arrest on police officers if the arrest was made on the basis of a valid warrant or on probable cause, but a verdict of not guilty was returned. Thus, an acquittal is not tantamount to a finding of no reasonable grounds for arrest.[13]

Stop and Frisk

Field interrogation or **stop and frisk** procedures can be a useful mechanism for police officers in areas where crime rates are high or where the potential risks for crime seem visibly present. In fact, it is not uncommon for police to stop on the street persons whose behavior seem suspicious, to detain them briefly by questioning for identification purposes, and to frisk (conduct a limited search by running the hands over the outer clothing) those whose answers or conduct suggest criminal involvement or threaten police safety.

Before the Supreme Court finally clarified the legal status of stop and frisk procedures in *Terry v. Ohio* (see Exhibit 8.2),[14] the authority for stop and frisk came from individual department directives, state judicial policy, police discretionary practices, and legislative statutes. In *Terry*, decided in 1968, the Supreme Court held that a police officer is not entitled to seize and search every person he sees on the streets and of whom he makes inquiries. Before placing a hand on the person of a citizen in search of anything, the officer must have constitutionally adequate, reasonable grounds for doing so.

Any evidence found during the course of a frisk that is contrary to the *Terry* decision falls under the long-standing **fruit of the poisonous tree**

> Stop and frisk is not uncommon where crime rates or the potential for crime is high.

> *Terry v. Ohio*

> Fruit of the poisonous tree

doctrine. Under this rule, evidence seized illegally is considered "tainted" and cannot be used against a suspect. Furthermore, subsequent evidence derived from the initially tainted evidence must also be suppressed.

Automobile Searches

As early as 1925, the Supreme Court established that due to the extreme mobility of motor vehicles, there were situations under which their warrantless search could be justified. In *Carroll* v. *United States*,[15] petitioner George Carroll was convicted of transporting liquor for sale in violation of the federal prohibition law and the Eighteenth Amendment. The contraband liquor used

---

EXHIBIT 8.2

Terry v. *Ohio*

At 2:30 P.M. on October 31, 1963, the attention of Cleveland police detective Martin McFadden was drawn to the activities of two men, Richard Chilton and John Terry, who were conversing at the intersection of two downtown thoroughfares. Periodically, one of the men would separate from the other, walk southwest along one of the streets, pause for a moment to peer into a particular store window, walk on a short distance, and then turn around and head back to the corner, pausing once again to look into the same window. The two men would then confer briefly before the second man would repeat the identical process of strolling down the street and looking into the very same store window. Detective McFadden observed Chilton and Terry repeat this reconnaissance ritual roughly a dozen times until a third man appeared, spoke with them briefly, and departed down one of the streets. Chilton and Terry resumed their pacing, peering, and conferring for another ten minutes, after which they departed together, following the path taken earlier by the third man.

At this point, the police detective was thoroughly convinced that Chilton and Terry were "casing a job, a stick-up." He followed them, and when they stopped to converse with the third man who had met them earlier on the street corner, he decided to intervene. Detective McFadden approached the three men, identified himself as a police officer, and asked for their names. When the men "mumbled something" in response to his inquiries, McFadden spun Terry around so he was facing the other two men, patted down the outside of his clothing, and felt what he believed to be a pistol. A more thorough search found that it was a .38-caliber revolver, and a frisk of the other two men revealed a revolver in Chilton's overcoat pocket. All three of the suspects were taken to the police station, where Chilton and Terry were formally charged with carrying concealed weapons.

Terry became an interesting case in law, for the prosecution argued that the guns had been "seized" in a "search" incident to a lawful arrest. The defense,

however, maintained that Detective McFadden had no probable cause for arrest and the guns ought to be suppressed as evidence obtained through illegal search and seizure. Not surprisingly, the court recognized that McFadden's search was *not* incident to a lawful arrest, for no arrest had been made prior to the search; rather, it was clearly a case of stop and frisk. In fact, it was the court's opinion that it "would be stretching the facts beyond reasonable comprehension" to find that the officer had probable cause to arrest the three men of attempted robbery *before* he patted them down for weapons. Nonetheless, the Ohio trial court did rule that Detective McFadden's method of obtaining the evidence had been lawful: he had a duty to investigate the observed suspicious activity and had an absolute right to protect himself by frisking for weapons.

Chilton and Terry were both convicted of the weapons charge, and Terry was sentenced to a term of one to three years in the state penitentiary. Two appellate courts in Ohio upheld Terry's conviction, and the U.S. Supreme Court

---

as evidence against him had been taken from his car by government agents acting without a search warrant. But the Supreme Court sustained Carroll's conviction against his contention that the seizure violated his Fourth Amendment rights. The Court determined that there had been probable cause for search. Chief Justice William Howard Taft explained the decision:

> The guaranty of freedom from unreasonable searches and seizures by the Fourth Amendment has been construed practically since the beginning of the government, as recognizing a necessary difference between a search of a store, dwelling house, or other structure in respect of which a proper official warrant readily may be obtained and a search of

granted *certiorari* (review) in 1967 in order to consider a number of questions concerning the constitutional validity of the stop and frisk practice. Showing rare solidarity, the High Court decided by an 8-to-1 margin to uphold a police officer's right to frisk and seize weapons under such circumstances. The Court ruled that Detective McFadden had reasonable grounds to believe that the "suspects" were armed and dangerous, that swift measures were necessary for the protection of himself and others, and that his frisk was appropriately limited to a patting down of the outer clothing until he felt weapons.

But central to the decision in *Terry* was the Court's general concern over police–citizen street encounters. Delivering the opinion of the Court on this issue, Chief Justice Earl Warren stated the following:

> Our first task is to establish at what point in this encounter the Fourth Amendment becomes relevant. That is, we must decide whether and when Officer McFadden "seized" Terry and whether and when he conducted a "search." There is some suggestion in the use of such terms as "stop" and "frisk" that such police conduct is outside the purview of the Fourth Amendment because neither action rises to the level of a "search" or "seizure" within the meaning of the Constitution. We emphatically reject this notion. It is quite plain that the Fourth Amendment governs "seizures" of the person which do not eventuate in a trip to the station house and prosecution for crime — "arrests" in traditional terminology. It must be recognized that whenever a police officer accosts an individual and restrains his freedom to walk away, he has "seized" that person. And it is nothing less than sheer torture of the English language to suggest that a careful exploration of the outer surfaces of a person's clothing all over his or her body in an attempt to find weapons is not a "search." Moreover, it is simply fantastic to urge that such a procedure performed in public by a policeman while the citizen stands helpless, perhaps facing a wall with his hands raised, is a "petty indignity." It is a serious intrusion upon the sanctity of the person, which may inflict great indignity and arouse strong resentment, and it is not to be undertaken lightly.

The *Terry* decision also provided standards for stop and frisk encounters, indicating that there had to be specific facts that could justify the police intrusion. In the words of Chief Justice Warren, there were five conditions that justified a stop and frisk action:

1. Where a police officer observes unusual conduct which leads him reasonably to conclude in light of his experience that criminal activity may be afoot;

2. and that the person with whom he is dealing may be armed and dangerous;

3. where in the course of investigating this behavior he identifies himself as a policeman;

4. and makes reasonable inquiry;

5. and where nothing in the initial stages of the encounter serves to dispel his reasonable fear for his own or others' safety . . .

Chief Justice Warren also emphasized, however, that the frisk was to be a limited search of the outer clothing in an attempt to discover weapons, and that the scope of any frisk or search associated with stop and frisk procedures was limited by the circumstances of the particular encounter.

SOURCE: Terry v. Ohio, 392 U.S. 1 (1968).

a ship, motor boat, wagon, or automobile for contraband goods, where it is not practicable to secure a warrant, because the vehicle can be quickly moved out of the locality or jurisdiction in which the warrant must be sought.

The Carroll Doctrine

Known as the **Carroll Doctrine**, the High Court's decision maintained that an automobile or other vehicle may, upon probable cause, be searched without a warrant even though in a given situation there might be time to obtain one. Subsequent rulings made clear the breadth of the Carroll Doctrine. In 1931, the Court upheld the search of a parked car as reasonable, since the police could not know when the suspect might move it.[16] The Carroll Doctrine was reaffirmed in 1970 when the Supreme Court held that a warrantless search of an automobile that resulted in the seizure of weapons and other evidence, but conducted at a police station many hours after the arrests of the suspects, was lawful.[17]

United States v. Ross

New York v. Belton

A related issue here involves how *extensive* the search of an automobile may be in the absence of a warrant. In *United States* v. *Ross*,[18] decided in 1982, the Supreme Court held that where police have probable cause to search an entire vehicle, they may do so, including containers and packages which may conceal the items being sought. Similarly, *New York* v. *Belton* a year earlier examined the scope of a vehicle search incident to arrest.[19] In *Belton* two principles were established. First, following a custodial arrest, police officers may search the entire passenger compartment of the vehicle as an incident of that arrest. Second, if during the course of the search any containers are found, they may be opened and searched. The decision in *Belton* seemed to impose no limits on the scope of a search of a vehicle's passenger compartment.

Police spot checks

Related to automobile searches are the random stopping of cars, and the searches and arrests that may follow. Known as *spot checks*, the random stopping of automobiles for the purpose of checking drivers' licenses and vehicle registrations has often been used as a form of proactive police patrol. One New York City patrolman reflected on this practice:

> You try to stop the cars and drivers that look suspicious, but other times you go the pot luck route to break the monotony and start with every 20th car. Some nights we'll stop just blue cars, and other times it'll be big cars or old cars or whatever. Other times we'll pull over just blacks, or white guys with beards.[20]

Spot checks can aid in the apprehension of criminals, as this Miami Beach police officer found:

> Depending on the time of night and where you are, maybe you'll pick up something. A few weeks back I see this guy stopped at a light and I just don't like the looks of him . . . so I pull him over. . . . It ends up that the car is stolen and he's wanted in two other states on forgery charges.[21]

The reflections of these police officers point to the dangers of spot checks, for although they can result in the apprehension of some offenders, they also lend themselves to discriminatory enforcement procedures.

Delaware v. Prouse

The Supreme Court has taken a strong stand against random spot checks, as was indicated in ***Delaware*** v. ***Prouse***.[22] On November 30, 1976, at about 7:30 P.M., a New Castle County, Delaware, police officer stopped the automobile in which William J. Prouse was riding. The car belonged to Prouse, but he was not the driver. As the patrolman approached the vehicle, he smelled marijuana smoke, and when he came abreast of the window he observed marijuana on the floor of the automobile. Prouse was arrested and later indicted for illegal possession of the drug.

At a hearing on Prouse's motion to suppress the marijuana seized as a result of the stop, the New Castle County police officer characterized the stopping of the car as "routine," explaining that "I saw the car in the area and was not answering any complaints so I decided to pull them off." He further indicated that before stopping the vehicle he had not observed any traffic or equipment violations, nor was he acting in accordance with directives relating to spot checks of automobiles.

After the suppression hearing, the trial court ruled that the stop and detention had been wholly capricious and therefore violative of Prouse's Fourth Amendment rights. When the prosecution appealed, the Delaware Supreme Court ruled in favor of Prouse, and the case went on to the United States Supreme Court. The High Court granted *certiorari* in an effort to resolve the conflict between the Delaware Supreme Court decision and similar decisions in five other jurisdictions, and the opposite decision, which had been rendered in six jurisdictions, that the Fourth Amendment does *not* prohibit the kind of automobile stop that occurred.

Ultimately, the Supreme Court ruled that random spot checks were a violation of constitutional rights. In so doing, however, the Court did not preclude states from devising methods for making spot checks of drivers' credentials that do not involve the unconstrained exercise of police discretion, such as roadblock inspections (see Exhibit 8.3).

Fresh Pursuit

Warrantless arrest and search is permissible in the circumstance of **fresh**, or "hot" **pursuit**, which involves chasing an escaping criminal or suspect into a house — and consequently searching that house — or into an adjoining jurisdiction. In common law, fresh pursuit referred to the immediate pursuit of a person for the purpose of arrest — pursuit that continued without substantial delay from the time of the commission or the discovery of an offense. Thus, fresh pursuit is the following of a fleeing suspect who is endeavoring to avoid immediate capture.

In contemporary statutes the notion of fresh pursuit has been broadened considerably. In Tennessee, for example, which reflects the comparative legislation in most state jurisdictions, the law reads as follows:

> The term "fresh pursuit" shall include fresh pursuit as defined by the common law, and also the pursuit of a person who has committed a felony or who is reasonably suspected of having committed a felony. It shall also include the pursuit of a person suspected of having committed a supposed felony, though no felony has actually been committed, if there is reasonable ground for believing that a felony has been committed. Fresh pursuit as used herein shall not necessarily imply instant pursuit, but pursuit without unreasonable delay.[23]

Consent Searches

Warrantless searches may be undertaken by law enforcement officers when the person in control of the area or object consents to the search. But consent

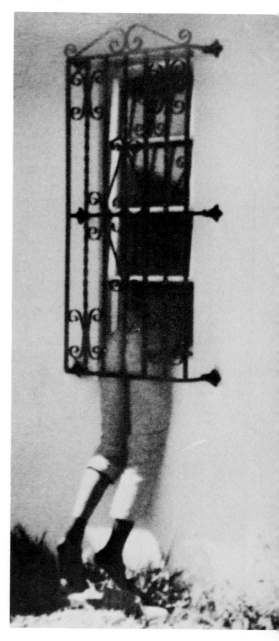

"Caught in the act" in Miami, this 16-year-old youth became stuck in the iron bars of the house he was trying to enter. He was able to call the emergency number for the police to rescue him and was charged with burglary and booked.

Spot Checks and Roadblock Inspections
Delaware v. Prouse

Accordingly, we hold that except in those situations in which there is at least articulable and reasonable suspicion that a motorist is unlicensed or that an automobile is not registered, or that either the vehicle or the occupant is otherwise subject to seizure for violation of law, stopping an automobile and detaining a driver in order to check his driver's license and the registration of the automobile are unreasonable under the Fourth Amendment. This holding does not preclude the State of Delaware or other States from developing methods for spot checks that involve less intrusion or that do not involve the unconstrained exercise of discretion. Questioning of all oncoming traffic at roadblock-type stops is one possible alternative. We hold only that persons in automobiles on public roadways may not for that reason alone have their travel and privacy interfered with at the unbridled discretion of the police officers. The judgment below is affirmed.
—Justice Byron White, speaking for the majority

The Court holds, in successive sentences, that absent an articulable, reasonable suspicion of unlawful conduct, a motorist may not be subjected to a random license check, but that the States are free to develop "a method for spot checks that . . . does not involve the unconstrained exercise of discretion," such as questioning . . . all on-coming traffic at roadblock-type stops. . . . Because motorists, apparently like sheep, are much less likely to be "frightened" or "annoyed" when stopped en masse, a highway patrolman needs neither probable cause nor articulable suspicion to stop all motorists on a particular thoroughfare, but he cannot without articulable suspicion stop less than all the motorists. The Court thus elevates the adage "misery loves company" to a novel role in Fourth Amendment jurisprudence. The rule becomes "curiouser and curiouser" as one attempts to follow the Court's explanation for it. . . . On the other side of the balance, the Court advances only the most diaphanous of citizen interests. Indeed, the Court did not say that these interests can never be infringed by the state, just that the state must infringe them en masse, rather than citizen by citizen. To comply with the Fourth Amendment, the state need only subject all citizens to the same anxiety and inconvenience to which it now subjects only a few.
—Justice Williams Hubbs Rehnquist, in dissent

SOURCE: Delaware v. Prouse, 24 CrL 3079 (1979).

searches can often precipitate complex and problematic legal issues, since a consent to search waives a person's right to the Fourth Amendment protection against unreasonable search and seizure. Thus, in a consent search, neither probable cause nor a search warrant is required, but when using evidence obtained through such a search the burden of proving consent becomes the responsibility of the prosecution. The issues involved are (1) *who* can give consent to search what, (2) *what* constitutes free and voluntary consent, and (3) is there a principle of *limited* consent?

Ordinarily, courts are unwilling to accept blindly the simple waiver of a defendant's Fourth Amendment right and require the state to prove that the consent was voluntarily given. In *Wren* v. *United States,*[24] the United States Court of Appeals ruled that a consent was indeed "voluntary" when the search was expressly agreed upon or invited by the person whose right was involved. *United States* v. *Matlock* expanded the range of voluntary consent to third parties who possessed common authority with the defendant over the property or premises to be searched.[25] In *Bumper* v. *North Carolina,*[26] the

These three photos, clockwise from upper left, show hot pursuit from the point of view of the officers involved.

issue of coercion by law enforcement officers was addressed. In *Bumper,* the police had obtained the consent of the defendant's grandmother to search her house in connection with a crime he was suspected of committing. But the police had incorrectly informed the woman that they had a lawful search warrant, and it was on that premise that she had consented to the search. The Court ruled that it was *not* a constitutionally valid consent. Finally, in *Schneckloth* v. *Bustamonte,*[27] the Supreme Court ruled that police officers are not required to advise the persons whose consent they are seeking that they are not obliged to give consent.

Although *Wren, Matlock,* and *Schneckloth* offer police wide latitude and discretion in the area of consent searches, the Supreme Court has also ruled that voluntary consents are also, to some degree, limited consents. The Court has ruled that a search based on voluntary consent must be limited to those items connected to the crime that triggered the desire to search and to other items clearly connected to that crime.[28]

Other Warrantless Searches

In addition to lawful arrest, stop and frisk, automobile searches, fresh pursuit, and consent, there are numerous other instances in which the search warrant requirement has been waived. Some examples are private searches, border searches, electronic eavesdropping, and searches of abandoned property and open fields.

Private Searches

As early as 1921, the Supreme Court ruled in *Burdeau* v. *McDowell* that the Fourth Amendment protects individuals only against searches and seizures by government agents, not against such actions undertaken by private individuals not acting in concert with law enforcement authorities.[29]

Border Searches

Although a series of rulings in the mid-1970s made it clear that warrantless searches of persons entering the United States at its borders violated the Fourth Amendment guarantee, *United States* v. *Martinez-Fuerte* in 1976 established that border patrol officers need not have probable cause or a warrant before they stopped cars for brief questioning at fixed checkpoints.[30]

Electronic Eavesdropping

Subsequent to *Katz* v. *United States* in 1967,[31] in which the Supreme Court ruled that conversations intercepted through warrantless electronic eavesdropping were in violation of the Fourth Amendment, Congress authorized the passage of the Omnibus Crime Control and Safe Streets Act of 1968, which included a provision involving electronic surveillance. The new act represented statutory authorization for the federal use of wiretaps and other eavesdropping devices through the issuance of warrants that could be approved only by the attorney general of the United States or his designated assistant.

Abandoned Property

In the 1960 case of *Abel* v. *United States*,[32] the Supreme Court spelled out an "abandoned property exception" to the warrant rule. In *Abel*, a hotel manager had given consent to an FBI agent to search a room that had been previously occupied by the petitioner. During the search, incriminating evidence was found in a wastepaper basket. The Court held that once Abel vacated the room the hotel had exclusive right to its possession and could freely give a consent to search.

Open Fields

As early as 1924, in *Hester* v. *United States*,[33] the Supreme Court established an "open fields exception" to the warrant rule. The Court reaffirmed the *Hester* ruling in two 1984 cases stating that landowners have "no reasonable expectation of privacy because open fields do not provide the setting for those intimate activities that the Fourth Amendment is intended to shelter from Government interference or surveillance."[34]

The "Plain View" Doctrine

Pertinent to this discussion of warrantless search and seizure is the highly controversial **"plain view" doctrine**, examined by the Supreme Court in *Harris* v. *United States* in 1968.[35] In *Harris*, the Court ruled that anything a police officer sees in plain view when he has a right to be where he is, is not the product of a search and is therefore admissible as evidence. In the *Harris* case, James E. Harris's automobile had been observed leaving the scene of a robbery in Washington, D.C. The vehicle was traced, and Harris was later arrested near his home as he was getting into his car. The arresting officer made a quick inspection of the car and then took his suspect to the police station.

Harris v. *United States* examined the "plain view" doctrine in 1968.

After some discussion, a decision was made to impound the car as evidence. Harris's vehicle was towed to the station house about 90 minutes after the arrest, arriving there with its doors unlocked and its windows open. Then it began to rain.

According to police procedures in the District of Columbia, the arresting officer in instances such as these is required to thoroughly search the impounded vehicle, remove any valuables, prepare a written inventory, and submit a report detailing the impounding. The officer undertook his search, and tied a property tag to the steering wheel. After this was done, he began to close up and lock the auto. When he opened the front door on the passenger side for the purpose of rolling up the window the officer for the first time observed a registration card, which lay face up on the metal stripping over which the door closes. The card, which was in "plain view," belonged to the victim of the robbery.

Harris moved to suppress the registration card on the grounds that its seizure was not contemporaneous with his arrest. In the Supreme Court's opinion, however, the observation of the card was not the outcome of a search, but rather, came about from a measure to protect the vehicle while in police custody. As such, the seizure was lawful.

Although the Court made the nature of "plain view" relatively clear in this case, a few police officers have apparently perjured themselves in using the doctrine as a mechanism for justifying illegal searches. If one were to sit in

EXHIBIT 8.5 (Cont'd)

Coolidge v. New Hampshire

car, she was told that both cars had been "impounded," and that the police would provide transportation for her. Some time later, the police called a towing company, and about two and a half hours after Coolidge had been taken into custody the cars were towed to the police station. It appears that at the time of the arrest the cars were parked in the Coolidge driveway, and that although dark had fallen they were plainly visible both from the street and from inside the house where Coolidge was actually arrested. The 1951 Pontiac was searched and vacuumed on February 21, two days after it was seized, again a year later, in January 1965, and a third time in April 1965.

At Coolidge's subsequent jury trial on the charge of murder, vacuum sweepings, including particles of gun powder, taken from the Pontiac were introduced in evidence against him, as part of an attempt by the State to show by microscopic analysis that it was highly probable that Pamela Mason had been in Coolidge's car. Also introduced in evidence was one of the guns taken by the police on their Sunday evening visit to the Coolidge house — a .22-caliber Mossberg rifle, which the prosecution claimed was the murder weapon. Conflicting ballistics testimony was offered on the question whether the bullets found in Pamela Mason's body had been fired from his rifle. Finally, the prosecution introduced vacuum sweepings of the clothes taken from the Coolidge house that same Sunday evening, and attempted to show through microscopic analysis that there was a high probability that the clothes had been in contact with Pamela Mason's body. Pretrial motions to suppress all this evidence were referred by the trial judge to the New Hampshire Supreme Court, which ruled the evidence admissible. The jury found Coolidge guilty and he

was sentenced to life imprisonment. The New Hampshire Supreme Court affirmed the judgment of conviction, and we granted *certiorari* to consider the constitutional questions raised by the admission of this evidence against Coolidge at his trial.

The Decision

In his appeal to the Supreme Court, Coolidge maintained that the warrant authorizing the seizure and subsequent search of his 1951 Pontiac automobile was invalid because it had not been issued by a "neutral and detached magistrate." The Court agreed, and the conviction was reversed.

Discussion

Six of the justices agreed that the warrant authorizing the seizure and subsequent search of Coolidge's automobile was invalid. The warrant had not been issued by a "neutral and detached" judicial officer as the Fourth Amendment required, but rather, by the state attorney general, who was actively prosecuting the case and was, in effect, a law enforcement officer.

The state of New Hampshire, however, also proposed several distinct theories to bring the seizure of the Pontiac within one or another of the exceptions to the warrant requirement.

1. *Arrest-Search Theory.* The State's first theory was that the seizure of Coolidge's automobile and its subsequent

search were "incident" to a lawful arrest. The Supreme Court disagreed since Coolidge was arrested inside the house and the car was outside. A warrantless search incident to arrest extends only to the area under the possession and control of the person being arrested — the search must be confined to the immediate vicinity of the arrest and contemporaneous with the arrest. The search met neither the first condition nor the second. In addition to Coolidge being inside the house, his automobile was not searched for the first time until two days later.

2. *The Probable Cause–Seizure Theory.* Citing *Carroll v. United States* (267 U.S. 132 [1925]) and *Chambers v. Maroney* (399 U.S. 42 [1970]), the State put forth the theory of warrantless probable cause searches of automobiles. Using the logic of *Carroll,* it was argued that there was a basic difference between searching a premises such as a house or store, and that of a vehicle; it would not be practicable to secure a warrant because the vehicle could be moved and the evidence lost. But the automobile exception in *Chambers v. Maroney* stressed the issue of emergency circumstances where the danger of the removal of the car and the evidence was potential. The Court, however, found no real emergency since the police had known for some time the

probable role of the automobile in the crime. The Court stated its opinion on this matter:

And surely there is nothing in this case to invoke the meaning and purpose of the rule [the automobile exception] — no alerted criminal bent on flight, no fleeting opportunity on an open highway after a hazardous chase, no contraband or stolen goods or weapons, no confederates waiting to move the evidence, not even the inconvenience of a special police detail to guard the immobilized automobile. In short, by no possible stretch of the legal imagination can this be made into a case where "it is not practicable to secure a warrant" . . . and the "automobile exception" despite its label, is simply irrelevant.

3. *The Plain View – Seizure Theory.* The state's third theory in support of the warrantless seizure and search of Coolidge's automobile was that the auto itself was an "instrumentality of crime" and as such might be seized because it was "in plain view." The Court ruled against this position, stating that all plain view searches, unless characterized by the following limitations, are indeed general searches, and as such are prohibited by the Fourth Amendment:

(1) plain view *alone* is not enough to justify the warrantless seizure; there must be prior justification of some kind for the police to be at the location where the evidence appears in plain view; (2) the discovery of the evidence in plain view must be inadvertent.

Furthermore, the Court stated:

In the light of what has been said, it is apparent that the "plain view" exception cannot justify the police seizure of the Pontiac car in this case. The police had ample opportunity to obtain a valid warrant; they knew the automobile's exact description and location well in advance; they intended to seize it when they came upon Coolidge's property.

One final issue confronted by the Court was whether Mrs. Coolidge's action of handing over to the police the rifle and articles of clothing belonging to her husband was a *voluntary consent*. The Court ruled that it was:

In assessing the claim that this course of conduct amounted to a search and seizure, it is well to keep in mind that Mrs. Coolidge described her own motive as that of clearing her husband, and that she believed that she had nothing to hide. She had seen her husband himself produce his guns for two other policemen earlier in the week, and there is nothing to indicate that she realized that he had offered only three of them for inspection on that occasion. The two officers who questioned her behaved, as her own testimony shows, with perfect courtesy. There is not the slightest implication of an attempt on their part to coerce or dominate her, or, for that matter, to direct her actions by the more subtle techniques of suggestion that are available to officials in circumstances like these. To hold that the conduct of the police here was a search and seizure would be to hold, in effect, that a criminal suspect has constitutional protection against the

adverse consequences of a spontaneous, good-faith effort by his wife to clear him of suspicion.

Comment

Six justices agreed that the search warrant was invalid; five agreed that the seizure of the automobile could not be justified under the Fourth Amendment; *all* agreed that the exclusionary rule did not apply to the rifle — the alleged murder weapon — that Mrs. Coolidge had turned over to the police. In addition, numerous justices manifested conflicting opinions of the Fourth Amendment's warrant clause. Despite these strong differences of opinion, however, *Coolidge* nevertheless represents a clear example of detailed judicial review of complex law and facts. At the same time, *Coolidge* also served to reiterate rather than solve the conflicts over *Mapp*. The chief justice found this case to be a graphic illustration of what he termed "the monstrous price we pay for the exclusionary rule in which we seem to have imprisoned ourselves."

SOURCE: Coolidge v. New Hampshire, 403 U.S. 443 (1971).

The retreat from *Mapp* began instead less than three years later, with *United States* v. *Calandra*,[57] decided on January 8, 1974. In *Calandra*, the Court ruled that the exclusionary rule was not applicable to the presentation of illegally obtained evidence at grand jury proceedings.

In 1976, the Court's decision in *Stone* v. *Powell* practically closed the federal courtroom doors to state prisoners convicted by means of illegal searches and seizures.[58] Under the common law principle of *habeas corpus*, state prisoners who had allegedly been convicted and incarcerated through illegally secured evidence could appeal to the federal courts. In *Powell*, the Court ruled that federal courts were under no constitutional obligation to use the writ of *habeas corpus** to order release of persons who argued that their convictions in state courts had been obtained with illegally seized evidence. So long as the state provided an opportunity for a full and fair hearing of the

---

*Habeas corpus is explored at length in Chapter 16.

EXHIBIT 8.6

United States v. Leon

In *United States* v. *Leon*, a California district court judge issued a search warrant based on information from a confidential source and a lengthy police investigation. The warrant authorized the search of three houses and several automobiles. The subsequent search produced large quantities of cocaine and methaqualone. Defendants filed a pretrial motion to suppress the evidence seized in the search on the grounds that the affidavit was insufficient to establish probable cause. The district court granted part of the motion and the U.S. Court of Appeals for the Ninth Circuit affirmed. The government's petition for *certiorari* presented only the question of whether a "good faith" exception to the exclusionary rule should be adopted.

Justice White, writing for the majority, reversed the decision of the court of appeals and finally announced the long-awaited good faith exception to the exclusionary

rule. The majority based its decision on two independent grounds. First, it said that the Fourth Amendment does not contain any expressed provisions precluding the use of evidence obtained in violation of its commands. Once the illegal search is completed, the wrong prohibited by the Fourth Amendment is "fully accomplished" and "the exclusionary rule is neither intended nor able to cure the invasion of the defendant's rights which he has already suffered." The judicially created rule acts only to safeguard Fourth Amendment rights through its deterrent effect.

Second, the majority said that the question of whether a party's Fourth Amendment rights were violated is a separate issue from the question of whether the exclusionary rule should be imposed. In *Leon*, only the latter question had to be resolved. The Court reasoned that it would be resolved by "weighing the costs

and benefits of preventing the use . . . of inherently trustworthy tangible evidence." The Court noted that the costs exacted by the exclusionary rule were "substantial." Excluding relevant, probative evidence impedes the "truthfinding" function of judge and jury, which further results in the objectionable consequence that "some guilty defendants may go free. . . ." Such a benefit to guilty defendants is particularly offensive to the criminal justice system when the illegal acts of law enforcement are minor and were done in good faith. Therefore, the indiscriminate application of the exclusionary rule under such circumstances might result in "disrespect for the law and the administration of justice." Thus, after applying a cost–benefit analysis test, the Court concluded that the exclusionary rule should be modified to allow introduction of unconstitutionally obtained evidence where officers acted in "reasonable good faith belief that

defendant's challenge to the evidence, the Court held, there was no obligation at the federal level to use the *habeas corpus* to enforce the exclusionary rule.

A further setback for the exclusionary rule came in 1984 with the Supreme Court's long anticipated enunciation of the "**good faith**" **exception.** The announcement came in ***United States v. Leon*** and *Massachusetts* v. *Sheppard*,[59] two cases involving defective search warrants. In *Leon*, the leading case, probable cause to support the warrant was lacking, yet this defect had not been ascertained by the prosecutors who reviewed the application, the magistrate who approved the warrant, or the officers who executed the search in accordance with its authorization (see Exhibit 8.6). In *Sheppard*, an inappropriate warrant form had been used. Moreover, it had been improperly filled out. Trial courts had held that these defects required the suppression of evidence seized under the Fourth Amendment's exclusionary rule. Disagreeing with this result, the Supreme Court adopted a good faith exception to the rule in *Leon* and then applied the exception in *Sheppard*, thus allowing the evidence obtained as a result of the warrants to be admissible.

The "good faith" exception to the exclusionary rule

United States v. Leon

such a search or seizure was in accord with the Fourth Amendment."

The majority further supported this new exception in those areas where the deterrent effect of the exclusionary rule would not be achieved. In those situations, the benefits of the rule "would not outweigh its costs." "In short . . . the Court has applied, in deciding whether exclusion is appropriate in a particular case, attempts to mark the point at which the detrimental consequences of illegal police action became so attenuated that the deterrent effect of the exclusionary rule no longer justifies its cost." This balancing approach provides strong support for adopting a good-faith modification.

The Court concluded that even if the rule effectively "deters *some* police misconduct . . . it can not be expected and should not be applied, to deter objectively reasonable law enforcement activity." Excluding evidence will not in any appreciable way further the ends of the exclusionary rule where the officer's conduct is objectively reasonable. "This is

particularly true when an officer acting with good faith has obtained a search warrant from a . . . magistrate and acted within its scope."

Under this rule, suppression of evidence would be an appropriate remedy when the issuing magistrate was misled by information that the affiant knew was false. This exception would also not apply when the issuing magistrate disregards his role in such a manner that "no reasonable well-trained officer should rely on the warrant." Nor would the police be acting in objective good faith if the affidavit was "so lacking of probable cause as to render official belief in its existence unreasonable."

The majority concluded that this good-faith exception was not intended to signal an unwillingness to enforce Fourth Amendment requirements. Nor would it preclude judicial review concerning the constitutionality of searches and seizures.

SOURCE: J. Michael Hunter, "Is the Exclusionary Rule a Relic of the Past? *Leon, Sheppard,* and 'Beyond,'" *Ohio Northern Law Review* 12 (November 1985). Reprinted by permission of the author.

Dick Wright, Scripps-Howard Newspapers

Custodial Interrogation

No person . . . shall be compelled in any criminal case to be a witness against himself.   —from the Fifth Amendment

In all criminal prosecutions the accused shall enjoy the right . . . to have the assistance of counsel for his defense.   —from the Sixth Amendment

The Fifth Amendment

Confessions, the Supreme Court stated more than a century ago in *Hopt* v. *Utah,*[60] are "among the most effectual proofs of the law," but by constitutional implication they are admissible as evidence only when given voluntarily. This has long since been the rule in the federal courts where the **Fifth Amendment** clearly applies. A confession, whether written or oral (but now usually recorded), is simply a statement by a person admitting to the violation of a law. In *Hopt,* the Court stressed that for a confession to be valid it had to be *voluntary,* defining as involuntary or coerced any confession that "appears to have been made, either in consequence of inducements of a temporal nature . . . or because of a threat or promise . . . which, operating upon the fears or hopes of the accused . . . deprive him of that freedom of will or self-control essential to make his confession voluntary within the meaning of the law." In 1896, the Court restated this position, ruling that the circumstances surrounding the confession had to be considered in order to determine if it had been voluntarily made.[61]

Twining v. New Jersey

The inadmissibility of involuntary confessions, however, did not apply to the states. The 1908 decision in *Twining* v. *New Jersey* specifically emphasized this.[62] In the *Twining* case, defendants Albert C. Twining and David C. Cornell, executives of the Monmouth Safe and Trust Company, were indicted by a New Jersey grand jury for having knowingly displayed a false paper to a bank examiner "with full intent to deceive him" as to the actual condition of their firm. At trial, Twining and Cornell refused to take the stand, and presiding judge Webber A. Heisley commented both extensively and adversely on this point. To the jury Heisley stated:

> Because a man does not go upon the stand you are not necessarily justified in drawing an inference of guilt. But you have a right to consider the fact that he does not go upon the stand where a direct accusation is made against him.[63]

The jury returned a verdict of guilty, at which point Twining and Cornell appealed to the U.S. Supreme Court. They contended that the exemption from self-incrimination was one of the privileges and immunities which the Fourteenth Amendment forbade the states to abridge, and that the alleged compulsory self-incrimination constituted a denial of due process. In an 8-to1 decision, the Court ruled against Twining and Cornell, stating that the privilege against self-incrimination was "not fundamental in due process of law, not an essential part of it."

Twining was not a case of forced confession in the strictest sense of the term, for no confession had actually occurred. But as an issue in self-incrimination, the notion of a potentially involuntary confession was inferred, and the resulting decision in 1908 was that *state* defendants did not enjoy the Fifth Amendment privilege against compelled self-incrimination.

Brown v. Mississippi

Although more than half a century would pass before the Supreme Court would specifically apply the Fifth Amendment privilege against state action, the Court, through its unanimous decision in *Brown* v. *Mississippi,*[64] did forbid states in 1936 to use coerced confessions to convict persons of crimes.

In *Brown,* three black men were arrested for the murder of a white man. At trial, they were convicted solely on the basis of their confessions, and sentenced to death. But the confessions had been coerced. The defendants had been tied to a tree, whipped, twice hanged by a rope from a tree, and told that the process would continue until they confessed. And although the use of torture to elicit the confessions was undisputed, the convictions were affirmed by the Mississippi Supreme Court.

On appeal to the U.S. Supreme Court, Mississippi defended its use of the confessions extracted through beatings and torture by citing the earlier *Twining* decision — that state defendants did not enjoy the Fifth Amendment privilege. The Court agreed with *Twining,* but rejected the Mississippi defense maintaining that the state's right to withdraw the privilege of self-incrimination was not the issue. In speaking for the Court, Chief Justice Charles Evans Hughes saw a distinction between "compulsion" as forbidden by the Fifth Amendment, and "compulsion" as forbidden by the Fourteenth Amendment's due process clause:

> The compulsion to which the Fifth Amendment refers is that of the processes of justice by which the accused may be called as a witness and required to testify. Compulsion by torture to extort a confession is a different matter. . . .
>
> Because a state may dispense with a jury trial, it does not follow that it may substitute trial by ordeal. The rack and torture chamber may not be substituted for the witness stand. . . . It would be difficult to conceive of methods more revolting to the sense of justice than those taken to procure the confessions of these petitioners, and the use of the confessions thus obtained as the basis for conviction and sentence was a clear denial of due process.

In the years that followed, the Supreme Court reversed numerous decisions in which confessions had been compelled, examining in every instance

---

EXHIBIT 8.7

The Fourteenth Amendment

All persons born or naturalized in the United States, and subject to the jurisdiction thereof, are citizens of the United States and of the State wherein they reside. No State shall make or enforce any law which shall abridge the privileges or immunities of citizens of the United States; nor shall any State deprive any person of life, liberty, or property, without due process of law; nor deny to any person within its jurisdiction the equal protection of the laws. . . .

the totality of circumstances surrounding the arrest and the interrogation procedures. The Court's philosophy made it clear that coercion could be psychological as well as physical. As summarized by Justice Felix Frankfurter in 1961:

> Our decisions . . . have made clear that convictions following the admission into evidence of confessions which are involuntary . . . cannot stand. This is so not because such confessions are unlikely to be true but because the methods used to extract them offend an underlying principle in the enforcement of our criminal law: that ours is an accusatorial and not an inquisitorial system — a system in which the State must establish guilt by evidence independently and freely secured and may not by coercion prove its own charge against an accused out of his own mouth.[65]

The Prompt Arraignment Rule

Just before the turn of the twentieth century, the Supreme Court had implied that delay in charging a suspect with a crime might be one of the factors in determining whether a confession had been voluntary or not.[66] A number of federal statutes served to clarify the Court's intent. Their purpose was to prevent federal law enforcement agents from using postarrest detention as a way of exacting confessions through interrogation, and from justifying illegal arrests through confessions subsequently obtained by means of prolonged questioning.

McNabb v. United States

But the rules had no compelling force until 1943, when the Supreme Court ruled in *McNabb* v. *United States* that confessions obtained after "unreasonable delay" in a suspect's arraignment could not be used as evidence *in a federal court*.[67] In *McNabb*, five Tennessee mountaineers were arrested when federal agents closed in on their moonshining operations, and during the course of the raid one of the agents was killed. Two of the defendants were convicted of second-degree murder on the strength of their confessions and were sentenced to 45 years' imprisonment. Their incriminating statements had come after *three days* of questioning in the absence of any counsel and before they were charged with any crime. The Court overturned the *McNabb* convictions, not on the basis of the Fifth Amendment, but on the

Prompt arraignment

existing **prompt arraignment** statutes as well as on the High Court's general power to supervise the functioning of the federal judicial system. Speaking for the Court, Justice Frankfurter addressed the purpose of the ban on unnecessary delay between arrest and arraignment:

> This procedural requirement checks resort to those reprehensible practices known as the "third degree" which though universally rejected as indefensible, still find their way into use. It aims to avoid all the evil implications of street interrogation of persons accused of crime. It reflects not a sentimental but a sturdy view of law enforcement. It outlaws easy but self-defeating ways in which brutality is substituted for brains as an instrument of crime detection.

Mallory v. United States

The Federal Rules of Criminal Procedure subsequently incorporated this rule. In *Mallory* v. *United States*,[68] almost 15 years after *McNabb*, the High Court reaffirmed its prompt arraignment mandate by nullifying the death sentence imposed on a convicted rapist who "confessed" to the crime during a delay of more than 18 hours between his arrest and arraignment. The defendant, Andrew Mallory, had been arrested in the District of Columbia, and during his long period of interrogation no attempt was made to bring official charges against him — even though arraigning magistrates were available in the same building throughout the period of questioning.

In both *McNabb* and *Mallory,* the Supreme Court did not rule on whether or not the confessions had been obtained voluntarily. Rather, the cases were decided on the basis of the Court's authority to police the federal judicial system. But the Court's decision in *Mallory* received fierce criticism. By reversing the conviction on the basis of the prompt arraignment rule, the Court was saying that any evidence gathered during the delay had been acquired unlawfully, and hence was inadmissible — even if it included a confession that was indeed voluntary.

The *McNabb – Mallory* prompt arraignment rule, however, would not stand the test of time. At the state level, the example set by the federal courts was never fully followed. And even the decisions in *McNabb* and *Mallory* were ultimately diluted. Less than a month after *Mallory* had been handed down, a subcommittee of the House Judiciary Committee began hearings to reverse the Supreme Court decision. Although no "corrective" legislation came out of the House, in 1968 Congress incorporated a section into the Omnibus Crime Control and Safe Streets Act that related directly to *Mallory.* The act modified the *Mallory* decision to provide that a confession made by a person in the custody of law officers was not to be inadmissible as evidence *solely* because of delay in arraigning the defendant if the confession were found to be voluntary, if the weight to be given the confession were left to jury determination, and if the confession were given within six hours immediately following arrest. The measure also provided that confessions obtained after this six-hour limit could be admissible if the presiding trial judge found the further delay to be not unreasonable.[69]

Confessions and Counsel

Prior to the 1960s, the Fifth Amendment privilege against self-incrimination and the **Sixth Amendment** right to counsel were not effectively linked. The *Brown* v. *Mississippi* decision in 1936 had ruled on the inadmissibility of confessions obtained by physical compulsion. In delivering the Court's opinion in that case, Chief Justice Hughes also highlighted the constitutional issue that "the state may not deny to the accused the aid of counsel." But in 1958, the Court's decision in *Crooker* v. *California* held that confessions could be both voluntary and admissible even when obtained from a suspect who was denied the opportunity to consult with legal counsel during interrogation by the police.[70] Through *Brown* and *Crooker,* the Court was taking a firm stand on coerced confessions but nevertheless was limiting the right to counsel.

The Sixth Amendment

With the criminal law revolution of the 1960s, under the stewardship of Chief Justice Earl Warren, a series of Supreme Court decisions ensued that served to unite more fully the provisions of the Fifth and Sixth Amendments and at the same time strengthen defendants' rights. In 1964, the Court reversed its position in *Crooker,* declaring in *Massiah* v. *United States* that an indicted person could not be properly questioned or otherwise persuaded to make incriminating statements in the absence of his or her attorney.[71] Shortly thereafter, the Court's decision in *Malloy* v. *Hogan* finally extended the privilege against self-incrimination to state defendants.[72] At the same time, it laid the groundwork for its most important decision of the 1964 term, ***Escobedo* v. *Illinois*** (See Exhibit 8.8).[73]

Escobedo v. Illinois

The *Escobedo* decision required that an accused be permitted to have an attorney present during police interrogation. The majority view held that the adversary system of justice had traditionally been restricted to the trial stage, and that the system was long overdue to be hauled back into the earlier stages of criminal proceedings. It was also contended, however, that the *Escobedo* decision need not affect the powers of the police to investigate unsolved crimes. But when "the process shifts from investigatory to accusatory," the Court stated, "when its focus is on the accused and its purpose is to elicit a confession, our adversary system begins to operate, and, under the circumstances here, the accused must be permitted to consult with his lawyer."

The four dissenting justices were not convinced, and the overall tenor of their opinions was that the decision would hamper criminal law enforcement.

EXHIBIT 8.8

Escobedo v. Illinois

Danny Escobedo

On the night of January 19, 1960, Manuel Valtierra, the brother-in-law of 22-year-old Danny Escobedo, was fatally shot in the back. Several hours later Escobedo was arrested without a warrant and was interrogated for some 15 hours. During that period he made no statements to the police, and was released after his attorney had obtained a writ of *habeas corpus.* Eleven days after the shooting of Valtierra, Escobedo was arrested for a second time and again taken to a police station for questioning. Shortly after Escobedo was brought to the Chicago police station, his attorney also arrived but the police would not permit him to see his client. Both the attorney and Escobedo repeatedly requested to see each other, but both were continually denied the privilege. Escobedo was told that he could not see his attorney until the police had finished their questioning. It was during this second period of interrogation that Escobedo made certain incriminating statements that would be construed as his voluntary confession to the crime.

Across the country police and prosecutors alike echoed the feelings of the dissenting justices. To interrogate a suspect behind closed doors in order to secure a confession was an aspect of policing based on centuries-old custom and usage and a deeply entrenched police practice. No longer would the well-developed "third degree" and sometimes melodramatic "good guy – bad guy" interrogation routines be as readily possible.

Miranda v. Arizona

In the final analysis, *Escobedo* seemed to raise more questions than it answered regarding police conduct during arrest and interrogation. In the Court's discussion of the conditions that existed in Danny Escobedo's inter-

Danny Escobedo was convicted of murder and sentenced to a 22-year prison term. On appeal to the state supreme court of Illinois, Escobedo maintained that he was told that "he would be permitted to go home if he gave the statement and would be granted an immunity from prosecution." The statement in question referred to the complicity of his four codefendants, who had all been arrested on the murder charge. The Illinois Supreme Court reversed Escobedo's conviction, but the state petitioned for, and the court granted, a rehearing of the case. The decision was again reversed, sustaining the trial court's original conviction, and Escobedo still faced the 22-year prison term. Escobedo's counsel appealed further, and the U.S. Supreme Court granted *certiorari*.

On June 22, 1964, the Court ruled in favor of Danny Escobedo by a 5-to-4 decision. In delivering the opinion of the Court, Justice Arthur Goldberg noted that it was based on five pivotal facts in the interrogation.

We hold, therefore, that where . . .

[1] the investigation is no longer a general inquiry into an unsolved crime but has begun to focus on a particular suspect,

[2] the suspect has been taken into police custody,

[3] the police carry out a process of interrogations that lends itself to eliciting incriminating statements,

[4] the suspect has requested and been denied an opportunity to consult with his lawyer, and

[5] the police have not effectively warned him of his absolute constitutional right to remain silent,

the accused has been denied "the assistance of counsel" in violation of the Sixth Amendment of the Constitution as "made obligatory upon the states by the Fourteenth Amendment" . . . and that no statement elicited by the police during the interrogation may be used against him in a criminal trial.

SOURCE: Escobedo v. Illinois, 378 U.S. 478 (1964).

rogation and that led to a reversal of his conviction, was it being suggested that *all* of these conditions had to be met in order for a confession to be admissible? Were police required to warn suspects of their right to remain silent? If a suspect requested counsel but none was at hand, could a police interrogation continue? If a suspect did not wish counsel, what then? And most importantly, how were the police to determine when an investigation began to "focus," to use the Court's term, on a particular suspect?

Given these unsettled issues, by January 1966, two separate United States courts of appeals had interpreted *Escobedo* in diametrically opposed ways. As referee of the conflict, the U.S. Supreme Court sifted through some 170 confession-related appeals,[74] granting *certiorari* to four cases: *Miranda v. Arizona, Vignera v. New York, Westover v. United States,* and *California v. Stewart.*[75] Known by its leading case, *Miranda* (see Exhibits 8.9 and 8.11), the package consolidated the appeals of four persons, all convicted on the basis of confessions made after extended questioning by police officers in which the defendants' right to remain silent had not been made known to them. In all four cases, the crimes for which the defendants had been convicted involved major felonies — Miranda had been convicted of kidnapping and rape, Vignera had been convicted of robbery in the first degree, Westover had been convicted of bank robbery, and Stewart had been convicted of robbery and first-degree murder. The convictions were reversed by the Supreme Court, and from this decision came the well-known *Miranda* warning rules, which every police officer must state to a suspect prior to any questioning:

1. "You have a right to remain silent."
2. "Anything you say can and will be used against you in a court of law."
3. "You have a right to consult with a lawyer and to have the lawyer present during any questioning."
4. "If you cannot afford a lawyer, one will be obtained for you if you so desire."

The reactions to *Miranda,* even from within the Supreme Court, were immediate. Four justices prepared a dissenting opinion, and it has been reported as well that Justice Harlan, his face flushed and his voice occasionally faltering with emotion, denounced the decision orally from the bench, terming it "dangerous experimentation" at a time of a "high crime rate that is a matter of growing concern" and a "new doctrine" without substantial precedent, reflecting "a balance in favor of the accused."[76]

Beyond the chambers of the Supreme Court, the *Miranda* decision was bitterly attacked for what was considered a handcuffing of the police in their efforts to protect society against criminals. It was asserted that more than three-fourths of the convictions in major crimes depended on confessions; and police officers and prosecutors across the country, together with some courts, echoed the belief of New York City's police commissioner, Patrick V. Murphy, that "if suspects are told of their rights they will not confess."[77]

At least one study, however, has suggested that *Miranda* had little or no effect on law enforcement. In New Haven, Connecticut, for example, some police simply did not comply with the decision in many cases.[78] Detectives gave the *Miranda* warnings only about 20 percent of the time, and few suspects were ever informed of their right to counsel. In instances when the warnings *were* given, the detectives had a number of ways to nullify their effect. Some altered the wording slightly: "Whatever you say may be used *for*

EXHIBIT 8.9

Miranda v. Arizona

Ernesto Miranda, a 23-year-old Mexican with less than a ninth-grade education, was arrested at his home in Phoenix on March 13, 1963, and taken to a local police station for questioning. He was suspected of having kidnapped and raped an 18-year-old woman. At the Phoenix police station, Miranda was placed in a lineup and identified by the victim, after which he was interrogated for two hours. At the close of the interrogation, the questioning officers emerged with a written confession signed by Miranda. The confession was admitted at trial, over Miranda's objections, and he was convicted of kidnapping and rape and received a 20-to-30 year sentence on each count. On appeal to the Arizona Supreme Court the conviction was affirmed.

The U.S. Supreme Court's decision reversed Miranda's conviction, based on its view of the relationships between custodial interrogation and genuinely voluntary confessions, combined with the constitutional rights of suspects as promulgated by the Fourth, Fifth, Sixth, and Fourteenth Amendments. In the Court's opinion, custodial interrogation was inherently coercive, and the procedures for advising suspects of their rights — if present — were rarely sufficiently clear.

In a 5-to-4 majority decision, Chief Justice Earl Warren offered the following statement:

Our holding will be spelled out with some specificity in the pages which follow but briefly stated it is this: the prosecution may not use statements, whether exculpatory or inculpatory, stemming from custodial interrogation of the defendant unless it demonstrates the use of procedural safeguards effective to secure the privilege against self-incrimination. By custodial interrogation, we mean questioning initiated by law enforcement officers after a person has been taken into custody or otherwise deprived of his freedom of action in any significant way. As for the procedural safeguards to be employed, unless other fully effective means are devised to inform accused persons of their right of silence and to assure a continuous opportunity to exercise it, the following measures are required. Prior to any questioning, the person must be warned that he has a right to remain silent, that any statement he does make may be used as evidence against him, and that he has a right to the presence of an attorney, either retained or appointed. The defendant may waive effectuation of these rights, provided the waiver is made voluntarily, knowingly and intelligently. If, however, he indicates that he wishes to consult with an attorney before speaking there can be no questioning. Likewise, if the individual is alone and indicates in any manner that he does not wish to be interrogated, the police may not question him. The mere fact that he may have answered some questions or volunteered some statements on his own does not deprive him of the right to refrain from answering any further inquiries until he has consulted with an attorney and thereafter consents to be questioned.

SOURCE: Miranda v. Arizona, 384 U.S. 436 (1966).

---

or against you in a court of law." Others inserted some qualifying remarks: "You don't have to say a word, but you ought to get everything cleared up," or "You don't have to say anything, of course, but you can explain how . . . "

The Erosion of *Miranda*

During his presidential campaign in 1968, Richard M. Nixon promised to appoint men to the Supreme Court who would be less receptive to the arguments of criminal defendants and more responsive to the needs and reasoning of law enforcement officers. The first of the Nixon appointees, Warren Burger, came in early 1969. Burger was a conservative appeals court judge, and he replaced the retiring Earl Warren as the Court's chief justice. Burger clearly espoused "law and order" concepts, which made him attractive to the Senate Judiciary Committee, and he was known in Washington circles as

Nixon's "hatchet man." As the new chief justice, he announced from time to time to the other justices exactly which previous decisions the Court now had to overrule — *Miranda, Mapp, Chimel,* and others — and he eyed closely the votes that might be marshalled achieve that result.[79] In 1970, Burger was joined on the bench by another Nixon appointee, Harry A. Blackmun, and in 1971 by Lewis F. Powell and William H. Rehnquist — the four comprising what quickly became known as the "Nixon Court." *Miranda* itself was not overturned, but in the 1970s the Court clearly began a retreat from *Miranda.*

Harris *v.* New York *(1971)*

In *Harris* v. *New York,*[80] by a 5-to-4 vote, the Court held that although statements made by a defendant during interrogation and before he was advised of his rights could not be used as evidence against him, those statements could nevertheless be used to impeach his credibility as a witness if he took the stand in his own defense and made statements conflicting with those made before trial.

Michigan *v.* Tucker *(1974)*

In *Michigan* v. *Tucker,*[81] the Court upheld the prosecutions's use of a witness whose identity was revealed during an interrogation contaminated by *Miranda* violations. Police had arrested Tucker for rape but failed to advise him of his right to free counsel. While being questioned, Tucker provided the name of a witness who could document his activities at the time of the crime. When contacted, the "alibi's" statements seriously incriminated Tucker.

Michigan *v.* Mosley *(1975)*

In *Michigan* v. *Mosley,*[82] the Court ruled that although a suspect's assertion of his right to silence must terminate police questioning about one crime, it does not foreclose subsequent police efforts, after an interval and a second reading of his rights, to question him about another crime.

United States *v.* Mandujano *(1976)*

In *United States* v. *Mandujano,*[83] the Court refused to require that *Miranda* warnings be given to grand jury witnesses before they testified — even though they might be potential defendants.

Oregon *v.* Mathiason *(1977)*

In *Oregon* v. *Mathiason,*[84] an Oregon state police officer left a note at the defendant's apartment requesting that he contact him. Mathiason later called the officer and met him at the police station. The officer informed Mathiason that he was not under arrest, but that he *was* a suspect in a burglary. Mathiason confessed to the crime, at which point the officer advised him of his rights and taped his confession. The Court held that Mathiason's rights had not been violated since he was not in custody when his incriminating statements were initially made.

The Supreme Court faced only one serious challenge to *Miranda* during the 1970s, in **Brewer v. Williams** (see Exhibit 8.10),[85] at the close of the decade, *Miranda* had yet to be overthrown. During the 1980s, however, further erosion of *Miranda* became apparent.

Brewer v. Williams

EXHIBIT 8.10

Brewer v. Williams

On Christmas Eve, 1968, in Des Moines, Iowa, 10-year-old Pamela Powers was abducted, raped, and strangled to death. Two days later Robert Williams, who had recently escaped from a mental institution and who resided at the Des Moines YMCA where the child had been abducted, surrendered to police in Davenport, Iowa, some 160 miles away. Williams had surrendered at the advice of his lawyer, Henry McKnight, and when it was learned that a detective would be transporting Williams back to Des Moines, McKnight insisted that no interrogation take place during the trip. The police agreed.

Knowing that Williams was a religious man, the detective addressed him as "Reverend" during the trip; he did not interrogate Williams, but presented him with a series of statements referred to in the record as the "Christian burial speech":

I want to give you something to think about while we're traveling down the road. . . . Number one, I want you to observe the weather conditions, it's raining, it's sleeting, it's freezing, driving is very treacherous, visibility is poor, it's going to be dark early this evening. They are predicting several inches of snow for tonight, and I feel that you yourself are the only person that knows where this little girl's body is, that you yourself have only been there once, and if you get a snow on top of it you yourself may be unable to find it. And, since we will be going right past the area on the way into Des Moines, I feel that we could stop and locate the body, that the parents of this little girl should be entitled to a Christian burial for the little girl who was snatched away from them on Christmas Eve and murdered. And I feel we should stop and locate it on the way in rather than waiting until morning and trying to come back out after a snowstorm and possibly not being able to find it at all.

Shortly after the detective's "Christian burial speech," Williams directed the officer to Pamela Powers's dead and frozen body.

Williams was convicted of murder, in spite of his counsel's objections to the admission of the evidence resulting from the incriminating statements Williams made during the trip. The Iowa Supreme Court affirmed the conviction, and on appeal to the U.S. Supreme Court, Iowa's attorney general, along with the National District Attorneys Association and Americans for Effective Law Enforcement, requested that the court overrule *Miranda*.

By a 5-to-4 decision, the Supreme Court ruled that Williams had not waived his right to counsel during his ride from Davenport to Des Moines, and that the detective's "Christian burial speech" constituted "custodial interrogation." Chief Justice Warren Burger castigated his more liberal colleagues in open court, stating in his strongly worded opinion that "the result by the Court in this case ought to be intolerable in any society which purports to call itself organized society."

SOURCE: Brewer v. Williams, 430 U.S. 387 (1977).

New York v. Quarles (1984)

The erosion of *Miranda* continued in the 1980s.

In *New York* v. *Quarles*,[86] a "public safety" exception to *Miranda* was established. Benjamin Quarles was taken into custody shortly after a woman had approached the arresting officer and told him that she had been raped by an armed assailant. After frisking and handcuffing Quarles, the officer asked him where the gun was. Upon being told, he retrieved Quarles's pistol, but no *Miranda* warnings had been given prior to this questioning. The Court held that the officer's failure to read the *Miranda* warnings before seeking to locate the firearm was justified in the interests of public safety.

Berkemer v. McCarty (1984)

In *Berkemer* v. *McCarty*,[87] the defendant in the case had been arrested on a misdemeanor charge of drunk driving. In the absence of *Miranda* warnings, he was questioned about his condition, at which point he admitted consuming two beers and "several joints of marijuana." The Court stated that anyone subject to custodial interrogation is entitled to *Miranda* warnings, regardless of the severity of the alleged offense. However, the Court added, the roadside questioning of a motorist persuant to a routine traffic stop *does not*, in and of itself, constitute a custodial interrogation and thus does not require *Miranda* warnings.

Nix v. Williams (1984)

In *Nix* v. *Williams*,[88] a later chapter in the case of *Brewer v. Williams* created an "inevitable discovery" exception to the *Miranda* rule (see Exhibit 8.11).

Show-ups, Line-ups, and Exemplars

A final aspect of this discussion of police and the Constitution involves a variety of investigating techniques law enforcement officers employ to detect and identify criminal offenders. Among these are show-ups, line-ups, photographs, and other forms of "nontestimonial" material that the Supreme Court has allowed, given certain conditions, as admissible evidence.

The *show-up* is a procedure that generally takes place shortly after a crime has been committed when a victim or witness is taken to a police station and confronted with a suspect. In the show-up, the victim or witness is not offered an array of individuals from which a suspect is to be possibly chosen, as in a line-up. Rather, it is often a one-on-one confrontation, presented in such a context as "Is he the one?" *Show-up* is a term that is not consistently used by either the police or the courts; *line-up* is more popular. However, *show-up* does seem to be used more often in the context of one-on-one identifications. Here is an example of a show-up, described in the 1972 case of *Kirby* v. *Illinois*.[89]

> After Kirby and his alleged accomplice Ralph Bean were arrested, police officers brought Willie Shard, the robbery victim, to a room in a police station where Kirby and Bean were seated at a table

with two other police officers. Shard testified at trial that the officers who brought him to the room asked him if Kirby and Bean were the robbers and he indicated they were.

In the *line-up,* the suspect is placed together with several other persons and the victim or witness is then asked to pick out the suspect.

The constitutional issues in the use of line-ups and show-ups have generally focused on the fairness of these procedures, and on the suspects' and defendants' rights to counsel during identification. In *Foster* v. *California,*[90] for example, there was only one witness to a robbery. The suspect, who was six feet tall, was first placed in a line-up with two other men who were several inches shorter. Also, he was wearing a leather jacket similar to the one the witness had seen one of the robbers wearing. The witness thought the suspect was indeed the robber, but was not absolutely sure. Several days later another line-up was held, and the suspect was the only one in the second line-up who had been in the earlier one. At this point the witness positively identified the suspect as the robber. The Supreme Court did not allow this type of identification procedure to stand, stating that "in effect, the police repeatedly said to the witness, '*This* is the man.'"

United States v. Wade addressed the issue of a defendant's right to counsel during a line-up.[91] In *Wade,* the defendant had been shown to witnesses before trial at a postindictment line-up, without notice of the line-up to the accused or his attorney, and without his attorney present. The Court recognized in this case that the chances of an unfair identification were so great, either through inadvertence or design, that it ruled that a person who is subjected to a pretrial line-up or show-up is entitled to be represented by counsel at that time. Importantly, however, the *Wade* case referred only to postindictment line-ups, and not to those occurring in earlier phases of the criminal justice process.

With respect to nontestimonial exemplars, the Supreme Court has maintained a firm position:

- In *Schmerber* v. *California,*[92] the Court ruled that the forced extraction of a blood sample from a defendant who was accused of driving while intoxicated was admissible at trial.
- In *United States* v. *Dionisio,*[93] the Court held that a suspect could be forced to provide voice exemplars.
- In *United States* v. *Mara,*[94] the Court held that a suspect could be compelled to provide a handwriting exemplar.
- In *United States* v. *Ash,*[95] the Court held that the Sixth Amendment does not grant the right to counsel at photographic displays conducted for the purpose of allowing a witness to attempt an identification of an offender.

The position of the Court in these cases has been that the Fifth Amendment privilege protects an accused only from being compelled to testify against himself—that is, from evidence of a communicative nature. On the other hand, in *Winston* v. *Lee* the Court held that a suspect cannot be forced to undergo surgery to remove a bullet from his chest, even though probable cause exists that the surgery would produce evidence of a crime.[96]

United States **v. Wade**

Nontestimonial exemplars: Voice, blood, handwriting, and other specimens used as evidence.

EXHIBIT 8.11

Whatever Happened to . . .

Dollree Mapp

When the *Mapp* v. *Ohio* decision in 1961 extended the exclusionary rule to the states, Dollree Mapp's conviction for the illegal possession of obscene materials was overturned on the grounds of illegal search and seizure. Many years later, Mapp again came into contact with the law. On November 2, 1970, some two years after relocating from Cleveland to New York City, she was arrested by detectives of the Narcotics Division and the Safe, Loft, and Truck Squad of the New York Police Department. Mapp was suspected of dealing in stolen property, and the detectives, pursuant to a search warrant, raided her home and found 50,000 envelopes of heroin and stolen property valued at over $100,000. On April 23, 1971, she was convicted of the felonious possession of dangerous drugs and sentenced to a term of 20 years to life.

Throughout her trial, Mapp argued against the legality of the search warrant, but three lower courts as well as the federal court of appeals sustained her conviction. However, on December 31, 1980, New York Governor Hugh Carey commuted her minimum sentence, making her eligible for parole the following day.

Danny Escobedo

The Supreme Court's *Escobedo* v. *Illinois* decision in 1964 overturned Danny Escobedo's murder conviction on the grounds that his constitutional rights had been violated when police refused him access to an attorney before he confessed to the slaying of his brother-in-law.

Within two years of the High Court's decision, however, Escobedo was making regular appearances before Chicago magistrates. During 1966 and 1967, he was arrested on various charges of disorderly conduct, burglary, weapons violations, and drug sales. On the burglary and drug charges, Escobedo was convicted and received concurrent sentences of 22 and 20 years. He was ultimately paroled in 1975.

Escobedo made the headlines on several occasions during the 1980s. In 1984 he was sentenced to 12 years in prison on conviction of taking indecent liberties with a 13-year-old girl. While free on bond pending an appeal of that conviction, in 1985 he was arrested in Chicago on a charge of attempted murder.

Ernesto Miranda

The *Miranda* v. *Arizona* decision in 1966, which laid out the well-known "Miranda warning rules," did not end Ernesto Miranda's legal entanglements. In February 1967, he was tried again on the kidnapping and rape charges, for when the Supreme Court overturned his original conviction it had not quashed the indictment, and Miranda was granted a new trial. During his second trial, Miranda's common-law wife, Twila Hoffman, testified that he had admitted kidnapping and raping the victim. Miranda was convicted and sentenced to a 20- to 30-year term in state prison. He was paroled in 1972. Two years later, he was arrested on a gun charge and for possession of drugs, but the cases were dismissed due to Fourth Amendment violations.

Summary

The police have both investigative and arrest powers. Investigative powers include the power to stop and frisk, to order someone out of a vehicle, to question, and to detain. Arrest powers include the power to use force, to search, and to exercise seizure and restraint. The Constitution places restrictions on the exercise of these powers, but determining the specific intent of the Constitution in this behalf has been left to the courts.

Search and seizure refers to the search for and taking of persons and/or property as evidence of crime. The Fourth Amendment prohibits "unreasonable" searches and seizures. The Supreme Court has ruled on guidelines for the issuance of search warrants, searches incident to arrest, and the circumstances involving stop and frisk, fresh pursuit, random automobile checks, consent search, and "plain view" seizure.

In 1975, Miranda was returned for a brief period to Arizona State Prison for parole violation, but he was released later that year. In early 1976, at age 34, Ernesto Miranda was slain in a Phoenix skid row bar during a quarrel over a card game. When the police arrested the suspect in the killing, they appropriately recited the *Miranda* warning rules.

Robert Williams

After the High Court's 1977 ruling in *Brewer* v. *Williams* (see Exhibit 8.10), Robert Williams was returned to the Iowa courts for a second trial for the 1968 murder of 10-year-old Pamela Powers. At this new trial, evidence about Powers's body was admitted, but not Williams's involvement in its discovery. Williams was convicted of first-degree murder, and the Iowa Supreme Court affirmed. In subsequent *habeas corpus* proceedings, the federal district court, denying relief, agreed with the Iowa trial and appeals courts, that the victim's body would inevitably have been found. However, the U.S. Court of Appeals for the Eighth Circuit

reversed, holding that — even assuming that there is an "inevitable discovery" exception to the exclusionary rule — the state had not met the exception's requirement that it be proved that the police did not act in bad faith. At that point, the state of Iowa appealed the court of appeals decision to the United States Supreme Court. The case was *Nix* v. *Williams,* and the High Court's ruling came in 1984.

By a vote of 7 to 2, the Supreme Court endorsed the "inevitable discovery" exception. Chief Justice Warren Burger noted that some 200 volunteers had been searching for Pamela Powers's body at the very time that Williams led police to it, and that it would have been "inevitably discovered" by lawful means without his help. That being so, wrote Burger in the Court's opinion, it "would reject logic, experience and common sense" to apply the exclusionary rule and bar the evidence. Sixteen years after the Christmas Eve slaying of Pamela Powers, Robert Williams's life sentence for the crime was fully endorsed.

In 1970, nine years after her conviction was overturned by the Supreme Court on the grounds of illegal search and seizure, Dollree Mapp was arrested when police, armed with a search warrant this time, found heroin and stolen property in her home.

The Supreme Court's exclusionary rule prohibits in court the use of any evidence seized in violation of the Fourth Amendment ban against unreasonable search and seizure. In *Weeks* v. *United States* in 1914, the Court established the exclusionary rule for federal prosecutions; *Mapp* v. *Ohio* extended this rule to the states in 1961. Since *Mapp,* however, there has been dissatisfaction with the exclusionary rule. As a result, there has been a retreat from *Mapp.*

In criminal prosecutions, the Constitution prohibits forced confessions and guarantees the assistance of counsel. However, these restrictions were applied to the states only recently. *Brown* v. *Mississippi* in 1936 began a movement that culminated with *Escobedo* and *Miranda* during the 1960s. As with *Mapp,* there was dissatisfaction with the *Miranda* rule, and over the years its original strength has been diluted.

Key Terms

Questions for Discussion

1. Given the facts in *Chimel* v. *California,* could the prosecution have applied the doctrines of "plain view" and protective sweep?
2. What are the various rights of the accused during the pretrial phases of the criminal justice process?
3. Applying the concept of probable cause, what specifically was "unreasonable" about the searches and seizures in *Aguilar* v. *Texas* and *Mapp* v. *Ohio?*
4. What are your opinions of the reasonableness of the Supreme Court decisions in *Escobedo* v. *Illinois, Miranda* v. *Arizona,* and *Brewer* v. *Williams?*

For Further Reading

Abraham, Henry J. *Freedom and the Court: Civil Rights and Liberties in the United States.* New York: Oxford University Press, 1977.

Creamer, J. Shane. *The Law of Arrest, Search, and Seizure.* New York: Holt, Rinehart and Winston, 1980.

Ginger, Ann Fagan. *The Law, the Supreme Court, and People's Rights.* Woodbury, N.Y.: Barron's, 1973.

Kelder, Gary, and Alan J. Statman. "The Protective Sweep Doctrine: Recurrent Questions Regarding the Propriety of Searches Conducted Contemporaneously with an Arrest on or near Private Premises." *Syracuse Law Review* 30 (1979): 973–1092.

Notes

1. J. Shane Creamer, *The Law of Arrest, Search, and Seizure* (New York: Holt, Rinehart and Winston, 1980); p. 3.
2. Locke v. United States, 7 Cr. 339 (1813).
3. Dumbra v. United States, 268 U.S. 435 (1925).
4. Aguilar v. Texas, 378 U.S. 108 (1964); Spinelli v. United States, 393 U.S. 410 (1969).
5. Illinois v. Gates, 462 U.S. 213 (1983).
6. United States v. Robinson, 414 U.S. 218 (1973).
7. United States v. Watson, 423 U.S. 455 (1976).
8. Payton v. New York, 445 U.S. 573 (1980).
9. McQueen v. Heck, 41 Tenn. 212 (1860); Shelton v. State, 3 Tenn. Cr. App. 310, 460 S.W. (2d) 869 (1970).
10. Harris v. State, 206 Tenn. 276 (1960).
11. Lowery v. State, 39 Ala. 659, 107 So. 2d 366 (1958).
12. State v. Autheman, 47 Idaho 328, 274 P. 305, 62 A.L.R. 195 (1929); Appleton v. State, 61 Ark. 590, 33 S.W. 1066 (1896).
13. For example, Neal v. Joyner, 89 N.C. 287 (1883).
14. Terry v. Ohio, 392 U.S. 1 (1968).
15. Carroll v. United States, 267 U.S. 132 (1925).
16. Husty v. United States, 282 U.S. 694 (1931).
17. Chambers v. Maroney, 399 U.S. 42 (1970).
18. United States v. Ross, 456 U.S. 798 (1982).
19. New York v. Belton, 453 U.S. 454 (1981).
20. Personal communication, October 31, 1970.
21. Personal communication, June 19, 1975.
22. Delaware v. Prouse, 24 CrL 3079 (1979).
23. *Tennessee Code,* Title 40, Section 811.
24. Wren v. United States, 352 F 2d 617 (1965).
25. United States v. Matlock, 415 U.S. 164 (1974).
26. Bumper v. North Carolina, 391 U.S. 543 (1968).
27. Schneckloth v. Bustamonte, 412 U.S. 218 (1973).
28. United States v. Dichiarinte, 445 F 2d 126 (1921).
29. Burdeau v. McDowell, 256 U.S. 465 (1921).
30. United States v. Martinez-Fuerte, 428 U.S. 543 (1976).
31. Katz v. United States, 389 U.S. 347 (1967).

32. Abel v. United States, 362 U.S. 217 (1960).

33. Hester v. United States, 265 U.S. 57 (1924).

34. Oliver v. United States, US SupCt (1984) 35 CrL 3011; Maine v. Thornton, US SupCt (1984) 35 CrL 3011.

35. Harris v. United States, 390 U.S. 234 (1968).

36. Steven M. Greenberg, "Compounding a Felony: Drug Abuse and the American Legal System," in *Drugs and the Criminal Justice System,* ed. James A. Inciardi and Carl D. Chambers (Beverly Hills, Calif.: Sage, 1974), p. 200.

37. Gary Kelder and Alan J. Statman, "The Protective Sweep Doctrine: Recurrent Questions Regarding the Propriety of Searches Conducted Contemporaneously with an Arrest on or near Private Premises," *Syracuse Law Review* 30 (1979): 973–1092.

38. Weeks v. United States, 232 U.S. 383 (1914).

39. Adams v. New York, 192 U.S. 585 (1904).

40. National Commission on Law Observance and Enforcement, *Report on Prosecution* (Washington, D.C.: U.S. Government Printing Office, 1931), p. 24.

41. People v. Defore, 242 N.Y. 13 at 21 (1926).

42. Elder Witt, ed., *Guide to the U.S. Supreme Court* (Washington, D.C.: Congressional Quarterly, 1979), p. 549.

43. Wolf v. Colorado, 338 U.S. 25 (1949).

44. Henry J. Abraham, *Freedom and the Court: Civil Rights and Liberties in the United States* (New York: Oxford University Press, 1977), pp. 71–72.

45. Rochin v. California, 342 U.S. 165 (1952).

46. Rea v. United States, 350 U.S. 214 (1956).

47. Elkins v. United States, 364 U.S. 206 (1960).

48. Mapp v. Ohio, 367 U.S. 643 (1961).

49. *New York Times,* June 20, 1961, p. 1.

50. Arthur Niederhoffer, *Behind the Shield* (Garden City, N.Y.: Doubleday, 1967), p. 159.

51. Yale Kamisar, "Criminals, Cops, and the Constitution," *The Nation* 199 (November 9, 1964): 323.

52. Linkletter v. Walker, 381 U.S. 618 (1965).

53. Chimel v. California, 395 U.S. 752 (1969).

54. Creamer, *Law of Arrest, Search, and Seizure,* pp. 234–235.

55. See Bob Woodward and Scott Armstrong, *The Brethren: Inside the Supreme Court* (New York: Simon and Schuster, 1979), pp. 112–119.

56. Coolidge v. New Hampshire, 403 U.S. 443 (1971).

57. United States v. Calandra, 414 U.S. 338 (1974).

58. Stone v. Powell, 428 U.S. 465 (1976).

59. United States v. Leon, US SupCt (1984) 35 CrL 3273; Massachusetts v. Sheppard, US SupCt (1984) 35 CrL 3296

60. Hopt v. Utah, 110 U.S. 574 (1884).

61. Wilson v. United States, 162 U.S. 613 (1896).

62. Twining v. New Jersey, 211 U.S. 78 (1908).

63. Cited by Abraham, *Freedom and the Court,* p. 59.

64. Brown v. Mississippi, 297 U.S. 278 (1936).

65. Rogers v. Richmond, 365 U.S. 534 (1961).

66. Bram v. United States, 168 U.S. 532 (1897).

67. McNabb v. United States, 318 U.S. 332 (1943).

68. Mallory v. United States, 354 U.S. 449 (1957).

69. Elder Witt, *Guide to the U.S. Supreme Court,* p. 679. See also Richard Harris, *The Fear of Crime* (New York: Praeger, 1969).

70. Crooker v. California, 357 U.S. 433 (1958).

71. Massiah v. United States, 377 U.S. 201 (1964).

72. Malloy v. Hogan, 378 U.S. 1 (1964).

73. Escobedo v. Illinois, 378 U.S. 478 (1964).

74. Abraham, *Freedom and the Court,* p. 144.

75. Miranda v. Arizona, Vignera v. New York, Westover v. United States, California v. Stewart—all 384 U.S. 436 (1966).

76. *New York Times,* June 14, 1966, p. 1.

77. Robert F. Cushman, *Cases in Constitutional Law* (Englewood Cliffs, N.J.: Prentice-Hall, 1979), p. 400.

78. Richard Ayres, "Confessions and the Court," in *The Ambivalent Force: Perspectives on the Police,* ed. Arthur Niederhoffer and Abraham S. Blumberg (Hinsdale, Ill.: Dryden, 1976), pp. 286–290.

79. William O. Douglas, *The Court Years: 1939-1975* (New York: Random House, 1980), p. 231.

80. Harris v. New York, 401 U.S. 222 (1971).

81. Michigan v. Tucker, 417 U.S. 433 (1974).

82. Michigan v. Mosley, 423 U.S. 96 (1975).

83. United States v. Mandujano, 425 U.S. 564 (1976).

84. Oregon v. Mathiason, 429 U.S. 492 (1977).

85. Brewer v. Williams, 430 U.S. 387 (1977).

86. New York v. Quarles, Us SupCt (1984) 35 CrL 3135.

87. Berkemer v. McCarty, US SupCt (1984) 35 CrL 3192.

88. Nix v. Williams, Us SupCt (1984) 35 CrL 3119.

89. Kirby v. Illinois, 406 U.S. 682 (1972).

90. Foster v. California, 394 U.S. 440 (1969).

91. United States v. Wade, 388 U.S. 218 (1967).

92. Schmerber v. California, 384 U.S. 757 (1966).

93. United States v. Dionisio, 410 U.S. 1 (1973).

94. United States v. Mara, 410 U.S. 19 (1973).

95. United States v. Ash, 413 U.S. 300 (1973).

96. Winston v. Lee, US SupCt (1985) 53 U.S.L.W. 4367.

9

Beyond the Limits of the Law: Police Crime, Corruption, and Brutality

There is more law in the end of a policeman's nightstick than in any decision of the Supreme Court.

— Alexander "Clubber" Williams, 1881

There is no reason to assume that the corrupt cop is any more psychologically or socially abnormal than you or me.

— Carl B. Klockars, 1983

The .38 service revolver is a police officer's final authority.

— from *Cops*, by Mark Baker, 1985

The problem lies in the fact that policing is rich in opportunities for corruption — more so than in most, if not all other occupations. The police officer stands at the front lines of the criminal justice system in a nation where crime rates are high and where the demands for illegal goods and services are widespread. These conditions, combined with a range of numerous other variables, create a situation in which police officers are confronted daily with opportunities for accepting funds in lieu of fully discharging their duties.

Police corruption

Police corruption occurs in many forms, but observers and researchers of police behavior tend to agree that it is most manifest in nine specific areas:[12]

1. meals and services
2. kickbacks
3. opportunistic theft
4. planned theft
5. shakedowns
6. protection
7. case fixing
8. private security
9. patronage

Meals and Services

Free or discount meals are available to police officers in almost every American city.[13] A number of restaurant chains have a policy of providing meals to officers on a regular basis, and these are tabulated daily, with records kept so they can demonstrate their goodwill to both the department and the city. Numerous diners, coffee shops, and other small restaurants have a similar policy, but in these the policy is maintained for the sake of **"police presence"** in the establishment. Many owners of diners and restaurants feel that if they can attract officers, it will extend a measure of security to their place of business. Unquestionably, it does; holdups are much less likely to occur at locations regularly visited by police, and if a crime or altercation happens nevertheless, police response is typically more rapid. Such deterrent presence is also "purchased" by other types of establishments — hardware stores, dry cleaners, small food shops, clothing outlets, liquor stores, and the like — generally by offering members of the police force goods and services at discount prices.

"Police presence"

However, in some places the providing of meals, goods, and services at reduced rates or even at no cost is forced through implicit or direct coercion. In such instances, shopkeepers are reluctant to donate food or "gifts" of any sort to officers, yet they understand that it is expected of them. They comply out of fear — fear that the patrolman will "look the other way" when trouble occurs, and fear that the local precinct will search harder for violations of some kind on the business premises. For example, a Brooklyn, New York, liquor store owner reported the following incident to the author:

> Less than two weeks after I opened this place, two cops walk in and tell me they're from this sector. Then they start fingering some bottles of Scotch so I ask them if they need any help. They ask me if I give special discounts and I say no, everything is already marked down. With that they just give me a funny look and walk out of the store. I guess it made them mad, 'cause from then on I never got any cooperation from the police.

strangulation during an epileptic seizure. During a search of the deceased's room in an effort to locate personal papers that might identify his next of kin, the officers found some $18,000 in small bills. The two officers divided the money equally between themselves.

Opportunistic theft is not restricted to expensive appliances, individual pieces of jewelry, or even thousands of dollars in cash. As described in Exhibit 9.1, such thefts can also involve millions of dollars.

Planned Theft

Planned theft as a variety of police corruption refers to the direct involvement of police in predatory criminal activities. During the last two decades, either through complicity with criminals or as undertaken directly by police, it has

case is stored by the department until final disposition of all legal proceedings. Whether the merchandise is a lock of hair, a diamond watch, a 97-foot yacht, or a multimillion-dollar cache of narcotics, it is marked as evidence and stored. So it was with the 97 pounds of heroin seized in the French connection. The drugs were marked and sealed as evidence, and assigned to a bin in the N.Y.P.D. property clerk's office.

Sometime between 1962 and 1972, the narcotics disappeared from the property clerk's office. A full audit revealed that 81 of the original 97 pounds were missing, as were 88 pounds of heroin and 31 pounds of cocaine from other cases. In the period from 1962 to 1972, person or persons unknown managed to substitute sacks of sugar for 200 pounds of heroin and cocaine, by forging a detective's name to withdraw drugs "for a court hearing."

This means that for some time the N.Y.P.D. had been one of New York's major suppliers of

drugs. To this day, the heroin and cocaine losses from the property clerk's office remain a mystery.

SOURCES: Patrick V. Murphy and Thomas Plate, *The Commissioner: A View from the Top of American Law Enforcement* (New York: Simon and Schuster, 1977); Robert Daley, *Target Blue: An Insider's View of the N.Y.P.D.* (New York: Delacorte Press, 1973); *TV Feature Film Source Book* (New York: Broadcast Information Bureau, 1978).

The "French Connection" was broken up in 1962 as the result of the efforts of two New York City police detectives, Eddie Egan and Sonny Grosso. At the bust, which netted nearly 97 pounds of heroin, Egan (right) handcuffs drug kingpin Jacques Angelvin (left).

occurred in Denver, Des Moines, Chicago, Nashville, New York, Philadelphia, Buffalo, Birmingham, Cleveland, New Orleans, Miami, and numerous other cities. A recent case involved a Greenville, South Carolina, police officer who was routinely stealing from establishments he was assigned to protect. The officer was found to be burglarizing homes and businesses along his patrol route regularly.[16] Similar examples appear throughout police literature.

Characteristically, however, planned theft by police officers, unlike some other forms of corruption, is rarely tolerated by police departments. Although there might be passive support for such activity, as soon as knowledge of this type of criminal enterprise becomes known to the public, even corrupt departments generally react in a forceful manner.[17]

Shakedowns

The "shakedown" racket

Shakedowns are forms of extortion in which police officers accept money from citizens in lieu of enforcing the law. The term *shakedown* has its roots in the nineteenth century British underworld. A "shakedown" was a temporary substitute for a bed, as was common in many an English prostitute's room. Hence, her quarters also became known as a shakedown. Commonplace in the underworld of the time was the practice of an extortion scheme that had several variations, usually involving the collective efforts of sneak thieves, prostitutes, and other types of criminals. In a typical situation, an attractively dressed female approached a country gentleman, explaining that she was a victim of circumstances and was thus forced for the first time in her life to accost a man. After naming a modest sum for her charms, he would accompany her to her room, bolting the door. While he engaged in sexual relations with the young woman, a wall panel would slide open from which a thief would enter, replace the money in the victim's pocket with paper, and silently exit. After the theft had taken place, a sound would be heard that the woman would claim to be her husband. The gentleman would quickly dress and hastily leave through a rear door, unaware that he had been robbed. It was from rackets such as this that most forms of extortion became known as shakedowns — appropriately named after the place where they occurred: the "shakedown," the prostitute's room.[18]

Police have been known to shake down tavern owners by threatening to enforce obscure liquor laws, and restaurant owners and shopkeepers by threatening to enforce health regulations and zoning violations. Perhaps most common, however, are shakedowns involving traffic violations. For example, the victim of one police shakedown reported the following story:

> It was on the New Jersey turnpike on a Monday night, and it was dark and raining and I just couldn't see a damn thing — so I decide to drive off the highway and rest until things let up. All of a sudden I see the red lights of a squad car behind me. It seems that I was going the wrong way on an exit ramp. . . .
>
> Well, the trooper gives me this long story as to how dangerous my driving was and all that could have happened, but then tells me that a twenty could square things.[19]

Shakedowns were once common in Chicago, according to reporter and author Mike Royko:

> It was a typical night for the Chicago police in early 1960. They were out making money. Some were making big money. Others took in smaller sums, but it added up. If a two-man squad could stop just six or

seven good traffic violators in one night, that was an extra fifty dollars in the wallet when midnight came. Some were so hungry they'd take anything. An old man who worked in a poultry store was stopped for running a light. He was broke, but when the policeman found that he worked in a poultry store, he made the old man promise to return to the same spot the following night with a chicken.[20]

Protection

The protection of illegal activities by police has been known in this country for well over a century. Such protection usually involves illegal goods and services such as prostitution, gambling, narcotics, and pornography, and the resulting corruption is typically well organized. In Mayor Richard Daley's Chicago, such corruption was apparent throughout the police hierarchy, according to Royko:

> Some taverns paid him to stay open beyond the 2 A.M. closing hour. He was less expensive than a 4 A.M. license. Others paid him to assure that if a bartender worked a customer over, the customer would be charged with assault. He didn't keep it all: the detectives on his shift got some, and the lieutenant in a little office in the back got more. And his collection was small change compared to what the captain's bag man picked up during the day.
>
> The captain's bag man made the rounds of the bookies, the homosexual bars, the hotels and lounges that were headquarters for prostitution rings. That's where the real money was, but the captain didn't keep it all. He got some, but most of it went to the ward committeeman. That's why the captain was running the station: the ward committeeman had put him there because he trusted him to collect the payoffs and give an honest accounting and a fair split. If he didn't, the ward committeeman would call downtown to headquarters and have the captain transferred to a paper-shuffling job somewhere. Not that this was likely to happen: the captain knew what he was supposed to do, or the ward boss wouldn't have had him promoted through the ranks all the way to captain.[21]

Police corruption in the form of protection of illegal activities was apparently most widespread, prior to the investigation by the Knapp Commission during the early 1970s, in New York City. The Commission found that more than half of New York's almost 30,000 officers took part in corrupt practices during 1971, much of which involved protection rackets (see Exhibit 9.2).

Case Fixing

As a form of corruption, case fixing has appeared at all levels of the criminal justice process and has involved not only police, but bailiffs, court personnel, members of juries, prosecutors, and judges. Fixing a case with a police officer, however, is the most direct, and often the least complicated and least expensive method. The most common form involves a bribe to an officer in exchange for not being arrested—a practice most typically initiated by pickpockets, prostitutes, gamblers, narcotics users, the parents of juvenile offenders, members of organized crime, and sometimes burglars. Case fixing can also take the form of an officer perjuring himself or herself on the witness stand, reducing the seriousness of a charge against an offender, or agreeing to drop an investigation prematurely by not pursuing leads that might produce evidence supporting a criminal charge.[22]

EXHIBIT 9.2

Some Findings of the Knapp Commission

We found corruption to be widespread. It took various forms depending upon the activity involved, appearing at its most sophisticated among plainclothesmen assigned to enforcing gambling laws. In the five plainclothes divisions where our investigations were concentrated we found a strikingly standardized pattern of corruption. Plainclothesmen, participating in what is known in police parlance as a "pad," collected regular bi-weekly or monthly payments amounting to as much as $3,500 from each of the gambling establishments in the area under their jurisdiction, and divided the take in equal shares. The monthly share per man (called the "nut") ranged from $300 and $400 in midtown Manhattan to $1,500 in Harlem. When supervisors were involved they received a share and a half. A newly assigned plainclothesman was not entitled to his share for about two months, while he was checked out for reliability, but the earnings lost by the delay were made up to him in the form of two months' severance pay when he left the division.

Evidence before us led to the conclusion that the same pattern existed in the remaining divisions which we did not investigate in depth. This conclusion was confirmed by events occurring before and after the period of our investigation. Prior to the Commission's existence, exposures by former plainclothesman Frank Serpico had led to indictments or departmental charges against nineteen plainclothesmen in a Bronx division for involvement in a pad where the nut was $800. After our public hearings had been completed, an investigation conducted by the Kings County District Attorney and the Department's Internal Affairs Division — which investigation neither the Commission nor its staff had even known about — resulted in indictments and charges against thirty-seven Brooklyn plainclothesmen who had participated in a pad with a nut of $1,200. The manner of operation of the pad involved in each of these situations was in every detail identical to that described at the Commission hearings, and in each almost every plainclothesman in the division, including supervisory lieutenants, was implicated.

Corruption in narcotics enforcement lacked the organization of the gambling pads, but individual payments — known as "scores" — were commonly received and could be staggering in amount. Our investigation, a concurrent probe by the State Investigation Commission and prosecutions by Federal and local authorities all revealed a pattern whereby corrupt officers customarily collected scores in substantial amounts from narcotics violators. These scores were either kept by the individual officer or shared with a partner and, perhaps, a superior officer. They ranged from minor shakedowns to payments of many thousands of dollars, the largest narcotics payoff uncovered in our investigation having been $80,000. According to information developed by the S.I.C. and in recent Federal investigations, the size of this score was by no means unique.

Corruption among detectives assigned to general investigative duties also took the form of shakedowns of individual targets of opportunity. Although these scores were not in the huge amounts found in narcotics, they not infrequently came to several thousand dollars.

Uniformed patrolmen assigned to street duties were not found to receive money on nearly

Here in Bogotá [Colombia], you can buy your way out of an arrest with a carton of Marlboro. **—American diplomat, 1982**

Traffic-ticket fixing is likely the most common form of case fixing, and often it does not involve any monetary payment.[23] In some jurisdictions, simply "knowing" someone on the police force is all that is needed to have a summons discharged, and in other instances a call to a police chief can be effective. There may also be long-standing complex arrangments. In Brooklyn, New York, a "protected" gambling establishment had no facilities for

so grand or organized a scale, but the large number of small payments they received present an equally serious if less dramatic problem. Uniformed patrolmen, particularly those assigned to radio patrol cars, participated in gambling pads more modest in size than those received by plainclothes units and received regular payments from construction sites, bars, grocery stores and other business establishments. These payments were usually made on a regular basis to sector car patrolmen and on a haphazard basis to others. While individual payments to uniformed men were small, mostly under $20, they were often so numerous as to add substantially to a patrolman's income. Other less regular payments to uniformed patrolmen included those made by after-hours bars, bottle clubs, tow trucks, motorists, cab drivers, parking lots, prostitutes and defendants wanting to fix their cases in court. Another practice found to be widespread was the payment of gratuities by policemen to other policemen to expedite normal police procedures or to gain favorable assignments.

Sergeants and lieutenants who were so inclined participated in the same kind of corruption as the men they supervised. In addition, some sergeants had their own pads from which patrolman were excluded.

Although the Commission was unable to develop hard evidence establishing that officers above the rank of lieutenant received payoffs, considerable circumstantial evidence and some testimony so indicated. Most often when a superior officer is corrupt, he uses a patrolman as his "bagman" who collects for him and keeps a percentage of the take. Because the bagman may keep the money for himself, although he claims to be collecting for his superior, it is extremely difficult to determine with any accuracy when the superior actually is involved.

Of course, not all policemen are corrupt. If we are to exclude such petty infractions as free meals, an appreciable number do not engage in any corrupt activities. Yet, with extremely rare exceptions, even those who themselves engage in no corrupt activities are involved in corruption in the sense that they take no steps to prevent what they know or suspect to be going on. . . .

It must be made clear that—in a little over a year with a staff having as few as two and never more than twelve field investigators—we did not examine every precinct in the Department. Our conclusion that corruption is widespread throughout the Department is based on the fact that information supplied to us by hundreds of sources within and without the Department was consistently borne out by specific observations made in areas we were able to investigate in detail.

SOURCE: Commission to Investigate Allegations of Police Corruption, and the City's Anti-Corruption Procedures, *The Knapp Commission Report on Police Corruption,* August 3, 1972.

customer parking, forcing bettors to park illegally. After numerous complaints to the local police captain, an arrangement was structured:

> You see, there's always been pressure on the cops to enforce the traffic laws down here, so there's no way I could get them to stop "writing." Now, for a $25 ticket for double parking, the customer gives me $5. At

the end of the day the money and a list of the ticket numbers goes over to the desk sergeant. As I understand things, 50 percent goes to the captain, 20 percent to the sergeant, and the rest goes to someone downtown. . . . We're talking sometimes too about as many as 80 to 90 tickets a week.[24]

Private Security

Corruption in the form of private security involves providing more police protection or presence than is required by standard operating procedures.[25] Examples might include checking the security of private premises more frequently and intensively than is usual, escorting businesspeople to make bank deposits, or providing more visible police presence in stores or establishments in order to keep out undesirables. In such instances, payoffs are less likely to be made in cash but more typically in goods, services, and favors.

Some officers hire themselves out as bodyguards. A Miami Beach officer who weighed more than 250 pounds and who was proficient with weapons, in the martial arts, and in stunt driving often placed himself at the disposal of cocaine dealers who were carrying large amounts of cash and drugs. He recently commented to a professional informant:

I'm as big as any fullback on the Dolphins, and they know I hit like one. Besides, they know I'm a cop . . . so they know it's best to stand clear.[26]

Patronage

Patronage can occur in a variety of ways, all of which involve the use of one's official position to influence decision making. Historically, patronage has meant making governmental appointments so as to increase one's political strength, and it has always been a part of political life in one form or another. Political patronage has been comically illustrated by journalist and author William Safire with a note allegedly written by New York political boss William Marcy Tweed to Pennsylvania politician Matthew Quay during the 1870s:

Dear Tit:
    The bearer understands addition, division, and silence. Appoint him!

Your friend,
Bill[27]

Although there may be ethical issues surrounding the practice of political patronage, it is not necessarily illegal in all of its forms. However, patronage clearly becomes corruption when payments are made for political favors. Within the ranks of policing, corruption by patronage can occur through the granting of promotions and transfers for a fee. Arranging access to confidential department records or agreeing to alter such records may also be construed as patronage. In addition, influencing department recommendations regarding the granting of licenses is patronage.

Patronage can emerge in other ways as well. Within a police department itself, for example, inside people have been payed to falsify attendance records, influence the choice of vacations and days off, report officers as on duty when they are not, and provide passing grades in training programs and promotion exams.

Police Violence

Officer, would you be terribly upset if your suspect here should accidentally get himself a broken jaw?   —a New York detective, 1964

He called me a racist pig! So I hit him.   —a Miami patrolman, 1976

Always carry a throwaway.*   —an Oakland plainclothesman, 1981

Police violence in the form of brutality, unwarranted deadly force, and other mistreatment of citizens is not uncommon in American history. Commentaries documenting the growth and development of both the urban metropolis and the rural frontier testify amply to the unwarranted use of force throughout the ranks of policing. Law enforcement records in the trans-Mississippi West provide numerous examples of the "shoot first and ask questions later" philosophy of many American lawmen. Moreover, the brutal and sadistic applications of the policeman's nightstick to demonstrate that "might makes right" appears often in the histories of urban police systems.

In 1903, New York City magistrate and former police commissioner Frank Moss commented:

> For three years, there has been through the courts and the streets a dreary procession of citizens with broken hands and bruised bodies against few of whom was violence needed to effect an arrest. Many of them had done nothing to deserve an arrest. In a majority of such cases, no complaint was made. If the victim complains, his charge is generally dismissed. The police are practically above the law.[28]

Moss was expressing his frustrations as both a member of the bench and a police reformer about a problem that was widespread during his time, but which received little attention. And the ambivalence over police violence has continued throughout the better part of the twentieth century.

It was not until the 1960s that the issue of police misconduct in the forms of brutality and deadly force assumed any public and political urgency, and this can be attributed to two phenomena. The first was the "criminal law revolution" carried on by the Supreme Court under the leadership of Chief Justice Earl Warren. The second was the findings of the Kerner Commission—the National Advisory Commission on Civil Disorders.

Brown v. *Mississippi* in 1936 established the Court's position on brutality, at least as far as coerced confessions were concerned.[29] It was the first time a state conviction was overturned because it had been obtained by using a confession extracted by torture. But the importance of *Brown* remained unnoticed for 25 years, until the High Court finally developed some hard and fast rules concerning the methods of interrogation of suspects while in police custody. *Rogers* v. *Richmond* in 1961, *Greenwald* v. *Wisconsin*, *Georgia* v. *Sims* and *Florida* v. *Brooks* in 1968 asserted that the Fourteenth Amendment bars confessions when "the methods used to extract them offend the underlying principle in the enforcement of our criminal law," especially those which reflect "shocking displays of barbarism."[30]

Police violence in U.S. history

Brown v. Mississippi

---

* A *throwaway* is generally an unregistered, untraceable pistol (or sometimes a knife) carried by some police officers. In the event of an accidental or unwarranted shooting of a citizen by an officer, the throwaway is placed on or in the vicinity of the body of the victim. The police officer then claims that the shooting was in self-defense.

| EXHIBIT 9.3 |

Drug Trafficking and Police Corruption

The corrupting power of drug money is one of the obvious reasons why this number one crime problem must be conquered.
—FBI Director William H. Webster, 1985

Drug abuse is generally understood in terms of a limited number of issues. First, it is a public health problem. Illicit drugs, whether narcotics, stimulants, depressants, or hallucinogens, have been found to cause a range of physical and psychosocial complications. Drug abuse can place at risk the productivity of a potentially large segment of the population. Second, there is the link between drug abuse and the crime rate. The connection between drug use and street crime has been well documented, for the drug-taking and drug-seeking activities of narcotics addicts and other types of drug users indeed affect the rates of burglaries, larcenies, and robberies. Further, the drug trafficking and distribution marketplace has increased the profits and power of criminal syndicates, and violent crime has come to be closely associated with the

The Kerner Commission investigated the causes of urban violence that took place in the summer of 1967.

While the Supreme Court examined police violence within the context of the brutality of squad room interrogations, the Kerner Commission targeted the wider issue of street justice in all of its varied and callous forms. Known more formally as the National Advisory Commission on Civil Disorders, its purpose was to investigate the causes of the rioting and destruction that occurred in Detroit, Los Angeles, Newark, New York, and 20 other urban areas during the summer of 1967. The commission concluded that there were numerous causes but ranked as the primary stimuli police practices in patrolling urban ghettos. Aggressive preventive patrol, combined with police misconduct in the forms of brutality, unwarranted use of deadly force, harassment, verbal abuse, and discourtesy were sources of aggravation among

competition that seems to exist at all levels of the drug distribution network.

Yet drug use and trafficking have a larger effect on the social, economic, and political organization and functioning of a nation or community. In South America, for example, cocaine trafficking has exacerbated the effects of inflation, altered economic planning, affected property values and inflated wages, and swung government power toward wealthy drug dealers. In *all* nations where drug use and trafficking are commonplace, the corruption of individuals

Increased cocaine-related corruption and violence among police is one of the effects of the rise in popularity and price of the drug. One recent example is the investigation and arrest of four Miami, Florida, policemen on charges of homicide and cocaine trafficking. Clockwise from upper left: Arturo de la Vega, charged with trafficking; Armando Estrada, Armando Garcia, and Roman Rodriguez, charged with the drowning murder of two cocaine smugglers.

is widespread, particularly of those charged with enforcement of the drug laws.

For as long as drug enforcement has been a part of American policing, there has been drug-related corruption. Some police officers have accepted bribes in lieu of enforcing the drug laws; others have directly participated in the actual trafficking of illegal substances. Yet the problem was rarely widespread and never endemic to any given police force. All of this seemed to change, however, with the arrival of the cocaine era of the 1980s.

The high price of cocaine, and the billions of dollars accumulated by cocaine traffickers, have brought about the wholesale corruption of law enforcement in some communities. In New York City and other urban areas, the number of police officers charged with selling drugs or involved with drug-related graft and extortion markedly increased during the 1980s. In Miami and other parts of south Florida, cocaine-related corruption became so commonplace that by 1985 reports of new scandals no longer received

extensive media coverage. In Key West, the involvement of police officers and administrators in cocaine trafficking became so enduring and pervasive that in 1985 federal prosecutors accused that city's entire police department of being a "continuing criminal enterprise." Even the FBI became tarnished by the cocaine trade when one of its agents accepted almost $1 million in bribes and skimmed 42 kilos from a load of cocaine he helped to seize.

So out of control has cocaine-related corruption become that in 1983 a high-ranking U.S. Department of Justice official stated:

It really represents a major threat to the integrity of government institutions in this country. We're finding politicians, police chiefs, sheriffs, and even assistant U.S. attorneys — people at all levels — corrupted by this stuff.

SOURCES: Wilmington (Delaware) *News-Journal*, October 6, 1983, p. A3; *New York Times*, June 24, 1984, p. 21; *Miami Herald*, March 15, 1985, p. 1C; *New York Times*, March 16, 1985, p. 7; *USA Today*, March 18, 1985, p. 8A; James A. Inciardi, *The War on Drugs: Heroin, Cocaine, Crime, and Public Policy* (Palo Alto, Calif.: Mayfield, 1986).

blacks, and complaints of such practices were found in all of the locations studied.[31]

Brutality

Although the Supreme Court and the Kerner Commission were significant in giving greater attention and public visibility to police violence during the 1960s, the nation already had an awareness of the problem, for the subject had been the focus of rigorous study.

In 1949, for example, sociologist William A. Westley surveyed police officers in Gary, Indiana, asking the question: "When do you think a police-

If his honor asks how come the suspect has his jaw wired and a few broken teeth, tell him the asshole tripped and fell in a sewer. — Boston police officer, 1985

man is justified in roughing a man up?"[32] Seventy-four officers responded, and the major reasons given covered a variety of areas:*

- Disrespect for police   27%
- When it is impossible to avoid   17%
- To obtain information   14%
- To make an arrest   6%
- For the hardened criminal   5%
- When you know the person is guilty   2%
- For sex criminals   2%

Systematic observations in Boston, Chicago, and Washington, D.C., during 1966 reflected similar patterns. Observers were placed with police in the three cities, and they found that almost half of the assaults occurred when citizens openly defied police authority. Another third were precipitated by encounters with drunks, homosexuals, and drug users.[33] During the period 1963 through 1967, a team of three parole officers observed more than a hundred incidents of police brutality within just one police precinct in Brooklyn, New York. The majority of the occurrences were during police–citizen encounters or interrogations. They resulted from indications of disrespect for police or failure to cooperate with officers. The violence was generally limited to pushing suspects around or "roughing them up." However, there were also many more serious situations, including the following:

- The prime suspect in an assault against a police officer was placed in a four-foot detention "cage" in the detectives' squad room. During his

---

* These percentages must be viewed with some caution. Most of the officers responded "never" to the question asked, and of the balance, many gave multiple answers. Thus, although the percentages total to 73, considerably fewer officers felt that roughing someone up was justified.

three-hour detention, detectives periodically opened the cage door and repeatedly kicked the suspect in the stomach, groin, and kidneys. A total of eight officers and detectives participated in the assaults. The suspect was finally released for lack of evidence but had to be taken to a hospital emergency room for having "fallen down a flight of stairs," as the official report stated.

- A "burglary in progress" report was dispatched to all radio cars in the precinct. When detectives arrived at the premises in question — a twelve-story apartment building — a black male who was found there was taken to the roof of the building and hung over the side by a rope fastened to his belt until he confessed to the offense.

- Two detectives entered a neighborhood tavern on a Saturday night to question the bartender as to the whereabouts of a specific suspect. During the conversation, a customer coming back from the men's room bumped into one of the detectives. The detective asked him, "Why don't you at least excuse yourself?" In reply, the customer said, in Spanish, "Police are shit." The two detectives then simultaneously hit him in the head and stomach with their fists, giving him a broken jaw and three fractured ribs.

- A local narcotics peddler was seen dropping small envelopes into a storm sewer as police officers approached him. With the evidence gone, the officers began prodding him with their nightsticks. When he raised his arms to defend himself, he was knocked to the ground, kicked, and arrested for assaulting a police officer.

- A suspect was brought to the detectives' squad room for questioning about a series of armed robberies. After three hours of fruitless interrogation, the suspect's pants were removed, a wire coat hanger was wrapped around his scrotum and testicles and twisted. He confessed.[34]

National attention has focused more recently on allegations of police brutality in Jacksonville, Miami, Houston, Philadelphia, Los Angeles, San Francisco, San Antonio, and New York City. Among the more conspicuous of these have been Houston and San Antonio, where there were isolated incidents of torturing prisoners, and New York, where it was alleged in 1985 that officers in one precinct had systematically assaulted, beaten, and burned a number of suspects.[35] The New York cases received international attention after five officers were arrested, having been charged with using an electric stun gun on drug suspects during interrogations.[36]

The causes of police brutality

In the past, **police brutality** was considered to be a practice limited only to those few sadistic officers who were seen as "bad apples." However, more recent commentaries suggest that police violence is the result of norms shared throughout a police department, and that it is best understood as an unfortunate consequence of the police role. Police are given the unrestricted right to use force in situations where their evaluation of the circumstances demands it. Yet this mandate has never been precisely defined or limited. Moreover, some officers show characteristics of the police "working personality": the feeling of constant pressure to perform, along with elements of authoritarianism, suspicion, racism, hostility, insecurity, and cynicism. Police norms that emphasize solidarity and secrecy allow a structure in which incidents of brutality and other misconduct will not draw the condemnation of fellow officers.

The "watchman's style" of policing may contribute to police brutality.

Also contributing to the existence of police brutality is the type of policing described by political scientist James Q. Wilson as the "watchman's style."[37] Watch-style departments tend to be located in the older American cities, where there are high concentrations of poor and minority citizens combined with machine politics. In such cities, police officers act primarily as reluctant maintainers of order. They ignore many minor problems—those involving the poor, gambling, traffic violations, misdemeanors, juvenile rowdiness, and domestic disputes. Officers act tough in serious situations, but in most others they often follow the path of least resistance, which is generally to render curbstone justice. Furthermore, many officers tend to be poorly trained, and the departments rarely meet even the most minimum standards for planning, research, and community relations. The consequence of this watch style is undefined boundaries and expectations of police behavior that become manifested in the form of organized corruption, discriminatory arrests, and unnecessary police violence.

Going beyond the "working personality" and the "watchman's style" as factors contributing to unnecessary police violence, sociologist Richard J. Lundman has focused on three additional issues related to violence that apply to most police organizations:

1. police perceptions that citizen acceptance of police authority is fundamental to effective policing
2. police judgments of the "social value" of certain citizens
3. the conservative nature of police decision making[38]

Police Authority

Because authority is both central and essential to the police roles of enforcing the law and keeping the peace, persons who question or resist that authority represent a challenge to officers, detectives, and the organizations they represent. Challenges are not taken lightly; they are seen as barriers to effective policing. Often police use intense verbal coercion to establish their authority quickly. Should that fail, some use physical force to elicit compliance from citizens. A Baltimore, Maryland, patrol officer recalled the following incident:

> I pulled this kid over one Sunday night for a defective tail light and I asked him for his license and registration. When he started making excuses I told him very clearly: "Look kid, it's late, you're a hazard to other motorists, and I don't want any of your shit!" When he continued to whine about getting a ticket I grabbed him by the jaw and told him that he'd either quit stalling or get his ass kicked from here to kingdom come.[39]

Judgments of Social Value

In the view of many law enforcement officers, certain citizens — drunks, juvenile gang members, homosexuals, sex offenders, drug users, hardened criminals — have little to contribute to society. Many officers do not consider such people worth protecting, or they protect them using different norms than those that guide their policing of other citizens. Some police even single these people out for physical abuse. A Delaware state police officer put it this way: "So what if we knocked him around a little; he was nothing but a dirty junkie."[40]

Police Decision Making

Since police work requires officers to make quick decisions, often on the basis of only fragmentary information, both officers and their superiors tend to defend the use of violence as a means of rapid problem resolution. As Richard J. Lundman has pointed out, many members of the criminal justice system and the public at large also hold this view.[41] He cites the example of *Chicago Daily News* journalist John O. Linstead, who was assaulted by police officers during the 1968 Chicago Democratic convention. Linstead observed police beating three bystanders and intervened in the situation by shouting obscenities at the officers. They turned on him. The officers were charged with the assault, and the evidence against them was overpowering. But the jury returned a verdict of not guilty, and the judge congratulated them with the following comment:

> The language that Mr. Linstead used . . . was vile and degrading to the officers. He charged some of the officers with committing incest with their mothers in the lowest gutter language, which I suggest would be provoking in such a manner that any red-blooded American would flare up.[42]

Deadly Force

In common law, police were authorized to use deadly force as a last resort to apprehend a fleeing felon. This common law rule dates back to the Middle Ages, when all felonies were punishable by death, and thus the killing of the felon resulted in no greater consequence than that authorized for the punishment of the offense. This "shoot to kill" doctrine based on common law principles persists in one form or another in many jurisdictions throughout the United States, for there are few operational guidelines in the use of deadly force by police. The *Code of Alabama* illustrates this point: "An officer may use reasonable force to arrest, but is without privilege to use more force than is necessary to accomplish the arrest."[43]

A Kentucky police officer fires at a fleeing suspect's car.

Tennessee v. Garner

The lack of specificity in such codes, and in similar case and statutory laws, demonstrates that the decision to use deadly force for making an arrest largely remains a matter of discretion. All jurisdictions permit officers to use lethal force in defense of themselves, and most allow firing on a fleeing felon. Yet prior to *Tennessee* v. *Garner*[44] in 1985, the conditions under which such force could be applied to a fleeing felon were variable. Some jurisdictions required the suspect to be a "known" felon; others required that the officer be a witness to the felony; and still others permitted deadly force when the officer had a "reasonable belief" that the fleeing individual committed the felony in question. In *Garner*, the Supreme Court held that deadly force against a fleeing felon was proper *only* when it was necessary to prevent the escape *and* if there was probable cause to believe that the suspect posed a significant threat of death or serious physical injury to the officer or others (see Exhibit 9.4). Alternatively, an officer cannot use deadly force to apprehend a misdemeanant, but in some jurisdictions the very act of fleeing is a felony — thus permitting deadly force in misdemeanor situations.

The killing of Arthur McDuffie by police

The number of civilians killed each year by "police intervention" has reached as many as 600,[45] but for the longest time the problem went unnoticed in many parts of the United States. The killing of Arthur McDuffie by Miami police in December 1979, however, more fully rekindled concern over the deadly force issue. At first, police reports of the incident aroused little suspicion. At 1:59 on the morning of December 17, a lone black male was said to have crashed his motorcycle while dodging police at speeds up to 100 miles per hour. He supposedly battled with policemen, who tried to subdue him with nightsticks. He died four days later of head injuries.[46]

When a review of the case showed several inconsistencies, police officials began an investigation. The victim had been Arthur McDuffie, a 33-year-old insurance salesman and ex-Marine. A reconstruction of the case suggested that McDuffie had a suspended driver's license, and may have indeed tried to elude the police. When he finally slowed down, the police pulled him from his vehicle; one officer held him while the others "taught him a lesson." McDuffie suffered six severe head wounds, with the killing blow struck squarely between his eyes.[47]

Indicted for manslaughter in the case were four white patrolmen, all of whom had been previously cited in civilian complaints of brutality. On May 17, 1980, the officers were acquitted by an all-white jury, and the response was the worst outbreak of racial violence the country had seen since 1967. Angry blacks took to the streets of Miami chanting McDuffie's name and charging that his death was only one of many recent incidents in which police escaped punishment for brutalizing black citizens. After three days of racial fury, 15 persons were dead, and the city had suffered a financial toll of some $200 million.[48]

The controversy in Miami was twofold: one part focused on the use of deadly force, and the other suggested that blacks had been singled out as victims. On this latter issue, more than one research investigation had come to a similar conclusion. For example:

Arthur McDuffie

- For the period 1965 through 1969, the racial distribution of killings by police was 43 percent white, 42 percent black, 13 percent Spanish-American, and 2 percent Asian or Native American.[49]
- In Philadelphia, from 1950 to 1960, 88 percent of the victims in police killings of civilians were black.[50]
- In Chicago, during 1969 and 1970, the death rate among blacks resulting from the police use of deadly force was 5.35 per 100,000 — some 6.3 times higher than the white rate.[51]
- In New York from 1970 to 1973, 73 percent of the 248 persons killed by police were minority group members.[52]

Other studies have reflected similar findings,[53] including a more recent effort in Miami which found that during the period 1956 through 1983, most victims of fatal police shootings were black — despite the fact that blacks composed less than one-fifth of the population.[54]

Data such as these readily show that minority group members are statistically overrepresented among the victims in police killings. But an explanation of the phenomenon is less clear. Radical sociologist Paul Takagi states that "police have one trigger finger for whites and another for blacks," suggesting that police are engaged in a form of genocide against minority groups.[55] This, however, seems to be a naive oversimplification of a very complex issue, for many factors are operating simultaneously. Another explanation is that communities get the number of killings by police that they deserve.[56] Researchers Richard Kania and Wade Mackey found that police killings are statistically associated with violent crimes in a community, and they argue that "the police officer is reacting to the community as he perceives it." A third view is the "bad apple" theory, which puts the blame on a few uncontrollable police officers.[57]

In all likelihood, however, the reasons for the disproportionate number of minority group members killed by police involve all of these explanations.

Every society gets the kind of criminal it deserves. What is equally true is that every community gets the kind of law enforcement it insists on.
—**Robert F. Kennedy, 1964**

Furthermore, the excessive use of deadly force in general — whether focused on minority groups or on others — is necessarily tied to the more pervasive problem of police brutality and the very reasons for its persistence.

Controlling Police Misconduct

Without question, policing is rich in opportunities for corruption, brutality, the abuse of discretionary powers, the violation of citizens' rights, and other forms of misconduct. Furthermore, "policing the police" is difficult, for a

---

EXHIBIT 9.4

Tennessee *v.* Garner

On the evening of October 3, 1974, Memphis police officers Elton Hymon and Leslie Wright were dispatched to answer a "prowler inside call." Upon arriving at the scene they saw a woman standing on her porch gesturing toward the adjacent house, indicating that she had heard glass breaking and that "someone" was breaking in next door. Officer Hymon went behind the house, heard a door slam, and saw someone run across the back yard. The fleeing suspect, Edward Garner — a 15-year-old eighth-grade student — stopped at a chain-link fence at the edge of the yard. With the aid of a flashlight, Officer Hymon was able to see Garner's face and hands. Hymon saw no sign of a weapon, and although not certain, was "reasonably sure" that the suspect was unarmed. While Garner was still crouched at the base of the fence, Officer Hymon shouted, "Police, halt!" and took a few steps forward. At this point Garner began to climb over the fence. Convinced that if Garner made it over the fence he would elude capture, Officer Hymon shot him. The bullet hit Garner in the back of the neck, causing a wound that proved to be fatal. Ten dollars and

a purse taken from the house were found on his body.

In using deadly force to prevent the escape, Officer Hymon was acting under the authority of a Tennessee statute which provided that " . . . if, after notice of intention to arrest the defendant, he either flee[s] or forcibly resist[s], the officer may use all the necessary means to effect the arrest."

The victim's father, Cleamtee Garner, brought an action to the federal district court on the grounds that the shooting had violated his son's constitutional rights under the Fourth, Fifth, Sixth, Eighth, and Fourteenth Amendments. Seeking damages, Mr. Garner named Hymon, the police department and its director, and the mayor and city of Memphis as defendants. The district court dismissed Garner's claims, concluding that the Tennessee statute was constitutional and that Officer Hymon had employed the only reasonable and practicable means of preventing Edward Garner's escape. The court of appeals agreed that Officer Hymon had acted in good-faith reliance on the Tennessee statute, but it ruled in favor of Garner in that the

---

variety of reasons. Corruption generally occurs in the most covert of circumstances and involves a willingness and cooperation on the part of many citizens. In addition, the victims of the misconduct — of the brutality, abuse of discretionary powers, and violations of due-process rights — are often reluctant, prevented, or otherwise indisposed to making the misconduct fully public. Further, police operations are in many ways invisible to disciplinary mechanisms, since officers operate alone or in small teams — beyond the observation of departmental supervisors. Finally, the "legitimation" at the administrative levels of the internal policing of certain abusive practices,

deadly-force statute was flawed since it failed to distinguish between felonies of different magnitude. The state of Tennessee, which had intervened in the case to defend the constitutionality of its statute, appealed the decision to the U.S. Supreme Court.

The High Court ruled in favor of Cleamtee Garner, holding the Tennessee statute to be unconstitutional in that it authorized the use of deadly force against an apparently unarmed, nondangerous suspect. The Court emphasized that deadly force may not be used unless it is necessary to prevent the escape of a suspect for whom there is reasonable cause to believe a significant threat of death or serious physical injury to the officer or others exists:

[a] Apprehension by the use of deadly force is a seizure subject to the Fourth Amendment's reasonableness requirement. To determine whether such a seizure is reasonable, the extent of the intrusion on the suspect's rights under that Amendment must be balanced against the governmental interests in effective law enforcement. The balancing process demonstrates that, notwithstanding probable cause to seize a suspect, an officer may not always do so by killing him. The use

of deadly force to prevent the escape of all felony suspects, whatever the circumstances, is constitutionally unreasonable.

[b] The Fourth Amendment, for purposes of this case, should not be construed in light of the common-law ruling allowing the use of whatever force is necessary to effect the arrest of a fleeing felon. Changes in the legal and technological context mean that the rule is distorted almost beyond recognition when literally applied. Whereas felonies were formerly capital crimes, few are now, or can be, and many crimes classified as misdemeanors, or nonexistent, as common law are now felonies. Also, the common-law rule developed at a time when weapons were rudimentary. And, in light of the varied rules adopted in the States indicating a long-term movement away from the common-law rule, particularly in the police departments themselves, that rule is a dubious indicium of the constitutionality of the Tennessee statute. There is no indication that holding a police practice such as that authorized by the statute unreasonable will severely hamper effective law enforcement.

[c] While burglary is a serious crime, the officer in this case could not reasonably have believed that the suspect posed any threat. Nor does the fact that an unarmed suspect has broken into a dwelling at night automatically mean he is dangerous.

A Florida National Guardsman directs traffic away from a district in Miami where fires burn out of control and looting goes on during riots sparked by a "not guilty" verdict for four policeman charged with the beating death of Arthur McDuffie.

combined with the elements of secrecy and solidarity that are characteristic of all police organizations, inhibit many police agencies from making instances of misconduct a matter of public record.

This is not to say, however, that police abuses cannot be brought under greater control. There are many mechanisms that can affect police behavior for the better, including the legislature, the community, and the police system itself.

Legislative Control

Although the Civil Rights Act of 1964, was a decision of Congress, it is actually implemented by the courts; as such it is not a direct legislative control over police behavior. However, state and local legislative bodies can have a specific impact on the conduct of law enforcement through a reevaluation of certain laws that create the potential for police violations and corruption.

Throughout the history of the United States, criminal justice has been all but paralyzed by the problem of overcriminalization due to the legislation of morality and the overregulation of civilian conduct. The laws that impose restrictions on alcohol consumption, drug use, prostitution, gambling, and other "victimless" crimes, combined with the numerous public health and other regulations over certain business enterprises, are typically the areas in which police corruption occurs. Thus, if legislatures are to control police conduct, they must begin by decriminalizing these victimless crimes. That anything will be done in this area seems unlikely, however. The continued existence of many of the victimless crimes that generate the potential for corruption is the result of legislative unwillingness to repeal them for fear of committing political suicide. Nevertheless, a few changes have occurred. The possession of small amounts of marijuana for personal use has been decriminalized in several jurisdictions; gambling laws have been relaxed through the establishment of state-run lotteries and off-track betting; prostitution has been legalized in one jurisdiction and reduced to a minor violation in others; and a number of the unreasonable restrictions placed on business owners, landlords, and the building construction industry have been eliminated.

By contrast, Section 1983 of the Civil Rights Act of 1871 authorizes suits for damages for violations of one's constitutional rights. By invoking Section 1983, an individual can hold a law enforcement agency or municipality liable for an incident of police misconduct. (For a closer look at such suits, see Exhibit 9.5.)

Civilian Review Boards

The influence of citizens on police behavior is most evident in small communities. There is closer contact between the police and members of the community, officers are typically longtime residents of the locations they patrol, police officials are often dependent on public support for their departmental finances and tenure, and police behavior in general has a higher grass-roots visibility. Further, the opportunities for police abuse are less widespread in small cities, towns, and rural areas. The reverse seems to be true in large urban centers, where community control over policing is almost totally absent. There have been a number of suggestions made over the years concerning how to counter this problem, including "putting the cop back on the beat," sensitivity training for police recruits, and the establishment of civilian review boards to enforce police discipline. More than a decade ago, author Arthur I. Waskow offered a three-part formula for placing control of the police system in the hands of the citizenry:

> *First*, police forces should be restructured along neighborhood lines with control over each force residing in elected officials from the neighborhood; *second*, organizations should be developed to protect those who are policed; and *third*, community control should be established informally by changing the police "profession" so that police are not isolated from the rest of the community.[58]

Waskow's suggestions are likely correct, at least from a technical point of view. But they are based on an idealized concept of police–community relations and are probably unworkable. The paramilitary character of police organizations, the conservative nature of police decision making, and the elements of the police culture that stress secrecy and solidarity, all combine to create a situation where police would be highly resistant to outside control. The experience with civilian review boards illustrates this point.

Prior to 1958, all the power to discipline law enforcement personnel was in the hands of police departments, generally in the form of some internal review committee composed of one or more police officials. But during the late 1950s and early 1960s, concern about this system surfaced when the United States Commission on Civil Rights found that many blacks felt powerless to do anything about police malpractice. These revelations were later confirmed by a number of studies conducted by the American Civil Liberties Union (ACLU), the National Association for the Advancement of Colored People (NAACP), and the University of California, which pointed to a range of dissatisfactions with internal police review boards: (1) They could not be impartial in judging fellow officers; (2) the procedures for filing complaints were so cumbersome that they discouraged citizen reporting; (3) they made no effort to solicit complaints; (4) they insulated police officers and departments from public accountability; and (5) they rarely disciplined officers, thus giving the impression that they were simply whitewash efforts.[59] The ACLU also found

EXHIBIT 9.5

Police Malpractice Suits

Physicians are not the only defendants in malpractice suits. In recent years, more citizens have been suing police departments for the misuse of deadly force and for ineptitude and carelessness that result in the injury and death of innocent bystanders.

The greater tendency for courts to compensate victims or their families for injuries and "wrongful deaths" at the hands of the police is an outgrowth of several historical factors. First was the steady erosion of the doctrine of **sovereign immunity,** the principle that the state cannot be sued in its own courts or in any other court without its consent and permission. This erosion began during the 1960s when Section 1983 of the Civil Rights Act of 1871 was recognized to be an appropriate way of bringing suit against state officers in prisoners' rights cases (see Chapter 16). A second factor was the U.S. Supreme Court's ruling in *Monell* v. *New York City Department of Social Services* in 1978.[a] Although *Monell* focused on a maternity leave policy rather than a criminal justice issue, the conclusion of the Court was that cities and other local governments could be sued directly under Section 1983 for damages if the action alleged to be unconstitutional implemented or executed a policy statement, ordinance, regulation, or decision officially adopted and promulgated. by that body's officers. In employing Section 1983 and *Monell*, the suits alleging police

malpractice have involved such issues as deadly force, innocent bystanders, and failure to protect citizens.

Cases evolving from police misuse of deadly force have been numerous. *Tennessee* v. *Garner* was the first such case to reach the Supreme Court (see Exhibit 9.4). A more notorious case, however, was *Prior* v. *Woods* in 1981,[b] which resulted in a $5.7 million award— one of the largest in police malpractice history. On the morning of July 31, 1979, 24-year-old David Prior was parked in front of his home in a Detroit suburb. Two police officers had been briefed earlier that David would be staying in his van in an effort to catch a thief who had twice stolen stereo equipment from the vehicle. Mistaken for a burglar, however, Prior was shot and killed by two police officers.

Beyond the issue of the misuse of deadly force, there have been other types of police malpractice cases. *Biscoe* v. *Arlington* in 1984 and *Grandstaff* v. *Borger* in 1985 both dealt with loss of life or serious injury to innocent bystanders.[c] In *Biscoe*, $5 million was awarded to Alvin B. Biscoe and his wife stemming from an incident that occurred in 1979. While waiting to cross a street in downtown Washington, D.C., Mr. Biscoe lost both his legs after he was hit by a car involved in a high-speed police chase. In *Grandstaff*, an award of $1.4 million went to the family of a man who had been mistaken for a fugitive and was killed in a barrage of gunfire. In both cases, the awards were grounded in the logic of *Monell*, that the constitutional injury was an outgrowth of an "official policy." The official policy in the *Biscoe* case was clear, for high-speed chases were sanctioned by the offending police department without regard to potential risk of harm to bystanders. In *Grandstaff* the showing of "official policy" was based on the inadequate training of the police officers involved in the shooting.

Sorichetti v. *City of New York* and *Thurman* v. *Torrington*,[d] both in 1985, focused on police failure to protect citizens. For the most part, however, citing the Supreme Court's position on sovereign immunity as stated in *South* v. *Maryland* in 1856,[e] the courts have ruled that state and municipal governments generally may not be held liable for failure to protect individual citizens from harm caused by criminal conduct. However, the courts have also recognized a "special relationship" exception to this rule. In *Sorichetti*, a case in which a woman sued the New York City Police Department for its failure to protect her daughter from the mother's estranged husband, such a "special relationship" existed. Liability was imposed for injuries the father inflicted on his daughter since the police department knew of the father's violent history and of a court order issued against him, but failed to follow up assurances it gave Mrs. Sorichetti

that it would investigate the child's welfare. *Thurman* involved a similar circumstance. Tracey Thurman was a battered wife who sued the police for failing to act on her complaints regarding her estranged husband's violations of a stay-away order, which resulted in a severe beating.

The impact of these and other court decisions has been felt at several levels. On the one hand, police agencies have begun to address the policies and practices that lead to malpractice suits. On the other, losing such cases has been disasterous for some local governments, especially small towns with little or no insurance. The City of South Tucson, Arizona, for example, had to file for bankruptcy in 1984 after the state appellate courts upheld a $3.6 million judgment in a police negligence case. The award was almost $1 million more than the town's entire annual budget.[f]

SOURCES:
a. Monell v. New York City Department of Social Services, 436 U.S. 658 (1978).
b. Prior v. Woods: see *National Law Journal*, November 2, 1981, p. 5; also, *New York Times*, May 12, 1985, p. 39.
c. Biscoe v. Arlington: 80-0766; *National Law Journal*, May 13, 1985, p. 1; Grandstaff v. City of Borger, CA 5 (1985) 37 CrL 1085.
d. Sorichetti v. City of New York, NY CtApp (1985) 37 CrL 1067; Thurman v. Torrington, USDC DConn (1985) 37 CrL 2329; *National Law Journal*, July 15, 1985, p. 6; *USA Today*, June 26, 1985, p. 1A.
e. South v. Maryland, 59 U.S. 394 (1856).
f. *National Law Journal*, May 13, 1985, p. 36.

that in an effort to protect the reputation of their departments, the internal affairs units and other special police squads that were structured for "policing the police" employed a host of reprehensible tactics to discourage citizens from filing complaints against officers. In New York City, they threatened complainants with criminal libel; in Cleveland, they forced them to take lie detector tests; and in Philadelphia, Washington, D.C., and Los Angeles, they took them into custody on charges of resisting arrest, disorderly conduct, or some other minor offense. Other departments intimidated witnesses, deprived complainants of access to departmental files, or otherwise acted as though the citizens were on trial.[60]

Led by the ACLU, the NAACP, and other citizen groups, public opinion urged police authorities to shift the responsibility for handling complaints to citizen-controlled outside review boards. The boards envisioned were to serve several purposes:

1. They would restrain those officers who engaged in brutality, harassment, and other abusive and even illegal practices.
2. By insuring a thorough and impartial investigation of all complaints, they would protect other officers against malicious, misguided and otherwise unfounded accusations.

3. They would provide blacks and other minority group members an avenue of redress, which would help restore their dwindling confidence in the police departments.

4. They would explain police procedures to citizens, review enforcement requirements with police, and initiate a genuine dialogue in place of mutual recrimination.[61]

Proposals for **civilian review boards** incensed most police officers, and were bitterly fought by such organizations as the International Association of Chiefs of Police (IACP), the International Conference of Police Associations (ICPA), and the Fraternal Order of Police (FOP). Despite opposition, however, a few cities did establish civilian review boards. The first was set up in Philadelphia, on October 1, 1958, but from its inception its potential for objective judgment was severely compromised. Philadelphia's five-person Police Advisory Board had no investigatory staff of its own and had to rely on the police department's community relations unit to investigate all complaints.

Civilian review boards met with police opposition.

Cincinnati, Los Angeles, Seattle, Detroit, Newark, San Diego, Hartford, Baltimore, and San Francisco managed to defeat proposals for civilian review boards. New York City, however, was successful in establishing a board, at least for a time. Mayor John V. Lindsay, who owed his election in large part to the city's black and Puerto Rican populations, established the Civilian Complaint Review Board by executive order in July 1966.[62] The New York board was somewhat unique, for it was actually a "civilian-dominated" review board composed of four citizens and three police officials. Within four months of its inception, however, the New York Patrolmen's Benevolent Association (PBA) prevailed on the voters to approve a proposition that would put the city's new board out of business, and it did. The following year, Philadelphia Mayor James Tate disbanded his city's Police Advisory Board — ending the existence of civilian review boards across America.[63]

The likelihood of any reemergence of civilian review boards is remote, at least for the present.* The experience demonstrated that they had a debilitating effect on police morale, that they were viewed by police as a mechanism for appeasing the more radical elements in minority group areas, and, according to some police groups, that they served only as a wedge between the police and the community. Furthermore, both the President's Commission on Law Enforcement and Administration of Justice in 1967 and the National Advisory Commission on Criminal Justice Standards and Goals in 1973 labeled the boards as unworkable.[64]

Police Control

Control of police misconduct directly from within police departments is generally of two types, preventive and punitive.

Preventive control manifests itself in several areas, all of which involve numerous alterations in the structure and philosophy of a police department.

---

*A number of cities do have civilian committees that are often called "civilian review boards," but these are not fully independent of the police department. In Kansas City, for example, there is an Office of Civilian Complaints. However, complaints received by the civilian staff are investigated by the police department's internal affairs division. Detroit's civilian Board of Police Commissioners is a more independent body, but its powers are severely limited. See Samuel Walker, *The Police in America* (New York: McGraw-Hill, 1983), pp. 239–240.

First, the policy of *internal accountability* holds members of a law enforcement agency responsible for their own actions as well as for those of others. It is based on a clear communication of standards to which officers and officials will be held accountable, and an articulation of "who will be responsible for whom." Second, internal accountability becomes workable only under *tight supervision* of police officers by administrators, precinct commanders, and other control staff. Tight supervision involves direct surveillance of officers' work time and work products by field commanders, combined with daily logs documenting officer activity. Third, preventive control can affect areas of police misconduct through an *abolition of corrupting procedures.* Every large police department and many smaller ones have numerous formal procedures that inadvertently encourage corruption. For example, some policies imply levels of productivity that are all but impossible to achieve by legitimate means; others create pressures for financial contributions by officers that they attempt to "earn back" in corrupt ways. Vice investigators and detectives, for instance, often must "purchase" leads from informers, but funds for such purposes may be limited or unavailable. Similarly, criminal investigation work may require the use of personal autos with no provisions for expense reimbursement.

Sociologist Lawrence W. Sherman has noted that subsequent to the police scandals in Oakland during the 1950s and in New York as an outgrowth of the Knapp Commission, preventive controls along these lines were implemented.[65] In both cities, reform executives established policies of internal accountability aimed at diffusing the responsibility for control of misconduct both vertically and horizontally throughout the police departments. Concomitantly, these policies were swiftly enforced. In Oakland, for example, a detective commander lost five days' pay for failing to thoroughly investigate a corruption allegation; a sergeant was suspended for failing to investigate a prisoner's complaint that officers had taken money from him; and another sergeant was suspended for letting one of his patrolmen work while intoxicated. Supervision was tightened, primarily through the extension of decision-making powers to lower levels in the police hierarchy and maintaining a lower ratio of line officers to supervisors.

The reform administration in New York also focused on its many potentially corrupting procedures. "Buy money" for purchasing narcotics, and funds for informers, were greatly increased and more rigidly controlled; the cost of using personal autos in surveillance work was reimbursed on a per-mile basis; and the use of arrest quotas to evaluate the productivity of vice investigators was abolished.

Punitive control falls into that area of policing known as internal affairs or *internal policing*—the purview of the so-called "shoo-fly" cops, who investigate complaints against police personnel or other actions involving police misconduct. Internal policing may be the responsibility of a single officer or detective, a small police unit, or an entire division or bureau, depending on the size of a department and its commitment to in-house review. Regardless of size, however, the responsibilities of internal affairs units generally include inquiries into the following:

"Shoo-fly" cops

1. allegations or complaints of misconduct made by a citizen, police officer, or any other person against the department or any of its members

2. allegations or suspicions of corruption, breaches of integrity or cases of moral turpitude from whatever source — whether reported to or developed by internal policing
3. situations in which officers are killed or wounded by the deliberate or willful acts of other parties
4. situations in which citizens have been killed or injured by police officers either on or off duty
5. situations involving the discharging of weapons by officers[66]

Internal policing began during the latter part of the nineteenth century, when headquarters roundsmen made inspections on a citywide basis and investigated corruption. They became known as "shooflies," a term taken from the argot of the professional underworld. The "shoofly" was originally a criminal's spy, who watched for police activity in order to warn the thief.[67] By 1900, detectives were also known as "shooflies," because in their nonuniformed investigative roles they spied on criminals.[68] During the tenure of Arthur Woods as commissioner of the New York Police Department which began in 1914, a confidential squad was organized to spy on the activities of police officers.[69] It was at that point that the shoo-fly cop more formally became a part of police argot.

It was not until the mid-1900s, however, that structured bureaus for internal policing came into being.[70] In the wake of a major scandal during the late 1940s, Los Angeles police chief William A. Worton formed the Bureau of Internal Affairs. Within a decade, Boston, Chicago, and Atlanta followed suit, and at the beginning of the 1960s New York City joined the trend when Commissioner Howard V. Leary established the Inspection Service Bureau, which brought together several units that had been separately monitoring the integrity and efficiency of the police.

The special internal control units and bureaus, although permanent fixtures in big-city policing, are not without their problems. Police rank and file have always despised the activities of the shoo-fly cops. Furthermore, internal affairs officers have sometimes been corrupt themselves, and others have been unwilling to tarnish the reputation of their departments by exposing corruption and incompetence. Finally, citizens have apparently been unwilling to file complaints and officers have been unwilling to testify against one another. The product of such difficulties is an acutely low level of efficiency.

Nevertheless, not all aspects of internal policing have been unsuccessful. Even in the more disorganized and inefficient of departments a certain level of misconduct has been detected and ferreted out. Without any internal control mechanisms, police organization would probably become chaotic.

Attempts to reduce police misconduct should not be limited to efforts by the legislature, review boards, and internal policing. These treat only the symptoms of the problem. More work in the area of police professionalization also seems warranted. However, this too is an area that is problematic, for there are differing conceptions of professionalism in law enforcement. Police understand professionalism to mean more tightly defined rules and regulations, increased central control, strict discipline, and obedience. In every other organization, professionalism means that a large measure of discretion is left to individuals, who respond to situations with a wealth of personal expertise born of long training and experience, which, rather than organizational rules and regulations, guide them in handling various situations. In law enforcement agencies, such professionalism would come from better trained and educated officers, more sophisticated police resources, closer attention to the needs for community service and police–community relations, and more efficient and detailed policies regarding police behavior in contacts with citizens.

Police professionalism

Properly understood, **police professionalism** implies that brutality and corruption are incompetent policing. And incompetence may be measured in terms of the following axiom: while the core of the police role is the right to use force, the skill in policing is the ability to avoid its use. With respect to corruption, professionalism engenders group norms of pride and dignity of occupation that make police intolerant of fellow officers who taint the profession.

There are reports that this notion of professionalism has taken hold in some police agencies. It should be recalled, for example, that Frank Serpico was one of the first police officers in New York City in recent years to publicly go against "the blue curtain of secrecy" in making disclosures about police corruption. That was in 1970 and 1971; a decade later, the situation had changed considerably. In 1981, there were 2,319 allegations of police misdeeds in New York City, and almost 20 percent of these reports were submitted by police officers.[71] The trend continued into 1982, and fellow officers were found to be less willing to cover up such police improprieties as accept-

ing bribes from narcotics dealers, possession and sale of narcotics, stealing drugs and money from suspects, and accepting money from business operators in exchange for favors.

Summary

Police misconduct falls primarily into two areas: corruption and violence. Police corruption reflects illegal activities for economic gain, including payment for services that police are sworn to do as part of their law enforcement role. Police violence, in the forms of brutality and the misuse of deadly force, involves the wrongful use of police power.

Police corruption can occur in many ways, but observers and researchers in the field of police behavior agree that it is most manifest in nine specific areas: meals and services, kickbacks, opportunistic theft, planned theft, shakedowns, protection, case fixing, private security, and patronage. Policing is rich in opportunities for corruption — more so than most, if not all, other occupations.

Police violence has been relatively visible throughout American history and has received much attention in recent years by the U.S. Supreme Court and the Kerner Commission. Studies have shown that police violence occurs most often when people show disrespect for officers and when police encounter certain types of offenders, as well as when police try to coerce confessions.

In the past, police brutality was considered to be a practice limited to a few sadistic officers. More recent commentaries suggest that it is widespread and an unfortunate consequence of the police role. Police violence also includes the improper use of deadly force — a "shoot-to-kill" doctrine based on common-law principles that persist in many law enforcement agencies.

Attempts to control police misconduct of all varieties have emanated from the legislature, from civilian review boards, and from police agencies themselves. Perhaps the most effective method is police professionalization, which views brutality as incompetent policing, and corruption as beneath the dignity of effective law enforcement agents.

Key Terms

civilian review boards **(297)**
the French Connection **(274)**
police brutality **(286)**

police corruption **(272)**
"police presence" **(272)**
police professionalism **(300)**

sovereign immunity **(294)**
Tennessee v. *Garner* **(288)**

Questions for Discussion

1. Is the problem of brutality so much a part of the police role that it can never be routed out? Why or why not?
2. In your community, what do you feel would be the best combination of activities for controlling police corruption?
3. Do you feel that corruption is *more* or *less* widespread in the ranks of policing than in other occupations and professions? Why?

4. What kinds of police misconduct have you observed? In each case, were they officer- or citizen-initiated?
5. Would you favor a civilian review board in your community? Why?

For Further Reading

Goldstein, Herman. *Police Corruption: A Perspective on its Nature and Control.* Washington, D.C.: The Police Foundation, 1975.

Kobler, Arthur L. "Police Homicide in a Democracy." *Journal of Social Issues* 31 (Winter 1975): 163–184.

Porter, Bruce, and Marvin Dunn. *The Miami Riot of 1980: Crossing the Bounds.* Lexington, Mass.: Lexington, 1984.

Sherman, Lawrence W. *Scandal and Reform.* Berkeley: University of California Press, 1978.

Notes

1. A.E. Costello, *Our Police Protectors* (New York: Author's Edition, 1885), pp. 364–365.

2. Herbert Asbury, *The Gangs of New York* (Garden City, N.Y.: Garden City, 1928), p. 235.

3. James F. Richardson, *The New York Police: Colonial Times to 1901* (New York: Oxford University Press, 1970), p. 204.

4. *Report of the Special Committee Appointed to Investigate the Police Department of the City of New York* (Albany: State of New York, Senate Documents, 1895), vol. I, pp. 30–32.

5. Lincoln Steffens, *The Autobiography of Lincoln Steffens* (New York: Harcourt, Brace, 1931), p. 209.

6. Lloyd Morris, *Incredible New York* (New York: Bonanza, 1951), p. 112; Edward Robb Ellis, *The Epic of New York City* (New York: Coward-McCann, 1966), p. 432.

7. M.R. Werner, *Tammany Hall* (Garden City, N.Y.: Doubleday, Doran, 1928), pp. 360–366.

8. Lawrence W. Sherman, *Scandal and Reform* (Berkeley: University of California Press, 1978), p. xxii.

9. Herman Goldstein, *Police Corruption: A Perspective on Its Nature and Control* (Washington, D.C.: Police Foundation, 1975), p. 55.

10. Jonathan Rubinstein, *City Police* (New York: Farrar, Straus and Giroux, 1973), p. 400.

11. *The Knapp Commission Report on Police Corruption* (New York: Braziller, 1972).

12. See, for example, Richard J. Lundman, *Police and Policing* (New York: Holt, Rinehart and Winston, 1980), pp. 142–148; Herman Goldstein, *Policing a Free Society* (Cambridge, Mass.: Ballinger, 1977), pp. 194–195; Thomas Barker and Julian Roebuck, *An Empirical Typology of Police Corruption: A Study in Organizational Deviance* (Springfield, Ill.: Charles C. Thomas, 1973); Rubinstein, *City Police.*

13. This discussion is based on Sherman, *Scandal and Reform;* Rubinstein, *City Police;* and on personal observations and contacts with police in New York City, Tampa, Philadelphia, Miami, and San Francisco.

14. Personal communication, May 15, 1974.

15. The events described were reported to the author by victims, police officers, and detectives in several cities.

16. *Miami Herald,* October 30, 1982, p. B1.

17. Lundman, *Police and Policing,* p. 148; Barker and Roebuck, *Empirical Typology of Police Corruption,* p. 36.

18. James A. Inciardi, *Careers in Crime* (Chicago: Rand McNally, 1975), p. 29.

19. Personal communication, March 25, 1974.

20. Mike Royko, *Boss: Richard Daley of Chicago* (New York: Signet, 1971), p. 111.

21. Royko, *Boss,* p. 108.

22. See, for example, *New York Times,* August 12, 1984, p. 30.

23. Lundman, *Police and Policing,* p. 147.

24. Personal communication, March 1970.

25. Goldstein, *Policing a Free Society,* p. 194.

26. Anonymous communication, March 13, 1981.

27. William Safire, *Safire's Political Dictionary* (New York: Random House, 1978), p. 517.

28. Cited by Albert J. Reiss, Jr., "Police Brutality—Answers to Key Questions," *Trans-Action* 5 (1968): 10.

29. Brown v. Mississippi, 297 U.S. 278 (1936).

30. Rogers v. Richmond, 365 U.S. 534 (1961); Greenwald v. Wisconsin, 390 U.S. 519 (1968); Georgia v. Sims, 385 U.S. 538 (1968); Florida v. Brooks, 389 U.S. 413 (1968).

31. *Report of the National Advisory Commission on Civil Disorders* (New York: E. P. Dutton, 1968).

32. William A. Westley, *Violence and the Police* (Cambridge, Mass.: MIT Press, 1970), p. 122.

33. Reiss, "Police Brutality,"

34. Personal communications, 1963-1967.

35. Wilmington (Delaware) *News-Journal,* October 14, 1983, p. A5; *Time,* May 13, 1985, p. 59; *Newsweek,* May 6, 1985, p. 59.

36. *Manchester Guardian Weekly,* June 23, 1985, p.9.

37. James Q. Wilson, *Varieties of Police Behavior* (New York: Atheneum, 1975), pp. 140-171.

38. Lundman, *Police and Policing,* pp. 161–164.

39. Personal communication, May 13, 1981.

40. Personal communication, August 28, 1978.

41. Lundman, *Police and Policing.*

42. *Newsweek,* June 23, 1969, p. 92.

43. Livingston v. Browder, 51 Ala. App. 366, 285 So.2nd 923 (1973).

44. Tennessee v. Garner, US SupCt (1985) 36 CrL 3233.

45. *Justice Assistance News,* April 1980, p. 2.

46. *U.S. News & World Report,* August 27, 1979, p. 27.

47. *Time,* January 21, 1980, p. 32.

48. *U.S. News & World Report,* June 2, 1980, pp. 19–22.

49. Arthur L. Kobler, "Police Homicide in a Democracy," *Journal of Social Issues* 31 (Winter 1975): 163–184.

50. Gerald D. Robin, "Justifiable Homicides by Police Officers," *Journal of Criminal Law, Criminology and Police Science,* June 1963, pp. 225–231.

51. Ralph Knoohirizen, Richard P. Fahey, and Deborah J. Palmer, *The Police and Their Use of Fatal Force in Chicago* (Evanston, Ill.: Chicago Law Enforcement Study Group, 1972).

52. Betty Jenkins and Adrienne Faison, *An Analysis of 248 Persons Killed by New York City Policemen* (New York: New York Metropolitan Applied Research Center, 1974).

53. David Jacobs and David Britt, "Inequality and Police Use of Deadly Force: An Empirical Assessment of a Conflict Hypothesis," *Social Problems* 26 (April 1979): 403–412; Lennox S. Hinds, "The Police Use of Excessive and Deadly Force: Racial Implications," in *A Community Concern: Police Use of Deadly Force*, ed. Robert N. Brenner and Marjorie Kravitz (Washington, D.C.: U.S. Department of Justice, 1979), p. 7–11.

54. *Miami Herald*, March 27, 1983, p. 18A.

55. Paul Takagi, "A Garrison State in a 'Democratic' Society," *Crime and Social Justice* 1 (Spring–Summer 1974): 27–33; "Death by 'Police Intervention,'" in *A Community Concern,* ed. Brenner and Kravitz, pp. 31–38.

56. Richard Kania and Wade Mackey, "Police Violence as a Function of Community Characteristics," *Criminology* 15 (May 1977): 27–48.

57. Kobler, "Police Homicide in a Democracy."

58. Arthur I. Waskow, "Community Control of the Police," *Trans-Action* 7 (December 1969): 4–7.

59. Paul Chevigny, *Police Power: Police Abuses in New York City* (New York: Vintage, 1969), p. 260; David H. Bayley and Harold Mendelsohn, *Minorities and the Police: Confrontation in America* (New York: Free Press, 1971), pp. 127–135.

60. Robert M. Fogelson, *Big City Police* (Cambridge, Mass.: Harvard University Press, 1977), pp. 283–284.

61. Fogelson, *Big City Police.*

62. For an interesting perspective on the Lindsay administration and its attempts to make New York a more livable city, see John V. Lindsay, *The City* (New York: Norton, 1970).

63. Fogelson, *Big City Police*, p. 286.

64. President's Commission on Law Enforcement and Administration of Justice, *The Challenge of Crime in a Free Society* (Washington, D.C.: U.S. Government Printing Office, 1967), p. 103; National Advisory Commission on Criminal Justice Standards and Goals, *Police* (Washington, D.C.: U.S. Government Printing Office, 1973), p. 472.

65. Sherman, *Scandal and Reform*, pp. 120–145.

66. George D. Eastman, ed., *Municipal Police Administration* (Washington, D.C.: International City Management Association, 1969), pp. 203–204.

67. Langdon W. Moore, *His Own Story of His Eventful Life* (Boston: L.W. Moore, 1893), pp. 287–289.

68. Hutchins Hapgood, *The Autobiography of a Thief* (New York: Fox, Duffield, 1903), p. 265.

69. Thomas A. Reppetto, *The Blue Parade* (New York: Free Press, 1978), p. 162.

70. Fogelson, *Big City Police,* p. 179.

71. *New York Times,* April 11, 1982, p. 43.

Part

3

The Courts

*The Supreme Court in session in
the 1930s. This photograph by
Dr. Erich Salomon, a pioneer in
candid news photography, is
believed to be the only one ever
taken while the justices were
actually hearing a case.*

10

This Is the House That Justice Built: The Structure of American Courts

CITIZEN: *Where's the courthouse?*
POLICE OFFICER: *Which one?*
CITIZEN: *The criminal court, please.*
POLICE OFFICER: *Which one?*
CITIZEN: *Huh?*
POLICE OFFICER: *There's the police court, county court, circuit court, trial court, superior court, and appeals court!*
CITIZEN: *The trial court, I guess.*
POLICE OFFICER: *Which one?*

As America evolved into a nation, the court emerged as an integral part of life in most communities. It was at the local courthouse that celebrations were held and emergencies brought to the attention of the populace. Courthouses provided mustering places during the War of Independence and Civil War, and victories and reverses were first announced by broadsheets posted on their doors. Because they were often built before any churches, they frequently served as meeting places — for religious services, dances, and town council assemblies — as well as fulfilled their primary function, the dispensation of justice. And courthouses were places for exchanging the news and meeting old friends.

In matters of law, the procedure was clear and simple. The courthouse stood at the center of town. There, the local justice of the peace decided on all aspects of civil disputes and minor criminal transgressions. With the more serious issues of crime, law, and justice, the procedure — at least in its more outward aspects — was just as clear. Once each month, on "court day," a judge of some higher authority would visit the community and dispose of these weightier matters.

As towns became cities, the procedures became somewhat less simple, but not by a great deal. Since there were more people, and hence more problems, there were more courts. For civil matters, there were counterparts of the rural justices of the peace; for less serious criminal affairs, there were police and magistrates' courts; and for the serious, pressing problems of law and order, there was a more permanent higher court.[1]

As the nation grew more populous and more mature, so too did its system of courts. By the late nineteenth century, American courts reflected a bewildering mosaic of names, types, structures, and functions. The old courthouse still stood, the rural justices of the peace and the urban magistrates still decided on certain matters of law, and the county courts, night courts, and higher courts still operated. But along with these one could also find mayors' courts, municipal courts, probate courts, chancery courts, superior courts, and various levels of appeals and supreme courts. Some local town and county courts were consolidated into circuits and districts; numerous areas had general sessions and special sessions courts; and legal practitioners spoke in terms of appeals courts and trial courts, higher courts and lower courts, superior courts and inferior courts. And over all was a **dual court system** that had evolved throughout America after the signing of the Declaration of Independence — at the state level and at the federal. Without question, "finding the courthouse," or at least the *right* courthouse, had become a perplexing problem.

Today, the situation is no less knotty, even when the courts handling civil matters exclusively are eliminated from consideration. In fact, it has become even more intricate. No two state court systems are identical, and the names of the courts tend to vary regardless of function. The purpose of this chapter is to unravel these complexities of American court configuration and to analyze the roles of the various courts in criminal justice processing.

The State Courts

This is the house that justice built,
this is the castle of fair play;
this is the place where wise men sit,
for the law and truth they belay.

The drums of crime, of lust and strife,
these are the souls we see;
in the righteous house that justice built,
here on this star-spangled street.

— Anonymous, c. 1980

These few lines of verse, found scribbled on a restroom wall in the basement of the Ross County Courthouse in Chillicothe, Ohio, are expressive of a role that many state courts play in the administration of justice. Exactly what type of justice the author of these words had in mind, however, is only open to speculation, for the particular courthouse in which they appeared houses many different types of courts. The writings are somewhat curious and paradoxical as well. Some of the words and even whole lines seem to have been taken from a Milton MacKaye article published in the *New York Evening Post* half a century earlier on January 10, 1930.[2] The paradox is in the fact that MacKaye's commentary was hardly one that praised the "righteous house that justice built." Rather, as a firsthand description of a busy magistrate's court in New York City, it was part of a series entitled "The Magistrate Racket" and addressed only the dismal aspects of the American court system. Or perhaps the anonymous author's poetic celebrations were written in a spirit of sarcasm, for there are thousands of tribunals across the United States — small and large, rural and urban — and a number of them are quite chaotic in their approach to the administration of justice.

Ross County courthouse,
Chillicothe, Ohio

State Court Infrastructure

Characteristic of the state court systems are that no two are exactly alike and that the names of the various courts vary widely regardless of function. For example, all states have major trial courts devoted to criminal cases. In Ohio and Pennsylvania, these are called courts of common pleas; in California, they are known as superior courts; in New York, they are supreme courts — a designation typically used elsewhere for appeals courts. Moreover, while Michigan's major trial courts use the label of circuit court, within the corporate limits of the city of Detroit they are called the recorder's court.

The many names, functions, and types that characterize state court structures have resulted from the fact that each state is a sovereign government insofar as the enactment of a penal code and the setting up of enforcement machinery are concerned. Thus, in each of the 50 jurisdictions, the court systems grew differently—sometimes in an unplanned, sporadic way—generally guided by different cultural traditions, demographic pressures, legal and political philosophies, and needs for justice administration. Yet, despite this apparent confusion, there is nevertheless a clear-cut structure within all the state court systems. State judiciaries are divided into three, four, and sometimes five specific tiers, each having separate functions and jurisdictions.

As outlined in Exhibit 10.1, the courts of last resort are at the uppermost level, occupying the highest rung in the judicial ladder. These are the appeals courts. Virtually all states have a court of last resort, but depending on the jurisdiction, the specific name will vary—supreme court, supreme court of appeals, or perhaps simply court of appeals. In addition, in states such as Texas and Oklahoma, there are two courts of last resort, one for criminal cases and one for all others.

Immediately below the courts of last resort in more than half the states are the intermediate appellate courts. Located primarily in the more populous states, these courts have been structured to relieve the case-load burden on the highest courts. Like the highest courts, they are known by various names; often the names are similar to those of the courts above them in the hierarchy (appeals courts), as well as below them (superior courts).

The major trial courts are the courts of general jurisdiction, where felony cases are heard. All states have various combinations of these, and depending on the locale, they might be called superior, circuit, district, or some other designation.

The lower courts, often referred to in legal nomenclature as inferior, misdemeanor, minor, or courts of limited jurisdiction, exist in numerous combinations in every state. Variously named county, magistrate, police, municipal, justice of the peace, and justice courts, as well as dozens of other designations, they are the entry point for most defendants being processed through the criminal justice system, and the only level at which infractions and most misdemeanors are processed.

The *jurisdiction* of each court varies by geography, subject matter, and hierarchy. Courts are authorized to hear and decide disputes arising within specific political boundaries—a city, borough, township, county, or group of counties. In addition, some courts are limited to specific matters—for example, misdemeanors or civil actions versus all other types of cases. There are family courts that decide on juvenile and domestic relations matters, probate courts whose jurisdiction is limited to the handling of wills and the administration of decedents' estates, and many others. Jurisdiction can also be viewed as limited, original, and appellate:

1. *Courts of limited jurisdiction*, the lower courts, do not have powers that extend to the overall administration of justice, they do not try felony cases, and they do not possess appellate authority.
2. *Courts of original jurisdiction*, the major trial courts, have the power and authority to try and decide any case, including appeals from a lower court.
3. *Courts of appellate jurisdiction*, the appeals courts, are limited in their jurisdiction to decisions on matters of appeal from lower courts and trial courts.

Lower courts have often been labeled inferior courts. Some have alleged that this designation comes from the lesser quality of justice and courtroom professionalism apparent in them. The term *inferior*, however, actually refers to the fact that the jurisdiction of these courts is limited.

Levels of jurisdiction in state courts

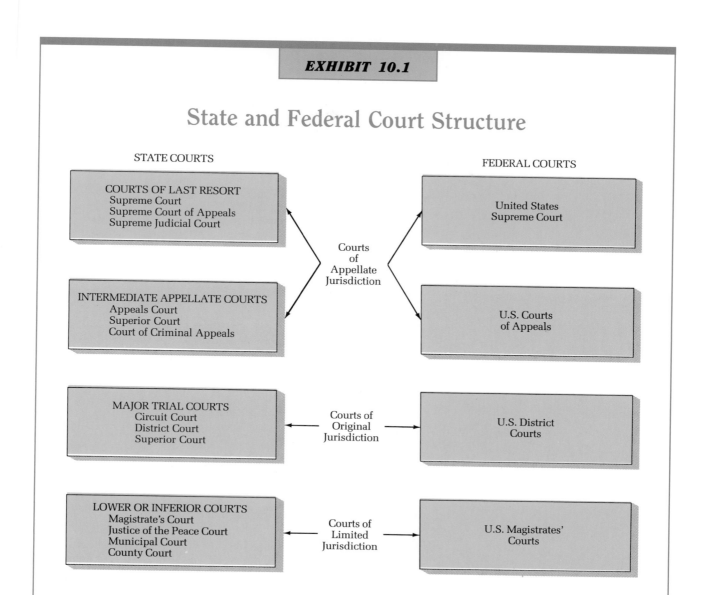

EXHIBIT 10.1

State and Federal Court Structure

STATE COURTS

FEDERAL COURTS

COURTS OF LAST RESORT
Supreme Court
Supreme Court of Appeals
Supreme Judicial Court

United States
Supreme Court

Courts
of
Appellate
Jurisdiction

INTERMEDIATE APPELLATE COURTS
Appeals Court
Superior Court
Court of Criminal Appeals

U.S. Courts
of Appeals

MAJOR TRIAL COURTS
Circuit Court
District Court
Superior Court

Courts of
Original
Jurisdiction

U.S. District
Courts

LOWER OR INFERIOR COURTS
Magistrate's Court
Justice of the Peace Court
Municipal Court
County Court

Courts of
Limited
Jurisdiction

U.S. Magistrates'
Courts

Court systems may be simple or complex in their organizational structure. The state of Florida has a simple four-tier court system of organization (see Exhibit 10.2). The county courts are the courts of limited jurisdiction and the circuit courts are those of original jurisdiction. The supreme court and the district courts of appeal are two levels of appellate jurisdiction. This system can be contrasted with the complexity of the system in New York State, which also has a four-tier system (see Exhibit 10.3). The two lowermost levels are the courts of limited jurisdiction, which are separated by discrete functions and geography. The supreme courts are the courts of original jurisdiction, and the upper courts, like those of Florida, are the appellate courts.

In the pages that follow, each level of the state court system is examined in more detail. The greatest amount of discussion will be about the lower courts, for it is there that most defendants begin judicial processing. The chief function of the trial court—the criminal trial—is addressed in a separate chapter.

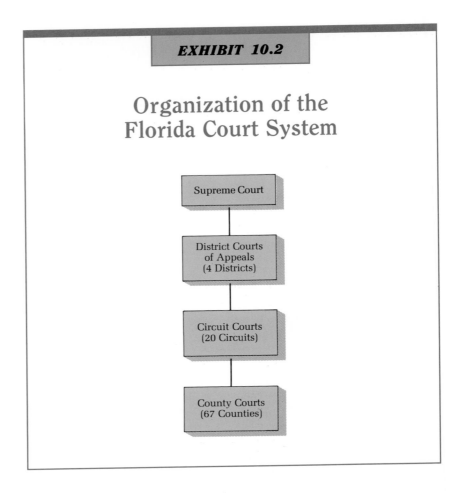

Organization of the Florida Court System

Supreme Court

District Courts of Appeals (4 Districts)

Circuit Courts (20 Circuits)

County Courts (67 Counties)

Courts of Limited Jurisdiction

The lower criminal courts represent a stepchild of the American judicial system.
—H. Ted Rubin, 1976

Courts of limited jurisdiction are the entry point for judicial processing.

The **courts of limited jurisdiction**, or **lower courts**—more than 13,000 in number across the nation—are the entry point for criminal judicial processing. They handle all minor criminal offenses, such as prostitution, drunkenness, petty larceny, disorderly conduct, and the myriad violations of traffic laws and city and county ordinances. In addition, they hear most civil cases and conduct inquests. For defendants charged with felonies, the lower courts have the authority to hold initial appearances and preliminary hearings, and to make bail decisions.

In matters of minor law violation, the lower court conducts all aspects of the judicial process—from initial appearance to sentencing. Given the large number of felony cases that are initially processed in this part of the state court structure, the lower courts ultimately deal, in one way or another, with more than 90 percent of all criminal cases.

Historically, the lower courts have been the most significant, yet typically the most neglected, of all the courts. The significance of these courts to the administration of justice lies not only in the sheer number of defendants who pass through them, but also in their jurisdiction over many of the

EXHIBIT 10.3

Organization of the New York State Court System

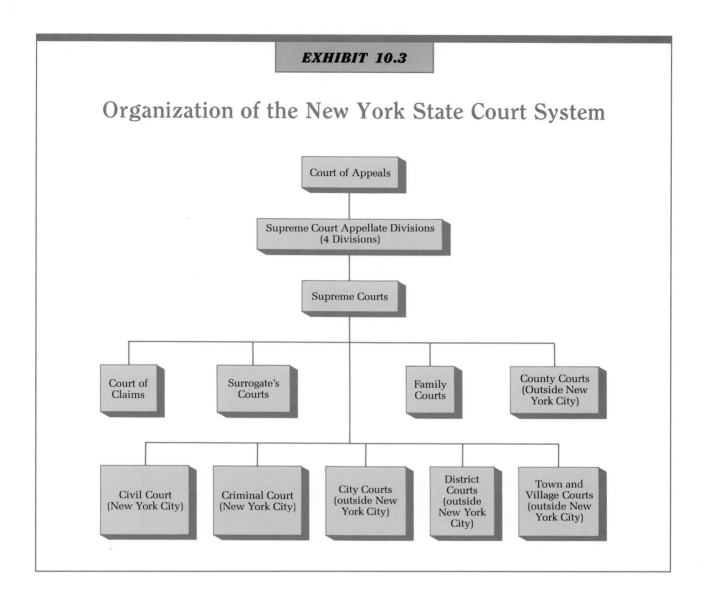

offenses that represent the initial stage of an individual's criminal career. As pointed out by the President's Commission on Law Enforcement and Administration of Justice, most convicted felons have prior misdemeanor convictions, and although the likelihood of diverting an offender from a career in crime is greatest at the time of his or her first brush with the law, the lower courts do not deal effectively with those who come before them.[3]

In 1919, in his address to the members of the New York Bar Association, the late Supreme Court Justice Charles Evans Hughes commented on the proper role of the lower courts:

> The Supreme Court of the United States and the Court of Appeals will take care of themselves. Look after the courts of the poor, who stand most in the need of justice. The security of the Republic will be found in the treatment of the poor and the ignorant; in indifference to their misery and helplessness lies disaster.[4]

"I'm afraid this is a matter for the lower court . . ."

Drawing by Arnie Levin, *National Law Journal.*

Trial *de novo*: A new trial, on appeal from a lower court to a court of general jurisdiction.

Problems with justice of the peace courts.

Although Justice Hughes might have been better advised to make his reference not only to the poor but also to the millions of others who pass through the lower courts each year, his point was well intentioned and unquestionably correct. But in the decades that followed, few changes in the lower courts seem to have occurred. In 1967, for example, reporter Howard James of the *Christian Science Monitor* remarked on the state of the lower courts:

> I have seen a wide gap between what we say is true about justice in the United States and what is really true. If I am entitled to an opinion, it is that what I have found in the minor courts has major impact on the problems our society faces today.[5]

And as recently as the 1970s, the National Advisory Commission on Criminal Justice Standards and Goals echoed the impressions of both Hughes and James, and outlined the three major problems that continued to plague the lower courts: (1) neglect by bar associations, the higher courts, and the government agencies; (2) the volume and nature of their case loads; and (3) the **trial *de novo*** system.[6] (See Exhibit 10.4.)

With the beginning of the 1980s, little has changed with respect to the operations of the lower courts. However, there are some differences in the nature of these enduring problems between rural and urban lower courts.

Justice of the Peace Courts

Justice of the peace courts, which are similar to aldermans' and mayors' courts, developed at a time when a lack of effective transportation and communication tended to isolate small communities, thus preventing them from having a quick means for hearing minor criminal cases and for exercising local community authority. The **justice of the peace** was generally not required to be an attorney, and was typically best known as the person who performed marriages. The justice was either appointed or elected and usually had strong community ties. He heard ordinance violations, issued search and arrest warrants, determined bail, arraigned defendants, and processed civil cases involving limited dollar amounts.[7]

The problems with this judicial system were, and still are, numerous. First, justices of the peace, referred to as JPs, not only had minimal, if any, legal training, but in addition dealt with legal matters in saloons and in filling stations where they worked, or in other undignified settings.

Second, methods of compensation were problematic. In some jurisdictions the JP was paid from the court costs he would assess convicted offenders. If the defendant was acquitted, the JP could assess no costs. Thus it was in the justice's interest to convict as many persons as possible.

In recent years, justice of the peace courts have been eliminated in some states, and have been upgraded in others. But many of the difficulties still persist. For example, although *Tumey* v. *Ohio* in 1927 declared that the practice of paying JPs from costs assessed defendants only when they were convicted was unconstitutional,[8] the President's Commission on Law Enforcement and Administration of Justice found the practice to be still current in some areas. Furthermore, as recently as 1977, the U.S. Supreme Court invalidated a Georgia law that provided JPs with a $5 fee for each search warrant they issued to the police.[9]

The lack of legal training among justices of the peace and the undignified nature of their court settings still endures in several jurisdictions. Reports

EXHIBIT 10.4

The Problems of the Lower Courts

The lower courts of most states share three problems.

The first is their position on the bottom rung of the judicial ladder, which results in neglect by those forces that should be scrutinizing and aiding the level of court performance — bar associations, the state supreme court, the press, government agencies, and citizen groups. The neglect is so severe that members of the legal profession and of the judiciary often are unaware of the number, names, functions, or identity of the judges of the lower courts. The inferior status of the lower courts and the traditional view that their work is ministerial, monotonous, and legally unchallenging also is reflected in the use of part-time support personnel, low salaries, and inadequate facilities. As a result, the lower courts generally tend to attract prosecutors, defense counsel, clerks, and judges of a caliber lower than normally encountered in the courts of general jurisdiction.

The second problem is the volume and nature of the case load. The overwhelming part of the case load of the lower courts consists of traffic violations and public intoxication prosecutions. These cases seldom raise any issue that requires consideration and decision and they encourage perfunctory, summary dispositions, often referred to as assembly-line justice. Assembly-line justice minimizes the likelihood that cases will be heard fully and fairly and virtually precludes any meaningful correctional disposition.

The third problem is the trial *de novo* system. This precludes effective review and monitoring of the work and decisions of the lower courts by appellate tribunals, and enables judges of the lower courts, unlike their general jurisdiction judicial counterparts, to operate with improper procedures and under erroneous assumptions of the substantive law.

SOURCE: National Advisory Commission on Criminal Justice Standards and Goals, *Courts* (Washington, D.C.: U.S. Government Printing Office, 1973), pp. 161–162.

by the *New York Times* and CBS-TV found that in South Carolina and other states, the average JP had only a high school education and some had never opened a law book; their courtrooms included kitchens, barns, and porches; and their dispensing of justice was only a part-time endeavor.[10] Similarly, the Louisiana constitution of 1921, still in effect today, provides that "Justices of the Peace shall be of good moral character, freeholders and qualified electors, able to read and write the English language correctly, and shall possess such other qualifications as may be prescribed by law."[11] Legal training was not considered a prerequisite for dispensing justice.

Conditions that led to the development and growth of justice of the peace courts no longer exist. Modern means of transportation and communication have eliminated the total isolation of even the most remote rural outposts. But as long as JPs can convince the electorate and legislature that their closeness to the community and its interests is advantageous, the justice of the peace court will continue to exist. JP courts persist, for example, throughout Delaware, not only in rural areas but also in the densely populated metropolitan county of New Castle.

Alternatives to the JP courts in rural America are the county courts and their variants, which do not involve the more negative aspects of the justice of

The Law West of the Pecos

In history and folklore, Judge Roy Bean of the West Texas frontier is a familiar character. Books have been written about him, and the 1972 Warner Brothers production *The Life and Times of Judge Roy Bean* cast actor Paul Newman as the colorful seat of the rural bench. Although Bean was hardly a Paul Newman lookalike, he was a caricature and exaggeration of everything that could possibly be wrong with a rural magistrate, and his methods of distributing justice were indeed a satirical rendition of the justice of the peace court.

Born in the hills of Mason County, Kentucky, in 1825, Roy Bean's early life hardly reflected the qualities and experiences one would hope to find in a person charged with making decisions in the cause of justice. In 1847 he shot a man in a barroom brawl; several years later, he killed a Mexican army officer in a gun duel over a woman, after which he was hanged (but survived); during the Civil War he operated with Confederate irregulars; and following the war he was a blockade runner in San Antonio.

Bean's career in frontier justice began in 1882 when he drifted across the Pecos River into West Texas, dispensing whiskey from a tent. First at a place called Eagle's Nest on the Rio Grande,

and later beside a railroad bed that ran through Dead Man's Canyon just north of the Mexican border, he plied his trade as a saloonkeeper. His saloon was called the "Jersey Lilly," and the spot was Langtry, Texas—both named after actress Lily Langtry, whom Bean idolized but had never met.

The records of Pecos County, Texas, document that Roy Bean was appointed justice of the peace on August 2, 1882, by the county commissioner's court, and that he fully qualified for the position by submitting a $1,000 bond on December 6, 1882.

As a rural magistrate, he dispensed both justice and beer from the same bar, frequently interrupting his court to serve liquor. He knew little of law or criminal procedure, and his methods of handling cases were often bizarre. Once he reportedly fined a dead man $40 for carrying a concealed weapon; on another occasion he threatened to hang a lawyer for using profanity in the courtroom (the attorney had stated that he planned to *habeas corpus* his client). And in one memorable trial Judge Bean freed a man accused of murdering a Chinese railroad worker because he could not find any law that made it a crime "to kill a Chinaman."

Bean's antics became so widely known that passengers passing through Langtry often stopped to look at the "Law West of the Pecos," as the judge called himself. These visits sparked more tales, which encouraged Bean to hand down more of his infamous "decisions." In fact, he spent much of his time working on the diffusion of his own legend.

But the "Law West of the Pecos" was anything but just, for Bean was ignorant, biased, and corrupt. He allowed his jurors (when he had them) to drink profusely before considering a verdict; he pocketed most of the fines he collected; he confiscated money and property from bodies brought to him in his role as coroner; he stuffed ballot boxes to ensure his reelection; and although he could hang a horse thief without batting an eye, when his friends were accused of murder, leniency always prevailed.

Besides his involvement—or lack of involvement—with law and order, Roy Bean spent much of his time worshiping Lily Langtry. As legend tells it, his most precious moment came in the spring of 1888, when the woman whose tattered picture he carried in his pocket played in San Antonio. Free of alcoholic fumes and in a front row seat, Bean watched the

the peace system. As lower courts, they handle minor offenses, civil issues, and the pretrial aspects of felony processing. County justices usually have at least some legal training; the dispensing of justice occurs in more formal courts of law staffed by judges, clerks, and other personnel on state or county payrolls; and the trappings of fees for service are absent. But as with all the lower courts, they tend to reflect the shortcomings characteristic of courts of limited jurisdiction.

woman who had tortured his mind for years. But no one would introduce him to her, and sadly he returned to Langtry and his "Jersey Lilly," thinking only of a love he could never have.

For the next eight years he continued his antics in frontier justice, until he finally overstepped his bounds. In 1896, after a count of votes cast for Bean proved their number to be well in excess of the Langtry population, he was removed from the bench. For the next seven years, until his death in 1903, Bean continued as a saloonkeeper, having failed to achieve his lifelong dream of meeting Miss Langtry. Ironically, only months after his death, she visited his saloon while on a tour through Texas. The Langtry townspeople gave Bean's revolver to Lily, and she kept it until her own death in 1929. Today, Roy Bean's "Jersey Lilly" still stands, and Langtry remains a small town in Texas with a population of some 75 persons.

SOURCES: Horace Bell, *On the Old West Coast* (New York: William Morrow, 1930); C.L. Sonnichsen, *Roy Bean: Law West of the Pecos* (Old Greenwich, Conn.: Devin-Adair, 1943).

Judge Roy Bean's combined courthouse and saloon, the "Jersey Lilly," in Langtry, Texas. Named for his idol, the actress Lily Langtry, it was the setting for Bean's wild-west justice from 1882 until 1903.

Municipal Courts

The urban counterpart of the justice of the peace and county courts are the municipal courts, also called magistrate's courts. In jurisdictions where the judicial system has formally separated the processing of criminal and civil cases, these lower courts may be known as criminal courts or police courts.

The functions of the municipal courts are the same as those of the county courts, and many of the problems are similar. But municipal courts have the added difficulty of large case loads and assembly-line justice. Some magistrates, in the face of heavy work loads, exercise wide discretion in ordering certain cases dismissed and in abbreviating the law. In addition, with lesser offenses such as prostitution, drunkenness, and loitering, groups of defendants are processed en masse and dispensed with quickly.

During the early 1920s, legal scholars Roscoe Pound and Felix Frankfurter participated in an analysis sponsored by The Cleveland Foundation of criminal justice administration in that midwestern city. Their report included a scathing denunciation of Cleveland's municipal court, noting that it was devoid of any quality and commenting that it was not unlike an early nineteenth-century police court.[12] Some 50 years later, H. Ted Rubin, former judge and assistant executive director of the Institute for Court Management in Denver, Colorado, returned to the Cleveland Municipal Court and described it as follows:

> **The Criminal Division of the Cleveland Municipal Court is located in the Police Building at 21st and Payne. The courtroom is well worn, crowded, and noisy. Row on row of benches are peopled with defendants out on bail, witnesses, friends and relatives of defendants, attorneys, social service personnel, and others. Most attorneys sit at the several counsel tables at the front of the room. The judge is flanked by a representative of the clerk's office to his right and two police officers. To his left is his bailiff. An assistant police prosecutor is present on one end of the judge's bench, an assistant county prosecutor on the other. A stenotype reporter was added during April 1971, and sits along the bar in front of the judge immediately next to the defendants and counsel who appear. The arraignments, hearings, and conferences which occur at the bench are largely inaudible beyond the second or third row of the spectator gallery. Witnesses generally testify from standing positions off to the side of the judge. There is little dignity to the setting. Jailed defendants are brought in and out from a door behind the judge and off to his right. People leaving the courtroom go out a door in the front of the room and off to the judge's left, where outside noise enters the courtroom as the door opens and closes.[13]**

According to Rubin the situation in the Cleveland Municipal Court in the early 1970s can be considered mild when compared with that in the New York criminal courts of the early 1980s. The criminal court in Brooklyn, New York, for example, is a court of limited jurisdiction that handles minor criminal offenses as well as pretrial processing of all felony cases. Observations made during 1980 and 1981 showed a chaotic system of justice.[14] On a Monday morning during the summer of 1981 in one particular courtroom that dealt almost exclusively with preliminary hearings and arraignments of felony cases, the rows of benches were packed with hundreds of spectators. Presumably, these were the families, friends, and acquaintances of the defendants, together with other interested parties, and possibly sightseers. Although many sat in a dignified manner, attempting to follow the proceedings, others

Conditions in the criminal court in Brooklyn, New York

conversed, ate, slept, played cards, read, or attended to other matters. Children played at their mothers' feet; an artist sketched the posture of the magistrate; and a Brooklyn College student read an accounting text while his female acquaintance attempted to solve the mystery of a Rubik's cube.

The rumble of sound made paying attention to the matters of the court impossible. Only those in the first few rows of the courtroom, which were reserved for attorneys, could hear the words of the judge, defendant, prosecutor, bailiff, and defense. An occasional thunderclap of laughter or crying or boisterousness would alert the clerk to remind the crowd that it was a court of law.

Along the aisles, sides, and rear walls of the courtroom were dozens of police, parole, and probation officers. They complained that the docket was crowded again that day, that their case would not be heard for at least three hours: "There goes another day off," said one patrolman. Another responded, "Doesn't pay to make an arrest any more."

Just beyond the rail that separated the bench from the spectators was the quarters of the Legal Aid lawyers. It was a long table piled high with case materials. Court personnel huddled around the table to discuss cases during the proceedings, while defendants, mothers, fathers, spouses, attorneys, police officers, and probation and parole officers hung over the rail to glance at the materials, plead their cases, or otherwise elicit information.

To the left of the magistrate's bench was a door that led to the detention pens where defendants awaited their turn. To the right of the bench, within the courtroom, was another holding area, where the faces of the accused were grim and their hands cuffed.

Justice was swift and to the point. A preliminary hearing in a felony case took only ten minutes, or five, or two. In one hearing, after the charges of robbery, assault, and possession of a deadly weapon were read, the following exchange took place:

MAGISTRATE: Son, do you understand the charges as they have been read?
DEFENDANT: Yes, sir.
MAGISTRATE: How do you plead?
DEFENDANT: Not guilty, sir.
MAGISTRATE: Is the state's case ready?
PROSECUTOR: Yes, your honor.
MAGISTRATE: Is the defense's case ready?
ATTORNEY: Yes, your honor.
MAGISTRATE: Bind him over for trial!

The entire proceeding lasted a total of 27 seconds. In another case:

MAGISTRATE: Where's your lawyer?
DEFENDANT: I don't know, he was supposed to be here.
MAGISTRATE: Postponement.

With that the magistrate rose to his feet, called the court to order, chastised those present for the misdeeds of those who had failed to be in the court, addressed the fact that justice could not be otherwise served, and called a recess.

Other urban courts reflect similar styles of criminal processing. The basic problem stems from case overloads, and the result is often shorthand

Too often, when our citizens seek a dignified place of deliberation in which to resolve their controversies, they find instead aesthetic revulsion. They bear witness — not to dignity, but to deterioration, not to actual justice delivered, but to the perception of justice denied or, worse, justice degraded. — Sol Wachtler, Chief Judge, New York State, 1985

justice. Defendants may not be accorded the full range of procedural safeguards, and the several millions who appear annually before the urban courts run the risk of conviction and sentence in situations in which constitutional guidelines may not be fully observed.

Major Trial Courts

Major trial courts, or courts of original jurisdiction, try all criminal and civil cases.

The major **trial courts**, or **courts of original jurisdiction**, are authorized to try *all* criminal and civil cases. Such courts, numbering in excess of 3,000 across the nation, handle about 10 percent of the defendants originally brought before the lower courts who are charged with felonies and serious misdemeanors (the balance having been already disposed of at the lower court level).

In terms of nomenclature, distinctions between some types of lower courts and trial courts can often be confusing. They may be called circuit, district, superior courts, or they may have other titles (see Exhibit 10.6). But there are some exceptions. For example, Indiana has both circuit courts and superior courts, and in Indianapolis the court is simply called "Criminal Court." While many county courts may be part of a state's lower courts, as described earlier, other county courts may actually be circuit or district courts and hence are major trial courts. Also, a given county courthouse may often

---

EXHIBIT 10.6

The State Felony Courts

Circuit Court

Alabama, Arkansas, Florida, Hawaii, Illinois, Indiana,* Kentucky, Maryland, Michigan, Mississippi, Missouri, Oregon, South Carolina, South Dakota, Tennessee, Virginia, West Virginia, Wisconsin

Court of Common Pleas

Ohio, Pennsylvania

District Court

Colorado, Idaho, Iowa, Kansas, Louisiana, Minnesota, Montana, Nebraska, Nevada, New Mexico, North Dakota, Oklahoma, Texas, Utah, Wyoming

Superior Court

Alaska, Arizona, California, Connecticut, Delaware, District of Columbia, Georgia, Indiana,* Maine, Massachusetts, New Hampshire, New Jersey, North Carolina, Rhode Island, Vermont, Washington

Supreme Court

New York

---

* Concurrent jurisdiction for felonies.

SOURCE: U.S. Department of Justice, U.S. Bureau of Census, *The National Survey of Court Organization* (Washington, D.C.: U.S. Government Printing Office, 1973).

serve as both a lower court and a trial court. For example, when several counties are politically grouped together in a **judicial circuit**, it is customary for a judge to hold court in each county in turn. The judge moves from county to county within the circuit, and the local county courthouse becomes the circuit court during the judge's term there; the phrase "riding the circuit" derives from this practice.[15]

The administration of criminal justice in the major trial courts tends to be less problematic than it is in the courts of limited jurisdiction. Judges are lawyers and members of the bar, and hence are better equipped to deal with the complex issues of felony cases: most are salaried, full-time justices and are not tarnished by the fee-for-service payment structure; the adjudication process is generally cloaked in the formalities of procedural criminal law and due process; and as courts of original jurisdiction, the trial courts are **courts of record**, which means a full transcript of the proceedings is made for virtually all cases. However, this does not mean that the trial courts are without difficulties. As seen in later chapters, there are procedural problems involving bail, indictment, plea negotiation, sentencing, and judicial discretion that can affect the fairness of trial court justice.

As a final note here, some comment seems warranted to illustrate more fully the separate roles and relationships between the lower and trial courts. The criminal case processing in the city of Kalamazoo, Michigan (shown in Exhibit 10.7), generally reflects what is typical throughout the nation. *All* felonies and misdemeanors begin in the lower court, called the district court in that jurisdiction. While the misdemeanor cases remain in the lower court through sentencing, felony processing shifts to the circuit court, the major trial court, at arraignment. This is in contrast to jurisdictions in which the *entire* felony process occurs in the trial court. The felony case flow in Marietta, Georgia (see Exhibit 10.8), is an example of this latter type of processing.

Appellate Courts

In law and criminal justice, the word *appeal* refers to the review by a higher court of the judgment of a lower court. Thus, **appellate jurisdiction** is restricted to matters of appeal and review; it cannot try cases as in the courts of original jurisdiction. However, this is not to say that the work load of these courts is light. Filings for appeal emerge not only from criminal cases, but from civil matters as well. In fact, the majority of appeals come out of civil suits. In the area of domestic relations alone, for example, the number of appeals filed requesting reviews of decisions rendered in matters of child custody rights, dependent support, alimony, and property settlement runs into the tens of thousands.

As a result, there are intermediate courts of appeal in more than half the states. If an attorney complies with the court's rules for appealing a case, the court must hear it. (This assumes that the matter is appealable — an issue discussed in Chapter 13.)

The intermediate courts of appeal serve to relieve the state's highest court from hearing every case. An unfavorable decision from an intermediate appeals court, however, does not automatically guarantee a hearing by the state supreme court, the court of last resort in each state. It has the power to choose which cases will be placed on its docket — a characteristic of the highest court in every jurisdiction.

EXHIBIT 10.7

Steps in the Criminal Process in Kalamazoo, Michigan

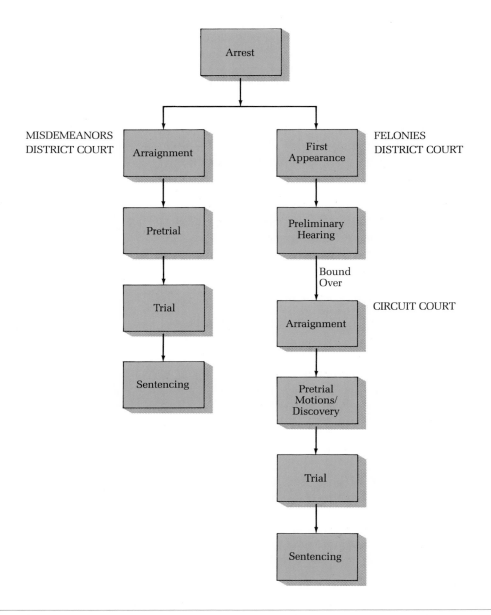

SOURCE: Law Enforcement Assistance Administration, *A Cross-City Comparison of Felony Case Processing* (Washington, D.C.: U.S. Government Printing Office, 1979), p. 92.

EXHIBIT 10.8

Steps in the Felony Process in Marietta, Georgia

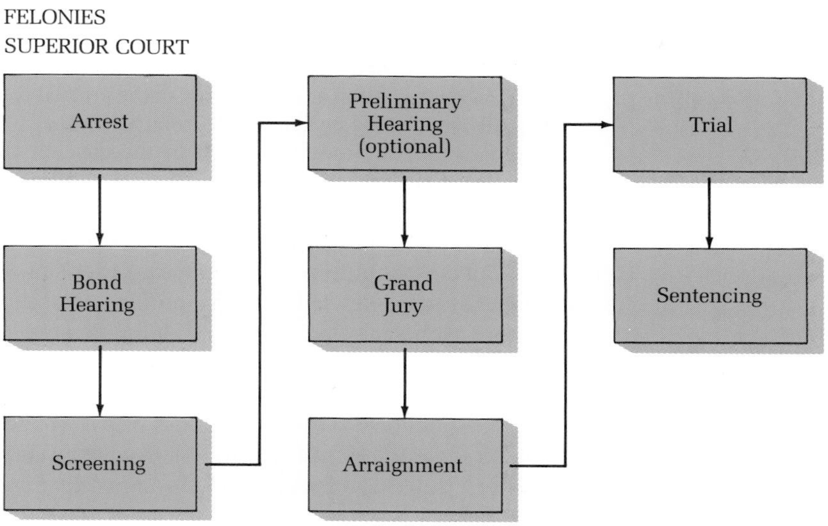

FELONIES
SUPERIOR COURT
Arrest
Bond Hearing
Screening
Preliminary Hearing (optional)
Grand Jury
Arraignment
Trial
Sentencing

SOURCE: Law Enforcement Assistance Administration, *A Cross-City Comparison of Felony Case Processing* (Washington, D.C.: U.S. Government Printing Office, 1979), p. 82.

Reform and Unification of State Courts

The state courts have many problems. There are awkward matters of procedure, but more pertinent to this discussion are problems of organization, structure, and deployment.

For most of the twentieth century, various federal, state, and city commissions and foundations have examined the state courts, and their recommendations for reorganization have remained unchanged through the years:

- unify felony and misdemeanor courts
- create single, unified state court systems
- centralize administrative responsibility
- abolish the justice of the peace courts
- increase judicial personnel
- improve physical facilities

Perhaps the most pressing issue in this regard is the matter of court unification. As a more recent study by the National Advisory Commission on Criminal Justice Standards and Goals has emphasized:

> **State courts should be organized into a unified judicial system financed by the State and administered through a statewide court ad-**

ministrator or administrative judge under the supervision of the chief justice of the State supreme court.

All trial courts should be unified into a single trial court with general criminal as well as civil jurisdiction. Criminal jurisdiction now in courts of limited jurisdiction should be placed in these unified trial courts of general jurisdiction, with the exception of certain traffic violations. The State supreme court should promulgate rules for the conduct of minor as well as major criminal prosecutions.

All judicial functions in the trial courts should be performed by full-time judges. All judges should possess law degrees and be members of the bar.

A transcription or other record of the pretrial court proceedings and the trial should be kept in all criminal cases.

The appeal procedure should be the same for all cases.[16]

Court unification, however, is more easily recommended than implemented. Some unification has occurred in Arizona, Illinois, North Carolina, Oklahoma, and Washington, and each year other states entertain proposals for a unified system. But few such proposals have been adopted due to the political, philosophical, and pragmatic dimensions involved. Local governments wish to retain control of their local courts; some judges fear that they would lose their status and discretion; nonlawyer judges fear that they would lose their jobs; political parties fear a loss of patronage opportunities; local municipalities fear the loss of revenues derived from court fines and fees; and many lawyers, judges, and prosecutors in all jurisdictions are simply resistive to change.[17]

The problem of overloaded court dockets is even more pervasive than court unification, for the costs that would be involved in expanding staff and facilities are well beyond the resources and willingness of most jurisdictions. Further, it seems that the overloading is only getting worse. Over the last decade the number of cases filed in state courts of general and limited jurisdiction has increased by 4 percent annually. During 1983 alone, there were almost 85 million filings, and although the majority of these were traffic cases quickly disposed of, there were still more than 25 million civil, criminal, and juvenile matters that required the courts' attention (see Exhibit 10.9). In addition to these, there were almost 200,000 cases filed at the appellate level.[18]

The Federal Judiciary

The judicial power of the United States shall be vested in one Supreme Court, and in such inferior courts as the Congress may from time to time ordain and establish.
— The Constitution of the United States

Unlike the state court systems, the federal judiciary has a unified structure with jurisdiction throughout the United States and its territories. But the federal court system is also complex. It has a four-tier structure similar to that in most of the states (see Exhibit 10.10). Although it handles fewer cases than the states, its scope is considerably greater. It has the responsibility for the enforcement of the following:

1. all federal codes (criminal, civil, and administrative) in all 50 states, U.S. territories, and the District of Columbia

Distribution of Cases Filed in Courts of General and Limited Jurisdiction in 1983

TYPE OF CASE

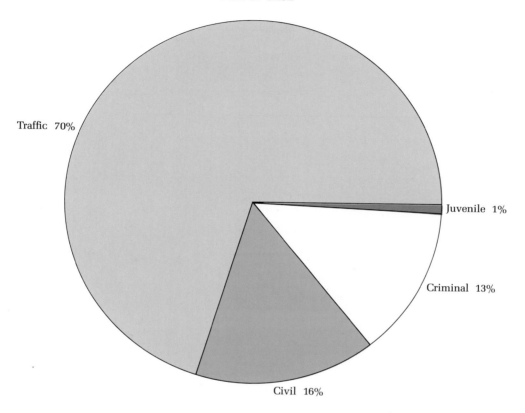

Traffic 70%

Juvenile 1%

Criminal 13%

Civil 16%

TOTAL 100%

Note: There were 80,580,851 cases filed during 1983 in 46 states and the District of Columbia. An additional 4 million cases are estimated for Indiana, Mississippi, Ohio, and Nevada, from which data were unavailable.

SOURCE: *Case Filings in State Courts, 1983.* Bureau of Justice Statistics Bulletin. October, 1984.

2. local codes and ordinances in the territories of Guam, the Virgin Islands, the Canal Zone, and the Northern Mariana Islands

In addition, the U.S. Supreme Court has ultimate appellate jurisdiction over the federal appeals courts, the state courts of appeal, the District of Columbia Court of Appeals, and the Supreme Court of Puerto Rico.

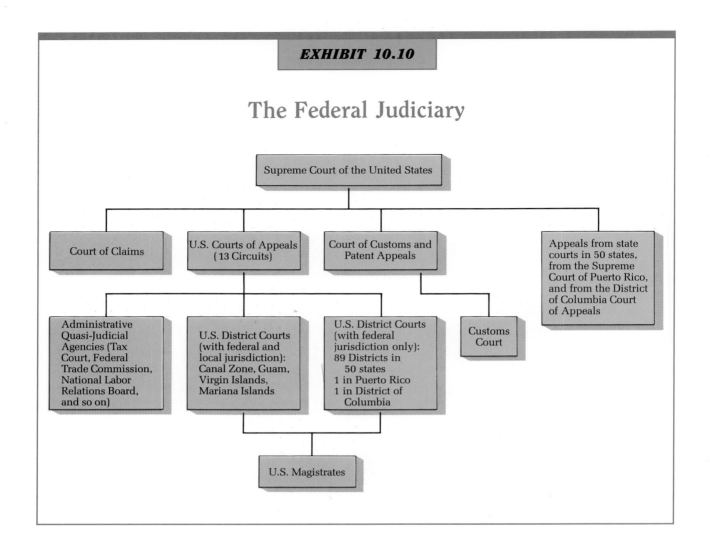

EXHIBIT 10.10

The Federal Judiciary

Supreme Court of the United States

Court of Claims

U.S. Courts of Appeals (13 Circuits)

Court of Customs and Patent Appeals

Appeals from state courts in 50 states, from the Supreme Court of Puerto Rico, and from the District of Columbia Court of Appeals

Administrative Quasi-Judicial Agencies (Tax Court, Federal Trade Commission, National Labor Relations Board, and so on)

U.S. District Courts (with federal and local jurisdiction): Canal Zone, Guam, Virgin Islands, Mariana Islands

U.S. District Courts (with federal jurisdiction only): 89 Districts in 50 states 1 in Puerto Rico 1 in District of Columbia

Customs Court

U.S. Magistrates

U.S. Commissioners' and U.S. Magistrates' Courts

Historically, U.S. commissioners occupied positions comparable to justices of the peace in the state court systems. Established by an act of Congress at the beginning of the twentieth century, commissioners had the authority to issue search and arrest warrants, arraign defendants, fix bail, hold preliminary hearings, and try petty offense cases on certain federal reservations. Many of the criticisms leveled at the justice of the peace system, however, were also applicable to the U.S. commissioners' courts. In 1967, the President's Commission on Law Enforcement and Administration of Justice found that 30 percent of the more than 700 commissioners were not lawyers, that all but seven had outside employment due to the part-time nature of the work, that commissioners' private businesses often took precedence over official duties, and that the number of commissioners in many districts had no relation to the number that might be needed. The President's Commission concluded by recommending that the system be either abolished or drastically altered.[19]

The phaseout of U.S. commissioners and the establishment of U.S. magistrates

On the basis of the commission's findings, together with an examination of the situation by the Senate Judiciary Committee, the federal Magistrate's Act, passed by Congress in 1968, provided for a three-year phasing out of the office of the U.S. commissioner. The act also established **U.S. magistrates** — lawyers whose powers are limited to trying lesser misdemeanors, setting bail in more serious cases, and assisting the district courts in various legal matters.[20] In 1976, their authority was expanded to include the issuance of search and arrest warrants, the review of civil rights and *habeas corpus* petitions, and the conducting of pretrial conferences in both civil and criminal hearings. Magistrates can be both full-time and part-time jurists and all are appointed by the federal district court judges.

United States District Courts

The sword of human justice is about to fall upon your guilty head.
— Isaac C. Parker, federal district court judge, 1876

The U.S. district courts were created by the federal Judiciary Act, passed by Congress on September 24, 1789. Originally there were 13 courts, one for each of the original states, but by the early 1980s there were 95 — 89 distributed throughout the 50 states, and one each in the District of Columbia, Puerto Rico, Guam, the Canal Zone, the Virgin Islands, and the Northern Mariana Islands.

The **U.S. district courts** are the trial courts of the federal system and the District of Columbia — the courts of original jurisdiction. They have dominion over cases involving violations of federal laws, including bank robbery, civil rights abuses, mail fraud, counterfeiting, smuggling, kidnapping, and crimes involving transportation across state lines. The district courts try cases that involve compromises of national security, such as treason, sedition, and espionage; handle selective service violations, copyright infringements, and jurisdictional disputes; and try violations of the many regulatory codes, such as violations of the Securities and Exchange Acts, the Endangered Species Acts, the Meat and Poultry Inspection Acts, and the Foreign Agent Registration Act, among many others. In addition, district court case loads include numerous civil actions and petitions filed by state and federal prisoners.

Each district court has between one and 27 judges, depending on the case load, with over 400 judgeships authorized by law. In most cases, a single judge presides over trials, and a defendant may request that a jury be present. In complex civil matters, a special three-judge panel may be convened. In addition to U.S. magistrates, each court has numerous other officers attached to it: a U.S. attorney, who serves as the criminal prosecutor for the federal government; several assistant U.S. attorneys; a U.S. marshal's office; and probation officers, court reporters, clerks, and one or more bankruptcy judges.

Throughout the 1970s and into the 1980s, the district courts have had to function under near-crisis conditions. The work load has increased dramatically, from 122,624 cases in 1970 to almost 300,000 by 1983. And although the level of criminal cases has remained relatively stable — from 30,000 to 40,000 filings each year dealing with everything from traffic offenses to significant violations of the U.S. Criminal Code (see Exhibit 10.11) — the number of district court judges has not been expanded in proportion to the work load. In 1970, there were 331 judges with an average load of 370 cases. In 1983, there were 484 judges with average loads of almost 600 cases, reflecting an increase of some 60 percent over the 13-year period.[21] To keep pace with the work load almost 300 new judges would have to be hired, and it

U.S. district courts are trial courts of the federal judiciary.

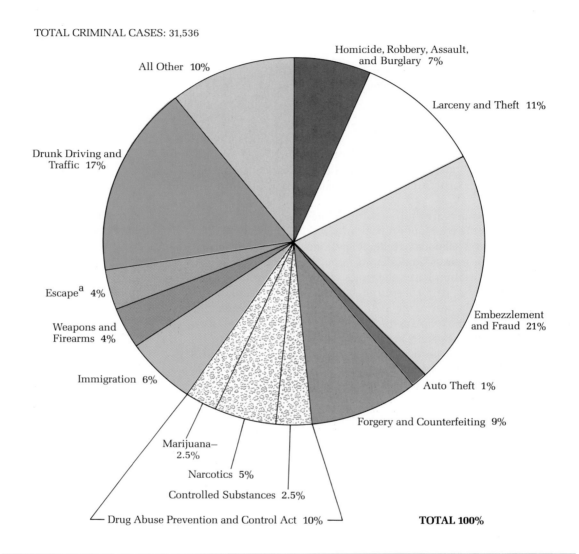

EXHIBIT 10.11

Criminal Cases Filed in U.S. District Courts

TOTAL CRIMINAL CASES: 31,536

Homicide, Robbery, Assault, and Burglary 7%

Larceny and Theft 11%

All Other 10%

Drunk Driving and Traffic 17%

Embezzlement and Fraud 21%

Escape[a] 4%

Weapons and Firearms 4%

Auto Theft 1%

Immigration 6%

Forgery and Counterfeiting 9%

Marijuana— 2.5%

Narcotics 5%

Controlled Substances 2.5%

Drug Abuse Prevention and Control Act 10%

TOTAL 100%

Note: Figure includes all offenses reported filed in federal district courts in accordance with reporting changes necessitated by the implementation of provisions of the Speedy Trial Act of 1974 (P.L. 93-619, approved January 3, 1975).

[a] Escape from custody, aiding or abetting an escape, failure to appear in court, and bail jumping.

SOURCE: Clerk, Administrative Office of the United States Courts.

is unlikely that there are that many highly qualified attorneys in the United States that would be willing to work for the salary offered. In 1983, a district court judge earned $73,100.* Although this is no trifling salary when compared to the average national income, it is more than 100 percent below that of other persons in the legal profession with similar credentials and experience. In 1980, Chief Justice of the United States Supreme Court Warren E. Burger stated that the pay system for federal judges was "the most pressing problem in the administration of justice,"[22] but Congress failed to respond by substantially increasing judicial salaries, and it is doubtful that it will in the near future. District court judges are already among the highest paid officials in the federal government, and if their salaries were raised significantly, many other federal salaries would have to be raised as well. The public, increasingly disenchanted with government spending and unmanageable budget deficits, probably would not stand for it.

United States Courts of Appeals

Appeals from the U.S. district courts move up to the next step in the federal judicial hierarchy, the **U.S. courts of appeals.** There are 13 of these courts, with more than 100 authorized judgeships. Each court is located in a *circuit*—a specific judicial jurisdiction served by the court, as defined by given geographical boundaries. For example, the U.S. Court of Appeals of the First Circuit is located in Boston and serves the district courts located in Maine, Massachusetts, New Hampshire, Rhode Island, and Puerto Rico (see Exhibit 10.12).

U.S. courts of appeals hear cases from the U.S. district courts.

The 13 courts of appeals hear some 30,000 cases each year involving both criminal and civil matters.[23] The cases heard are those appealed from the U.S. district courts—*not* those from state supreme or appeals courts. Almost all cases are heard by three-judge panels; a few are heard *en banc,* or "in bank," meaning the full bench of judges authorized for the court considers the appeal. In only three instances can a case appealed from one of the district courts bypass the court of appeals and go directly to the U.S. Supreme Court:

1. when the ruling under appeal was decided by a special three-judge district court hearing
2. when the case involves a federal statute declared unconstitutional by a district court, and the United States is a litigant
3. when the issue under review is deemed to be of such importance that it requires immediate settlement

The United States Supreme Court

The Supreme court is a virtual Tower of Babel, from which no definitive principles can be clearly drawn. — William Rehnquist, U.S. Supreme Court Justice, 1981

The **U.S. Supreme Court,** also known as the Court, High Court, and High Tribunal, is the highest court in the nation. It stands at the apex of the federal

Nine justices sit on the Supreme Court bench.

* In 1970, the salary of district court judges was $40,000, roughly equivalent to $119,000 in 1986 dollars.

EXHIBIT 10.12

The Thirteen Federal Judicial Circuits

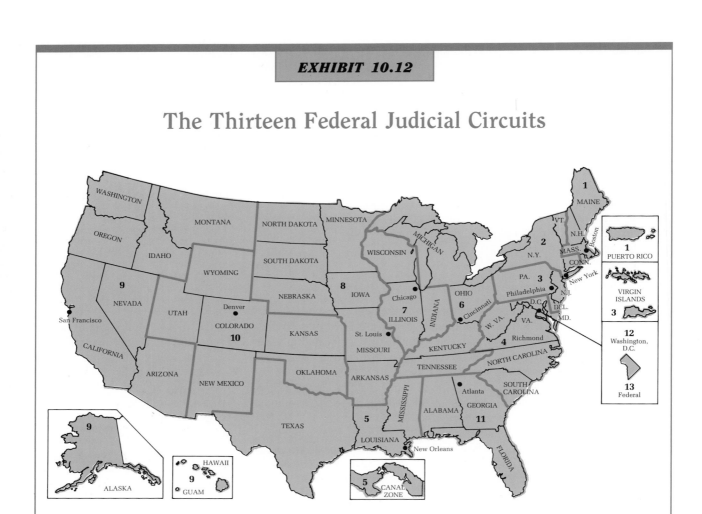

judiciary and is truly the court of last resort. The High Court is composed of nine justices: one chief justice and eight associate justices, who serve for life. They are nominated by the president of the United States and must be confirmed by the Senate.

The Origins of the Supreme Court

The Court was provided for by the Constitution, but only in the briefest of terms. Article III placed the judicial power of the United States in a supreme court and inferior federal courts: Section 1 of the article noted that the justices would hold their posts during "good behavior," and Section 2 outlined the range of judicial power. In contrast to Articles I and II of the Constitution, which spell out with considerable detail the powers and prerogatives of the Congress and the executive branch, what was stated for the nation's highest court was no more than a terse outline. Moreover, the Court had a slow start.

On September 24, 1789, President George Washington signed the Judiciary Act, which actually created the Supreme Court, into law, and sent to the Senate for confirmation the names of the first chief justice and five associate justices. However, one of these declined, another accepted but never attended, and three others either resigned or died before the close of the Court's first decade. John Jay of New York, the first chief justice, spent much of his tenure abroad and resigned in 1795. Two other men followed him as chief justice within 10 years — John Rutledge of South Carolina, as an unconfirmed recess appointment in 1795, and John Marshall of Virginia in 1801. (For later, more controversial appointments to the High Court, see Exhibit 10.13.)

The status of the first terms of the Court during the 1790s were also ambiguous and comparatively minor.[24] Only three of the six justices were present for the Court's opening session on February 1, 1790, but there was no business other than the appointment of a clerk. In fact, during the Court's first three years, no judicial decisions were made, and in 1792 Chief Justice John Jay reportedly described the post of a Supreme Court justice as "intolerable."[25]

Although the early terms of the Court saw few significant decisions, the justices themselves were kept busy. When the Judiciary Act of 1789 created the Supreme Court and the 13 district courts, it also established three judicial circuits, each composed of the geographical areas covered by several of the district courts. Twice annually, within each of the circuits, circuit court sessions were held to handle some of the more serious federal cases. But the Judiciary Act had not provided for a set of judges for the federal circuit courts. Thus, the chief justice and his five associate justices were required to travel throughout the country to hold circuit court where and when necessary, a situation that lasted for almost a full century.

Above: supreme court chambers, Southampton, New York. Below: the Supreme Court of the United States.

Marbury v. Madison

Marbury v. Madison

The full establishment of Supreme Court power occurred during the early decades of the nineteenth century under the leadership of John Marshall, chief justice from 1801 through 1835. Just two years after Marshall assumed his post, the Court announced its decision in *Marbury* v. *Madison*,[26] and in so doing it claimed, exercised, and justified its authority to review and nullify acts of Congress that it found to conflict with the Constitution.

Marbury v. *Madison* in 1803 was a dispute over presidential patronage that had escalated into a contest for authority between Congress and the Supreme Court. The case emerged from the bitter presidential election of 1800, when Republican Thomas Jefferson defeated Federalist John Adams. Unwilling to relinquish the power they had held since the beginning of the Union, the Federalists sought to entrench themselves in the federal judiciary. John Marshall's appointment had been part of that entrenchment. In addition, the lame duck Congress, just prior to Adams's leaving office as president, approved legislation creating 16 new district court judgeships. Furthermore, it authorized Adams to appoint as many justices of the peace for the newly created District of Columbia as he deemed necessary, and it reduced the number of Supreme Court justices from six to five at the next vacancy. This latter move was intended to deprive Jefferson of a quick appointment to the bench.

Adams named and Congress confirmed the 16 district court judges and 42 justices of the peace. On his last night in office, Adams signed the commissions for the new justices of the peace and had them taken to Marshall, then secretary of state, who was to affix the Great Seal of the United States and deliver them to the appointees. The Seal was affixed, but not all of the commissions were delivered.

William Marbury, an aide to the secretary of the Navy, was one of four men who had not received their commissions. At President Jefferson's request, Secretary of State James Madison refused deliverance of the commissions. Marbury asked the Supreme Court to issue a writ of *mandamus* ordering Madison to give the four men their commissions. A **writ of *mandamus*** is simply a command to perform a certain duty, and the Judiciary Act of 1789 had authorized the Supreme Court to issue such writs to officers of the federal government.

Writ of *mandamus*

Chief Justice Marshall found himself in a dilemma, with the authority of the Supreme Court at stake. If the High Court ordered delivery of the commission, Madison could refuse to obey the order, which seemed likely, and the Court had no means to enforce compliance. If the Court did not issue the writ, it would mean surrendering to President Jefferson's point of view. Either way, the Court would be conceding its power.

In what has been called a "masterwork of indirection, a brilliant example of Marshall's capacity to sidestep danger while seeming to court it, to advance in one direction while his opponents are looking in the other,"[27] the chief justice made a cunning decision. First, he ruled that once the president had signed the commissions and the secretary of state had recorded them, the appointments were complete and valid. Second, he ruled that a writ of *mandamus* was the proper tool to require the new secretary of state to deliver the commissions. These actions served to rebuke Madison, and Jefferson by implication. Marshall then turned to the question of jurisdiction, to whether the High Court had the authority to issue the writ. He concluded that it did not. Marshall stated that the Congress could not expand or contract the jurisdic-

EXHIBIT 10.13

Scorecard of the High Court Appointments
Whites 101, Blacks 1; Men 101, Women 1

When President George Washington made his nominations for the United States Supreme Court in 1790, his six selections for the Court's first bench reflected the tenor of the times—all were white, male, and Protestant. It would be almost half a century before this barrier would even begin to be breached.

The first Roman Catholic to get a seat on the Supreme Court was Roger Brooke Taney, the son of a Maryland plantation owner. Taney had been nominated by President Andrew Jackson to fill the seat left vacant by the death of Chief Justice John Marshall.

Another 80 years passed before the barrier against Jews was finally breached. In 1916, President Woodrow Wilson filled a vacant seat with Louis Dembits Brandeis, a prominent Boston lawyer and the son of Jewish immigrants from Bohemia. There was vicious opposition to Brandeis's nomination, but he was confirmed nevertheless by a Senate vote of 47 to 22.

In 1932, Benjamin Nathan Cardozo was seated on the Supreme Court by President Herbert Hoover. Cardozo's parents were descendants of Sephardic Jews who had settled in New York—one of whom had authored the words at the base of the Statue of Liberty. Cardozo's so-called Jewish seat was successively held by Felix Frankfurter (1939–1962), Arthur Goldberg (1962–1965), and Abe Fortas (1965–1969).

The barrier against blacks fell in 1967, with President Lyndon B. Johnson's appointment of Thurgood Marshall, a former U.S. court of appeals judge.

And after almost two centuries, the barrier against women also finally fell. It came in 1981, with the vacancy left by the retirement of Associate Justice Potter Stewart, who had been a member of the Bench since 1958. The "brethren's" first "sister" was Sandra Day O'Connor, an Arizona court of appeals judge nominated by President Ronald Reagan in fulfillment of a campaign promise.

Curiously, the current High Court has three "minority" members—one woman (O'Connor), one black (Marshall), and one Catholic (William J. Brennan). But the Court has six other members, and, as in 1790, all are white, male, and Protestant.

Roger Brooke Taney
1836–1864

Sandra Day O'Connor
1981–

Louis Dembits Brandeis
1916–1939

Benjamin Nathan Cardozo
1932–1938

Thurgood Marshall
1967–

tion of the Supreme Court, and that Congress had acted unconstitutionally and exceeded its power when, in Section 13 of the Judiciary Act of 1789, it had authorized the Court to issue such writs in original cases ordering federal officials to perform particular acts.

Although this matter of jurisdiction served to absolve the Jefferson administration of installing several of President Adams's appointments, the real significance of *Marbury* v. *Madison* was the establishment of the Court's power to review acts of Congress.

The *Marbury* decision is considered by many to have been the most important ruling in Supreme Court history, for without it, the Court may never have summoned itself up from its constitutional vapors.

Marbury v. Madison **established the Supreme Court's power to review acts of Congress.**

The Jurisdictional Scope of the Supreme Court

In the words of the Constitution, the jurisdiction of the Supreme Court is broad but not unbounded. As stated in Article III, Section 2:

> The judicial power shall extend to all cases, in law and equity, arising under this Constitution, the laws of the United States, and treaties made, or which shall be made, under their authority; to all cases affecting ambassadors, other public ministers and consuls; to all cases of admiralty and maritime jurisdiction; to controversies to which the United States shall be a party; to controversies between two or more States; between a State and citizens of another State; between citizens of the same State claiming lands under grants of different States, and between a State, or the citizens thereof, and foreign States, citizens or subjects.

Thus the Constitution outlined eight jurisdictional areas for the Supreme Court, but its main function was as guardian of the Constitution.

As defined by the Constitution and spelled out in the Judiciary Act of 1789, the Supreme Court has two kinds of jurisdiction over cases — original and appellate. The Court's original jurisdiction usually involves suits between two states, issues that test the constitutionality of state laws, and matters relating to ambassadors. In such instances, the Supreme Court can serve as a trial court. In its appellate jurisdiction, the High Court resolves conflicts that raise "substantial federal questions" — typically related to the constitutionality of some lower court rule, decision, or procedure.

Selection of Cases

As the final tribunal beyond which no judicial appeal is possible, the Supreme Court has the discretion to decide which cases it will review. However, the Court must grant its jurisdiction in *all* instances in which:

- a federal court has held an act of Congress to be unconstitutional
- a U.S. court of appeals has found a state statute to be unconstitutional
- a state's highest court of appeals has ruled a federal law to be invalid
- an individual's challenge to a state statute on federal constitutional grounds is upheld by a state supreme court

In all other instances, as provided by the Judiciary Act of 1925, the Supreme Court decides whether or not it will review a particular case.

The Supreme Court does not have the power and authority to review all decisions of the state courts in either civil or criminal matters. Its jurisdiction extends only to those cases where a federal statute has been interpreted or a defendant's constitutional right has allegedly been violated. Furthermore, a petitioner must exhaust all other remedies before the High Court will consider reviewing his or her case (see Exhibit 10.14). That is, should a matter of "substantial federal question" emerge in a justice of the peace court, for example, the first review would not be in the Supreme Court. Rather it would be heard as a trial *de novo* in the state trial court. Following that would be an appeal to the intermediate court of appeals (in those states where they exist), and then an appeal to the state's highest court. Only then is it eligible for review by the Supreme Court. A similar process occurs with respect to the federal court structure.

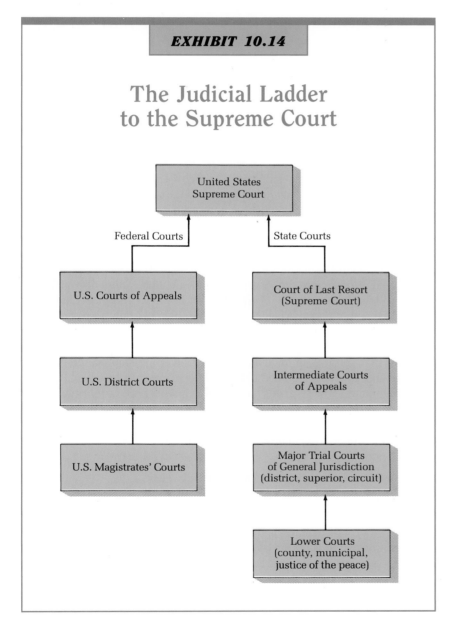

EXHIBIT 10.14

The Judicial Ladder to the Supreme Court

United States
Supreme Court

Federal Courts   State Courts

U.S. Courts of Appeals

Court of Last Resort
(Supreme Court)

U.S. District Courts

Intermediate Courts
of Appeals

U.S. Magistrates' Courts

Major Trial Courts
of General Jurisdiction
(district, superior, circuit)

Lower Courts
(county, municipal,
justice of the peace)

Writ of *certiorari*

The Rule of Four

The High Court's authority to exercise its own discretion in deciding which cases it will hear is known as its *certiorari power,* and comes from the **writ of *certiorari,*** a writ of review issued by the High Court ordering some lower court to "forward up the record" of a case it has tried in order that the Supreme Court can review it.

Prior to this granting of *certiorari,* the potential case must pass the **Rule of Four;** that is, a case is accepted for review only if four or more members of the High Court feel that it merits consideration by the full Court.

The Supreme Court accepts for review only cases in which its decision might make a difference to the appellant, and as stated earlier, only those of "substantial federal question." It does not operate as a court of last resort to correct the endless number of possible errors made by other courts. Rather, it marshals its time and energy for the most pressing matters. Currently, between 4,000 and 5,000 cases are filed annually for review by the Supreme Court. However, the Court limits itself to deciding less than 200 cases with full opinions each term.

Affirming, Reversing, and Remanding

When the Supreme Court affirms a case, it has determined that the action or proceeding under review is free from reversible prejudicial or constitutional error and that the judgment appealed from shall stand. Thus, if a conviction appealed from a lower court is *affirmed,* the conviction remains in force.

A Supreme Court decision that *reverses* or overturns a defendant's conviction or sentence does not necessarily free the appellant or impose a lighter penalty. Rather, it *remands* or returns the case to the court of original jurisdiction for a proper judgment. Upon reversing and remanding, the trial court has several options, depending on the nature of the case. Many of the criminal cases that receive Supreme Court attention revolve around the constitutional issues of illegal search and seizure, illegal confessions, and other matters that might invoke the exclusionary rule. In such instances, the court of original jurisdiction can order a new trial, but cannot introduce the "tainted" evidence. In many of these cases, however, the prosecution may decide that without such evidence the state would have only a weak case, and it dismisses the charges. In other circumstances, the Supreme Court decision may require a *change of venue* because of pretrial publicity or community hostility that resulted in an unfair original hearing. The change of venue requires that any new trial be held in a different county or judicial district. Other Supreme Court reversals have ordered institutional authorities to remedy unconstitutional conditions of incarceration, and have required that trial courts resentence certain defendants on the grounds that the original sentences constituted cruel and unusual punishment.

The Supreme Court's Mounting Problems

When the first Supreme Court convened in 1790, its role as guardian of the Constitution had only been recently conceived. At the same time, the country itself was new, with 13 states and fewer than four million citizens. The work of the High Court in those early days was simple. In its first three years it decided no cases, and during the next two years the six justices ruled on only four matters.

As the United States grew in size, complexity, and maturity, and a greater emphasis was placed on due process, human rights, and civil liberties, more and more cases began to work their way up through the appellate system (see, for example, Exhibit 10.15). By 1985, the number of justices on the Bench had increased by 50 percent, from six to nine. But, in the almost two centuries since the Court's inception, the population the Court was serving had expanded by 235 million—an increase of some 6,000 percent.

During the term ending in the summer of 1985, more than 4,000 petitions had been received by the Court, a rate of more than 70 each week. With the crush of appeals, the nine justices have been forced to rely more and more on their clerks to review cases, and a greater number of appeals have been rendered without written opinions. Furthermore, the Court has had to become more selective in the cases it chooses to hear; or, as the former dean of

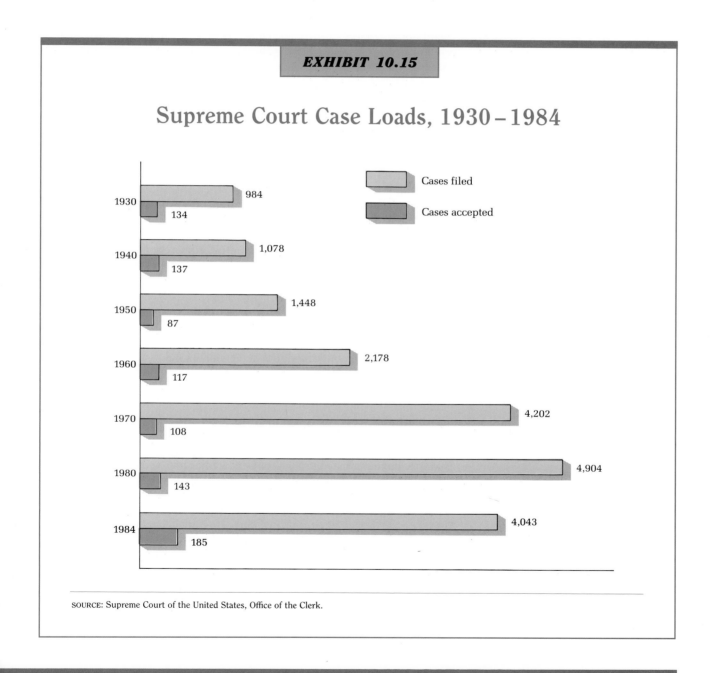

EXHIBIT 10.15

Supreme Court Case Loads, 1930–1984

Cases filed

Cases accepted

1930 — 984 / 134
1940 — 1,078 / 137
1950 — 1,448 / 87
1960 — 2,178 / 117
1970 — 4,202 / 108
1980 — 4,904 / 143
1984 — 4,043 / 185

SOURCE: Supreme Court of the United States, Office of the Clerk.

Harvard Law School, Erwin N. Griswold, characterized it, the justices have been forced into "rationing justice"—ruling in only a smattering of cases, while leaving citizens without guidance on an array of questions.[28]

In 1981, Chief Justice Warren E. Burger commented that the Supreme Court's overwhelming burden of cases comprised many minor matters. The Court had become "mired in trivia" as Burger put it.[29] For example, as noted earlier, it must consider *all* challenges to the constitutionality of state laws, even if they affect only a few persons. The Chief Justice has asked Congress to end the Court's mandatory jurisdiction over all cases, but this, it seems, would come into conflict with the basis of the *Marbury* v. *Madison* decision of 1803. Burger and others have also discussed the creation of a "national court of appeals" for key cases the Supreme Court has no time to deal with.

The increased Court work load comes not only from the simple mathematics of population growth and from the greater emphasis and awareness of civil liberties, but also from the Supreme Court's very performance. When *Mapp* v. *Ohio* in 1961 extended the exclusionary rule to the states,[30] for example, the Court opened the door to thousands of appeals involving various aspects of illegal search and seizure (see Chapter 7). Although the *Mapp* decision was clear enough in its spirit and central holding, it offered lower state and federal courts no guidance as to the specific criteria that make a search violative of the Fourth Amendment. For example, *Mapp* shed no light on such important questions as whether searches of automobiles following a traffic arrest were valid, whether search warrants issued on the basis of anonymous tips were justifiable, or whether one spouse could waive the Fourth Amendment rights of the other and consent to a search of the home. Indeed, the Court did not even tell the lower courts if the *Mapp* decision should be regarded as retroactive, that is, applicable to cases where the trial occurred before *Mapp*. In light of the confusion surrounding *Mapp*, then, it is not surprising that research has disclosed that no two state supreme courts have reacted to *Mapp* in the same way. Some state high courts implemented *Mapp* in a very receptive fashion, while others responded to post-*Mapp* legal questions in as restrictive a manner as possible.[31]

Studies of the impact of Supreme Court decisions demonstrate that a similar phenomenon has occurred in the aftermath of every major Supreme Court decision affecting the rights of defendants. Like *Mapp*, decisions such as *Escobedo* v. *Illinois* and *Miranda* v. *Arizona* actually created more legal questions than they answered.[32] In the field of criminal law, as in all areas of law, the Court simply cannot hear enough cases to spell out all of the corollary principles that may derive from its major decisions. The very nature of the Court's work permits the justices to do little more than formulate general policy. The pressures generated by heavy case loads and the necessity to write majority opinions that usually represent a compromise among the divergent viewpoints of individual justices make it highly likely that the Court's decisions will be uncertain and ambiguous.

The Supreme Court's holdings have been especially vague in the field of corrections law, thereby leading to what some observers have termed a "deluge" or "avalanche" of prisoners' petitions filed in federal and state courts. Prior to the 1960s, the courts followed a policy of declining jurisdiction over cases brought by prisoners. This policy, generally known as the *hands-off doctrine*,* reflected the view that a convicted prisoner was a "slave of the

---

* The hands-off doctrine is discussed in Chapter 16.

state," without enforceable rights. However, beginning in 1961, the High Court announced a series of decisions that signaled the impending demise of the hands-off doctrine and greatly expanded the right of access to the courts for American prisoners. With the doors to the judicial process opened to them, prisoners have brought thousands of suits, challenging either their original convictions or the conditions of their confinement. Although most prisoners' suits are dismissed as frivolous or without factual basis, inmates have won hundreds of courtroom victories in cases involving such issues as brutality, racial discrimination, improper medical care, nutritionally inadequate food, censorship of letters, restrictions on the free exercise of religion, and failure to follow due-process guidelines in disciplinary proceedings. By 1980, the courts had declared prisons in 15 states to be in violation of the Eighth Amendment's cruel and unusual punishment clause, and similar suits were pending in numerous other states. Correctional administrators, like their colleagues in law enforcement and judicial circles, have often complained that Supreme Court and lower court decisions are anything but precise and fail to tell them exactly what it takes to run a prison system that will withstand judicial scrutiny.[33]

Stanford University Law School professor Gerald Gunther has noted that there seems to be a direct correlation between the growing number of Supreme Court law clerks and Court opinions that are getting longer, are filled with tangents, and in that sense are somewhat more confusing.[34] The clerks

The members of the Supreme Court. Seated, from left: Justice Thurgood Marshall, Justice William J. Brennan, Jr., Chief Justice William H. Rehnquist, Justice Byron R. White, Justice Harry A. Blackmun. Standing: Justice Sandra Day O'Connor, Justice Lewis F. Powell, Jr., Justice John Paul Stevens, Justice Antonin Scalia.

are being relied on more and more to prepare first drafts of Court opinions. As recent law school graduates, they often focus on issues of personal intellectual interest that may be only minimally related to the decision at hand, and they are short on in-depth analysis. The heavy case load prevents the justices from thrashing out their differences and finding a common ground, and in the rush of time, a clerk's inconsistencies can slip by. Perhaps this was the reason for the virtual "Tower of Babel," as Justice Rehnquist put it, that occurred at the close of the 1980–1981 term. For example, because the law was too broad, the Court struck down as an unconstitutional infringement of free speech a San Diego ordinance banning billboards. In the process, however, seven justices with differing views on the ordinance agreed that states and cities do have the right to prohibit strictly commercial billboards.[35]

Summary

The American court system has come to be a bewildering mosaic of names, structures, and functions. There are justice of the peace and municipal courts, county and city courts, superior and inferior courts, trial and appellate courts, plus a host of others. The confusion comes from a variety of sources — no two state court systems are identical, the names of courts vary regardless of function, and there are various levels of jurisdictional authority.

State court structure includes appeals courts, intermediate appellate courts (in more than half the states), major trial courts, and courts of limited jurisdiction. Court jurisdiction varies by geography, subject matter, and hierarchy. The federal judiciary reflects a structure similar to that of the states.

The United States Supreme Court stands at the apex of the federal judiciary and is the highest court in the nation. The Constitution provided the High Court with both original and appellate jurisdiction. Its original jurisdiction covers suits between two states, issues that test the constitutionality of state laws, and matters relating to ambassadors. In its appellate jurisdiction, the Court resolves conflicts that raise "substantial federal questions."

In recent years the Supreme Court has become overburdened by a crush of appeals. This problem has occurred mostly as a result of the greater emphasis on due process, human rights, and civil liberties.

Key Terms

appellate jurisdiction (321)
courts of limited jurisdiction (312)
courts of original jurisdiction (320)
courts of record (321)
dual court system (308)
judicial circuit (321)

justice of the peace (314)
lower courts (312)
Marbury v. *Madison* (332)
Rule of Four (336)
trial courts (320)
trial *de novo* (314)

U.S. courts of appeals (329)
U.S. district courts (327)
U.S. magistrates (327)
U.S. Supreme Court (329)
writ of *certiorari* (336)
writ of *mandamus* (332)

Questions for Discussion

1. What type of restructuring would be most efficient to unify the state court systems?
2. What are the major problems with the lower courts, and how might these be remedied?
3. What are the similarities and differences between rural and urban lower courts?

4. How would Chief Justice Burger's suggestion to end the Supreme Court's mandatory jurisdiction over all challenges to the constitutionality of state laws conflict with the decision in *Marbury* v. *Madison*?

For Further Reading

Feeley, Malcolm M. *The Process Is the Punishment: Handling Cases in a Lower Criminal Court.* New York: Russell Sage, 1979.

McCloskey, Robert G. *The American Supreme Court.* Chicago: University of Chicago Press, 1960.

Posner, Richard A. *The Federal Courts: Crises and Reform.* Cambridge: Harvard University Press, 1985.

Notes

1. For a retrospective overview of the charm of the early American courthouse, see Richard Pare, ed., *Court House* (New York: Horizon Press, 1978).

2. The MacKaye material is reprinted, in part, in Raymond Moley, *Our Criminal Courts* (New York: Minton, Balch, 1930), pp. 5–9. MacKaye's essay included the following:

   This is the house that justice built. This is the castle of fair play. This is the place where wise men shall sit and contemplate our human jealousies, our petty quarrels, our wrong-doings. This, by the grace of God, is a magistrate's court.

   Set squarely down in a backwater street, it is not, for some disappointing reason, impressive. But the spangled parade of a city's life passes here, gaudy and gay, drab and mean. The push of ambition, the drums of crime, the blare of pretension, and keen quiet tragedy . . .

   This, then, is a magistrate's court set down on the backwater street.

3. President's Commission on Law Enforcement and Administration of Justice, *Task Force Report: The Courts* (Washington, D.C.: U.S. Government Printing Office, 1967), p. 29.

4. *Proceedings of the 42nd Annual Meeting of the New York State Bar Association*, 1919, pp. 240–241, as quoted in the President's Commission, *Task Force Report*, p. 29.

5. Howard James, *Crisis in the Courts* (New York: David McKay, 1971), p. 55.

6. National Advisory Commission on Criminal Justice Standards and Goals, *Courts* (Washington, D.C.: U.S. Government Printing Office, 1973), pp. 161–162.

7. H. Ted Rubin, *The Courts: Fulcrum of the Justice System* (Pacific Palisades, Calif.: Goodyear, 1976), p. 49.

8. Tumey v. Ohio, 273 U.S. 510 (1927).

9. President's Commission, *Task Force Report: The Courts*, p. 34; Connally v. Georgia, 429 U.S. 245 (1977).

10. *New York Times*, June 2, 1975, p. 16; "60 Minutes," CBS-TV, February 22, 1976.

11. Rubin, *The Courts*, p. 51.

12. The Cleveland Foundation, *Criminal Justice in Cleveland* (Cleveland: The Cleveland Foundation, 1922), pp. 627–641.

13. H. Ted Rubin, *The Felony Processing System, Cuyahoga County, Ohio* (Denver: Institute for Court Management, 1971), pp. 16–17.

14. These observations were made by the author.

15. Murray S. Stedman, *State and Local Governments* (Cambridge, Mass.: Winthrop, 1979), p. 156.

16. National Advisory Commission, *Courts*, p. 165.

17. David W. Neubauer, *America's Courts and the Criminal Justice System* (North Scituate, Mass.: Duxbury, 1979), pp. 65–66.

18. *Case Filings in State Courts, 1983*, Bureau of Justice Statistics Bulletin, October, 1984.

19. President's Commission, *Task Force Report: The Courts*, p. 36.

20. Institute of Judicial Administration, *A Guide to Court Systems* (New York: Institute of Judicial Administration, 1971), p. 13.

21. See Richard A. Posner, *The Federal Courts: Crises and Reform* (Cambridge, Mass.: Harvard University Press, 1985).

22. *U. S. News & World Report*, December 22, 1980, p. 68.

23. Richard A. Posner, p.352.

24. See Robert G. McCloskey, "James Wilson," in *The Justices of the United States Supreme Court, 1789–1969: Their Lives and Major Opinions*, 4 vols., ed. Leon Friedman and Fred L. Israel (New York: Chelsea House and R. R. Bowker, 1969), vol. 1, p. 93.

25. Charles Warren, *The Supreme Court in United States History*, 2 vols. (Boston: Little, Brown, 1926), vol. 1, p. 89.

26. Marbury v. Madison, 1 Cr. 138 (1803).

27. Robert G. McCloskey, *The American Supreme Court* (Chicago: University of Chicago Press, 1960), p. 40.

28. *U.S. News & World Report*, March 26, 1979, p.33.

29. *U.S. News & World Report*, January 12, 1981, p. 7.

30. Mapp v. Ohio, 367 U.S. 643 (1961).

31. See Bradley C. Canon, "Reactions of State Supreme Courts to a U.S. Supreme Court Civil Liberties Decision," *Law and Society Review*, vol. 8, no. 1 (Fall 1973): 109–134.

32. Escobedo v. Illinois, 378 U.S. 478 (1964); Miranda v. Arizona, 384 U.S. 436 (1966). See Stephen L. Wasby, *The Impact of the United States Supreme Court* (Howard, Ill.: Dorsey, 1970); and Theodore L. Becker and Malcolm M. Feeley, eds., *The Impact of Supreme Court Decisions*, 2nd ed. (New York: Oxford University Press, 1973).

33. Kenneth C. Haas and Anthony Champagne, "The Impact of *Johnson* v. *Avery* on Prison Administration," *Tennessee Law Review*, vol. 43, no. 2 (Winter 1976–1977): 275–306.

34. *U.S. News & World Report*, March 26, 1979, p. 33.

35. *Time*, July 13, 1981, p. 52.

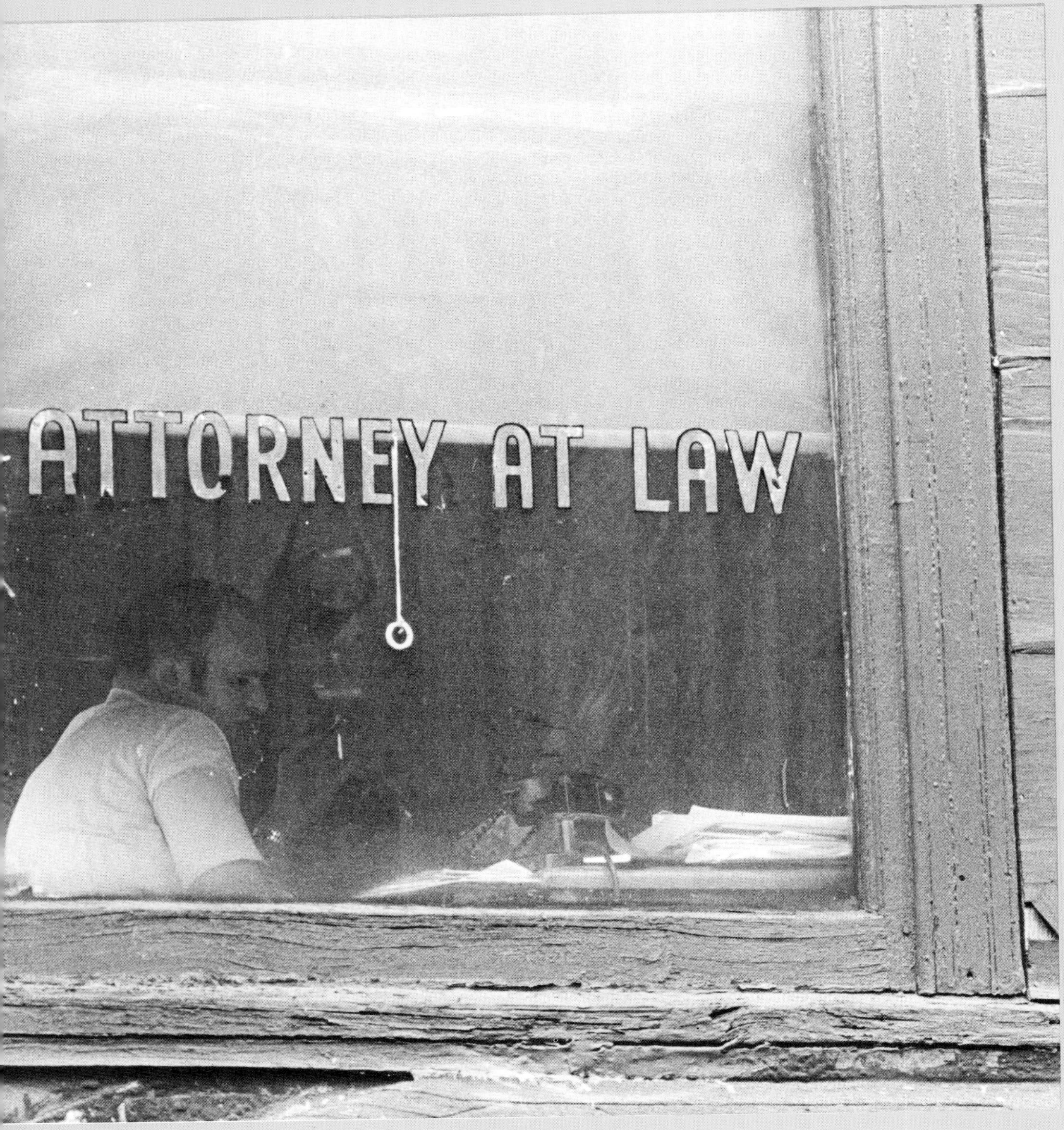
ATTORNEY AT LAW

11

Judges, Prosecutors, and Other Performers at the Bar of Justice

Justice is the great interest of man on earth.

— Daniel Webster, 1845

Injustice is relatively easy to bear; what stings is justice.

— H. L. Mencken, 1922

Everyone loves justice in the affairs of others.

— Italian proverb

Bailiffs and Sheriffs

Each courtroom is assigned a *bailiff* or *sheriff,* whose formal duties are to announce the arrival and departure of the judge and to maintain order in the courtroom. In addition, as local custom may dictate, they serve as messengers for lawyers and other court officials; they keep track of prosecutors, attorneys, and witnesses in order that they be present when their cases come up; and in some instances, they serve as information sources for defendants — advising them which court they belong in, where their attorney might be found, and if asked, what the outcome of the case might be.[38]

The Court Clerk

Every court has a clerk, whose responsibilities include "calling the calendar" (calling up the next case before the judge), updating the defendants' files, exercising control over the court's files, and ensuring the security of evidence that is in the custody of the court. In the small lower courts, there may be only one clerk for the entire courthouse. In larger jurisdictions, each courtroom may have its own *court clerk,* plus several courthouse file clerks who help maintain the court's records, collect any fines and court costs imposed, and prepare the daily calendars.

Although the title may convey otherwise, the court clerk occupies a position of considerable importance, especially the chief clerk of a large court system. Often the clerk's post is occupied by young attorneys who use it as a stepping-stone to the prosecutor's office. Not only does it give the incumbent exposure to the routine of the courthouse, but it also provides experience in some areas of law, since many clerks are empowered to prepare formal writs and process documents issued by the court.

Court Reporters and Court Stenographers

A *court reporter* or *court stenographer* is present at almost every judicial proceeding to report and (perhaps) transcribe matters of record. The mechanics of court reporting have changed considerably over time. In years past most reporters were expert stenographers who used a manual shorthand system to fashion verbatim accounts (transcripts) of proceedings. Manual shorthand writers are almost extinct, having been replaced by machine writers. Machine writers use a device that resembles a small typewriter with which to imprint coded letters on a tape. The tape may be translated visually, or it may be optically scanned. Alternatively, the keystrokes may be used to create a cassette from which a computer is instructed to transcribe.

Enormous sums have been spent on installing electrical equipment with which to record judicial proceedings, and some courtrooms are even designed to accommodate such systems. Although cost effective when compared to live reporter costs — some reporters earn as much as $200 a day or more — the product has proved cost defective. Objectionable comments of witnesses and counsel, extraneous noises, and privileged communications are regularly recorded — none of which is easily edited. More importantly, there is no court reporter present to interrupt proceedings when language is unclear, garbled, or barely audible.

Computer-assisted reporting and transcription have revolutionized the profession. Not only are transcripts more accurate; but preparation and delivery times have been reduced appreciably. Today's court reporter must be a computer-compatible writer, a far cry from the Scribes of Israel.

Witnesses

Almost all criminal proceedings have witnesses — one or more of three principal types: the police witness, the lay witness, and the expert witness.

A *police witness* is generally an arresting officer who has some knowledge of the facts of the case through his or her presence at the scene of the crime during or soon after its commission. The police witness would be called to testify if the officer had observed some part of the offense (for example, having seen the accused perpetrating the crime), or pertinent events in its aftermath (for example, having observed the accused fleeing from the scene of the crime). Police also serve as witnesses when they present the results of an investigation that led to the arrest of the defendant.

The *lay witness* is a citizen bystander or victim who has some personal knowledge relevant to the case. The lay witness is permitted to testify only on facts directly ascertained through sensory perception. Thus, the citizen cannot be a witness if his or her knowledge of the case is based on conjecture or opinion.[39]

The *expert witness* is called into court to provide technical information and opinions about matters of which the judge or jury may have no knowledge. To qualify as an expert, the witness must offer testimony in an area in which the general public has little or no understanding, and must have established qualifications and authority in that area. The decision whether someone qualifies as an expert witness is made by the trial judge. A psychiatrist, for example, may serve as an expert witness to testify as to the accused's mental competency to stand trial; an authority on ballistics may serve as an expert witness to comment on whether a bullet was fired from a certain weapon; or, for a less common example, a specialist in earth science may serve as an expert witness to establish whether mud on an accused's clothing and shoes matches the soil where a murder victim's body was found.

Coroners and Medical Examiners

The *coroner* is an appointed or elected county official whose chief function is to investigate the cause of all deaths that have occurred in the absence of witnesses, where there has been evidence of violence, or that have occurred under any suspicious circumstances. The office of coroner is an English invention dating from the twelfth century, when the entire realm was considered to be the property of the king. The term derives from *corona*, meaning crown, and the coroner was second only to the king in power and dignity. He was a man of substance who was considered to be capable of mature judgment; his duties included adjudicating not only on matters of violent and suspicious death but also on questions of property ownership.[40]

The American coroner system is a relic of its early English counterpart. Currently, the office of coroner in most communities is a political position like that of mayor or sheriff, and the potential incumbent needs no qualification other than that of eligibility to run on the predominant party ticket. To perform his duties, the coroner appoints a number of deputies, a forensic pathologist — sometimes with an assistant who specializes in toxicology or ballistics — and a scattering of part-time physicians.

The coroner does not hold a judicial position in the strictest sense, but quasi-judicial functions are nevertheless present. The coroner is authorized, for instance, to conduct *inquests,* which are legal inquiries into deaths where accident, foul play, or violence is suspected. The inquest in many ways is similar to a trial, although it is not governed by the precise procedure. The

The police witness

The lay witness

The expert witness

The coroner's role

coroner conducts the inquest, subpoenas witnesses and documents, cross-examines witnesses under oath, introduces evidence, and receives testimony — all with a jury present. Should the inquest suggest "just cause" and a suspect exists, the coroner issues an arrest warrant or moves for the prosecutor to request a warrant from a magistrate.

Criticisms of the coroner system

The coroner system in the United States has been heavily criticized for both corruption and incompetence. The coroner has often been the recipient of a patronage position, either through direct appointment or placement on the ballot. Coroners usually have no background in either medicine or law; the physicians who work as adjuncts to the office are not necessarily required to have any medico-legal training; and if a forensic pathologist is appointed as a coroner's deputy, he or she is generally a newly qualified medic with little experience.

The medical examiner is free from political control and is a forensically trained physician.

As a result, many jurisdictions have abolished the office of coroner and substituted the office of *medical examiner,* thus divorcing the system from political control and influence. The medical examiner is a licensed physician with training in forensic pathology who is appointed by government authority on a nonpartisan basis. He or she carries out only the medical aspects of any investigation, not the quasi-judicial functions, which are handled by the courts.[41]

The medical examiner system was first installed in Massachusetts as early as 1877 and is currently used in almost half the states. It also functions in the metropolitan areas of some states where the coroner system still persists. And in addition, some jurisdictions, such as Los Angeles County, have medical examiner – coroner systems, in which the coroner's office is headed by a medical examiner.[42]

Auxiliary Court Personnel

Depending on the jurisdiction, the size of the court, and the traditions of a given legal community, a range of additional figures may provide support services for the criminal judicial process. Both the prosecutor's and public defender's offices may have a number of *secretaries, aides,* and *investigators,* who assist in the collection of evidence and the preparation of cases. There are *court officers,* or perhaps *police officers assigned to the court,* or *correction officers* who maintain custody over detainees who are making court appearances. Also, since many courts have various types of pretrial diversion programs, there may be any number of *pretrial service representatives.* Or similarly, since pretrial release often occurs, *bail bondsagents* are also visible in the court process.

Finally, there are a number of highly significant figures in the court process that have not yet been mentioned, primarily because they are discussed in detail in later chapters. These are *probation officers, grand juries,* and *trial juries.*

The Right to Counsel

. . . in all criminal prosecutions, the accused shall enjoy the right . . . to have the assistance of counsel for his defense.   —from the Sixth Amendment

The Sixth Amendment

Despite the rather unambiguous language of the **Sixth Amendment,** for almost a century and a half after the framing of the Constitution only persons

6. See Richard W. Watson and Rondal G. Downing, *The Politics of the Bench and the Bar* (New York: Wiley, 1969).

7. *U.S. News & World Report,* December 19, 1973, p. 22.

8. *National Law Journal,* May 27, 1985, pp. 1, 26–28.

9. John R. Schmidhauser, *Judges and Justices: The Federal Appellate Judiciary* (Boston: Little, Brown, 1979), p. 75.

10. New York City Criminal Court Act, Laws of 1962, Chapter 697, Section 22 (1).

11. Wayne R. LaFave, *Arrest: The Decision to Take a Suspect into Custody* (Boston: Little, Brown, 1965), p. 515.

12. Advisory Committee on the Prosecution and Defense Functions, *The Prosecution Function and the Defense Function* (New York: American Bar Association, 1970), pp. 17–134.

13. President's Commission on Law Enforcement and Administration of Justice, *Task Force Report: The Courts* (Washington, D.C.: U.S. Government Printing Office, 1967), p. 5.

14. National Advisory Commission on Criminal Justice Standards and Goals, *Courts* (Washington, D.C.: U.S. Government Printing Office, 1973), p. 20.

15. George F. Cole, "The Decision to Prosecute," *Law and Society Review* 4, no. 3 (1970): 331–343. See also Eric D. Poole and Robert H. Regoli, "The Decision to Prosecute in Felony Cases," *Journal of Contemporary Criminal Justice* 2 (March 1983): 18–21.

16. See Joan E. Jacoby, *The Prosecutor's Charging Decision: A Policy Perspective* (Washington, D.C.: U.S. Department of Justice, 1977).

17. Kenneth C. Davis, *Discretionary Justice* (Baton Rouge: Louisiana State University Press, 1969), p. 170.

18. United States v. Cowen, 524 F. 2d 785 (1975).

19. See Arthur Rosett and Donald R. Cressey, *Justice by Consent: Plea Bargains in the American Courthouse* (Philadelphia: J. B. Lippincott, 1976).

20. *Miami Herald,* August 22, 1982, p. 11A; *Time,* August 30, 1982, p. 22.

21. National Advisory Commission, *Courts,* p. 46.

22. Brady v. United States, 397 U.S. 742 (1970).

23. Santobello v. New York, 404 U.S. 257 (1971).

24. Henderson v. Morgan, 426 U.S. 637 (1976).

25. Tollett v. Henderson, 411 U.S. 258 (1973).

26. Bordenkircher v. Hayes, 434 U.S. 357 (1978).

27. Hunter v. Fogg, 616 F. 2d 55 (2d Cir. 1980).

28. State v. Barton, 609 P. 2d 1353 (Wash. 1980).

29. Larson v. State, 614 P. 2d 776 (Alaska 1980).

30. See Advisory Committee, *Prosecution Function and the Defense Function,* pp. 141–309; Paul W. Wice, *Criminal Lawyers: An Endangered Species* (Beverly Hills: Sage, 1978).

31. Wice, *Criminal Lawyers,* p. 143.

32. Anthony C. Friloux, "Motion Strategy—The Defense Attack," Speech before the National College of Criminal Defense Lawyers, Houston, Texas, 1975, cited by Wice, *Criminal Lawyers,* p. 148.

33. For example, see Jack Ladinsky, "Careers of Lawyers, Law Practice, and Legal Institutions," *American Sociological Review* 27 (February 1963).

34. Abraham S. Blumberg, *Criminal Justice: Issues and Ironies* (New York: New Viewpoints, 1979), pp. 242–246.

35. Blumberg, *Criminal Justice,* p. 245.

36. Blumberg, *Criminal Justice,* p. 243.

37. Murray A. Schwartz, quoted in John Kaplan, *Criminal Justice* (Mineola, N.Y.: Foundation Press, 1973), p. 261.

38. Malcolm M. Feeley, *The Process Is the Punishment: Handling Cases in a Lower Criminal Court* (New York: Russell Sage, 1979), p. 121.

39. See Delmar Karlen, *The Citizen in Court* (Hinsdale, Ill.: Dryden, 1964).

40. Frank Smyth, *Cause of Death* (New York: Van Nostrand Reinhold, 1980), pp. 32–34.

41. William J. Curran, A. Louis Mc Garry, and Charles S. Petty, *Modern Legal Medicine, Psychiatry, and Forensic Science* (Philadelphia: F. A. Davis, 1980), pp. 51–56.

42. Curran et al., *Modern Legal Medicine,* p. 55.

43. The full story of the Scottsboro boys can be found in Dan T. Carter, *Scottsboro: A Tragedy of the American South* (New York: Oxford University Press, 1969).

44. Powell v. Alabama, 287 U.S. 45 (1932).

45. See Howard N. Meyer, *The Amendment That Refused to Die* (Boston: Beacon, 1978).

46. Johnson v. Zerbst, 304 U.S. 458 (1938).

47. Townsend v. Burke, 334 U.S. 736 (1948).

48. Betts v. Brady, 316 U.S. 455 (1942).

49. Uveges v. Pennsylvania, 335 U.S. 437 (1948).

50. Moore v. Michigan, 355 U.S. 155 (1957).

51. Hamilton v. Alabama, 368 U.S. 52 (1961).

52. Carnley v. Cochran, 369 U.S. 506 (1962).

53. Gideon v. Wainwright, 372 U.S. 335 (1963).

54. Anthony Lewis, *Gideon's Trumpet* (New York: Vintage, 1966), pp. 5–6.

55. Lewis, *Gideon's Trumpet,* p. 4.

56. See Meyer, *Amendment That Refused to Die.*

57. Douglas v. California, 372 U.S. 353 (1963).

58. Massiah v. United States, 377 U.S. 201 (1964); Escobedo v. Illinois, 378 U.S. 478 (1964); Miranda v. Arizona, 384 U.S. 694 (1966); United States v. Wade, 388 U.S. 218 (1967).

59. Coleman v. Alabama, 399 U.S. 1 (1970).

60. Argersinger v. Hamlin, 407 U.S. 25 (1972).

61. Mc Mann v. Richardson, 397 U.S. 759 (1970).

62. Ross v. Moffitt, 417 U.S. 600 (1974).

63. Scott v. Illinois, 440 U.S. 367 (1979).

64. Lawrence A. Benner and Beth Lynch Neary, *The Other Face of Justice* (Chicago: National Legal Aid and Defender Association, 1973), p. 13.

65. *Criminal Defense Systems,* Bureau of Justice Statistics Special Report, August 1984.

66. Harry P. Strumpf, "Law and Poverty: A Political Perspective," *Wisconsin Law Review* (1968): 698–699.

67. *Time,* October 3, 1983, p. 83; *U.S. News & World Report,* October 31, 1983, pp. 66–67.

68. See Charles L. Markmann, *The Noblest Cry: A History of the American Civil Liberties Union* (New York: St. Martin's Press, 1965).

69. See Michael Moore, "The Right to Counsel for Indigents in Oregon," *Oregon Law Review* 44 (1965): 255–300; Lee Silverstein, *Defense of the Poor* (Chicago: American Bar Association, 1965).

70. *Report of the Attorney General's Committee on Poverty and the Administration of Federal Criminal Justice* (Washington, D.C.: U.S. Government Printing Office, 1963), p. 40.

71. *Criminal Defense Systems,* supra note 65.

72. *The National Law Journal,* October 5, 1981, p. 1.

73. State v. Myles, 389 So. 2d 12 (1981).

74. *U.S. News & World Report,* March 13, 1978, p. 63.

75. *New York Times,* July 19, 1981, p. 20.

12

The Business of the Court: From First Appearance Through Trial

Courtroom: a place where Jesus Christ and Judas Iscariot would be equals, with the betting odds in favor of Judas.

— H. L. Mencken

The task of the trial court is to reconstruct the past from what are at best second-hand reports of the facts.

— Jerome Frank, U.S. court of appeals judge

A common theme in the discussions of many social critics and legal reformers is the chaotic state of criminal justice in the United States. They often refer to the organization and administration of justice as a "nonsystem," because the police, the courts, and the correctional process have no common goals, cooperative attitudes, or central direction. They claim that America's courts are at the brink of disaster: backlogs are colossal, work loads are always increasing, and the entire design is misshapen and understaffed. Furthermore, it is often argued that the administration of criminal justice has underscored the notions of due process and defendants' rights to such an exaggerated degree that criminals are all too quickly and easily dispersed to again prey on law-abiding citizens.

Of course, to suggest that the legal process is not working is clearly absurd. After all, each year millions of offenders are arrested and convicted, and a significant number are incarcerated. Others are dismissed or exonerated, presumably because of lack of evidence or because of their innocence, but dismissing and releasing the arrested under such circumstances is unquestionably a legitimate function of the court.

When the serious observer takes the time to examine what actually happens in the criminal courts, what is remarkable is not how badly they seem to function, but how well. As inefficient and unjust as it may appear, courthouse justice generally does an effective job of separating the innocent from the guilty. Although most of those who are guilty of crimes are never arrested, most of those coming to the courts who should be convicted *are* convicted, and most of these who should be punished *are* punished. Further, there is no evidence to support the contentions that repealing the exclusionary rule, eliminating plea bargaining, legislating mandatory prison terms for serious offenders, or reducing judges' freedom to determine length of sentences would produce any significant reduction in the rate of crime in the streets. On this point, journalist Charles E. Silberman has argued persuasively:

- It is *not* true that the courts have been hamstrung by the exclusionary rule or other decisions of the Warren Court; except for drug cases, few convictions are lost because "tainted" evidence is excluded from court.

- It is *not* true that the courts are more lenient than they used to be; the available data indicate that a larger proportion of felons are incarcerated now than in the 1920s.

- It is *not* true that disparate sentencing practices undermine the deterrent power of the criminal law. Within any single court system, the overwhelming majority of sentences — on the order of 85 percent — can be predicted if one knows the nature of the offense and of the offender's prior record.

- It is *not* true that plea bargaining distorts the judicial process. Contrary to popular impression, plea bargaining is not a recent innovation, nor is it the product of heavy case loads; it has been the dominant means of settling criminal cases for the last century.

- Most important of all, it is *not* true that the guilty escape punishment; when charges are dropped, it usually is because the victim refuses to press charges, or because the prosecutor lacks the evidence needed to sustain a conviction.[1]

This should not suggest that the administration of justice in the United States, and particularly the processing of defendants through the criminal courts, have no problems. The courts indeed *are* overcrowded and under-staffed, plea bargaining *does* result in lighter sentences for many offenders and in guilty records for some innocents, and the rigid adherence to constitutional safeguards *does* allow some dangerous criminals to return to freedom. But it is important to keep in mind that many of these phenomena are the direct result of the U.S. Constitution's regard for individual rights and civil liberties. On the one hand, perfect protection of the accused does mean imperfect protection of society. On the other, a system of justice that has no miscarriages is not a workable one; a system that automatically checkmates every defendant seeking equity and justice is hardly fair-minded and dispassionate. Speaking before the House of Commons in 1947, Sir Winston Churchill remarked: "Democracy is the worst form of government except all those other forms that have been tried from time to time." So it might also be argued about a system of justice based on the adversary process and grounded in "due process of law."

Perhaps the greatest difficulties with criminal judicial processing come from its very complexity. Defendants are arrested and booked. There is an initial appearance, with or without preliminary hearing, at which point pretrial release is considered and "probable cause" is determined. Through an information or indictment the charges are formalized. Should the evidence warrant it, defendants then face arraignment. There, before the presiding magistrate, the charges are read and a plea is entered. And perhaps throughout these pretrial phases plea negotiation has been discussed. Taking the process further, there are pretrial motions, jury selection, and the drama of the criminal trial. At its conclusion there is a verdict, posttrial motions, sentencing, and perhaps an appeal. In all, it is a complex of proceedings with due-process safeguards at every juncture. It is hardly a speedy process. But its very lack of speed is relevant because determining the innocence or guilt of the accused is important to ponder — and to ponder at length. As distinguished attorney and legal writer Charles Rembar has poignantly remarked: "Speedy justice is not the ultimate aim; just justice is."[2]

The courts are the final strongholds of feudalism in the United States.
—**Harvey A. Siegal, 1983**

Bail and Pretrial Release

Excessive bail shall not be required. . . .   — from the Eighth Amendment

For a defendant, bail is the bottom line of a criminal case.
 — Steven Phillips, former assistant district attorney, Bronx County, New York

Bail: Security posted guarantee that a defendant in a criminal proceeding will appear and be present in court as required.

Bail is a form of security guaranteeing that a defendant in a criminal proceeding will appear and be present in court at all times as required. Thus, bail is a guarantee: in return for being released from jail, the accused guarantees his or her future appearance by posting funds or some other form of security with the court. When the defendant appears in court as required, the security is returned; if he fails to appear, the security is forfeited.

The bail system as we know it today has its roots deep in English history, well before the Norman Conquest in 1066. It emerged at a time when there were few prisons, and the only places secure enough to detain an accused awaiting trial were the dungeons and strong rooms in the many castles around the countryside. Magistrates often called upon respected local noblemen to serve as jailers, trusting them to produce the accused on the day of trial. As the land became more populated and the castles fewer in number, magistrates were no longer able to locate jailers known to them. Volunteers were sought, but to ensure that they would be proper custodians, they were required to sign a bond. Known as private sureties, these jailers would forfeit to the king a specified sum of money or property if they failed to live up to their obligations of keeping defendants secure and producing them in court on the day required.[3] As the system was transferred to the New World, it shifted from a procedure of confinement to one of freedom under financial control. In current practice, it is the accused that posts the bond, or has some third party — a **surety** — post it in his or her behalf.

The accused posts a bond, or a surety posts it in his or her behalf.

The Right to Bail

The Eighth Amendment to the United States Constitution clearly specifies that "excessive bail shall not be required," but the extent to which the accused have any "right" to bail is a matter still under contention. The statutory right of federal defendants to have bail set in all but capital cases was established by the Judiciary Act of 1789. Furthermore, the Supreme Court held in *Hudson* v. *Parker* that a presumption in favor of granting bail exists in the Bill of Rights. Justice Horace Gray wrote in 1895:

> The statutes of the United States have been framed upon the theory that a person accused of crime shall not, until he has been fully adjudged guilty in the court of last resort, be absolutely compelled to undergo imprisonment or punishment, but may be admitted to bail, not only after arrest and before trial, but after conviction and pending a writ of error.[4]

But Justice Gray's words carried no firm guarantees for all criminal defendants seeking release on bail. Only one year before, the Court had ruled in *McKane* v. *Durston* that the Eighth Amendment's bail provision placed limits only on the federal courts, and did not apply to the states.[5] Since that time, the Supreme Court has decided relatively few cases involving bail, mainly because it is an issue that is moot by the time the case reaches the appellate stage of the criminal process. At the state level, the vast majority of state constitutions grant an absolute right to bail in noncapital cases.[6] However, constitutional or statutory rights to have bail set have never in practice meant an absolute right to freedom before trial. In years past, judges invariably insisted on cash bail or a surety bond from a bail bondsman. If the defendant could not afford it, he or she remained in jail awaiting trial — for days, months, and sometimes even years.

In its principal bail ruling, **Stack v. Boyle** in 1951,[7] the Supreme Court left unsettled the constitutional status of a defendant's *right* to bail (see Exhibit 12.1). But the Court did address the issue of "excessive bail," ruling that the fixing of bail must be based on standards relevant to the purpose of

Stack v. Boyle

EXHIBIT 12.1

The Right to Bail: Neither Excessive nor Absolute

Stack v. Boyle, 342 U.S. 1 (1951)

In *Stack,* twelve petitioners had been accused of conspiring to violate the Alien Registration Act of 1940. Known also as the Smith Act, it made unlawful, among other things, advocating the overthrow of the United States government by force. Bail had been set by a federal district court judge in amounts that varied from $2,500 to $100,000, and after motions made by several of the defendants were considered, the court reset bail at a uniform $50,000 for all twelve accused. In setting bail in that amount, however, the district judge had no knowledge of whether the defendants would be poor bail risks. His only basis for setting bail at such a high level was the record of a previous case in the same court where four persons convicted of violating the Smith Act had forfeited their bail. The appeal to the U.S. Supreme Court argued that the bail as set was "excessive" within the meaning of the Eighth Amendment.

The Court ruled that bail had not been fixed by proper methods, but rather that it had

been fixed chiefly by consideration of the nature of the offense and did not take into account the difference in circumstances among different defendants. Speaking for the Court, Chief Justice Fred M. Vinson stated it this way:

> This traditional right to freedom before conviction permits the unhampered preparation of a defense, and serves to prevent the infliction of punishment prior to conviction. . . . Unless this right to bail before trial is preserved, the presumption of innocence, secured only after centuries of struggle, would lose its meaning.
> The right to release before trial is conditioned upon the accused's giving adequate assurance that he will stand trial and submit to sentence if found guilty. . . . Bail set at a figure higher than at an amount reasonably calculated to fulfill this purpose is "excessive" under the Eighth Amendment. . . .

Carlson v. Landon, 342 U.S. 524 (1952)

In *Carlson,* several alien communists had been detained in federal custody prior to a final determination on their deportation. Their application for bail was

denied by the United States attorney general acting under provisions of the Internal Security Act of 1950. In a 5-to-4 decision, the Court affirmed the attorney general's actions, ruling that the Eighth Amendment did not guarantee all persons detained by federal authority the right to be released on bail. Writing for the majority, Justice Stanley F. Reed concluded with this comment:

> The bail clause was lifted . . . from the English Bill of Rights Act. In England that clause has never been thought to accord a right to bail in all cases, but merely to provide that bail shall not be excessive in those cases where it is proper to grant bail. When this clause was carried over into our Bill of Rights, nothing was said that indicated any different concept. The Eighth Amendment has not prevented Congress from defining the classes of cases in which bail shall be allowed in this country. Thus, in criminal cases, bail is not compulsory where the punishment may be death. Indeed, the very language of the Amendment fails to say all arrests must be bailable. We think, clearly, here that the Eighth Amendment does not require bail be allowed under the circumstances of these cases.

ensuring the presence of the defendant at trial. One year later, in *Carlson* v. *Landon*,[8] however, the Court held that inasmuch as the Eighth Amendment fails to state that all offenses are bailable, Congress may define the classes of *federal* offenses in which bail shall be allowed.

Discretionary Bail Setting

In theory, the purpose of bail is to ensure that the accused appear in court for trial. With this in mind, the magistrate is required to fix bail at a level calculated to guarantee the defendant's presence at future court hearings. This view has grown out of the historical forms of bail, as well as from the adversarial premise that a person is innocent until proven guilty and therefore ought not suffer confinement while awaiting trial. At the same time, however, there is the belief that more important than bail is the matter of societal protection. Should potentially dangerous defendants who might commit additional crimes be free to roam the community prior to trial? Judges often answer this problem by setting bail so high for some defendants that in practice, bail becomes a mechanism for preventive detention.

In most jurisdictions, those arrested for minor misdemeanors can be released almost immediately by posting bail at the police station where they are booked. In these cases, there are fixed bail schedules and the size of the bond is relatively small. For serious misdemeanors and felonies, the amount of bail required is left to the discretion of the judge. Research has demonstrated, however, that decisions determining the size of bail are neither random nor arbitrary.

Bailing criteria   By statute and case law, most jurisdictions have certain criteria that need to be considered in determining bail. The New York Criminal Procedure Law, for example, lists seven items that must be weighed by the presiding magistrate:

1. The principal's character, reputation, habits and mental condition;
2. His employment and financial resources; and
3. His family ties and the length of his residence if any in the community; and
4. His criminal record, if any; and
5. His previous record if any in responding to court appearances when required or with respect to flight to avoid criminal prosecution; and
6. If he is a defendant, the weight of the evidence against him in the pending criminal action and any other factor indicating probability or improbability of conviction . . .
7. If he is a defendant, the sentence which may be . . . imposed upon conviction.[9]

Despite the presence of specific criteria such as these, in practice there are typically only three factors that are considered in bail setting. By far, the most important is the *seriousness of the crime;* the assumption is that the more severe the offense the greater the likelihood of forfeiture of bail. The second factor is the defendant's *prior criminal record;* the rationale for this is that recidivists (repeat offenders) have a higher probability of forfeiting bond. In conjunction with these two factors is the *strength of the state's case.* Here the premise is that the greater the chance of conviction, the stronger the accused's interest in fleeing.[10]

Thus, if the state has a strong case against an accused with a prior felony record, and the current offense was a dangerous crime, then unquestionably, the bail set would be high.

The Bail Bond Business

Once bail has been set, there are three ways it can be exercised. First, the accused may post the full amount of the bond in cash with the court. Second, many jurisdictions allow a defendant (or family and friends) to put up property as collateral and, thus, post a property bond. In either case, the money or property is returned when all court appearances are satisfied, or they are forfeited if the defendant fails to appear.

Neither cash bail nor property bonds are commonly used, however. Most defendants seldom have the necessary cash funds to meet the full bond, and the majority of courts require that the equity in the property held as collateral be at least double the amount of the bond. Thus the most common method — the third alternative — is to use the services of bail bondsmen.

Clustered around urban courthouses across the nation are the storefront offices of the bail bondsmen. Often aglow with bright neon lights, their signs boldly proclaim: BAIL BONDS — 24-HOUR SERVICE. Or sometimes, during the late night hours on local television, the viewer is confronted with the most unlikely of commercials: "Are you in trouble? Call ———, 24-hour bail bond services!" In either case, the message is quite clear, that freedom is available — for a price.

Bail bondsmen, also referred to as commercial bondsagents, are essentially small business entrepreneurs who serve as middlemen with the courts. For a nonrefundable fee, they post a surety bond with the court, and if the defendant fails to appear at trial, the bondsagent is responsible for the full amount of the bond.

Defendants without the funds or property necessary to meet the full amount of bail seek out a bondsman, for the actual out-of-pocket costs usually amount to only 10 percent of the established bail. Furthermore, in actual practice the bondsman rarely posts a cash surety with the court. Let us assume, for example, that defendant Smith's bail is set at $10,000. His bondsman charges him a nonrefundable fee of $1,000, since 10 percent is the prevailing rate. The bondsman then purchases a surety bond from an insurance company, which typically costs 30 percent of the fee collected. Smith's cost for pretrial freedom is $1,000, of which $700 becomes the property of the bondsman — whether or not Smith ever appears in court again. If Smith should "jump bail," the insurance company, in theory, pays the forfeiture.

Smith's case, however, is an idealized typical one, and would proceed smoothly as described only if he was considered a good bail risk. If he were not, it is unlikely that the insurance company would provide a bond, or that the bondsman would even accept him as a client. In general, the bondsagent views four types of defendants as poor risks:

1. *first felony offenders,* because they are likely to panic and leave the community
2. *recidivists* whose new offenses are more serious than previous ones
3. *violent offenders,* because they can represent a personal threat to the bondsagent

Poor bail risks

4. *those whose bail has been set at a high level,* because forfeiture would result in large financial losses, as well as damage to the agent's reputation with the insurance companies

In assessing a client's reliability, the bondsman inquires into his or her criminal record, family situation, employment history, roots in the community, and anything else that would suggest that the defendant has some type of "investment" in the social system. If the client is considered a bad risk, he will be rejected; if he is a marginal risk, the bondsman may require him to post collateral — such as his house, car, or some other resource — in addition to the fee.

Criticisms of the Bail System

For decades, the bail system has been the subject of continuing criticism. In 1931, the National Commission on Law Observance and Enforcement launched a strong attack on bail procedures, noting that the amount of bail set was arbitrarily determined; that bondsmen were unreliable and sometimes corrupt, and that they played too important a role in the administration of justice; and that bonds were easily forfeited, but in only a small portion of the cases were the forfeitures ever collected.[11] The findings and overall sentiments of the commission were not unlike those of the Cleveland Foundation's analysis of crime and justice in 1922, *The Missouri Crime Survey* in 1926, the *Survey of the Administration of Criminal Justice in Oregon* in 1932, and the President's Commission on Law Enforcement and Administration of Justice in 1967.[12]

Bail tends to discriminate against the poor.

Criticisms of the bail system continue, although they vary from one jurisdiction to the next. First, bail tends to discriminate against the poor. When cash bail is set at a high level, it results in the pretrial confinement of many "low risk" defendants who do not have the funds either to post bond or retain a bondsman. Second, despite the Eighth Amendment safeguard against excessive bail, bail setting is totally discretionary on the part of the judge; many courts set bail at unreasonably high levels. Third, since bail is generally determined at the initial appearance, the court has little time to investigate the background of the accused and, hence, cannot adequately determine the nature of risk. Fourth, bail is often manipulated into an instrument for preventive detention. As a measure of community protection against offenders who are viewed by the courts as risks to the social welfare and safety, bail is set so high that it can rarely be met.[13]

Deficiencies in the bail bond industry

As to the criticisms leveled against the bail bond industry decades ago, most still apply today. First, as with the bail system in general, commercial bail bond operations also discriminate against the indigent. As a penalty for being poor, the defendant is forced to buy his freedom for a fee, which is nonrefundable — whether or not he appears for trial, and whether or not he is completely exculpated.

Second, the very structure of bail bonding serves to defeat the basic assumption that underlies the cash bail system. In current practice, most defendants pay a 10 percent fee to the bondsagent, who then secures a bond from an insurance company. The financial risks of forfeiture are transferred to the agent and the insurance company, eliminating the defendant's financial penalty. The fact that the bondsman's fee is not returnable under any circumstances further reduces any incentives to appear.

Third, the bondsman is in effect an agent of the court and plays a crucial role in determining who will receive pretrial release. Even though it is the judge who sets bail, in the reality of many defendants the court makes a determination of "bail eligibility." The bail bondsman's right to deny his services, to set his fee, to raise premiums, and to require collateral gives him the power to veto the court's bail decision.

Fourth, the bail bond industry tends to promote corruption. Clients are secured through advertising and referrals, and the referral network produces a situation ready-made for unscrupulous practices. Some bondsmen enter into collusive agreements with lower-level judges to set unnecessarily high bail or to increase the bondsagent's bail fee. For his part, the magistrate may receive a kickback or an illegal "gift" from the bondsman. At the same time, the magistrate returns the favor, granting to a favored few bonding firms permission to solicit clients at local lockups. Furthermore, through the magistrate–bondsman arrangement, the charging of illegal fees is both encouraged and protected. Similarly, court clerks, bailiffs, defense attorneys, public defenders, and police have been known to "steer" defendants to specific bondsmen in return for a kickback. Such corruption can even extend into government. In 1968, for example, the Pennsylvania Crime Commission discovered that the mayor of Chester, Pennsylvania, had personally orchestrated the division of the bail bond market. All police captains had been instructed to call specific bonding firms, and the kickbacks stretched from the police department to the mayor's office.[14]

Fifth, although many surety bonds are secured through insurance and are fortified by collateral, most bondsmen suffer no direct financial losses if the defendant fails to appear at trial. Nevertheless, it is in a bondsman's best interests that his clients do appear; otherwise, relationships with the court and insurance carriers will weaken. The methods used by some bondsmen to insure appearance have been both unethical and illegal, including threats, violence, and abduction.

Sixth, the requirement to pay high fees for bonding has led many defendants to commit new crimes while out on bail.

Seventh, bail bondsmen have extraordinary legal powers over bailed defendants who "jump bond" and flee. When a bond is issued, the client is required to sign a contract waiving the right to extradition and allowing the *bondsman*—or his agent or deputy—to retrieve him from wherever he has fled. This results in law enforcement powers that exceed those of police officers. Bondsmen need no warrants, nor are they prevented from taking bond jumpers across state lines. Worse, since most bondsmen are ill equipped to seek out bond jumpers personally, they use professional "skip tracers," who are essentially armed bounty hunters (see Exhibit 12.2).

Eighth, and finally, failure to appear in court means that the entire amount of the bond is forfeited. Yet in many jurisdictions, forfeited bonds regularly go uncollected. The reason for this is the judge's discretionary power to vacate outstanding bonds, and it is often in the court's best interests to "go easy" on the bondsmen. Without the bail bond industry, the courts would be faced with a large jail population, and costs for pretrial detention would be prohibitive. The courts tend to do what they can to keep the bail bonding business healthy. In California, to encourage bondsmen to seek out their absconded clients, a grace period of 180 days is allowed before bonds are forfeited. And in St. Louis, most bonds are vacated. In one year alone, for example, of 318 bonds that should have been forfeited, some 304 were set aside by the court.[15]

In addition to forfeiture of bail, failure to appear in court as required entails other consequences. A *capias,* or *bench warrant,* is issued by the court

Bench warrant: A written order, issued by the court, authorizing a defendant's arrest.

EXHIBIT 12.2

From Bounty Hunters to "Skip Tracers"

It is noon. The sun blazes down on a deserted, dusty street. Two men step casually from the shadows to face each other. Both are unshaven and a bit disheveled; their lips are drawn back in a sneer, and they walk arrogantly forward looking neither to the right nor the left. Suddenly, hands flash down, and there is a thunderous roar of gunfire. When the smoke clears, one man stands alone, gun in hand. The other lies dead in the street. It is a scene often depicted in films of the American West. Sometimes the victor is Wyatt Earp, Wild Bill Hickok, or John Wesley Hardin. But often it is the bounty hunter, charged with bringing back his quarry "dead or alive."

There is a modern counterpart to the story. It is a rainy Sunday afternoon in Manhattan. The streets are deserted, except for a late-model Ford LTD parked at the end of the block. Inside sits a heavy-set man in his early fifties. He wears jeans, black boots, a wool shirt, and a hunting jacket whose pockets are filled with cigars. He is armored with a bulletproof vest and has a shotgun at his side. The man is Stan Rivkin, and he is watching the door of a tenement house halfway down the block. Somewhere inside the building is another man — wanted for drug-dealing and the attempted murder of a police officer. He is also wanted for jumping bail in California, and there is a price on his head. That is why Stan Rivkin sits, waits, and watches. Rivkin is a *"skip tracer,"*[a] a modern-day bounty hunter working for a bail bondsagent. In capturing bail-jumpers Rivkin has more authority than any law enforcement officer in the United States. He can enter a house without a warrant; he can arrest a bail-jumper in any state and return him to court without the formalities of extradition. The Constitution has been suspended for him.

Stan Rivkin's extraordinary powers of arrest come from a century-old Supreme Court decision. In *Taylor* v. *Taintor,*[b] argued in 1873, the Court described the common law power of the bondsagent:

> **When bail is given, the principal is regarded as delivered to the custody of his sureties. Their dominion is a continuance of the**

authorizing the defendant's arrest. Furthermore, bail jumping represents a new offense and carries criminal penalties. In Maryland, for example, which is typical of most jurisdictions, "failure to surrender after forfeiture of bail" can result in a new felony charge with penalties of five years' imprisonment with or without a $5,000 fine:

> **Any person who has been admitted to bail . . . in any criminal case in this State who forfeits the bail . . . and willfully fails to surrender himself within thirty days following the date of forfeiture shall be sentenced as provided herein. If the bail . . . was given in connection with a charge of felony or pending an appeal *certiorari, habeas corpus,* or post conviction proceeding after conviction of any offense, the person shall be fined not more than $5,000 or imprisoned in the penitentiary for not more than five years or both. If the bail . . . was given in connection with a charge of committing a misdemeanor, the person shall be fined not more than $1,000 or imprisoned for not more than one year, or both.[16]**

Pretrial Detention

For defendants, the principal difficulty with the bail system is its relationship to financial well-being. Although most bail premiums paid to bondsmen are 10 percent of the face amount of the bond, rates as high as 20 percent have been

original imprisonment. Whenever they choose to do so, they may seize him and deliver him up to their discharge; and if it cannot be done at once, they may imprison him until it can be done. They may exercise their rights in person or by agent. They may pursue him into another state; may arrest him on the Sabbath; and if necessary, may break and enter his house for that purpose. The seizure is not made by virtue of due process. None is needed.

In place now for more than a century in the United States, the powers of pursuit and arrest held by bail bondsagents, and their designated skip tracers, has neither been revoked nor altered by the Supreme Court.

SOURCES:
a. *Parade*, August 5, 1984, p. 11.
b. Taylor v. Taintor, 83 U.S. 66 (1873).

Modern-day bounty hunters like Stan Rivkin, shown here with his shotgun and Duke, his Doberman, have legal powers of arrest that surpass those of any law officer in the nation.

reported.[17] When bail is set at $1,000 or more, premiums of $100 to $200 become more than many defendants can afford. One study of bail practices in New York City found that 25 percent of all defendants failed to make bail at $500, 45 percent failed at $1,500, and 63 percent failed at $2,500.[18] In other jurisdictions the proportion of defendants facing felony charges that were unable to make bail ranged as high as 93 percent.[19] The result of bail, then, has been the arbitrary punishment of hundreds of thousands of persons, many of whom were innocent of any crimes. Here are some examples:

- A man was jailed on a serious charge. . . . He could not afford bail and spent 101 days in jail until a hearing. Then the complainant admitted the charge was false.
- A man could not raise $300 bail. He spent 54 days in jail waiting trial for a traffic offense, for which he could have been sentenced to no more than five days.
- A man spent two months in jail before being acquitted. In that period, he lost his job, and his car, and his family was split up.[20]

Then there was the Charlottesville, Virginia, case in 1981 in which a man was jailed for 14 days because he could not raise $250 for bail. The only difficulty was that he had been arrested for abusive and insulting language, a misdemeanor offense that carried no jail sentence.[21]

The legal consequences of pretrial detention

In addition to depriving a defendant of freedom, **pretrial detention** prevents the accused from locating evidence and witnesses, and from having more complete access to counsel. It disrupts employment and family relations. It coerces defendants into plea negotiation in order to settle the matter more rapidly. Most importantly, however, pretrial detainees are confined in city and county jails — the worst penal institutions in the country. They are overcrowded, unsanitary, and poorly equipped. Few have sufficient space for inmates to confer with counsel or visit with families. Defendants awaiting trial are indiscriminately mixed with convicted felons, with a result, as Justice William O. Douglas once remarked, "equivalent to giving a young man an M.A. in crime."[22] Finally, jails are populated by many violent offenders, and scores of detainees each year are beaten, raped, and murdered.

Preventive Detention

Stack v. *Boyle* in 1951 made it explicitly clear that the purpose of bail is "to assure the defendant's attendance in court when his presence is required." At the same time, the Supreme Court also noted that bail is not "a means for punishing defendants nor protecting public safety." In these words, the High Court has made its position on **preventive detention** unmistakable, at least by implication; at the same time, however, it has not ruled whether the practice is constitutionally impermissible. As a result, many magistrates use bail as a mechanism for preventive detention. For those who are considered dangerous offenders or where there is a likelihood of repeated crimes during the pretrial period, prohibitively high money bail is set for the ostensible purpose of insuring an accused's appearance in court. In fact, despite the implication in *Stack* v. *Boyle,* as of 1985 the District of Columbia, the entire federal system, and 32 states had laws permitting judges to consider an accused's danger to the community in setting pretrial release conditions.[23] In the federal system, this was promulgated by the new Bail Reform Act of 1984 (see Exhibit 12.3).

The legal consequences of pretrial detention, whether preventive or otherwise, can be disastrous. Research has demonstrated repeatedly that detainees are more likely to be indicted, convicted, and sentenced more harshly than released defendants. A study based on 3,459 cases from New York's Court of General Sessions highlighted the fact that when the nature of the offense, previous record, and other factors were roughly equivalent, detainees were more often convicted and sentenced to prison than released defendants.[24] Furthermore, in its work on pretrial release the American Bar Association noted that studies in Philadelphia, New York, and the District of Columbia all indicated that the conviction rate for jailed defendants materially exceeded that of bailed defendants.[25] In terms of the sentences imposed on those convicted, the bailed defendant was far more likely to receive probation; his jailed counterpart, having been unable to confer more fully with his counsel, seek out witnesses and evidence in his own behalf, and most importantly, prevented from demonstrating his reliability in the community, went to prison more frequently.

There are some factors, such as strong evidence of guilt or a serious prior criminal record, that necessarily lead to high bail and hence detention. These factors, of course, and not just pretrial detention, can also cause a court to find a defendant guilty and sentence him to prison rather than give him probation. However, one study that took these factors into consideration as well still found a strong relationship between detention and unfavorable disposition.[26]

EXHIBIT 12.3

The Bail Reform Act of 1984

During early 1983, President Ronald Reagan sent a 44-point crime package to Congress as part of his commitment to engineer changes in the American system of justice. The result was the Comprehensive Crime Control Act of 1984 (CCCA), legislation which Reagan hoped would shift the balance away from suspects toward victims and the state.[a] Although CCCA contained provisions that brought about numerous changes in federal criminal law, what had an immediate impact was its opening chapter, the Bail Reform Act of 1984.

Under the new bail law, federal judges could assess an accused's danger to other persons and the community in making temporary release decisions. Moreover, pursuant to the findings of a detention hearing, bail could be denied outright to defendants if there was an indication that they would not show up for trial. As such, certain aspects of the act represented an endorsement of preventive detention.

A key feature of the act was its establishment of a "no-bail presumption" in certain types of cases. In other words, the court could deny bail on the presumption that certain kinds of defendants, such as drug traffickers, were unlikely to appear for trial. Furthermore, when this presumption was triggered, the burden of rebuttal fell on the accused. This provision was especially welcomed by federal prosecutors in South Florida who had been plagued with repeated instances of bail jumping in cocaine trafficking cases. Known in the Miami courts as the "Colombian dismissal," it was not uncommon for a trafficker to put up $1 million in cash bail, then go to Miami International Airport and take a one-way flight to Bogota.[b]

During the first six months after the Bail Reform Act was put into force, 820 requests for pretrial detention were made in the federal courts, of which more than three-fourths were granted.[c] Moreover, there were numerous constitutional challenges to the new law:

- In *U.S.* v. *Hazzard*,[d] argued less than two months after the act's passage, the preventive detention provision was tested. The court held that the government's interest in protecting the community by preventing further crime was sufficiently weighty to override an accused's interest in pretrial release.

- In *U.S.* v. *Aiello*,[e] a drug trafficking case involving defendants with ties in Sicily, the no-bail presumption was examined. The court remarked that the presumption feature saves a court the need for introducing evidence on certain general matters about which Congress made its own findings while drafting the Bail Reform Act. For example, the court need not show that narcotics traffickers generally devote their full attention to their business, that they have connections in other countries, and that most can tap large financial resources to make bail and effect escape.

- In *U.S.* v. *Jessup*,[f] the no-bail presumption in drug trafficking cases passed constitutional muster at the appellate level.

- In *U.S.* v. *Motamedi*,[g] a federal appellate court ruled that the "preponderance of evidence" standard was all the Bail Reform Act required the government to meet in order to obtain pretrial detention of defendants on grounds that they would otherwise flee. In the "preponderance" standard, evidence need not be "beyond a reasonable doubt." Rather, it simply must be of greater weight and more convincing than that which is offered in opposition.

SOURCES:

a. *Comprehensive Crime Control Act of 1984*. Public Law 98-473, October 12, 1984.

b. James A. Inciardi, *The War on Drugs: Heroin, Cocaine, Crime, and Public Policy* (Palo Alto, Calif.: Mayfield, 1986).

c. *National Law Journal,* July 8, 1985, p. 20.

d. U.S. v. Hazzard, 36 CrL 2217, 598 F.Supp. 1442 (1984).

e. U.S. v. Aiello, 36 CrL 2218, 598 F.Supp. 740 (1984).

f. U.S. v. Jessup, 36 CrL 2445, CA 1 (1985).

g. U.S. v. Motamedi, 37 CrL 2394, CA 9 (1985).

There is an additional problem with preventive detention. Some courts have used it as a method of punishing defendants for the crimes for which they were charged. This is a serious abuse of judicial discretion, for punishment without conviction is patently illegal. Nevertheless, there are differing opinions on the matter. Former New York City Mayor John V. Lindsay once made this comment:

> Defendants are subjected to the Red Queen's jurisprudence: first the punishment, then the trial. They do time before they are found guilty of the crime.[27]

On the other side, a South Carolina justice of the peace remarked not too many years ago, "It is for violation and a good reminder not to do it again."[28] More to the point, from New York City comes this remark:

> THE COURT: Now, these boys, as I see it, have gone beyond children's acts. This is something that shows they don't know when to stop. Maybe a couple of days in jail may solve the problem. I'm going to set $5,000 bail on each. Now, I'm leaving word that if a bond is presented, the matter is to be sent back to me, and I'll tell you right now, if they put up $5,000 bail, I'll make it $10,000, and if they put up ten, I'll make it

A holding cell in New York City's infamous Manhattan House of Detention, known as the "Tombs"

$25,000. I want these boys to spend one or two nights in jail. Maybe that is the answer.[29]

Release on Recognizance

At the beginning of the 1960s, increasing dissatisfaction with the bail bond system led to experimentation with alternative forms of pretrial release. Early in the decade, New York industrialist Louis Schweitzer's concern for youths who were detained while awaiting trial led to his establishment of the Vera Foundation (named after Schweitzer's mother). The foundation, later called the Vera Institute of Justice,[30] conducted an experiment with pretrial release based on the notion that "more persons can successfully be released . . . if verified information concerning their character and roots in the community is available to the court at the time of bail determination."[31] Known as the Manhattan Bail Project and begun in 1961, the effort was made possible through the cooperation of the New York criminal courts and law students from New York University. The students interviewed defendants, looking for information that would support a recommendation for pretrial release: (1) present or recent residence at the same address for six months or more; (2) current or recent employment for six months or more; (3) relatives in New York City with whom the defendant was in contact; (4) no previous conviction of a crime; and (5) residence in New York City for 10 years or more. For those who met the criteria, the students would recommend **release on recognizance (ROR)** to the judge. ROR simply meant that the defendant would be released on his or her own obligation without any requirement of money bail. The obligation was one of record entered into before the court with the condition to appear as required. If the judge agreed with the project's recommendation, the accused was released, subject to some follow-up contacts to ensure that the defendant knew when he or she was due to make a court appearance. Not all defendants were eligible for ROR. Those arrested for such charges as murder, robbery, rape, and other serious crimes were excluded, as were defendants with long criminal histories.

The Vera Institute's pioneer effort in release on recognizance was an immediate success in that four times as many defendants were released. Follow-up studies demonstrated that few released defendants defaulted on their obligation, and the ROR programs modeled after the Manhattan Bail Project were also deemed successful (see Exhibit 12.4).

Within a decade after the Vera Institute initiated the first ROR program, some 90 others were operational in 39 states and the District of Columbia, and Connecticut and Delaware operated theirs statewide.[32]

Along with ROR, other forms of pretrial release emerged. Several jurisdictions established 10 percent cash bond plans. Under the Illinois program, adopted in 1964 and the first in the nation, the court sets bail as it normally would. However, the defendant is permitted to deposit 10 percent of the bond with the court, eliminating the need for a bondsman. When the accused appears for trial, 90 percent of the deposit is returned with the remainder retained to support the operating costs of the program.[33] For example, should bail be set at $1,000, the defendant deposits a $100 cash bond with the court; when he appears for trial, $90 is returned to him. In this way, the financial incentive to appear shifts from the bondsman to the accused.

The size of the deposit and the proportion that is returned varies from one jurisdiction to another. Some require only a 5 percent deposit; others, such as Atlantic City, New Jersey, return the entire deposit upon appearance.

The Manhattan Bail Project

Release on recognizance (ROR): The release of an accused on his or her own obligation rather than on a monetary bond.

The 10 percent cash bond plan

The New York, Philadelphia, and San Francisco ROR Projects

The Manhattan Bail Project

The Vera Institute's ROR program in New York City pioneered this form of pretrial release. A 1964 report on the Vera program provided the following figures:

The results of the Vera Foundation's operation show that from October 16, 1961, through April 8, 1964, out of 13,000 total defendants, 3,000 fell into the excluded offense category, 10,000 were interviewed, 4,000 were recommended and 2,195 were paroled. Only 15 of these failed to show up in court, a default rate of less than seven-tenths of 1 percent. Over the years, Vera's recommendation policy has become increasingly liberal. In the beginning, it urged release for only 28 percent of the defendants interviewed; that figure has gradually increased to 65 percent. At the same time, the rate of judicial acceptance of recommendations has risen from 55 percent to 70 percent. Significantly, the district attorney's office, which originally concurred in only about half of Vera's recommendations, today agrees with almost 80 percent. Since October 1963, an average of 65 defendants per week have been granted parole on Vera's recommendations.

The Philadelphia Common Pleas and Municipal Court ROR Program

The Philadelphia program, modeled on the Manhattan Bail Project, provides for release on a promise to appear at trial of certain arrested persons whose ties to the community suggest that it is reasonable to expect them to appear when directed. The program is a device to eliminate the necessity for money bail and applies to all felonies and misdemeanors.

Arrested persons are interviewed at the police station by the staff of a pretrial services program, who obtain and verify information regarding the accused. The information sought includes residence, family ties, employment,

Whatever the arrangement, the purposes were to make bail possible for those who were not eligible for ROR and at the same time to eliminate the bondsman from the administration of bail.

Both the 10 percent cash bond and the ROR programs have been successful, and a larger portion of defendants are released who might otherwise have awaited trial in detention facilities. Nevertheless, there have been some minor difficulties. Observations in the criminal courts in Miami, Florida, demonstrated that drug users were discriminated against when it came to ROR decisions. When a prosecutor was confronted on the matter, he responded:

> You're not going to get me to cut this junkie loose. He can always get somebody to bail him out. . . . If he gets back on the streets

and prior record. The interviewer submits copies of his or her report to the court, the district attorney, the public defender, and the ROR program agency. A point system that places values on ties to the community is applied to each accused, and from that system a recommendation is made to the court as to whether the accused qualifies for ROR. The judge at arraignment can then either accept or reject the recommendation.

The ROR investigators verify more thoroughly the information concerning defendants who are detained after arraignment. Further interviews may also be conducted. Where warranted, the interviewer may recommend that a petition be filed on behalf of the defendant requesting the court either grant ROR or reduce bail. The pretrial services staff also follows up on persons released on ROR. Each released defendant is obligated to report by telephone to the ROR main office. ROR staff also contact defendants to remind them of their court date.

In the first year of the program ROR staff interviewed 36,252 arrested persons and initially recommended ROR for 17,175, or 47.4 percent. The court granted ROR to 13,041 of those recommended for such release and not otherwise discharged from custody.

During the same year, ROR defendants had a total of 24,790 court appearances scheduled, and only 7.4 percent failed to appear, of which [only] 5.6 percent were willful failures.

The San Francisco Bail Project

The ROR program in San Francisco is modeled after the Vera Institute program and the results have been similar. From August 1, 1964, to July 31, 1968, 6,377 persons were released on their promise to appear. Ninety percent returned for trial and only 1 percent evaded justice altogether.

SOURCE: Quoted from National Advisory Commission on Criminal Justice Standards and Goals, *Corrections* (Washington, D.C.: U.S. Government Printing Office, 1973), p. 109.

and robs some poor bastard for his next fix, at least it won't be on my conscience. If he can't make bail, then he can sit in the can for a few weeks and clean himself up.[34]

For misdemeanants, numerous jurisdictions have adopted citation release programs. In Oakland, California, for example, police officers are authorized to issue citations in lieu of arrests for misdemeanor crimes on the basis of six subjective criteria:

Citation release

Continue: Is the offense likely to continue?
Care: Is the accused in need of medical care, as in the case of drunks or prostitutes?
Identification: Is it inadequate?

Investigation: Is further investigation needed?

Risk: Is the accused a bad risk in the officer's view?

Refuses: Does the accused refuse to sign the citation?

If the answers to all of these questions are no, the field or station-house officer is authorized to release the accused.[35] The Miami, Florida, police department has a similar project, modeled after the Oakland plan. New York City has its Desk Appearance Ticket Program, which involves possible release following fingerprinting, record and warrant checks, and the accused's written promise to appear in court. In all, these citation programs have fugitive rates of less than 10 percent.[36]

The Grand Jury

It must be remembered that a proceeding before a grand jury is an inquest and not a trial. If defendants are treated as having any right to be heard, the whole affair is likely to cease to be an *ex parte* proceeding resulting in a charge which can be fully met at the trial, but to become a litigation in which each side has the right to offer evidence, and an indictment can only be found if the evidence on the whole case preponderates against the defendants. Such it is believed was never the function of the Grand Inquest. — Judge Augustus Hand, 1922

Information: A formal charging document drafted by a prosecutor and tested before a magistrate.

Indictment: A formal charging document returned by a grand jury, based on evidence presented to it by the prosecutor.

Presentment: A written notice of accusation issued by a grand jury, based on its own knowledge and observation.

Grand jury: A body of persons who have been selected according to law and sworn to hear the evidence against accused persons and determine whether there is sufficient evidence to bring those persons to trial, to investigate criminal activity generally, and to investigate the conduct of public agencies and officials.

Hurtado v. California

Following the initial court proceedings, prosecution is instituted by an information, indictment, or presentment. The **information** is a document filed by the prosecutor that states the formal charges, the statutes that have been violated, and the evidence to support the charges. The filing of the information generally occurs at the preliminary hearing and the judge determines whether there is "probable cause" for further processing. The **indictment** is a formal charging document returned by a grand jury, based on evidence presented to it by the prosecutor. Slightly different from the indictment is the **presentment,** which is a written notice of accusation issued by a grand jury. The presentment comes not from evidence and testimony provided by the prosecution, but rather from the initiative of the grand jury, based on its own knowledge and observation. In actual practice, however, the terms *indictment* and *presentment* have come to be substantially interchangeable.

The **grand jury** system apparently originated in England in 1166, when King Henry II required knights and other freemen drawn from rural neighborhoods to file with the court accusations of murder, robbery, larceny, and harboring of known criminals. In time, as the common law developed, the English grand jury came to consist of not fewer than 12 or more than 23 men. Furthermore, not only did they tender criminal accusations, but they considered them from outsiders as well. The jurors heard witnesses and, if convinced that there were grounds for trial, returned an indictment.[37] Historically, therefore, the purposes of the grand jury were to serve as an investigatory body and to act as a buffer between the state and its citizens in order to prevent the Crown from unfairly invoking the criminal process against its enemies.

After the American Revolution, the grand jury was incorporated into the Fifth Amendment to the Constitution, which provides that "no person shall be held to answer for a capital or otherwise infamous crime, unless on a presentment or indictment of a grand jury." Despite this Fifth Amendment guarantee, however, the Supreme Court ruled in *Hurtado v. California* more than a century ago that the grand jury was merely a form of procedure that the states could abolish at will (see Exhibit 12.5).[38]

The American grand jury has retained the common law size from 12 to 23 persons, and the jury's purposes remained unchanged: to investigate and to protect citizens from unfair accusations. Currently, most of the states and

---

EXHIBIT 12.5

Hurtado v. California

In the early days of the Republic, due process was construed not as compliance with the fundamental rules for fair and orderly legal proceedings, but more simply as a limitation on governmental procedure. In terms of criminal procedure, it was presumed to be the procedures spelled out in the Bill of Rights. In the 1878 case of *Davidson* v. *New Orleans* (96 U.S. 97), however, the Supreme Court rejected the notion that due process required adherence to a fixed list of prescribed procedures. Rather, it explained that the meaning of due process would be determined "by the gradual process of judicial inclusion and exclusion." Furthermore, the Court had already decided in 1856 in *Murray's Lessee* v. *Hoboken Land and Improvement Co.* (18 How. 272) that "due" process did not necessarily mean "judicial" process. But if due process procedures were not necessarily "judicial," shouldn't they not then be the common law procedures listed in the Bill of Rights? This was the argument in *Hurtado* v. *California*.*

In 1882, Joseph Hurtado was accused of killing a man named José Stuardo. In a California court, Hurtado was convicted and sentenced to hang. Some years earlier, in 1879, California's constitution had dropped the grand jury system,

substituting the prosecutor's information in its place. Hurtado's attorneys objected, claiming that their client was forced to trial without having been indicted and thus denied "due process of law."

The Supreme Court upheld Hurtado's conviction and death sentence, stating that the grand jury is merely a form of procedure the states can abolish at will. Furthermore, the Court ruled, the due process clause of the Fourteenth Amendment did not encompass any of the fundamental rights that were enumerated in the first ten amendments.

Thirteen years later in the 1897 case of *Chicago, Burlington & Quincy Railroad Co.* v. *City of Chicago* (167 U.S. 226), the Court held that it had been narrow-sighted in *Hurtado,* nullifying the justification for its holding in that decision. However, it never overturned *Hurtado,* and states that joined the Union later failed to adopt the grand jury system, doing so without Supreme Court interference.

As if to underscore its belief that grand juries serve a useless purpose in the administration of justice, the Supreme Court has followed a path of almost complete noninterference with grand jury actions.

---

* Hurtado v. California, 110 U.S. 516 (1884).

---

the federal system use grand juries, and members are generally selected from voting registers. However, many of the territories west of the Mississippi that achieved statehood late in the nineteenth century did not adopt the grand jury system, choosing instead the prosecutor's information (see Exhibit 12.6).

Operation of the Grand Jury

Investigatory and accusatory grand juries

There are essentially two types of grand juries: *investigatory* and *accusatory*. The investigatory grand jury (which must be specially impaneled as such) looks into general allegations of unlawful activity within its jurisdiction in an effort to discover if there is enough information to justify initiating criminal

---

EXHIBIT 12.6

Accusatory Grand Juries by Jurisdiction and Type of Case

Type of Case	Jurisdiction
All cases	Alaska, Arkansas, Iowa, New Jersey, North Carolina, Oregon, South Carolina, Tennessee
Felonies	Alabama, Delaware, District of Columbia, Georgia, Hawaii, Illinois, Kentucky, Maine, Massachusetts, Minnesota, Mississippi, New Hampshire, New York, North Dakota, Ohio, Pennsylvania, Rhode Island, Texas, Vermont, West Virginia, Wisconsin
Capital or life imprisonment offenses	Connecticut, Florida, Louisiana
No grand jury	Arizona, California, Colorado, Idaho, Indiana, Kansas, Maryland, Michigan, Missouri, Montana, Nebraska, Nevada, New Mexico, Oklahoma, South Dakota, Utah, Washington, Wyoming

Notes:

In the federal system, grand juries are used only in felony cases.

In Delaware and Kentucky, grand juries are used also for serious "public offenses," such as crimes committed by public officials.

In Minnesota, grand juries are used only in those felonies that carry a sentence of ten years or longer.

All states maintain grand juries for investigative purposes.

In Indiana, the grand jury is permitted by law, but its use is at the discretion of the prosecutor or the court.

---

prosecutions against anyone. An investigatory grand jury may sit for as little as one month and as many as 18 months, and most often examines suspicions and allegations regarding organized crime and official corruption. More common is the accusatory grand jury, a body impaneled for a set period of time — generally three months — that determines whether there is sufficient evidence against persons already charged with particular crimes to warrant criminal trials. It is the indictment by the accusatory grand jury that parallels the prosecutor's filing of an information, and it is the accusatory grand jury that serves as a screening body to decide whether cases already in the early stages of the criminal justice process are worthy of being tried.

Since grand juries are either investigating or accusing bodies, and do not determine guilt or innocence, many of the elements of due process are absent. For example:

- Grand jury sessions are private and secret.
- Witnesses, having been subpoenaed by the prosecutor, are sworn and heard one by one, and excused as soon as they are finished testifying.
- Ordinarily the accused is not present, unless compelled to testify or invited to serve as a witness.
- In most jurisdictions, the defense counsel has no right to be present; if present, the defense counsel has no right to cross-examine witnesses.
- In some jurisdictions, written transcripts are not required.

When the members of a grand jury agree that an accused should be tried for a crime, they issue a **true bill**. That is, they endorse the validity of the charge or charges specified in the prosecutor's bill, thus returning an indictment. When they fail to find probable cause, they issue *no bill* and the accused is released. Since the grand jury proceeding is not a trial, only a majority vote — not a unanimous one — is required for a true bill.

True bill: A grand jury's endorsement of the charge or charges specified in the prosecutor's bill.

Grand Jury Procedure and the Supreme Court

Prosecutors have wide discretion in the conduct of grand jury proceedings. They may introduce almost any evidence to support their cases, for the Supreme Court has generally refused to impose substantive limits on a grand jury's exercise of discretion. One exception to this course occurred in 1906, in *Hale* v. *Henkel*.[39] In this decision, the Court ruled that "a grand jury may not indict upon current rumors or unverified reports." At the same time, however, the justices did agree that indictments could be based on other information — however unreliable — as long as it was not called "rumor." The Court's position on this latter point became more explicit half a century later in the 1956 case of *Costello* v. *United States*.[40]

Costello v. United States

The principal in the case was Frank Costello, a member of organized crime. Costello was well known to the federal judiciary — he was an associate of such underworld figures as Charles "Lucky" Luciano and Vito Genovese, and had been the star witness in the Kefauver Committee hearings in 1951. Furthermore, as a syndicate racketeer who had consolidated gambling interests throughout the United States during the 1930s, he had the continuous attention of the Internal Revenue Service.

Early in the 1950s, Frank Costello was indicted by a federal investigatory grand jury for willfully attempting to evade payment of federal income taxes for the years 1947 through 1949. The indictments, however, were based on hearsay evidence. Three FBI agents who had no personal knowledge of Costello's finances appeared before the grand jury and "summarized his net worth on the basis of witnesses who were not called to testify." The agents produced "exhibits," which included newspaper stories about Costello's activities. They also made "computations" based on the "exhibits" to demonstrate that Costello and his wife had received a far greater income during those years than they had reported.

After a trial in which 144 witnesses testified and 368 exhibits were introduced, Costello was convicted. The Supreme Court upheld the indictments against Costello, and in so doing, established a precedent that grand juries may issue indictments based on hearsay evidence—evidence learned through others and not within the personal knowledge of the witness offering it as testimony. In delivering the Court's opinion in *Costello,* Justice Hugo L. Black wrote the following:

> Neither the Fifth Amendment nor any other constitutional provision prescribes the kind of evidence upon which grand juries must act. The grand jury is an English institution, brought to this country by the early colonists and incorporated in the Constitution by the Founders. There is every reason to believe that our constitutional grand jury was intended to operate substantially like its English progenitor. The basic purpose of the English grand jury was to provide a fair method for instituting criminal proceedings against persons believed to have committed crimes. Grand jurors were selected from the body of the people and their work was not hampered by rigid procedural or evidential rules. In fact, grand jurors could act on their own knowledge and were free to make their presentments or indictments on such information as they deemed satisfactory. . . .
>
> If indictments were to be held open to challenge on the ground that there was inadequate or incompetent evidence before the grand jury, the resulting delay would be great indeed. The result of such a rule would be that before trial on the merits a defendant could always insist on a kind of preliminary trial to determine the competency and adequacy of the evidence before the grand jury. This is not required by the Fifth Amendment.

United States v. Calandra

In *United States v. Calandra,* almost two decades later,[41] the Court addressed the role of the exclusionary rule in grand jury proceedings. The case involved the search of John Calandra's place of business in Cleveland, Ohio. Federal agents, armed with a valid search warrant, were seeking evidence of bookmaking records and gambling paraphernalia. They found none, but during the course of the search they did discover evidence of a loan-sharking operation. Subsequently, a special federal grand jury was convened and Calandra was subpoenaed to answer questions based on the evidence seized. Calandra refused on Fifth Amendment grounds, as well as on the basis that the search and seizure exceeded the scope of the warrant and was in violation of the Fourth Amendment. The district court ordered the evidence suppressed and the U.S. court of appeals affirmed, holding that the exclusionary rule may be invoked by a witness before a grand jury to bar questioning based on illegally obtained evidence.

On an appeal to the United States Supreme Court brought by the prosecution, the lower court ruling was reversed. The Court based its decision to allow the evidence to be used upon what it found to be the purpose of the exclusionary rule: "The rule is a judicially-created remedy designed to safeguard Fourth Amendment rights generally through its deterrent effects rather than a personal constitutional right of the party aggrieved."

> In deciding whether to extend the exclusionary rule to grand jury proceedings, we must weigh the potential injury to the historic role and functions of the grand jury against the potential benefits of the rule as applied in this context. It is evident that this extension of the exclusionary rule would seriously impede the grand jury. Because the grand jury does not finally adjudicate guilt or innocence, it has traditionally been allowed to pursue its investigative and accusatorial functions unimpeded by the evidentiary and procedural restrictions applicable to a criminal trial. Permitting witnesses to invoke the exclusionary rule before a grand jury would precipitate adjudication of issues hitherto reserved for the trial on the merits and would delay and disrupt grand jury proceedings. . . .

Grand Juries on Trial

Historically, the grand jury was created to stand between government and the citizen as a protection against unfounded charges and unwarranted prosecutions. Critics maintain, however, that the grand jury process has now become an instrument of the very prosecutorial misconduct it was intended to buffer the citizen against.

One complaint concerns the *ex parte* nature of grand jury proceedings. An ex parte is a "one-party" proceeding, meaning that the accused and his or her attorney are not permitted to be present during the grand jury hearing. Under this circumstance, the accused cannot cross-examine witnesses, or object to testimony or evidence.

Ex parte proceedings

Criticisms leveled against grand juries also suggest abuses of their power as they relate to the granting of "immunity." The Fifth Amendment protects individuals against self-incrimination. Traditionally, the government could compel a witness to testify and still protect his or her Fifth Amendment privilege by providing **transactional immunity.** This meant the witness was granted immunity against prosecution in return for testifying. Pursuant to a federal statute in 1970, however, the government adopted a new form of immunity, **use immunity.** This is a limited immunity that prohibits the government only from using a witness's compelled testimony in a subsequent criminal proceeding. If a grand jury witness has been granted use immunity, his compelled testimony cannot be used against him as direct evidence or as an "investigatory lead" in a subsequent criminal proceeding. At the same time, the prosecutor has an affirmative duty to prove that the evidence he or she proposes to use against the immunity-granted witness was derived from a source wholly independent of the compelled testimony. However, as supported by the Supreme Court's 1972 decision in *Kastigar v. United States*,[42] a witness can be indicted on the basis of evidence gathered because of, but "apart" from, his testimony. For example, if a grand jury witness has been given use immunity and his compelled testimony reveals that he was a participant in a bank robbery, the witness may nevertheless be prosecuted for that crime *if* the prosecution is able to produce at trial evidence wholly independent of the witness's grand jury testimony. In the final analysis, then, use immunity is not total immunity.

Transactional immunity: Immunity against prosecution given to a grand jury witness in return for testifying.

Use immunity: A limited immunity that prohibits the government only from using a grand jury witness's compelled testimony in a subsequent criminal proceeding.

Grand juries also possess **contempt power,** which can be used to compel witnesses to provide testimony needed for criminal investigations. Witnesses who refuse to testify can be jailed for an indefinite period of time until they

Contempt power of grand juries

"purge" themselves of contempt by providing the requested information.* This would seemingly result in the abridgement of certain constitutional guarantees. However, the Supreme Court's decision in *Branzburg* v. *Hayes* in 1972 forced journalists to testify before a grand jury when subpoenaed.[43] Some journalists have gone to jail, rather than reveal their confidential sources because they believe that to do so would erode the freedom of the press, protected by the First Amendment. Furthermore, some critics have maintained that the grand jury's contempt power has been used to intentionally punish political dissidents. Activist Anne Strick has argued this point:

> The grand jury, in other words, strips the citizen of almost all constitutional protection; denies him almost all reasonable aid; and then confronts him with the investigatory resource and prestige of an entire state or federal government. Far from protecting the innocent, the grand jury more often offers the innocent no chance to protect themselves from their accusers no matter how false the evidence may be. The witness who resists goes to jail.[44]

The Plea

After the formal determination of charges through either the information or indictment the defendant is arraigned, at which time he or she is asked to enter a plea. The four basic pleas, as noted in Chapter 5, are not guilty, guilty, *nolo contendere,* and standing mute. There is also the special plea of not guilty by reason of insanity.

Plea of Not Guilty

The plea of not guilty, the most common entry at arraignment, places the full burden on the state to move ahead and prove beyond a reasonable doubt the case charged against the defendant. Under the principles of American jurisprudence, even the "guilty" are morally and legally entitled to make such a plea. In the adversary system of justice, it is the right of everyone charged with a crime to rely on the presumption of innocence. *Standing mute* at arraignment by failing or refusing to enter a plea is presumed to be an entry of not guilty.

Guilty Plea

The guilty plea, whether negotiated or not, has several consequences, as pointed out by the National Advisory Commission on Criminal Justice Standards and Goals:

> Such a plea functions not only as an admission of guilt but also as a surrender of the entire array of constitutional rights designed to protect a criminal defendant against unjustified conviction, including the right to remain silent, the right to confront witnesses against him, the right to a trial by jury, and the right to be proven guilty by proof beyond a reasonable doubt.[45]

---

* Although the jailing for contempt can be indefinite, it is usually limited to the period that the grand jury is in session.

The entry of a plea of guilty serves to surrender numerous constitutional rights, including those guaranteed under the Fifth and Sixth Amendments. It is for this reason that observers and attorneys were surprised when Mark David Chapman — accused in the slaying of ex-Beatle John Lennon on December 8, 1980 — entered a guilty plea in a New York court in June 1981.[46] As is the case with virtually all guilty pleas, Chapman's plea to the criminal charge led directly and immediately to a conviction on the underlying crime.

Nolo Contendere

The *nolo contendere* plea is essentially a plea of guilty.

The *nolo contendere* plea, which means "no contest," or, more specifically, "I will not contest it," is essentially a guilty plea. It carries with it the surrendering of certain constitutional rights, and conviction is immediate. However, there is one important difference between a *nolo contendere* and a guilty plea. With *nolo contendere,* there is technically no admission of guilt, which protects the accused in civil court should the victim subsequently sue for damages. In a 1977 case, for example, the noted motorcycle daredevil Evel Knievel entered such a plea after being charged with assaulting his former press agent. Knievel's conviction, then, could not automatically be used against him if the agent later sued for injuries and any lost income resulting from the assault.[47]

The *nolo contendere* plea is not an automatic option at arraignment. It is acceptable in the federal courts and in about half the states, and may be entered only at the discretion of the judge and the prosecutor. Generally, this plea is entered for the benefit of the accused, but in at least one instance, it carried an unintended consequence for perhaps the whole nation. On August 7, 1973, the *Wall Street Journal* reported that Spiro T. Agnew — at the time vice president of the United States under Richard Nixon — was the target of an investigation by U.S. Attorney George Beall in Maryland concerning allegations of kickbacks by contractors, architects, and engineers to officials of Baltimore County. The alleged violations of conspiracy, extortion, bribery, and tax statutes were supposed to have extended from the time Agnew was a Baltimore County executive in 1962 through his years in the vice presidency. After several sessions of plea negotiation between Agnew's attorneys and the Justice Department, it was agreed that Agnew would resign the vice presidency and plead *nolo contendere* to a single charge of income tax evasion. In return, the Justice Department would not proceed with indictment on the other charges. On October 10, 1973, Agnew announced his resignation and entered his plea. It was accepted by Federal District Judge Walter Hoffman, and Agnew received a $10,000 fine and three years' unsupervised probation.

Seven years later, Judge Hoffman recalled the case and remarked that accepting Agnew's plea had been a "wise decision." Had he not accepted the plea, Agnew would have been indicted, tried, and, upon conviction, probably would have appealed. This would have meant that the case would still have been pending when President Nixon resigned from the presidency on August 9, 1974. As Hoffman put it, "When Nixon resigned, Agnew would automatically have been President of the United States."[48]

Insanity Plea

The plea of not guilty by reason of insanity is generally not to the advantage of the accused, for it is an admission of guilt with the contention that the commission of the crime is not culpable in the eyes of the law because of the insanity of the defendant at the time he or she committed the act. More typically, a dual plea of not guilty *and* not guilty by reason of insanity is entered, which implies, "the burden is on the government to prove that I did the act upon which the charge is based, and, even if the government proves that at trial, I still claim I am not culpable because I was legally insane at the time."[49]

Not all jurisdictions have a separate insanity plea, nor do all have the dual plea of not guilty – not guilty by reason of insanity. In these instances, a plea of not guilty is entered and it is the burden of the defense to raise the issue of insanity. However, even in jurisdictions where the statutes allow the insanity plea, the accused and his or her counsel must present an *affirmative defense*. In law, this defense amounts to something more than just a mere denial of the prosecution's allegations. Thus, while the burden of proving the guilt of the accused is on the state, evidencing insanity at the time of the commission of the offense generally rests with the defendant.

Since the early 1970s, there has been considerable opposition to the insanity plea, and courts and legislatures have been pressured to limit, redefine, and even abolish the insanity defense. The opposition is based on the belief that such a plea and defense is an easy route by which defendants in grisly murders, bizarre sex crimes, and attempts on the lives of national figures (such as the assassination attempt on President Ronald Reagan in 1980 by John W. Hinckley, Jr.) can hope to avoid punishment. During the fall of 1981, for example, an Associated Press – NBC News poll demonstrated that 87 percent of the public felt that too many murderers were using insanity pleas to avoid a prison sentence, and almost 70 percent would have banned insanity defenses altogether in murder cases.[50]

However, studies suggest that the general public drastically overestimates the incidence of successful insanity pleas, primarily because the insanity cases are among the most highly publicized. In reality, comparatively few defendants enter pleas of not guilty by reason of insanity. Furthermore, the insanity defense rarely wins. During 1978, of the more than two million criminal cases disposed of in state and federal courts, less than one-tenth of 1 percent of the defendants were institutionalized after successful insanity pleas. Furthermore, only one in four insanity pleas led to acquittals, and the majority of these involved misdemeanor charges.[51]

Nevertheless, legislators have continued to press for changes. In 1979, Montana abolished the insanity defense, and in 1982 Idaho enacted a similar statute. Moreover, Georgia and Michigan have adopted "guilty but mentally ill" laws. Under these regulations, which other states are considering, defendants found guilty but mentally ill go to prison. If they require psychiatric treatment, they receive it in the penitentiary.

Pleas of Statute of Limitations

Every state has laws known as "statutes of limitations," which bar prosecution for most crimes after a certain amount of time has passed; that is, the suspect must be accused within a reasonable period of time after the offense was committed. The reasons for these statutes are numerous. After the passage of time, for example, a defendant may be unable to establish his whereabouts at the time of the crime, or evidence or witnesses supporting his innocence might be lost. Similarly, after long periods of time, those guilty of crimes may be unable to gather evidence to support their defense or to mitigate their conduct. Furthermore, during the long period of time since the offense the offender may have become a law-abiding citizen who presents no further threat to the community, and conviction and sentencing would serve little purpose.

Statutes of limitations can be quite complex. Generally, such statutes do not apply to murder prosecutions. Furthermore, statutes for other offenses may be *tolled* (suspended) by reason of numerous circumstances, such as the defendant's absence from the state. And finally, in most jurisdictions the plea of statute of limitations must be entered at arraignment, otherwise the accused will be deemed to have waived that particular defense.[52]

Double Jeopardy

To restrain the government from repeatedly prosecuting an accused for one particular offense, the prohibition against **double jeopardy** — two trials for one offense — was included in the Constitution. The Fifth Amendment provides in part: "Nor shall any person be subject for the same offense to be twice put in jeopardy of life or limb."

The Supreme Court has held that this guarantee protects the accused against both multiple prosecutions for the same offense and multiple punishments for the same crime. However, to whom and when the Fifth Amendment guarantee applies are matters that have taken the Supreme Court almost two centuries to clarify.

United States v. *Perez* in 1824 denied double jeopardy protection in cases where a jury failed to agree on a verdict.[53] In 1896, the Court ruled in *United States* v. *Ball* that if a conviction is set aside for some reason other than insufficient evidence, the defendant may be tried again for the same offense.[54] *Wade* v. *Hunter* in 1949,[55] following a similar line, declared that the double jeopardy clause did not apply in certain circumstances of mistrial.

In the 1922 case of *United States* v. *Lanza,*[56] the Court addressed the issue of double jeopardy and dual sovereignty. In *Lanza,* the defendant had been convicted of violating Washington state's prohibition law. He had then been indicted on the same grounds for violating the federal prohibition law. In a 6-to-3 vote, the Court ruled that the Fifth Amendment double jeopardy clause protected only against repeated prosecutions by a single sovereign government. The Court's opinion, which approached the state of Washington and the federal government as separate sovereignties deriving power from different sources, was that the second indictment had been a valid one. The *Lanza* rule was reaffirmed in the 1959 case of *Abbate* v. *United States,*[57] but in *Waller* v. *Florida* 11 years later,[58] the Court ruled that a city and a state were not separate sovereignties.

The application of the double jeopardy clause to state criminal trials was rejected by the Supreme Court in the 1937 case of **Palko v. Connecticut.**[59] Some three decades later, however, in **Benton v. Maryland** — the last announced decision of the Warren Court — the majority opinion declared that the double jeopardy clause applied to the states through the due process clause of the Fourteenth Amendment.[60] (See Exhibit 12.7.) Finally, in **Downum v. United States,**[61] the Court declared that double jeopardy begins at the point where the second trial jury is sworn in.

Under state statutes, pleas of not guilty on double jeopardy grounds can be of two types: *autrefois* acquit and *autrefois* convict.[62] The accused can plead *autrefois acquit* (formerly acquitted) if he or she was acquitted of the identical charge involving the same set of facts on a previous occasion before a

The Fifth Amendment protection against double jeopardy protects an accused from both multiple prosecutions for the same offense and multiple punishments for the same crime.

Palko v. Connecticut
Benton v. Maryland

Downum v. United States

Autrefois acquit

court of competent jurisdiction. Or the accused can plead *autrefois convict* (formerly convicted) if he or she was convicted of the identical charge involving the same set of facts on a previous occasion before a court of competent jurisdiction.

Pretrial Motions

All pleas of not guilty (other than those dismissed on statute of limitations or double jeopardy grounds) result in the setting of a trial date. Prior to the actual commencement of the trial, however, and sometimes prior to arraignment, both the defense and the prosecution may employ a number of motions. A *motion* is a formal application or request to the court for some action, such as an order or rule. The purpose of motions is to gain some legal advantage, and most are initiated by the defense. The number and type of motions vary by

---

EXHIBIT 12.7

The States and Double Jeopardy

Palko v. Connecticut, 302 U.S. 319 (1937)

The petitioner, Frank U. Palko, had been indicted by the state of Connecticut for murder in the first degree for the fatal shooting of two policemen. The trial jury, however, found him guilty of only second-degree murder, for which he was sentenced to life imprisonment. The state appealed the conviction to the Court of Errors—Connecticut's highest court—charging that the action of the trial court (convicting on the lesser count) constituted an "error of law to the prejudice of the state." The Court of Errors agreed, reversed the judgment, and ordered a new trial. Subsequently, Palko was convicted of murder in the first degree and sentenced to death.

Palko appealed to the United States Supreme Court contending that "whatever is forbidden by the Fifth Amendment is forbidden by the Fourteenth

also." The Court rejected Palko's argument, stating that the Fifth Amendment's double jeopardy prohibition was not a fundamental right and did not apply to state criminal prosecutions. Frank Palko was subsequently executed by electrocution.

Benton v. Maryland, 395 U.S. 784 (1969)

Thirty-two years after *Palko*, in 1969, the Court again considered whether the double jeopardy clause was applicable to the states. The petitioner, John Benton, had been indicted for burglary, larceny, and housebreaking. At trial, he was convicted of burglary, acquitted on the larceny charge, and not tried on the housebreaking. He was then sentenced to 10 years on the burglary conviction.

Both the indictment and conviction were set aside by a subsequent change in the state

law, and Benton was given the option of being retried or leaving his conviction for burglary intact. He chose to be retried, but at his second trial he was tried again not only for the burglary but for the larceny as well. He was convicted and sentenced on both counts, and appealed to the U.S. Supreme Court on double jeopardy grounds.

In a 6-to-2 majority decision, the Court overruled *Palko*. Justice Thurgood Marshall stated his opinion:

Our recent cases have thoroughly rejected the *Palko* notion that basic constitutional rights can be denied by the States so long as the totality of the circumstances does not disclose a denial of "fundamental fairness." Once it is decided that a particular Bill of Rights guarantee is "fundamental to the American scheme of justice," . . . the same Constitutional standards apply against both the State and Federal Governments. *Palko*'s roots had thus been cut away years ago. We today only recognize the inevitable.

---

the nature and complexity of the case, and it is the court's role to decide whether each should be granted or denied. Without question, the court's decisions in these matters can have a considerable impact on the outcome of a proceeding.

Motion for Discovery

It is always in the best interests of the defense to know in advance what witnesses and kinds of evidence the prosecution plans to introduce at trial. The *motion for discovery* is a request to examine the physical evidence, evidentiary documents, and lists of witnesses in the possession of the prosecutor. Although some jurisdictions may resist such a motion, discovery is a matter of constitutional law. The Supreme Court's decision in the 1963 case of *Brady* v. *Maryland* held that a prosecutor's failure to disclose evidence favorable to the accused upon request violates due process.[63] However, in *Moore* v. *Illinois* some years later,[64] the Court also ruled that there was no constitutional requirement for the prosecution to fully disclose the entire case file to the defense.

Motion for Change of Venue

Venue, from the Latin meaning "neighborhood," refers to the county or district—not the jurisdiction—wherein a case is to be tried. A *motion for a change of venue* is a request that the trial be moved from the county, district, or circuit in which the crime was committed to some other place. The jurisdiction does not change; the original trial court simply moves if the motion is granted.

Either the defense or the prosecution can introduce such a motion. Typically, however, it is a move made by the defense in the case of sensational or highly publicized crimes when it is felt that the accused cannot obtain a fair trial in the particular locale of the court.

Motion for Suppression

Mapp v. *Ohio, Escobedo* v. *Illinois,* and *Miranda* v. *Arizona* collectively served to make suppression one of the most common of pretrial motions in criminal cases.[65] The *motion for suppression* is a request to have evidence excluded from consideration. Typically, it is filed by the defense to prohibit evidence that was obtained as the result of an illegal search and seizure or wiretap, or to challenge the validity of a confession.

Motion for a Bill of Particulars

A *bill of particulars* is a written statement that specifies additional facts about the charges contained in the information or indictment. As a motion filed by the defense, it is a request for more details from the prosecution. The motion is not made for the purpose of discovering evidence or of learning exactly how much the prosecution knows, and it is not designed to suggest an insufficient indictment. Rather, the *motion for a bill of particulars* asks for details about what the prosecution claims in order to give the accused fair notice of what must be defended. For example, if a neighborhood bookie who operates illegal lotteries and off-track betting schemes is charged with possession of gambling paraphernalia, the defense might wish to know which of the confiscated

Bill of particulars: A written statement that specifies additional facts about a charge.

materials (policy slips, betting cards, and so on) the prosecutor intends to use as the basis of his or her action.

Motion for Severance of Charges or Defendants

Many legal actions involve multiple charges against one defendant. The accused may have been arrested, for example, for a number of different crimes resulting from a single incident—an auto theft, for example, followed by destruction of property, resisting arrest, and assault upon a police officer. Or the accused may be charged with multiple counts of the same offense— perhaps several sales of dangerous drugs during a given period of time. In both instances, and for the sake of expediency, the prosecution may consolidate these multiple charges into a single case. The defense, however, may feel that different tactics are required for dealing with each charge. Thus, the *motion for severance of charges* requests that each specific charge be tried as a separate case.

Similarly, many proceedings involve more than one person charged with participation in the same crime—perhaps four codefendants in a bank robbery. There are times when the best interests of one or more of the accused are served by separate trials. Defendant Smith, for example, may wish a trial by jury; defendant Jones may wish to place the blame on his codefendants. Thus, the *motion for severance of defendants* requests that one or more of the accused be tried in separate proceedings.

Motion for Continuance

The *motion for continuance* requests that the trial be postponed to some future date. Such a motion is filed by the defense or the prosecution on the grounds that there has not been sufficient time to prepare the case. There may, for example, have been difficulty in gathering evidence or locating witnesses. This motion is used by some defense attorneys as a stalling tactic to enhance the accused's chances. As one of Brooklyn, New York's "Court Street lawyers" commented:

> If you can delay a case long enough, victims' memories begin to fail, witnesses begin to lose interest, and the court wants to move on to other things. Sometimes you end up working out a better plea, and on two separate occasions we actually managed to get the cases dismissed because of lack of witnesses.[66]

Motion for Dismissal

As a matter of common practice, at arraignment, defense attorneys make a *motion for dismissal* of charges on the grounds that the prosecution has failed to produce sufficient evidence to warrant further processing. Justified or not, this is an almost automatic motion filed by most defense attorneys. In practically all instances, however, such a motion is denied by the judge. There are other situations, though, where the motion for dismissal is fully warranted and is granted by the presiding magistrate. A previously granted motion for suppression, for example, may have weakened the state's case. Here it could be the defense *or* the prosecution who files the motion. Furthermore, in jurisdictions where prosecutors do not have full authority to issue a *nolle prosequi,* the dropping of charges must be sought through a judicial dismissal.

Other pretrial motions may include requests to inspect grand jury minutes, to determine sanity, or to discover statements made by prosecution witnesses. By far, however, the most common are the motions for suppression and dismissal.

It should be emphasized here that if a motion by the defense results in the dismissal of a case, the prosecution has the legal authority to reinstate the case. Charges can be filed, dismissed, and refiled, for there is no double jeopardy connected with the pretrial process. As noted in *Downum* v. *United States* and reaffirmed by the Supreme Court in *Serfass* v. *United States*,[67] in a jury trial, jeopardy attaches when the jury is impaneled and sworn; in a bench trial, jeopardy attaches when the court begins to hear evidence.

Speedy and Public Trial

In all criminal prosecutions, the accused shall enjoy the right to a speedy and public trial. . . . . —from the Sixth Amendment

It is no surprise that the right to a **speedy trial** appears in the Constitution of the United States. Without it, persons accused of crimes would have no protection against indefinite incarceration prior to coming to trial. Like all

Defendants have the constitutional right to a speedy trial, provided by the Sixth Amendment.

The witness stand in the Edgefield County courthouse, Edgefield, South Carolina

other provisions in the Bill of Rights, the guarantee of a speedy trial is a measure devised solely to ensure the rights of individual defendants, rather than to protect the state from delays that might be caused by the accused.

Putting the speedy trial clause of the **Sixth Amendment** into practice, however, has been difficult. First, since the early days of the Constitution, the criminal justice system has become more complex. Many procedural steps have been added to criminal proceedings in order to guarantee a fair hearing for the accused. Second, more persons are accused of violations of the law each year, making delays inevitable. Furthermore, in many metropolitan areas where crime rates are high, it is difficult for some defendants to receive any trial at all, not to mention a speedy one. Third, the criminal law has become more detailed and elaborate. Some state statutes have become so highly specific that the evidence-gathering process in many cases has evolved into a time-consuming task. Fourth, the requirement that the judicial contest be conducted with promptness must be balanced against the right of an accused as well as of a prosecutor to have ample time to prepare their cases before going to trial. Fifth, some trials are inexcusably delayed by either the prosecution or the defense for the purpose of achieving their own objectives. A prosecutor, for example, may seek several continuances, hoping to put off a trial until an accused's codefendant is convinced to "strike a deal" and become a witness for the state. A defense attorney may employ the same delaying tactics in anticipation of witnesses' loss of interest in the case. Sixth, some delays result from little more than prosecutors' apathy or lack of concern for defendants' rights and humanity. A case that received national publicity in 1975 involved a New York truck driver awaiting trial on charges of two counts of vehicular homicide. After spending some 14 months in jail, he was finally freed when it was disclosed that two assistant district attorneys had known for the entire period that eyewitnesses corroborated the accused's claim that he was not the driver of the vehicle in question.[68] And seventh, there is no consensus among the states as to the meaning of "speedy trial." Statutory time limits vary by jurisdiction and by the nature of the offense charged. Here are three examples:

- In California, the period between arraignment and trial must not exceed 56 days.[69]
- In Alabama, the time limit between arrest and trial is set at 12 months for misdemeanors, three years for all felonies — except capital offenses, for which there is no limit.[70]
- In Maine, there is a flexible standard of "unnecessary delay" — whatever that might mean.[71]

The Supreme Court and Speedy Trial

The Constitution offers no clues as to what its framers had in mind when they incorporated the concept of "speedy trial" into the Bill of Rights. As a result, the Supreme Court has attached a standard of *reasonableness* to the right, which represents an attempt at a balancing of interests — weighing the effects of delays against their causes and justifications. The Court emphasized this posture, as early as 1905, when in *Beavers* v. *Haubert* it ruled that the right to a speedy trial was only a "relative" matter "consistent with delays and dependent on circumstances."[72]

In many of the Court's subsequent decisions, the particulars of individual cases seem to have been addressed rather than more encompassing policy issues. With the onset of the 1970s, however, the Supreme Court rulings in a series of cases did provide some guidelines for trial courts. The first of these was *Barker* v. *Wingo*,[73] decided in 1972. Until that time, both federal and state courts operated under the assumption that an accused's failure to demand a speedy trial meant that he was essentially unopposed to any accumulating delays. In *Barker,* the Court rejected this thesis, holding that passive compliance does not amount to a waiver of the Sixth Amendment right. Furthermore, although the Court was unwilling to announce any specific time frame for what would constitute delay, it did identify a variety of factors that trial courts should examine in determining whether the right to a speedy trial had been denied: the length of the delay, the reason for the delay, the defendant's assertion of his right, and prejudice to the defendant.

The following year, in *Strunk* v. *United States,*[74] the Supreme Court unanimously held that if a defendant is denied a speedy trial, "the only possible remedy" is for the charges to be dismissed. Later in the decade, in *United States* v. *Lovasco,*[75] the Court made clear that the Sixth Amendment right did not apply to delays before a person is accused of a crime, but rather, only to the interval between arrest and trial.

Speedy Trial and the States

Speedy trial, a constitutional guarantee since the framing of the Bill of Rights, was not made applicable to the states until recently. The vehicle was ***Klopfer v. North Carolina,***[76] decided in 1967.

Klopfer v. North Carolina

The petitioner in this somewhat unusual case was Peter H. Klopfer, a professor of zoology at Duke University. Klopfer had been indicted by the state of North Carolina for criminal trespass as the result of a sit-in at a segregated motel and restaurant. At trial, however, the jury failed to agree on a verdict. This resulted in a mistrial, thus necessitating a new trial. But after a year had passed and the second trial had not been ordered, Professor Klopfer demanded that his case either be tried immediately or dismissed. Rather than complying with the petitioner's demands, the presiding judge instead granted the prosecutor's request for a *nolle prosequi.* At the time, this allowed the prosecutor to place the indictment in an inactive status without bringing it to trial — and thus retaining it for use at *any* time in the future. On appeal to the North Carolina Supreme Court, Klopfer argued that the trial judge's action denied his Sixth Amendment right, which he regarded as applicable to the states. The Carolina appeals court ruled that a defendant's right to a speedy trial did not encompass "the right to compel the state to prosecute him." Thus, still in limbo with his "suspended" trespass indictment, Klopfer petitioned the United States Supreme Court.

The Court ruled in favor of Professor Klopfer, and more. First, it unanimously struck down the recalcitrant North Carolina law that allowed indefinite postponement of a criminal prosecution without dismissal of an indictment. And second, Chief Justice Earl Warren explained that the North Carolina procedure

> clearly denies the petitioner the right to a speedy trial which we hold is guaranteed to him by the Sixth Amendment. . . . We hold here that the right to a speedy trial is as fundamental as any of the rights secured by the Sixth Amendment.

In so stating, the Court extended the speedy trial clause to the states.

The Speedy Trial Act of 1974

The Speedy Trial Act reduced delays in federal trials.

The ruling in *Barker* v. *Wingo* prompted Congress — against the advice of both the Justice Department and the federal judges — to pass the **Speedy Trial Act** of 1974 in an effort to demand a reduction in delays in *federal* trials. Under the sponsorship of Senator Sam J. Ervin of North Carolina, the act established a 100-day deadline between arrest and trial.

The Speedy Trial Act was phased in gradually, not becoming fully effective until June 30, 1980. Currently, under its mandate, failure to bring a case to trial within the 100 day deadline — except in a few rigidly defined situations — results in dismissal of charges.

The Right to a Public Trial

The Sixth Amendment right to a public trial derives from English common law.

The Sixth Amendment provides not only for a speedy trial, but for a **public trial** as well — a guarantee with its roots in our heritage of English common law.

The traditional Anglo-American distrust for secret trials evolved from the notorious use of the practice by the Spanish Inquisition, the English Star Chamber court,* and the French monarchy's use of the *lettre de cachet.*† In the hands of despotic groups, these institutions became instruments of political and religious suppression through their ruthless disregard of the accused's right to a fair trial.

Although all jurisdictions have adopted the Sixth Amendment right to a public trial through state constitutions, by statute, or by judicial decisions, there have been exceptions in the recent past. *In re Oliver,*[77] decided in 1948, was one of the very few cases addressed by the Supreme Court on the right to a public trial. The issue in *Oliver* stemmed from the actions of a Michigan judge serving in the role of a one-person grand jury. The judge's actions were described in the High Court's opinion:

> In the case before us, the petitioner was called as a witness to testify in secret before a one-man grand jury conducting a grand jury investigation. In the midst of petitioner's testimony the proceedings abruptly changed. The investigation became a "trial," the grand jury became a judge, and the witness became an accused charged with contempt of court — all in secret. Following a charge, conviction, and sentence, the petitioner was led away to prison — still without any break in the secrecy. Even in jail, according to undenied allegations, his lawyer was denied an opportunity to see and confer with him. And that was not the end of the secrecy. His lawyer filed in the state supreme court this *habeas corpus* proceeding. Even there, the mantle of secrecy enveloped the transaction and the state supreme court ordered him sent back to jail without ever having seen a record of his testimony, and without knowing all that took place in the secrecy of the judge's

---

* In England during the Middle Ages, the Star Chamber was a meeting place of the King's counselors in the palace of Westminster — so called from the stars painted on its ceiling. The Court of the Star Chamber developed from the proceedings traditionally carried out by the king and his council, and typically dealt with equity matters. In the fifteenth century under the Tudors, the jurisdiction of the court was extended to criminal matters. Faster and less rigid than the common law courts, Star Chamber proceedings tended to be harsh at times, and they were ultimately abolished by Parliament in 1641. (It was from this court that the 20th Century-Fox film *Star Chamber,* in 1983, drew its title.)

† A part of seventeenth-century French law, the *lettre de cachet* was a private, sealed document issued as a communication from the king which could order the imprisonment or exile of an individual without recourse to the courts.

chambers. In view of this nation's historic distrust of secret proceedings, their inherent dangers to freedom, and the universal requirement of our federal and state governments that criminal trials be public, the Fourteenth Amendment's guarantee that no one shall be deprived of his liberty without due process of law means that at least an accused cannot be thus sentenced to prison.

The Court further held that the failure to give the accused a reasonable opportunity to defend himself against the contempt charge was a denial of due process of law. Yet curiously, despite the justice's pronouncement in behalf of the petitioner, *Oliver* did not expressly incorporate the Sixth Amendment right to a public trial within the meaning of the Fourteenth Amendment. This did not occur until 30 years later, in a footnote to *Duncan* v. *Louisiana,*[78] discussed in the next section.

The Jury

As a criminal prosecution approaches the trial date, a pretrial hearing is held, at which point the pretrial motions are heard and dealt with by the judge. At the same time, the court also asks whether the accused wishes a trial by judge or a trial by jury.

The trial by judge (or judges), more commonly referred to as a *bench trial,* is one in which the decision of innocence or guilt is made by the presiding judge. In some jurisdictions the decision regarding trial by judge may be dictated by state requirements. Under Tennessee statutes, for example, the accused is not prevented from waiving his right to a trial by jury;[79] in Idaho, however, this waiver is permitted only in nonfelony cases.[80]

Bench trials

When defendants are in a position to exercise a choice, there are several circumstances under which the bench trial would probably be more desirable. For example, the crime may be so reprehensible or so widely publicized that finding a neutral jury could be difficult if not impossible. Or the nature of the defense may be too complex or technical for persons untrained in law to fully comprehend. Also, the presiding judge may have a previous record of favorable decisions in like cases. In addition, there is the possible effect of the defendant's appearance and past record on the jury:

> The general appearance of the defendant may be such that a jury may become more prejudiced against him. The defendant may have a serious past criminal record subjecting him to possible impeachment should he take the witness stand in his own defense, and the probability of the jury convicting the defendant on his past record rather than on the evidence contended in the present charge is great. Or the defendant may be a part of an organized criminal syndicate, or minority group of which local feeling is against, and the jury may convict the accused by association rather than on the facts of the case. A judge is considered less inclined to be affected by any of these situations than a jury.[81]

The reasons for selecting a trial by jury are perhaps even more compelling. The jury serves as a safeguard against overzealous prosecutors and biased judges, and it affords the accused the benefit of commonsense judgment as opposed to the perhaps less sympathetic reactions of a single magistrate. More important to the defendant, it has been empirically documented that the odds for acquittal are better with a jury than with a judge. The widely acclaimed University of Chicago Jury Study during the 1960s demonstrated, for example, that the conviction rate by judges was some 83.3 percent, as opposed to the lesser 64.4 percent by juries.[82]

The Right to Trial by Jury

The trial by jury is a distinctive feature of the Anglo-American system of justice, dating back more than seven centuries. When the Magna Carta was signed in the year 1215, it contained a special provision that no freeholder would be deprived of life or property except by judgment of his or her peers. This common law principle was incorporated into the Constitution of the United States. Article III contains this simple and straightforward statement: "The trial of all crimes, except in cases of impeachment, shall be by jury." Article III is reaffirmed by the Sixth Amendment, which holds that "in all criminal prosecutions, the accused shall enjoy the right to a speedy and public trial by an impartial jury."

In federal cases, where Article III applies directly, the Supreme Court has been unrelenting in its view that a jury in criminal cases must contain twelve persons and reach a unanimous verdict.

Curiously, however, for almost two centuries after the framing of the Constitution, the right to a trial by jury "in all criminal prosecutions" was not fully binding in state trials. Despite Article III and the Sixth Amendment, some state statutes denied the right to many defendants. What ultimately brought *Duncan v. Louisiana* the right to a jury trial to the states was ***Duncan v. Louisiana,***[83] decided in 1968.

The setting was Plaquemines Parish, Louisiana, an oil-rich community some 50 miles northwest of New Orleans. At the time, Plaquemines Parish had long been bossed by the skillful political leader Leander H. Perez, a virulent segregationist whose philosophies and opinions seemingly influenced local folkways. Gary Duncan, a 19-year-old black, had been tried in the local court on a charge of simple battery — a misdemeanor punishable by a maximum of 2 years' imprisonment and a $300 fine. His crime had involved no more than slapping the elbow of a white youth. He was convicted, fined $150, and sentenced to 60 days in jail. Duncan had requested a trial by jury, but this was denied on the authority of the Louisiana constitution, which granted jury trials only in cases where capital punishment or imprisonment at hard labor could be imposed. Duncan appealed to the U.S. Supreme Court, contending that his right to a jury trial was guaranteed by the Sixth and Fourteenth Amendments.

In a 7-to-2 decision, the Court ruled in favor of Duncan, thus incorporating the Sixth Amendment right to a jury into the due process clause of the Fourteenth Amendment. In the words of Justice Byron White:

> Because we believe that trial by jury in criminal cases is fundamental to the American scheme of justice, we hold that the Fourteenth Amendment guarantees a right of jury trial in all criminal cases which — were they to be tried in federal court — would come within the Sixth Amendment's guarantee. Since we consider the appeal before us to be such a case, we hold that the Constitution was violated when appellant's demand for jury trial was refused.

In spite of this holding, the matter was not fully resolved — not for Gary Duncan and not for thousands of defendants who would be requesting jury trials. The Supreme Court's ruling in *Duncan* had reversed the Louisiana trial court's conviction of Gary Duncan. This mandated either a dismissal of the simple battery charge or a new trial. But the Louisiana court refused to comply with either alternative, thus leaving Duncan under a continuing threat of further prosecution. This situation remained unchanged for three years, until the federal courts could effectively command Plaquemines Parish to dispose of the case.[84]

The other unresolved issue related to a segment of Justice White's opinion in *Duncan*. He had pointed out that so-called petty offenses were traditionally tried without a jury. That would continue to be so, but beyond that, he offered no distinction between serious and petty offenses in state cases. Two years later the Court brought this matter to rest in *Baldwin* v. *New York*,[85] when it defined a petty offense as one carrying a maximum sentence of six months or less.

Jury Selection

Historically, trial juries — sometimes referred to as *petit juries* to differentiate them from grand juries — have typically consisted of 12 jurors. In all federal prosecutions 12-member juries are required, but not in all state prosecutions (see Exhibit 12.8). In *Williams* v. *Florida*,[86] decided in 1970, the Court ruled that it was proper for states to use juries composed of as few as six persons, at least in noncapital cases, and some eight years later it reaffirmed this decision when it rejected the use of a five-person jury in the state of Georgia.[87]

Jury selection involves a series of procedural steps, beginning with the preparation of a master list of eligible jurors. Eligibility requirements gener-

The steps in jury selection

EXHIBIT 12.8

State Provisions on Jury Size in Criminal Prosecutions

Twelve-Member Juries Required

Alabama, Hawaii, Illinois, Maine, Maryland, New Jersey, North Carolina, North Dakota, Rhode Island, Vermont, West Virginia, Wisconsin

Juries of Fewer Than Twelve Members Specifically Authorized

Alaska, Arizona, Colorado, Connecticut, Florida, Georgia, Idaho, Indiana, Iowa, Kansas, Kentucky, Louisiana, Massachusetts, Michigan, Minnesota, Mississippi, Missouri, Montana, Nebraska, New Hampshire, New Mexico, New York, Ohio, Oklahoma, Oregon, South Carolina, South Dakota, Tennessee, Texas, Utah, Virginia, Washington, Wyoming

Juries of Fewer Than Twelve Members Permitted by Agreement

Arkansas, California, Delaware, Nevada, Pennsylvania

SOURCE: Based on data from National Center for State Courts, *Facets of the Jury System: A Survey* (1976), pp. 41–44.

Cat Mousam, who was listed as an occupant on her owners' door, was duly counted by the Boston census taker and later summoned for jury duty. Her owners, social workers wise to bureaucratic ways, used the portion of the summons set aside for reasons to decline to serve to declare that "Cat Mousam is not qualified to serve as a juror because she is a cat." Accordingly, notice came back from the Massachusetts jury commissioner that Cat Mousam would indeed be excused from duty. Reason: "Language." She and another cat in the household had been listed on the rolls as nurses ages 29 and 32.

The *voir dire* is an oath sworn by a juror regarding his or her qualifications. The *venire* is a writ that summons jurors.

ally include citizenship and literacy. In addition, there are restrictions against minors, persons with serious felony convictions, and occupational groups such as physicians, attorneys, police officers, legislators, the clergy, and several others, depending on the rules of the jurisdiction. Others, such as the aged, disabled, mothers with young children, and persons whose employers will not allow it, may be exempted from jury service on the basis of hardship. Not too many exemptions can be allowed, in preparing the master list, however, because an "impartial" jury in constitutional terms means a representative cross-section of a community's citizens. This is why the Supreme Court in 1975 struck down a Louisiana law that barred women from juries unless they specifically requested, in writing, to participate.[88]

In current practice, the basis of the master list in many communities is the local voter registration roll. This source, at least in theory, is considered to be representative of the population. It does not systematically exclude persons on the basis of age, sex, ethnicity, political affiliation or socioeconomic status. Furthermore, it is readily available. However, studies of voting behavior have demonstrated that registration lists are highly biased as sources of jury pools. From 30 percent to 50 percent of those eligible in various jurisdictions do not register to vote. Furthermore, one study undertaken during the late 1970s found the registration rates for persons with incomes of less than $3,000 to be only 61.2 percent, compared to 85 percent for those earning over $15,000.[89] Similarly, members of racial minorities, young people, and the poorly educated more frequently ignore the electoral process, or have been excluded from it by legal or extralegal means. To mitigate this difficulty, some communities have initiated the use of multiple-source lists, supplementing voter registration lists with additional names drawn from rosters of licensed drivers, and telephone directories.

The Venire

From the master list of eligible jurors, names are randomly selected for the *venire*. The *venire,* or *venire facias,* is the writ that summons jurors. More commonly, however, the *venire* refers to the list of potential jurors who are eligible for a given period of service. These summoned jurors become members of a jury pool, and they are interviewed to confirm their eligibility and availability. Those who remain in the pool are paid for their time; the current nationwide average rate is $15 per day.

The procedure through which members of the jury pool become actual trial jurors begins with the selection of a jury *panel.* In a felony prosecution that requires 12 jurors, as many as 30 are selected for the panel. Their names are drawn at random by the clerk of the court, and from there they move on to the *voir dire* examination.

The Voir Dire

A *voir dire,* meaning "to speak the truth," is an oath sworn by a prospective juror regarding his or her qualifications as a juror. The *voir dire* examination involves questioning by the prosecutor, defense attorney, and sometimes the judge in order to determine a candidate's fitness to serve as a juror. The inquiry focuses on the person's background, familiarity with the case, associations with persons involved in the case, attitudes about certain facts that might arise during the trial, and any other matters that may reflect upon his or her willingness and ability to judge the case fairly and impartially.

A potential juror who is deemed unacceptable to either the prosecutor or the defense is eliminated through either the challenge for cause or the peremptory challenge.

The *challenge for cause* means that there is a sound legal reason to remove a potential juror, and whoever makes such a challenge — either the defense attorney or the prosecutor — must explain to the judge the nature of the concern. Typically, challenges for cause allege that the prospective juror would be incapable of judging the accused fairly. Such challenges are controlled by statute, and the decision to remove a juror is vested with the court. Also, there is technically no limit on the number of challenges for cause that may be made (see Exhibit 12.9).

A *peremptory challenge* is an objection to a prospective juror for which no reason must be assigned. It can be made for any reason or no reason at all and is totally within the discretion of the attorney making it. Peremptory challenges generally reflect the biases and strategies of the defense and the

Challenge for cause

Peremptory challenge

EXHIBIT 12.9

Challenges for Cause: An Excerpt from a Statute

1. A challenge for cause is an objection to a prospective member of the jury and may be made only on the gound that:

(a) He does not have the qualifications required by the judiciary law; or

(b) He has a state of mind that is likely to preclude him from rendering an impartial verdict based upon the evidence adduced at the trial; or

(c) He is related within the sixth degree by consanguinity or affinity to the defendant, or to the person allegedly injured by the crime charged, or to a prospective witness at the trial, or to counsel for the people or for the defendant; or that he is or was a party adverse to any such person in a civil action; or that he has complained against or been accused by any such person in a criminal action; or that he bears some other

relationship to any such person of such nature that it is likely to preclude him from rendering an impartial verdict; or

(d) He is to be a witness at the trial; or where a prosecutor's information was filed at the direction of a grand jury, he was a witness before the grand jury or at the preliminary hearing; or

(e) He served on a trial jury in a prior civil or criminal action involving the same conduct charged; or where a prosecutor's information was filed at the direction of a grand jury, he served on the grand jury which directed such filing.

2. All issues of fact or questions of law arising on the challenge must be tried and determined by the court. . . .

SOURCE: State of New York, Criminal Procedure Law, Laws 1970, Chapter 996, Section 360.25.

prosecution. Clarence Darrow, perhaps the greatest defense attorney of the twentieth century, once advised his colleagues to avoid affluent jurors, "because, next to the Board of Trade, the wealthy consider the penitentiary to be the most important of all public buildings.[90] In contrast is an excerpt from a training manual for Texas district attorneys:

WHAT TO LOOK FOR IN A JUROR

A. Attitudes

1. You are not looking for a fair juror, but rather a strong biased, and sometimes hypocritical individual who believes that defendants are different from them in kind, rather than degree.

2. You are not looking for any member of a minority group which may subject him to oppression—they almost always empathize with the accused.

3. You are not looking for the free thinkers and flower children. . . .[91]

During the 1974 trial of James Richardson, a black man charged with the murder of a white police officer in New York City, the noted defense attorney William M. Kunstler used most of his preemptory challenges to eliminate from the jury as many whites as possible. At the same time, assistant district attorney Steven Phillips used his peremptory challenges in an effort to stack the jury with a large number of conservative, law-and-order black jurors. In addition, Phillips eliminated one juror solely on the basis that he was a longtime admirer of Kunstler's flamboyance and apocalyptic rhetoric.[92]

The jury consists of twelve persons chosen to decide who has the better lawyer.
—Robert Frost

In short, many attorneys use these challenges to try to obtain partial jurors, not impartial ones; they hope to impanel jurors sympathetic to their side. This was certainly the case in the late 1960s trial of Black Panther Warren Wells, charged with the murder of a police officer. Wells's first two trials resulted in hung juries: 10-to-2 and 11-to-1 for acquittal. At his third trial, however, he was convicted. The guilty verdict was reached by an all-white jury put together by the district attorney by using all of his peremptory challenges to eliminate blacks from the jury.[93] The practice of systematically

"The jury will disregard the witness's last remarks."

excluding minorities from juries has been sanctioned by the Supreme Court in 1965 through its ruling in *Swain* v. *Alabama*.[94] In 1986, the Supreme Court overruled *Swain* in part, holding that prosecutors may not exclude blacks from juries because of concern that they will favor a defendant of their own race.[95]

The *voir dire* examination continues until the required number of jurors has been selected. In many jurisdictions where the 12-person jury is used, as many as 14 may be accepted. The additional two jurors serve as alternates. They sit through the entire trial and are available to take the place of a regular jury member should he or she become ill, be forced to withdraw, or become disqualified while the trial is in process. Potential jurors who are successfully challenged return to the original jury pool, and new ones are drawn from the panel and subjected to *voir dire* (see Exhibit 12.10). Those ultimately selected are sworn in and become the trial jury.

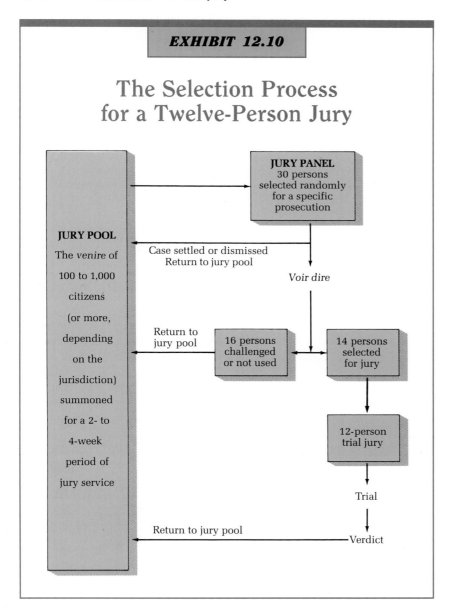

EXHIBIT 12.10

The Selection Process for a Twelve-Person Jury

JURY PANEL
30 persons selected randomly for a specific prosecution

JURY POOL
The *venire* of 100 to 1,000 citizens (or more, depending on the jurisdiction) summoned for a 2- to 4-week period of jury service

Case settled or dismissed
Return to jury pool

Voir dire

Return to jury pool

16 persons challenged or not used

14 persons selected for jury

12-person trial jury

Trial

Return to jury pool

Verdict

The *voir dire* can be brief or it can be time-consuming. In prosecutions of misdemeanors and many felonies where there has been little pretrial publicity and trial proceedings are anticipated to be fairly routine, there may be few challenges and the *voir dire* may last only a few hours or even less. In other cases, the examination can continue for days, weeks, or even months. When Black Panthers Bobby Seale and Ericka Huggens were tried in a New Haven, Connecticut, courtroom in 1971 on a charge of murdering a fellow Panther, the process was even more time consuming. The *voir dire* lasted for more than four months, and a total of 1,035 prospective jurors were interrogated.[96]

It is the challenges for cause that lengthen the *voir dire* proceedings. Any and every potential juror can be thus challenged. Peremptory challenges, on the other hand, are controlled by statute. In New York, for example, the maximum permitted is three, except in such serious cases as murder, where as many as 20 are allowed, and where there are multiple defendants.

The *voir dire* can be crucially important part of a criminal proceeding. Its purpose is to do more than merely choose a fair and impartial jury — as significant as this may be. Its primary functions are to educate the citizen as to the role of the juror and to develop jury – attorney rapport. Moreover, the *voir dire* provides the defense and the prosecution with the opportunity to attempt to influence jurors' attitudes and perhaps their later vote. One prosecutor put it this way:

> There is much more to a *voir dire* than the simple process of questioning and selecting jurors. In addition to the gamesmanship and psychology, a *voir dire* is an opportunity for the attorneys to educate their juries about the theories of their cases. It is also an opportunity to plant seeds of doubt that they hope will produce a favorable verdict. It is a chance to predispose jurors to be receptive to the attorney's case.[97]

The Criminal Trial

That's what's wrong with our legal system, ya need evidence!
— Archie Bunker, 1982

The trial is the climax of the criminal proceeding and it begins as soon as the jury is sworn in. The only matter that remains in doubt before commentary and testimony can begin is the judge's decision as to whether or not to sequester the jurors for the entire trial. **Sequestration** involves removal of the jurors (and alternates, if any) from all possible outside influence. They are housed in a hotel or motel for the duration of the trial; they are forbidden all visitors; and the newspapers they read, as well as the television programs they watch, are fully censored.

Few juries are sequestered for an entire trial, for most criminal prosecutions fail to generate a line of newspaper copy or even a second of television news time. Only if there is continuing media coverage that has the potential for influencing a juror's decision is sequestration ordered. If the judge does so rule, however, sequestration places a tremendous hardship on the jury members. One recent commentator spoke of the total isolation resulting from sequestration:

> Jurors were driven to their homes on January 15, the first evening after they had been selected to serve, so that they could get a week's worth of clothing. They were returned to their homes for clean clothing on

Sequestration: The removal of the jurors (and alternates, if any) from all possible outside influences.

January 20 and January 27. . . . Each juror was accompanied by a marshal on each trip . . . and even the windows of the vans [were] covered with paper so a juror [could not] see a newspaper headline at a newsstand. The jurors also were escorted by marshals to two theater productions and to one dinner at a restaurant away from their hotel. . . . The jurors were allowed no visits by relatives and were allowed telephone conversations only after a deputy marshal dialed the number, cautioned the answering party against discussing the case, and listened in on a second telephone that had a cut-off button to be used if either party violated the restrictions.[98]

The procedures used in criminal trials are for the most part the same throughout the United States, and the process consists of the following steps:

- opening statements
- presentation of the state's case
- presentation of the defense's case
- rebuttal and surrebuttal
- closing arguments
- charging the jury
- deliberation and verdict

In bench trials, this process is altered only minimally. First, those steps involving the jury are eliminated. Second, the tactics and strategies of the defense and prosecuting attorneys are simplified and much of the dramatic effect is removed.

Opening Statements

The first step in a trial proceeding is the reading of the criminal complaint by the court clerk, followed by opening statements — first by the prosecution and then by the defense.

The prosecutor's statement is an attempt to provide the jury with an outline of the case and how the state intends to prove, beyond a reasonable doubt, that the defendant did indeed commit the crime or crimes charged in the indictment. This outline generally includes a description of the crime, the defendant's role in it, and a discussion of the evidence and witnesses to be presented. In addition, the prosecutor is likely to address the meaning of "beyond a reasonable doubt." Reasonable doubt is fair doubt based upon reason and common sense and growing out of the testimony of the case; it is doubt arising from a candid and impartial investigation of all the evidence and testimony presented. The purpose of the prosecutor's analysis here is to distinguish between reasonable doubt and vague apprehension, and at the same time to emphasize that the state's object is to prove guilt beyond a *reasonable* doubt — not beyond *all* doubt.

Although the prosecutor has considerable freedom as to what is said in the opening statement, no references may be made to evidence that is known to be inadmissible, and no comment may be made concerning the defendant's prior criminal record (if any exists). To make such a comment would be considered a *prejudicial error* — an error of such substance that it compromises the rights of the accused. Prejudicial errors that cannot be corrected by any action by the court are often the bases for appeals. Furthermore, they can

Prejudicial errors can result in judicial action, appeals, or a mistrial.

result in a **mistrial,** a discharging of the jury without a verdict. A mistrial is the equivalent of no trial at all.*

The defense attorney's opening statement is an address to the jury that focuses on how the defense will show that the state has a poor case, and that proof of guilt beyond a reasonable doubt cannot be demonstrated. It is not uncommon for defense attorneys to stress that the accused is innocent until proven guilty, and that the burden of proof is fully on the prosecution.

Defense attorneys and prosecutors often vary their strategies for opening statements, as dictated by the nature of the case, evidence, and witnesses. One approach is to keep opening remarks short and vague, letting the particulars of the case emerge during the course of the trial. Such a tactic makes few promises to the jury, but it allows flexibility. Such flexibility can be important because it enables the attorney, during the final summation, to structure an argument uncompromised by promises that he or she could not deliver. An alternative is a detailed opening statement, eloquently expressed and forcefully presented, that conditions the jury to accept the evidence that is ultimately delivered. This can be a risky technique, but it is highly rewarding if the promises made can be kept during the course of the trial.[99]

In a jury trial, the prosecutor always delivers an opening statement. Without it, the jurors would have no framework within which to consider the evidence and testimony. The defense attorney, however, may choose to make no statement at all — out of necessity perhaps, if the defense strategy cannot be determined until the content of the state's case is revealed; or as part of the strategy, which is not to be revealed until the proper time. Opening statements are infrequently used in bench trials; they are less effective, since the seasoned judge has handled perhaps hundreds of similar cases in the past.

Presentation of the State's Case

In order to give the accused the opportunity to provide an informed defense, it is the state that presents its case first in the adversary system of justice. The prosecutor begins by presenting evidence and questioning witnesses.

The Rules of Evidence

Generally, **evidence** is any species of proof, through the medium of witnesses, records, documents, concrete objects, and circumstances. Specifically, evidence is of four basic types:

There are four basic types of evidence: real, testimonial, direct, and circumstantial.

1. *Real evidence* is physical objects, such as a murder weapon, stolen property, fingerprints, the physical appearance of the scene of the crime, the physical appearance of a person when exhibited to the jury, wounds, or other items. Real evidence may be the original objects, or facsimile representations, such as photographs, models of the crime

---

* It should be noted that it is not only the prosecutor who can make prejudicial errors resulting in a mistrial. In a 1981 Washington, D.C., rape case, a mistrial was declared when the judge learned that two jurors had been drinking heavily during the trial arguments (*Time,* May 18, 1981, p. 29). In a 1983 narcotics case, also in the District of Columbia, trial proceedings were terminated when it became apparent that one of the jurors was deaf and had heard none of the testimony (*National Law Journal,* December 5, 1983, p. 43). In a 1984 Ohio capital murder trial, the presiding county court judge ordered a mistrial when one juror had grabbed and frightened two others during deliberations (*National Law Journal,* March 5, 1984, p. 10). The failure to order a mistrial when warranted is grounds for appeal (see Chapter 13).

scene, tire tracks, or other duplicates of objects that are either unavailable or unusable in their original form.

2. *Testimonial evidence* is the sworn, verbal statements of witnesses. All real evidence is accompanied by testimonial evidence, in that objects presented in evidence are explained by someone qualified to discuss them. Conversely, however, not all testimonial evidence is accompanied by real evidence.

3. *Direct evidence* is eyewitness evidence. Testimony that a person was seen painting a fence, for example, is direct evidence that the person painted a fence.

4. *Circumstantial evidence,* or indirect evidence, is evidence from which a fact can be reasonably inferred. Testimony that a person was seen with paint and a paint brush in the vicinity of a newly painted fence is circumstantial evidence that the person painted the fence.

These four types necessarily overlap, since all are ultimately presented through testimony. Furthermore, *all* evidence must be competent, material, and relevant. Evidence is *competent* when it is legally fit for admission to court. The testimony of an expert witness on a scientific matter is deemed competent, for example, if the court accepts his or her credentials as a reflection of proficiency in the subject area. In contrast, testimonial evidence on ballistics presented by an automobile mechanic would be considered incompe-

All evidence must be competent, material, and relevant.

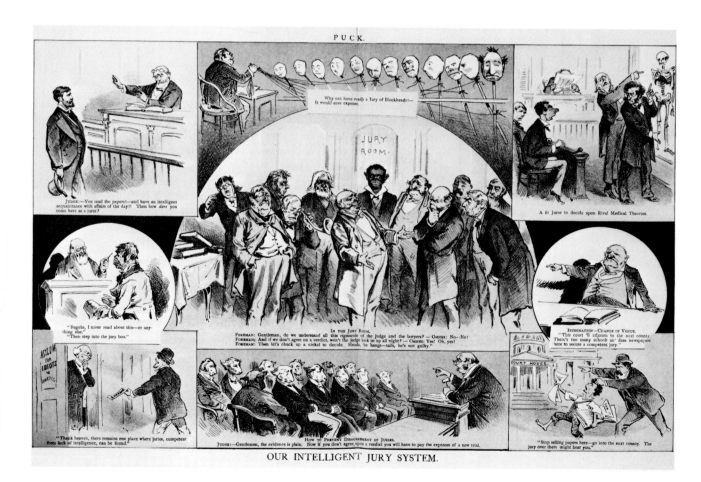

OUR INTELLIGENT JURY SYSTEM.

tent; or an individual who has been convicted of perjury might be considered incompetent to testify. In common law, a person was considered to be "incompetent" to testify against his or her spouse, under the theory that by being compelled or even allowed to do so would undermine the marriage and thus be detrimental to the public welfare. In 1980, however, the Supreme Court ruled in *Trammel* v. *United States* that a criminal defendant could no longer invoke the "privilege against adverse spousal testimony," as long as the testimony is voluntary and does not compromise a confidential marital communication.[100]

Evidence can be deemed incompetent if it is based on hearsay. Under most circumstances the hearsay rule prohibits a witness from testifying about statements not within his or her personal knowledge — that is, about secondhand information. There are two exceptions to this rule. The first is an admission of criminal conduct made by the defendant to the witness. Such hearsay testimony is allowed because the accused is present in court to challenge it. The other exception is the "dying declaration" of a crime victim that has been told to or overheard by the witness; it is based on the presumption that a person who is about to die will not lie.[101]

To be admissible in a court of law, evidence must also be material and relevant, and there is only a slight distinction between the two. Evidence is *material* when it has a legitimate bearing on the decision of the case. Evidence is *relevant* when it is applicable to the issue in question. For example, evidence of a defendant's bad character on previous occasions is immaterial (unless he is submitting his good character in evidence). By contrast, the fact that an accused has stolen property in the past is irrelevant to whether or not he has murdered someone (assuming, of course, that he is not being tried on multiple charges of theft and murder).

Examination of Witnesses

The state's presentation begins with the *direct examination* of witnesses. This consists only of eliciting facts from the witness in some chronological order. The first witness called is generally one who can establish the elements of the crime. Subsequent witnesses introduce physical, direct, and indirect evidence, and expert testimony.

After the prosecutor has completed his interrogation of a witness through direct examination, the defense is permitted (but not required) to cross-examine the witness. The purpose of *cross-examination* is to discredit the testimony, by either teasing out inconsistencies and contradictions or attacking the credibility of the witness. The prosecution can ask further questions of the witness through a *redirect examination,* as can the defense with a *recross-examination.* This examination procedure continues until all of the state's witnesses have been called and evidence presented.*

Objections

During the examination of any witness, whether it be by the prosecutor or the defense counsel, the opposing attorney can *object* to the introduction of evidence or testimony that he or she considers to be incompetent, immaterial,

---

* Redirect examinations and recross-examinations are limited — redirect only to matters emanating from the cross, and recross only to matters emanating from the redirect.

or irrelevant. Objections can also be made to "leading questions" (ones that inherently instruct or at least suggest to the witness how to answer), to eliciting witness's opinions and conclusions, to being argumentative, and to "badgering" (abusing) a witness.

If the objection is *sustained* (consented to), the examiner is ordered to withdraw the question or cease the mode of inquiry, and the jury is instructed to disregard whatever was deemed inappropriate. If the objection is *overruled* (rejected), the examining attorney may continue with the original line of questioning.

Motion for Directed Verdict

Following the presentation of the state's case, it is not uncommon for the defense attorney to enter a motion for a *directed verdict*. With this, the defense moves that the judge enter a finding of acquittal on the grounds that the state failed to establish a *prima facie* case of guilt against the accused. If the judge so moves, he directs the jury to acquit the defendant. Even in the absence of a motion by the defense, the trial judge can order a directed verdict. Furthermore, the judge can do so not only on the grounds that the state failed to prove its case, but also because the testimony of the prosecution witnesses was not credible or because the conduct of the prosecutor was not proper. Conversely, *a judge cannot direct the jury to convict the accused.*

Prima facie **case: A case supported by sufficient evidence to warrant submission to the jury for the rendering of a verdict.**

Presentation of the Defense's Case

When the U.S. Supreme Court spoke of "the dead hand of the common law rule of 1789" many decades ago,[102] it was referring to a provision of the Judiciary Act of 1789 that noted that codefendants were not entitled to testify in each other's behalf. The provision seemingly was a remnant of a pre-eighteenth-century English common law principle that denied defendants charged with treason or felonies the right of having witnesses testify in their defense. This restriction in the Judiciary Act, however, seemed to contradict somewhat a component of the Sixth Amendment providing that in all criminal prosecutions the accused shall enjoy the right "to have compulsory process for obtaining witnesses in his favor." *Compulsory process* refers to the subpoena power that can force a witness into court to testify. In 1918, the Supreme Court extended the compulsory process clause, without limitation, to federal defendants.[103] In *Washington* v. *Texas,*[104] decided in 1967, the Court extended this right to the states.

This compulsory process clause rests at the foundation of the presentation of the defense's case. During this presentation the counsel for the accused calls witnesses to testify in support of the not-guilty plea. It is also at this point that the counsel for the accused has the opportunity to offer **evidence in chief**—that is, the first or direct examination of a witness.

Evidence in chief: The first or direct examination of a witness.

At the outset, the defense attorney has the option of presenting many, some, or no witnesses or evidentiary elements on behalf of the accused. In addition, the defense must decide whether the accused will testify on his or her own behalf. The Fifth Amendment right against self-incrimination does not require it, but if the defendant does so choose, the prosecution then has the option of cross-examination.

Once these matters are decided, the defense's presentation follows the procedures outlined for the state's presentation: direct examination, cross-examination, redirect examination, and recross-examination. In addition, the rules of evidence and right to make objections apply equally to the defense as to the prosecution.

It is a common misconception that during this stage of the trial the burden of proof shifts to the defense. *This is not so.* The responsibility of proving guilt beyond a reasonable doubt always remains with the prosecution. What shifts to the defense is the "burden of going forward with the evidence."[105] This means that since the prosecution has presented its suit to the jury, it becomes the defense's responsibility to offer its own argument for the jury to consider.

Rebuttal and Surrebuttal

When the defense "rests" (concludes its presentation), the prosecutor may elect to introduce new witnesses or evidence in an effort to refute the defense's case. Known as the *prosecutor's rebuttal,* the same format of examination and cross-examination, redirect and recross-examination is followed. In turn, the counsel for the accused may put forth a *surrebuttal,* which is a rebuttal of the prosecutor's rebuttal.

Closing Arguments

The *summation,* or closing arguments, gives each side the opportunity to recapitulate all the evidence and testimony offered during the trial. The arguments are made directly to the jury, and the defense emphasizes a posture of innocence while the state proffers the opposite view.

The summation ceremonies begin with the defense attorney, who points out any weaknesses or flaws in the prosecutor's theory and evidence. Counsel for the accused argues that proof "beyond a reasonable doubt" has not been established, and reminds the jurors that they will have to live with their decision and consciences for the rest of their lives. Since the burden of proof rests with the state, the prosecutor is entitled to the final argument. For both the defense and the prosecution, perhaps the most vital element to be offered is *persuasion.* One prosecutor made just this point:

> Summing up in a criminal trial is a throwback to an earlier age. It is one of the few arts left in which time is of no consequence. Standing before twelve people, a lawyer can be brief or lengthy — the choice is his own; there are no interruptions, and a captive audience. All that matters are those twelve people; they must be persuaded, or everything that has gone before is in vain. Summation is the one place where lawyers do make a difference; if an attorney can be said to "win" or "lose" a case, the chances are that he did so in his closing argument to the jury.
>
> The appeal of a summation may be to the heart, the intellect or the belly — or to all of them. There are as many different ways of summing up as there are trial lawyers, and there is no one correct way to deliver a summation, or to learn how to give one. It is largely a matter of instinct and of experience. Either you are able to reach out and move people with your words or you are not, and that is all there is to it.[106]

Charging the Jury

The **charge to the jury** is an order by the judge that directs the jurors to retire to the jury room, consider the facts of the case and the evidence and testimony presented, and from their deliberations return a just verdict. Regarded by many as the single most important statement made during the trial, it includes instructions as to the possible verdicts, the rules of evidence, and the legal meaning of "reasonable doubt." The instructions contained in the charge, furthermore, are often arrived at through consultation by the defense and the prosecution with the judge, and from statutory instructions as contained in the jurisdiction's code of criminal procedure.

In some states, the judges are permitted to review thoroughly all the evidence that has been presented to the jury. They are free to summarize, for example, the testimony of each witness. This can be useful to jurors, especially if the trial has been long and complex. But it also can be hazardous, for a judge has opinions about innocence and guilt, and these can inadvertently influence the jury.

In North Carolina, for example, although the statute governing instructions to the jury does not require the judge to state the evidence, it does not prohibit it either:

> In instructing the jury, the judge must declare and explain the law arising on the evidence. He is not required to state the evidence except to the extent necessary to explain the application of the law to the evidence.[107]

The rule goes on to forbid the judge from expressing opinions as to the accused's culpability, the strengths and weaknesses of evidence, and whether or not some fact was proven. Any violations of this rule could result in a mistrial. Clearly, it would have tremendous impact on the jury if the judge were to state the following, for example:

> The jury should bear in mind that while the accused has maintained that he was at a neighborhood cocktail party at the time of the offense, it seems strange that he cannot remember the name of a single person — *not one* — who was also at the party, or where the party even took place.

Such a statement would be highly prejudicial in any jurisdiction and would likely result in a mistrial. Nevertheless, the North Carolina statute, like similar ones in many other jurisdictions, gives the judge tremendous latitude for expression. If the judge believes the defendant is guilty, he or she might give more time and emphasis to the most damaging evidence; if the judge views the accused as innocent, he or she might give more consideration to the testimony of defense witnesses. As a result, complete objectivity can be difficult to achieve.

Even more difficult to present seems to be instructions that juries can fully understand. Because the nuances of the law are so complex the instructions can take hours to deliver. In a Justice Department study conducted in 1981, moreover, it was found that in half the cases jurors had been confused by the judges' instructions.[108]

Finally, the members of the jury are instructed that they cannot communicate with anyone as to the facts of the case. Further sequestration might be ordered, which would place the jurors under the supervision of a court officer until a verdict is reached.

Jury Deliberations

Every jury has a *foreman* or *forewoman,* who serves as the nominal leader of the group. He or she is chosen by the jurors during the trial or after retirement to the jury room. In New York the first juror selected in the *voir dire* becomes the leader. Whether this person becomes the *actual* leader is another matter, depending on personality factors and the dynamics of group interaction.

Once the jury has retired, it is traditional for the foreman to sit at the head of the table and call for a vote. With the exceptions of Oregon and Louisiana, unanimous verdicts are required by law (see Exhibit 12.11). If such a verdict is acquired, the deliberations are finished. Typically, however, it is not that simple. In one study undertaken by the University of Chicago, for example, one vote was all that was necessary to reach a unanimous verdict in only 30 percent of the cases.[109]

The "hung" jury

Should deliberations fail to generate a unanimous decision, the dilemma is referred to as a deadlocked or "hung" jury. There are several consequences of such a situation: the jury is dismissed in open court, the judge declares a mistrial, and the prosecution can either retry the case or dismiss the charges. Deadlocked juries result from differences of opinion over the strengths and weaknesses of evidence, varying perceptions of innocence and guilt, and the meaning of "reasonable doubt." The deadlocked jury is not a common occur-

---

Nonunanimous Juries

Johnson v. Louisiana, 406 U.S. 356 (1972)

In *Johnson,* the petitioner was convicted of robbery under a Louisiana statute that permitted a defendant in a *noncapital* case to be found guilty by a vote of 9 out of 12 jurors. The Supreme Court upheld the Louisiana law, noting that want of jury unanimity is not to be equated with the existence of a reasonable doubt concerning the accused's guilt. Justice Byron White wrote for the majority:

This Court has never held jury unanimity to be a requisite of due process of law. . . . Of course, the State's proof could perhaps be regarded as more certain if it had convinced all 12 jurors instead of only nine. . . . But the fact remains that nine jurors—a substantial majority of the jury—were convinced by the evidence. In our view disagreement of three jurors does not alone establish reasonable doubt.

Apodaca v. Oregon, 406 U.S. 404 (1972)

In the Oregon case, decided the same day as *Johnson,* Robert Apodaca and codefendants Cooper and Madden were convicted of, respectively, assault with a deadly weapon, burglary, and grand larceny. Each was found guilty by a separate jury, but in all three the decisions were less than unanimous: 11-to-1, 10-to-2, and 11-to-1.

The petitioners argued that a jury trial under the Sixth Amendment, made mandatory on the states by virtue of the due-process clause of the Fourteenth Amendment, required a unanimous verdict in order to give substance to the reasonable-doubt standard. The Court rejected their contention, with the same reasoning declared in *Johnson.*

Burch v. Louisiana, 441 U.S. 130 (1979)

In both *Johnson* and *Apodaca,* the Court limited by implication the use of nonunanimous verdicts to noncapital cases. Furthermore, the Court noted that a "substantial majority" in each case had voted for conviction. In *Burch,* seven years later, the defendant appealed a criminal conviction by a 5-to-1 vote of a six-person jury. In this case, however, the Court ruled that a jury as small as six persons must reach its verdict unanimously in order to convict for a nonpetty offense. As Justice William Rehnquist declared:

Lines must be drawn somewhere if the substance of the jury trial right is to be preserved.

---

rence. Reports indicate that only 6 percent of all criminal trials end with a hung jury,[110] with most resulting in a negotiated consensus.[111]

Verdict and Judgment

When the jury reaches a verdict, it returns to the courtroom to announce its decision: "We, the jury, duly impaneled and sworn, find the defendant guilty [or not guilty] as charged." In cases involving multiple counts, the jury may find the accused guilty of some charges and innocent of others.

One of the more enduring issues in criminal trials is the problem of **jury nullification**. It occurs when juries do not follow the court's interpretation of the law in every instance, disregard what they have been told about the law or certain aspects of evidence, consider the application of certain laws to be unjust, refuse to convict because they consider the penalties too severe, or otherwise "nullify" or suspend the force of strict legal procedure.

Jury nullification can be both inadvertent or by design. If a verdict of guilty is returned and it is the court's opinion that it is an erroneous decision,

Jury nullification: The refusal or marked reluctance on the part of a jury to convict, because of the severe nature of the sentence involved.

EXHIBIT 12.12

A Most Unpredictable Jury

Some years ago, a man was tried in a California court for the murder of his wife. The state's case was quite convincing, but one thing was missing — the victim's body. This was the basis of the defense's case, and no evidence or testimony was presented on behalf of the accused.

In a dynamic summation performance, the counsel for the defense soared to eloquent heights of oratory, repeating that with the absence of the body of the alleged victim, it could not be proven that a crime had been committed. "You must find my client innocent for one simple reason," he shouted. Then, dropping to a breathless whisper, he added, "His wife is still alive. In fact — she just walked into the courtroom!"

At once, the heads of all the jurors and spectators turned only to see that not a soul had entered the chambers. But the attorney had made his point. How could

proof beyond a reasonable doubt be concluded if the jurors suspected that the defendant's wife might still be alive.

Everyone agreed that it was a brilliant ploy, and after less than an hour's deliberation, the jury returned with a verdict. Yet, to the amazement and disbelief of all those present, the jury had found the accused guilty of murder.

When the trial was over and the jury dismissed, the bewildered defense counsel confronted the first few jurors he saw. "How," he asked, "could you find a man guilty when you weren't even sure his wife was dead? Hadn't everyone turned to look for her in the back of the courtroom?"

"Yes," answered one of the jurors, "everybody except your client."

SOURCE: Based on a story in Melvyn Bernard Zerman, *Beyond a Reasonable Doubt: Inside the American Jury System* (New York: Crowell, 1981), pp. 10–13.

the judge can refuse to abide by it. He can *direct* the jury to acquit, or "arrest" the guilty verdict and enter a judgment of acquittal. However, a trial judge does *not* have the authority to direct a jury to convict or enter a judgment arresting a verdict of not guilty.

Polling the jury

Lastly, jurors can be *polled*. At the request of the defense or the prosecution, the judge (or the bailiff) asks each juror if the verdict announced is his or her individual verdict. Polling the jury is done to determine whether any juror has been pressured by fellow jury members into voting a particular way.

Posttrial Motions

With a judgement of not guilty, the defendant is immediately released — unless other charges are still pending. With a guilty verdict, most jurisdictions allow the defense to file motions to set aside the judgement or to file motions for a new trial.

Motion in arrest of judgment

The *motion in arrest of judgment* asks that no judgment be pronounced because of one or more defects in the record of the case. Possible defects include the following: (1) The trial court had no jurisdiction over the case; (2) the verdict included conviction on a charge that was not tested in the indictment or information; or (3) there was error "on face of the record." This last term refers to any faults of procedure that may have occurred during the pretrial process.

Motion for a new trial

The *motion for a new trial,* which can be made only by the defense, can be based on numerous grounds: (1) The jury received evidence outside of the courtroom; (2) the jury was guilty of misconduct during deliberations; (3) the court erred in overruling an objection or permitting the introduction of certain evidence; (4) the jury charge was made improperly; (5) the prosecution was guilty of misconduct; (6) there is a suspicion of *jury tampering* (bribes or threats made to a juror to influence his or her vote); and (7) newly discovered evidence is available for review.

If either motion is sustained, new proceedings will be initiated. Any new trial that results, however, does not represent double jeopardy, for the defendant's motion is an allegation that the proceedings should be declared utterly invalid.

Summary

The movement of defendants through the criminal courts is complex. The process is characterized by many stages and checks and balances while beset with numerous difficulties. Early in the process is the matter of pretrial release. Bail has been the traditional mechanism of temporary release. The amount of bail set is determined by a number of factors, including the seriousness of the crime, the defendant's prior criminal record, and the strength of the state's case. The bail system has been heavily criticized on the grounds that it discriminates against the poor and that the bail bond industry promotes inequity and corruption.

Stack v. *Boyle* noted that bail was not a means for punishing defendants or protecting society, but rather of assuring the accused's attendance in court. Nevertheless, high bail is often set for the purposes of preventive detention. Moreover, for those who cannot make bail, pretrial detention has negative effects on their criminal processing. Release on recognizance has become a popular alternative to bail and has been generally effective.

Following the initial court proceedings, an information or indictment initiates prosecution. The indictment is handed down by a grand jury, whose purpose is to investigate and to protect citizens from unfair accusations. Since grand juries do not determine guilt or innocence, many of the elements of due process are absent. The Supreme Court has generally refused to impose substantive criteria on the grand jury's exercise of discretion.

After the formal determination of charges, the defendant is arraigned, at which time he or she is asked to enter a plea. The basic pleas are those of guilty, not guilty, *nolo contendere,* and standing mute. In addition, there are the insanity plea, pleas of statute of limitations, and the issue of double jeopardy.

Prior to the actual trial a number of motions can be filed by the defense or prosecution: discovery, change of venue, suppression, bill of particulars, severance, continuance, and dismissal. Then there is the matter of a "speedy trial" as guaranteed by the Sixth Amendment. There are many legitimate reasons for delays in formally trying a defendant, but the Supreme Court has held that if a defendant is denied a speedy trial, the remedy is dismissal of the charges.

Criminal defendants have a constitutional right to a trial by jury, a right extended to the states through *Duncan* v. *Louisiana* in 1968. Potential jurors are selected from voter registration rolls or multiple source lists. The *voir dire* examination functions to determine a candidate's fitness to serve, and jurors can be eliminated through challenges by the defense and prosecution.

The criminal trial has many steps: opening statements, presentation of the state's and defense's case, rebuttal and surrebuttal, closing arguments, charging the jury, and deliberation and verdict. There may be posttrial motions for arrest of judgment or for a new trial.

Key Terms

bail (394)
Benton v. *Maryland* (417)
charge to the jury (438)
contempt power (413)
double jeopardy (417)
Downum v. *United States* (417)
Duncan v. *Louisiana* (426)
evidence (434)
evidence in chief (437)
grand jury (408)
Hurtado v. *California* (408)
indictment (408)

information (408)
jury nullification (441)
Klopfer v. *North Carolina* (423)
mistrial (434)
nolo contendere (415)
Palko v. *Connecticut* (417)
presentment (408)
pretrial detention (402)
preventive detention (402)
public trial (424)
release on recognizance
   (ROR) (405)

sequestration (432)
Sixth Amendment (422)
speedy trial (421)
Speedy Trial Act (424)
Stack v. *Boyle* (395)
surety (394)
transactional immunity (413)
true bill (411)
United States v. *Calandra* (412)
use immunity (413)
venire (428)
voir dire (428)

Questions for Discussion

1. Do Justice Gray's remarks in *Hudson* v. *Parker* at least imply (1) that all defendants have a right to bail, and (2) that defendants have some right to remain at liberty until all mechanisms of appeal have been exhausted? Why?

2. How might a bench trial versus a jury trial alter the opposing attorneys' strategies and tactics?
3. Given the respective roles of the defense and the prosecution, is the deliberate seeking of biased jurors legal or ethical?

4. What ought to constitute the "substantial majority" test that was mentioned by the Court in *Johnson* v. *Louisiana* and *Apodaca* v. *Oregon?*

5. What are the potential consequences of a defendant's waiver of rights?

For Further Reading

Frankel, Marvin E., and Gary P. Naftalis. *The Grand Jury: An Institution on Trial.* New York: Hill and Wang, 1977.

Goldfarb, Ronald. *Ransom: A Critique of the American Bail System.* New York: Harper & Row, 1965.

Kalven, Harry, and Hans Zeisel. *The American Jury.* Boston: Little, Brown, 1966.

Phillips, Steven. *No Heroes, No Villains: The Story of a Murder Trial.* New York: Vintage, 1978.

Wice, Paul. *Freedom for Sale.* Lexington, Mass.: Lexington, 1974.

Zerman, Melvyn B. *Beyond a Reasonable Doubt: Inside the American Jury System.* New York: Crowell, 1981.

Notes

1. Charles E. Silberman, *Criminal Violence, Criminal Justice* (New York: Random House, 1978), pp. 254–255.
2. Charles Rembar, *The Law of the Land: The Evolution of Our Legal System* (New York: Simon and Schuster, 1980), p. 95.
3. See Luke Owen Pike, *A History of Crime in England,* vol. 1 (London: Smith, Elder, 1873–1876), pp. 57–60; Ernst W. Puttkammer, *Administration of Criminal Law* (Chicago: University of Chicago Press, 1953), pp. 99–100.
4. Hudson v. Parker, 156 U.S. 277 (1895).
5. McKane v. Durston, 153 U.S. 684 (1894).
6. Patricia M. Wald, "The Right to Bail Revisited: A Decade of Promise Without Fulfillment," in *The Rights of the Accused,* ed. Stuart S. Nagel (Beverly Hills, Ca.: Sage, 1972), pp. 175–205.
7. Stack v. Boyle, 342 U.S. 1 (1951).
8. Carlson v. Landon, 342 U.S. 524 (1952).
9. *New York Criminal Procedure Law,* Section 510.30.
10. See Paul Wice, *Freedom for Sale* (Lexington, Mass.: Lexington, 1974); Frederick Suffet, "Bail Setting: A Study of Courtroom Interaction," *Crime and Delinquency* (October 1966): 318–331.
11. National Commission on Law Observance and Enforcement, *Report on Prosecution* (Washington, D.C.: U.S. Government Printing Office, 1931), pp. 89–92.
12. The Cleveland Foundation, *Criminal Justice in Cleveland* (Cleveland: Cleveland Foundation, 1922); Missouri Association for Criminal Justice, *The Missouri Crime Survey* (New York: Macmillan, 1926); Wayne L. Morse and Ronald H. Beattie, *Survey of the Administration of Criminal Justice in Oregon* (Eugene: University of Oregon Press, 1932); President's Commission on Law Enforcement and Administration of Justice, *Task Force Report: The Courts* (Washington, D.C.: U.S. Government Printing Office, 1967).
13. See Frederick Suffet, "Bail Setting"; Wice, *Freedom for Sale.*
14. Robert P. Rhodes, *The Insoluble Problems of Crime* (New York: Wiley, 1977), p. 216.
15. See Wice, *Freedom for Sale;* Daniel Freed and Patricia Wald, *Bail in the United States* (Washington, D.C.: National Conference on Bail and Criminal Justice, 1964); Forrest Dill, "Discretion, Exchange and Social Control: Bail Bondsmen in Criminal Courts," *Law and Society Review* 9 (Summer 1975): 639–674.
16. *Annotated Code of Maryland,* Article 27, Section 12B.
17. Freed and Wald, *Bail in the United States,* pp. 23–24.
18. Caleb B. Foote, "A Study of the Administration of Bail in New York City," *University of Pennsylvania Law Review* 102 (March 1958): 693.
19. President's Commission, *Task Force Report: The Courts,* p. 37.
20. President's Commission, *Task Force Report: The Courts,* p. 38.
21. *National Law Journal,* June 29, 1981, p. 9.
22. *New York Times,* April 4, 1963, p. 37.
23. *National Law Journal,* July 8, 1985, p. 20.
24. Freed and Wald, *Bail in the United States,* p. 47.
25. Advisory Committee on Pretrial Release, *Standards Relating to Pretrial Release* (New York: American Bar Association, 1968), p. 3.
26. Anne Rankin, "The Effect of Pre-Trial Detention," *New York University Law Review* 39 (June 1964): 641.
27. Statement by Mayor John V. Lindsay, Administrative Board of the Judicial Conference of the State of New York, October 9, 1970.
28. *New York Times,* June 2, 1975, p. 16.
29. Ronald Goldfarb, *Ransom: A Critique of the American Bail System* (New York: Harper & Row, 1965), p. 47.
30. For more on the Vera Foundation and the Vera Institute of Justice, see its ten-year report, 1961–1971, *Programs in Criminal Justice Reform* (New York: Vera Institute, 1972); and *Further Work in Criminal Justice* (1977), its later five-year report.
31. Charles E. Ares, Anne Rankin, and Herbert Sturtz, "The Manhattan Bail Project," *New York University Law Review* 38 (January 1963): 68.
32. National Advisory Commission on Criminal Justice Standards and Goals, *Corrections* (Washington, D.C.: U.S. Government Printing Office, 1973), p. 108.
33. Tyce S. Smith and James W. Reilley, "The Illinois Bail System: A Second Look," *John Marshall Journal of Practice and Procedure,* Fall 1972, p. 33.
34. Personal observations by the author in the Dade County courts, May to August 1973.
35. National Advisory Commission on Criminal Justice Standards and Goals, *Police* (Washington, D.C.: U.S. Government Printing Office, 1973), pp. 83–84.
36. National Advisory Commission, *Police,* pp. 83–84.

37. Marvin E. Frankel and Gary P. Naftalis, *The Grand Jury: An Institution on Trial* (New York: Hill and Wang, 1977), pp. 3–17.

38. Hurtado v. California, 110 U.S. 516 (1884).

39. Hale v. Henkel, 201 U.S. 43 (1906).

40. Costello v. United States, 350 U.S. 359 (1956).

41. United States v. Calandra, 414 U.S. 338 (1974).

42. Kastigar v. United States, 406 U.S. 441 (1972).

43. Branzburg v. Hayes, 408 U.S. 665 (1972).

44. Anne Strick, *Injustice for All* (New York: Penguin, 1978), p. 175.

45. National Advisory Commission, p. 12.

46. *Time,* July 6, 1981, p. 12.

47. *New York Times,* December 9, 1977, p. D1.

48. *New York Times,* October 5, 1980, p. 33.

49. Thomas C. Marks and J. Tim Reilly, *Constitutional Criminal Procedure* (North Scituate, Mass.: Duxbury, 1979), p. 136.

50. *National Law Journal,* May 3, 1982, p. 11.

51. *National Law Journal,* May 3, 1982, p. 11.

52. David A. Jones, *The Law of Criminal Procedure* (Boston: Little, Brown, 1981), p. 398.

53. United States v. Perez, 9 Wheat. 579 (1824).

54. United States v. Ball, 163 U.S. 662 (1896).

55. Wade v. Hunter, 336 U.S. 684 (1949).

56. United States v. Lanza, 260 U.S. 377 (1922).

57. Abbate v. United States, 359 U.S. 187 (1959).

58. Waller v. Florida, 397 U.S. 387 (1970).

59. Palko v. Connecticut, 302 U.S. 319 (1937).

60. Benton v. Maryland, 395 U.S. 784 (1969).

61. Downum v. United States, 372 U.S. 734 (1963).

62. See, for example, *Code of Alabama,* 1975, Title 15, Section 15-4.

63. Brady v. Maryland, 363 U.S. 83 (1963).

64. Moore v. Illinois, 408 U.S. 786 (1972).

65. Mapp v. Ohio, 367 U.S. 643 (1961); Escobedo v. Illinois, 368 U.S. 478 (1964); Miranda v. Arizona, 384 U.S. 436 (1966).

66. Personal communication, September 15, 1971.

67. Serfass v. United States, 420 U.S. 377 (1975).

68. *New York Times,* May 21, 1975, p. 1.

69. *California Penal Code,* Section 1382 (1).

70. *Code of Alabama,* Title 15, Section 3-1.

71. State v. Brann, 292 A. 2d 173 (Me. 1972).

72. Beavers v. Haubert, 198 U.S. 77 (1905).

73. Barker v. Wingo, 407 U.S. 514 (1972).

74. Strunk v. United States, 412 U.S. 434 (1973).

75. United States v. Lovasco, 431 U.S. 783 (1977).

76. Klopfer v. North Carolina, 386 U.S. 213 (1967).

77. In re Oliver, 333 U.S. 257 (1948).

78. Duncan v. Louisiana, 391 U.S. 145 (1968).

79. *Tennessee Code Annotated,* Title 40-2504.

80. *Idaho Code,* Title 19-1902.

81. Gilbert B. Stuckey, *Procedures in the Criminal Justice System* (Columbus, Ohio: Merrill, 1976), p. 91.

82. Harry Kalven and Hans Zeisel, *The American Jury* (Boston: Little, Brown, 1966), pp. 56–60.

83. Duncan v. Louisiana, 391 U.S. 145 (1968).

84. Perez v. Duncan, 404 U.S. 1071, *certiorari* denied (1971).

85. Baldwin v. New York, 399 U.S. 66 (1970).

86. Williams v. Florida, 399 U.S. 78 (1970).

87. Ballew v. Georgia, 435 U.S. 223 (1978).

88. Taylor v. Louisiana, 419 U.S. 522 (1975).

89. Laura Rose Handman, "Underrepresentation of Economic Groups in Federal Juries," *Boston University Law Review* 57 (January 1977): 198–224.

90. Melvyn B. Zerman, *Beyond a Reasonable Doubt: Inside the American Jury System* (New York: Crowell, 1981), p. 181.

91. Zerman, *Beyond a Reasonable Doubt,* p. 181.

92. Steven Phillips, *No Heroes, No Villains: The Story of a Murder Trial* (New York: Vintage, 1978), pp. 132–138.

93. Ann Fagan Ginger, *Minimizing Racism in Jury Trials* (Berkeley, Calif.: National Lawyers Guild, 1969), pp. 157–160.

94. Swain v. Alabama, 380 U.S. 202 (1965).

95. *New York Times,* May 1, 1986, p. A1.

96. *New York Times,* March 12, 1971, p. 1.

97. Phillips, *No Heroes, No Villains,* pp. 136–137.

98. Noted by Zerman, *Beyond a Reasonable Doubt,* pp. 147–148.

99. See, for example, Phillips, *No Heroes, No Villains;* Seymour Wishman, *Confessions of a Criminal Lawyer* (New York: Times Books, 1981).

100. Trammel v. United States, 445 U.S. 40 (1980).

101. Jones, *Law of Criminal Procedure,* p. 475.

102. Rosen v. United States, 245 U.S. 467 (1918).

103. Rosen v. United States, 245 U.S. 467 (1918).

104. Washington v. Texas, 388 U.S. 14 (1967).

105. Marks and Reilly, *Constitutional Criminal Procedure,* p. 147

106. Phillips, *No Heroes, No Villains,* pp. 196–197.

107. *General Statutes of North Carolina,* Laws of 1977, Chapter 15A-1232.

108. *New York Times,* June 7, 1981, p. 25.

109. D. W. Broeder, "The University of Chicago Jury Project," *Nebraska Law Review* 38 (May 1959): 744–760.

110. Zerman, *Beyond a Reasonable Doubt,* p. 102.

111. See Kalven and Zeisel, *American Jury.*

13

Sentencing, Appeal, and the Judgment of Death

All I can say is, forgive them, Father, for in their ignorance they know not what they do.

> —Convicted murderer Anthony Antone, moments before his execution in Florida's electric chair in 1984

I'm not kidding. Capital punishment may not be much of a deterrent against murder, but the sight of a few corpses swinging from a scaffold might work with drug dealers.

> —*Newsweek* columnist James J. Kilpatrick, 1986

Even in this staged version of an executioner's final preparations, death by injection is a sentence to give one pause for reflection.

A fter conviction, the business of the court is not complete. First there is the matter of sentencing, and second there is the potential for appellate review.

What makes both sentencing and appeal significant is that in all prior phases of justice administration the purpose is to establish, beyond a reasonable doubt, the criminal liability of the defendant. The adversary system of American jurisprudence, grounded in due process of law, is structured from arrest through trial on the premise that the accused is innocent until proven guilty. Upon conviction, of course, the accused *has* been proven guilty. At sentencing, the court's obligation to criminal law and judicial procedure suddenly shifts from impartial and equitable litigation to the determined imposition of sanctions. On appeal, the court also deals, at least in most circumstances, with those who have been proven guilty, but who are requesting decisions on errors they claim were made in procedure or judgment.

In either case, the court's position is arduous and challenging. It must mediate among the functions of justice, the statutory authority of law, the assurances of due process, the needs for correctional application, the burdens of a congested justice system, the urgency of political realities, the essentials of legal ethics, and the demands for community protection.

Without question, sentencing is the most controversial aspect of criminal justice processing. Appellate review, although somewhat less visible, can also generate considerable controversy. And perhaps of greatest concern is the judgment of death, a criminal sanction that cuts across both sentencing and appellate decision making.

Sentencing

Life for life, eye for eye . . .   — Exodus 21:22 – 23

What should be done with criminal offenders after they have been convicted? The answer is a difficult one for a sentencing judge, because the administration of justice has a variety of conflicting goals: the rehabilitation of offenders, the discouragement of potential lawbreakers, the isolation of dangerous criminals who pose a threat to community safety, the condemnation of extralegal conduct, and the reinforcement of accepted social norms. Objectives as varied as these tend to generate such contradictory suggestions as the following:

"The punishment should fit the crime."
"The public demands a prison sentence."
"The purpose of justice is individualized sentencing."
"The sentence should be a warning to others."
"Rehabilitate the offender so he can be returned to society."
"Lock him up and throw away the key."

The burden of the judge is to choose among one or more of these various goals while subordinating all others.

Sentencing Objectives

Throughout the history of the United States, there has been no single and clearly defined rationale to serve as a guiding principle in sentencing. For 200 years, the public has alternated between revulsion at inhumane sentencing practices and prison conditions on the one hand, and overly compassionate treatment on the other. While the former practices are denounced as "barbaric" and "uncivilized" and the latter as "coddling criminals," the fate of convicted offenders has repeatedly shifted according to prevailing national values and current perceptions of danger and fear of crime. As a result, sentencing objectives are based on at least four competing philosophies: retribution, isolation, deterrence, and rehabilitation.

Retribution

Retribution is societal vengeance. It is concerned exclusively with making the punishment fit the crime, and is as old as recorded history. It can be found in Genesis (27:45), Exodus (21:23–25), and Leviticus (25:17–22), with such prescriptions as "When one man strikes another and kills him, he shall be put to death," and "Eye for eye, tooth for tooth, hand for hand, foot for foot, burning for burning, wound for wound . . . " Retribution was also the basis of punishment under Mosaic law — that there should fall upon the offender what he had done to his neighbor.

Retribution rests on the notion that criminals are wicked, evil people who are responsible for their actions and deserve to be punished. At the same time, however, it asserts that the *state* shall act as the instrument of the community's collective revenge, thus incorporating the idea that the victims of crime cannot make reprisals against the offending parties.

As a sentencing philosophy, retribution presents an ethical dilemma. In a democratic society built on the principles of individual rights and civil liberties, criminal penalties based on "getting even" represent a contradiction in values. Furthermore, many libertarian ideals in modern society foster the notion that "making criminals suffer for the sake of suffering" is barbaric and uncivilized. As a result, although human instincts have tended to demand vengeance, there have been few twentieth-century advocates of the retribution theory of punishment. Most recently, however, there has been a resurgence of this posture, referred to as a "just deserts" philosophy. Stated

A criminal is executed by an elephant at Baroda, India.

Retribution is societal vengeance.

"Just deserts"

simply, the philosophy is that criminal sanctions should be imposed because the offender "deserves" them. "Just deserts" implies retribution, vengeance, and revenge, but with its current label the theme has been receiving wider attention since — at least semantically — it is less emotion laden.[1]

Isolation

Isolation is the removal of the offender from society.

Unlike retribution, **isolation** is simply the removal of dangerous persons from the community.[2] Also referred to as the "restraint" or "incapacitation" philosophy, its object is community protection rather than revenge. By removing the offender from society through execution, imprisonment, or exile (as is the case with the *deportation* of foreign nationals upon conviction of certain crimes), the community is thus protected from further criminal activity. (See Exhibit 13.1.)

As with retribution, isolation as a punishment philosophy is problematic. If the goals are crime prevention and community protection, then the sanctions would have to be quite severe to be effective. Regardless of the

---

EXHIBIT 13.1

The Isolation of Habitual Offenders and Sexual Psychopaths

Isolation of a relatively permanent nature evolved during the early part of this century under what has often been referred to as the "Baumes laws." In 1926, restrictive penal legislation was sponsored by a New York State penal committee headed by Senator Caleb H. Baumes. The laws provided for an increase in penalty with each successive felony offense and an automatic life sentence for the fourth offense. The term *Baumes laws* became widely applied to similar **habitual offender laws** passed in other states. Virtually all jurisdictions in the United States now have some form of habitual offender laws. Most have statutes similar to the New York codes, which now can provide for life imprisonment for a third felony offense. Some states go one step further; in Texas, for example, a sentence of up to 99 years may be mandated for some second felony offenders.

Comparable to the habitual offender laws are the sexual psychopath laws and sex offender acts, which also call for sentences of extended isolation. Such legislation came into being as the result of alarm over widely publicized sex crimes. The first of these laws appeared in Michigan in 1935, and by the 1950s they were apparent in many jurisdictions. They allowed prosecutors to initiate proceedings against a defendant to have him placed in an institution for an indeterminate length of time if there was sufficient reason to believe that he

---

offense, life imprisonment with no parole and execution are the only forms of restraint that can guarantee the elimination of future offenses against the community. The alternative—temporary incarceration until such times as the community can be reasonably assured the offender will no longer commit crimes—is impossible to predict. In addition, there is an economic dimension. As the guiding principle of sentencing, isolation would require the costly construction of many more prison facilities, plus the annual costs of supporting an expanded population of inmates, combined with the increased expense of new custodial personnel.

In current practice, isolation as a premise for sentencing is not uncommon. The National Advisory Commission on Criminal Justice Standards and Goals has noted the following, however, about prisons as vehicles for offender restraint:

> **They protect the community but that protection is only temporary. They relieve the community of responsibility by removing the offender, but they make successful reintegration of the offender into the community unlikely.[3]**

was sexually dangerous. The indeterminate period, furthermore, could range anywhere from one day to life, and some did not even require proof that a crime had been committed.

The sexual psychopath laws were ultimately deemed to have little value, primarily because they were enacted out of hysteria and provided little community protection. The vicious acts of child molesting and sadomasochistic rape that they targeted were behavior that could be neither predicted nor prevented, and many offenders rarely repeated their crimes. Over time, the laws were either revoked or ignored, but in some jurisdictions they nevertheless remain in force. In Illinois, for example, the Sexually

Dangerous Persons statute currently reads:

All persons suffering from a mental disorder, which mental disorder has existed for a period of not less than one year, immediately prior to the filing of the petition hereinafter provided for, coupled with criminal propensities to the commission of sex offenses, and who have demonstrated propensities toward acts of sexual assault or acts of sexual molestation of children, are hereby declared sexually dangerous persons.

SOURCES: State of New York, Penal Law, 40–70.10; Texas Penal Code, Section 12.42; Illinois Codes, 38-105-3; Alan H. Swanson, "Sexual Psychopath Statutes: Summary and Analysis," *Journal of Criminal Law, Criminology and Police Science* 51 (July–August 1960): 215–235.

Deterrence

Deterrence makes an example of persons convicted of crimes.

The most widely held justification for punishment is reducing crime. Thus, as a sentencing philosophy, **deterrence** refers to the prevention of criminal acts by making examples of persons convicted of crimes. Deterrence can be both general and specific. General deterrence seeks to discourage would-be offenders from committing crimes; specific deterrence is designed to prevent a particular convicted offender from engaging in future criminal acts.

The notion of punishment as a deterrent is best illustrated in the words of an eighteenth-century judge who reportedly stated to a defendant at sentencing, "You are to be hanged not because you have stolen a sheep but in order that others may not steal sheep."[4] Belief in the efficacy of deterrence, however, seems mainly based on conjecture, faith, and emotion, and there is overwhelming evidence to suggest that the deterrent effect of punishment is, at best, weak.[5] Increased crime rates in the nation's cities as well as high levels of recidivism among many offender populations are ample evidence of this. On the other hand, the philosophy of specific deterrence does seem to have an impact on the behavior of many white-collar criminals and first-time misdemeanants whose arrests and convictions cause them embarrassment and public disgrace, and threaten their careers and family life. General deterrence can be applied to similar populations for certain types of criminal activity. During the 1970s, for example, when many jurisdictions made it a misdemeanor to patronize a prostitute, a U.S. Department of Justice employee commented:

> Almost every weekend I'd go to downtown D.C., to Atlantic City, or Times Square and shack up with some sleazy hooker. . . . No more, babe! That's all I need, getting busted for sleeping with a whore. . . . So much for a career in Justice.[6]

Rehabilitation

Rehabilitation seeks to reintegrate the offender into society.

From a humanistic point of view, the most appealing basis for sentencing and justification for punishment is that future crime can be prevented by changing the offender's behavior. The **rehabilitation** philosophy rests on the premise that persons who commit crimes have identifiable reasons for doing so, and that these can be discovered, addressed, and altered. Rehabilitation suggests to the offender that "crime does not pay" and that "there is a better way." Its aim is to modify behavior and reintegrate the lawbreaker into the wider society as a productive citizen.

The goal of rehabilitation has wide support, for in contrast with other sentencing philosophies, it takes a positive approach to eliminating offense behavior. Unlike the false hope of deterrence or the temporary measures of retribution and isolation, proponents argue that rehabilitation is the only humanitarian mechanism for altering the criminal careers of society's casualties.

Yet the efficacy of rehabilitation has been seriously questioned. Some suggest that since the causes of crime are not fully understood, efforts at behavioral change are of questionable value. Others maintain that since the availability of rehabilitative services in many institutions and community-based programs is either minimal or nonexistent, then "correction" as such has only little limited practical potential. Still a third group espouses a "nothing works'' philosophy, arguing that rehabilitation has not demonstrated and never will demonstrate its ability to prevent or reduce crime.[7]

Statutory Sentencing Structures

Regardless of the sentencing philosophy of the presiding judge, the actual sentence imposed is influenced to some degree by the statutory alternatives that appear in the penal codes, combined with the facilities and programs available in the correctional system. Thus, the competing objectives of retribution, isolation, deterrence, and rehabilitation may be diluted to some degree since the judicial sentencing responsibility must be carried out within the guidelines provided by legislative sentencing authority.

Executions by beheading — a potent deterrence — took place in China at the turn of the century.

The **statutory sentencing** guidelines, which have generally evolved over long periods of time and often reflect the changing nature of legislative philosophy, appear in each state's criminal code. No two state codes are quite alike — the punishments they designate for specific crimes vary, and the methods establishing the parameters for sentencing can also differ. Furthermore, some statutes give judges wide latitude in sentencing, while others do not. In some states — Tennessee, for example — the penal code designates the range of punishments for each specific crime. Others, such as Idaho, follow the Tennessee model for some crimes, but extend almost total discretion to the judge for others. And in other states, such as New York, crimes are first classified according to their severity (for example, rape in the first degree is a class B felony, while incest is a class E felony) and then assigned punishments according to their felony or misdemeanor class.

Although statutory guidelines provide a range of sentencing alternatives, judges also have discretion in many instances to deviate from the legislative norm, on the premise that sentences should be individualized. Conversely, there are situations in which sentencing discretion can be taken away from the judge. For example, a person convicted of rape in the first degree in the state of New York faces a statutory period of imprisonment of no less than 6 years and no more than 25 years, since the crime is a class B felony. Assume that the judge imposes the maximum of 8 to 25 years, his or her philosophy being that the defendant is a dangerous criminal from which society must be protected for as long as is legally possible. Under Section 70.40 of the New York penal law, however, this offender can be released on parole after serving the minimum sentence — 8 years. In addition, under Section 241 of the New York correction law, the governor always has the power to reduce a sentence or grant a pardon. Although these contingencies are highly unlikely with a violent crime such as forcible rape, they have occurred with less serious felonies, countermanding the original designs of the sentencing judge.

A judge's authority and discretionary power to determine a sentence is, in a few jurisdictions, delegated by statute to the jury — but only for certain types of crimes. North Carolina, for example, is one of several southern states in which the jury makes the sentencing decision in capital cases. In addition, 13 jurisdictions provide for jury-determined sentences in some noncapital cases. The wisdom of this practice, however, has been called into serious question. Author Melvyn Zerman has commented that the sentencing decision is the most formidable demand that can be made of a jury, and that it often occurs at a time when the jurors are both mentally and physically weak.[8] Even more to the point, the National Advisory Commission on Criminal Justice Standards and Goals has argued:

> **The practice has been condemned by every serious study and analysis in the last half century. Jury sentencing is nonprofessional and is more likely than judge sentencing to be arbitrary and based on emotions rather than the needs of the offender or society. Sentencing by juries leads to disparate sentences and leaves little opportunity for development of sentencing policies.[9]**

Sentencing Alternatives

Whatever theory of sanctions ultimately guides the sentencing of the defendant, and depending on the statutory requirements of the jurisdiction, the alternatives for the presiding judge include fines, probation or some other community-based program, imprisonment, or the death penalty.

Fines

Fines are imposed either in lieu of or in addition to incarceration or probation. They are the traditional means of dealing with most traffic infractions and many misdemeanors, and the sentence "$30 or 30 days" has often been heard in courtrooms across America over the years. The following illustrate the use of fines in contemporary statutes:

- In Maryland, larceny of goods valued at less than $100 — a misdemeanor — calls for (1) return of the goods stolen or repayment of their full value to the owner, and (2) a fine of not more than $100, and/or (3) imprisonment of not more than 18 months.[10]
- In New York, exposure of a female — a "violation" with the curiously worded definition of "clothed in such a manner that the portion of her breast below the top of the areola is not covered" — calls for (1) a fine not to exceed $250, or (2) imprisonment of not more than 15 days.[11]

Fines can also be imposed for felonies, instead of or in addition to some other sentence. They can involve many thousands of dollars, and sometimes twice the amount of the defendant's gain from the commission of the crime. However, since *Williams* v. *Illinois* in 1970 and *Tate* v. *Short* the following year,[12] the use of fines has been curtailed somewhat. In *Williams,* the Supreme Court ruled that no jurisdiction could hold a person in jail or prison beyond the length of the maximum sentence merely to work off a fine they were unable to pay — a practice that was allowed at that time in 47 states. In *Tate,* the Court held that the historic "$30 or 30 days" sentence was an unconstitutional denial of equal protection. The Court's unanimous decision maintained that limiting punishment to a fine for those who could pay, but expanding punishment for the same offense to imprisonment for those who could not, was a violation of the Fourteenth Amendment.

$30 or 30 days

For a convicted offender who receives a sentence of imprisonment, there are numerous types of sentence on the statute books; some have elicited considerable controversy. Sentences can be *indeterminate, determinate, definite, "flat," "fixed," indefinite, intermittent,* or *mandatory,* plus a host of other names, many of which have been confused and mislabeled in the literature. In practice, there are three major types: the indeterminate, the determinate, and the definite sentence.

The Indeterminate Sentence

The most common sentence is the **indeterminate sentence,** which has a fixed minimum and a fixed maximum term for incarceration, rather than a definite period. The actual amount of time served is determined by the paroling authority. Sentences of 1 to 5 years, 7½ to 15 years, 10 to 20 years, or 15 years to life are indeterminate.

The statutory sentencing guidelines for forcible rape in New York and Idaho are truly indeterminate (see Exhibit 13.2). For example, the crime of

Indeterminate sentence: A sentence of incarceration having a fixed minimum and a fixed maximum term of confinement.

EXHIBIT 13.2

Alternative Sentencing Guidelines

The definitions of crimes and their corresponding statutory sentencing guidelines vary widely from state to state. This is illustrated in the following contrasting approaches toward forcible rape in the states of Idaho, Tennessee, and New York.

From the Idaho Code, Title 18:

18-6101. Rape defined. Rape is an act of sexual intercourse accomplished with a female under either of the following circumstances:

1. Where the female is under the age of eighteen (18) years.

2. Where she is incapable, through lunacy or any other unsoundness of mind, whether temporary or permanent, of giving legal consent.

3. Where she resists but her resistance is overcome by force or violence.

4. Where she is prevented from resistance by threats of immediate and great bodily harm, accompanied by apparent power of execution; or by any intoxicating narcotic, or anaesthetic substance administered by or with the privity of the accused.

5. Where she is at the time unconscious of the nature of the act, and this is known to the accused.

6. Where she submits under the belief that the person committing the act is her husband, and the belief is induced by artifice, pretense or concealment practiced by the accused, with intent to induce such belief.

18-6104. Punishment for rape. Rape is punishable by imprisonment in the state prison not less than one (1) year, and the imprisonment may be extended to life in the discretion of the District Judge, who shall pass sentence.

From the Tennessee Code, Title 39:

39-3701. Rape defined. Rape is the unlawful carnal knowledge of a woman, forcibly and against her will. Carnal knowledge is accomplished by the commencement of a sexual connection, and proof of emission is not required.

39-3702. Punishment for rape. Whoever is convicted of the rape of any female under twelve (12) years of age shall suffer death by electrocution. Whoever is convicted of the rape of any female over the age of twelve (12) years shall be punished by imprisonment in the penitentiary for life or for a period of not less than ten (10) years.

From the New York Code, Chapter 40:

130.25 Rape in the third degree. A male is guilty of rape in the third degree when:

1. He engages in sexual intercourse with a female who is incapable of consent by reason of some factor other than being less than seventeen years old; or

2. Being twenty-one years old or more, he engages in sexual intercourse with a female less than seventeen years old.

Rape in the third degree is a class E felony.

130.30 Rape in the second degree. A male is guilty of rape in the second degree when, being eighteen years old or more, he engages in sexual intercourse with a female less than fourteen years old.

Rape in the second degree is a class D felony.

130.35 Rape in the first degree. A male is guilty of rape in the first degree when he engages in sexual intercourse with a female:

1. By forcible compulsion; or

2. Who is incapable of consent by reason of being physically helpless; or

3. Who is less than eleven years old.

Rape in the first degree is a class B felony.

70.00 Sentence of imprisonment for felony. For a class B felony, the term shall be fixed by the court, and shall not exceed twenty-five years;

For a class D felony, the term shall be fixed by the court, and shall not exceed seven years;

For a class E felony, the term shall be fixed by the court, and shall not exceed four years.

70.02 Sentence of imprisonment for a violent felony offense. For a class B felony, the term must be at least six years, and must not exceed twenty-five years; and . . . the minimum period of imprisonment . . . must be fixed by the court at one-third of the maximum term imposed and must be specified in the sentence.

rape in the first degree in the New York law calls for a period of incarceration of not less than 6 years and not more than 25 years, with the minimum fixed at one-third of the maximum. Within those guidelines, the judge can impose a sentence, for example, of 7 to 21 years. Thus, the offender must serve at least 7 years, after which the paroling authority may release him at *any* time prior to the completion of his maximum sentence.

The philosophy behind the indeterminate sentence is based on a purely correctional model of punishment, the underlying premise being that the sentence should meet the needs of the defendant. After incarceration begins, at least in theory, the rehabilitation process is initiated, and the inmate should be confined until there is substantial evidence of "correction." At that point, it becomes the responsibility of the paroling authority to assess the nature and extent of such rehabilitation, and release the defendant if the evidence so warrants it. Thus, the indeterminate sentence rests on the notion that the length of imprisonment should be based on progress toward rehabilitation:

1. Criminals are personally or socially disturbed or disadvantaged and therefore their commission of crime cannot be considered a free choice. If this is the case, then setting terms commensurate with the severity of the crime is not logical.
2. Indeterminate sentences allow "effective" treatment to rectify socio-psychological problems, which are the root of crime.
3. Readiness for release varies with the individual and can only be determined when the inmate is in the institution, not before.[13]

(All of these contentions are disputable and are not widely held in penological and criminological circles.)

In its purest form, the indeterminate sentence would involve a term of one day to life, but this is rarely found in current statutes. Confusion emerges in that some refer to this last example as the "indefinite" sentence, while others use the terms *indefinite* and *indeterminate* interchangeably.

In recent years, the practice of indeterminate sentencing has received considerable criticism. For example, the following arguments have been made against this form of sentencing:

- Since the causes of crime and criminal behavior are not readily understood, they cannot be dealt with under the premise of indeterminate sentencing.
- Rehabilitation cannot occur within the prison setting, regardless of the nature of the sentencing.
- The indeterminate sentence is used as an instrument of inmate control, put into practice through threats of disciplinary reports and hence, extended sentences.
- Sentences within the indeterminate model can vary by judge and by jurisdiction, resulting in unfair and disparate terms of imprisonment.
- An offender's uncertainty as to how long his or her prison term may endure can lead to frustration, violence, and riot.[14]

Criticisms of indeterminate sentencing

The Determinate Sentence

The growing concerns over indeterminate sentencing have generated considerable interest in the **determinate sentence.** Known also as the "flat," "fixed" or "straight" sentence, it has no set minimum or maximum, but rather, a fixed

Determinate sentence: A sentence of incarceration for a fixed period of time.

period of time. The term of the determinate sentence is established by the legislature — say, 15 years — thus removing the sentencing discretion of the judge. However, under determinate sentencing guidelines, the court's discretion to choose between prison, probation, a fine, and some other alternative is not affected. Only the length of the sentence is taken away from judicial discretion, if the judge imposes imprisonment.

In some instances, the determinate sentence can, in effect, become an indeterminate sentence. Under determinate sentencing statutes, inmates are still eligible for parole after a portion of their terms have been served. Thus, in a state where parole eligibility begins after one-half of the term has expired, a determinate sentence of 10 years really ranges from a minimum of 5 years to a maximum of 10.

The Definite Sentence

Definite sentence: A sentence of incarceration having a fixed period of time with no reduction by parole.

The first application of indeterminate sentencing policies in the United States appeared in 1924 at New York's House of Refuge.[15] Prior to that time, a regular feature of incarceration was the **definite sentence** — one having a fixed period of time with no reduction by parole. This type of sentence fell out of favor, however, because those interested in rehabilitation found it to be too rigid and insensitive to defendants' individual characteristics and needs.

In contemporary statutes, the definite sentence is occasionally seen with respect to punishments for minor misdemeanors. It is rarely imposed with felonies, however, although life sentences with no eligibility for parole are in a sense definite sentences. For example, in Delaware,

> **any person who is convicted of first-degree murder shall be punished by death or by imprisonment for the remainder of his or her natural life without benefit of probation or parole or any other reduction.**[16]

The diminished appeal of the indeterminate sentence in recent years, combined with the growing concerns over street crime and the "coddling of criminals," has led to renewed interest in definite sentencing guidelines. In 1975, Maine became the first state to abandon the indeterminate sentencing system. At the same time, it also abolished parole. Under its new "flat" sentencing laws, terms of imprisonment are, in effect, definite sentences.

Other Sentencing Variations

In addition to the three basic sentences of imprisonment — the indeterminate, the determinate, and the definite — a number of variations and adaptations have been receiving increased attention in recent years.

In New York and several other jurisdictions there is the sentence of intermittent imprisonment. Under the New York statute, the **intermittent sentence** is a term to be served on certain days or periods of days as specified by the court.[17] For example, a defendant who pleaded guilty to the felonious possession of 74 pounds of marijuana was sentenced to an intermittent term of 60 days, to be served on consecutive weekends, followed by five years' probation.[18] It is a sanction used in instances where the nature of the offense warrants incarceration, but where the defendant's characteristics and habits suggest full-time imprisonment to be inappropriate. It should also be noted that a sentence of intermittent imprisonment is *revocable*. That is, should the offender fail to report to the institution on the days specified, he or she can be returned to court and resentenced to a more traditional term of imprisonment.

Intermittent sentence: A sentence to periods of confinement interrupted by periods of freedom.

Also, a variety of determinate sentence known as the **mandatory sentence** has been the subject of extensive discussion since the middle of the 1970s. Mandatory sentences limit judicial discretion; they are penal code provisions that require the judge to sentence persons convicted of certain specified crimes to prison terms. Under these statutes, which are intended to guarantee that recidivists, violent offenders, and other serious criminals face the strictness and certainty of punishment, neither probation nor other alternative sentences are permitted. One illustration of the mandatory sentence is the Massachusetts Gun Control Law, which requires imprisonment of no less than 1 year and no more than 2½ years for the illegal possession of a firearm.[19] In addition, due to the persistent high rates of auto theft in Massachusetts, that state imposes mandatory sentences for those felonies as well.[20]

Mandatory sentence: A statutory requirement that a certain penalty shall be set and carried out in all cases upon conviction for a specified offense or series of offenses.

The growing appeal of this form of sanction became most evident in 1979. During that year, 18 states enacted some form of mandatory sentencing statutes.[21] This brought the total number of states with such provisions to 27, with others considering similar adoptions.

Although some people would argue that mandatory sentences could be construed as cruel and unusual punishment in violation of the Eighth Amendment, more and more states are adopting mandatory sentencing provisions in their penal laws. Furthermore, the most recent statement on this issue came from the Attorney General's Task Force on Violent Crime in 1981, which urged the widespread adoption of mandatory sentences for a significant range of offenses.[22]

Finally, there have been some unique variations in sentencing imposed by judges across the country on the basis of "letting the punishment fit the crime." For example:

- In 1984, a Tennessee farmer who had assaulted his mistress was sentenced to buy a new car — *for his wife*.[23]
- In 1981, a San Francisco judge sentenced a local prostitute to spend 90 days in a convent with the Sisters of the Good Shepherd.[24]
- For first-time shoplifters, an East Brunswick, New Jersey, magistrate imposes a $300 fine and 4½ hours of lectures by a supermarket manager.[25]
- In Oswego, New York, a man convicted of using obscene language against a police officer was sentenced in 1981 to have his mouth washed out with soap.[26]
- In Florida, Virginia, and Texas during 1982, several sentencing judges invoked the "law of the old West," when they offered several convicted defendants the choice of either incarceration or "getting out of town."[27]

And then there is a most controversial sentence for convicted rapists — castration (see Exhibit 13.3).

Disparities in Sentencing

Sentencing disparities have long since been a major problem in criminal justice processing. The basis of the difficulty is threefold:

1. the structure of indeterminate sentencing guidelines
2. the discretionary powers of sentencing judges
3. the mechanics of plea bargaining

The statutory minimum and maximum terms of imprisonment combined with fines, probation, or other alternatives to incarceration create a number of sentencing possibilities for a specific crime. With judicial discretion in sentencing, sanctions can vary widely according to the jurisdiction, the community, and the punishment philosophy of a particular judge. The dynamics of plea bargaining enable various defendants accused of the same crime to be convicted and sentenced differently. These problems exist, furthermore, both within an individual court and across jurisdictions, since sentencing statutes can differ drastically from one state to the next.

Consider, for example, the range of sentences possible for conviction of burglary in the first degree (or its equivalent) in the following states:

- *Idaho:* imprisonment for not less than 1 year nor more than 15 years, or probation[28]
- *New York:* imprisonment for not less than 3 years and not more than 25 years, or probation, or a fine[29]
- *West Virginia:* imprisonment for not less than 1 year nor more than 10 years, or probation (for a first felony conviction)[30]

- *Delaware:* 3 to 30 years' imprisonment, or a suspended sentence, or probation, or a fine (payable in installments)[31]
- *Maryland:* imprisonment for not more than 20 years, or probation[32]
- *Alabama:* imprisonment for not less than 10 years, or probation[33]

Just within these few jurisdictions, the potential for disparate sentences is obvious. In Delaware, for example, the sentence imposed upon conviction for first-degree burglary can range from a fine to 30 years' imprisonment. Minimum terms of imprisonment extend from a low of 1 year in Idaho to a high of 10 years in Alabama. And the maximum term allowable can range from 10 years (West Virginia) to 30 years (Delaware), to perhaps even life (Alabama).

Statistical comparisons of sentencing tendencies in various jurisdictions demonstrate that disparities are indeed widespread. In the Detroit Recorder's Court, for example, sentencing dispositions were sampled from ten judges over a 20-month period. It was found that one judge imposed prison terms upon as many as 90 percent of the defendants he sentenced, while another ordered such sentences in only 35 percent of his cases. Another magistrate consistently imposed prison sentences twice as long as those of the most lenient judge; and judges who were the most severe for certain crimes were the most lenient in others.[34] Similarly, forgers sentenced by federal judges in the Southern District of New York (Manhattan) received sentences that were an average of 20 months longer than those imposed in the Eastern District of New York (Brooklyn and Long Island).[35] Recent analyses have also demonstrated that a conviction for automobile theft in West Virginia will result in more time in prison than a rape conviction in 16 other states, and that South Carolina prisoners sentenced for armed robbery end up doing more time in the penitentiary than convicted murderers in six other states.[36] For example, a Miami woman shot and killed her lover in 1984 after he slapped her in the face. After being charged with murder, she pleaded guilty to manslaughter and was placed on probation.[37] By contrast, there was the case of Roger Trenton Davis, convicted in Virginia in 1973 for "possession with intent to distribute" nine ounces of marijuana. The judge imposed a term of 40 years—a sentence which the Supreme Court upheld in 1982.[38]

With the examples of sentencing disparity noted here, it might be argued that the judges might have been dealing with crimes of varying degrees of seriousness and with offenders who were deserving of more or less punishment; but other data tend to contradict such an argument. In one study, conducted by the Federal Judicial Center during 1974, each of 50 federal judges from the Second Circuit were given 20 identical presentence reports drawn from actual cases, and asked to render sentences. The outcome clearly indicated disparate sentencing. In one case involving a defendant convicted of extortion, the sentences ranged from 3 years' imprisonment, at one end, to 20 years plus a $65,000 fine, at the other.[39] Later during the 1970s, 41 New York judges drawn from across the state participated in a similar experiment, and the results further confirmed disparate sentencing practices (see Exhibit 13.5).[40] During the early 1980s, a similar study was conducted by the Justice Department with 264 federal judges. A major highlight of the findings was that for the same hypothetical offense, the recommended sentences ranged from probation to 20 years' imprisonment.[41]

The consequences of disparities in sentencing can be significant, and not only for the convicted, but also for the court and correctional systems and the entire administration of justice. First, the wide variations in sentencing

Disparities in sentencing are widespread.

The consequences of disparate sentencing

EXHIBIT 13.3

Castrating the Rapist

Since violent people beget other violent people, castration would prevent a second generation.
—Woody Aydlette, 1983

One may think of castration as a penalty for rape to be associated with the unusual punishments of antiquity, but it has a recent history in the United States. Scores of sex offenders were castrated in California during the 1930s and 1940s. Moreover, in the early 1970s a Colorado man facing a 40-year term for rape and child molestation volunteered for and underwent surgical castration, with a prior agreement with the judge that probation would be granted in exchange.

More recently, however, the issue became an emotional and legal debate of national proportions following a trial in the small town of Anderson, South Carolina. In April 1983, three men committed what was described as a heinous crime. They had raped a 23-year-old woman in a motel room for six hours, tortured her with a cigarette lighter, and photographed her in the various sex acts into which she was forced. The victim lost a total of four pints of blood; her hospitalization lasted several days; and it is probable that she will suffer emotional scars for the rest of her life. After their conviction in 1983, presiding judge C. Victor Pyle gave the defendants—ages 27, 21, and 19—a shocking choice: accept a 30-year prison sentence, or submit to surgical castration and go free.

Immediately, there were moral, legal, ethical, medical, and constitutional questions and arguments raised. Judge Pyle's

sentence also became the center of an emotional debate. There was considerable support for the idea of castrating rapists; many people even held that castration alone was not a severe enough punishment. Representative Woody Aydlette of South Carolina put it, "In my humble opinion, Judge Pyle's sentence was a masterful piece of creativity and imagination." Yet many people were opposed to the idea. Physicians held that while castration might prevent a rapist from having children, it might not prevent intercourse. For after all, male hormones which restore both libido and potency are available in artificial form by pill or injection.

Criminologists and women's rights advocates had long since argued that castration does not even begin to solve the problem of rape, a crime that is a sexual expression of aggression, not an aggressive expression of sexuality. And there was support for this position in the very case that initiated the debate. The motive behind the rape, at least in part, was a kind of blackmail: the victim had brought a paternity suit against one of the men, and he was trying to pressure her, with the help of his friends, to drop the suit.

Professor Alan Dershowitz of Harvard Law School commented on a different aspect of the debate:

When Judge C. Victor Pyle recently gave three convicted rapists the "choice" between 30 years' imprisonment and surgical castration, he was acting more like a mikado* than an American judge. . . .

Supporters of Judge Pyle will argue that castration was not the

---

* A Japanese emperor.

Drawing by David Seavey, *USA Today*, December 5, 1983, p. 10A.

sentence imposed. The defendants were given a *choice* between imprisonment and castration.

But the illusion of choice should not salvage the constitutionality of the sentence. Were judges permitted to circumvent the Constitution by allowing choices, it would be a simple matter for an American mikado to achieve his "object all sublime." He would impose severe traditional sentences and then give the defendant the "choice" of accepting less severe, but unconstitutional, alternate punishments that "fit the crime."

The possibilities are limitless: 10 years imprisonment or convert to Baptism; five years or move to another state; three years or 60 lashes; one year or quit the National Organization for Women; six months or vote Republican.

In the aftermath of the sentence, all three defendants filed appeals. However, Roscoe Brown, the oldest of the three, quickly dropped his appeal and asked to be castrated so as to get out of prison. Judge Pyle delayed ruling on the matter until the final disposition of the other defendants' appeals. Roscoe Brown then filed a petition for a writ of *mandamus* with the South Carolina Supreme Court to force the judge to carry out the sentence. Later, the other two defendants asked that their appeals be dismissed so they also could choose castration. On February 13, 1985, after hearing oral arguments on the *mandamus* request, the justices of the South Carolina Supreme Court voided the entire sentence on grounds that it violated the Eighth Amendment ban on cruel and unusual punishment, and remanded the case for resentencing.

Although it would appear that, at least for a time, the issue of surgical castration for rapists has been put to rest, there was still the matter of *chemical* castration. In 1983, a San Antonio man convicted of rape avoided imprisonment, by means of a negotiated plea, by agreeing to submit to injections of Depo-Provera — a synthetic female hormone that in men shrinks the testicles and reduces the sex drive. The chemical castration was carried out with no apparent legal entanglements.

SOURCES: Brown v. State, SC SupCt (1983) 36 CrL 2463; *Newsweek*, September 5, 1983, p. 69; Wilmington (Delaware) *News-Journal*, November 27, 1983, p. A17; *New York Times*, December 11, 1983, p. 35; *Time*, December 12, 1983, p. 70; Philadelphia *Inquirer*, January 1, 1984, pp. 1A, 2A, 14A; *USA Today*, December 5, 1983, p. 10A; *National Law Journal*, March 4, 1985, p. 9.

make a mockery of the principle of evenhanded administration of the criminal law, thus calling into question the very philosophy of justice in America. Second, disparities have a rebound effect on plea bargaining and court scheduling. On the one hand, defendants may opt for a negotiated plea rather than face trial before a judge known to be severe. On the other, substantial delays often result from the granting of continuances sought by defense attorneys who hope that numerous reschedulings will ultimately bring their cases before lenient judges. Known as "judge-shopping," the practice is so wide-

A Consequence of Sentencing Disparity?

One of the more celebrated cases of disparate sentencing practices involved the conviction of a 20-year-old youth on charges of conspiracy to commit a felony and assault with the intent to rob. The year was 1924, and the youth, although AWOL from the U.S. Navy, had no prior criminal record. His codefendant, Edgar Singleton, was a 31-year-old former convict and umpire for a local baseball team.

The two had collaborated to rob a grocery store in Mooresville, Indiana, but the victim resisted, the attempt was thwarted, and both were quickly arrested.

Fearing the strictness and certainty of punishment handed down at the county court in Martinsville, Indiana, Singleton obtained a change of venue, received a term of 2 to 10 years, and was paroled after less than two years. The youth, however, threw himself on the mercy of the local court, but nevertheless received sentences of 2 to 14 years and 10 to 20 years.

Embittered by unequal justice and the inequitable sentence, the youth rebelled against his warders at the Indiana State Reformatory. He attempted escape on three occasions, was charged with numerous disciplinary violations, and as a result was denied parole when first eligible in 1929. Later that year, he was transferred to Indiana State Prison, where he met a score of experienced criminals who taught him the fine art of bank robbery.

On May 22, 1933, just a few days before his thirtieth birthday, after having spent his entire young adult life in prison, he was finally paroled. Based on the tutelage provided by his inmate associates, he began a professional career in bank robbery. During the next 13 months, he engineered a score of armed holdups at banks and stores across the Midwest. His efforts netted him many hundreds of thousands of dollars, but in the process he killed at least 15 people. On July 2, 1934, as a young man of only 31 years, FBI agents shot him to death as he exited a theater in Chicago, Illinois. His name was John Dillinger.

SOURCES: L. L. Edge, *Run the Cat Roads* (New York: Dembner, 1981); J. Edgar Hoover, *Persons in Hiding* (Boston: Little, Brown, 1938); Jay Robert Nash, *Bloodletters and Badmen* (New York: M. Evans, 1973); John Toland, *The Dillinger Days* (New York: Random House, 1963).

EXHIBIT 13.5

Disparate Sentencing

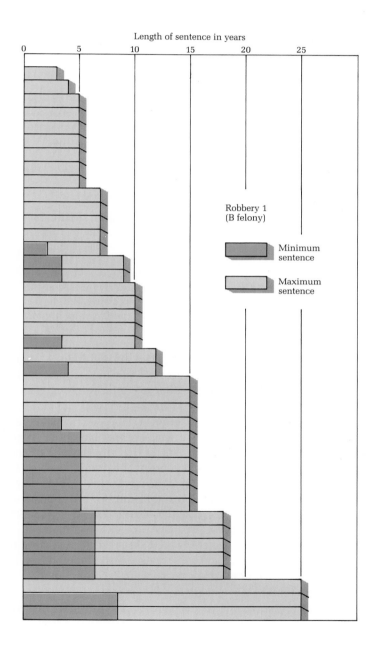

Length of sentence in years

Robbery 1
(B felony)

Minimum sentence

Maximum sentence

In a study of 41 New York judges from across the state, the judges were asked to review files on actual cases and then indicate the sentences they would impose.

In this case, an elderly man was robbed at gunpoint by a heroin addict. The defendant was convicted of first-degree robbery. He was unemployed, lived with his pregnant wife, and had a minor criminal record. His actual sentence was 0–5 years. Each bar in the figure represents one judge's hypothetical sentence.

SOURCE: *New York Times*, March 30, 1979, p. B3.

spread that at one time in the District of Columbia court of general sessions, giving a defendant the judge of his or her choice became part of the plea negotiation arrangements.[42] Third, prisoners compare their sentences, and an inmate who believes that he or she received an unfair sentence or was the victim of judicial prejudice often becomes hostile, resistant to correctional treatment and discipline, and even riot-prone. Fourth, the image of the courts and of the process of justice is even further denigrated.

Sentencing Reform

There have been a number of strong criticisms on the matter of sentencing disparities. Four decades ago, U.S. attorney general Robert H. Jackson commented:

> It is obviously repugnant to one's sense of justice that the judgment meted out to an offender should be dependent in large part on a purely fortuitous circumstance: namely, the personality of the particular judge before whom the case happens to come for disposition.[43]

More recently, federal judge Marvin E. Frankel of the Southern District of New York commented:

> The sentencing powers of the judges are, in short, so far unconfined that, except for frequently monstrous maximum limits, they are effectively subject to no law at all. Everyone with the least training in law would be prompt to denounce a statute that merely said the penalty for crimes "shall be any term the judge sees fit to impose." A regime of such arbitrary fiat would be intolerable in a supposedly free society, to say nothing of being invalid under our due-process clause. But the fact is that we have accepted unthinkingly a criminal code creating in effect precisely that degree of unbridled power.[44]

The criticisms of both Attorney General Jackson and Judge Frankel, as well as those of numerous others, are directed not only toward judicial discretion, but also toward the penal statutes that make far-reaching discretion possible. Criminal laws that allow jurists to impose terms of "not more than" 5 years, or 10 years, or 30 years proclaim, in effect, that sentencing judges are answerable only to their consciences. The measures that have been proposed or adopted in various jurisdictions to remedy the problem of sentencing disparities remove that key phrase "not more than" from the penal laws, reducing judicial discretion. Mandatory sentencing statutes, with their stipulations of fixed penalties, are in part the result of calls for better community protection, but they also clearly decrease the court's discretion. Mandatory sentence statutes, however, are not a panacea for either crime control or sentencing disparities, for they can easily increase prosecutorial discretion, court delays, and overcrowded prison conditions. Furthermore, they almost totally eliminate the rehabilitative goals of individualized justice.

A less extreme model for eliminating the abuses of discretion is the **presumptive fixed sentence,** now under consideration in several jurisdictions. The objectives of presumptive sentencing are (1) to reduce disparities by limiting judicial discretion without totally eliminating it, and (2) to increase community protection by imposing a sentence the offender is required to serve.

Presumptive sentencing

More stringent than the indeterminate sentence but less rigid than the determinate sentence, the presumptive fixed sentence is a good combination of the two. A state legislature would set a minimum and maximum term, with a limited range, for a particular crime. The judge would impose a fixed determinate sentence within that range, decided on the bases of mitigating circumstances and the offender's characteristics. This sentencing scheme also eliminates the need for parole.[45]

For example, a presumptive sentence for the crime of burglary in the first degree might have a lower legislative limit of three years and an upper limit of 10, with a fixed sentence of five years as set by the judge. Through this model, imprisonment becomes mandatory, a defined range of terms is established by statute, and a degree of judicial discretion remains. At the same time, such disparity-producing guidelines as Delaware's 3 to 30 years' imprisonment for the same crime, or Alabama's imprisonment "for not less than" 10 years, or other terms "as the judge sees fit to impose" would be eliminated.

Sentencing institutes, councils, and guidelines also have been introduced in the hope of influencing judicial discretion. Sentencing institutes, initiated at the federal level in 1958, are designed to generate interest in formulating policies and criteria for uniform sentencing procedures. Periodically convened in the form of one- and two-day workshops, they typically involve mock sentencing experiments followed by discussions of any observed disparities. Sentencing councils, which were started in 1960 in the federal court for the Eastern District of Michigan, are also intended to reduce disparities. The council includes three judges who examine the cases awaiting sentence and make recommendations to the sentencing judge. Sentencing guidelines are based on the actual sentencing behavior of judges. Statistical tables are constructed that reflect the average sentences imposed by judges in a specific jurisdiction, broken down by the seriousness of the crime and the characteristics of the offender. These guideline tables make it possible for a judge to know in advance of sentencing a case what his or her peers have done in similar circumstances. Such tables are intended to curb disparities by structuring discretion on the judges' common experience.

Sentencing institutes

Sentencing councils

Sentencing guidelines

None of these approaches, however, has been particularly effective.[46] The institutes are poorly attended, the councils have been only rarely adopted, and the guidelines are cumbersome and have appeared only periodically in a few jurisdictions. The reason for the limited attendance and adoption is, for the most part, judicial opposition. Sentencing is the one area of court processing where judges are in total command and can freely exercise their power and authority—capacities they are not likely to relinquish easily. One judge expressed his opposition this way: "To do away with judicial sentencing is to improperly delegate a responsibility that is rightfully and inherently a part of the judiciary."[47]

The Sentencing Process

Sentencing is generally a collective decision-making process that involves recommendations of the prosecutor, the defense attorney, the judge, and sometimes the presentence investigator. In jurisdictions where sentence bargaining is part of the plea negotiation process, the judge almost invariably imposes what has been agreed upon by the prosecution and the defense.

In the federal system and the majority of state jurisdictions, a **presentence investigation** may be conducted prior to actual sentencing. This is

Before sentence is passed, a presentence investigation of the defendant's situation may be made.

undertaken by the court's probation agency or presentence office, and the resulting report is a summary of the defendant's present offense, previous criminal record, family situation, neighborhood environment, school and educational history, employment record, physical and mental health, habits, associates, and participational activities. The report may also contain comments as to the defendant's remorse, and recommendations for sentencing by the victim, the prosecutor, and the officer who conducted the investigation.

Presentence reports vary in detail and length depending on the resources and practices of the jurisdiction. The statutes requiring the use of such reports are of three basic types:

1. those that make it a matter of judicial discretion;
2. those that make it mandatory for certain types of cases — such as felonies, or where the defendant is a recidivist, or where the offense is punishable by a year or more imprisonment; and,
3. those that make it mandatory if probation is to be the disposition.[48]

The value of presentence reports

Although presentence investigations are not mandatory in all jurisdictions, the American Bar Association has recommended that they be used for every criminal case.[49] Furthermore, as noted by the Administrative Offices of the U.S. Courts, the value of presentence reports goes well beyond their use in determining appropriate sentences. For example:

- They aid probation and parole officers in their supervision of offenders.
- They aid correctional personnel in their classification, treatment, and release programs.
- They furnish parole boards with useful information for release decision making.
- They can serve as a data base for systematic research.[50]

Allocution: The right of a convicted offender to address the court personally prior to the imposition of sentence.

Following the submission of the presentence report to the judge, a sentencing hearing is held. In common law, and in most jurisdictions, a convicted offender has the right to address the court personally prior to the imposition of sentence. Known as **allocution,** this practice is available so that the court can identify the defendant as the person judged guilty, the defendant can be given the opportunity to plead a pardon, move for an arrest of judgment, or indicate why judgment ought not be pronounced. The specific matters a defendant might state at the allocution are limited and would not include attempts to reopen the question of guilt. Rather, some of the claims included in allocutions have been that the offender has become insane since the verdict was rendered,* that he or she has received a pardon for the offense in question, that the defendant is not the person against whom there was a finding of guilt, and in the case of a woman, especially if a death sentence is to be pronounced, that the punishment be adjusted or deferred because of a possible pregnancy.[51]

Under Rule 32 (a) of the Federal Rules of Criminal Procedure, allocution is required. However, the failure of a federal judge to allow a defendant to address the court under Rule 32 (a) is not considered an error of constitutional

---

* Under the system of due process, the law will not punish a person who is unable to understand why he or she is being punished. If such is the case, the sentence must be deferred until understanding and reason have returned.

dimension.[52] Such a denial might result only in a remanding of the case for resentencing. Allocution only rarely produces a deferral of punishment.

The presiding judge then imposes the sentence. As noted earlier, the most typical sanctions include fines, imprisonment, probation, or some combination thereof, or death. In instances where the defendant receives multiple sentences for several crimes, the judge may order that terms of imprisonment be served concurrently or consecutively. *Concurrent sentences* are those that are served simultaneously. For example, if the defendant is convicted of both burglary and assault, and is given two terms of five years' imprisonment to be served concurrently, both terms are satisfied after five years. *Consecutive sentences* are successive — one after another.

Concurrent and consecutive sentences

As noted earlier in the discussions of bail and pretrial detention, it often happens that a defendant comes before a judge for sentencing having already spent weeks, months, and sometimes even years in a local jail or detention facility awaiting trial. This period of detention, referred to as "jail time," is generally deducted from the period of imprisonment imposed. When the conviction is for a misdemeanor or minor felony and the period of pretrial detention closely matches the probable term of imprisonment, the judge may impose a sentence of "time served." That is, the accumulated jail time represents the sentence, and the defendant is released. When the jail time spent awaiting trial is not counted as part of the final sentence, it is commonly referred to as "dead time."

The Death Penalty in the United States

Death cases are indeed different in kind from all other litigation. The penalty, once imposed, is irrevocable.   — Justice John Paul Stevens, 1981

For the greater part of U.S. history, the death penalty was used as a punishment for crime, with little thought given to its legitimacy or justification. It was simply accepted as an efficient mechanism for dealing with criminal offenders. When the framers of the Constitution incorporated the **Eighth Amendment ban** against cruel and unusual punishment, the death penalty itself was apparently not an issue. From the earliest days of the colonial experience, capital punishment was considered neither cruel nor unusual. Under the criminal codes of 1642 and 1650 enacted for the New Haven colony, for example, a total of eleven offenses — some of which do not even appear as misdemeanors in contemporary statutes — called for the death sentence:

The Eighth Amendment ban against cruel and unusual punishment

1. If any person within this Government shall by direct, express, impious or presumptuous ways, deny the true God and His attributes, he shall be put to death.
2. If any person shall commit any wilful and premeditated murder he shall be put to death.
3. If any person slayeth another with a sword or dagger who hath no weapon to defend himself; he shall be put to death.
4. If any man shall slay, or cause another to be slain by lying in wait privily for him or by poisoning or any other such wicked conspiracy; he shall be put to death. . . .

5. If any man or woman shall lie with any beast or brute creature by carnal copulation they shall be put to death, and the beast shall be burned.

6. If any man lieth with mankind as he lieth with a woman, they shall be put to death, unless the one party were forced or be under fourteen years of age, in which case he shall be punished at the discretion of the Court of Assizes.

7. If any person forcibly stealeth or carrieth away any mankind; he shall be put to death.

8. If any man bear false witness maliciously and on purpose to take aways a man's life, he shall be put to death.

9. If any man shall traitorously deny his Majesty's right and titles to his Crowns and Dominions, or shall raise armies to resist his authority, he shall be put to death.

10. If any man shall treacherously conspire or publickly attempt to invade or surprise any town or towns, fort or forts, within this Government, he shall be put to death.

11. If any child or children, above sixteen years of age, and of sufficient understanding, shall smite their natural father or mother, unless thereunto provoked and forced for their self-protection from death or maiming, at the complaint of said father and mother, and not otherwise, there being sufficient witnesses thereof, that child or those children so offending shall be put to death.[53]

The electric chair.

Within such a context, execution upon conviction of numerous crimes was indeed quite usual. The definition of what was cruel punishment similarly eluded rigid guidelines. Consider, for example, the punishment for treason under the English common law — the very sanction that the leaders of the American Revolution risked by signing the Declaration of Independence:

That you and each of you, be taken to the place from whence you came, and from thence be drawn on a hurdle to the place of execution where you shall be hanged by the neck not till you are dead; that you be severally taken down, while yet alive, and your bowels be taken out and burned before your faces — that your heads be then cut off, and your bodies cut into four quarters, to be at the king's disposal. And God have mercy on your souls.[54]

What the framers likely had in mind, however, were the many more grisly forms of execution that had periodically appeared throughout human history. Down through the ages criminals have been burned at the stake, crucified, boiled in flaming oil, impaled, and flayed, to name only a few. Or, take the case of Mithridates of ancient Persia:

He was encased in a coffin-like box, from which his head, hands, and feet protruded, through holes made for that purpose; he was fed with milk and honey, which he was forced to take, and his face was smeared with the same mixture; he was exposed to the sun, and in this state he remained for seventeen days, until he had been devoured alive by insects and vermin, which swarmed about him and bred within him.[55]

The Death Sentence, 1864–1967

On January 20, 1864, William Barnet and Sandy Kavanagh were executed in the Vermont State Prison for the crime of murder. During the slightly more than 100 years that followed, through 1967, there were a total of 5,707 state-imposed death sentences carried out across the country.[56] Few of these executions (less than 1 percent) occurred prior to 1890, but the number then began to grow rapidly (see Exhibit 13.6). The imposition of the death penalty reached its peak during the 1930s, with more than 1,500 executions during that decade alone. The numbers then began to decline, from 1,174 during the 1940s to less than 200 by the 1960s.

This extensive use of the death penalty is explained, at least in part, by the number of states with capital statutes in their penal codes and the proportion of offenses that were punishable by death. In 1961, for example, of 54 jurisdictions (including the 50 states, the District of Columbia, Puerto Rico, and the federal civil and military authority), 48 carried capital statutes; for homicide in 47 jurisdictions; for kidnapping in 37; for treason in 25; for rape in 20; for carnal knowledge in 16; for robbery in 10; for perjury (in a capital case) in nine; for bombing in seven; for assault (by a life-term prisoner) in five; for train robbery, burglary, or arson in four; for train wrecking in three; and for espionage in two.[57] In addition, 19 jurisdictions carried a variety of special statutes whereby the death sentence could be imposed for such offenses as aiding a suicide and forcing a woman to marry (in Arkansas), performing an abortion and advising abortion to a woman (in Georgia), lynching (in Kentucky), attempt or conspiracy to assault a chief of state (in New Jersey), use of a machine gun in a crime of violence (in Virginia), and child stealing (in Wyoming), to name but a few. In addition, the death penalty was the mandatory sentence for some offenses (typically homicide and treason) in 27 jurisdictions.

The state calls its own violence law, but that of the individual, crime. — Max Stirner

I don't enjoy handing out death sentences, but I haven't lost any sleep over them. — Thomas M. Coker, Jr., circuit court judge, Broward County, Florida, 1982

EXHIBIT 13.6

Executions under State Authority, 1860s–1960s

Decade	Number of Executions	Percentage	Developmental Period
1860s and earlier*	12	0.2	Dormancy period
1870s	18	0.3	
1880s	26	0.5	
1890s	154	2.7	Growth period
1900s	275	4.8	
1910s	625	11.0	
1920s	1,030	18.0	
1930s	1,520	26.6	Peak period
1940s	1,174	20.6	Period of decline
1950s	682	12.0	
1960s	191	3.3	
Total	5,707	100.0	

* Includes two executions in the District of Columbia during the 1850s.

SOURCE: Based on figures from William J. Bowers, *Executions in America* (Lexington, Mass.: D.C. Heath, 1974), and from Negley K. Teeters and Charles J. Zibulka, "Executions Under State Authority: 1864–1967," in *Executions in America*, ed. Bowers.

The first execution by electrocution took place at Auburn Prison, Auburn, New York, on August 6, 1890. The prisoner, William Kemmler, was executed for murder.

Statutes calling for the death penalty varied widely from one jurisdiction to the next. In the District of Columbia, Connecticut, Delaware, Massachusetts, and New Hampshire, for example, capital punishment could be imposed only in the case of murder. In Rhode Island the death penalty was restricted even further to the crime of murder when committed by a prisoner serving a life sentence. In contrast, there were 22 capital statutes in the federal criminal codes, and a dozen or more in the states of Alabama and Arkansas.

Capital Punishment and Discrimination

In 1967, the President's Commission on Law Enforcement and Administration of Justice commented that the death penalty "is most frequently imposed and carried out on the poor, the Negro, and the members of unpopular groups."[58] Such an observation was no surprise to those who had watched closely the pattern of the imposition of capital punishment over the years, or to the many blacks, especially in the South, who had been systematically victimized by death sentences for well over a century and a half. In Virginia during the 1830s, for example, there were five capital crimes for whites but at least 70 for blacks.[59] In 1848 the Virginia legislature required the death

---

EXHIBIT 13.7

A Frontier Judge Imposes Death
Judicial Candor or Racial Discrimination?

Jose Manuel Miguel Xaviar Gonzales, in a few short weeks it will be spring. The snows of winter will flee away. The ice will vanish. And the air will become soft and balmy. In short, Jose Manuel Miguel Xaviar Gonzales, the annual miracle of the years will awaken and come to pass, but you won't be there.

    The rivulet will run its soaring course to the sea. The timid desert flowers will put forth their tender shoots. The glorious valleys of this imperial domain will blossom as the rose. Still, you won't be here to see.

    From every tree top some wild woods songster will carol his mating song. Butterflies will sport in the sunshine. The busy bee will hum happy as it pursues its accustomed vocation. The gentle breeze will tease the tissels of the wild grasses, and all nature, Jose

Manuel Miguel Xaviar Gonzales, will be glad but you. You won't be here to enjoy it because I command the sheriff or some other officers of the county to lead you out to some remote spot, swing you by the neck from a knotting bough of some sturdy oak, and let you hang until you are dead.

    And then, Jose Manuel Miguel Xaviar Gonzales, I further command that such officer or officers retire quickly from your dangling corpse, that vultures may descend from the heavens upon your filthy body until nothing shall remain but bare, bleached bones of a cold-blooded, copper-colored, blood-thirsty, throat-cutting, chili-eating, sheep-herding, murdering son-of-a-bitch.

SOURCE: From the judge's decision in *United States* v. *Gonzales* (1881), United States District Court, New Mexico Territory Sessions.

penalty for any offense committed by a black for which three or more years' imprisonment might be imposed as punishment for a white.[60] Pursuant to the South Carolina Black Codes in 1825, burning at the stake was permitted and even carried out—a punishment that had originally been reserved for executing heretics in medieval Europe.[61] And from 1882 through 1903 at least 1,985 blacks were hanged or burned alive by the Ku Klux Klan and other southern lynch mobs—often when there was no offense at all or the mere suspicion of one.[62]

Even the most superficial analysis of executions under civil authority reflects a clear overrepresentation of blacks. In 1965, for example, sociologist Marvin E. Wolfgang and law professor Anthony Amsterdam began a study to determine the relationship between ethnicity and sentencing for rape in eleven southern and border states where rape was a capital offense. Their findings supported the notion that blacks were treated with undue severity:

> Among the 823 blacks convicted of rape, 110, or 13 percent, were sentenced to death; among the 442 whites convicted of rape, only 9, or 2 percent, were sentenced to death. *The statistical probability that such a disproportionate number of blacks could be sentenced to death by chance alone is less than one out of a thousand.*[63] [emphasis added]

There were 3,859 prisoners executed under civil authority in the United States from 1930 through 1967 (see Exhibit 13.8). When these cases are studied, it becomes even more evident that capital punishment was used as an instrument for racial discrimination. In this period, some 55 percent of those executed for all crimes were either black or members of some other minority group. Of the 455 executed for rape alone, 90 percent were nonwhite.

Cruel and Unusual Punishment

Historically, the Supreme Court's position on the death penalty has been grounded in the broader issue of "cruel and unusual" punishment as prohibited by the Eighth Amendment. When adopting the Eighth Amendment ban, it is likely that the framers of the Constitution had intended to outlaw punishments that were outside both the mainstream of penalties typically imposed in the new nation and the moral judgments of the people. Thus the purpose of the amendment may have been to prevent any return to the screw and the rack, rather than to outlaw any sanctions then in common use. But this can be viewed only as conjecture, for the High Court itself, for more than a century, offered little as to the nature and scope of the ban.

The notion that punishment *could* be cruel and unusual was argued by at least one of the justices in 1892. The case was *O'Neil* v. *Vermont*,[64] in which the petitioner stood to serve 19,914 days (almost 55 years) in jail for 307 separate illegal sales of liquor. The Court found that since the Eighth Amendment did not limit the states, no federal question was involved, and the sentence imposed by the Vermont court was affirmed. However, in a strong dissenting opinion, Justice Stephen J. Field argued that punishment would necessarily be cruel and unusual when it did not fit the crime to which it was attached.

After *O'Neil*, the issue remained dormant for almost two decades until *Weems* v. *United States*,[65] decided in 1910. The case was significant for the Eighth Amendment ban, for in its ruling the Court struck down a sentence

When a man knows he is to be hanged in a fortnight, it concentrates his mind wonderfully. — Samuel Johnson, 1777

Weems v. United States

EXHIBIT 13.8

Prisoners Executed under Civil Authority, by Race and Offense, 1930–1967

Year	Total				White				Black				Other Races			
	Total	Murder	Rape	Other Offenses*	Total	Murder	Rape	Other Offenses	Total	Murder	Rape	Other Offenses	Total	Murder	Rape	Other Offenses
All years	3,859	3,334	455	70	1,751	1,664	48	39	2,066	1,630	405	31	42	40	2	0
1967	2	2	0	0	1	1	0	0	1	1	0	0	0	0	0	0
1966	1	1	0	0	1	1	0	0	0	0	0	0	0	0	0	0
1965	7	7	0	0	6	6	0	0	1	1	0	0	0	0	0	0
1964	15	9	6	0	8	5	3	0	7	4	3	0	0	0	0	0
1963	21	18	2	1	13	12	0	1	8	6	2	0	0	0	0	0
1962	47	41	4	2	28	26	2	0	19	15	2	2	0	0	0	0
1961	42	33	8	1	20	18	1	1	22	15	7	0	0	0	0	0
1960	56	44	8	4	21	18	0	3	35	26	8	1	0	0	0	0
1959	49	41	8	0	16	15	1	0	33	26	7	0	0	0	0	0
1958	49	41	7	1	20	20	0	0	28	20	7	1	1	1	0	0
1957	65	54	10	1	34	32	2	0	31	22	8	1	0	0	0	0
1956	65	52	12	1	21	20	0	1	43	31	12	0	1	1	0	0
1955	76	65	7	4	44	41	1	2	32	24	6	2	0	0	0	0
1954	81	71	9	1	38	37	1	0	42	33	8	1	1	1	0	0
1953	62	51	7	4	30	25	1	4	31	25	6	0	1	1	0	0
1952	83	71	12	0	36	35	1	0	47	36	11	0	0	0	0	0
1951	105	87	17	1	57	55	2	0	47	31	15	1	1	1	0	0
1950	82	68	13	1	40	36	4	0	42	32	9	1	0	0	0	0
1949	119	107	10	2	50	49	0	1	67	56	10	1	2	2	0	0
1948	119	95	22	2	35	32	1	2	82	61	21	0	2	2	0	0
1947	153	129	23	1	42	40	2	0	111	89	21	1	0	0	0	0
1946	131	107	22	2	46	45	0	1	84	61	22	1	1	1	0	0
1945	117	90	26	1	41	37	4	0	75	52	22	1	1	1	0	0
1944	120	96	24	0	47	45	2	0	70	48	22	0	3	3	0	0
1943	131	118	13	0	54	54	0	0	74	63	11	0	3	1	2	0
1942	147	115	25	7	67	57	4	6	80	58	21	1	0	0	0	0
1941	123	102	20	1	59	55	4	0	63	46	16	1	1	1	0	0
1940	124	105	15	4	49	44	2	3	75	61	13	1	0	0	0	0
1939	160	145	12	3	80	79	0	1	77	63	12	2	3	3	0	0
1938	190	154	25	11	96	89	1	6	92	63	24	5	2	2	0	0
1937	147	133	13	1	69	67	2	0	74	62	11	0	4	4	0	0
1936	195	181	10	4	92	86	2	4	101	93	8	0	2	2	0	0
1935	199	184	13	2	119	115	2	2	77	66	11	0	3	3	0	0
1934	168	154	14	0	65	64	1	0	102	89	13	0	1	1	0	0
1933	160	151	7	2	77	75	1	1	81	74	6	1	2	2	0	0
1932	140	128	10	2	62	62	0	0	75	63	10	2	3	3	0	0
1931	153	137	15	1	77	76	1	0	72	57	14	1	4	4	0	0
1930	155	147	6	2	90	90	0	0	65	57	6	2	0	0	0	0

* Includes 25 executed for armed robbery, 20 for kidnapping, 11 for burglary, 6 for sabotage, 6 for aggravated assault, and 2 for espionage.

SOURCE: U.S. Department of Justice, *Capital Punishment 1976* (Washington, D.C.: U.S. Government Printing Office, 1978).

involving a heavy fine, 15 years at hard labor, the wearing of chains, the lifelong loss of certain rights, plus several other sanctions — all for the offense of making false entries in official records.

By 1958, the Court had agreed that the constitutional prohibition could have no fixed and unchanging meaning. Rather, any challenges brought to the Court must necessarily be viewed in terms of "evolving standards of decency":

> The exact scope of the constitutional phrase "cruel and unusual" has not been detailed by this Court. . . . The basic concept underlying the Eighth Amendment is nothing less than the dignity of man. While the State has the power to punish, the Amendment stands to assure that this power be exercised within the limits of civilized standards. Fines, imprisonment and even execution may be imposed depending upon the enormity of the crime, but any technique outside the bounds of these traditional penalties is constitutionally suspect. . . . The Court [has] recognized . . . that the words of the Amendment are not precise, but that their scope is not static. The Amendment must draw its meaning from the evolving standards of decency that mark the progress of a maturing society.[66]

Death and the Supreme Court

On the issue of capital punishment per se, the Supreme Court's interpretation of the Eighth Amendment has remained flexible. As to the method of execution, the Court offered some preliminary guidelines more than a century ago. In *Wilkerson* v. *Utah*,[67] decided in 1878, the justices agreed that public shooting was neither cruel nor unusual. At the same time, however, it was noted that the constitutional amendment would oppose such punishments as drawing and quartering, burning alive, and other punishments of torturous death. *In re Kemmler*,[68] decided in 1890, held that death by electrocution reflected humane legal intentions, and hence did not offend the Eighth Amendment.

Subsequent to *Kemmler,* the Court remained essentially silent on the constitutionality of capital punishment for almost eight decades. In *Trop* v. *Dulles*,[69] decided in 1958, a plurality of four justices held that expatriation was a cruel and unusual punishment, but noted that this holding did not necessarily apply to the death penalty.

Meanwhile, throughout the 1950s and well into the 1960s, the NAACP Legal Defense and Education Fund combined its efforts with those of the American Civil Liberties Union (ACLU) to wage an all-out legal attack against capital punishment. The two organizations came to the aid of many prisoners who had been sentenced to death. Briefs were prepared, appeals were filed, and data on the disproportionate use of the death penalty for black offenders were collected. And the courts reflected an increasing willingness to review capital cases and to reverse lower court decisions, with the result that many state authorities became reluctant to schedule and perform executions.

In 1963, Justice Arthur J. Goldberg suggested that capital punishment may be a per se violation of the Eighth Amendment. Although he was not speaking for the majority of the Court at the time, his statement, combined with mounting pressure for a decision on the constitutionality of the death penalty, served to further NAACP–ACLU effort. The penalty was ultimately challenged on a variety of legal grounds, and on June 3, 1967, the impending execution of more than 500 condemned prisoners throughout the country came to a halt, while courts and governors waited to see what the High Court would decide.

Witherspoon v. Illinois

The first of these challenges reached the Supreme Court in ***Witherspoon* v. *Illinois*,**[70] and the decision in 1968 was the first indication that the death penalty might be in trouble. In *Witherspoon,* an Illinois court had permitted a verdict of guilty and a sentence of death to be handed down by a jury from which the state had deliberately and systematically excluded all persons who had any scruples against capital punishment. The Court sustained Witherspoon's challenge, ruling that the "death-qualified jury" was indeed unconstitutional.

McGautha v. California

Witherspoon had not been a total victory for those opposed to capital punishment. They remained firmly optimistic, however, and the moratorium on

---

EXHIBIT 13.9

If at First You Don't Succeed . . .
The Strange Case of Willie Francis

Perhaps the most bizarre of the Supreme Court's death penalty cases involved Willie Francis, a Louisiana youth sentenced to death by electrocution.

The story began in November 1944 with the killing of Andrew Thomas, a pharmacist from St. Martinsville, Louisiana. Thomas was shot five times, and when his body was found by the police, a watch and a wallet containing $4 were missing.

While the quest for Thomas's killer was under way in Louisiana, an unrelated search was in progress some 200 miles southwest, in Port Arthur, Texas. The Texas case involved narcotics, and during the course of the investigation a 15-year-old black youth named Willie Francis was arrested—mistakenly thought to be the accomplice of a suspected drug dealer.

During interrogation by Port Arthur police, Francis admitted to the murder of Andrew Thomas. Francis was then turned over to Louisiana authorities and tried for murder. Although there were no

witnesses to the crime and the murder weapon was lost, the prosecution's case was strong. Francis had confessed twice, and a dozen witnesses testified that his confessions had been voluntary. And Francis's case was weak. His two court-appointed attorneys called no witnesses in his behalf.

The trial lasted only three days, and the jury found the defendant guilty of murder. No transcript of the trial had been taken, no request for a change of venue had been made, no motion for a new trial had been entered, and no appeal had been filed. On the very next day Francis was sentenced to death, with his electrocution set for several months from then.

On May 3, 1946, Francis, now age 17, was strapped into the electric chair that had been trucked to St. Martinsville the previous night. Captain E. Foster of the Louisiana State Penitentiary, formally in charge of the execution, checked his dials, bid Francis goodbye, and threw the switch.

For a fraction of a second nothing happened. Then Francis jumped; he strained against the straps, and then groaned. But he didn't die! Frantically, Foster threw the switch again and again. For two minutes the procedure was repeated before a panel of horrified spectators.

The electrodes were then removed from Francis's body, and everyone in the jailhouse breathed a sigh of relief. He managed to get to his feet, and later said that he had felt only a small current of electricity.

Whatever miracle had saved Willie Francis from death caught the public's imagination. The story made headlines across the country, and the governor of Louisiana was engulfed with letters imploring him not to send the youth through the experience again.

Francis appealed to the United States Supreme Court, asking them to forbid the state a second execution attempt because it would constitute "cruel and unusual punishment" in violation of the Eighth Amendment.

---

executicns continued as other challenges were prepared for Supreme Court review. The abolition movement eagerly awaited the ruling in **McGautha v. California,**[71] a case that argued that leaving the choice between life imprisonment or death to the total discretion of a jury was a violation of the due-process clause of the Fourteenth Amendment. Decided in 1971, the Court held in *McGautha:*

> In light of history, experience, and the present limitations of human knowledge, we find it quite impossible to say that committing to the untrammeled discretion of the jury the power to pronounce life or death in capital cases is offensive to anything in the Constitution.

McGautha seemed to be a fatal blow to the movement dedicated to the abolition of capital punishment, and it was widely viewed as the Supreme

McGautha v. California

The death penalty is the final resort to truly evil crime.
—Texas prison guard, 1981

Speaking for the majority opinion, Justice Stanley F. Reed commented:

The fact that petitioner has already been subjected to a current of electricity does not make his subsequent execution any more cruel in the constitutional sense than any other execution. The cruelty against which the Constitution protects a convicted man is cruelty inherent in the method of punishment, not the necessary suffering involved in any method employed to extinguish life humanely. The fact that an unforeseeable accident prevented the prompt consummation of the sentence cannot, it seems to us, add an element of cruelty to a subsequent execution.

On May 9, 1946, Willie Francis was again strapped into the electric chair. The switch was thrown, and on this occasion his coffin could be used, and the crowd was not disappointed.

SOURCES: Louisiana ex. rel. Francis v. Resweber, 329 U.S. 459 (1947); Barrett Prettyman, *Death and the Supreme Court* (New York: Harcourt, Brace & World, 1961).

Willie Francis

Court's final word on the death penalty. Furthermore, with no new cases pending before the Court on the issue, and with the right of juries to discretionarily impose the death sentence firmly guaranteed, it appeared unlikely that any Eighth Amendment argument could prevail. However, as the states began preparations for executing the more than 600 prisoners that had accumulated on death row, the Court suddenly announced that it would hear a group of cases involving the Eighth Amendment ban on cruel and unusual punishment.

Furman *v.* Georgia

Furman v. Georgia

In the fall of 1971, *Furman* v. *Georgia, Jackson* v. *Georgia,* and *Branch* v. *Texas* were brought before the High Court on the challenge that the death sentences ordered were "cruel and unusual" because of the arbitrary and discriminatory manner in which such sanctions had been imposed in the past for the crimes of murder and rape. The leading case was **Furman v. Georgia,**[72] which involved the death sentence following William Furman's conviction for a murder that had occurred during the course of a burglary attempt. The decision as to whether Furman's sentence should be life or death had been left to the jury, and his conviction and sentence had been affirmed by all of the Georgia courts.

The Supreme Court's *Furman* decision on June 29, 1972, was a most complex one. It was announced in a nine-opinion *per curium* (unsigned) opinion that summarized the narrow argument of the five justices in the majority. In addition, each of the nine justices issued a separate concurring or dissenting opinion. Only Justices Brennan and Marshall were willing to hold that capital punishment was unconstitutional per se. Justices Douglas, Stewart, and White adopted a more narrow view, arging that the state statutes in question were unconstitutional because they offered judges and juries no standards or guidelines to consider in deciding between life and death. As Justice Stewart put it, the result was that the punishment of death was tantamount to being "struck by lightning." In other words, all state and federal death penalty statutes were deemed too arbitrary, capricious, and discriminatory to withstand Eighth Amendment scrutiny. The position taken by Justice Douglas, Stewart, and White represented the common ground of agreement with Justices Brennan and Marshall, thus constituting the five-justice majority.

The four dissenting justices were Burger, Blackmun, Powell, and Rehnquist — all appointed to the High Court by President Richard Nixon. All four dissenting opinions emphasized the view that in a democracy, issues such as capital punishment should be decided by the legislative branch of government — the people's representatives — and not by the courts. Chief Justice Burger also accused the justices in the majority of "overruling *McGautha* in the guise of an Eighth Amendment adjudication." He also asked rhetorically whether those in the majority would be willing to sanction mandatory death penalty laws on the grounds that such laws would eliminate the harmful effects of excessive jury discretion. Although the chief justice may have scored some debating points, the effect of *Furman* was nevertheless to invalidate every death penalty statute in the United States.

Where the Court had rejected a Fourteenth Amendment due process challenge to jury imposition of the death sentence in *McGautha,* it upheld an Eighth Amendment argument in *Furman.* What represented a majority opinion in *Furman* was neither a statement against capital punishment nor an argument against a jury's authority to decide upon the death sentence. Rather, it was an attack on state statutes that allowed a jury to reach a finding of an accused's guilt and then, in the absence of any guidance or direction, decide on whether that person should live or die.

Gregg v. Georgia

By effectively invalidating all existing state death penalty statutes, *Furman* also served to remove over 600 persons from death row. But the Court's decision in *Furman* did provide two avenues by which states could enact new capital punishment laws. First, they could establish a two-stage procedure: a trial at which the question of culpability could be determined, followed by an additional proceeding for those found guilty, during which evidence might be presented to make the decision for death or life more informed and procedurally sound. Second, states could remove the discretion from the jury by making death the mandatory punishment for certain crimes.

In the wake of *Furman,* 35 states passed new capital statutes. Ten chose the mandatory route while 25 selected the two-stage procedure. By 1976,

Have you noticed that right-to-life people are in favor of capital punishment?
—Gore Vidal, 1979

An execution chamber with electric chair

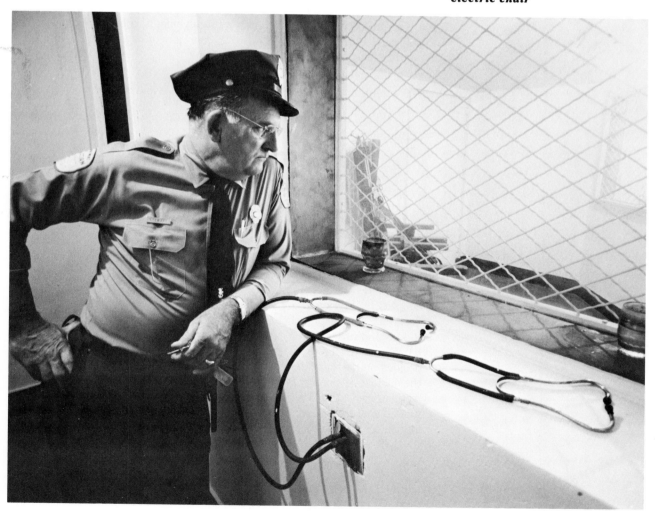

both approaches were brought before the Supreme Court, and the constitutionality of the death penalty was again argued.

Gregg v. Georgia　　The issue in **Gregg v. Georgia**[73] was Georgia's new bifurcated trial structure: following a conviction of guilt in first-degree murder cases, the nature of punishment was decided in a separate proceeding. The Georgia statute required the judge or jury to consider any aggravating or mitigating circumstances in the life-or-death decision, including the following conditions:

- The defendant had a prior conviction for a capital felony or a substantial history of serious assaultive criminal convictions.
- The murder was committed during the course of a rape, an armed robbery, a kidnapping, a burglary, or arson.
- The defendant created a grave risk of death to more than one person.
- The defendant killed for profit.
- The victim was a judicial officer or a prosecutor killed during or because of his exercise of official duty.
- The victim was a police officer, corrections employee, or fireman who was engaged in the performance of his duties.
- The defendant directed another person to kill as his agent.
- The murder was committed in a wantonly vile, horrible, or inhumane manner because it involved torture, depravity of mind, or an aggravated battery.
- The defendant was a prison escapee.
- The murder was committed in an attempt to avoid arrest.[74]

By a 7-to-2 majority, the decision in *Gregg* upheld the Georgia law, reasoning that

> **the new Georgia sentencing procedures, by contrast, focus the jury's attention on the particularized nature of the crime and the particularized nature of the individual defendant. While the jury is permitted to consider any aggravating or mitigating circumstances, it must find and identify at least one statutory aggravating factor before it may impose a penalty of death. In this way is the jury's discretion channeled. No longer can a jury wantonly and freakishly impose the death sentence; it is always circumscribed by the legislative guidelines.**

In two companion cases the Court also upheld similar procedures adopted by Florida and Texas (and presumably 22 additional states), thus declaring capital punishment laws constitutional as long as they provided judges and juries with clear and fair criteria when deciding whether to sentence an offender to death.[75] However, in *Woodson* v. *North Carolina,*[76] decided on the same day, the Court struck down state laws that made death the mandatory penalty for first-degree murder. The Court's position was that mandatory death penalty statutes "simply papered over the problem of unguided and unchecked jury discretion" and failed to allow for differences in individual defendants and crimes.

Post-*Gregg* Developments

During the years following the decision in *Gregg,* the Supreme Court continued in its refusal to hold categorically that the death penalty per se constituted cruel and unusual punishment. However, in a series of rulings from 1977 through 1980, the Court did place limitations on the imposition of capital sentences (see Exhibit 13.10). In **Coker v. Georgia**,[77] decided in 1977, it was held that the death sentence could not be imposed for rape, because such punishment was grossly disproportionate to the injury caused the victim. And without expressly stating so, the Court strongly implied in *Coker* that a death sentence was inappropriate except as punishment for murder. In a series of Ohio cases, decided in 1978, the Court ruled against a state statute that required jury consideration of aggravating circumstances, but not mitigating circumstances, in the imposition of capital sentences.[78]

Coker v. Georgia

In *Godfrey* v. *Georgia*,[79] decided in 1980, the High Court continued to clarify its holding in *Gregg*. In *Godfrey*, the petitioner had murdered his wife and mother-in-law in the presence of his daughter. The killings had occurred as the result of "heated arguments" that Godfrey felt had been induced by his mother-in-law, and stemmed from a host of marital differences of opinion.

Godfrey v. Georgia

EXHIBIT 13.10

Major Supreme Court Cases Involving the Death Penalty

Case	Ruling
Witherspoon v. Illinois, 391 U.S. 510 (1968)	States cannot exclude from juries in capital cases *all* persons opposed to the death penalty.
McGautha v. California, 402 U.S. 183 (1971)	State statutes that leave the decision to impose the death penalty to the discretion of the jury are not a violation of due process.
Furman v. Georgia, 408 U.S. 238 (1972)	Statutes that leave arbitrary and discriminatory discretion to juries in imposing death sentences violate the Eighth Amendment ban on cruel and unusual punishments.
Gregg v. Georgia, 428 U.S. 153 (1976)	The death penalty is not, in itself, cruel and unusual punishment. Further, a two-part proceeding—one for the determination of innocence or guilt and the other for determining the sentence—is constitutional and meets the objections noted in *Furman*.
Woodson v. North Carolina, 428 U.S. 280 (1976)	State laws that make death the mandatory penalty for first-degree murder are unconstitutional.
Roberts v. Louisiana, 431 U.S. 633 (1977)	State laws that make death the mandatory penalty for the killing of a police officer during the performance of his or her duties are unconstitutional.
Coker v. Georgia, 433 U.S. 583 (1977)	Death is an excessive penalty for the crime of rape.
Godfrey v. Georgia, 446 U.S. 420 (1980)	Aggravating circumstances, as contained in death penalty statutes, cannot be interpreted too broadly.

Immediately after the homicides, Godfrey telephoned the local sheriff, confessed to the crimes, led authorities to the slain bodies, and stated that the scene was "hideous." Godfrey was convicted, and pursuant to the revised Georgia law as tested in *Gregg,* both murders were found to be accompanied by one of the "aggravating circumstances": the killings were committed in a "wantonly vile, horrible, or inhumane" manner because they involved "depravity of mind." Thus, the jury imposed a death sentence.

Upon Court review, Godfrey's death sentence was vacated on grounds that the jurors were given too much discretion under the state's statutory guidelines for capital cases. A plurality of justices maintained, specifically, that the Georgia statute had been interpreted too broadly, that the "depravity of mind" clause was a "catch all" phrase for cases that did not fit other statutory circumstances. Finally, although Justices Marshall and Brennan concurred with the ruling, they reiterated their minority view that the death penalty was unconstitutional under all circumstances and remarked that *Gregg* was doomed to failure.

The Return of Capital Punishment

On June 2, 1967, Luis José Monge was put to death in Colorado for the crime of murder. He was the last person to be executed in the United States prior to the suspension of capital punishment later that year, and for a full decade capital punishment ceased to exist throughout the United States. With the decision of *Gregg,* however, made on the eve of the nation's 200th birthday, the Supreme Court upheld the constitutionality of capital punishment. By 1977, more than 400 persons were on death row, with the first execution occurring during the early weeks of that year.

The prisoner was Gary Mark Gilmore, a convicted murderer who had been sentenced to death by a Utah court.[80] The Gilmore case attracted national headlines, not only because it was the first probable execution in a decade, but also because of the many bizarre events associated with it. The initial sensation came late in 1976 when Gilmore fired his attorneys, abandoned his appeal, and requested that his execution be carried out at the earliest possible date. He even appeared before the justices of the U.S. Supreme Court to argue that he had a "right to die."

Attorneys then petitioned the Utah courts, indicating that Gilmore was insane, that he was incapable of representing himself, and that his "death wish" was "tantamount to suicide." But the state court rejected this argument, and all pending appeals were dismissed. Gilmore's mother then petitioned the U.S. Supreme Court, maintaining that her son was incompetent to waive his right to appeal. The stay of execution she requested was denied, however, on the basis that she had no legal standing to seek relief for her son.

The case of Gary Mark Gilmore then began to take on a tragically comic air. On the morning of November 16, 1976, Gilmore attempted suicide by taking an overdose of sedatives. At almost the same moment, some 40 miles south of the prison in a small apartment just outside Provo, Utah, 20-year-old Nicole Barrett also took an overdose of drugs. The "suicide pact" had been arranged as part of a pathetic love affair that Gilmore had been carrying on with the young mother of two. But Gilmore survived the ordeal, as did Ms. Barrett.

Counsel was then appointed to help Gilmore secure an execution date. It was later revealed that this attorney had a financial interest in Gilmore's death,

If they are serious about using the death penalty as a deterrent, they should let the people see it. Televise it on the networks.
— James Autry, executed in Texas in 1984

having secured the exclusive right to act as the condemned man's biographer and agent; a six-figure contract had been negotiated for publication and motion picture rights to the story of Gilmore's life and death. GARY GILMORE T-shirts also appeared, and the media "bidding wars" began for exclusive interviews and stories.

Independent legal groups challenged the courts with collateral legal suits, but angered over the new delays, Gilmore staged yet another unsuccessful suicide attempt. The Supreme Court elected not to intervene in any further litigation, and an execution date was finally set. As the day approached, the media and pro- and anti-death groups began a death watch outside the walls of the prison. During his final hours, Gilmore refused any interviews. There was another stay of execution, but it lasted only a few short hours. Gilmore was scheduled to die before a firing squad, and while he was being led to the execution chamber, mobile television crews attempted to position themselves to record the gunshots signaling Gilmore's demise. When asked by Warden Samuel W. Smith if he had any last words, Gilmore offered nothing philosophical or dramatic — simply, "Let's do it!" Finally, just after dawn on January 17, 1977, Gilmore was strapped to a wooden chair in a cold and shadowy prison warehouse. At 8:07 A.M., a signal was given to marksmen hidden behind a cubicle 30 feet from the prisoner. Four .30-caliber bullets ripped through his chest, and Gary Mark Gilmore became the first person to be executed in an American prison in almost a decade.[81]

Murderer Gary Mark Gilmore, under tight security, is on his way to court to receive judgment on the date of his execution by firing squad.

Methods of Execution

In a series of decisions spanning the period 1878 through 1953, the Supreme Court has upheld as constitutional such methods of execution as hanging, shooting, electrocution, and the use of lethal gas.

As of 1986, 37 states had a death penalty in force (see Exhibit 13.11). A number of states allowed for more than one mode of execution, including lethal gas. While electrocution is generally instantaneous, the use of cyanide gas is considered by many to be more humane. The well-known "gas chamber," however, also seems to be a grim process. An eyewitness described the execution of Luis José Monge in 1967:

> According to the official execution log unconsciousness came more than five minutes after the cyanide splashed down into the sulphuric acid. Even after unconsciousness is declared officially, the prisoner's body continues to fight for life. He coughs and groans. The lips make little pouting motions resembling the motions made by a goldfish in a bowl. The head strains back and then slowly sinks down to the chest. And in Monge's case, the arms, though tightly bound to the chair, strained through the straps and the hands clawed torturously as if the prisoner were struggling for air.[82]

In three states — Delaware, Montana, and New Hampshire — the official method of execution is hanging. Such was also the case in the state of Washington, but this was eliminated in 1981 when the supreme court of Washington declared hanging to be "a cruel and barbarous act offensive to civilized standards of decency."[83] In Delaware, many a defense attorney has vividly described execution via the hangman's noose in an attempt to sway

EXHIBIT 13.11

Inmates on Death Row, Total Executed since 1976, and Methods of Execution

State	Number of Inmates	Number Executed	Method
Alabama	80	1	Electrocution
Alaska	No death penalty		
Arizona	62	0	Gas
Arkansas	29	0	Injection, electrocution
California	177	0	Gas
Colorado	1	0	Gas
Connecticut	0	0	Electrocution
Delaware	4	0	Hanging
District of Columbia	No death penalty		
Florida	230	13	Electrocution
Georgia	106	6	Electrocution
Hawaii	No death penalty		
Idaho	14	0	Injection, firing squad
Illinois	83	0	Injection
Indiana	33	2	Electrocution
Iowa	No death penalty		
Kansas	No death penalty		
Kentucky	25	0	Electrocution
Louisiana	46	7	Electrocution
Maine	No death penalty		
Maryland	20	0	Gas
Massachusetts	No death penalty		
Michigan	No death penalty		
Minnesota	No death penalty		
Mississippi	46	1	Gas, injection
Missouri	38	0	Gas
Montana	5	0	Injection, hanging
Nebraska	13	0	Electrocution

The switch for Georgia's electric chair

State	Number of Inmates	Number Executed	Method
Nevada	29	2	Injection
New Hampshire	0	0	Hanging
New Jersey	17	0	Injection
New Mexico	5	0	Injection
New York	No death penalty		
North Carolina	54	2	Gas, injection
North Dakota	No death penalty		
Ohio	57	0	Electrocution
Oklahoma	55	0	Electrocution, firing squad, injection
Oregon	0	0	Injection
Pennsylvania	74	0	Electrocution
Rhode Island	No death penalty		
South Carolina	40	1	Electrocution
South Dakota	0	0	Injection
Tennessee	50	0	Electrocution
Texas	212	10	Injection
Utah	5	1	Firing squad, injection
Vermont	0	0	Electrocution
Virginia	28	4	Electrocution
Washington	6	0	Injection
West Virginia	No death penalty		
Wisconsin	No death penalty		
Wyoming	3		Gas, injection
Total	1,649	50	

Note: Number of inmates on death row as of January 1, 1986.
SOURCE: Bureau of Justice Statistics; NAACP Legal Defense and Educational Fund, Inc.

The gallows at Washington State Penitentiary, Walla Walla. The noose into which the prisoner's head is placed hangs over a trap door. The prisoner is strapped to the board at left, and then the trap door is sprung.

If there were a death penalty, more people would be alive.
— Nancy Reagan, 1982

jurors away from imposing a death sentence. This was most effectively done in the case of Mark McKinney, convicted of a 1980 homicide:

> He will walk 13 steps to the gallows. He will stand, and a hood, black in color, will be placed over his head. A noose with 13 knots will be dropped over his shoulders and filled around his neck.
> There will be an executioner, whom we do not know, who will stand removed, and Mark will stand over a trap door. The executioner will push a button which will cause the trap door to spring open, and Mark will drop between four to six feet. The rope will constrict around his neck, causing him to die.[84]

For inmates sentenced to death under federal statutes, the method of execution is governed by the law of the state in which the punishment is to be carried out.

"The Ultimate High"

Among the most virulent arguments regarding the nature of execution emerged in 1977 when a number of states enacted statutes that put to rest their electric chairs, gas chambers, and gallows. In their place was death by lethal injection, referred to by many death row inmates as "the ultimate high."

Proponents of the new process argued that it would be a more palatable way of killing — it would be instantaneous, and the prisoner would simply fall asleep.[85] Opponents denied its humanity, arguing that sticking a needle into a vein can be tricky, with the prospect of repeated attempts upon a struggling prisoner posing "a substantial threat of tortuous pain."[86] The American Medical Association also took a stand on the matter, instructing its members not to take part in such executions, arguing that the role of the physician was to protect lives, not take them.[87]

Despite the arguments, the new method of execution went forward. On December 7, 1982, Charles Brooks, Jr., was put to death in Huntsville, Texas, becoming the first person to die by a state-sanctioned lethal injection. First a catheter was placed into the vein of his left arm through which a saline solution flowed — a sterile salt water used routinely as a medium for drug injections. Brooks was then given doses of barbiturates and potassium chloride, which paralyzed him, stopped his breathing, and guaranteed his death.[88] Ironically, on Brooks's arm above the catheter through which the deadly concoction flowed was a tattoo that read, "I was born to die."

The lethal injections were temporarily halted in 1983 when a federal appeals court ordered the Food and Drug Administration to determine whether the drugs were painless and could be used for executions. In 1984, the Supreme Court agreed to review the matter.[89] However, just prior to granting *certiorari,* Chief Justice Burger postponed the effect of the appeals court ruling,[90] permitting states to carry out their scheduled lethal injections. Meanwhile, as the High Court denied appeals to several death row inmates, Justices Thurgood Marshall and William Brennan personally condemned the use of electrocution in executions.[91]

The Death Penalty Debate

The arguments for or against capital punishment historically have revolved around the issues of economics, retribution, public opinion, community protection, deterrence, irreversibility, discrimination, protection of the criminal justice system, and cruel and unusual punishment.

The **economic argument** for capital punishment holds that execution is far less expensive than maintaining a prisoner behind bars for the remainder of his or her natural life. Death sentences are invariably appealed, and these too can be costly. One estimate of California's expense in the case of Caryl Chessman, who was eventually executed, totaled more than half a million dollars.[92] For Gary Gilmore, the 78 days preceding his death cost the state of Utah, in addition to food, clothing, and supervision, at least $98,568 — over $60,000 to keep him alive during his suicide attempts and another $18,330 for convalescent care, $19,000 in overtime payments for secretaries and deputies on execution day, $513 for a charter flight to Denver where a last-minute stay of execution was overturned, and $725 to pay for the six-man firing squad.[93] And not only was *Gilmore* a case in which the dealth penalty was imposed, but one in which the condemned argued for his "right to die." Furthermore, these figures did not include expenses incurred by Gilmore's family, the NAACP Legal Defense Fund, the American Civil Liberties Union, and other groups and individuals who fought for his life.

The **retribution argument** asserts that the kidnapper, the murderer, and the rapist, as vile and despicable human beings, deserve to die. This is

The needle used in Texas for executions by injection. The first such execution in the U.S. took place there on December 7, 1982, of murderer Charles Brooks, Jr.

EXHIBIT 13.12

"Enough Electrical Energy to Light 800 Lights in the Average Home"

The condemned prisoner undergoing electrocution at Sing Sing Prison is given one shock of . . . alternating current at an average starting potential of approximately 2,000 volts. This voltage is immediately reduced at the end of three seconds to the neighborhood of 500 volts where it is held for an additional period of 57 seconds. . . .

This initial force sends a starting current of 8 to 10 amperes through the human body, which causes instantaneous death and unconsciousness by its paralysis and destruction to the brain. The current is then cut down under the lower voltages to from 3 to 4 amperes in order to avoid burning the body and at the same time to hold paralysis of the heart,

respiratory organs, and brain at a standstill for the remaining period of execution. This insures complete destruction of all life.

As the switch is thrown into its socket there is a sputtering drone, and the body leaps as if to break the strong leather straps that hold it. Sometimes a thin gray wisp of smoke pushes itself out from under the helmet that holds the head electrode, followed by the faint odor of burning flesh. The hands turn red, then white, and the cords of the neck stand out like steel bands. . . .

If temperatures are taken during and immediately after an application of electricity it will be found that the electrodes making the contact may reach a temperature high enough to melt

copper . . . and that the average body temperature will be in the neighborhood of 140 degrees . . . and that the temperature of the brain itself approaches the boiling point of water. . . .

Although it would be absolutely impossible to revive any person after electrocution in Sing Sing's death chair, an autopsy is immediately performed as provided by law. Thus justice grinds out its grist; the hand of the law drops a living man or woman into the death-house hopper, where the chair and the surgeons' knives and saws convert it into the finished product — a grisly corpse.

SOURCE: Lewis E. Lawes, *Life and Death in Sing Sing* (Garden City, N.Y.: Garden City, 1928), pp. 170–171, 188–190.

simply a matter of individual opinion, and differences in philosophy appear even within the Supreme Court. In *Furman,* Justice Thurgood Marshall spoke against this position. At the same time, however, the Court stated that while retribution was no longer a dominant objective, "neither is it a forbidden objective nor one inconsistent with our respect for the dignity of men."

Public opinion has been a motivating factor in the recent reenactment of death penalty statutes. When the California Supreme Court declared the state's death penalty law unconstitutional in February 1972, letters and telegrams opposing the decision poured into the legislature and governor's office. In a referendum held later that year, five months after *Furman,* California voters overwhelmingly approved an amendment to the state constitution that made capital punishment mandatory for selected crimes.[94] And more recently, a Gallup poll conducted during 1985 found that 72 percent of all Americans favored the death penalty for murder.[95]

The **community protection argument** made by supporters of the death penalty maintains that such a "final solution" is necessary to keep the murderer from further ravaging society. Counter to this position is the claim that life imprisonment could achieve the same goal. Yet, as has been pointed out by the President's Commission on Law Enforcement and the Administration of Justice and others, paroled murderers have lower rates of recidivisim than other classes of offenders.[96]

Related to this is the **deterrence argument,** held by retentionists, that capital punishment not only prevents the offender from committing additional crimes, but deters others as well. With respect to deterrence in general, the work of Franklin E. Zimring and Gordon J. Hawkins demonstrated that punishment is an effective deterrent for those who are not predisposed to commit crimes, but a questionable deterrent for those who are criminally inclined.[97] A number of studies have also been done on the deterrent effects of capital punishment. One research strategy for such studies has been to compare the homicide rates in states that have death penalty provisions with states that do not. Another has been to examine murder rates in given areas both before and after an execution. And still a third approach has been to analyze crime rates in general as well as murder rates in particular in jurisdictions before and after the abolition of capital punishment. Regardless of the nature and logic of the inquiry applied, the studies have consistently produced no evidence that the death penalty deters homicide.[98]

The **irreversibility argument** put forth by those opposed to the death penalty contends that there is always the possibility that an innocent person might be put to death. Retentionists maintain that although such a risk might exist, there are not documented cases of such an occurrence in recent years. But as Roy Calvert, the leading figure in the English abolition movement during the 1930s, has noted, "The fact that few errors of justice come to light in connection with capital offenses should not lead us to suppose that such mistakes do not occur."[99]

In fact, there have indeed been numerous errors of justice of this type (see, for example, Exhibit 13.13). Hugo Adam Bedau, a prominent American researcher on the topic, compiled information on 74 cases occurring in the United States from 1893 through 1962, in which a wrongful conviction of criminal homicide has been alleged and, in most cases, proved beyond a reasonable doubt.[100] Bedau's data show that of the 74 convictions, a death sentence was imposed in 31 and actually carried out in 8 convictions.

One could readily argue that since most of these convictions were ultimately reversed and the defendant's life spared, the moral is easily dodged.

Yet the very same reasoning can be used to support the irreversibility argument — that wrongful convictions do indeed happen, and only through luck and circumstance have many of the victims managed to escape death. An illustration of this is the case of Isidore Zimmerman, an instance of judicial error that came to light after Bedau's research. On June 5, 1937, at age 19, Zimmerman was arrested along with several other youths for the crime of murder in the first degree. Ten months later he was convicted and sentenced to death. From April 1938 through January 1939, Zimmerman lived on Sing Sing's death row. During that time 13 men were electrocuted, including one of his codefendants. Only two hours before his scheduled execution, New York's Governor Herbert H. Lehman commuted the sentence to life imprisonment. For the next 23 years, Zimmerman was simply a number in New York's maximum-security prison population. During a three-year stay at Attica State Prison, from 1947 through 1950, he spent eight months in solitary confinement.

In February 1962, Zimmerman was released from prison upon a ruling of the state appeals court granting a writ of *coram nobis*,* setting aside his original conviction and directing a new trial. On March 13, 1967, almost 30 years after his arrest on the murder charge, the indictment was dismissed, the original conviction having been obtained on the basis of suppressed evidence and perjured testimony.[101]

The **discrimination argument** against capital punishment contends that the death penalty is a lottery system, with the odds stacked heavily against those less capable of defending themselves. As Justice Thurgood Marshall wrote in his concurring opinion in *Furman* v. *Georgia*:

> It also is evident that the burden of capital punishment falls upon the poor, the ignorant, and the underprivileged members of society. It is

---

* *Coram nobis* is a writ used to obtain review of a judgment for the purpose of correcting errors of fact.

Margie Velma Barfield, put to death in North Carolina on November 2, 1984, was the first woman executed in the United States in 22 years. Barfield had confessed to several murders. She was convicted in the poisoning death of her fiancee, whose beer she had laced with ant poison at a Rex Humbard religious rally in 1978.

Isidore Zimmerman, who spent nearly 24 years in prison for a murder he did not commit, also spent 20 years battling New York State in the courts over his wrongful conviction and confinement. In 1983, at age 66, he was finally awarded $1 million, only to die of a heart attack just a few weeks later.

Whatever can be said about the death penalty, it cannot be said that it causes otherwise unavoidable death. —Ernest van den Haag, 1983

There is no great difficulty to separate the soul from the body, but is not so easy to restore life to the dead. —Musharrif-uddin, 1258

the poor, and the members of minority groups who are least able to voice their complaints against capital punishment. Their impotence leaves them victims of a sanction which the wealthier, better-represented, just-as-guilty person can escape. So long as the capital sanction is used only against the forlorn, easily forgotten members of society, legislators are content to maintain the status quo, because change would draw attention to the problem and concern might develop. Ignorance is perpetuated and apathy soon becomes its mate, and we have today's situation.

The most recent statistics available on the social characteristics of death row inmates suggest that the death penalty continues to be administered in a

---

EXHIBIT 13.13

Capital Punishment and Errors of Justice

It is generally believed that gross errors of justice occurred in the cases of Caryl Chessman, and Nicola Sacco and Bartolomeo Vanzetti. Chessman was convicted of kidnapping and rape, and Sacco and Vanzetti were found guilty of murder. All were sentenced to die; all were eventually executed; and in retrospect, there is evidence and sentiment that all may have been innocent. But in these cases the presumption of error is based only on suspicion. There are less well known persons, however, about whose executions the evidence of judicial miscarriage is somewhat stronger.

Massachusetts, 1898

Jack O'Neil was convicted for the murder of Hattie McCloud and hanged on January 7, 1898. As he went to his death, he stated calmly, "I shall meet death like a man and I hope those who see me hanged will live to see the day when it is proved I am innocent— and it will be, some time." Several months later, a soldier attached to the Sixth Massachusetts Militia

received a fatal wound while fighting in Cuba during the Spanish-American War. On his deathbed, he confessed to the crime and cleared O'Neil.

New York, 1914

Frank Cirofici, along with co-defendants Harry Horowitz, Jacob Seidenshmer, and Louis Rosenberg were convicted in the murder of gambler Herman Rosenthal—a gangland execution orchestrated by a Brooklyn police lieutenant. The four were electrocuted in the Sing Sing Prison death house on April 13, 1914. According to a statement made by Warden Clancy of Sing Sing, Cirofici's accomplices admitted while in prison that he had not even been at the scene of the crime.

New York, 1916

Thomas Bambrick was convicted of murder, sentenced to death, and executed on October 7, 1916, in Sing Sing's electric chair. Only

---

selective and discriminatory manner. As of January 1, 1985, over 40 percent of those under the sentence of death were black, and nearly all of those on death rows across the United States were indigents—too poor to afford private counsel—who had to rely on a state-supplied attorney.[102] The federal courts have rejected this claim, however, even when arguments have been grounded in precise statistical studies. In *McCleskey* v. *Zant*,[103] a 1984 Georgia case, the U.S. district court held that statistical data "are incapable of producing evidence on whether racial factors play a part in the imposition of the death penalty in any particular case."

The **protection of the criminal justice system argument** against capital punishment holds that equity in the administration of justice is hindered by

I go to sleep and I dream of me sitting down in that chair. I mean it's such a fearful thought. Me walking down the tier, sitting down in it, them hooking it up and turning it on. . . . I can wake up, my heart's beating fast, I'm sweating like hell, just like I'd rinsed my head in water. . . . I feel I'm gonna have a heart attack. —**Alabama death row prisoner, 1978**

hours before his death, evidence was discovered that convinced Warden Thomas Mott Osborne of his innocence. Efforts to reach the governor for a stay of execution failed, and the death sentence was carried out on schedule.

New York, 1920

Known only as "Russell" (as identified by Sing Sing's warden, Lewis E. Lawes), the accused was executed for the murder of a police officer. Subsequent to the electrocution, his "accomplice" admitted that Russell had not been involved.

New York, 1930

Stephen Grezschowiak, Max Rybarczyk, and Alex Bogdanoff were convicted of murder, sentenced to death, and executed in Sing Sing Prison on July 17, 1930. Bogdanoff, who admitted his guilt, insisted that the other two were not involved in the crime and had been mistakenly identified by eyewitnesses.

New York, 1936

Everett Applegaite and Frances Creighton were executed for the murder of Applegaite's wife. Some weeks after the execution, evidence surfaced that Applegaite had been falsely implicated by Creighton. (Frances Creighton was one of only seven women to be executed in the history of the Sing Sing death house.)

New York, 1937

George Wing Chew was convicted of murder and executed on June 10, 1937. According to Sing Sing's Warden Lawes, Chew had been found guilty through a false identification and perjured testimony.

SOURCES: Raymond Bye, *Capital Punishment in the United States* (Philadelphia: Committee of Philanthropic Labor, 1919), pp. 77–78; Sara Ehrmann, "For Whom the Chair Waits," *Federal Probation* 26 (March 1962): 14–25; Hugo Adam Bedau, ed., *The Death Penalty in America* (Chicago: Aldine, 1964), pp. 440–452; William J. Bowers, *Executions in America* (Lexington, Mass.: Lexington, 1974), pp. 296–312.

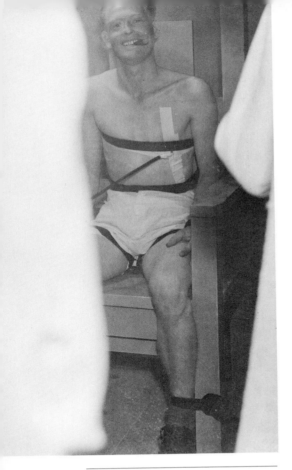

Murderer Jack Sullivan, sentenced to death in the gas chamber at Arizona State Prison in 1936, awaits his execution. Taped to his chest is a stethoscope. Less than two minutes after the cyanide gas swirled around his head, he was pronounced dead.

Killing human beings is an act so awesome, so destructive, so irremediable that no killer can be looked upon with anything but horror, even when that killer is the state. — Henry Schwarzschild, American Civil Liberties Union, 1981

the very bearing of capital statutes. As noted by the President's Crime Commission:

> Whatever views one may have about the efficacy of the death penalty as a deterrent, it clearly has an undesirable impact on the administration of justice. The trial of a capital case is a stirring drama, but that is perhaps its most dangerous attribute. Selecting a jury often requires several days; each objection or point of law requires excessive deliberation because of the irreversible consequences of error. The jury's concern with the death penalty may result in unwarranted acquittals and there is increased danger that public sympathy will be aroused for the defendant, regardless of his guilt of the crime charged.[104]

And finally, the **cruel and unusual punishment argument** maintains that the death penalty is a violation of the constitutional right guaranteed by the Eighth Amendment. Abolitionists and retentionists differ, however, in their interpretations of the "cruel and unusual punishment" clause. The former hold that capital punishment *in all circumstances,* is cruel and unusual. The latter insist that a sentence of death is forbidden by the Eighth Amendment only when it is a disproportionate punishment for the crime committed. These conflicting views were the bases for the Supreme Court's rulings in both *Furman* and *Gregg.*

Capital Punishment in the 1980s

By the end of 1980, a total of 714 persons were under the sentence of death in the United States, and during the following year the death row population increased to over 900. By the beginning of 1986, this figure had climbed to more than 1,600* (see Exhibit 13.14). And as the growing number of offenders awaiting death increased, so too did the number of executions. During the first six years after the reinstatement of capital punishment in 1976, there were only six executions. Then, there were 5 in 1983, 21 in 1984, and 18 in 1985. Ernest van den Haag, Professor of Jurisprudence and Public Policy at Fordham University — who supports the death penalty — estimated during the latter part of 1985 that by 1990 the number of executions would rise to 100 a year.[105] Van den Haag based his prediction on the fact that many death row inmates had exhausted their appeals. In addition, during the first half of the 1980s the Supreme Court decided on one case that served to curtail an avenue for appeal and on another that clamped down on the lengthy appeals process. In *Pulley* v. *Harris,*[106] decided by the Court in 1984, petitioner Robert Alton Harris had claimed that California's capital punishment statute was invalid under the Constitution because it failed to require the California Supreme Court to compare his sentence with others imposed in similar capital cases and thereby determine whether they were proportionate. The U.S. Supreme Court held that Harris's claim was without merit, ruling that the Eighth Amendment ban against cruel and unusual punishment does not require, as an invariable rule in every case, comparative proportionality review of capital sentences by an appellate court. In *Barefoot* v. *Estelle,*[107] decided a year earlier, the Court said, in effect, that federal appeals courts may compress the time they take to consider appeals as long as all the issues are covered adequately and on their merits. While the ruling in *Barefoot* mandated nothing, it suggested to federal appeals courts the adoption of rules under which

* As of January 1, 1986, there were 1,649 prisoners on death row nationally.

stays of execution could be granted. Moreover, it noted that stays of execution were not automatic upon filing petitions of *certiorari*.

Yet these decisions in no way indicated that the High Court had made up its mind on the death penalty. Quite the contrary. As public sentiment pushed for a more rapid imposition of the death penalty, the Justices argued among themselves about the merry-go-round of litigation that had come to characterize capital punishment cases. And too, although the pace of executions had increased, the American death house remained a warren of segregated convicts preparing briefs while rehearsing the day of their final judgment and ceremony of death.

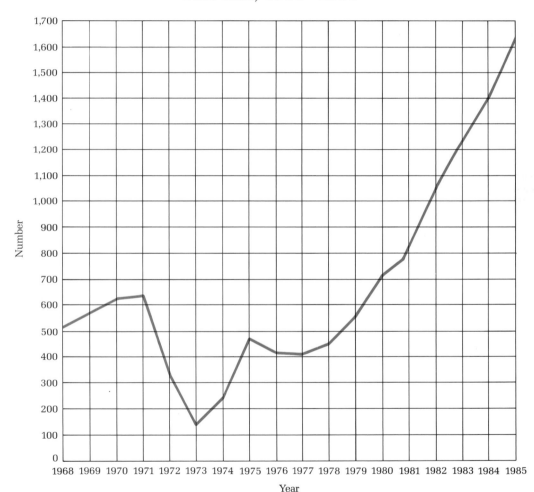

EXHIBIT 13.14

The Number of Persons on Death Row
Year End, 1968–1985

SOURCES: Bureau of Justice Statistics; NAACP Legal Defense and Education Fund, Inc.

EXHIBIT 13.15

Lockhart v. McCree

In *Witherspoon* v. *Illinois,* decided in 1968, the U.S. Supreme Court held that in capital cases states cannot exclude from juries *any* persons opposed to the death penalty. To do so, the Court argued, would result in a jury that could not speak for the community. Constituted as such, a jury would be "death-qualified" and thus represent a violation of due process. But the justices held that jurors could be excluded for cause if their scruples against the death penalty were so strong that they would automatically vote against the imposition of capital punishment *regardless of the evidence.* Such jurors have become known as "*Witherspoon* excludables." Moreover, the ruling applied only to juries involved in sentencing decisions, leaving open the question of whether "death qualification" tainted a guilty or not-guilty verdict. *Lockhart* v. *McCree,* decided by the Court in 1986, addressed this latter issue.

In 1978, Ardia McCree had been charged with capital felony murder. In accordance with Arkansas law, the trial judge at *voir dire* removed for cause, over McCree's objections, those prospective jurors who stated that they could never vote for the imposition of the death penalty. McCree was convicted, and although the prosecution had requested a capital sentence, the jury set the punishment at life imprisonment without the possibility of parole. On appeal before the Eighth Circuit Court of Appeals,[a] McCree argued two points. First, he claimed that the removal for cause of the "*Witherspoon* excludable" prospective jurors violated his

right under the Sixth and Fourteenth Amendments to have his guilt or innocence determined by an impartial jury selected from a representative cross-section of the community. Second, McCree maintained that the absence of the "*Witherspoon* excludables" slanted the jury in favor of conviction. He produced the findings of a variety of studies which suggested that the juries in question were indeed conviction-prone.

When the court of appeals ruled in favor of McCree, sending the matter to the U.S. Supreme Court, *Lockhart* suddenly became the most important death penalty case of the 1980s. Only days before the Court finally released its opinion on May 5, 1986, there were more than 1,700 inmates housed on death rows nationally, most of whom had been convicted by "death-qualified" juries. An affirmation of the circuit court decision would have meant new trials for several hundred inmates awaiting execution.

To the bewilderment of civil libertarians, the Court ruled against McCree by a 6-to-3 majority. It was the opinion of the Court that the "death qualification" process does not cast doubt on the impartiality of anyone chosen to be on a jury, and that the Constitution does not require that a trial jury hold a balance of viewpoints or attitudes.

At the heart of the Court's decision was the issue of whether the Sixth Amendment required that a jury represent a fair cross-section of a community:

The essence of a "fair cross-section" claim is the systematic exclusion of a "distinctive" group in the community.

In our view groups defined solely in terms of shared attitudes that would prevent or substantially impair members of the group from performing one of their duties as jurors, such as the "*Witherspoon* excludables" at issue here, are not "distinctive groups" for fair cross-section purposes.

"Death qualification," unlike the wholesale exclusion of blacks, women, or Mexican-Americans from jury service, is carefully designed to serve the state's concededly legitimate interest in obtaining a single jury that can properly and impartially apply the law to the facts of the case at both the guilt and sentencing phases of a capital trial.

As to the many studies that addressed the purported conviction-prone nature of "death-qualified" juries,[b] the Court had examined them closely. But, said Justice Rehnquist:

We have serious doubts about the value of these studies in predicting the behavior of actual jurors. In addition, two of the three "new" studies did not even attempt to simulate the process of jury deliberation, and none of the "new" studies was able to predict to what extent, if any, the presence of one or more "*Witherspoon* excludables" on a guilt-phase jury would have altered the outcome. . . .

We will assume . . . that "death qualification" in fact produces juries somewhat more "conviction-prone" than "non-death-qualified" juries. We hold, nonetheless, that the Constitution does not prohibit the States from "death qualifying" juries in capital cases.

SOURCES:
a. Lockhart v. McCree, 38 CrL 4014 (1985).
b. Brief for *Amicus Curiae,* American Psychological Association in Support of Respondent, *Lockhart* v. *McCree,* on Writ of *Certiorari* to the United States Court of Appeals for the Eighth Circuit.

Jimmy Lee Gray in his death row cell in Mississippi State Prison. Executed on September 2, 1983, Gray had been convicted of raping a 3-year-old girl and murdering her by suffocation in mud.

Appellate Review

An appeal is when you ask one court to show its contempt for another court.
— Finley Peter Dunne

This brief utterance from the essays of the early twentieth-century American journalist and humorist Finley Peter Dunne, although cynical and irreverent in tone, is essentially what an appeal is all about. More accurately, an **appeal** is a complaint to a superior court of an injustice done or error committed by a lower court, whose judgment or decision the higher tribunal is called upon to correct or reverse.

Appeal

Despite the fact that appellate procedures exist throughout the federal and all of the state court structures, the right of appeal was unknown in common law, and such a right was not incorporated into the Constitution. Furthermore, the constitutionality of a state's denial of appellate review has never been decided by the United States Supreme Court, and the High Court has often noted, *in dicta,** on many occasions that such review is not constitutionally required.[108]

---

* *In dicta* are expressions in an opinion of the court that are not necessarily to support the decision.

The Defendant's Right to Appeal

At the appellate stage, the presumption of innocence has evaporated, and it becomes the defendant's obligation to show why a conviction should be overturned. Thus the nature of the adversary system changes, the burden of proof shifting from the prosecution to the defense.

All jurisdictions have procedural rules requiring that objections to the admission (or exclusion) of evidence, or to some other procedure, be made by the defense either at a pretrial hearing or at the time evidence or other procedure becomes an issue at trial. Failure to make a timely objection results in an automatic forfeiture of the claim for appeal purposes. Such a requirement has been instituted in order that trial judges can make rules and develop facts that will appear in the record and thus enable the appeals court to conduct an adequate review.

The Plain Error Rule

Plain errors are subject to appellate review.

The notable exception to the timely objection requirement is the **plain error rule,** incorporated into *Federal Rules of Criminal Procedure* and with an equivalent in all state jurisdictions. Under this rule, "plain errors or defects affecting substantial rights" of defendants become subject to appellate review even though they may not have been properly raised at trial or during some prior appeal.[109] Thus, a denial of the right to counsel at trial, the admission of an involuntary confession, or the negation of some other constitutional guarantees — even in the absence of a timely objection — are considered "plain errors" and hence appealable.

The Automatic Reversal Rule

Certain constitutional errors are subject to automatic reversal.

On numerous occasions, the Supreme Court has held that certain constitutional errors are of such magnitude that they require *automatic reversal* of a conviction: hence, the **automatic reversal rule.** The Fourteenth Amendment guarantee of due process, for example, ensures the defendant a fair trial before an impartial judge. Pursuant to this guarantee, the Court ruled in *Tumey* v. *Ohio,*[110] decided in 1927 by a unanimous vote, that an accused is denied due process when tried before a judge with a direct, personal, pecuniary interest in ruling against him. At issue in *Tumey* was the fact that the petitioner had been tried in a city court, whose judge was the mayor, and from which fines were deposited in the city treasury. The High Court found the lower court's error to be of such significance that it mandated an automatic reversal of Tumey's conviction. Similarly, the Court considers as automatically reversible such *plain* errors as the use of an involuntary confession at trial, and the denial of counsel at trial in violation of its holding in *Gideon* v. *Wainwright.*[111]

The Harmless Error Rule

A denial of a constitutional right can at times be a harmless error not subject to reversal on appeal.

In *Chapman* v. *California,*[112] decided in 1967, the Supreme Court established the **harmless error rule,** holding that a denial of a federal constitutional right can at times be of insufficient magnitude to require a reversal of a conviction on appeal. Known also as the *Chapman* rule, the "harmless error" doctrine has been applied by the Supreme Court and other appellate courts in numerous areas of constitutional dimension: evidence seized in violation of the Fourth Amendment, denial of counsel at a preliminary hearing, in-court identifications based on invalid pretrial identification procedures, and obtaining a confession from a defendant after indictment without expressly informing the defendant of his right to counsel.[113] When a court considers an error to be harmless, it is indicating that the mistake was not prejudicial to the rights of the accused and thus made no difference in the subsequent conviction or sentence.

The Invited Error Rule

Although uncommon, there have been instances where during the course of a proceeding, the defense requests the court to make a ruling that is actually erroneous, and the court does so. Under the **invited error rule,** the defense cannot take advantage of such an error on appeal or review.[114]

On appeal or review, the defense cannot use an erroneous ruling it has requested the court to make.

The Prosecution's Right to Appeal

Neither the federal government nor the states may appeal the acquittal of a defendant. Nor can the prosecution appeal the conviction of some lesser offense (say, murder in the second degree or manslaughter) when the original indictment was for a greater one (murder in the first degree). In either case, such an action is barred by the double jeopardy clause of the Fifth Amendment. However, there are two instances in which the prosecution may initiate appellate review. Should a defendant successfully appeal and his or her conviction is reversed on some matter of law, the prosecution may contest the correctness of that legal ruling to the next higher court or even to the United States Supreme Court. Such was the case in *Delaware* v. *Prouse*,[115] which involved a seizure of marijuana following a random "spot check" of the defendant's driver's license and vehicle registration. Upon conviction, the defendant appealed to the Delaware Supreme Court, which overturned the lower court ruling on the basis of illegal search and seizure. The prosecution then appealed to the United States Supreme Court, to argue the constitutionality of the state's random license check practices. (See Chapter 8.)

Alternatively, some jurisdictions permit the prosecution to initiate appeals from both convictions *and* acquittals, solely for the purpose of correcting any legal errors that may have occurred during trial.[116]

Appellate Review of Sentences

Although appeals are commonly filed to review either real or imagined errors in court procedure, sentences, for the most part, are unappealable. This is so because each jurisdiction has statutes that mandate a range of penalties for each specific crime. Although a convicted offender might consider the sentence imposed to be unfair, as long as it falls within statutory guidelines, it is *legal.*

There are, however, a number of circumstances under which sanctions have been appealed and reversed, including when: (1) the sentence was not authorized by statute and thus was illegal; (2) the sentence was based on sex, ethnicity, or socioeconomic status and was, therefore, a violation of due process; (3) the sentence had no relationship to the purposes of criminal sanctions; and (4) the sentence was cruel and unusual. Note that in these four potential instances, the bases for appeal are not simply issues of sentencing "excess," but rather, straightforward matters of constitutional rights.

It has been argued for many decades that all sentences should be subject to some form of appeal. The fact that sentences are discretionary within a jurisdiction's statutory guidelines and, as such, are lawful should not automatically suggest that they are therefore unappealable. Discretion, after all, can be abused. Furthermore, as Judge Marvin E. Frankel has maintained:

> The contention that sentencing is not regulated by the rules of "law" subject to appellate review is an argument for, not against, a system of appeals. The "common law" is, after all, a body of rules evolved through the process of reasoned decision of concrete cases, mainly by appellate courts. English appellate courts and some of our states have been evolving general, legal "principles of sentencing" in the course of reviewing particular sentences claimed to be excessive. One way to begin to temper the capricious unruliness of sentencing is to institute the right of appeal, so that appellate courts may proceed in their accustomed fashion to make law for this grave subject.[117]

Currently, only about fourteen states have appellate bodies that generally review a term handed down by a sentencing judge. State appeals courts, on the other hand, are generally reluctant to review sentences. Not wishing to "second guess" the sentencing judge, these higher courts feel that the magistrate who presided at the trial and pronounced the sentence had the most information available and was in the most qualified position to determine the penalty.

Finally, although the U.S. Supreme Court has reviewed many sentences where the issue at stake was of constitutional magnitude, only once did the justices require a sentencing judge to explain the bases of the penalty imposed. The case was *North Carolina* v. *Pearce*,[118] in which the defendant, who was retried by the same judge after his original conviction was reversed, was reconvicted and sentenced more severely than he was after the first conviction. The Court ruled that in such circumstances, the reasons for the more severe sentence must be placed in the record, the logic being that the due-process clause of the Fourteenth Amendment forbids the imposition of a harsher sentence for the purpose of discouraging defendants from exercising their rights of appeal.

The Appeal Process

After conviction, appeals are not automatic. There are specific procedural steps that must be followed. First, within a specified period of time (from 30 to 90 days) subsequent to conviction, the petitioner must file with the court a notice of appeals. Second, and again within a specified period of time, the petitioner must submit an "affidavit of errors" setting forth the alleged errors or defects in the trial (or pretrial) proceedings that are the subjects of the appeal. If these requirements are followed, the higher court must review the case.[119] Appeals are argued on the basis of the affidavit of errors, and sometimes through oral argument. In either case, the subject matters of the appeal must be limited to the contents of the original proceeding. Thus, no new evidence or testimony can be presented, for an appeal is not a trial. However, if new evidence is discovered that was unknown or unknowable to the defense at the time of the trial, that can be made the *basis* of an appeal.*

---

* There are other mechanisms through which cases can be reviewed, such as collateral review proceedings and writs of *habeas corpus*. These are generally initiated after the defendant's sentence has commenced. They are discussed in Chapter 16, under prisoners' rights and postconviction remedies.

Summary

After the verdict, the business of the court is not complete. First there is the matter of sentencing. Throughout American history, there has been no single and clearly defined rationale to serve as a guiding principle in sentencing. As a result, even contemporary sentencing objectives are seemingly based on at least four competing philosophies: retribution, isolation, deterrence, and rehabilitation. Sentencing alternatives include fines, probation or some other community-based program, imprisonment, or the death penalty.

The death penalty is the most terminal form of punishment. When the framers of the Constitution incorporated the Eighth Amendment ban against cruel and unusual punishment, the death penalty was apparently not at issue. Under colonial philosophy, capital punishment was considered neither cruel nor unusual.

The Supreme Court's interpretation of the Eighth Amendment has been flexible. The Court has ruled on various forms of punishment but has generally been silent regarding the constitutionality of capital punishment. *Furman* v. *Georgia* in 1972 invalidated state death penalty statutes on Eighth Amendment grounds, but it enabled the states to enact new capital punishment laws. Executions resumed, and the number of persons on death rows across the nation began to grow. Meanwhile, the death penalty debate continues, with arguments for and against capital punishment revolving around issues of economics, retribution, public opinion, community protection, deterrence, irreversibility, discrimination, and cruel and unusual punishment.

At the appellate stage of the criminal justice process, the presumption of innocence has evaporated with the finding of guilt. It then becomes the defendant's obligation to show why a conviction should be overturned. There are grounds on which the defense can initiate an appeal, but the prosecution cannot appeal the acquittal of a defendant because of the double jeopardy clause of the Fifth Amendment. However, should an accused successfully appeal and have his conviction reversed on some matter of law, the prosecution may contest the correctness of that legal ruling to the next highest court or even to the U.S. Supreme Court.

Key Terms

allocution (468)
appeal (495)
automatic reversal rule (496)
Coker v. *Georgia* (481)
community protection argument (488)
cruel and unusual punishment argument (492)
definite sentence (458)
determinate sentence (457)
deterrence (452)
deterrence argument (488)
discrimination argument (489)
economic argument (487)
Eighth Amendment ban (469)
Furman v. *Georgia* (478)

Gregg v. *Georgia* (480)
habitual offender laws (450)
harmless error rule (496)
indeterminate sentence (455)
intermittent sentence (459)
invited error rule (497)
irreversibility argument (488)
isolation (450)
mandatory sentence (459)
McGautha v. *California* (477)
plain error rule (496)
presentence investigation (467)
presumptive fixed sentence (466)
protection of the criminal justice system argument (491)
public opinion (488)

rehabilitation (452)
retribution (449)
retribution argument (487)
statutory sentencing (454)
Weems v. *United States* (473)
Witherspoon v. *Illinois* (476)

Questions for Discussion

1. Given the decision in *Tate* v. *Short,* is it constitutionally permissible to sentence an indigent to imprisonment for even a short period of time if the statutes permit the imposition of a fine? At the same time, which would be the more severe sentence — $1,000 fine for a person of moderate means or 30 days for an indigent defendant?

2. How might mandatory sentencing statutes lead to increased prosecutorial discretion and court delays?

3. What argument in favor of capital punishment seems most valid? Should capital punishment be abolished? Will it be?

4. Would mandatory sentencing statutes make the certainty of punishment more realistic? Would such sentences affect the crime problem?

For Further Reading

Bedau, Hugo Adam. *The Death Penalty in America.* Chicago: Aldine, 1964.

Haas, Kenneth C. "Reaffirming the Value of Life: Arguments Against the Death Penalty." *Delaware Lawyer,* 3 (Summer 1984), pp. 12–20.

van den Haag, Ernest, and John P. Conrad, *The Death Penalty: A Debate.* New York: Plenum Press, 1983.

Zimring, Franklin E., and Gordon J. Hawkins. *Deterrence.* Chicago: University of Chicago Press, 1973.

Notes

1. See Andrew von Hirsch, *Doing Justice: The Choice of Punishments* (New York: Hill and Wang, 1976), pp. 45–55, 143–149.

2. Paul W. Tappan, *Crime, Justice and Correction* (New York: McGraw-Hill, 1960), p. 255.

3. National Advisory Commission on Criminal Justice Standards and Goals, *Corrections* (Washington, D.C.: U.S. Government Printing Office, 1973), p. 1.

4. Quoted in Sanford H. Kadish and Monrad G. Paulsen, *Criminal Law and Its Processes* (Boston: Little, Brown, 1969), p. 85.

5. See Franklin E. Zimring and Gordon J. Hawkins, *Deterrence* (Chicago: University of Chicago Press, 1973).

6. Personal communication, January 6, 1978.

7. The issues for and against the rehabilitative approach are discussed at greater length in Part 4 of this text.

8. Melvyn Bernard Zerman, *Beyond a Reasonable Doubt: Inside the American Jury System* (New York: Crowell, 1981). p. 170.

9. National Advisory Commission on Criminal Justice Standards and Goals, *Courts* (Washington, D.C.: U.S. Government Printing Office, 1973), p. 110.

10. *Code of the Public General Laws of Maryland,* Article 27, Section 341.

11. State of New York, *Penal Law,* 40-70.15, 80.05, 245.01.

12. Williams v. Illinois, 399 U.S. 235 (1970); Tate v. Short, 401 U.S. 395 (1971).

13. Walter S. Carr, "Sentencing Practices, Problems, and Remedies," *Judicature* 53 (1969): 14.

14. See Marvin E. Frankel, *Criminal Sentences: Law Without Order* (New York: Hill and Wang, 1973); Karl Menninger, *The Crime of Punishment* (New York: Viking, 1968); von Hirsch, *Doing Justice;* Nigel Walker, *Sentencing in a Rational Society* (London: Penguin, 1972).

15. Harry Elmer Barnes, *The Repression of Crime* (New York: George H. Doran, 1926), p. 220.

16. *Delaware Code,* Title 11, Section 4209.

17. State of New York, *Penal Law,* 40-85.

18. People v. Warren, 79 Misc 2d 777, 360 NYS 2d 961 (1974).

19. *Massachusetts General Laws,* Chapter 269-10, Acts of 1974.

20. *New York Times,* June 22, 1977, p. B2.

21. *New York Times,* March 30, 1980, p. 27.

22. Attorney General's Task Force on Violent Crime, *Final Report* (Washington D.C.: U.S. Government Printing Office, 1981).

23. *National Law Journal,* November 19, 1984, p. 47.

24. *People,* January 1, 1981, p. 86.

25. *New York Times,* November 4, 1984, p. 57.

26. *National Law Journal,* October 5, 1981, p. 39.

27. *National Law Journal,* March 29, 1982, p. 47.

28. *Idaho Code,* 18-1403, 19-2601.

29. State of New York, *Penal Law,* 40-70.00, 80.00, 140.30.

30. *West Virginia Code,* Chapter 61, Section 3-11; Chapter 62, Section 12-2.

31. *Delaware Code,* Title 11, Sections 826, 4204-5.

32. *Code of the Public General Laws of Maryland,* Article 27, Sections 29, 641.

33. *Code of Alabama,* 13-2-40, 15-22-50.

34. President's Commission on Law Enforcement and Administration of Justice, *The Courts* (Washington D.C.: U.S. Government Printing Office, 1967), p. 23.

35. William Zumwalt, "The Anarchy of Sentencing in the Federal Courts," *Judicature* 57 (October 1973): 96–104.

36. *New York Times,* February 15, 1981, p. 43.

37. *Miami Herald,* January 13, 1984, p. 1D.

38. Hutto v. Davis, 454 U.S. 372 (1982). See also *High Times,* July 1983, pp. 32–37.

39. *National Observer,* September 14, 1974, p. 5.

40. *New York Times,* March 30, 1979, p. B3.

41. *National Law Journal,* April 5, 1982, p. 3.

42. President's Commission, *Courts,* p. 24.

43. President's Commission, *Courts,* p. 23.

44. Frankel, *Criminal Sentences,* p. 8.

45. Marvin Zalman, "The Rise and Fall of the Indeterminate Sentence," *Wayne Law Review* 24 (1978): 857.

46. See, for example, Frankel, *Criminal Sentences.*

47. Joseph Mattina, "Sentencing: A Judge's Inherent Responsibility," *Judicature* 57 (October 1973): 105.

48. National Advisory Commission, *Courts,* p. 326.

49. Advisory Committee on Sentencing and Review, *Standards Relating to Probation* (New York: American Bar Association, 1970), p. 32.

50. Administrative Offices of the U.S. Courts, Division of Probation, "The Selective Presentence Investigation Report," *Federal Probation* 38 (December 1974): 48.

51. Ernst W. Puttkammer, *Administration of Criminal Law* (Chicago: University of Chicago Press, 1953), p. 215.

52. Hill v. California, 368 U.S. 424 (1962).

53. Barnes, *Repression of Crime,* pp. 44–45.

54. George Ryley Scott, *The History of Capital Punishment* (London: Torchstream, 1950), p. 179.

55. Cited by Harry Elmer Barnes, *The Story of Punishment: A Record of Man's Inhumanity to Man* (Montclair, N.J.: Patterson Smith, 1972), p. 232.

56. Negley K. Teeters and Charles J. Zibulka, "Executions Under State Authority: 1864–1967," in *Executions in America,* ed. William J. Bowers (Lexington, Mass.: D. C. Heath, 1974), pp. 200–401.

57. Hugo Adam Bedau, *The Death Penalty in America* (Chicago: Aldine, 1964), p. 46.

58. President's Commission, *Courts,* p. 28.

59. C. Spear, *Essays on the Punishment of Death* (London: John Green, 1844), pp. 227–231.

60. David A. Jones, *The Law of Criminal Procedure* (Boston: Little, Brown, 1981), p. 543.

61. Jones, *Law of Criminal Procedure,* p. 544.

62. Richard Maxwell Brown, "Historical Patterns of American Violence," in *Violence in America: Historical and Comparative Perspectives,* ed. Hugh Davis Graham and Ted Robert Gurr (Beverly Hills, Calif.: Sage, 1979), p. 31.

63. Marvin E. Wolfgang and Marc Riedel, "Race, Judicial Discretion, and the Death Penalty," *Annals of the American Academy of Political and Social Science* 407 (May 1973): 129.

64. O'Neil v. Vermont, 114 U.S. 323 (1892).

65. Weems v. United States, 217 U.S. 349 (1910).

66. Trop v. Dulles, 356 U.S. 86 (1958).

67. Wilkerson v. Utah, 99 U.S. 130 (1878).

68. In re Kemmler, 136 U.S. 436 (1890).

69. Trop v. Dulles, *supra* note 66.

70. Witherspoon v. Illinois, 391 U.S. 510 (1968).

71. McGautha v. California, 402 U.S. 183 (1971).

72. Furman v. Georgia, Jackson v. Georgia, Branch v. Texas, 408 U.S. 238 (1972).

73. Gregg v. Georgia, 428 U.S. 153 (1976).

74. *Georgia Code,* 26-1101, 1311, 1902, 2001, 3301 (1972).

75. Profitt v. Florida, 428 U.S. 325 (1976); Jurek v. Texas, 428 U.S. 262 (1976).

76. Woodson v. North Carolina, 428 U.S. 280 (1976).

77. Coker v. Georgia, 433 U.S. 583 (1977).

78. Lockett v. Ohio, 438 U.S. 586 (1978); Bell v. Ohio, 438 U.S. 637 (1978).

79. Godfrey v. Georgia, 446 U.S. 420 (1980).

80. Gilmore v. Utah, 429 U.S. 1012 (1976).

81. This account on the Gilmore case is based on Louis R. Katz, *The Justice Imperative* (Cincinnati: Anderson, 1980); pp. 348–349; *New York Times:* January 18, 1977, pp. 1, 21; January 12, 1977, pp. 1, 12; January 11, 1976, pp. 1, 14; January 16, 1977, p. 1, 48; December 1, 1976, p. 18; January 17, 1976, pp. 1, 24.

82. Quoted in Austin Sarat and Neil Vidmar, "Public Opinion, The Death Penalty, and the Eighth Amendment: Testing the Marshall Hypothesis," *Wisconsin Law Review* (1976): 206.

83. State v. Frampton, 95 Wn 2d 469 (1981); *National Law Journal,* June 8, 1981, p. 4.

84. Wilmington (Delaware) *News-Journal,* February 17, 1985, p. A16.

85. *New York Times,* December 9, 1979, p. 73.

86. *National Law Journal,* September 14, 1981, p. 5.

87. *American Medical News,* July 11, 1980, p. 13.

88. *Time,* December 20, 1982, pp. 28–29. See also, *Texas Monthly,* February 1983, pp. 100–105, 170–176, 182.

89. Heckler v. Chaney, CADE, 35 CrL 4077 (1984).

90. O'Bryan v. Heckler, 35 CrL 4002 (1984).

91. *USA Today,* April 30, 1985, p. 3A.

92. Cited by Sue Titus Reid, *Crime and Criminology* (New York: Holt, Rinehart and Winston, 1979), p. 566.

93. *New York Times,* January 31, 1977, p. 12C.

94. *National Observer,* November 18, 1972, p. 2.

95. *New York Times,* February 3, 1985, p. 23.

96. President's Commission, *Courts,* p. 27.

97. Zimring and Hawkins, *Deterrence.*

98. See Thorsten Sellin, ed., *Capital Punishment* (New York: Harper & Row, 1967); Karl F. Schuessler, "The Deterrent Influence of the Death Penalty," *Annals of the American Academy of Political and Social Science* 284 (November 1952): 54–62; Hugo Adam Bedau and Chester M. Pierce, eds., *Capital Punishment in the United States* (New York: A M S Press, 1976), pp. 299–416.

99. Roy E. Calvert, *Capital Punishment in the Twentieth Century* (New York: G. P. Putnam's, 1936), p. 125.

100. Bedau, *Death Penalty in America,* pp. 434–452.

101. Isidore Zimmerman, *Punishment Without Crime* (New York: Manor, 1973).

102. William J. Bowers and Glenn L. Pierce, "Arbitrariness and Discrimination under Post-*Furman* Capital Statutes, *Crime and Delinquency* 26 (October 1980), pp. 563–635; Kenneth C. Haas, "Reaffirming the Value of Life: Arguments Against the Death Penalty," *Delaware Lawyer* 3 (Summer 1984), pp. 12–20; *USA Today,* August 26, 1985, p. 2A.

103. McCleskey v. Zant, 34 CrL 2429 (1984).

104. President's Commission, *Courts.*

105. *New York Times,* August 26, 1985, p. A12.

106. Pulley v. Harris, U.S. SupCt (1984) 34 CrL 3027.

107. Barefoot v. Estelle, 103 S.Ct. 3383 (1983).

108. For example, in McKane v. Durston, 153 U.S. 684 (1894); Griffin v. Illinois, 351 U.S. 12 (1956).

109. *Federal Rules of Criminal Procedure,* Rule 52 (b).

110. Tumey v. Ohio, 273 U.S. 510 (1927).

111. Gideon v. Wainwright, 372 U.S. 335 (1963).

112. Chapman v. California, 386 U.S. 18 (1967).

113. See Peter W. Lewis and Kenneth D. Peoples, *The Supreme Court and the Criminal Process* (Philadelphia: W. B. Saunders, 1978), p. 515.

114. Gresham v. Harcourt, 93 Tex. 149, 53 S. W. 1019.

115. Delaware v. Prouse, 440 U.S. 648 (1979).

116. Katz, *Justice Imperative,* p. 315.

117. Frankel, *Criminal Sentences,* p. 84.

118. North Carolina v. Pearce, 395 U.S. 711 (1969).

119. *Gilbert Criminal Law and Procedure* (New York: Matthew Bender, 1979), p. 460.10.

Part

4

Corrections

From Walnut Street to Alcatraz: The American Prison Experience

The mood and temper of the public with regard to the treatment of crime and criminals is one of the unfailing tests of the civilization of any country.

— Winston Churchill, 1910.

The public will grow increasingly ashamed of its cry for retaliation, its persistent demand to punish. This is its crime, our crime against criminals.

— Karl Menninger, 1968

Punishment — if not the only, or the first, or even the best means of making people obey laws — is ultimately indispensable.

— Ernest van den Haag, 1975

Historically and cross-culturally, the range of punishments imposed by societies has been vast. Over the centuries, the sanctions for even less serious crimes were exceedingly harsh, and the litany of punishments down through the ages has often been referred to as the story of "man's inhumanity to man."[1]

In early societies the death penalty was a universal form of punishment. It was commonly applied both as a deterrent and a means for removing an offender from the community. Criminal codes from the ancient East to the modern West included capital statutes for offenses as trivial as adultery and petty theft. As recently as the early nineteenth century in England there were 200 capital crimes — ranging from murder and rape to larceny and disturbing the peace. The methods of execution went well beyond the diabolical and macabre, and they were often performed in public.[2]

Corporal punishment, in the form of mutilation, branding, whipping, and torture, was also commonplace for a variety of punitive purposes. Mutilations were attempts to "let the punishment fit the crime": thieves and robbers lost their hands, perjurers and blasphemers had their tongues cut out or pierced with hot irons, and rape was punished by castration. Branding and whipping were noncapital sanctions to preserve discipline and to deter would-be offenders. Torture, a popular means for exacting confessions, included measures of gruesome ingenuity. The torture devices of medieval Europe, for example, were often monstrous. They included the *rack*, which stretched its victims, and the "Scavenger's Daughter," which rolled them into a ball:

> On the rack the prisoner seemed in danger of having the fingers torn from his hands, the toes from his feet, the hands from the arms, the feet from the legs, the forearms from the upper arms, the legs from the trunk. Every ligament was strained, every joint loosened in its socket; and if the sufferer remained obstinate when released, he was brought back to undergo the same cruelties with the added horror of past experience and with a diminished fortitude and physical power. In the Scavenger's Daughter, on the other hand, the pain was caused by an ingenious process of compression. The legs were forced back to the thighs, the thighs were pressed onto the belly, and the whole body was placed within two iron bands which the torturers drew together with all their strength until the miserable human being lost all form but that of a globe. Blood was forced out of the tips of the fingers and toes, the nostrils and mouth; and the ribs and breastbone were commonly broken in by the pressure.[3]

Banishment and transportation were alternatives to capital punishment. Banishment served to rid the community of undesirables, who were

The Ducking-Stool

never to return, under penalty of certain death. The most systematic form of banishment occurred in several European countries during the sixteenth through nineteenth centuries under a program of transportation to far-removed lands. England led the world in this practice, which it used to eliminate convicts from its shores as well as colonize what were considered inhospitable territories. From 1606 through 1775, tens of thousands of vagrants and thieves were shipped to the American colonies in the West Indies, and then to Australia following the discontinuance of transportation to the American colonies after the American Revolution.[4] In its most modern form, banishment has appeared as "deportation" of alien criminals, with examples including Charles "Lucky" Luciano and Xaviera Hollander ("the Happy Hooker")—both forced out of the United States after convictions on "morals" charges.

Other punishments have included forced labor, sterilization, excommunication from the church, loss of property and inheritance rights, disfigurement, and imprisonment.

The Roots of American Correctional Philosophy

With the growth of the American colonies, many of the punishments that had been common throughout medieval Europe found their way to the New World. Capital statutes endured for numerous offenses, as did banishment, and corporal punishments in the form of branding, flogging, and mutilation persisted.

Colonial Punishments

A curious variety of sanctions appeared in colonial tradition: the ducking stool, the stocks and pillory, the brank, the scarlet letter, and the bilboes. They were imposed for minor offenses, and although they are generally associated with early American life, most had originated in Western Europe as means to shame and humiliate offenders.[5]

The *ducking stool,* as its name implies, was a chair fastened to a long lever and situated at the bank of a river or pond. The victim, generally a village gossip or scold, was repeatedly submerged in the water before a jeering crowd. The *stocks and pillory,* common in almost every early New England community, were wooden frames with holes for the head, hands, and feet. They were located in the town square, and the culprit—generally a wife beater, petty thief, vagrant, Sabbath-breaker, drunkard, adulterer, or unruly servant—would be open to public scorn. Confinement in the stocks or pillory often resulted in much more than simple humiliation. The offenders were often whipped or branded while being detained, and most were pelted by passersby. Some were even stoned to death. Those secured to the pillory generally had their ears nailed to the frame, and were compelled to tear themselves loose (or have their ears cut off) when their period of detention concluded.

The *brank,* also called the "gossip's helm" and the "dame's bridle," was a cage placed about the head. It had a spiked plate or flat dish of iron that was placed in the mouth over the tongue thus inflicting severe pain if the offender spoke. As the structure of the device would suggest, it had been designed for gossips, perjurers, liars, and blasphemers, but in colonial New York it was also used for husband beaters and village drunkards.

Laying by the heels in the Bilboes.

The *scarlet letter,* made famous by Nathaniel Hawthorne's novel of the same name, was used for a variety of offenses. The adulterous wife wore an *A,* cut from scarlet cloth and sewn to her upper garments. The blasphemer wore a *B,* the pauper a *P,* the thief a *T,* and the drunkard a *D* (see Exhibit 14.1).

And finally there was the *bilboes,* wherein the citizen convicted of slander and libel was shackled by the feet to a wooden stake.

Punishment versus Reformation

Throughout English and American history, scholars and kings, philosophers and reformers, and legislators and statesmen have argued the merits of punishment versus reformation in the management and control of criminal of-

The Scarlet Letter.

EXHIBIT 14.1

Marian and the Elders

Nathaniel Hawthorne's *The Scarlet Letter,* published in 1850, is a story of Puritanism and pariahs in seventeenth-century Boston. Hester Prynne, having given birth to an illegitimate daughter, is scorned by her neighbors and forced by her church to wear a scarlet *A*—signifying "Adulteress"—as a token of her sin.

Surprisingly, Hawthorne's novel became the theme of an Oklahoma trial in 1984. The story began three years earlier in Collinsville, Oklahoma, a rural town some ten miles north of Tulsa. Marian Guinn, a member of the Collinsville Church of Christ and a divorced woman with four children, had begun a relationship with a local man who was also divorced. Almost immediately, Marian was confronted on the affair by the church elders, who demanded that she confess her transgression publicly. When she refused, the elders made a formal statement before the entire Collinsville Church of Christ congregation, denouncing her "fornication" and calling for

members to "withhold fellowship" from her. Marian Guinn then sued the church, alleging invasion of privacy and infliction of emotional stress.

At the 1984 trial, which took place in Tulsa, Guinn's attorney likened the church's action toward her client to that directed toward the fictional Hester Prynne. Of his client's affair he stated: "He was a single man. She was a single woman. And this is America." The elders argued that Ms. Guinn's soul was at stake, and that they had an absolute right to practice their religion as Church of Christ tradition dictated—which included the monitoring and disciplining of their 1.3 million adult members. The jury did not agree, and the court ruled in Marian Guinn's favor. The damage award of $390,000 turned out to be more than the Collinsville congregation's entire proceeds for six years.

SOURCES: Newsweek, February 27, 1984, p. 46; *New York Times,* March 11, 1984, p. 25; *USA Today,* March 12, 1984, p. 2A; *Miami Herald,* March 17, 1984, p. 8A; *Time,* March 26, 1984, p. 70; *National Law Journal,* April 2, 1984, p. 6.

fenders. Their views were shaped by the evolution of criminal law, alternative conceptions of justice, and changing social attitudes toward what might be appropriate responses to lawbreaking. The varying ideas and practices, however, all shared similar goals—the taking of vengeance, the reduction of crime, and the protection of self and society. Criminal sanctions focused on retribution, banishment, isolation, and death, and were based on the reasoning that offenders were enemies of society, that they deserved punishment, and that severe approaches would eliminate their potential for future crime. This *punishment ideology* has endured throughout recorded history.

During the eighteenth century—the Age of Enlightenment—a new ideology began to emerge. It was a reform movement that stressed the dignity and imperfections of the human condition; it recognized the harshness of

Marian Guinn in front of the Collinsville, Oklahoma, church she successfully sued for invasion of privacy and the infliction of emotional stress. In an action likened to Hawthorne's novel The Scarlet Letter, *church elders publicly denounced the divorced Guinn's relationship with a local man.*

criminal law and procedure; and it fought against the cruelty of many punishments and conditions of confinement. Among the leading European thinkers in the reform movement were Charles Montesquieu, François Voltaire, and Denis Diderot in France; Cesare Beccaria in Italy; and Jeremy Bentham, John Howard, Samuel Romilly, and Robert Peel in England (see Exhibit 14.2).[6]

EXHIBIT 14.2

Leading Figures in the Classical School

Montesquieu (1689–1755)

Charles-Louis de Secondat, Baron de La Brède et de Montesquieu, the French lawyer, philosopher, and man of letters, epitomized the Enlightenment's concern for the rights of humanity. His book, *The Spirit of the Laws,* and essay, "Persian Letters," condemned the barbarous injustice of the French penal code and advocated reforms that would make punishments less severe and more adapted to the crimes for which they were imposed.

Voltaire (1694–1778)

François-Marie Arouet, or Voltaire, the French humanist and satirist, was also the most versatile of the eighteenth-century philosophers. In his writings, he condemned the arbitrary powers of judges, the secret trial, and the use of torture, and he demanded that the purpose of the law be the protection of the citizen and that all persons should be equal before the law.

Diderot (1713–1784)

Denis Diderot, the French encyclopedist, novelist, dramatist, and art critic, was also a philosopher who attacked the orthodoxy of his time. He revolted against the unquestioning acceptance of tradition and authority, and in many of his works he heavily criticized the chaos and corruption in political institutions as well as the superstition and cruelty that pervaded penal practices.

Beccaria (1738–1794)

Cesare Bonesana, Marchese di Beccaria, the Italian economist and jurist, proposed a whole new concept for the administration of justice. His major work, *An Essay on Crimes and Punishments,* became the manifesto of the liberal approach to criminal law. It condemned capital punishment and torture, suggested that the law should be specific, and advocated the prevention of crime and rigid rules of criminal procedure.

Bentham (1748–1832)

Jeremy Bentham, the English jurist and philosopher, was the leader of English criminal law reform. He believed that punishment should be a deterrent. His "hedonistic calculus" argued that if punishments were designed to negate whatever pleasure or gain the criminal derived from crime, the crime rate would go down. This ethical doctrine was founded on the notion that the morality of actions is determined by utility, and appeared in his major work on the administration of justice, *Introduction to the Principles and Morals of Legislation.*

Howard (1726?–1790)

The name of John Howard, High Sheriff of Bedfordshire for almost two decades, became synonymous with English prison reform. His work, *State of Prisons,* was based on observations of prison conditions throughout England and continental Europe, and influenced the passage of the Penitentiary Act of 1779. This legislation resulted in England's first penitentiary, one that incorporated many principles of basic prison reform.

Romilly (1757–1818)

Sir Samuel Romilly, the English lawyer and law reformer, devoted his energies to changes in the harsh criminal codes. His efforts secured the repeal of many Elizabethan capital statutes and numerous other harsh and irrational laws. He also influenced the construction of the first modern English prison.

Peel (1788–1850)

Sir Robert Peel, the English statesman, member of Parliament, and prime minister, influenced legislation that reformed the criminal law. He established the Irish constabulary (called the "Peelers"), and pushed the legislation that created the London metropolitan police (the "bobbies")—both named after him.

The Classical School of Criminology

The principles of Montesquieu, Voltaire, and other Enlightenment philosophers with regard to criminal law and the administration of justice merged during the middle of the eighteenth century into what has become known as the **classical school of criminal law and criminology**. It has been called "classical" because of its historical significance as the first body of ideas before modern times that was coherently formulated to bring about changes in criminal law and procedure. At the basis of the classical tradition were the ideas that man was a self-determining being, acting on reason and intelligence, and therefore responsible for his behavior.

The classical school began as an outgrowth of the acquaintanceship between the young Italian economist **Cesare Beccaria** and Alessandro Verri, a prison official in Milan. Beccaria's numerous visits to Verri exposed him to the existing policies of criminal justice procedure. He found judges to be applying capricious and purely personal justice; he found criminal sanctions to be almost totally discretionary; he saw many magistrates exercising their power to add to the punishments nebulously prescribed by law; and he witnessed such tyrannical and brutal punishments as having criminals branded, mutilated, torn limb from limb, fed to animals, slowly starved, scalded, burned, hanged, enslaved, crucified, and stoned or pressed to death.

Outraged by the experience, Beccaria, at age 24, began writing what became one of the most significant books of his time. Two years later, in 1764, his *Dei delitti et delle pene* (*An Essay on Crimes and Punishments*) was published. It outlined a liberal doctrine of criminal law and procedure, and highlighted the following points:

> The classical school of criminal law and criminology began with Cesare Beccaria.

1. Since the criminal law placed restrictions on individual freedom, the law should be limited in scope. The function of the law was to serve the needs of a given society, not to enforce moral virtue, and as such, to prohibit an action necessarily increases rather than decreases crime.

2. In the administration of justice, the presumption of innocence should be the guiding factor, and at all stages in the criminal justice process the rights of the suspected, the accused, the convicted, and the sentenced should be protected.

3. The criminal law should define in advance both the offenses and their punishments. Thus there should be a complete written code of criminal law.

4. Punishment should be retributive: "Everyone must suffer punishment so far to invade the province of his own rights as the crime he has committed has penetrated into that of another."

5. The severity of punishment must be limited; it should be proportionate to the crime; it should not go beyond the point that already prevents the offender from further injuring others or beyond the point that already deters others.

6. The nature of the punishment should correspond with the nature of the offense; a fine would be appropriate for simple thefts, but corporal punishment and labor would satisfy crimes of violence.

7. There must be certainty of punishment; penalties must be applied with speed and certainty.

8. Punishment should not be used to make an example of the offender for society, nor should the punishment include reformatory measures,

since enforced reformation by its very nature is of little use. Furthermore, the punishment should be based on the objective criterion of the crime, and not varied to suit the personality of the offender.

9. "It is better to prevent crimes than to punish them" and prevention consists in a clear and limited code of laws, supplemented by the rewarding of virtue.[7]

Beccaria's reformist views were highly praised, for they appeared at a time when European jurists were ready to hear and implement the kinds of changes he had proposed. His arguments were incorporated into both English and French criminal codes, and among those inspired by Beccaria's work were the framers of the United States Constitution.

The classical school was not limited to the writing and influence of Cesare Beccaria. In England, such classicists as Jeremy Bentham, Samuel Romilly and John Howard sought to reform the infamous "bloody codes" — a system of laws that permitted execution for pickpocketing, cutting down trees on government parklands, setting fire to a cornfield, escaping from jail, and shooting a rabbit.

The "bloody codes"

However, the doctrine of free will, which dominated classical thinking, also served to generate weaknesses in its perspective. Its proponents argued that all behavior was based on *hedonism,* the pleasure–pain principle. People chose those courses of action that would give them the most pleasure and avoided those that would bring pain. Thus behavior was purposive, and punishment, they reasoned, should result in more pain than the pleasure received from the forbidden act. Moreover, this view applied equally to all citizens with no allowances for aggravating or mitigating circumstances. In spite of this flaw, the classical school did make contributions. It was instrumental in making the law impartial, in reducing the harshness of penalties, and with replacing the arbitrary powers of judges with a specified range of criminal sanctions.

The pleasure–pain principle

American Prisons in Perspective

The American prison system had its beginnings during the second half of the seventeenth century in Philadelphia. In 1682, William Penn, a religious reformer and the founder of Pennsylvania, made sweeping changes in the administration of justice in the territory under his control. He limited the death penalty in Pennsylvania to cases of murder, called for fines and imprisonment as penalties for most offenses, and urged flogging for adultery, arson, and rape. These were mild sanctions compared to the executions, brandings, mutilations, and other severe punishments that existed throughout the other colonies. Penn also influenced the construction of county jails, which were designed to be workhouses for convicted felons. The first of these was the High Street Jail in Philadelphia erected in 1682; others appeared in the decades that followed. But even before Penn's death in 1718, the workhouse idea failed due to overcrowding and inadequate conditions. As one observer described the situation:

William Penn

What a spectacle must this abode of guilt and wretchedness have presented, when in one common herd were kept by day and night prisoners of all ages, colors and sexes! No separation was made of the most flagrant offender and convict, from the prisoner who might, perhaps, be falsely suspected of some trifling misdemeanor; none of the old and hardened culprits from the youthful, trembling novice in crime; none even of the fraudulent swindler from the unfortunate and possibly the most estimable debtor; and when intermingled with all these, in one corrupt and corrupting assemblage were to be found the disgusting object of popular contempt, besmeared with filth from the pillory — the unhappy victim of the lash, streaming with blood from the whipping post — the half-naked vagrant — the loathsome drunkard — the sick, suffering from various bodily pains, and too often the unaneled* male-factor, whose precious hours of probation had been numbered by his earthly judge.[8]

The Walnut Street Jail

During the eighteenth century, the Quakers of Pennsylvania placed their commonwealth in the forefront of correctional history. In 1787, they formed the Philadelphia Society for Alleviating the Miseries of Public Prisons and quickly addressed the conditions of their local jails. In 1776, a new prison-workhouse opened on Philadelphia's Walnut Street to receive prisoners from the overcrowded High Street Jail. In 1790, influenced by the work of John Howard, the society transformed the new structure on Walnut Street into the first American penitentiary.

The **Walnut Street Jail** was both a prison and a workhouse, and covered some two acres of ground. Those convicted of the most serious crimes were confined without labor in 16 solitary cells, each 6 feet wide and 8 feet long, with an inner iron door, an outer wooden door, and wire across the single window. The prisoners were fed the rather peculiar diet of pudding made of molasses and maize. A large pipe extending from each cell to a sewer served as a toilet, while a stove in the corridor provided heat. Offenders confined for less serious crimes were lodged together in rooms 18 by 20 feet in size. Together they worked in a large stone structure at shoemaking, carpentry, weaving, tailoring, and nailmaking. Women worked at spinning cotton, preparing hemp and wool, washing, and mending. Vagrants and unskilled prisoners beat hemp or picked moss and oakum (jute fiber used for caulking ships). Male prisoners were credited with the prevailing wage but were charged the costs of their trials, fines, and maintenance. Women were not given wages, nor were they charged for their maintenance. No irons or guard weapons were permitted. Except for women prisoners, silence was enforced in the shops and at meals, but some low-toned conversation was permitted in the night quarters before bedtime. Religious instruction and weekly services were offered.[9]

Throughout the 1790s, the Walnut Street Jail was considered a model prison. Officials from other states and from throughout Europe visited to observe its cellular confinement pattern and workhouse program, returning to their homes to praise its design and procedures. By the beginning of the nineteenth century, however, Philadelphia's acclaimed jail had begun to deteriorate, primarily due to overcrowding. Work activity had become impossible to continue, discipline had become difficult, and riots were common.

The Separate System

The solitary confinement of hardened offenders in the Walnut Street Jail was based on the notion that recidivism could be prevented and offenders reformed

The Walnut Street Jail, the first American penitentiary

---

*Not having received the last rites of the church.

by eliminating evil association in congregate prison quarters. Confinement in an isolated cell would give the convict an opportunity to contemplate the evils of his past life, thereby leading him to resolve "in the spiritual presence of his Maker" to reform his future conduct.[10] More specifically, the defenders of this **separate system** argued, it possessed a number of wholesome virtues:

The virtues of the separate system

- the protection against possible moral contamination through evil association
- the invitation to self-examination and self-reproach in solitude
- the impossibility of being visited by anyone (other than an officer, a reformer, or members of the clergy)
- the great ease of administration of discipline
- the possibility of a great degree of individuality of treatment
- the minimal need for disciplinary measures
- the absence of any possibility of mutual recognition of prisoners after discharge
- the fact that the pressures of loneliness would make convicts eager to engage in productive labor, during which time they could be taught a useful trade[11]

Such was the basis for the construction of Western Penitentiary near Pittsburgh in 1826, and Eastern Penitentiary near Philadelphia in 1829. Eastern Penitentiary epitomized the Pennsylvania correctional philosophy,

Eastern Penitentiary,
Philadelphia, Pennsylvania

and its architecture was adapted to the principle of solitary confinement.[12] It had seven wards housing 844 individual cells, all radiating from a common center like the spokes of a wheel. To each individual cell on the lower floor of each ward was attached a small exercise yard, which the prisoner could visit twice daily for short periods of time. In the interim, he washed, ate, and slept in his cell, seeing no one other than the prison officials and reformers from the outside community. Massive walls surrounded the entire institution and divided its parts so as to eliminate all contact and make escape impossible.

Visitors from almost every nation in the Western world marveled at the construction and plan of Eastern Penitentiary, and recommended that the model be adopted in their home countries. In 1833, French writers Gustave de Beaumont and Alexis de Tocqueville commented on the reformative effects of the absolute solitude that Pennsylvania's separate system provided for its confined offenders:

> Generally, their hearts are found ready to open themselves, and the facility of being moved renders them also fitter for reformation. They are particularly accessible to religious sentiments, and the remembrance of their family has an uncommon power over their minds. . . . Nothing distracts, in Philadelphia, the mind of the convicts from their meditations; and as they are always isolated, the presence of a person who comes to converse with them is of the greatest benefit. . . . When we visited this penitentiary, one of the prisoners said to us: "It is with joy that I perceive the figure of the keepers, who visit my cell. This summer a cricket came into my yard; it looked like a companion. When a butterfly or any other animal happens to enter my cell, I never do it any harm.[13]

However, the abominable simplicity of the separate system was also a dehumanizing experience. As one commentator described it:

> He was given a hot bath, and a prison uniform. Then his eyes were bandaged, and he was led blindfolded into the rotunda, where, still not seeing, he heard the rules of the house explained by the superintendent. And still blindfolded, he was led to his living grave. The bandage was taken from his eyes. He saw a cell less than twelve feet long, less than eight feet wide, and if he was to live on the ground floor, he saw a little courtyard, the same size, highly walled, opening out of it, in which he sometimes might exercise. In that cell, and that courtyard, he stayed, without any change, for three, ten, twenty years or for life. He saw only the guard who brought his food to him, but who was forbidden to speak to him. He got no letters, saw none of his family. He was cut off from the world. When the cholera raged in Philadelphia in 1843, it was months before the prisoners got a hint that an epidemic had vistited the city. After the slave had been three days in his cell, he was allowed to work, if he wished, and the fact that nearly all prisoners asked for something to do proved to the inspectors that reform was beginning. If they did not choose to work they might commune with their corrupt hearts in a perfectly dark and solitary punishment cell.[14]

Despite its attractiveness to Europeans, the Pennsylvania plan never gained widespread popularity in the United States. It was the basis of temporary experimentation in New Jersey and Rhode Island, but by the latter part of the nineteenth century it had been abandoned, even in Pennsylvania.

The history of correction is a graveyard of abandoned fads.
—**Robert Martinson, 1976**

The Silent System

The silent system at
Auburn Prison

The demise of the separate system was due not so much to the destructive effects of long-term solitary confinement as to the emergence of a different pattern of prison administration in New York State. Known as the **silent system** and established at Auburn Prison in 1823, it was considered to be the most economically sound of penitentiary programs (see Exhibit 14.3). As opposed to the outside cells with individual exercise yards at Eastern penitentiary, prisoners at Auburn were confined in banks of inside cells each measuring only 7 feet by 3½ feet. Inmates were employed in congregate shops during the day under a rigid rule of absolute silence at all times, and with solitary confinement only at night. Hard labor was considered essential to the reformation of character and to the economic solvency of the prison. Perpetual silence was seen as mandatory while inmates were in close proximity in order to avoid

---

EXHIBIT 14.3

A Day at Auburn Prison

At Auburn we have a more beautiful example still of what may be done by proper discipline, in a prison well constructed. It is not possible to describe the pleasure which we feel in contemplating this noble institution, after wading through the fraud, and the material and moral filth of many prisons. We regard it as a model worthy of the world's imitation. We do not mean that there is nothing in this institution which admits of improvement; for there have been a few cases of unjustifiable severity in punishments; but, upon the whole, the institution is immensely elevated above the old penitentiaries.

The whole establishment, from the gate to the sewer, is a specimen of neatness. The unremitted industry, the entire subordination and subdued feeling of the convicts, has probably no parallel among an equal number of criminals. In their solitary cells they spend the night, with no other book but the Bible, and at sunrise they proceed, in military order, under the eye of the

turnkeys, in solid columns, with the lock march, to their workshops; thence, in the same order, at the hour of breakfast, to the common hall, where they partake of their wholesome and frugal meal in silence. Not even a whisper is heard; though the silence is such that a whisper might be heard through the whole apartment. The convicts are seated, in single file, at narrow tables, with their backs towards the center, so that there can be no interchange of signs. If one has more food than he wants, he raises his left hand; and if another has less, he raises his right hand, and the waiter changes it. When they have done eating, at the ringing of a little bell, of the softest sound, they rise from the table, form the solid columns, and return, under the eye of the turnkeys, to the workshops. From one end of the shops to the other, it is the testimony of many witnesses, that they have passed more than three hundred convicts, without seeing one leave his work, or turn his head to gaze at them. There is the

most perfect attention to business from morning till night, interrupted only by the time necessary to dine, and never by the fact that the whole body of prisoners have done their tasks, and the time is now their own, and they can do as they please. At the close of the day, a little before sunset, the work is all laid aside at once, and the convicts return, in military order, to the solitary cells, where they partake of the frugal meal, which they were permitted to take from the kitchen, where it was furnished for them as they returned from the shops. After supper, they can, if they choose, read Scripture undisturbed and then reflect in silence on the errors of their lives. They must not disturb their fellow prisoners by even a whisper.

SOURCE: From a letter by Lewis Dwight, founder of the Boston Prison Discipline Society, written shortly after the full implementation of the "silent system" at Auburn in 1823; cited by Harry Elmer Barnes, *The Story of Punishment: A Record of Man's Inhumanity to Man* (Montclair, N.J.: Patterson Smith, 1972), pp. 136–137.

their corruption of one another and to reduce any opportunities for the hatching of plots for insurrection, escape, or riot. Furthermore, all prisoners were totally separated from the outside world; communication with relatives and friends was forbidden.[15]

The attractiveness of the silent system was primarily due to its economic advantages. Small inside cells were cheaper to construct. Also, industrial production within a setting of large congregate work areas was far greater and more efficient than the limited output possible under the Pennsylvania plan of handicraft construction in separate confinement. The hard and unremitting labor, perpetual silence, and unquestioning obedience were maintained by severe corporal punishments such as flogging, the "douche," and the "water cure." Flogging was considered the most effective method of gaining compliance, and was generally done with a rawhide whip or a "cat" made of wire strands. The "douche" involved the continuous dumping of frigid water from a great height onto the body of the prisoner. The "water cure" was of several varieties. At times it consisted of a strong fine stream of water turned onto sensitive parts of the prisoner's body; on other occasions, water came only one drop at a time onto the prisoner's head, the process sometimes lasting for days. These were common punishments for breaking the silence rule. The technique of talking out of the side of one's mouth — often depicted in the gangster movies of the 1930s and 1940s — had its origin in "silent" prisons, where it was a means of getting around the silence rules.

Prison stripes and the **lock-step** were also features of prison life devised at Auburn. Striped uniforms served to degrade convicts and to make them conspicuous should they escape. The lock-step, which was originated for the purpose of making supervision easier, was a bizarre marching formation. Prisoners were required to line up behind one another, with their hands on the shoulders or under the arms of the person in front. The line then moved rapidly toward its destination as the prisoners shuffled their feet in unison, without lifting them from the ground with their eyes focused on the guard.

Prisoners marching in lock-step at Joliet Penitentiary, Illinois, in 1900

Another feature of Auburn was the "prison-within-a-prison," or "hole," which was an area where prisoners were put into total isolation for violation of some institutional rule.

Prison Industries

The Auburn model became the major pattern of prison administration for the rest of the nineteenth century. Sing Sing Prison in New York followed the Auburn plan in 1825, and more than 30 other states built similar institutions in the years that followed. However, the rule of absolute silence was soon relaxed, for conditions within most penitentiaries made it impractical. Not only had most of the institutions become overcrowded, but more importantly, the Industrial Revolution had arrived and factory workshop production had been introduced to exploit cheap inmate labor and to make the penitentiaries self-sustaining. Production became the paramount goal of prisons, and the necessity for communication within the industrial shops served to make the perpetual silence rule counterproductive.[16]

Contract labor, the piece-price system, the lease system, and the state account and state use systems of prison industry

Contract labor and the **piece-price system** were the earliest forms of prison industry. Under the contract system, the labor of the inmates was leased to an outside contractor, who furnished the machinery and raw materials and supervised the work. The only responsibility of the prison administration under such an arrangement was to guard the convicts. The piece-price system was a variation on this. Under this plan, the contractor supplied the raw material and received the finished product, paying the prison a specified amount for each unit produced. Under both plans the prisoners were invariably exploited, overworked, and otherwise abused. Contractors often shortchanged convicts in their work tallies, and prison officials were known to force inmates to work long hours, under deplorable conditions, and for little or no pay. Recalling his experiences at Michigan's Ionia Reformatory in 1889, an inmate at Illinois State Penitentiary wrote some four decades later:

> During my stay at this time there was a great deal of fighting, especially in the Cigar Shop, owing to the fact that the boys were continuously stealing cigars from each other to complete the task set them by the Contractors, as it was almost impossible to do what they demanded. In the Shoe Shop things were about the same, and a friend of mine, Tiny Prince, tried to cut off his finger in full view of all of us. Another man on the Shoe Contract took a hatchet and cut off his thumb because he was unable to do his task.

Here I will make a confession I have never made in my life before. The first finger of my left hand is gone. I have always let people think it got cut off accidentally in a machine. Well, it didn't. I cut it off myself like these other men did, in order to cripple myself so I could escape for a little while from the hell of that contract labor at Ionia. I did it by bracing a knife blade against my finger and pounding it with my shoe. That was how bad some of us hated the contract system.[17]

Even more vicious was the **lease system,** under which contractors assumed complete control over the prisoners, including their maintenance and discipline. Convicts were taken from the institutions and employed in agriculture, quarrying, bridge and road construction, mining, and in turpentine camps or sugar cane plantations. The forced labor resembled slavery, and prisoners received little, if any compensation for their work.[18]

Alternatives to the contract labor practices were the **state account** and **state use systems.** Under the state account plan, inmate production was directed and supervised by prison officials, the manufactured goods were sold on the open market, and the convicts received a small share of the profits. The state use plan produced articles in prison that were subsequently used in state-supported institutions and bureaus. Related to these was the public works system of prison labor, under which inmates were employed in the construction and repair of public streets, highways, and structures. The well-known Sing Sing Prison, for example, from which came such terms as

Warden T. M. Osborne and jailers in a cell block at Sing Sing, 1915

the "big house" and "up the river,"* was constructed by a team of 100 inmates from Auburn under the public works system.[19]

Most nineteenth-century prisons also included farming as a form of prison labor. As a separate form of the state use philosophy, prison agriculture was viewed as a necessary part of institutional procedure. The raising of crops and vegetables was a means of hard inmate labor, while at the same time it reduced the costs of inmate maintenance.

The Reformatory Era

From the institutional backwater of the mid-nineteenth century emerged a *treatment* philosophy of corrections. This was an ideology that viewed many forms of offense behavior as manifestations of various social "pathologies," psychological "maladies," and inherited "predispositions" that could be "corrected" by some form of therapeutic or rehabilitative intervention. This new treatment ideology led to the **reformatory era** in American corrections, which endured from 1870 through 1910. The influences that led to the reformatory idea came from numerous theorists and practitioners in many parts of the world, but the movement was affected most directly by the work of Captain Alexander Maconochie in Australia and Sir Walter Crofton in Ireland.

In 1840, Captain **Alexander Maconochie**, a geographer with England's Royal Navy, was placed in charge of Norfolk Island, a penal colony for habitual felons located 1,000 miles off the coast of Australia. Conditions were so bad at Norfolk that it has been said that "men who were reprieved wept with sorrow that they had to go on living, and those doomed to die fell on their knees and thanked God for the release that was to be theirs."[20] Maconochie eliminated the brutality of the system and implemented a correctional scheme that rested on five postulates:

The reformatory era in American corrections

Alexander Maconochie

1. Sentences should not be for a period of time, but for the performance of a determined and specified quantity of labor; in brief, time sentences should be abolished, and task sentences substituted;
2. The quantity of labor a prisoner must perform should be expressed in a number of "marks" which he must earn, by improvement of conduct, frugality of living, and habits of industry, before he can be released;
3. While in prison he should earn everything he receives; all sustenance and indulgences should be added to his debt of marks;
4. When qualified by discipline to do so he should work in association with a small number of other prisoners, forming a group of six or seven, and the whole group should be answerable for the conduct and labor of each member of it;
5. In the final stage, a prisoner, while still obliged to earn his daily tally of marks, should be given a proprietary interest in his own labor and be subject to a less rigorous discipline in order to prepare him for release into society.[21]

The "mark system"

This "apparatus," as Captain Maconochie called it, removed the "flat" term of imprisonment, and replaced it with a **"mark system,"** whereby an

---

* Sing Sing, for a short time known as Ossining Correctional Facility, is located on the eastern shore of the Hudson River, 30 miles north of New York City.

inmate could earn early release by hard work and good behavior. But the scheme was not looked upon favorably by Maconochie's superiors. He was removed as administrator after only a brief time, his accomplishments were disclaimed, and the colony quickly returned to its former brutalizing routine.

But what had occurred at Norfolk Island had not gone unnoticed. Drawing upon Maconochie's notion that imprisonment could be used to prepare a convict for eventual return to the community, **Sir Walter Crofton** of Ireland implemented what he called his "indeterminate system." Also known as the "Irish system," it called for four distinct stages of treatment: solitary confinement at monotonous work for two years, followed by congregate labor under a marking system that regulated privileges and determined the date of discharge, then by an intermediate stage during which inmates were permitted to work on outside jobs, and finally conditional release under a **"ticket-of-leave."**[22] This ticket, which could be revoked if the convict failed to live up to the conditions of his temporary release, was the first attempt at what has come to be known as *parole*.

Maconochie's "mark system" and Crofton's "Irish system" were overwhelmingly endorsed at the American Prison Congress in 1870. The result was the opening of the first reformatory in the United States in 1876, at Elmira, New York, as an institution for youths and young adults serving their first term of imprisonment. Zebulon Brockway, the first superintendent of Elmira, listed the essentials of a successful reformatory system:

Sir Walter Crofton's "Irish system"

"Ticket-of-leave," the first attempt at parole

1. The material structural establishment itself. . . . The general plan and arrangements should be those of the Auburn System plan, modified and modernized; and 10 percent of the cells might well be constructed like those of the Pennsylvania System structures. The whole should be supplied with suitable modern sanitary appliances and with abundance of natural and artificial light.

2. Clothing — not degradingly distinctive but uniform, yet fitly representing the respective grades or standing of the prisoners. . . . Scrupulous cleanliness should be maintained and the prisoners appropriately groomed.

3. A liberal prison dietary designed to promote vigor. Deprivation of food, by a general regulation, is deprecated. . . .

4. All the modern appliances for scientific physical culture; a gymnasium completely equipped with baths and apparatus; and facilities for field athletics.

5. Facilities for manual training sufficient for about one-third of the population. . . . This special manual training covers, in addition to other exercises in other departments, mechanical and freehand drawing; cardboard constructive form work; clay modeling; cabinet making; clipping and filing; and iron molding.

6. Trade instruction based on the needs and capacities of individual prisoners.

7. A regimental military organization with a band of music, swords for officers and dummy guns for the rank and file of prisoners.

8. School of letters with a curriculum that reaches from an adaptation of the kindergarten . . . up to the usual high school course; and, in addition, special classes in college subjects. . . .

9. A well-selected library for circulation, consultation and, for occasional semi-social use.

10. A weekly institutional newspaper, in lieu of all outside newspapers, edited and printed by the prisoners under due censorship.
11. Recreating and diverting entertainments for the mass of the population, provided in the great auditorium; not any vaudeville or minstrel shows, but entertainments of such a class as the middle cultured people of a community would enjoy. . . .
12. Religious opportunities . . . adapted to the hereditary, habitual, and preferable denominational predilection of the individual prisoners.
13. Definitely planned, carefully directed, emotional occasions; not summoned, primarily, for either instruction, diversion, nor, specifically, for a common religious impression, but, figuratively, for a kind of irrigation.[23]

The program established at Elmira quickly spread to other states, but the reformatory movement as a whole proved to be a relative failure and disappointment for its advocates. Many of Brockway's principles were never put into effect; prison employees were too conditioned to the punishment ideology to support the new concepts; safe and secure custody continued to be regarded as the most important institutional activity; the reformatories quickly became overcrowded and staff shortages prevented the development of academic programs; and, hard-core offenders were housed in the new structures, thus turning them into the more typical penal environments.[24]

By 1910 the reformatory experiment was abandoned. Nevertheless, it left an important legacy for corrections in the years to come. The indeterminate sentence, conditional release, educational programs, vocational training, and the other rehabilitative ideals fostered by the reformatory became fully a part of the correctional ideology of later decades.

The Twentieth-Century Industrial Prison

By the early years of the twentieth century, the American prison system had evolved into a growing number of Sing Sing and Auburn-type institutions. With many reflecting the architecture of medieval dungeons and Gothic castles, they were fortresslike structures, operated on the principles of mass congregate incarceration and rigid discipline and securtiy. Their most distinctive feature, furthermore, was the use of inmate labor for the production of industrial goods for sale on the open market. This practice was widely encouraged not only because of the belief in hard labor as a correctional tool, but also because of the economics of creating a self-sustaining prison system.

Yet as the industrial prison was developing into a prudent financial operation, so too was opposition to inmate labor. Prison industries under the contract, piece-price, lease, and state account systems were seen as threats to free enterprise. With the formation of the American Federation of Labor in 1880, labor and its political lobbyists organized a formal attack on the industrial prison. The culmination of the assault came during the years of the Great Depression with the passage of numerous federal and state statutes.[25] Even before the economic strains of the depression occurred, the *Hawes-Cooper Act* of 1929 disallowed certain prison-made goods from being shipped to other states. Put into force on January 1, 1934, the act, in effect, barred these products from interstate commerce. At the same time, 33 states produced legislation that prohibited the sale of prison goods on the open market. The

Opposition to inmate labor

Ashurst-Sumners Act in 1935 banned transportation companies from accepting inmate products for shipment into states where the local laws prohibited their sale. And the *Walsh-Healy Act,* signed into law by President Franklin D. Roosevelt on October 14, 1940, excluded almost all prison-made products from interstate commerce.

Humanitarian concerns as well aided in the demise of the prison industrial complex. Contract labor systems were often no more than exploitation motivated by corruption and greed. Although the philosophy of the time supported the notion that offenders needed discipline and hard labor to teach them the lessons of deterrence and salvation, reformers nevertheless opposed the misuse of convict workers.

The abolition of contract labor was in many ways desirable, but there was little to take the place of free-market prison enterprise. State use and public works programs survived, but a majority of convicts were left idle. The reduction in institutional self-support and maintenance led to the gradual decay of prison structures and conditions. Eventually many state penitentiaries began shifting back to their original purposes of punishment and custody.

After the depression years, through World War II, and into the second half of the twentieth century, there was great turmoil within state prison systems. Referred to as the "period of transition" in American corrections,[26] it was a time when clinicians and reformers were introducing new treatment ideas against a backdrop of growing apathy and decaying institutions. Some segments of the public subscribed to the rehabilitative goals of correctional ideology; others wished prisons to be no more than secure places to house criminal offenders.

The 1960s and 1970s reflected even greater contrasts. Emphasis was placed more on the needs of individual prisoners, and many of the ideas generated during the reformatory era were put into place. Academic and vocational programs were established; social casework and psychiatric treatment approaches were designed and implemented; many prison facilities were expanded; special institutions were built and equipped for youthful offenders; more concern was demonstrated for the separation of hard-core from amateur criminals; a variety of changes made prison life somewhat more humane and productive; and, state and federal judges reflected a greater awareness of prisoners' rights by providing easier access to the courts for those seeking remedies against cruel and unusual punishment. At the same time, however, there was growing unrest within the nation's institutions. The majority of state penitentiaries were still the walled fortresses of decades past — solemn monuments to the ideas of nineteenth-century penology. Prison administrators were faced with the contradictions of "rehabilitation" within a context of mass overcrowding, personnel shortages, and demands for better security. It was also a time of militancy and violence within the nation's correctional institutions. The awareness of prisoners' rights under conditions that seemed to be getting worse instead of better led to riots — in the East, the Midwest, the South, and the far West.

Through the first half of the 1980s, the future of the American prison system still remained unclear. Diagnosticians, reformers, social scientists, and civil libertarians continued their efforts to make prisons more humane, structured for the rehabilitation of offenders. Yet the growing "law and order" approach toward offenders combined with perceptions of inefficiency within the criminal justice system served only to harden public attitudes toward the treatment of criminals.

The Federal Prison System

The most diversified prison system in the United States emerged at the federal level, and many of the reforms and rehabilitative measures that were introduced in state institutions following the depression years were modeled after federal practices. The federal system is also the most recently developed, although its roots date back to the signing of the Declaration of Independence.

Beginning in 1776 and for more than a century, all federal offenders were confined in state and territorial institutions. The criminal law of the

United States government was not particularly well developed at that time, and the few federal prosecutions there were were limited to the areas of counterfeiting, piracy and other crimes on the high seas, and felonies committed on Indian reservations. By the 1880s, however, the number of federal prisoners in state penitentiaries numbered over 1,000 with an additional 10,000 housed in county jails. This situation created pressure on federal authorities to take a more active role in the field of corrections.[27]

The first federal penitentiaries were authorized by Congress in 1891, and by 1905 institutions were opened in Atlanta, Georgia, and Leavenworth, Kansas. In 1919, McNeil Island in Puget Sound off the coast of Washington State was designated as a federal facility; in 1924, a women's reformatory was constructed at Alderson, West Virginia, and during the following year a men's reformatory was authorized at the military reservation at Chillicothe, Ohio.

As a result of the Mann Act (1910), which prohibited the transportation of women in foreign and interstate commerce for immoral purposes; the Harrison Act (1914), which regulated the distribution and sale of narcotics; the Volstead Act (1919), which prohibited the manufacture, transportation, and sale of alcoholic beverages; and the National Motor Vehicle Theft Act (1919), which controlled the interstate transportation of stolen vehicles, the number of persons convicted of federal crimes during the 1920s grew rapidly. The result was the creation of the **Federal Bureau of Prisons,** signed into law on May 14, 1930. It called for the "proper classification and segregation of Federal prisoners according to their character, the nature of the crimes they have committed, their mental condition, and such other factors as should be taken into consideration in providing an individualized system of discipline, care, and treatment."[28]

> **The creation of the Federal Bureau of Prisons**

Subsequently, the bureau established a graded system of institutions including maximum-security penitentiaries for the close custody of the most serious felons, medium-security facilities for the better rehabilitative prospects, reformatories for young and inexperienced offenders, minimum-security open camps for those requiring little custodial control, detention centers for those awaiting trial and disposition, and a variety of halfway houses and community treatment centers. Despite the many negative opinions about its fortresslike **Alcatraz Island Penitentiary** (see Exhibit 14.4), the bureau evolved into the acknowledged leader in American correctional practice. By the early 1980s, the bureau had grown to the point where it operated an integrated system of 50 adult and juvenile correctional facilities nationwide.[29]

> **Alcatraz Island Penitentiary**

Jails and Detention Centers

JAIL: An unbelievably filthy institution in which are confined men and women serving sentences for misdemeanors and crimes, and men and women not under sentence who are simply awaiting trial. . . . A melting pot in which the worst elements of the raw material in the criminal world are brought forth blended and turned out in absolute perfection.
— Joseph F. Fishman, inspector of prisons, United States government, 1923

The jail is for the poor, the street is for the rich.   — Noah Pope, jail inmate

A jail is not a prison. **Prisons** are correctional institutions maintained by the federal and state governments for the confinement of convicted felons. **Jails** are facilities of local authority for the temporary detention of defendants awaiting trial or disposition on federal or state charges, and of convicted

> **A jail is not a prison.**

EXHIBIT 14.4

The "Rock"
Alcatraz Island Penitentiary

Would it not be well to think of having a special prison for racketeers, kidnappers, and others guilty of predatory crimes. . . . It would be in a remote place — on an island. . . .
— Homer S. Cummings, U.S. attorney general, August 1, 1933

During the early years of the Great Depression, an unusual crime wave spread across the American Midwest. Banks that had weathered the Crash of 1929 were being robbed at the rate of two a day. The outlaws operated with flair and skill. Armed with machine guns, they recreated a frontier pattern of rapid assault followed by elusive retreat. The millions of citizens caught in the drab round of idleness and poverty that characterized the times responded to the criminal exploits with acceptance and admiration. The bandits became folk heroes and such names as John Dillinger, Frank Nash, Charles "Pretty Boy" Floyd, Bonnie Parker, Clyde Barrow, and George "Baby Face" Nelson quickly found their way into American folklore. But to the Federal Bureau of Investigation they were "public enemies"; to FBI Director J. Edgar Hoover they were "public rats," "the lowest dregs of society," "vermin in human form," "slime," "vermin spewed out of prison cells," and "scum from the boiling pot of the underworld."

The crime wave, the public enemies, and the vibrant rhetoric ushered in a new phase in twentieth-century penology. It was a thesis built on the belief that some criminals were so incorrigible that they should be repressed and disciplined with absolute inflexibility. As U.S. Attorney General Homer S. Cummings announced during a national radio address on October 12, 1933:

For some time I have desired to obtain a place of confinement to which could be sent our more dangerous, intractable criminals. You can appreciate, therefore, with what pleasure I make public the fact that such a place has been found. By negotiation with the War Department we have obtained the use of Alcatraz Prison, located on a precipitous island in San Francisco Bay, more than a mile from shore. The current is swift and escapes are practically impossible. Here may be isolated the criminals of the vicious and irredeemable type.

Originally named by eighteenth-century Spanish explorers Isla de los Alcatraces (Island of Pelicans) after the birds that then roosted there, Alcatraz has an area of 12 acres and rises steeply to 136 feet above the bay. In 1859 a U.S. military prison was built on the island, and in March 1934 it was taken over by the Federal Bureau of Prisons.

Alcatraz became the most repressive maximum security facility in the nation. Its six guard towers, equipped with .30-caliber carbines and high-powered rifles, could observe every square foot of the island. Barbed-wire barriers dotted the shorelines, and each entrance to the cell house had a three-door security system.

There were 600 one-man cells, built into three-tiered cell blocks. Measuring 8 feet by 4 feet, each cell contained a fold-up bunk hooked to the wall, fold-up table and chair, shelf, wash basin, toilet, and shaded ceiling light. Cell block D was the disciplinary barracks — solitary confinement for the more difficult offenders. It included "the Hole," a series of smaller cells with solid steel walls, floors, and doors; there were no furnishings and its inmates were locked into total darkness.

Each day at Alcatraz began at 6:30 A.M. with the clanging of a bell and a burst of electric light. Inmates had 20 minutes to dress and make their beds. At 6:50 the bell sounded again and the guard counted the prisoners. A third bell signaled that the count was "right" — all prisoners accounted for. No inmate could wear a watch. Bells told the time. Fourth bell. Breakfast. 7 A.M. Bell, workshops. Midmorning. Bell. Recess. Bell. Work. 11:30. Bell. Count. Bell. Noon. Bell. Lunch. 1 P.M. Bell. Work. Midafternoon. Bell. Recess. Bell. Work. 4:30. Bell. Count. Bell. Supper. Bell. Back to cell. Bell. Count. Bell. 6:30. Bell. Lockup. 9:30. Bell. Lights out!

Recreation was limited to an exercise yard and a small library. There was no commissary. Prisoners were allowed three packs of cigarettes each week. Newspapers and radio were denied in order to intensify the sense of isolation. One letter could be written each week and three could be received, but with severe restrictions: Correspondence could

Alcatraz Island Penitentiary

not be carried on with nonrelatives, and the content was restricted to family matters. One visit per month, from a family member or attorney, was permitted. Work was limited to cooking, cleaning, maintenance, and laundry. Security was rigid, with one guard for every three inmates.

With its policy of maximum security combined with minimum privileges and total isolation for America's "public enemies," Alcatraz did have a number of underworld aristocrats and spectacular felons: Arthur "Doc" Barker, last surviving son of Ma Barker's murderous brood;

kidnappers George "Machine Gun" Kelly, Albert Bates, and Harvey Bailey; train bandit and escape artist Roy Gardner; Alvin Karpis, the most evasive bank robber of the 1930s; and bootlegger, murderer, and syndicate boss Al "Scarface" Capone. But for the most part, comparatively few big-time gangsters ever went to Alcatraz; many of the island's inmates were actually first offenders.

From its earliest days, the concept behind Alcatraz had generated considerable opposition from social scientists and prison administrators. It was closed in

1963 because it was too costly to operate and too typical of the retributive justice that no longer had any stature in the federal prison system. Today, Alcatraz Island Penitentiary is part of the Golden Gate National Recreation Area, having shifted over a four-decade period from a dead-end prison to a public tourist attraction.

SOURCES: E. E. Kirkpatrick, *Voices from Alcatraz* (San Antonio: Naylor, 1947); James A. Johnston, *Alcatraz Island Prison* (New York: Scribner's, 1949); John Kobler, *Capone: The Life and World of Al Capone* (New York: G. P. Putnam's, 1971); L. L. Edge, *Run the Cat Roads* (New York: Dembner, 1981).

offenders sentenced to short-term imprisonment for minor crimes. Historically, however, jails have been somewhat more than this — they have been used for the holding of many types of outcasts, suspects, and offenders.

Gaols, Hulks, and the Origins of American Jails

The jail is the oldest institution for incarcerating offenders, dating to perhaps as early as fourth-century England, when Europe was under the rule of the Roman Empire. But little is known of the jails of that period other than that they were places for the accused and that there were separate quarters for women and men.

Even more wretched were the notorious hulks of eighteenth- and nineteenth-century England. In 1776, when transportation to the American colonies was terminated, a series of acts passed by George III ordered that the excess prison populations be placed in *hulks,* abandoned or unusable sailing vessels, generally of the man-of-war (warship) variety, permanently anchored in rivers and harbors throughout the British Isles. Within, they were similar to prisons and other places of detention. For security, inmates were often chained in irons. Like the gaols, hulks were overcrowded and dirty, and they quickly degenerated into human garbage dumps.

Gaols   The American jail as we know it today is more likely rooted in the twelfth century, when places of detention had to be provided for prisoners awaiting trial in the English courts. Known as **gaols** (pronounced "jails"), they were often only a single room or two in a castle, market house, or the gaoler's own dwelling. The inmates were known as *gaolbirds* (jailbirds), from the large cagelike cells often used to confine groups of the prisoners like "birds in a cage."

By the seventeenth century, England's jails had come to house both accused and convicted criminals. In addition to those awaiting trial, the jails held minor offenders sentenced to short-term imprisonment; debtors who were detained until they paid their creditors; vagrants, beggars, and other rogues and vagabonds who were considered public nuisances; and prisoners awaiting transportation to the colonies, execution, mutilation, branding, or placement in the stocks or pillory. The conditions were abominable, and inmates were abused and exploited by their keepers. Furthermore:

> Devoid of privacy and restrictions, its contaminated air heavy with the stench of unwashed bodies, human excrement, and the discharges of loathsome sores, the gaol bred the basest thoughts and the foulest deeds. The inmates made their own rules, and the weak and the innocent were exposed to the tyranny of the strong and the vicious. Prostitutes plied their trade with ease, often with the connivance and support of the gaolers, who thus sought to supplement their fees. Even virtuous women sold themselves to obtain food and clothing, and frequently the worst elements of the town used the gaol as they would a brothel. Thus, idleness, vice, perversion, profligacy, shameless exploitation, and ruthless cruelty were compounded in hotbeds of infection and cesspools of corruption. These were the common gaols of England.[30]

The English jail tradition came with the colonists to the New World. Jails first appeared in the Virginia colony in 1626, and were established in Pennsylvania as promulgated by the *Charter and Laws* of the Duke of York on September 25, 1676.

> Every town shall provide a pair of stocks for offenders, and a pound for the impounding of cattle; and prisons and pillories are likewise to be provided in these towns where the several courts of sessions are to be holden.

Thus, the conventional English detention jail was introduced into America. The city and county jails in the colonies, and later in the states, maintained the characteristics of their prototypes. They were overcrowded and poorly maintained, prisoners were exploited by their warders, and both suspected and convicted offenders were kept unsegregated within their walls. It was not until the conversion of Philadelphia's Walnut Street Jail into a prison in 1790 and the development of the penitentiary system during the following century that jails and prisons across America became distinct custodial entities.

Contemporary Jail Systems

Jails, in current terminology, include a variety of facilities and structures. Depending on the jurisdiction and locale, they might be called "lockups," workhouses, detention centers, stockades, or town, city, and county jails. Regardless of the particular nomenclature, however, all are institutions of temporary or short-term detention. Some are small and able to hold only a few inmates; others can house many hundreds, even thousands, of prisoners.

Jail systems vary widely in terms of organization and jurisdictional authority. There are county jails under the jurisdiction of the local sheriff, and

The "lockup"

city jails under the authority of the chief of police. These are often independent units and not tied to any jail "system" as such. In some large communities, there are complex arrangements of authority between several segments of local government. In New York City, for example, each police precinct has its own "lockup," which holds suspects during the questioning and booking stages of processing. In this phase, the jailing authority is in the hands of the precinct captain and the city police commissioner. Prisoners are then shifted to one of many city jails or detention centers. These are located in several of New York's five counties and are under the single authority of the New York City Department of Correction. There are also statewide systems, such as in Alaska, Connecticut, Delaware, Rhode Island, and Vermont, where all jails fall under the authority of a single state agency. Finally, there is the federal system, with its numerous detention centers throughout the United States under the jurisdiction of the Federal Bureau of Prisons.

The Jail Population

The jail is the portal of the criminal justice system. Except for defendants who are bailed while still in initial police custody, most arrestees are placed in jail, even if only for a short period of time.

A police precinct lockup

According to a recent survey conducted by the Department of Justice, as of June 30, 1983, there were 3,338 jails across the nation holding a total of 223,551 inmates.[31] Of this population, 93 percent were men and slightly less than 1 percent were juveniles. The survey data also reflect the traditional, twofold function of the jail: a place for the temporary detention of the unconvicted and a confinement facility where many convicted persons, primarily misdemeanants, serve out their sentences. As of June 30, 1983, some 47 percent of the jail inmates were unconvicted, either not arraigned or arraigned and awaiting trial. The balance were either sentenced offenders or convicted offenders awaiting sentence.

Noah Pope's contention, noted at the beginning of this section, that "jail is for the poor, the street is for the rich"[32] was borne out in a jail survey conducted in 1978, for which more data were made available. At that time, although the majority of the jail inmates were employed prior to their arrest, their earnings were minimal. The median annual income of the surveyed inmates was $3,714 — well below the poverty level. Including those with no sources of funds, some 46 percent had incomes below $3,000, 68 percent had incomes below $6,000, and 82 percent had incomes below $10,000. Only 13.5 percent of the jail inmates reported earnings of $10,000 or more annually. Combining these figures with the facts that most had less than a high school education and were under age 30, it becomes clear that the U.S. jail population includes primarily the poor who are both young and uneducated.[33]

"The jails are getting overcrowded again . . . we'd better legalize something else."

Jail Conditions

For more than two centuries, jails have been described as "cesspools of crime," the "ultimate ghetto," "dumping grounds," and "festering sores in the criminal justice system." And what was said about American jails in the 1780s still applies in the 1980s.[34] Most jails were, and are still, designed to allow for a minimum of staff while providing secure confinement for inmates. Most cells are large, cagelike rooms that hold significant numbers of prisoners at any given time. Although some structures have separate quarters for violent offenders, "drunk tanks" for the intoxicated, and alternative facilities for youthful offenders, many maintain all inmates in common quarters. The only exception here is the separation of sexes, which is almost universal.

Sanitary facilities are generally poor and degrading, especially in older jails. Common open toilets prevent personal privacy; the large percentage of drunks and others who spew vomit and urine on the toilets and floors make for unhealthy and unwholesome circumstances; poor plumbing often results in repeated breakdowns and clogged facilities; and the inadequate availability of showers and washrooms inhibits personal cleanliness. To add to these potential health problems, many jails fail to provide appropriate medical care or even a physical examination at admission, thus increasing the possibility of disease.

Jails are poorly staffed. Whatever personnel is available is often untrained. This can result in a lack of attention to inmate needs and mistreatment by other prisoners or guards. As one offender in the Manhattan House of Detention — the infamous New York "Tombs" — reported some years ago:

> As they took me into the Tombs I asked to see a doctor. "I have a bad case of piles [hemorrhoids]," I said. The guard tells me to turn around, and then he just kicks me in the ass.[35]

The jail has often been described as the "ultimate ghetto" of the American criminal justice system.

EXHIBIT 14.5

The Raymond Street Jail
Brooklyn's Gothic Horror

New York's Raymond Street Jail, officially known as King's County Jail, was for more than 80 years an example of desperately poor conditions in a fortresslike setting. Considered the worst jail ever built in New York, Raymond Street's damp, cavelike cells smelled of human waste and provided no fresh air, little light, and a haven for the vermin that lived side by side with the prisoners. Although these conditions are an extreme example of those in jails generally, they are found to some degree in many jails nationwide; warehousing replaces recreation and rehabilitation as the guiding philosophy of most jails.

Six o'clock in the morning,
the waiter comes around;
a slice of bread and butter,
that weighs a half a pound.

The coffee's like tobacco java,
the bread is hard and stale,
and that's the way they treat
   the boys
in Raymond Street's nice jail.

This short chorus, sung to the melody of the Irish patriotic and revolutionary song *The Wearing of the Green,* was periodically heard on the streets of Brooklyn, New York, during the early years of the twentieth century. But it never fully described the conditions that existed in the Raymond Street Jail for more than 80 years. Officially known as Kings County Jail, this grim "gothic castle" was erected in 1879 and immediately received criticism for the barbaric circumstances within its walls.

My first visit to Raymond Street Jail was in 1962. I was a newly assigned parole officer, directed to interview a parole violator who was being detained there. After I entered the jail's massive doors, my attention was immediately drawn to a series of brown paper bags, carefully hung from a ceiling pipe by long strands of wire. I later learned that the bags contained the guards' lunches, positioned like that to keep them out of the reach of vermin.

As I moved to the interior of the facility, being escorted to the cell where the parolee was quartered, I was reminded of the medieval dungeons of the old Robin Hood movies. The jail was like a gloomy cave; the air was stale, thick with the smell of urine, sweat, and excrement; and the walls and floors were damp. The environment seemed more suitable for snakes, bats, and owls than for people, for in competition with the inmates for space was a noticeable population of healthy mice, roaches, and other small creatures.

After being led through the bowels of Raymond Street Jail, I was finally brought to the person I had requested to see. His name was Bernard. "Benny," as the guards called him, was 33 years old. In 1951, he had been arrested for opening a garage door and stealing a bicycle. Charged with breaking and entering and grand larceny, he was convicted the following year, sentenced to 7½ to 15 years, and transferred to Sing Sing Prison. Not only had it been his first conviction, but his first arrest as well.

At Sing Sing, Benny had hardly been a model prisoner. His long record of minor disciplinary reports served to deny him early parole. After nine years he ultimately earned his release, but within three weeks he was cited for parole violation, arrested, and returned to Sing Sing. He was released after nine more months, again to be cited for violation of parole within only a short period. On this occasion he was arrested for disorderly conduct and resisting arrest — that was what I was there to find out about. As a parolee under the supervision of the state, Benny had had a parole violation warrant lodged against him, so he could not be bailed.

Benny's cell looked like a small cave. The door was of strap iron, which ran both up and down and side to side, leaving openings of only about one square inch, and providing little fresh air to breathe or light for seeing. We spoke in an adjacent room. He told me his story. I related that the parole board would make a decision after he was tried on the new charges.

Thirty-eight days later he entered a plea of guilty and was sentenced to time served. Then his violation report went to the parole board, and they ordered him to be released. I returned again to Raymond Street to remove the warrant on Benny. As we walked out together, he told me that he would rather die than go back to Raymond Street. He had spent 1,512 hours in that dark, cramped, slimy, smelly, vermin-infested jail with no fresh air, exercise, or recreation, "all for calling a cop a son of a bitch."

In 1963, Raymond Street Jail was ordered closed, bringing an end to what was considered the worst jail in New York's history. The following year the building was razed. The site is now occupied by Brooklyn Hospital. As for Benny, his fate was no better than that of the Raymond Street Jail. In 1966 he was arrested for petty theft. Unable to make bail, he was detained in the New York Tombs, where he hanged himself.

SOURCE: James A. Inciardi.

Rikers Island Penitentiary

Most jail inmates have little to do with their time. Some of the larger detention centers have libraries and exercise areas, but in the main, recreational and academic facilities are not provided. Furthermore, the concepts of "treatment" and "rehabilitation" are not part of the American jail tradition. New York City's Rikers Island Penitentiary is the largest penal colony in the nation. It consists of six facilities, each holding a separate population of offenders and a total daily inmate count of almost 8,000. Built in 1933 to house sentenced offenders, some of its cell blocks are the length of a football field. One of its facilities is a house of detention for men. With respect to both the detainees and the inmates serving time, an official at Rikers made the following comment about rehabilitative treatment:

> This is neither a country club, a finishing school, nor a psychiatric facility. It's a prison, and that's all. The people here won't and can't be rehabilitated. They just get three "squares" [meals] a day, a clean place to shit, and a chance to do their time . . . nothing more, but nothing less.[36]

Yet even this was an overstatement. A 1975 inquiry into the growing number of inmate suicides, disturbances, and grievances in the Rikers Island detention facility found an absence of privacy, widespread unsanitary surroundings, "hot" meals that were being served cold, and daily food expenditures of $1.38 per inmate.[37]

New York's famous City Prison, "The Tombs," was of Egyptian style and made of solid granite. This illustration of the building dates from 1850.

Conditions apparently remained much the same in the 1980s. After having served a 90-day sentence for possession of narcotics in 1984, a Brooklyn, New York, heroin user said about Rikers:

> You have to see it from the inside to really appreciate what doing time there is like. It's such a damn shit hole . . . bad food, crowded, gang fights, stabbings, killings, everybody having to smell each other's farts. . . . And worst of all, you spend most of the time just hanging around, waiting out your time, trying to put something over on the next guy, and nobody really caring one way or another.[38]

A correction officer at Rikers Island indicated in 1985:

> It's such a gem of a place. Everything and everyone there is scum — the inmates, most of the staff, the conditions, the administration. . . . Oh, they're trying to make changes. There's always some new directive coming down the line, but the whole system is so foregone that trying to do something is like trying to dig fly shit out of a sugar bowl with your feet.[39]

In fairness to those sheriffs, police chiefs, wardens, and other jail administrators who have made attempts to upgrade the personnel and conditions in the facilities under their authority, it must be stated here that not all detention centers across America suffer from all of these deficiencies. There are many jurisdictions that have provided the funds for the construction of modern, humane jails. Recent court decisions have legislated change in others. And too, there are independent jailers and wardens who have extended themselves to make the best of what otherwise might have been intolerable situations.

There have been numerous suggestions for improving local jails, including state inspection; the provision of social casework services; the development of educational, medical, and drug treatment programs; the use of volunteers to structure and supervise recreational services; and reorganization and cost sharing by state and local governments.[40] Some of these approaches are beginning to be implemented.

In the final analysis, most of the problems of jails stem from overcrowding. It was once estimated that the daily population of American jails could be reduced by 50 percent, without endangering the public, by making these changes:

1. the wider use of release on recognizance
2. preferential trial scheduling for those in jail
3. the use of citations rather than jail terms for more offenses
4. the creation of installment plans for those who go to jail because they cannot pay their fines
5. the use of work-release for jail inmates[41]

Although these alternatives have been implemented widely in many jurisdictions, apparently they have not been enough. The jail population of 223,551 inmates represented a 41 percent increase since 1978, up from 158,394.[42] Perhaps in years to come the jail population will begin to decline as a result of the newest detention innovation — the electronic jail (see Exhibit 14.6).

EXHIBIT 14.6

Electronic Jails:
The Future of Confinement?

Although many solutions to the problems associated with prison overcrowding have been implemented throughout the nation, none is likely to be more controversial than the suggestion that homes be turned into prisons.[a] This was the suggestion made in 1983 by district judge Jack Love, of Albuquerque, New Mexico.

This was not the first time this suggestion had been made in the United States in modern times, but it was the first time technology had been developed expressly for electronically monitoring people in their own homes. Following a brief experiment with home incarceration in New Mexico (or "house arrest" as it is known in some foreign countries), interest began to spread rapidly throughout the United States. Soon Pride, Inc., a nonprofit organization that handles probationers in West Palm Beach, Florida, was using electronic monitoring devices on some of its clients. At nearly the same time, Kentucky's general assembly considered a bill in 1984 that would permit this new type of incarceration for misdemeanors.[b] Kentucky, with one of the highest jail incarceration rates in the United States, found strong support for the idea among its citizens, and in May 1985, Kenton County's Fiscal Court started a home incarceration program using electronic monitoring. This was the first county in the United States to use the system as a way to reduce jail overcrowding. Now several states, including Oregon, Michigan, New York, Illinois,

Indiana, Oklahoma, Utah, California, and Virginia, are either using home incarceration with electronic monitoring or are seriously considering its use.

This idea is attractive to many in the criminal justice system and the general public. Electronic confinement is simple to understand and implement, requiring only that a monitor be strapped on a convicted person who has a telephone at home. With the aid of a small transmitter plugged into a 120 volt AC outlet, a signal can be sent over the telephone to a computer that records when the person comes and goes from home. By knowing a person's work and home schedule, correction officials can keep very close tabs on their behavior.[c]

Home incarceration is also economically attractive when compared to the cost of constructing new jails and prisons. In addition, some jurisdictions have devised a weekly rental fee by which those under house arrest pay according to their income to be on the system. In Covington, Kentucky, people who cannot pay may also be sentenced to home incarceration. Thus the system keeps offenders out of overcrowded jails and at home with their families—and allows them to stay in the workforce to pay taxes and contribute to their means of confinement.

Critics of home incarceration argue that it could lead to spreading the criminal justice net so that half of the population is in jail while the other half monitors

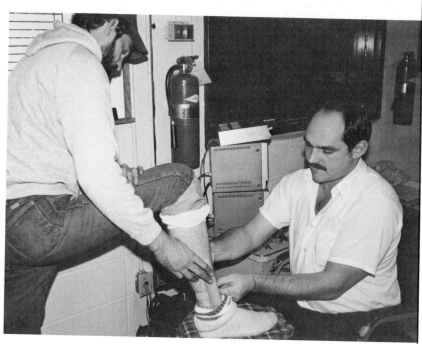

them. Others are concerned that turning homes into prisons with electronic monitoring devices is frighteningly similar to the tactics of Big Brother in George Orwell's novel *1984*. Indeed, the monitors can be altered so that monitoring personnel can hear and see what the detainee is doing. If electronic confinement were to grow out of control, it could radically alter our conceptions of freedom, privacy, and community.

The technology is available for tracking people and monitoring their behavior.[d] If fear, ignorance, and economic interests have contributed to explain our responses to criminals in the past, we can only hope that home incarceration is an exception to the rule.

An electronic monitoring device, attached to the detainee's leg, used in home incarceration

a. Richard A. Ball, and J. Robert Lilly, "Home Incarceration: An International Alternative to Total Incarceration," *International Journal of Comparative and Applied Criminal Justice* 2 (Winter 1985): 85–97.

b. Richard A. Ball and J. Robert Lilly, "Giving Birth to Electronic Shackles in Kentucky: A Case Study in Creating Law," paper presented at the annual meeting of the American Society of Criminology, Cincinnati, Ohio, 1984.

c. Richard A. Ball and J. Robert Lilly, "The Potential Use of Home Incarceration with Drunken Drivers," *Crime and Delinquency* (forthcoming).

d. Gary T. Marx, "I'll Be Watching You," *Dissent* (Winter 1985): 26–34; Gary T. Marx, "The New Surveillance," *Technology Review* 45 (May–June 1985): 43–48.

SOURCE: J. Robert Lilly and Richard A. Ball. Reprinted by permission of the authors.

Summary

Throughout history, the range of punishments has been vast. At one time, the death penalty was an almost universal form of punishment. Corporal punishment, particularly in the forms of whippings and torture, was also widespread. During the Age of Enlightenment a new ideology began to emerge in a reform movement spirited by the work of Montesquieu, Voltaire, Diderot, Beccaria, Bentham, Howard, Romilly, and Peel. Particularly influential was Beccaria's liberal doctrine of criminal law and procedure, which emphasized the principle of free will.

The American prison experience began during the eighteenth century in Philadelphia. The Walnut Street Jail was the nation's first penitentiary. Throughout the 1790s its structure and separate system characterized it as a model prison. This was subsequently rivaled by New York's silent system as it emerged at Auburn Prison in 1823.

The work of Alexander Maconochie in Australia and Sir Walter Crofton in Ireland influenced America's reformatory era. The first reformatory was at Elmira, New York, but by 1910 this correctional experiment was abandoned. As corrections moved from the mid-1800s into the early years of this century, the American prison system had evolved into an expanding hoard of maximum-security institutions. This period first witnessed active prison industries, then idle convict populations. Following the depression years, new treatment ideas were introduced against a backdrop of growing apathy and decaying institutions. The 1960s and 1970s saw even greater contrasts — an emphasis on individual prisoners' needs and rights in settings of unrest and mass overcrowding.

Key Terms

Alcatraz Island Penitentiary (525)
Alexander Maconochie (520)
Cesare Beccaria (511)
classical school of criminal law
   and criminology (511)
contract labor (518)
corporal punishment (506)
Federal Bureau of Prisons (525)

gaol (528)
jail (525)
lease system (519)
lock-step (517)
"mark system" (520)
piece-price system (518)
prison (525)
reformatory era (520)

separate system (514)
silent system (516)
Sir Walter Crofton (521)
state account system (519)
state use system (519)
"ticket-of-leave" (521)
Walnut Street Jail (513)

Questions for Discussion

1. How did the Industrial Revolution affect the evolution of prisons in the United States?
2. Could the purposes of Alcatraz, as stated by Attorney General Cummings, be achieved by some other penal policies?

3. Which of Beccaria's ideas are reflected in current conceptions of due process?
4. How might the alternative conceptions of bail reform affect the jail problem?

For Further Reading

Ball, Richard A., and J. Robert Lilly, "Home Incarceration: An International Alternative to Total Incarceration." *International Journal of Comparative and Applied Criminal Justice* 2 (Winter 1985): 85–97.

Goldfarb, Ronald. *Jails: The Ultimate Ghetto of the Criminal Justice System.* Garden City, N.Y.: Anchor, 1976.
McKelvey, Blake. *American Prisons: A History of Good Intentions.* Montclair, N.J.: Patterson Smith, 1977.

Notes

1. Harry Elmer Barnes, *The Story of Punishment: A Record of Man's Inhumanity to Man* (Montclair, N.J.: Patterson Smith, 1972).

2. The public execution endured into the twentieth century, even in the United States. The last such event, at least in this country, occurred with the hanging of 22-year-old Ramsey Bethea in Owensboro, Kentucky, on August 14, 1936. News dispatches stated that some 20,000 spectators witnessed the execution. See Negley K. Teeters, "Public Executions in Pennsylvania, 1682 to 1834," *Journal of the Lancaster County Historical Society* (Spring 1960): 117.

3. Luke Owen Pike, *A History of Crime in England*, vol. 2 (Montclair, N.J.: Patterson Smith, 1968), pp. 87–88.

4. See George Rusche and Otto Kirchheimer, *Punishment and Social Structure* (New York: Columbia University Press, 1939).

5. See Alice Morse Earle, *Curious Punishments of Bygone Days* (Montclair, N.J.: Patterson Smith, 1969).

6. For a discussion of the leading thinkers in the eighteenth-century reform movement, see Leon Radzinowicz, *Ideology and Crime* (New York: Columbia University Press, 1966).

7. George B. Vold, *Theoretical Criminology* (New York: Oxford University Press, 1958), pp. 14–18; Radzinowicz, *Ideology and Crime*, pp. 6–14.

8. Cited by Harry Elmer Barnes, *The Evolution of Penology in Pennsylvania* (Indianapolis: Bobbs-Merrill, 1927), p. 64.

9. Orlando F. Lewis, *The Development of American Prisons and Prison Customs, 1776–1845* (Albany: Prison Association of New York, 1922), pp. 26–28.

10. Harry Elmer Barnes, *The Repression of Crime* (New York: George H. Doran, 1926), p. 162.

11. Barnes, *Repression of Crime*.

12. See Negley K. Teeters and John D. Shearer, *The Prison at Philadelphia: Cherry Hill* (New York: Columbia University Press, 1957); William Crawford, *Report on the Penitentiaries of the United States* (Montclair, N.J.: Patterson Smith, 1969), pp. 1–2.

13. Gustave de Beaumont and Alexis de Tocqueville, *On the Penitentiary System in the United States and Its Application to France* (Carbondale: Southern Illinois University Press, 1964), p. 83.

14. Margaret Wilson, *The Crime of Punishment* (New York: Harcourt, Brace, 1931), pp. 219–220.

15. Lewis, *Development of American Prisons*, pp. 80–95.

16. See Blake McKelvey, *American Prisons: A History of Good Intentions* (Montclair, N.J.: Patterson Smith, 1977), 116–149.

17. Charles L. Clark and Earle Edward Eubank, *Lockstep and Corridor: Thirty-five Years of Prison Life* (Cincinnati: University of Cincinnati Press, 1927), p. 30.

18. See J. C. Powell, *The American Siberia* (Chicago: H. J. Smith, 1891).

19. McKelvey, *American Prisons*, p. 14.

20. John V. Barry, "Alexander Maconochie," *Journal of Criminal Law, Criminology, and Police Science* 47 (July-August 1956): 145–161.

21. John V. Barry, "Captain Alexander Maconochie," *The Victorian Historical Magazine* 27 (June 1957): 5.

22. McKelvey, *American Prisons*, p. 37.

23. Zebulon Brockway, *Fifty Years of Prison Service* (Montclair, N.J.: Patterson Smith, 1969), pp. 419–423.

24. Harry Elmer Barnes and Negley K. Teeters, *New Horizons in Criminology* (Englewood Cliffs, N.J.: Prentice-Hall, 1959), p. 428.

25. Frank Flynn, "The Federal Government and the Prison Labor Problem in the States," *The Social Science Review* 24 (March, June 1950): 19–40, 213–236.

26. Harry E. Allen and Clifford E. Simonsen, *Corrections in America* (New York: Macmillan, 1981), pp. 51–53.

27. Paul W. Tappan, *Crime, Justice, and Correction* (New York: McGraw-Hill, 1960), p. 619.

28. 18 *U.S. Code 907*, cited by Tappan, *Crime, Justice and Correction*, p. 620.

29. U.S. Department of Justice, Bureau of Justice Statistics, *Justice Agencies in the United States* (Washington, D.C.: U.S. Government Printing Office, 1980).

30. Robert G. Caldwell, *Criminology* (New York: Ronald Press, 1965), p. 495.

31. *The 1983 Jail Census*, Bureau of Justice Statistics Bulletin, November 1984.

32. Cited by Ronald Goldfarb, *Jails: The Ultimate Ghetto of the Criminal Justice System* (Garden City, N.Y.: Anchor, 1976), p. 3.

33. U.S. Department of Justice, Bureau of Justice Statistics, *Profile of Jail Inmates: Sociodemographic Findings from the 1978 Survey of Inmates of Local Jails* (Washington, D.C.: U.S. Government Printing Office, 1980).

34. See Goldfarb, *Jails;* George Ives, *A History of Penal Methods* (Montclair, N.J.: Patterson Smith, 1970); Joseph F. Fishman, *Crucibles of Crime: The Shocking Story of the American Jail* (Montclair, N.J.: Patterson Smith, 1969); *Newsweek*, August 18, 1980, pp. 74, 76.

35. Personal communication, June 1966.

36. Personal communication, August 1974.

37. *New York Times*, May 8, 1977, p. 6.

38. Personal communication, November 1984.

39. Personal communication, October 1985.

40. C. Ronald Huff, *The Baltimore Jail Project: An Experiment in the Coordination of Legal Services* (Washington, D.C.: American Bar Association, 1978); Benedict S. Alper, *Prisons Inside-Out: Alternatives in Correctional Reform* (Cambridge, Mass.: Ballinger, 1974); Hans Mattick, "The Contemporary Jails of the United States: An Unknown and Neglected Area of Justice," in *Handbook of Criminology*, ed. Daniel Glaser (Chicago: Rand McNally, 1974), pp. 777–848.

41. Richard A. McGee, "Our Sick Jails," *Federal Probation* 35 (March 1971): 4–5.

42. *The 1983 Jail Census*.

15

Penitentiaries, Prisons, and Other Correctional Institutions: A Look Inside the Inmate World

A prison is a house of care,
  a place where none can thrive;
A touchstone true to try a friend
  a grave for one alive.
Sometimes a place of right,
  sometimes a place of wrong.
Sometimes a place of rogues and thieves
  and honest men among.

—Inscription on Tolbooth Prison, Edinburgh, Scotland, 1817

Total institutions are places that furnish barriers to social interchange with the world at large.[1] In total institutions, large groups of persons live together, day and night, in a fixed area and under a tightly scheduled sequence of activities imposed by a central authority. In total institutions there are "subjects" and "managers." Subjects are the large class of individuals who have restricted contact with the world outside the walls. Managers, who are socially integrated into the outside world, are the small class that supervise the subjects. In total institutions the social distance between subjects and managers is great and communication is restricted. Each group conceives of the members of the other in terms of narrow, hostile stereotypes, resulting in the development of alternative social and cultural worlds that remain in continuous conflict with one another. In total institutions there is an elaborate system of formal rules intended to achieve the organization's official aim and to maintain the distance between subjects and managers. Correctional institutions are total institutions organized to protect the community against what are conceived to be intentional dangers to it. Correctional institutions include penitentiaries and reformatories, as well as a multitude of training schools, ranches, farms, and camps. Regardless of the designations, however, all are generally referred to as "jails" or "prisons"— two words that have quite distinct meanings for the professional, although probably not for the lay public.

Types of Prisons

It has been traditional in the United States to divide correctional institutions into three or more levels of custody, according to their construction and measures of custody and control.

Maximum-Security Prisons

The best-known prisons in the United States are likely Sing Sing, Attica, San Quentin, Leavenworth, Joliet, and the now-closed Alcatraz Island Penitentiary. These are **maximum-security** prisons. They are walled fortresses of concrete and steel and house the most serious, most aggreesive, and most incorrigible of offenders.

Maximum-security prisons hold the most aggressive and incorrigible offenders.

Most maximum-security prisons have a common design. Housing anywhere from many hundreds to several thousands of inmates, secure custody and control are the guiding principles. They are enclosed by massive concrete walls, sometimes as high as 30 feet, or by a series of double or triple perimeter fences topped with barbed wire and often electrically charged. Located along the outer-perimeter walls are well-protected guard towers, strategically placed to provide guards with open fields of fire and observation of prison yards and the outside areas surrounding the prison. New York's Green Haven Correctional Facility (called Green Haven Prison until 1970, when the state legislature's epidemic of wishful thinking decreed that "prisons" henceforth would be "correctional facilities," "guards" would be "correction officers," and "wardens" would be "superintendents") is typical, if not an exaggeration, of this high-control design. Built as a military prison during World War II and acquired by New York in 1949, Green Haven was designed to be an "escape-proof" institution. Its outer wall of reinforced concrete is 30 feet high, almost three feet thick, and is said to go 30 feet below the ground. Its twelve towers, reaching to 40 feet above the ground, are evenly positioned along the mile-long wall around the perimeter of the prison. Tower guards, armed with an array of shotguns, rifles, and tear gas guns, have a sweeping view of both sides of the wall. The towers also provide focused surveillance of "no man's land," a 100-foot-wide stretch of open space between the inner and outer walls of the prison across which nothing and no one can pass unobserved. No one has ever managed to escape over the wall at Green Haven.[2]

A characteristic feature of the maximum-security prison is the inside cell block. **Inside cells** are constructed back to back, with corridors running

New York's Green Haven Prison

Inside cells are a feature of maximum-security facilities.

High-polish bronze bars of the temporary holding cells greet visitors at "The Walls," the oldest unit in the Texas prison system. This 140-acre complex derives its name from its massive stone perimeter wall, completed in the 1850s.

Operating under the watchful eyes of the central administration offices — unlike the twenty or so other plantation-style institutions in East Texas — life at the Walls comes close to fitting the official "keep 'em busy, keep 'em safe" ideology. There is little violence, few accusations of brutality. Many inmates view assignment here as the next best thing to freedom. Others view it as a haven for "wimps" and "broke dicks" unable to cope with life in the "real" world of southern prisons.

A woman guard at the Oregon State Penitentiary

Most guards have nothing to do but stand guard; they do not use inmates productively any more than they themselves are used productively by prison managers. —Donald R. Cressey, 1965

tent, and self-confident. Moreover, as the eminent criminologist Robert G. Caldwell once described him:

> The guard . . . occupies a pivotal and strategic position in the prison. Upon his competence and loyalty, upon his resourcefulness and skill, depend both the safety of the prison and the spirit of the inmates. He is the first line of attack in case of escapes and the most immediate instrument for the proper handling of the prisoners. He must enforce the rules and regulations. He must be on the alert to detect signs of uprisings and to prevent the introduction of contraband into the prison and its circulation among the inmates. He must count the prisoners under his charge several times each day. He must patrol his gallery and periodically inspect the cells there. He must administer to the inmates' needs and make reports regarding their condition and behavior. During the day he must supervise the prisoners while they are at work and play and as they march from place to place. At night he must lock them in, see that the lights are out, and make certain that all is secure.[12]

Within such a setting, "a closed and timeless world where days, weeks, and months have little to distinguish them," [13] and faced with few means for carrying out his custodial duties, he must resort to a number of unconventional mechanisms for maintaining the internal order of the prison. Some become brutal and sadistic. A few become indispensable to the inmate black market, providing illegal services and contraband or serving as "mules" to carry drugs into the prison. And still others develop a system of punishments and rewards to exact inmate compliance. Most prison guards, however, use the spirit of compromise to accomplish their mission. They overlook a number of infractions. Inmates may be allowed to remain out of their cells without authorization, to pass letters back and forth, to cook food stolen from the prison kitchen, to smoke in unauthorized areas, or to possess trivial contraband items. In return, they are expected to refrain from violence, to perform their assigned tasks, and to be civil toward the guards.[14] As one officer from a New Jersey prison put it:

> You could write these guys up [prepare a disciplinary report] every day of the week. They're all into something. . . . But you have to bend some if you want to get your job done. . . .
> Yesterday I caught this one with a "dropper" [a wire device connected to the light socket, used for boiling water]. It's not allowed because you could electrocute yourself, but he's smart enough not to do that. I could have taken it and cited him, but I just told him to take it down. He'll remember. . . . Next time I tell him to get in line he'll move. . . . It's like the old saying, "grease the floor and you slide easier." [15]

Institutional Routines

When they locked me in my cell that very first day it suddenly hit me all at once. "This is it, asshole," I said to myself, "you're gonna die in this place." I was scared, lonely, and depressed and really feeling sorry for myself. But I didn't die. I became just like all the other shitheads, pissholes, and zombies — playing the games, doing the time, falling into the routine . . . sleep, eat, work, sleep, eat, work, "yes sir," "no sir," "I'm sorry sir," "I must have been mistaken sir. . . ."
— Former inmate, Leavenworth Penitentiary

At the beginning of 1985, there were almost 470,000 persons housed in federal and state correctional institutions in the fifty states, the District of Columbia, and the U.S. territories.[16] Most of the prison inmates were white (51 percent), and 46 percent were black, the balance including native Americans, Pacific islanders, Alaskan natives, and Asians.*

The institutions in which these prisoners were being held included the full range of correctional facilities—from maximum-security walled fortresses, to minimum-security cottages and reformatories, to "open" forestry camps and ranch settlements. The physical conditions of these institutions also covered the entire range of alternatives—from the best to the worst that the American prison system has to offer. Although many new correctional facilities have been built over the years, the majority are old and in varying stages of decay, with conditions that are often appalling.

Change is a rare occasion in prison—sameness is the law. The same people with the same crime, the same colored clothes with the same stripe, the same brown-suited guards with the same orders, the same food on the same day, the same disciplinary slips with the same verdicts (guilty), the same bed in the same cell night after night. —Anonymous prison inmate, 1971

Prison Facilities

In 1975, studies by the Federal Bureau of Prisons revealed that of the 577 state institution in operation at that time, 47 percent had been built since 1949, 32 percent dated from the period 1924–1948, and the balance had been put into operation during 1923 or earlier.[17] Furthermore, 24 of the prisons— most of them large maximum-security facilities—had been in

---

* This distribution varies from one prison to another. In federal prisons, which contain only about 10 percent of the nation's convict population, whites are preponderant; in some state prisons, blacks alone, or blacks and Hispanics as a joint group, are overwhelmingly in the majority.

continuous use since before 1874. By the 1980s, with proper upkeep of the institutions difficult, further deterioration had become apparent. Today, Clinton Prison in New York, Joliet in Illinois, and California's San Quentin are more than 125 years old; Michigan's Jackson Prison and Pennsylvania's Eastern Penitentiary have been housing inmates for a century and a half; and if current trends in prison use continue, both Auburn and Sing Sing in New York may celebrate their bicentennials as still-operational institutions. All of these ancient institutions have made improvements over the years: many of the original cell blocks have been abandoned or modernized, new structures have been added, and sanitary and other facilities have been renovated to reflect more humanitarian standards. Nevertheless, in their basic order and design, the more than 100 correctional institutions built during the nineteenth and early twentieth centuries, together with the many more built during the 1920s and 1930s, continue to operate as grim monuments to the penal philosophy of the unyielding past.

Based on 1984 U.S. General Accounting Office data, it can be estimated that there are some 140,000 cells and slightly more than 2,000 dormitories and cottages housing the nation's current population of 470,000 convicts.[18] The vast majority of these cells, upwards of 90 percent, are designed to house one inmate. Depending on the age and size of the prison, its level of security, the state in which it is located, and correctional policy, the size and physical arrangements of the cells vary. Most have toilets, sinks, and pull-down bunks or cots for sleeping. Chairs, tables or desks, lockers, and other amenities are standard in some institutions but not in others. The resources available within prisons also vary, and may include a library, television and game room, barber shop, gymnasium, athletic field, workshops, commissary, classrooms, chapel, and perhaps a theater. Prisons also have visiting rooms, but visits by family members are friends are rigidly controlled, and each institution has different policies regarding the number and length of the visits inmates are permitted.

Collectively, these resources combined with the buildings and open spaces that house them — everything, that is, within the prison walls — are referred to as the "physical plant" of the institution.

Classification

The prison experience generally begins with classification. In its broadest sense, **classification** is the process through which the educational, vocational, treatment, and custodial needs of the offender are determined. At least theoretically, it is the system by which a correctional agency reckons differential handling and care, and fits the treatment and security programs of the institution to the requirements of the individual.

The most rudimentary forms of correctional classification were seen when the practice developed of imprisoning people after conviction. Separating the guilty from the not-guilty was itself a process of classifying those accused of criminal behavior. The separation of debtors from criminals was a type of classification by legal status. Early forms of classification included the separation of men from women, youth from adults, and first offenders from habitual criminals. The reformatory movements of the late nineteenth century, the differentiation between maximum- versus medium- and minimum-security prisons, and the designation of Alcatraz as a superpenitentiary for the most incorrigible felons were all examples of rudimentary classification schemes. As correctional systems continued to evolve, the separation of the feebleminded, the tubercular, the venereally diseased, the sexually perverted, the drug addicted, and the aged and crippled from the general prison population or into special institutions was also based on the principle of classification.

Currently, classification goes beyond the mere separation of offenders on the basis of age, sex, custodial risk, or some other factor. It is now based on diagnostic evaluation and treatment planning, followed by placement into the recommended institutional programs or one type of correctional facility as opposed to another. The extent to which classification schemes are used tends to vary, however, not only from state to state but also among institutions within the same jurisdiction. Furthermore, there are numerous different organizational structures within which classification may occur: reception and orientation units, classification committees, and reception-diagnostic centers.

Reception and Orientation Units

Some jurisdictions have reception units or *classification clinics* within the institutions. Staffed by psychologists, social workers, or other professionals, these units carry out a series of diagnostic studies and make recommendations to institutional authorities regarding the custodial, medical, vocational, and treatment needs of each incoming inmate. Classification clinics also provide orientation programs for new prisoners, providing them with an overview of institutional life, routine, rules and regulations, and custodial and correctional expectations.

The reception unit system, although generally characterized by high-quality diagnostic work, suffers from a number of defects, which have called its usefulness into serious question.[19] Reports submitted to administrative authorities are often ignored and recommendations are not followed. There are rarely effective linkages between these units and the institutional program components; this results in discrepancies between classification and placement. Furthermore, these units generally lack research personnel, thus preventing follow-up to determine whether the classification process is actually working.

Classification Committees

Whereas the reception unit operates autonomously and its recommendations are not binding on institutional authorities, classification committees, composed of both professional and administrative personnel, have emerged as integrated classification systems. A classification committee may be chaired by the warden or deputy warden and may include institutional social workers, psychologists, chaplains, medical officers, teachers, vocational and recreational supervisors, and others. The decisions of the committee are binding on the administration, and any changes in the recommended program must be approved by the committee.[20]

The integrated committee is the most widely used classification system in contemporary institutions. Its important advantages are that it permits professional and administrative personnel to work together in determining inmate needs, and at the same time it allows each group of personnel to gain some understanding of the problems the other faces. Even this integrated committee structure, however, has problems. The classification committee processes *all* inmates, and time constraints restrict the discussion of issues and interactions with individual inmates. Since committee members drawn from administrative and program personnel have other duties and responsibil-

The integrated committee is widely used.

ities, their commitment to the classification process is segmented. These time and work load pressures combine to overroutinize the classification process, resulting in recommendations based overwhelmingly on case-file material, with little or no personal contact with the inmates under review. The National Advisory Commission on Criminal Justice Standards and Goals summarized the problem:

> The demands of time, program routine, and workload — and the institutionalization of personnel themselves — prevent effective performance of service. The result is that a large number of ranking institutional personnel are tied up in a process that accomplishes very little in effective programming for the individual inmate.[21]

Reception Centers

Reception center: A central receiving institution where all felony offenders sentenced to a term of imprisonment are committed for orientation and classification.

The **reception center,** or diagnostic center, is a central receiving institution where all felony offenders sentenced to a term of imprisonment are committed for orientation and classification. These specialized facilities are relatively new in American corrections, dating from the 1940s when they were established in New York, California, and the federal system.

The purpose of these centers is to delegate the responsibility of classification to the authority of the correctional system, rather than to a specific institution. This standardizes the classification process statewide and provides for a facility and staff whose sole functions are classification and orientation. Furthermore, as a mandate of the state's correctional policy, it makes the diagnostic recommendations binding on the authorities of the individual institutions to which the classified inmates are ultimately sent. At the reception center, the newly sentenced inmates are intensively studied for a period of 20 to perhaps 90 days. The ensuing recommendations include not only custodial and treatment plans, but also a statement as to which correctional facility the inmates should be sent.

Critical reactions to and opinions of the reception center concept have been mixed. In 1973, the National Advisory Commission on Criminal Justice Standards and Goals maintained that reception-diagnostic centers were obsolete and urged that they be discontinued, for the following reasons:

1. They started prisoners in the most confining, most severe, and most depressing part of the state's correctional system;
2. they employed an impersonal assembly-line procedure;
3. they produced excessive information that was often not used after custodial placement;
4. they kept prisoners for too long; and,
5. they drained the state's correctional system of its best professional personnel to staff the centers, therefore placing a premium on diagnosis rather than on treatment.[22]

In contrast, the American Correctional Association has strongly endorsed the reception-diagnostic center concept, urging that it be established in all fifty states.[23] The association feels that only by using this system can a good diagnosis and treatment plan be developed for each inmate. In its view, the system's pivotal position within a state's correctional structure helps to ensure that recommendations will be implemented at the receiving institutions.[24]

A nineteenth-century convict transportation cage

The Classification Process

Three factors generally combine to dictate how intensive the classification process will be: the personnel available; the inmate workload; and whether it occurs in a reception and orientation unit of a prison facility, through an integrated classification committee, or at a separate reception-diagnostic center. The procedure may range from a physical examination and a single interview to an extensive series of psychiatric and psychological tests, academic and vocational evaluations, orientation sessions, medical and dental checkups, and numerous personal interviews. Some classification programs may also include analyses of athletic abilities and recreational interests, and contacts with religious advisors.

Subsequent to the testing and interview period, reports are prepared by the various diagnosticians and incorporated into the inmate's case file. Summaries of the prisoner's social and family background, work history, criminal record, prior institutionalization (if any), current offense, and any other relevant background data are also included. A classification board or committee then evaluates the case, and makes its recommendations. This board can range from one counselor or social worker to as many as 15 persons, including teachers, psychologists, physicians, researchers, members of the administrative and custodial staffs, and persons from numerous other fields. This board then integrates and discusses the various data, and plans the inmate's correctional career. It also takes responsibility for *reclassification* should the inmate's needs or situation change.

Trends in Classification

During recent decades, there have been experiments with new approaches to classification. The *treatment team concept,* begun in 1958 at the Air Force

Retraining Facility at Amarillo, Texas, and used later at the Federal Correctional Institution at Ashland, Kentucky, provides for the continuity of care that is lacking in traditional classification and treatment planning. In the team approach, a counselor, a teacher, and a custodial officer become a "team" for each individual inmate. The team takes over the duties of classification, coordinates the treatment plan, and handles disciplinary problems. The same team may be assigned to all the inmates in a particular dormitory or cell block. Its major benefit has been to make academic and custodial staff more treatment-oriented, and counseling staff more sensitive to custodial issues by virtue of their collective involvement in the correctional and prison management processes.[25]

Contract classification has been reported by Warden A. J. Murphy of the Oklahoma State Penitentiary at McAlester as gaining favor among both inmates and staff.[26] The basic process is similar to other forms of classification, but the recommendations are in the form of a contract signed by the inmate and the chair of the classification committee. Inmate "needs" and requirements are spelled out in the document, and when these are achieved, such benefits as lower security, additional privileges, and recommendation for early parole are awarded.

With the exploding growth of technological literacy across the United States, *computerized classification* has recently been introduced as a diagnostic tool. First implemented by the U.S. Bureau of Prisons during the late 1960s,[27] and later refined in Kentucky, the process is based on a "screening" system designed to measure an inmate's potential for aggressive behavior, depression and suicidal tendencies; intellectual status, vocational skills and interests, socialization, criminal sophistication, and physical and mental health. As explained by its designers:

> The new system consists of a 20-minute, structured caseworker interview and a series of questionnaires, checklists, and interest and ability tests requiring approximately two hours for completion. These data are optically scanned and computer processed, and a detailed printout comparing each inmate with the total population of inmates that have been previously classified is provided.[28]

Prison Programs

Institutional programs include a variety of activities, all of which can have an impact, either directly or indirectly, on the rehabilitation of offenders and their successful reintegration into the free community. There are *treatment programs,* for example, which focus on behavioral change. These attempt to remove what are often considered "defects" in an inmate's socialization and psychological development and that are necessarily responsible for some lawbreaking behaviors. There are *academic and vocational programs,* which attempt to provide inmates with the skills necessary for adequate employment after release. There are *recreational programs,* which have humanitarian, medical, social-psychological, and custodial motives; they are structured to ease the pressures of confinement, making inmates more receptive to rehabilitation and less depressed, hostile, and asocial. There are *work programs,* which serve many of the humanitarian and rehabilitative needs of the offender, yet at the same time are related to the successful economic functioning of the institution. And finally, there are *medical and religious programs,* which also have implications for institutional management and reintegration of the offender into the community.

Health and Medical Services

The number and types of programs and services available to inmates vary widely by both jurisdiction and institution. Every prison has some form of health and medical program, although some are quite rudimentary. All reception centers have comprehensive medical facilities, with separate hospital units and some with well-equipped operating rooms. Similar facilities are also present in the larger prisons and reformatories.

Smaller institutions use a range of medical and health alternatives. Some have small hospital units with a full-time physician or nurse, and paraprofessionals that are on hand for the day-to-day care of minor illnesses and injuries. Where a physican is not a full-time member of the institutional staff, one is drawn from the local community to visit on a routine basis. All but the largest prisons and reception centers contract out for the services of dentists and opticians.

The importance of sufficient medical care for prison inmates cannot be overstated. Poor diet, alcoholism and drug abuse, and histories of inadequate medical attention are disproportionately evident among those entering the nation's correctional system. There is also the increasing problem of AIDS (acquired immune deficiency syndrome) (see Exhibit 15.2). Furthermore, the potential for the rapid spread of even the most minor illnesses is high within a population that is confined in such close quarters. The prison medical unit also has responsibility for monitoring sanitary conditions and inmate dietary needs, for these too are directly related to the well-being of the institution as a whole.

Religious Programs

The availability of spiritual services to prison inmates has a long history in American correction. Solitary meditation was the theoretical basis of reform in Philadelphia's Walnut Street Jail almost two centuries ago, and penitence was encouraged by frequent visits by missionaries and local clerics. Over the years, various Christian denominations and other religious organizations have devoted their time to the spiritual needs of inmates and many have provided ongoing programs of religious instruction.

Contemporary institutions generally retain Protestant, Roman Catholic, and sometimes Jewish chaplains, or at least a nondenominational cleric, on a full- or part-time basis, for religious counseling and worship services. In some small institutions where there are no educational programs or rehabilitative services, the prison chaplain represents the only available treatment component.

Opinions as to the usefulness of religious programs in prisons are decidedly mixed. They have been praised by wardens as anchors of law and order, by chaplains as powerful treatment forces, and by some inmates as sources of inspiration and cushions against despair. At the same time, however, they have been heavily criticized. Many prison administrators view religious counseling as useless and the cause of trouble and dissension; inasmuch as some jurisdictions prohibit the searching or questioning of the clergy, chaplains have also been viewed as potential security risks. Many chaplains

Prisoners and AIDS

Because of how the deadly virus is transmitted (by sexual activity and through contaminated blood products), acquired immune deficiency syndrome, or AIDS, has become a special problem in contemporary prison settings. Homosexuals account for nearly three out of four men who contract AIDS, but they are not particularly associated with the types of crimes that result in a prison sentence. On the other hand, intravenous drug users *are*.

Some 30 percent of the nation's prison inmates have histories of intravenous heroin use; higher proportions occur in those parts of the country where heroin use is more widespread. The highest rates of heroin use appear to be in the Northeast and in Florida, a fact that seems to correlate with the incidence of AIDS in prisons. In the latter part of 1985, for example, although Colorado had not reported a single case of the disease within its system of more than 17,000 inmates, New York had 196 cases; New Jersey had 73; and Florida had 17, with 40 or more having early symptoms.

Although prison physicians are uncertain over how quickly the AIDS virus can be transmitted in a prison setting, whether through drug use or sexual activity, they believe that the incubation period is three to five years. This suggests that the extent of the problem will not be known for a number of years. Yet even one AIDS case in a prison presents a problem for both inmates and institutional physicians and officials. To date, inmates who are "known" AIDS victims are routinely segregated in isolation or special units of prison hospitals. In either case, they quickly become the pariahs of the prison system. As for the rest, a health administrator at Sing Sing recently commented:

We have been trying to educate both our prisoners and employees about AIDS and how one gets it, but I think many people here are afraid they have done things that would make them candidates to contract the virus.

SOURCES: *Prisoners and Drugs,* Bureau of Justice Statistics Bulletin, March 1983; *New York Times,* August 11, 1985, p. 22; *New York Times,* October 20, 1985, p. 51.

look on their own programs as dull and unrealistic, and given the remote locations of many correctional facilities the prison chaplaincy has become one of the positions least sought after by ministers. Inmates often consider the programs to be empty, insincere, stale, and platitudinous; as a result, few make use of them.[29] As one inmate expressed it: "If there is a God, he sure as hell was not on my side."[30] Many of these issues have become further complicated by the current conflicts within organized religion.[31] As more and more members of the clergy drift from the conservative pastures of orthodox theology and its uncompromising acceptance of tradition, the role of the prison chaplain has become a frustrating one. Recognizing the inequities of institutional life, many wish to act on behalf of inmates' legitimate interests. Yet the domination of correctional policies that see prisons as coercive environments have thwarted the hopes of numerous chaplains to serve as activist ministers of dissent.

Education Programs

Most Americans have confidence in education as a mechanism for upgrading skills and understanding, for shaping attitudes, and for promoting social adjustment. It is not surprising then that academic education and vocational training are regarded as the primary programs in correctional institutions.

In *academic education* programs, the emphasis is on the acquisition of basic knowledge and communicative skills. Most institutions have some sort of prison school, and in most state correctional systems education for inmates is a matter of legislative mandate. Courses of instruction vary from one institution to the next, ranging from literacy programs to high school equivalency studies to college level learning with degree-awarding curricula.[32]

Prison schools, however, are beset with numerous difficulties. Many institutions are short on classroom facilities and useful teaching aids; there is a lack of qualified instructors, which forces a reliance on rejects from the public school system and on inmate teachers, scores of whom are undereducated; many inmates lack motivation, which results in teachers being pressured to make the classes effortless and to complete false reports on inmate progress; and the realities of prison discipline and security often interfere with inmates' courses of instruction or curtail enrollments. And in addition to these issues there is another problem:

> The classes held in most institutions are conventional and relatively old fashioned, in contrast to the learning innovations available to students at all levels on the outside. Most prisoners have had little formal education and probably resisted whatever teaching they were exposed to. Material that bored them as children or as truant teenagers is not likely to hold them enthralled as adults. What these mature felons do not need are "Dick and Jane" readers or other textbooks designed for children. But because of the low priority and minimal funds assigned to education in most institutions, it is these useless texts that prisoners are offered, often by public schools that no longer use them. Small wonder that most prison programs are neither accredited nor enthusiastically supported by inmates. The surprising fact is that some educational services not only survive, but even contribute to inmate rehabilitation.[33]

Vocational training programs focus on preparing inmates for meaningful postrelease employment. Most of the larger institutions and many small ones have a number of such programs, including automobile repair and maintenance, welding, sheet metal work, carpentry and cabinet making, plumbing and electricity, and radio and television repair. As with academic programs, these too have some problems. Many prison shops are poorly equipped and lack the appropriate technical staff; in others the machinery and fittings have long since become outmoded; and in still a third group, the training is in fields where work is unavailable in the outside world. Furthermore, inmates acquiring skills in such areas as plumbing, electrical work, carpentry, and masonry are often barred upon release from joining unions because of their criminal records. Even more frustrating is the fact that some institutional programs continue to train inmates in spheres that have virtually no relevance to the job market.[34] One inmate remarked not long ago:

> I came in here a laborer and I will go out a laborer. They taught me how to make [license] tags, but where else can I go to make tags? I got news for you, baby. In six months you'll have me back makin' those tags.[35]

Despite the many difficulties, the profile of academic education and vocational training programs in contemporary corrections is not entirely bleak. The administrators of many institutions have encouraged community volunteers and local school districts to aid in tutoring the more motivated inmates; prison routines have been more flexible for those wishing to attend classes; federal funds have been allocated for the upgrading of many prison schools; self-taught programmed courses of instruction in elementary and secondary school subjects have become more available; and a growing number of prison systems are introducing college degree-granting programs. Furthermore, the need for more relevant vocational education has also been recognized. Numerous correctional facilities are upgrading prison shop equipment; others are implementing new programs in more timely fields such as graphic communications and computer operation and technology.

Prison Labor and Industry

Closely related to vocational training in correctional institutions are the prison work and industrial programs. At least in theory, these can provide numerous opportunities for inmates

- to earn wages while serving their terms
- to develop regular work habits
- to gain experience in machine operation, manufacturing, and other specialized skills
- to ease the boredom of institutional confinement

The print shop at the State Penitentiary of New Mexico at Santa Fe

Despite these praiseworthy possibilities, most prison work programs generally fail to provide most, if not all, of these opportunities. First, many penitentiaries and other correctional institutions have no such programs. Those that do are open to less than 25 percent of the prison population and they provide wages that are extremely low. During the mid-1970s, for example, work in prison industries paid from 4 cents to 85 cents per hour.[36] Little has changed since that time. The 1982 wages in New York State correctional facilities ranged from a low of 35 cents to a high of only $1.45 per day.[37] Second, the jobs made available to inmates are typically dull and irrelevant. The major industries include printing and the production of auto tags, road signs, brooms, clothing, and similar articles. Furthermore, many nonindustrial prison jobs are restricted to such meaningless tasks as cleaning, laundry, and other simple maintenance work.

There are many reasons for this situation. First, state use is the chief outlet for prison-made products. As noted in Chapter 14, this situation is the result of state and federal legislation that barred prison industrial production from competing with private enterprise. Second, prison industrial plants are costly to construct, equip, maintain, and keep up to date. And third, to house an inmate in a correctional institution is prohibitively expensive. In 1975, such costs ranged from $700 per inmate per year in Mississippi to $7,000 in Montana.[38] The double-digit inflation of the late 1970s through 1981 pushed the annual expenditures per inmate to $10,000 in some jurisdictions and to as much as $25,000 in others, with the national average set at $16,000 by 1984.[39] This rebounds on prison inmates in that their wages are kept low, with most of the profits going into state treasuries.

On the more optimistic side, not all states and institutions suffer equally from these problems. A number of prisons have modernized their industrial plants or constructed totally new ones in an effort to make inmate work more instructive, meaningful, and efficient. Florida's Union Correctional Institution, for example, has its own inmate-operated slaughterhouse and cement block plant. In Texas, where local laws do not prohibit the sale of its prisons' products in markets within the state, prison industries have moved into some highly technical areas and generate many millions of dollars each year.

Chief Justice Warren E. Burger has repeatedly argued, throughout the first half of the 1980s, that as an alternative to the present system prisons be changed from "warehouses" for criminals to "factories with fences":

> Most prison inmates, by definition, are maladjusted people. Place that person in a factory, whether it makes ballpoint pens, hosiery, cases for watches, parts of automobiles, lawn mowers, computers, or parts of other machinery; then pay that person some reasonable compensation, and charge something for room and board and keep, and we will have a better chance to release from prison a person able to secure gainful employment.[40]

The Chief Justice also noted, however, that achieving such a goal would require the conversion of prisons into places of education and training and into factories for production, and in the process, repealing laws that limit prison industry production, limiting any form of discrimination against prison products, and working to change the attitudes of organized labor and business leaders toward the use of prison inmates to produce goods or parts. Given the ever-changing economic scene of the mid 1980s, however, combined with the already highly competitive markets brought about by increasing foreign imports, it is questionable whether such drastic changes will actually be made.

Clinical Treatment Programs

Academic education and vocational training are often viewed as the primary rehabilitative tools a correctional institution has to offer. It is felt that if inmates can learn the necessary skills and training to secure and maintain gainful employment after release, then their need to return to careers in crime will be eliminated, or at least reduced. In this sense, academic and vocational programs can also be viewed as treatment programs, for correctional treatment has generally meant the explicit activities designed to alter or remove conditions operating on offenders which are responsible for their behavior.[41] In a more clinical sense, however, institutional treatment programs are those efforts specifically oriented towards helping inmates resolve those personal, emotional, and psychological problems that are related to their lawbreaking behavior.

Counseling, social casework, psychological and psychiatric services, and *group therapy* represent the core of clinical treatment programs in prisons. Counseling refers to the relationship between the counselor and the prisoner-client in which the counselor attempts to understand the prisoner-client's problems and to help him or her solve the problems by discussing them together, rather than by giving advice or admonition.[42] Social casework is a process of professional services that (1) develops the prisoner-client's case history, (2) deals with immediate problems involving personal and familial relationships, (3) explores long-range issues of social adjustment, and (4) provides supportive guidance for any anticipated plans or activities.[43] Psychological and psychiatric services provide more intensive diagnosis and treatment aimed at (1) discovering the underlying causes of individual maladjustments, (2) applying psychiatric techniques to effect improved behavior, and (3) providing consultation to other staff members.[44]

These three modes of treatment involve direct interaction between clini-

To put people behind walls and bars and do little or nothing to change them is to win a battle but lose a war. It is wrong. It is expensive. It is stupid. —Chief Justice Warren Burger, 1984

I would say there are two basic complaints by prisoners about prison. First: the monotony of prison routine. Second: the numerous ways you are made to feel you are finished as a man. —William R. Coons, 1971

Clinical treatment programs

cian and prisoner-patient on an individual, one-to-one basis. Treatment in a group setting includes one or more clinicians plus several prisoner-patients. Group treatment programs have been variously referred to as "group psychotherapy," "group therapy," "group guided interaction," "group counseling," and numerous other terms that are often used interchangeably. However, only two basic kinds of therapy are actually involved when the "group" label is used: group psychotherapy, which is individual therapy in a group setting; and "group" therapy in its truest sense, which is designed to change groups, not individuals.[45]

The more common of the two in the prison setting is "group" therapy. In terms of its underlying approach and philosophy:

> This treatment stratagem focuses on groups as the "patient." It assumes that specific persons exhibit unfavorable attitudes, self-images, and the like because of the associational network in which they are involved. Because the person's interactional associates are extremely meaningful to him, any attempt to change the person without altering those groups with which he associates is likely to fail. Accordingly, group therapy proceeds on the premise that entire groups of persons must be recruited into therapy groups and changed. In addition, it is argued that treatment in which an individual's close associates are

A Vietnam veterans' group therapy session at Washington State Prison: helping prisoners deal with delayed-stress syndrone

includes these directives: "Don't be nosy," "Don't put a guy on the spot," and "Keep off a man's back." There are no justifications for failing to comply with these rules.

2. *Keep out of quarrels or feuds with fellow inmates.* This is expressed in the directives, "Play it cool," "Do your own time."

3. *Don't exploit other inmates.* Concretely, this means, "Don't break your word," "Don't steal from the cons," "Don't welsh on debts," and "Be right."

4. *Don't weaken; withstand frustration or threat without complaint.* This is expressed in such directives as, "Don't cop out" (cry guilty), "Don't suck around," "Be tough," and "Be a man."

5. *Don't give respect or prestige to the custodians or to the world for which they stand.* Concretely, this is expressed by "Don't be a sucker," and "Be sharp." [81]

Although the inmate code is violated regularly, most prisoners adhere to its major directives. But they do so not because it represents a "code of honor," but for other, more serious considerations — the very same reasons why professional thieves follow the underworld code:

> Honor among thieves? Well — yes and no. You do have some old pros who might talk about honor, but they're so well heeled and well connected that they can afford to be honorable. But for most people, it's a question of "do unto others" — you play by the rules because you may need a favor someday, or because the guy you skip on, or the guy you

rap to the cops about — you never know where he'll turn up. Maybe he's got something on you, or maybe he ends up as your cell-mate, or he says bad things about you — you can't tell how these things could turn out.[82]

The Sources and Functions of the Inmate Social System

The deprivation model

There is little consensus as to how the inmate subculture evolves behind prison walls. One explanation for it has been the *deprivation model;* that is, upon entering prison, inmates are faced with major social and psychological problems resulting from the loss of freedom, status, possessions, dignity, autonomy, security, and personal and sexual relationships. The inmate subculture emerges through prisoners' attempts to adapt to the deprivations imposed by incarceration. The subculture is a mechanism — through mutual cooperation — for reducing the pains of isolation, obtaining and sharing possessions, regaining dignity and status, developing meaningful relationships, and enjoying some personal security.[83]

The importation model

Another model, the *importation model,* views inmates as doing considerably more than simply responding to immediate, prison-specific problems. Cultural elements are "imported" into the prison from the outside world. Prisoners bring with them their values, norms, and attitudes, and these become the content of the inmate subculture.[84]

Both models seem to be crucial to the inmate subculture. On the one hand, the deprivation thesis serves to explain the emergence and persistence of the subculture. The pains and deprivations of imprisonment represent the stimulus for the formation of a social system that provides status, security, and solidarity. On the other, much of the richness of the subculture comes from the norms of the various underworlds and the experiences of inmates within other, outside criminal subcultures. (See Exhibit 15.3.)

Whether its sources are deprivation, importation, or both, the inmate social system functions not only for its members, but for the prison as a whole. More specifically, the inmate social system is a mechanism for controlling the behavior of prisoners. Without it, the custodial administration could not fully maintain order. Within most correctional institutions, both guards and inmates play specific roles. Guards provide inmates with illegitimate opportunities for obtaining needed goods and services. In return, inmates exercise control over their peers. Thus a level of accommodation develops, and each becomes captive and captor to the other. Guards play their roles of accommodation in order to avoid disruptions in prison order and routine. The inmate social system polices its members so that custodial accommodation will not be withdrawn.[85]

The Social Order of Women's Prisons

Most studies of prison communities and inmate social systems have been undertaken in men's institutions, and the findings are not fully applicable to women's prisons. Fewer women are convicted of crimes, and a greater proportion of these who are found guilty are placed on probation. Those who do receive terms of imprisonment have typically been convicted of homicide, check forgery, shoplifting, and violations of the narcotics laws, with few serving time for burglary and robbery. Women's prisons have an even greater proportion of minority group members than have institutions for men, but fewer women have had prior prison experiences. Finally, the cottage system is

EXHIBIT 15.3

Social Roles and Prison Argot

Prisoners' relationships to the inmate social system are reflected in the roles they take on in the institution and are reflected in the labels they are given by their peers. These labels are part of the general prison argot.

Like other groups that are devoted to specialized activities or purposes separate from those of the wider society, prisoners' communication patterns include the verbal camouflage and symbolism of argot. This artificial language expresses the specific behavioral orientations of the prison community. It emphasizes the attitudes and values of the inmate world while downgrading those of the prison administration and of "straight" society. Furthermore, it represents a means for expressing feelings not normally communicated by traditional language. Perhaps most importantly, prison argot is also a distinguishing system serving to designate the social roles played by the various members of the inmate world. In every prison community, for example, there are:

"Rats" and "squealers": Those who deny the primary value of inmate cohesion by betraying fellow prisoners.

"Center-men": Inmates who take on the attitudes and opinions of the official; they are named after the "center," which is the official seat of government of the institution.

"Gorillas": Prisoners who increase their material goods in prison by the use of force.

"Merchants": Inmates who refuse to share their scarce goods; they exploit the needs of their peers by selling instead of giving.

"Wolves," "punks," and "fags": Labels that refer to the various homosexual roles. *Wolves* play the masculine role in homosexual relations while *fags* play the female role and have given up their claims to masculinity; *punks* are masculine except during the sex act, taking on the feminine role out of fear ("punks are made but fags are born").

"Ball busters": Inmates who openly defy guards.

"Toughs" and "hipsters": Among those who frequently fight with other inmates, *toughs* are admired masculine types who fight both the weak and the strong, while *hipsters* are generally bullies.

"Real men": Those who endure the rigors of imprisonment with dignity.

"Square Johns": Inmates with only minimal, if any, involvement in systematic crime; they actively participate in prison treatment programs and identify with conventional norms.

"Right guys": Inmates who avoid contact with staff or treatment programs; they aspire to criminal vocations, and they fully ascribe to illegitimate standards.

"Politicians": Sophisticated criminals who use skill and wit to manipulate other inmates and staff.

"Outlaws": Criminals who confront their victims and always emphasize force.

"Dings": Inmates whose concerns and behaviors lack the consistency necessary to be assigned to one of the above roles.

In addition, guards are known as "hacks" and "screws," inmates who submit to hard work are "suckers," and the place where prisoners talk about the world of crime and penitentiary life is called the "yard." There are hundreds more.

Although most, if not all, of these social roles emerge within every correctional institution, the specific labels — "rats," "wolves," "dings" — vary from place to place and change over time.

SOURCES: Peter G. Garabedian, "Social Roles and Processes of Socialization in the Prison Community," *Social Problems* (Fall 1963): 139 – 152; James A. Inciardi, *Careers in Crime* (Chicago: Rand McNally, 1975), p. 56; Gresham M. Sykes, *The Society of Captives: A Study of a Maximum Security Prison* (New York: Atheneum, 1965), pp. 84 – 105.

the model more typically followed in women's prisons. Although few women inmates are confined in cells, the more "open" nature of the women's institution often requires more frequent security checks and, hence, close custodial supervision. All of these factors combine to affect the character of the social order of female correctional institutions.

In some ways, the social system in women's prisons is similar to that in the all-male penitentiary. There are social roles, argot, an inmate code, and accommodation between captive and captor. But in other ways the social system of women inmates is not as clearly defined, for it is a microsociety made up of four main groups.[86] There are the "squares" from conventional society, who are having their first experience with custodial life. Many of these are members of the middle class. They see themselves as respectable persons and view prisons as places to which only "criminals" go. Their convictions have generally been for embezzlement or situational homicides. There are the "professionals," who are career criminals and who view incarceration as an occupational hazard. Expert shoplifters fall into this group. They adopt a "cool" approach to prison life that involves taking maximum advantage of institutional amenities without endangering their chances for parole or early release. The third group, and perhaps the largest is made up of habitual criminals, who have had numerous experiences with prison life since their teenage years. Some are prostitutes who have assaulted and robbed their clients, many are thieves, and others are chronic hard drug users and sellers. For them, institutional life provides status and familial attachments. Finally, there is the custodial staff, which reflects the same values and attributes as in men's institutions.[87]

This microsociety seems to be changing. The growth of coeducational institutions over the last decade has served to remove many of the less serious offenders from the sex-segregated women's prisons. Furthermore, with the emancipation of women during the 1970s and early 1980s, more are engaging in "male-type" crimes, a larger number are being arrested and convicted, and a greater proportion are being sentenced to terms of imprisonment.[88]

The Effectiveness of Correctional Treatment

What works?   — Robert Martinson, 1974

With few and isolated exceptions, the rehabilitative efforts that have been reported so far have no appreciable effect on recidivism.   — Martinson, 1974

Is it treatment or our evaluation methods which have failed?
— Susan B. Long, 1979

The treatment approach to the management and control of criminal offenders was used in the United States early in its history, and by the middle of the twentieth century the idea of "changing the lawbreaker" had become a dominant force in correctional thinking. Most offenders were still "punished," but at the same time classification exercises assigned them to "programs" and "supervision" designed for their "reintegration" into law-abiding society.

Yet throughout the history of corrections in America there has also been a tendency among advocates of both the punishment and treatment philosophies to commit themselves to unproven techniques. Correctional and reform approaches were often founded on intuition and sentiment, rather than on an awareness of prior success or failure. This began to change, however, when the rehabilitative ideal emerged as a strong force in correctional thinking. Attempts were made not only to test the efficacy of existing programs, but also to design and evaluate experimental and innovative approaches. Research strategies were devised, outcome measures were specified, data were prudently collected and judiciously analyzed, and the findings were invariably circulated.

Throughout the 1950s and for the better part of the 1960s, a vast body of literature began to accumulate offering testimony on the successes and failures of therapeutic approaches. In the main, however, they projected a rather gloomy outlook for the rehabilitative ideal. One of the early disappointments, for example, was the well-known Cambridge-Somerville Youth Study. Begun in 1935 and often described as the most energetic experiment in the prevention of delinquency, it attempted to test the impact of intensive counseling on young male delinquents. For ten years the research continued, using an experimental group of youths who had access to counseling and a control group who did not. When the findings of the experience were published in 1951, it was learned that there were no significant differences between the outcomes of the treatment and the control groups. This led the evaluators to the natural conclusion that there was no evidence that counseling could make a positive contribution to the rehabilitation of delinquents.[89] In subsequent years, numerous researchers in Europe and the United States surveyed the field of correctional evaluation. Their conclusions were overwhelmingly negative — that the treatment of offenders had questionable results.[90] But still, the focus on treatment continued and the findings of the studies were ignored by all but the social-behavioral research communities.

The Cambridge-Somerville Youth Study

Prisons don't rehabilitate, they don't punish, they don't protect, so what the hell do they do?
— E. G. Brown, Jr., 1976

This apparent disregard of negative results could be readily understood. The research had typically been carried out by members of the academic community. The findings were prepared in a technical format, and, perhaps more importantly, they appeared almost exclusively in professional and scientific journals, government reports, academic symposia, and books published by university presses. For the general public and the nation's legislators and opinion makers, these sources of information were as remote as medieval parchments hidden in the cellars and garrets of some ancient moated castle. And too, many of the more pessimistic pronouncements were published during the enthusiasm of the 1960s — amidst the vigor of John F. Kennedy's "American Camelot" and the optimism of the Great Society years.

"Camelot" was a reference to the glamour of the Kennedy years. The White House image was that of the legendary court, complete with its handsome king and beautiful queen, and its shining knights, its feudal lords, and its courtiers and fools. At the same time, as a reflection of this, the nation seemed to be asserting itself in a new era under the protectorship of its revered charismatic leader.* Even more important, however, were the Great Society years of President Lyndon B. Johnson, who had declared in 1964: "We have

---

* It was not until after Kennedy's assassination in 1963 that the "Camelot" label was actually used. In an article entitled "For President Kennedy: An Epilogue," which appeared in *Life* magazine after Kennedy's death, author Theodore H. White reported Jacqueline Kennedy as saying:

At night, before we'd go to sleep, Jack liked to play some records; and the song he loved most came at the very end of this record. The lines he loved to hear were:

Don't let it be forgot
That once there was a spot,
For one brief shining moment
That was known as Camelot.

The lines were from "Camelot," a popular Broadway musical of the time about King Arthur and the knights of the Round Table. Mrs. Kennedy also said that "there'll never be another Camelot," and the image caught the imagination of a nation grief-stricken over the President's tragic death.

been called upon — are you listening? — to build a great society of the highest order, a society not just for today or tomorrow, but for three or four generations to come." The Great Society, the President explained, rested on abundant liberty for all, and it demanded an end to poverty and racial injustice.

But all of this began to fade quickly, followed by a series of events that turned the nation's attention to the effectiveness of correctional treatment.

The Martinson Report

We should not fool ourselves that the "hard rocks" will emerge from the cesspools of American prisons willing or able to conduct law-abiding lives.
— David Bazelon, federal judge, 1985

During the late 1960s and early 1970s, the Great Society image began to tarnish. The programs to abolish poverty and racial injustice had not lived up to their expectations. There were riots, many were angered over American involvement in Vietnam, and crime rates were increasing at a rapid pace. Furthermore, there was growing opposition to the many Supreme Court decisions that some claimed, and others denied, were "handcuffing police" and "coddling criminals." During much of this period, researchers in New York had been undertaking a massive evaluation of prior efforts at correctional intervention.

The idea for the research went back to early 1966, when the New York State Governor's Special Committee on Criminal Offenders decided to commission a study to determine what methods, if any, held the greatest promise for the rehabilitation of convicted offenders. The findings of the study were to be used to guide program development in the state's criminal justice system. The project was carried out by researchers at the New York State Office of Crime Control Planning, and for years they analyzed the literature on hundreds of correctional efforts published between 1945 and 1967.

The findings of the project were put together in a massive volume that was published in 1975.[91] Prior to the appearance of the in-depth report, an article by one of the researchers, Robert Martinson, was published in *The Public Interest* entitled "What Works? — Questions and Answers About Prison Reform."[92] In it he reviewed the purpose and scope of the New York study and implied that with few and isolated exceptions, *nothing works!*

"What works?"

There was little that was really new in Martinson's article. In 1966, Professor Walter C. Bailey of the City University of New York had published the findings of a survey of 100 evaluations of correctional treatment programs with the final judgment that "evidence supporting the efficacy of correctional treatment is slight, inconsistent, and of questionable reliability.[93] The following year, Roger Hood in England completed a similar review which concluded that the different ways of treating offenders lead to results that are not very encouraging.[94] And in 1971, James Robison and Gerald Smith's analysis of correctional treatment in California asked the questions: "Will the clients act differently if we lock them up, or keep them locked up longer, or do something with them inside, or watch them more closely afterward, or cut them loose officially?" Their conclusion was a resounding "Probably not!"[95]

But the Martinson essay created a sensation, for it appeared in a visible publication and attracted popular media attention at a time when politicians and opinion makers were desperately searching for some response to the widespread public fear of street crime. Furthermore, as Harvard University's James Q. Wilson explained:

> Martinson did not discover that rehabilitation was of little value in dealing with crime so much as he administered a highly visible *coup de grace*. By bringing out into the open the long-standing scholarly skep-

ticism about most rehabilitation programs, he prepared the way for a revival of an interest in the deterrent, incapacitative, and retributive purposes of the criminal justice system.[96]

Martinson also created a sensation within the research and treatment communities—mostly negative. He was criticized for bias, major distortions of fact, and gross misrepresentation.[97] And for the most part, his critics were correct. Martinson had failed to include all types of treatment programs; he tended to ignore the effects of some treatment programs on some individuals; he generally concentrated on whether the particular treatment method was effective in *all* the studies in which it was tested; and he neglected to study the new federally funded treatment programs that had begun after 1967.

In all fairness to Martinson, though, his work cannot be overlooked. While he may have been guilty of overgeneralization, most correctional treatment programs *were* demonstrating little success, and indeed, many were *not* working. Furthermore, his essay had an impact in other ways. It pushed researchers and evaluators to sharpen their analytical tools for the measurement of success and failure. Yet simultaneously, it ushered in an "abolish treatment" era characterized by a "nothing works" philosophy.

The "nothing works" philosophy

The Value of Correctional Treatment

Going beyond the "what works" and "nothing works" rhetoric of the 1970s and early 1980s, questions still remain as to how effective correctional treatment really is. Probably no one actually knows.

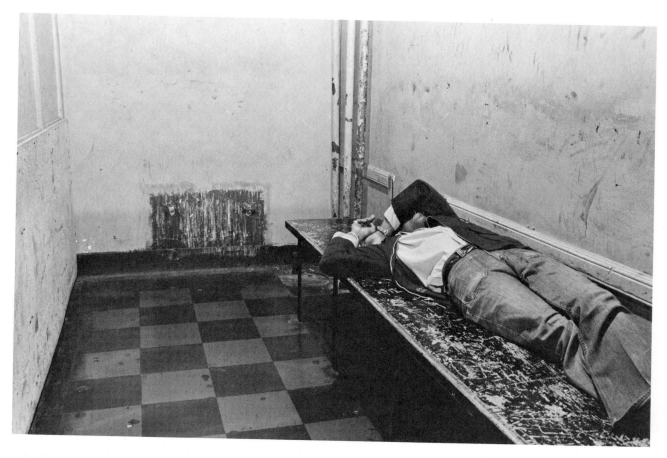

Several years ago, sociologist Susan B. Long began looking at the matter in another way by questioning whether it was "treatment" or "evaluation methods" that were failing.[98] This, furthermore, is a question that clinicians in the drug abuse field have been asking for years.[99]

In all likelihood, Long is more correct in her question than Martinson and his critics were in their evaluations. Most realistically, an overview of the various approaches to correctional treatment suggests that *everything is working and everything is failing*. By that it is meant that all correctional strategies — whether they be vocational training, academic education, penitence through prayer, recreation, group therapy, or whatever — seem to be working for somebody. However, correctional, therapeutic, and research technologies do not seem to be capable of accurately determining what rehabilitative approach is most effective for whom. Perhaps, then, the greatest problem is in the selection of offenders for delivery of particular correctional services. The poorest achievements may not be in the design of programs, but rather, in (1) the screening of offenders into treatment, (2) the focusing of the most appropriate programs upon those who need them most, (3) the failure to admit that there are persons who cannot be helped, and (4) the determination of when an offender has received the maximum benefits from any given technique.

Obstacles to Effective Correctional Treatment

Despite any advances in correctional techniques and program services, there are numerous obstacles that prevent most prisons from becoming effective agencies of rehabilitation:

1. Many institutions are old and antiquated.
2. Maximum-security prisons are, for the most part, too large or overcrowded.
3. Prison cells and many medium-security dormitories are unsuitable for human habitation.
4. Correctional institutions are typically understaffed and personnel often lack proper training.
5. The proper segregation of inmates is not widely enforced.
6. Inmate unemployment is common, and too many prisoners are assigned to what has become known as "idle company."
7. Institutional discipline is often too rigid.
8. Prison life tends to be monotonous and oppressive.
9. Parole policies are sometimes unfair or inefficient.
10. Comprehensive classification and program strategies are not universally available.
11. The prisonization and criminalization processes apparent in many correctional facilities bar many inmates from achieving any motivation for treatment.

By the mid-1980s, attempts at prison reform had accomplished little to remove these obstacles. Moreover, given the fiscal constraints on state and local governments, combined with sentencing philosophies that serve to increase the already overpopulated prisons, it would appear that the American penitentiary of the 1990s will resemble that of the 1970s and 1980s.

Summary

Total institutions such as prisons are places that furnish barriers to social interchange with the world at large. There are a variety of types of prisons differentiated by their level of security. Prisons are administratively structured like other large organizations. The physical facilities of correctional institutions vary from one place to another. Most prisons, however, are rather old, and many are deteriorated. As a result, upkeep tends to be difficult.

The prison experience begins with classification, a process through which the educational, vocational, treatment, and custodial needs of offenders are determined. Prison programs focus on health and medical services, religious needs, academic education and vocational training, labor and industry, recreation, and clinical treatment.

Aside from the loss of liberty itself, perhaps the most obvious deprivation associated with prison life is the loss of heterosexual activity. As a result, homosexual relationships and sexual assaults are not uncommon behind prison walls. The conjugal visit has been promoted as a means for reducing sexual frustrations in correctional institutions. Furthermore, coeducational facilities are being experimented with for the purpose of reducing both homosexuality and violence.

Every prison has an inmate social system, characterized by a specialized argot, social roles, and an inmate code. Exposure to the social system of the prison community begins almost immediately after the prisoner enters an institution. All new inmates become quickly aware of the norms and values that are shared by their fellow inmates. The internalization of these prison norms and values is known as prisonization.

Evaluative studies of correctional treatment programs have not been favorable to the notion of rehabilitation. Research findings during the 1960s and early 1970s resulted in a "nothing works" and "abolish treatment" era in corrections. By and large, however, every type of treatment program seems to work for someone. Research methodologies just cannot determine what treatment is most appropriate for whom.

Key Terms

classification (552)
conjugal visitation (568)
inmate code (572)
inside cells (543)
maximum security (542)

medium security (544)
minimum security (544)
open institutions (545)
prison community (571)
prisonization (571)

reception centers (554)
total institutions (542)

Questions for Discussion

1. In what ways is life in prison similar to that in the military or on the college campus?
2. What are the general characteristics of prison life?
3. Without making prisons into bordellos, what could be done to ease the sexual frustrations of prison life?
4. What steps should be taken to change prisons into environments more suitable for rehabilitation and reform?
5. What impact might the changing nature of female crime have on the social order of women's prisons?
6. What kinds of parallels are there between the prison community and certain groups in the outside world?

For Further Reading

Clemmer, Donald. *The Prison Community.* New York: Rinehart, 1958.

Giallombardo, Rose. *Society of Women: A Study of a Women's Prison.* New York: Wiley, 1966.

Goffman, Erving. *Asylums.* Garden City, N.Y.: Anchor, 1961.

Orland, Leonard. *Prisons: Houses of Darkness.* New York: Free Press, 1975.

Sherman, Michael, and Gordon Hawkins. *Imprisonment in America.* Chicago: University of Chicago Press, 1981.

Notes

1. Erving Goffman, *Asylums* (Garden City, N.Y.: Anchor, 1961), pp.1–8.

2. For a description of inmate life in Green Haven, see Susan Sheehan, *A Prison and a Prisoner* (Boston: Houghton Mifflin, 1978).

3. National Advisory Commission on Criminal Justice Standards and Goals, *Corrections* (Washington, D.C.: U.S. Government Printing Office, 1973), p. 345.

4. U.S. Department of Justice, Bureau of Justice Statistics, *Prisoners in 1984* (Washington, D.C.: U.S. Government Printing Office, 1985), p. 3.

5. Paul W. Tappan, *Crime, Justice, and Correction* (New York: McGraw-Hill, 1960), p. 653.

6. See Rose Giallombardo, *Society of Women: A Study of a Women's Prison* (New York: Wiley, 1966); Clarice Feinman, "Sex Role Stereotypes and Justice for Women," *Crime and Delinquency* 25 (January 1979): 87–94.

7. Blake McKelvey, *American Prisons: A History of Good Intentions* (Montclair, N.J.: Patterson Smith, 1977), pp. 150–196.

8. President's Commission on Law Enforcement and Administration of Justice, *Task Force Report: Corrections* (Washington, D.C.: U.S. Government Printing Office, 1967), p. 59.

9. *Manual of Correctional Standards* (College Park, Md.: American Correctional Association, 1966), p. 319.

10. Personal communication, October 29, 1972.

11. Eldridge Cleaver, *Soul on Ice* (New York: McGraw-Hill, 1968); George Jackson, *Soledad Brother: The Prison Letters of George Jackson* (New York: Bantam, 1970).

12. Robert G. Caldwell, *Criminology* (New York: Ronald Press, 1965), p. 576.

13. James B. Jacobs and Harold G. Retsky, "Prison Guard," *Urban Life* 4 (April 1974): 5–29.

14. Jacobs and Retsky, "Prison Guard"; Gresham M. Sykes, *The Society of Captives: A Study of a Maximum Security Prison* (New York: Atheneum, 1965), pp. 40–62; Edgar May, "Prison Guards in America: The Inside Story," *Corrections Magazine* 2 (December 1976): 3–5, 40, 45.

15. Personal communication, April, 1978.

16. U.S. Department of Justice, *Prisoners in 1984.*

17. U.S. Department of Justice, *Census of State Correctional Facilities, 1974* (Washington, D.C.: U.S. Government Printing Office, 1975).

18. U.S. General Accounting Office, *Federal, District of Columbia, and States Future Prison and Correctional Institution Populations and Capacities* (Washington, D.C.: General Accounting Office, February 27, 1984).

19. National Advisory Commission, *Corrections,* p. 206.

20. John Hepburn and Celesta A. Albonetti, "Team Classification in State Correctional Institutions: Its Association with Inmate and Staff Attitudes," *Criminal Justice and Behavior* 5 (March 1978): 63–73.

21. National Advisory Commission, *Corrections.*

22. National Advisory Commission, *Corrections,* p. 207.

23. American Correctional Association, *Handbook on Correctional Classification* (Cincinnati, Ohio: Anderson, 1978), p. 67.

24. For a bibliography of studies of reception centers, see American Correctional Association, *Handbook,* pp. 81–83.

25. Vernon Fox, *Introduction to Corrections* (Englewood Cliffs, N.J.: Prentice-Hall, 1977), pp. 209-210.

26. Cited by Sue Titus Reid, *Crime and Criminology* (New York: Holt, Rinehart and Winston, 1982), p. 546.

27. *United States Bureau of Prisons Policy Statement on the Case Management System* (Washington, D.C.: U.S. Bureau of Prisons, 1969).

28. Robert A. Baker et al., "A Computerized Screening System for Correctional Classification," *Criminal Justice and Behavior* 6 (September 1979): 270.

29. A. E. Kannewischer, "The Role of the Protestant Chaplain in Correctional Institutions," *American Journal of Correction* 19 (January–February 1957); *Final Report: Task Force Report on the Role of the Chaplain in New York City Correctional Institutions* (New York: New York City Correction Board, 1972).

30. Fox, *Introduction to Corrections,* p. 219.

31. Stuart D. Johnson, "The Correctional Chaplaincy: Sociological Perspectives in a Time of Rapid Change," *Canadian Journal of Criminology and Corrections* 14 (April 1972): 173–180.

32. See Benedict Alper, *Prisons Inside-Out* (Cambridge, Mass.: Ballinger, 1974), pp. 43–94.

33. Harry E. Allen and Clifford E. Simonsen, *Corrections in America* (New York: Macmillan, 1981), p. 392.

34. John Irwin, *Prisons in Turmoil* (Boston: Little Brown, 1980), p. 46; Gordon Hawkins, *The Prison: Policy and Practice* (Chicago: University of Chicago Press, 1976), pp. 116–118.

35. Neil M. Singer, "The Value of Inmate Power," *Journal of Research in Crime and Delinquency* (January 1976): 3–4.

36. Hawkins, *The Prison,* p. 119; see also *U.S. News & World Report,* June 20, 1977, p. 60.

37. Memorandum, State of New York, Department of Correctional Services, October 2, 1981.

38. Kenneth J. Lenihan, "The Financial Condition of Released Prisoners," *Crime and Delinquency* 21 (July 1975): 277.

39. *U.S. News & World Report,* January 4, 1982, p. 8; *USA Today,* June 21, 1984, p. 8A.

40. *New York Times,* December 17, 1981, p. B16. See also *Miami Herald,* June 25, 1984, p. 13A.

41. Don C. Gibbons, *Changing the Lawbreaker: The Treatment of Delinquents and Criminals* (Englewood Cliffs, N.J.: Prentice Hall, 1965), p. 136.

42. *Manual of Correctional Standards* (Washington, D.C.: American Correctional Association, 1969), p. 422.

43. *Manual of Correctional Standards,* p. 423

44. *Manual of Correctional Standards,* p. 423.

45. Gibbons, *Changing the Lawbreaker,* p. 150

46. Gibbons, *Changing the Lawbreaker,* p. 151.

47. Maxwell Jones, *The Therapeutic Community: A New Treatment Method in Psychiatry* (New York: Basic Books, 1953).

48. Lewis Yablonsky, *The Tunnel Back: Synanon* (New York: Macmillan, 1965).

49. For Clinton Prison, see Bruno M. Cormier, *The Watcher and the Watched* (Plattsburgh, N.Y.: Tundra, 1975); for the facility at Danbury; see Louis P. Carney, *Corrections: Treatment and Philosophy* (Englewood Cliffs, N.J.: Prentice-Hall, 1980), p. 203.

50. From Hans Toch, *Living in Prison: The Ecology of Survival* (New York: Free Press, 1977), p. 99.

51. Gustave de Beaumont and Alexis de Tocqueville, *On the Penitentiary System in the United States and Its Application in France* (Carbondale: Southern Illinois University Press, 1964), p. 173.

52. Leonard Orland, *Justice, Punishment, Treatment* (New York: Free Press, 1973), pp. 263–269.

53. Toch, *Living in Prison*, p. 100.

54. Allen and Simonsen, *Corrections in America*, pp. 57, 375

55. Allen and Simonsen, *Corrections in America*, pp. 57, 375.

56. Nick Pappas, *The Jail: Its Operation and Management* (Lompoc, Ca.: Federal Prison Industries, 1971), p. 23.

57. Toch, *Living in Prison*, p. 104.

58. Cited by Tom Wicker, *A Time to Die* (New York: Ballantine, 1975), p. 110.

59. Tappan, *Crime, Justice and Correction*, pp. 678–679.

60. Joseph Fishman, *Sex in Prison* (New York: National Library Press, 1934); Donald Clemmer, *The Prison Community* (New York: Rinehart, 1958), pp. 249–273; Sykes, *Society of Captives*; Peter C. Buffum, *Homosexuality in Prisons* (Washington, D.C.: U.S. Government Printing Office, 1972); John H. Gagnon and William Simon, "The Social Meaning of Prison Homosexuality," *Federal Probation* 32 (March 1968): 23–29.

61. Sykes, *Society of Captives*, pp. 95–99; Clemmer, *The Prison Community*; Leo Carroll, *Hacks, Blacks, and Cons: Race Relations in a Maximum Security Prison* (Lexington, Mass.: Heath, 1974).

62. Giallombardo, *Society of Women*; David Ward and Gene Kassebaum, *Women's Prisons* (Chicago: Aldine, 1965), pp. 80–101; Gagnon and Simon, "Social Meaning of Prison Homosexuality"; Reid, *Crime and Criminology*, pp. 588–599.

63. *Ibid.*

64. Gene Kassebaum, "Sex in Prison," *Psychology Today*, January 1972, p. 39.

65. "Sexual Assaults in Prison," from *Report on Sexual Assaults in a Prison System and Sheriffs Vans* (1968), cited in *Crime and Justice: The Criminal Under Restraint*, ed. Leon Radzinowicz and Marvin E. Wolfgang (New York: Basic Books, 1977), p. 223. See also Susan Brownmiller, *Against Our Will: Men, Women, and Rape* (New York: Simon and Schuster, 1975) p. 257–268; Ted Morgan, "Entombed," *The New York Times Magazine*, February 17, 1974, p. 19; Jared Stout, "Quaker Tells of Rape in D.C. Jail," *Washington Star-News*, August 25, 1973; David L. Aiken, "Ex-Sailor Charges Jail Rape, Stirs Up Storm," *The Advocate*, September 26, 1973, p. 5.

66. Daniel Lockwood, "Issues in Prison Sexual Violence," in Michael Braswell, Steven Dillingham, and Reid Montgomery (eds.), *Prison Violence in America* (Cincinnati, Oh.: Anderson, 1985), pp. 89–96; Buffum, *Homosexuality in Prisons*, pp. 2–3; Allen and Simonsen, *Corrections in America*, pp. 182–183.

67. Brownmiller, *Against Our Will*, p. 258.

68. Leo Carroll, "Humanitarian Reform and Biracial Sexual Assault in a Maximum Security Prison," *Urban Life* 5 (January 1977): 422.

69. Brownmiller, *Against Our Will*, p. 268.

70. Columbus B. Hopper, *Sex in Prison* (Baton Rouge: Louisiana State University Press, 1968); *Time*, August 18, 1967, p. 49; *Time*, August 9, 1968, p. 68.

71. Pauline Morris, *Prisoners and Their Families* (New York: Hart, 1965), p. 90.

72. Donald Johns, "Alternatives to Conjugal Visits," *Federal Probation* 35 (March 1971): 48.

73. Norman S. Hayner, "Attitudes Toward Conjugal Visits for Prisoners," *Federal Probation* 36 (March 1972): 43.

74. J. G. Ross, E. Heffernan, J. R. Sevick, and F. T. Johnson, *Assessment of Coeducational Corrections* (Washington, D.C.: U.S. Government Printing Office, 1978).

75. *Newsweek*, January 11, 1982, p. 66.

76. *Newsweek*, January 11, 1982, p. 66; *Corrections Digest*, September 18, 1974, p. 2.

77. Sykes, *Society of Captives*, p. 82.

78. Sykes, *Society of Captives*, p. 83.

79. Clemmer, *The Prison Community*, p. 299.

80. For a review and commentary of the various studies and points of view of prisonization, see Hawkins, *The Prison*, pp. 56–80.

81. Gresham M. Sykes and Sheldon L. Messenger, "The Inmate Social System, " in *Theoretical Studies in the Social Organization of the Prison* (New York: Social Science Research Council, 1960), pp. 6–8.

82. James A. Inciardi, *Careers in Crime* (Chicago: Rand McNally, 1975), p. 70.

83. Sykes, *Society of Captives*, pp. 81–83.

84. John Irwin and Donald R. Cressey, "Thieves, Convicts, and the Inmate Culture," *Social Problems* 10 (Fall 1962): 143.

85. Richard A. Cloward, "Social Control in the Prison," in *Theoretical Studies in the Social Organization of the Prison* (New York: Social Science Research Council, 1960), pp. 35–48.

86. Esther Heffernan, *Making It in Prison: The Square, the Cool and the Life* (New York: Wiley, 1972).

87. For descriptive material on women's prisons, see Kathryn W. Burkhart, *Women in Prison* (New York: Doubleday, 1973).

88. See Susan K. Datesman and Frank R. Scarpitti, eds. *Women, Crime, and Justice* (New York: Oxford University Press, 1980).

89. Edwin Powers and Helen Witmer, *An Experiment in the Prevention of Delinquency* (New York: Columbia University Press, 1951).

90. See, for example, Walter C. Bailey, "Correctional Outcome: An Evaluation of 100 Reports," *Journal of Criminal Law, Criminology, and Police Science* 57 (June 1966): 153–160; Roger Hood, "Research on the Effectiveness of Punishments and Treatments," in European Committee on Crime Problems, *Collected Studies in Criminological Research* (Strasbourg: Council of Europe, 1967).

91. Douglas Lipton, Robert Martinson, and Judith Wilks, *The Effectiveness of Correctional Treatment: A Survey of Treatment Evaluation Studies* (New York: Praeger, 1975).

92. Robert Martinson, "What Works?—Questions and Answers About Prison Reform," *The Public Interest* 35 (Spring 1974): 22–54.

93. Bailey, "Correctional Outcome."

94. Hood, "Research on the Effectiveness of Punishments and Treatments."

95. James Robison, "The Irrelevance of Correctional Programs," *Crime and Delinquency* 17 (January 1971): 67–80.

96. James Q. Wilson, "'What Works?' Revisited: New Findings on Criminal Rehabilitation," *The Public Interest* 61 (Fall 1980): 3–17.

97. See, for example, Carl B. Klockars, "The True Limits of the Effectiveness of Correctional Treatment," *The Prison Journal* 55 (Spring–Summer 1975): 53–64; Ted Palmer, "Martinson Revisited," *Journal of Research in Crime Delinquency* 12 (July 1975): 133–152.

98. Cited by Reid, *Crime and Criminology*, p. 558.

99. See, for example, James A. Inciardi, "The Evaluation of Addiction Treatment," *The Addiction Therapist* 1 (Autumn 1975): 1–5.

16

Prison Conditions and Inmate Rights

A convicted felon . . . has, as a consequence of his crime, not only forfeited his liberty, but all of his personal rights except those which the law in its humanity accords to him. He is for the time being the slave of the State.

—Ruffin v. Commonwealth, 1871

Prisoners are not stripped of their constitutional rights, including the right to due process, when the prison gate slams shut behind them.

—United States ex rel. Gereau v. Henderson, 1976

Inmate no. 3409, buried in a small cemetery on the grounds of New York's Greenhaven Prison in 1962, remains but a number in death as in life. His name was John Baldwin.

Until only recently, the opinion expressed in *Ruffin* v. *Commonwealth*,[1] which maintained that prisoners have no legal rights, accurately reflected the judicial attitude toward correctional affairs. The conditions of incarceration and every aspect of institutional life were left to the unregulated discretion of the prison administration. Since prisoners were "slaves" of the state, privileges were matters of custodial benevolence, which wardens and turnkeys could "giveth or taketh away" at any time and without explanation. The courts, furthermore, maintained a steadfast hands-off position regarding correctional matters. They unequivocally refused to consider inmate complaints regarding the fitness of prison environments, the abuse of administrative authority, the constitutional deprivations of penitentiary life, and the general conditions of incarceration.

The "hands-off" doctrine

Not until the 1960s did the ideology expressed in *United States ex rel. Gereau* v. *Henderson* begin to take noticeable form.[2] The **"hands-off" doctrine** began to lose its vitality, and during that decade and the years that followed, prisoners were given the right to be heard in court regarding such matters as the widespread violence that threatened their lives and security, the problems of overcrowding, the nature of disciplinary proceedings, the conditions affecting health and safety, the regulations governing visitation and correspondence, and the limitations on religious observance, education, work, and recreation.

Attica

When the prisoners' rights movement began some two decades ago, the higher courts across America became the instruments of change in correctional policy. But only a few years after the movement had begun in earnest, there was a major event and human tragedy that served to dramatize the problems with prisons and the character of inmate life. That event was the inmate uprising at New York's **Attica** Correctional Facility on September 9, 1971. And although the riot at Attica occurred well over a decade ago, it continues to be a case study of the typical conditions and situations that tend to bring about most prison unrest — even now in the 1980s!

Attica, 1971

Condemned by the Wickersham Commission for its maintenance of Auburn and Clinton prisons, New York State will have an answer to charges of inhuman penal conditions when the new Wyoming State Prison opens at Attica within the next few months with its full quota of 2,000 convicts. Said to be the last word in modern prison construction, the new unit in the State's penal system will do away with such traditions as convict bunks, mess hall lockstep, bull pens, and even locks and keys.

In their places will be beds with springs and mattresses, a cafeteria with food under glass, recreation rooms and an automatic signal system by which convicts will notify guards of their presence in their cells. Doors will be operated by compressed air, sunlight will stream into cells and every prisoner will have an individual radio.
— *New York Times,* August 2, 1931

Perhaps because of the depression economy, or perhaps for other reasons, when Attica Prison opened during the latter part of 1931 it was hardly the convict's paradise alluded to by the *New York Times.* None of the facilities mentioned in the *Times* article were present. In fact, the style of imprisonment at Attica was no different from that found at Auburn and Sing Sing prisons a hundred years before. Men were locked in their cells, harshly disciplined under a system of rigid rules and regulations; the food was poor and medical services were lacking; and programs for inmate diversion and rehabilitation were almost nonexistent. Forty years after its opening, however, the *Times* would be given a second opportunity to write about Attica Prison.

Conditions at Attica

For prisoners at Attica in late 1971, "correction" meant little more than daily degradation and humiliation. They were locked in cells for 14 to 16 hours each day; they worked for wages that averaged 30 cents a day at jobs with little or no vocational value; and they had to abide by hundreds of petty rules for which they could see no justification. In addition, their mail was read, their radio programs were screened in advance, their reading material was restricted, their movements outside their cells were tightly regulated, they were told when to turn lights out and when to wake up, their toilet needs had to be taken care of in the full view of patrolling officers, and their visits from family and friends took place through a mesh screen and were preceded and followed by strip searches probing every opening of their bodies.

In prison, inmates found deprivations worse than they had encountered on the street: meals were unappetizing and not up to nutritional standards. Clothing was old, ill-fitting, and inadequate. Most inmates could take showers only once a week. State-issued clothing, toilet articles, and other personal items had to be supplemented by purchases at a commissary where prices did not reflect the meager wages inmates were given to spend. To get along in the prison's economy, inmates resorted to "hustling."

The sources of inmate frustration and discontent did not end there. Medical care, while adequate to meet acute health needs, was dispensed in a callous, indifferent manner by doctors who feared and despised most of the convicts they treated; inmates were not protected from unwelcome homosexual advances; even the ticket to freedom for most inmates — parole — was burdened with inequities or at least the appearance of inequity.

For officers, "correction" meant a steady but monotonous 40-hour-a-week job, with a pension after 25 years' service. It meant maintaining custody and control over an inmate population that had increasing numbers of young blacks and Puerto Ricans from the urban ghettos who were unwilling to conform to the restrictions of prison life and ready to provoke confrontation —men whom the officers could not understand and were not trained to deal with. It meant keeping the inmates in line, seeing that everything ran smoothly, and enforcing the rules. It did not mean, for most officers, helping inmates to solve their problems or to become citizens capable of returning to society. For the correction officers, who were always outnumbered by inmates, there was a legitimate concern about security; but that concern was not served by policies that created frustration and tension far more dangerous than the security risks they were intended to avert.

Above all, for both inmates and officers, "correction" meant an atmosphere charged with racism. Racism was manifested in job assignments, discipline, self-segregation in the inmate mess halls, and in the daily interactions of inmate and officer and inmate and inmate. There was no escape within the walls from the growing mistrust between white middle America and the residents of urban ghettos. Indeed, at Attica racial polarity and mistrust were magnified by the constant reminder that the keepers were white and the kept were largely black or Spanish-speaking. The young black inmate tended to see the white officer as a symbol of a racist, oppressive system that put him behind bars. The officer, his perspective shaped by his experience on the job, knew blacks only as belligerent unrepentant criminals. The result was a mutual lack of respect that made communication all but impossible.[3]

> **For both inmates and officers at Attica, "correction" meant an atmosphere charged with racism.**

The Dewer Incident

The majority of Attica's inmates were housed in four main cell blocks: A, B, C, and D Blocks. Each block had three tiers of cells, and each group of about 40 cells was referred to as a "company."

The uprising against the conditions in Attica was not the result of a planned revolt inspired by a core of inmate revolutionaries. Rather, it was the product of building dissatisfactions and frustrations and was sparked by two related incidents.

Tensions had been growing between inmates and correction officers amidst a setting of rising expectations of improved conditions. But the anticipated changes in the prison environment seemed to be slow in coming. During the summer of 1971 there had been a number of organized protest efforts, but these accomplished no more than the disciplining of the organizers.

On September 8, an incident occurred that provoked the particular resentment and anger of inmates in two companies of Block A. A misunderstanding in the exercise yard led to an unusually intense confrontation between officers and inmates, during which a lieutenant was struck by inmate Leroy Dewer. The officers were forced to back down. That evening, however, Dewer and another inmate were removed from their cells and placed in solitary confinement. It was widely believed that the two were subsequently beaten by several of the guards.

The Revolt

On the following morning, September 9, officers found the men of 5-company, to which one of the inmates involved in the Dewer incident belonged, to

During riots at Attica Prison, prisoners raise their hands in clenched fists in a show of unity.

be especially belligerent and troublesome. Thus, they decided to return the members of 5-company to their cells immediately after breakfast without allowing them their usual time in the exercise yard. This decision came at a point when the inmates were lined up in one of the prison's many "tunnels."

Attica's four cell blocks form a square enclosing a large open area. Narrow corridors ["tunnels"] running from the middle of one block to the block opposite divide the central area into four exercise yards. The "tunnels" intersect at a junction that is called "Times Square," inside of which is a locking device that controls access to all of the cell blocks.

As the inmates of 5-company were being escorted through the "tunnels" back to their cells, several attacked the officer on duty. Others joined in, and after an initial outburst of violence, the A Block inmates regrouped and set upon the locked gate at Times Square. A defective weld, unknown to officers and inmates alike, broke and the gate gave way. This gave the prisoners access to Times Square and the keys that unlocked the gates to all other directions. From Times Square the inmates spread throughout the prison, attacking officers, taking hostages, and destroying property.

By afternoon, the New York state police had regained control of part of the prison, but most of the inmates assembled in one of the exercise yards along with their 39 hostages, whom the rioters threatened to kill if their demands were not met.

The "tunnels" to "Times Square"

The Negotiations

Initially, the rebellious inmates released a series of five demands, including complete amnesty and safe transportation to a "nonimperialistic" country. These, however, were quickly rejected and more serious negotiations began. New York's Commissioner of Corrections Russell Oswald ultimately came up with a 28-point proposal that represented major advances in penal reform. It included a general liberalization of prison life, combined with provisions for more adequate food, political and religious freedom, realistic rehabilitation programs, reductions in cell time, removal of most communications censorship, recruitment of black and Hispanic correction officers, better education and drug treatment programs, and more adequate legal assistance services. In

A helicopter flies over Attica Prison, dropping tear gas as police rush in to attack rioting prisoners.

addition, Oswald agreed to recommend the application of the New York state minimum wage law standards to all work done by inmates.

But for four days the negotiations dragged on because of one major stumbling block: *amnesty.* During the initial revolt, one of the correction officers, William Quinn, sustained serious skull injuries at the hands of the inmates. Two days later he died. Without total amnesty, the inmates realized there would be murder charges — which would subject any prisoner already serving a life sentence to a possible death sentence.

The Assault

Governor Nelson Rockefeller was asked to make a personal appearance at Attica to help with the negotiations and prevent a bloodbath, but he refused. Instead, he authorized Commissioner Oswald to end the rebellion by force if necessary.

On the morning of September 13, 1971, a local state police troop commander planned and led an assault to retake Attica Prison. Within fifteen minutes, the Attica uprising was over. However, the armed state troopers had killed 29 inmates and 10 of the officer hostages, wounding hundreds more. Ironically, it was the bloodiest one-day encounter between Americans since the Civil War.[4]

In Pursuit of Prisoners' Rights

The Attica revolt was a dramatic symbol of the enduring struggle that had been developing for almost a decade. Prior to the 1960s, it was a matter of law that offenders were deemed to have forfeited virtually all rights and to have retained only those expressly granted by statute or correctional authority. Thus, inhuman conditions and practices were permitted to develop and continue in many correctional systems, despite the Eighth Amendment's ban on cruel and unusual punishment. The courts, furthermore, generally refused to intervene in correctional matters. Their justifications were twofold:

> Judges felt that correctional administration was a technical matter to be left to experts rather than to courts, which were deemed ill-equipped to make appropriate evaluations. And, to the extent that courts believed the offenders' complaints involved privileges rather than rights, there was no special necessity to confront correctional practices, even when they infringed on basic notions of human rights and dignity protected for other groups by constitutional doctrine.[5]

The Writ of *Habeas Corpus*

Whenever an individual is being confined in an institution under state or federal authority, he or she is entitled to seek *habeas corpus* relief. This is guaranteed by Article I, Section 9 of the United States Constitution, which states: "The privilege of the Writ of *Habeas Corpus* shall not be suspended." *Habeas corpus* relief also has statutory bases, in the Federal Habeas Corpus Act as well as in state *habeas corpus* laws.

By applying for a writ of *habeas corpus,* the person seeking relief is challenging the lawfulness of his confinement. *Habeas corpus* is a Latin term

Habeas corpus: A writ that directs the person holding a prisoner to bring him or her before a judicial officer to determine the lawfulness of imprisonment.

that means "you should have the body." In practice, *habeas corpus* relief involves a writ issued by a court commanding the person who holds another in captivity to produce the prisoner in court so that the legality of the prisoner's confinement can be adjudicated.[6]

Traditionally, the writ was limited to contesting the legality of confinement itself. However, in *Coffin v. Reichard*,[7] decided in 1944, the Sixth Circuit U.S. Court of Appeals held that, in the Sixth Circuit, suits challenging the *conditions* of confinement could be brought under the Federal *habeas corpus* statute. The court reasoned that:

> A prisoner is entitled to the writ of *habeas corpus* when, though lawfully in custody, he is deprived of some right to which he is lawfully entitled even in his confinement, the deprivation of which serves to make his imprisonment more burdensome than the law allows or curtails his liberty to a greater extent than the law permits.

Despite this ruling, existing law required (and continues to require) that the inmates of state institutions exhaust all state judicial and administrative remedies before they apply for the federal writ of *habeas corpus*. Thus, most prisoners remained (and continue to remain) effectively barred from the most direct mechanism for challenging the conditions of their confinement.

Civil Rights and Prisoners' Rights

The civil rights movement of the late 1950s and early 1960s created a climate more conducive to a serious reexamination of the legal rights of prisoners. The specific vehicle that opened the federal courts to inmates confined in state institutions was **Section 1983** of the Civil Rights Act of 1871, which provides:

> Every person who, under color of any statute, ordinance, regulation, custom, or usage of any State or Territory subjects, or causes to be subjected, any citizen of the United States or other person within the jurisdiction thereof to the deprivation of any rights, privileges, or immunities secured by the Constitution and laws shall be liable to the party injured in an action at law, suit in equity or other proper proceeding for redress.

The Section 1983 suit was resurrected by *Monroe* v. *Pape*.

The long-dormant Section 1983 was resurrected in ***Monroe* v. *Pape*,**[8] decided by the Supreme Court in 1961 and holding that citizens could bring Section 1983 suits against state officials to the federal courts without first exhausting state judicial remedies. However, in *Preiser* v. *Rodriguez*,[9] the Court held that although a Section 1983 is a proper remedy to make a constitutional challenge to the *conditions* of prison life, it could not be used to challenge the *fact* and *length* of custody.

The major advantages of a Section 1983 suit, as opposed to a *habeas corpus* petition, are that a Section 1983 suit does not require that available state remedies be exhausted before the federal district courts will have jurisdiction, and that an award of money damages is possible. However, the remedy of release from imprisonment is not available under a Section 1983 suit. As the High Court stated in *Preiser* v. *Rodriguez*, only the writ of *habeas corpus* could secure such release.

Legal Services in Prison

The state and its officers may not abridge or impair petitioner's right to apply to a federal court for a writ of *habeas corpus.* —*Ex parte Hull*, 1941

In *ex parte Hull*,[10] a state prison regulation required that all legal documents in an inmate's court proceedings must be submitted to an institutional official for examination and censorship before they are filed with the court. The Supreme Court found this and similar prison regulations invalid, holding that whether a petition is properly drawn and what allegations it must contain were issues for the court, not the prison authorities, to decide.

Johnson v. Avery

In spite of the rule established by *Hull*, an inmate's right of access to the courts proved to be more theoretical than actual. In many prison systems, disciplinary actions for inmates pursuing legal remedies or wholesale confiscation of a prisoner's legal documents were quite common. Furthermore, court access was either curtailed or totally inhibited because most prison officials withheld from inmates any services related to their legal needs. In most instances, inmates seeking remedies were provided with no more than a few outdated law books and occasionally the services of a notary public. Since most prisoners were indigent and lacked the funds to secure the help of an attorney, the courts were essentially closed to them. Many correctional institutions had "jailhouse lawyers"—inmates who claimed legal expertise and who provided advice and counsel to their fellow prisoners, with or without compensation. Yet even this aid was severely restricted by prison officials, thus further denying inmates their basic constitutional right of access.

Johnson v. *Avery* in 1969 acknowledged and resolved a number of these problems.[11] The case involved the constitutionality of a Tennessee prison regulation which provided that

> no inmate will advise, assist or otherwise contract to aid another, either with or without a fee, to prepare writs or other legal matters. . . . Inmates are forbidden to set themselves up as practitioners for the purpose of promoting a business of writing writs.[12]

The petitioner in *Johnson* was a jailhouse lawyer serving a life sentence who had spent almost a year in solitary confinement for repeatedly violating the rule against writ writing.

In its analysis of the Tennessee rule, the Supreme Court addressed the fact that many prisoners are illiterate and are frequently unable to find legal help from sources beyond the prison walls. Thus, the justices held that unless the state could provide some reasonable alternative type of legal assistance to inmates seeking postconviction relief, a jailhouse lawyer must be permitted to aid inmates in filing *habeas corpus* petitions.

Although the decision in *Johnson* was a significant one, it failed to delineate many of the specifics of inmates' mechanisms for legal access. In the years that followed, the courts began to address this vagueness:

> *Younger* v. *Gilmore*,[13] 1971 The state must maintain an adequate number of law books in prison libraries and other legal materials sufficient enough to inform prisoners of what is legally relevant.

Wolff v. *McDonnell,*[14] 1974   Inmates have a right to the legal assistance of a jailhouse lawyer not only for seeking *habeas corpus* relief, but also for filing civil rights actions against prison officials.

Procunier v. *Martinez,*[15] 1974   Regulations that prohibit law students and legal paraprofessionals from entering prisons to assist attorneys in case investigations do not satisfy the requirements of *Johnson* v. *Avery.*

Bounds v. *Smith,*[16] 1977   Even when prison policy permits mutual legal assistance among inmates, officials are nevertheless obligated to establish either a legal services program or a law library that will meet the needs of the inmate population.

Jailhouse Lawyers

The prison regulations that forbade inmates from assisting or receiving counsel from fellow inmates in the preparation of legal documents was an outgrowth of several factors. Initially, the rule was a reflection of the general custodial attitude toward prison inmates. That is, the convict was a ward of the state who possessed no civil rights, and the privilege of obtaining legal help from other convicts was simply unthinkable. In addition, there were a number of security issues involved. "Writ-writers," as they were often called, were seen as potential troublemakers. Officials often felt that the jailhouse lawyer, in advising inmates of their legal rights, might create dissatisfactions within the prison population that could lead to belligerence and revolt. Furthermore, the phenomenon of inmates conferring about legal matters was interpreted by some as plotting against administrative authority. Finally, there was the fear that jailhouse lawyers would provide their clients with inferior representation and false hopes of success while they flooded the courts with spurious claims.

Most of these administrative and custodial concerns had some basis in fact, but in general, the problems that jailhouse lawyers caused in correctional institutions were more often ones of inconvenience rather than of discipline and security. Since *Johnson* v. *Avery* and numerous subsequent state and federal court decisions, the activities of jailhouse lawyers in many jurisdictions have been relatively unrestricted.

During the past few years, public and private agencies have begun to furnish grants to law schools for the development of legal aid programs for prisons and jails. But as Justice William O. Douglas pointed out in his concurring opinion in *Johnson,* such programs rest on a shifting law school population and often fail to meet the daily needs and demands of inmates. As a result, the jailhouse lawyer has become a significant figure in the developing prisoners' rights movement. Moreover, the courts have continued to recognize the right established by *Johnson* v. *Avery.* In 1984, for example, a Wisconsin prisoner was charged with the unauthorized practice of law for helping two of his fellow inmates draft postconviction motions. Not only was the charge dismissed on the ground that his activity was constitutionally protected, but in a subsequent proceeding a federal jury assessed $22,000 in damages against his jailers for malicious prosecution.[17]

Constitutional Rights and Civil Disabilities

Historically, persons convicted of serious crimes could lose much more than their liberty or their lives. Under the early English common law an offender, in addition to his sentence, was also "attaint." Under this status, he lost all of his civil rights and forfeited his property to the Crown. Furthermore, his entire family was declared corrupt, which made them unworthy to inherit his property. The U.S. Constitution forbids bills of attainder,[18] and similar provisions against the attainder or its effects are found in the constitutions and statutes of the states. Yet in spite of these, every state has enacted civil disability laws that affect convicted offenders. Depending on the jurisdiction, civil disabilities may include losses of the rights to vote, hold public office, sit on a jury, be bonded, collect insurance or pension benefits, sue, hold or inherit property, receive worker's compensation, make a will, marry and have children, or even remain married. The most severe disability is the loss of all civil rights, or "**civil death.**" Under current Idaho statutes, for example:

> **18-310. A sentence of imprisonment in a state prison for any time less than for life suspends all the civil rights of the person so sentenced, and forfeits all public offices and all private trusts, authority or power during such imprisonment.**
>
> **18-311. A person sentenced to imprisonment in the state prison for life is thereafter deemed civilly dead.**

Technically, a civil right is a right that belongs to a person by virtue of his or her citizenship.* Since civil rights include constitutional rights, it would seem that state statutes and provisions that place civil disabilities on convicted and imprisoned offenders would be in direct conflict with the Constitution. However, the Supreme Court has not interpreted these statutes as complete denials of prisoners' civil rights, but as restrictions and conditions of their expression. And with respect to many rights that have some direct bearing on the Constitution, the Court's position in recent years has been to remove a number of these restrictions.

Religion

The First Amendment of the Constitution provides that "Congress shall make no law respecting an establishment of religion, or prohibiting the free exercise thereof." Generally, or at least historically, freedom of religion was rarely a problem in correctional institutions. In fact, participation in religious instruction and worship services was always encouraged. Infringements on this right began only with the rise of minority religions and the demands of their members to have the same rights as those of conventional faiths.

The leading cases involving religious expression occurred with the growing influence of the Black Muslim movement within prisons during the 1960s. Issues such as the right to attend services, obtain literature, and wear religious medals were raised by the Black Muslims because, unlike Protestant or Catholic inmates, the Black Muslims had been denied the right to engage in such practices. The threshold question was the recognition of the Muslim faith as a religion. This was quickly answered by a federal court in 1962 with its decision in *Fulwood* v. *Clemmer*,[19] and in subsequent cases,[20] with the assertion that Black Muslims retain the same constitutional protection offered to members of other recognized religions. However, although these cases established the Black Muslims' right to hold religious services, the

Bills of attainder

"Civil death"

---

* Other than the right to vote and freedom from being subject to deportation, civil rights also apply, generally, to noncitizen residents of the United States.

courts have refused to extend that right in specific circumstances. In some institutions and at certain times, for instance, assemblages of Black Muslims were considered by custodial authorities to be revolutionary in character and to represent "clear and present dangers" to security. In several decisions, the courts ruled that although Black Muslims had the right to worship, their right to hold religious services could be withheld if they represented potential breaches of security.[21]

Cruz v. Beto

Other cases involving religious freedom in prisons dealt with inmate access to clergy, special diets, and the right to wear religious medals. The only case to reach the U.S. Supreme Court, however, was *Cruz* v. *Beto* in 1972.[22] Cruz, a Buddhist, had been barred from using the chapel in a Texas prison and was placed in solitary confinement for sharing his religious material with other inmates. The Court ruled that the Texas action was "palpable discrimination" in violation of the equal protection clause of the Fourteenth Amendment. On the other hand, the federal courts have held that placing limits on the practice of "satanism" is not a violation of prisoners' First Amendment rights.[23]

Mail and Media Interviews

Prison officials in the United States have traditionally placed certain restrictions on inmates' use of the mails. These restrictions generally include limiting the number of persons with whom inmates may correspond, opening and reading incoming and outgoing material, deleting sections from both incoming and outgoing mail, and refusing to mail for an inmate or forward to an inmate certain types of correspondence. The reasons for these restrictions follow security and budgetary requirements. Contraband must be intercepted, escape plans must be detected, and material that might incite the inmate population in some way must be excluded. Furthermore, correctional budgets do not allow for the unlimited use of the mails. Prisons have also used the goal of rehabilitation to justify certain restrictions on inmate correspondence. The courts have generally accepted these justifications for mail censorship and limitation, and in years past rarely intervened in prison mail regulations. More recently, however, a range of situations have been examined by the courts, with major rulings in *Wolff* v. *McDonnell* and *Procunier* v. *Martinez*, both decided by the Supreme Court in 1974.[24]

In *Wolff,* at issue was whether prison officials could justifiably open correspondence from an inmate's attorney. The Court ruled that officials are permitted to open a communication from an attorney to check for contraband, but (1) it must be done in the presence of the inmate and (2) the contents must not be read. (*Wolff* is discussed in more detail later.) *Procunier* v. *Martinez* dealt with the broader issue of censorship of nonlegal correspondence. The Supreme Court held that prison mail censorship is constitutional only when two criteria are met: (1) the practice must further substantial government interests such as security, order, or rehabilitation; and (2) the restrictions must not be greater than necessary to satisfy the particular government interest involved.

The decision in *Procunier* also confirmed the earlier opinions of other courts with related matters. In the 1970 case of *Carothers* v. *Follette*,[25] a federal district court castigated officials at New York's Green Haven Prison for refusing to mail a letter from an inmate to his parents. The letter contained remarks critical about prison conditions. In the 1971 case of *Nolan* v. *Fitzpatrick*,[26] inmates contested the legality of a Massachusetts prison regu-

STATE LAW
EFFECTIVE 5-23-78
Section 2921.36 O.R.C.

PROHIBITS
Conveying onto the grounds of a detention facility or delivery of items to inmates thereof:

1. Any deadly weapons or parts thereof, or ammunition.
2. Any drugs.
3. Any intoxicating liquors.

FURTHERMORE
Whoever violates above section is subject to arrest by detention authorities!

PENALTY
A felony or a misdemeanor.

lation that totally banned letters to the news media. Officials claimed that such communications could inflame the inmates and, hence, endanger prison security. Furthermore, they maintained that complaint letters would retard rehabilitation and create administrative problems since they would encourage media representatives to seek interviews with inmates. *Procunier* specifically invalidated prison censorship of statements that "unduly complain" or "magnify grievances"; expressions of "inflammatory political, racial, or religious, or other views"; and matter deemed "defamatory" or "otherwise inappropriate." As the Court noted:

> These regulations fairly invited prison officials and employees to apply their own personal prejudices and opinions as standards for prisoner mail censorship. Not surprisingly, some prison officials used the extraordinary latitude for discretion authorized by the regulations to suppress unwelcome criticism. For example, at one institution under the Department's jurisdiction, the checklist used by the mailroom staff authorized rejection of letters "criticizing policy, rules or officials," and the mailroom sergeant states in a deposition that he would reject as "defamatory" letters "belittling staff or our judicial system or anything connected with the Department of Corrections." Correspondence was also censored for "disrespectful comments," "derogatory remarks," and the like.

However, in *Pell* v. *Procunier*,[27] also decided in 1974, the Supreme Court ruled that neither prisoners nor the press had a freedom of speech right to specific personal interviews. The Court noted that alternative channels of communication were open to inmates and would be protected by the earlier *Procunier* v. *Martinez* ruling.

Rehabilitative Services

There is agreement among many clinicians, legislators, and members of the general public that in addition to confinement, one purpose of imprisonment is rehabilitation. Furthermore, in the constitutions and statutes of many states, the rehabilitation of prison inmates is at least implied, if not directly stated. For example, the New York state correction law indicates:

> Correctional facilities shall be used for the purpose of providing places of confinement and *programs of treatment* for persons in the custody of the department. Such use shall be suited, to the greatest extent practicable, to the objective of assisting persons to live as law abiding citizens.[28] [emphasis added]

The courts, however, while supporting the rehabilitative ideal, have not defined rehabilitative treatment as a constitutional right. In *O'Connor* v. *Donaldson*,[29] decided in 1975 (a case involving the rights of institutionalized mental patients), the Supreme Court refused to decide on the matter of rights to treatment. Other courts have approached the issue more directly:

- *Wilson* v. *Kelley* in 1968 stated that the duty prison officials owed to an inmate was "to exercise ordinary care for his protection and to keep him safe and free from harm."[30]
- *Padgett* v. *Stein* more specifically ruled that there is no constitutional duty imposed on a government entity to rehabilitate prisoners.[31]

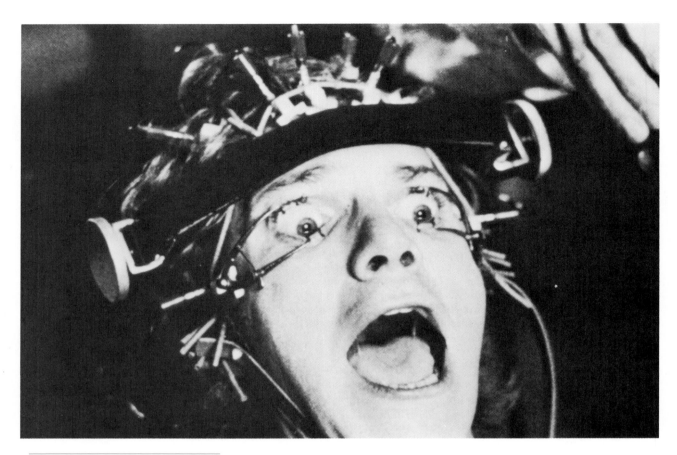

A Clockwork Orange

While the courts may not have extended constitutional status to the right to treatment, they have taken a strong stand against several "rehabilitative" practices of questionable moral and legal status. During the early 1970s, for example, a number of behavior modification techniques were imposed on inmates, ostensibly for their therapeutic value. Several of these techniques seemed to have been taken directly from Anthony Burgess's *A Clockwork Orange,* George Orwell's *1984,* and Aldous Huxley's *Brave New World.* Especially applicable to a number of these practices was the "Clockwork Orange" theme presented by Burgess. His story is set in a near-future semitotalitarian state in which thugs roam the streets of London engaging in assorted acts of intimidation and violence. Alex, a 15-year old psychopath, is caught by the police and subjected to "corrective brainwashing." He is bound to a chair and forced for weeks on end to view films of brutal violence until he himself becomes sickened by it. His destructive behavior is destroyed along with his will, and the State succeeds in transforming him into a "good," unthinking, obedient automaton. In the real-life parallel, Connecticut's maximum-security prison at Sommers instituted an electroshock program for habitual child molesters in 1973.[32] The "patient" viewed slides of children and adults, and received an electric shock every time a picture of a naked child appeared. The rationale of the program — as with the "corrective brainwashing" in *A Clockwork Orange* — was to repress the offender's ability to think of children as sex objects. In a similar case that reached the federal courts in 1973, severely nauseating injections were used to produce an aversion to minor infractions of prison rules.[33]

However, the courts have supported some prison requirements that mandate enrollment in certain institutional programs (such as class attendance by illiterate convicts) and disciplinary measures for those who refuse to participate.[34]

Medical Services

In principle, inmates have a right to "adequate" and "proper" medical care on several grounds. The right is protected by common law and state statutes, by the Civil Rights Act of 1964, by the due-process clause of the Fifth and Fourteenth Amendments, and by the Eighth Amendment ban against cruel and unusual punishment. Prisoners have made claims regarding the adequacy and nature of medical care received, improper and inadequate care, and the total denial of medical and health services.

In *Estelle* v. *Gamble* in 1976,[35] the U.S. Supreme Court enunciated its position on the medical rights of inmates:

Estelle v. Gamble

> **Deliberate indifference to serious medical needs of prisoners constitutes the "unnecessary and wanton infliction of pain" proscribed by the Eighth Amendment. This is true whether the indifference is manifested by prison doctors in their response to the prisoner's needs or by prison guards in intentionally denying or delaying access to medical care or intentionally interfering with the treatment once prescribed.**

Beyond this statement, the High Court has generally left the specifics of medical rights to the lower courts. The federal judiciary has taken the position that what amount of medical aid is "adequate" is largely dependent upon the facts of each case.[36] Thus, no uniform definition of "adequate" health care has been specified. Furthermore, in *Priest* v. *Cupp*,[37] an Oregon court made it clear that the constitutional prohibition against cruel and unusual punishment does not guarantee that an inmate will be free from or cured of all real or imagined medical problems while he or she is in custody. Thus, although prison officials cannot deny medical aid, inmates cannot expect perfect medical services.

Prison Discipline and Constitutional Rights

Many readers may be familiar with the story of *Papillon*. Written by French novelist Henri Charriere and produced as a motion picture in 1973 starring actors Dustin Hoffman and the late Steve McQueen, it told the story of two convicts confined to several French penal colonies and of the determination of one to escape. The colonies included several camps in French Guiana, and Devil's Island — a patch of rock less than a mile in circumference some 10 miles off the Guiana coast. Most striking in *Papillon* were the severe disciplinary procedures for escape attempts and other rule violations: slow starvation; confinement for years at a time in small, dark, vermin-infested cells; or even a short interlude with what Frenchmen called "the widowmaker" — the infamous guillotine.[38]

Many may think of such practices as utterly foreign to American soil, or at least far removed in time from contemporary standards. But only a few short years ago, long after the French penal colonies were abolished during World War II, discipline at least as barbaric as the Devil's Island tradition was practiced in the very heart of America.

The Arkansas Prison Scandal

In 1966, Winthrop Rockefeller, grandson of industrialist and philanthropist John D. Rockefeller, was elected governor of Arkansas. As a candidate, he had pledged to eliminate corruption in state government and to hire a professional penologist to reform the state prison system. The following year, Tom Murton, a professor of criminology from Southern Illinois University, was put in charge of the Arkansas prisons. (Murton was the real Warden Brubaker, as portrayed by actor Robert Redford in the 1980 Universal film *Brubaker*.)

What Murton found was a prison system that had been operated on fear for over a century.[39] The traditional methods of instilling inmate compliance included beatings, needles under the fingernails, starvation, and floggings with the "hide"—a leather strap five inches wide and five feet long. At Tucker Prison Farm, as recently as 1968, there was a contraption known as the "Tucker telephone" used to punish inmates and to extract information:

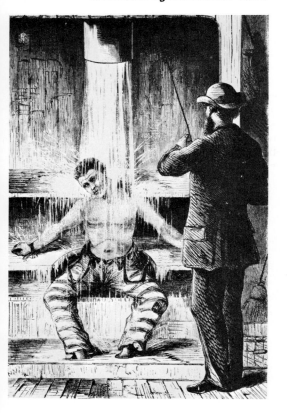

Punishment of prisoners at Sing Sing Prison included torture and death by the shower-bath.

> The telephone, designed by prison superintendent Jim Bruton, consisted of an electric generator taken from a crank-type telephone and wired in sequence with two dry-cell batteries. An undressed inmate was strapped to the treatment table at Tucker Hospital while electrodes were attached to his big toe and to his penis. The crank was then turned, sending an electrical charge into his body. In "long distance calls" several charges were inflicted—of a duration designed to stop just short of the inmate's fainting. Sometimes the "telephone" operator's skill was defective, and the sustained current not only caused the inmate to lose consciousness but resulted in irreparable damage to his testicles. Some men were literally driven out of their minds.[40]

For more than 50 years, many boasted that the Arkansas prison system was a symbol of efficiency, for no state appropriations were needed to support the convicts. But Murton found that this was so only because of the exploitation of inmate labor. Furthermore, the control of inmates, work assignments, promotion, food rations, bed assignments, visiting privileges, commissary privileges, laundry and clothing procedures, and the very survival of the inmate had been delegated to a select few powerful convicts who operated the prison. To make such a system operable, these "trustees" had been granted many privileges, including graft obtained from all inmate goods and services, freedom to sell liquor and narcotics, to gamble and loan money, to live in squatter shacks outside the prison and spend nights with female companions, and to profit from the illegal trafficking in prison produce. Thus, there were no traditional custodial officers. Rather, the institutions were run by a powerful structure of convict guards who used bribery and torture to maintain the status quo and to profit from the inmate slavery. In Arkansas's Cummins Prison Farm, it was alleged that inmates had been routinely murdered as punishment for disciplinary infractions and then buried in a remote cow pasture. The total number of these killings was estimated to be over 100.[41]

The barbaric conditions in the Arkansas prisons came to national attention in January 1968, as a result of Murton's discoveries and efforts at reform. However, for fear that Murton was damaging the image of Arkansas with the **Arkansas prison scandal,** on March 2, 1968, he was fired from his post and placed under house arrest. Governor Rockefeller at a press conference the following day simply explained that Murton had been a "poor prison administrator."

The Arkansas prison scandal

In the years following Murton's departure, the Arkansas prisons were in constant turmoil. On several occasions, inmates protesting prison conditions were shot at by prison officials.[42] Explanations for the continuing difficulties focused on racial conflicts and efforts at integration.

When the courts finally listened to the Arkansas prisoners, the savage discipline and inhumane conditions were more fully acknowledged. A federal court decision, *Holt v. Sarver* in 1970,[43] declared the entire Arkansas prison system to be in violation of the Eighth Amendment ban against cruel and unusual punishment (see Exhibit 16.1).

Holt v. *Sarver*

EXHIBIT 16.1

Arkansas State Penitentiary

For the ordinary convict a sentence to the Arkansas Penitentiary today amounts to a banishment from civilized society to a dark and evil world completely alien to the free world, a world that is administered by criminals under unwritten rules and customs completely foreign to free world culture.

After long and careful consideration the Court has come to the conclusion that the Fourteenth Amendment prohibits confinement under the conditions that have been described and that the Arkansas penitentiary system as it exists today, particularly at Cummins, is unconstitutional.

Such confinement is inherently dangerous. A convict, however cooperative and inoffensive he may be, has no assurance whatever that he will not be killed, seriously injured, or sexually abused. Under the present system the state cannot protect him.

Apart from physical danger, confinement in the penitentiary involves living under degrading and disgusting conditions. This Court has no patience with those who still say, even when they ought to know better, that to change those conditions will convert the prison into a country club; the Court has not heard any of those people volunteer to spend a few days and nights at either Tucker or Cummins incognito.

The peril and degradation to which Arkansas convicts are subjected to daily are aggravated by the fact that the treatment which a convict may expect to receive depends not at all upon the gravity of his offense or the length of his term. In point of fact, a man sentenced to life imprisonment for first-degree murder and who has a long criminal record may expect to fare better than a country boy with no serious record who is sentenced

to two years for stealing a pig.

It is one thing for the State to send a man to the penitentiary as a punishment for crime. It is another thing for the State to delegate the governance of him to other convicts and to do nothing meaningful for his safety, well-being, and possible rehabilitation. It is one thing for the State not to pay a convict for his labor; it is something else to subject him to a situation in which he has to sell his blood to obtain money to pay for his own safety, or for adequate food, or for access to needed medical attention.

However constitutionally tolerable the Arkansas system may have been in former years, it simply will not do today as the twentieth century goes into its eighth decade.

SOURCE: From the Supreme Court's opinion in Holt v. Sarver, 309 F. Supp. 362 (E. D. Ark. 1970).

Solitary Confinement

Solitary confinement has been variously referred to as "isolation" or "segregation" in "the hole" or in a "strip cell." It is the total separation of an inmate from the general prison population in a special cell of meager size and comfort, combined with the revocation of all prisoner privileges and constitutional rights, and often with a restricted diet or other physical abuse. Placement in "solitary" generally occurs for serious violations of prison regulations, such as escape attempts, forced homosexual advances, assaulting guards or other inmates, or being excessively troublesome.

The use of solitary confinement in the United States is as old as the nation's prison system, and its application is acknowledged in many state statutes. For example, Title 41 of the current *Tennessee Code* states:

> If any convict neglects or refuses to perform the labor assigned him, or wilfully injures any of the materials, implements, or tools, or engages in conversation with any other convict, or in any other manner violates any of the regulations of the penitentiary, he may be punished by solitary confinement for a period not exceeding thirty (30) days for each offense, at the discretion of the warden, or person acting in his place.[44]

As with other aspects of prisoners' rights, prior to the 1960s the courts maintained their hands-off doctrine with respect to inmate complaints concerning isolated confinement. During the past two decades, however, numerous actions concerning the practice have been brought to the courts by both state and federal inmates. Some suits have argued that the very practice of solitary confinement is unconstitutional. The federal courts, however, have flatly rejected this contention. In *Sostre* v. *McGinnis,*[45] for example, circuit judge Irving R. Kaufman remarked: "For a federal court . . . to place a punishment beyond the power of the state to impose on an inmate is a drastic interference with the state's free political and administrative processes."

Despite the courts' unwillingness to ban solitary confinement on constitutional grounds, they have taken a stand on how it can be imposed and administered. Using standards established by the Supreme Court for interpreting what constitutes cruel and unusual punishment,[46] the federal courts have examined the duration of an inmate's confinement, the physical conditions of the cell, the hygienic conditions of the inmate, the exercise allowed, the diet provided, and the nature of the infraction that resulted in punitive isolation.

The courts have been reluctant, however, to establish rigid criteria for deciding on the unconstitutionality of solitary confinement. In *Jordan* v. *Fitzharris,*[47] for example, the "strip cells" in California's Soledad Prison were deemed "cruel and unusual" due to their poor sanitary conditions. In contrast, in *Bauer* v. *Sielaff,*[48] since the inmate was not denied the minimum necessities of food, water, sleep, exercise, toilet facilities, and human contact, the Federal Court of the Eastern District of Pennsylvania held that the deprivation of a comb, pillow, toothbrush, and toothpaste for seven to ten days in a segregation cell with continuous lights, a few mice and roaches, and no reading material was not unconstitutional. Furthermore, although the stereotyped solitary confinement meal of "bread and water" has been disapproved of by the courts,[49] it has been deemed satisfactory when supplemented by a full meal every third day.[50]

The Lash

Whipping (or flogging) has been a common sanction in most Western cultures. In American tradition, it was used as a punishment for crimes and for preserving discipline in domestic, military, and academic environments. And curiously, although whipping has been viewed by most as uncivilized brutality, its final abolition in American penal practice has only been recent. In Delaware, for example, whipping was a constitutionally permissible punishment for specified crimes from the seventeenth through the twentieth centuries (see Exhibit 16.2). Furthermore, in many jurisdictions, flogging was a form of convict discipline.

The end of whipping as an official means of enforcing prison rules and regulations evolved from an Arkansas case, ***Jackson* v. *Bishop*,**[51] decided by a federal circuit court in 1968. In the Arkansas prison system, whipping was the primary disciplinary measure. Facilities for segregation and solitary confinement were limited, and inmates had few privileges that could be withheld from them as punishment. Prison regulations, furthermore, allowed whipping for such infractions as homosexuality, agitation, insubordination, making or concealing weapons, participating in or inciting a riot, and refusing to work when medically able to do so. Using the criteria of "broad and idealistic concepts of dignity, civilized standards, humanity, and decency," the court declared whipping to be a violation of the Eighth Amendment ban on cruel and unusual punishment, for the following reasons:

Jackson v. Bishop

> (1) We are not convinced that any rule or regulation as to the use of the strap, however seriously or sincerely conceived and drawn, will successfully prevent abuse. . . . (2) Rules in this area often seem to go unobserved. . . . (3) Regulations are easily circumvented. . . . (4) Corporal punishment is easily subject to abuse in the hands of the sadistic and the unscrupulous. (5) Where power to punish is granted to persons in lower levels of administrative authority, there is an inherent and natural difficulty in enforcing the limitations of that power. (6) There can be no argument that excessive whipping or an inappropriate manner of whipping or too great frequency of whipping or the use of studded or overlong straps all constitute cruel and unusual punishment. But if whipping were to be authorized, how does one, or any court, ascertain the point which would distinguish the permissible from that which is cruel and unusual? (7) Corporal punishment generates hate toward the keepers who punish and toward the system which permits it. It is degrading to the punisher and to the punished alike. It frustrates correctional and rehabilitative goals. . . . (8) Whipping creates other penological problems and makes adjustment to society more difficult. (9) Public opinion is obviously adverse. Counsel concede that only two states still permit the use of the strap.

Prison Disciplinary Proceedings

Throughout the history of corrections, disciplinary actions against prison inmates have often been arbitrary administrative operations controlled solely by wardens, their deputies, or other custodial personnel. Without a formal hearing, and at the discretion of an institutional officer, inmates could be placed in solitary confinement, lose some or all of their privileges, or be deprived of "good time" credits. Even in those correctional settings where disciplinary hearing committees were convened to review serious infractions

EXHIBIT 16.2

Delaware's Infamous "Red Hannah"

The semiannual whipping and pillorying of criminals convicted at the present term of the court, of theft and other crimes, took place on Saturday. The attendance was small, probably not exceeding one hundred people, most of whom were boys. The following are the names of the "candidates," and the offenses for which they were sentenced:

Joseph Derias, colored, horse stealing, 20 lashes, one hour in the pillory.

Scott Wilson, larceny of clothing, 20 lashes.

John Carpenter, colored, four cases of larceny (ice cream freezers, carriage reins, and a cow).

He received 10 lashes in each case.

John Conner, larceny of tomatoes, 5 lashes.

John Smith, colored, house breaking, 20 lashes.

John Brown, horse stealing, 20 lashes and one hour in the pillory.

—Delawarean, *May 27, 1876*

For centuries, the whipping post was a conspicuous part of Delaware's penal tradition. The first person to suffer the sanction was Robert Hutchinson, convicted of petty theft and sentenced to 39 lashes on June 3, 1679. Each town and county had its own whipping post, but the one that earned a prominent place in the history of American corrections was the notorious "Red Hannah." As the Wilmington *Journal Every Evening* once described it:

In days gone by, the whipping post down in Kent County stood out brazenly in the open courtyard of the county jail not far from the old state house. It looked like an old-time octagonal pump without a handle. It had a slit near the top of it in which the equally old-time pillory boards might be inserted when needed for punitive use. There also were iron shackles for holding the prisoners while they were being whipped. That whipping post was painted red from top to bottom. Negro residents bestowed upon it the name of "Red Hannah." Of any prisoner who had been whipped at the post it was said, "He has hugged Red Hannah!"

Red Hannah was a survivor. Despite public and local congressional pressure to ban whipping in the state, during the second half of the twentieth century, almost 300 years after Robert Hutchinson received his 39 lashes, old Red Hannah was still very much alive.

of prison regulations, decisions could be made entirely on the basis of a custodial officer's testimony. Evidence was generally not required, prisoners were rarely permitted to speak in their own behalf, and the rules of due process were typically ignored. When the prisoners' rights movement first brought these practices to the attention of the federal courts during the 1960s, the due-process clauses of the Fifth and Fourteenth Amendments were applied sparingly and only in specific circumstances. The position of the courts seemed to be that due process should prevent only "capricious" or

Old Red Hannah, Delaware's whipping post

In 1963, the statutes that permitted whipping were challenged in the Delaware Supreme Court. The case was *State* v. *Cannon,* and the presiding judge held that the use of flogging to punish certain crimes did *not* violate either state or federal bans on cruel and unusual punishment. However, Red Hannah was ultimately laid to rest in 1973, when the statute authorizing the use of the lash was finally repealed by the Delaware legislature.

SOURCES: Robert G. Caldwell, *Red Hannah: Delaware's Whipping Post* (Philadelphia: University of Pennsylvania Press, 1947); *Delawarean,* May 27, 1876, p. 3; *Journal Every Evening,* August 2, 1938, p. 8; State v. Cannon, 55 Del. 587 (1963).

"arbitrary" actions by prison administrators. In the 1966 case of *Landman* v. *Peyton,*[52] for example, a federal appeals judge stated:

> Where the lack of effective supervisory procedures exposes men to the capricious imposition of added punishment, due process and Eighth Amendment questions inevitably arise.

During the 1970s, however, the courts began to focus on the specific procedures used in prison disciplinary proceedings, seeking to resolve the wider issue of due-process requirements. The principal case was ***Wolff* v. *McDonnell*,**[53] decided by the U.S. Supreme Court in 1974. The ruling in *Wolff* held the following:

1. Advance written notice of the charges against an inmate must be provided to him at least 24 hours prior to his appearance before the prison hearing committee.
2. There must be a written statement by the fact finders as to the evidence relied upon and the reasons for the disciplinary action.
3. The prisoner should be allowed to call witnesses and present documentary evidence in his defense providing such actions would cause no undue hazards to institutional safety or correctional goals.
4. The inmate must be permitted representation by a counsel substitute (a fellow inmate or staff member) when the prisoner is illiterate or when the complexity of the case goes beyond the capabilities of the person being charged.
5. The hearing committee must be impartial (suggesting that those involved in any of the events leading up to the hearing — such as the charging or investigating parties — may not serve as members of the committee).

In establishing these requirements, the full spectrum of due process was *not* extended. The Court made it clear that neither retained or appointed counsel, nor the right to confrontation and cross-examination, were constitutionally required. The decision stressed some additional points. First, the ruling in *Wolff* did not apply retroactively. Second, in writing the Court's opinion, Justice White emphasized that the limitations on due process imposed by the decision were "not graven in stone"; future changes in circumstances could require further "consideration and reflection" of the Court. Third, the due-process requirements set forth applied only to proceedings that could result in solitary confinement and the loss of "good time." Left unresolved, however, were the procedures to be observed if other penalties were to be imposed.

Two years later, in the companion cases ***Meachum* v. *Fano*** and *Montanye* v. *Haymes*,[54] this issue was partially settled. In *Meachum*, inmate Fano was one of several prisoners charged with setting fires at a medium-security correctional facility in Massachusetts. As an outgrowth of a reclassification hearing that fell short of the due-process requirements set forth in *Wolff*, Fano was transferred to a maximum-security prison in another part of the state. At issue in the case were the transfer and the concomitant reduction in privileges that logically resulted from the relocation to a more rigidly controlled and custodially strict institution. In a strongly worded opinion that was a setback for prisoners, the Supreme Court held that the Fourteenth Amendment's due-process clause in and of itself does not entitle an inmate to a fact-finding hearing prior to his transfer from one correctional institution to another. The Court emphasized that this is so even when the conditions at the receiving facility are substantially less favorable to the prisoner than those existing in the institution from which he is transferred, provided that such conditions are within the sentence originally imposed by the trial court and do not otherwise violate the Constitution. *Montanye* v. *Haymes* carried this point even further. The due-process clause does not require hearings in connection with transfers whether or not they are the result of the inmate's misbehavior or may be labeled as disciplinary or punitive.

The essential difference between *Wolff* on the one hand, and *Meachum* and *Montanye* on the other, was the issue of an inmate's "liberty interest" and any "grievous loss" of that interest. The Fourteenth Amendment prohibits any state from depriving a person of life, liberty, or property without due process of law. Penal codes that provide for sentences of imprisonment deprive duly convicted offenders of their liberty, yet at the same time imply other liberty interests: confinement within the general prison population and access to "good time" credits. In *Wolff*, placement in punitive segregation and reduction in "good time" represented a "grievous loss" of these liberty interests. In *Meachum* and *Montanye*, such interests were not involved. As the Court explained it in *Meachum*:

> Given a valid conviction, the criminal defendant has been constitutionally deprived of his liberty to the extent that the State may confine him and to subject him to the rules of its prison system so long as the conditions of confinement do not otherwise violate the Constitution. The Constitution . . . does not guarantee that the convicted prisoner will be placed in any particular prison. . . . The conviction has sufficiently extinguished the defendant's liberty interest to empower the State to confine him in any of its prisons.

The Conditions of Incarceration

As crime rates rise, state legislators react by passing stiff laws requiring longer minimum prison sentences. Result: more prisoners stay longer in prisons that are already crammed well past their planned capacity. Tensions rise as up to five inmates crowd into one-man cubicles. Gang rule prevails, as the toughest convicts abuse and torment the meek or nonviolent, and guards on undermanned correction staffs fear to intervene.
— *Time*, June 8, 1981

Prisons are as safe as the inmates want them to be.
— Custodial official, Attica Correctional Facility, 1981

In here, not having a knife is a death sentence. — Inmate, Jackson Prison, 1981

The Arkansas prison scandal in 1968 pointed to many problems within that state's correctional system. Not only was there corruption and brutality, but as the Supreme Court noted, there was also confinement under degrading and disgusting conditions. Although Arkansas during the 1960s may have been unique in its sanctioned administration by convicts under a system of unwritten rules, its general prison conditions were not an isolated phenomenon. Similar problems of overcrowding and extreme physical danger were commonplace all across the nation.

In general, the courts have held that most aspects of prison life are dictated by the needs of security and discipline, thus giving custodial authorities wide discretion in their regulation of inmate comforts. At the same time, however, the federal courts have monitored some conditions of confinement, taking the position that while offenders are sent to prison for punishment,

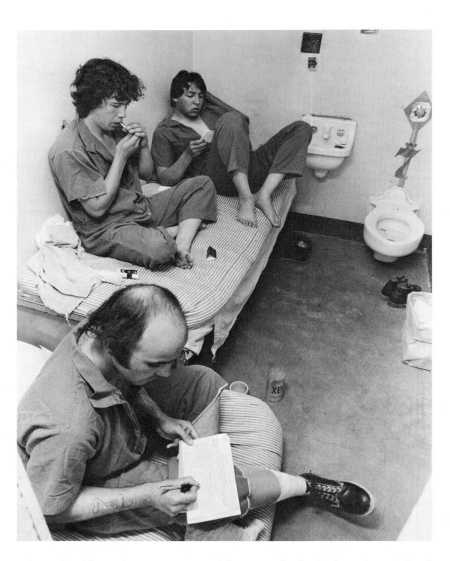

*Overcrowded conditions in
maximum security at New
Mexico State Prison*

prison should not impose extra punishments of a barbaric and uncivilized
nature. For example, prison overcrowding itself has not been declared unconstitutional. Yet, as was pointed out in *Costello* v. *Wainwright* in 1975,[55]
overcrowding can be a factor, when combined with other conditions, in declaring the circumstances of incarceration to be in violation of the Constitution. Thus, the federal courts have indicated that it is their duty to protect
inmates from conditions of confinement that serve to add punitive measures to
those already meted out by a sentencing court. The courts have also ruled, as

People v. *Lovercamp*

in the 1974 case of *People* v. *Lovercamp*,[56] that the situations and circumstances some inmates face inside prison walls may serve as a defense for the
crime of escape (see Exhibit 16.3).

The Texas Prison Suit

The people of Texas don't want prison reform.   — Senator Chet Brooks, 1981

The Texas prison suit, a matter that was in the courts for more than a decade,
reflects the kaleidoscope of conditions of confinement and attempts at prison

EXHIBIT 16.3

The Defense of Necessity and the Right to Escape from Prison

Rather early in the legal history of the offense of prison escape, it became clear that all departures from lawful custody were not necessarily escapes. Two and a half centuries ago it was written that if a prison caught fire and an inmate departed to save his life, then the necessity to save his life "excuseth the felony."[a] Yet despite this pre–Revolutionary War holding, the courts traditionally have not favored the defense of necessity in escape cases. The principal justification for this hostility has been the frequently expressed fear that the availability of the defense might lead to an increase in prison escapes. This consideration has led some courts to hold that even the most intolerable of prison conditions will never justify an escape.[b] In *People* v. *Lovercamp,* however, decided by the California Court of Appeals in 1974, the conditions under which the defense of escape might be used were established.

In *Lovercamp,* two women inmates had escaped from the California Rehabilitation Center and were promptly captured in a hayfield just a few yards away. They had been in the institution just a few months and during that time they had been threatened by a group of lesbian inmates who told them that they were to perform certain lesbian acts — the exact expression was "fuck or fight." They complained to prison authorities on several occasions but nothing was done. On the day of the escape, ten or fifteen of these lesbian inmates approached them and again offered the alternative — "fuck or fight." A fight ensued, and the two women were told that they would see the group again. Fearing for their lives, and on the basis of what occurred, the threats made, and the fact that the prison officials had not done anything for their protection, the two women felt that they had no choice but to leave the institution to save themselves.

In considering these facts, the court ruled:

We conclude that the defense of necessity to an escape charge is a viable defense. However, before Lovercamp becomes a household word in prison circles and we are exposed to the spectacle of hordes of prisoners leaping over the walls screaming "rape," we hasten to add that the defense of necessity to an escape charge is extremely limited in its application. . . . We hold that the proper rule is that a limited defense of necessity is available if the following conditions exist:

[1] the prisoner is faced with a specific threat of death, forcible sexual attack, or substantial bodily injury in the immediate future;

[2] there is no time for a complaint to the authorities or there exists a history of futile complaints which make any result from such complaints illusory;

[3] there is no time or opportunity to resort to the courts;

[4] there is no evidence of force or violence used towards prison personnel or other "innocent" persons in the escape; and

[5] the prisoner immediately reports to the proper authorities when he has attained a position of safety from the immediate threat.

In subsequent cases, although the courts have agreed that the *Lovercamp* criteria are generally relevant to the defense of necessity in escape cases, they have disagreed on the role that the criteria should play. As a result, three approaches have emerged.[c] Under the most restrictive approach, the jury is not permitted to consider the evidence offered in support of the defense if any one of the *Lovercamp* criteria has not been met. The second approach, that taken by the *Lovercamp* court, requires that all five criteria be met before illegal conduct will be excused, but allows the jury, rather than the judge, to make this determination. The third approach treats the *Lovercamp* criteria only as factors to be considered by the jury in assessing the credibility of the evidence offered to establish the defense. As such, under this third approach all of the *Lovercamp* criteria need not be met.

SOURCES:

a. 1 Hale P. C. 611 (1736).

b. Comment, "From Duress to Intent: Shifting the Burden in Prison Escape Prosecutions," *University of Pennsylvania Law Review* 127 (1979), pp. 1142–1173.

c. Case Comment, "Intent, Duress, and Necessity in Escape Cases," *Georgetown Law Journal* 68 (1979), pp. 249–266.

reform. Just a few years ago, the penitentiary system in the Lone Star state was the largest in the nation, with some 30,000 inmates at the close of 1980.* All 19 Texas prisons were built as maximum-security institutions, and they were designed as such to foster rigid discipline and inhibit escape. Overcrowding is a major problem. With only 14,000 cells for its tens of thousands of inmates, the system was operating at 230 percent of capacity. That represented a doubling of the prison population since 1974. The reasons for this overcrowding were numerous. In Texas, long sentences have always been the rule. As of 1980, almost 10 percent of the inmates were serving life sentences; an additional 45 percent had terms of 10 years or more. Since 1977, the Texas legislature has passed several laws ordering mandatory sentences for a variety of offenses and requiring inmates convicted of certain crimes to serve at least one-third of their terms before becoming eligible for parole. Furthermore, parole recommendations are frequently vetoed by executive authority. In 1980, for example, Texas Governor William Clements denied 2,241 of 7,886 parole recommendations, or more than 28 percent.

Overcrowding was not the only problem in the Texas prison system; there was also violence. During 1981, 11 prisoners were murdered by fellow inmates, and during one seven-day period, more than 70 inmates and guards were injured in a series of altercations.[57] Two factors contributing to this violence have been understaffing and the use of prisoners as building tenders,

* By the close of 1984 Texas ranked second, with 37,000 inmates. California was the largest, with over 43,000 inmates.

turnkeys, counters, and in supervisory roles. A Texas statute specifically prohibited the use of inmates in such administrative and supervisory capacities, but it was generally ignored by institutional officials. Furthermore, and ironically, for a long time these inmate supervisors *were permitted to carry weapons*—weapons that would have been denied them outside the prison walls.[58]

In June 1972, *Ruiz v. Estelle* was instituted as a class action suit in behalf of all past, present, and future Texas Department of Corrections (TDC) inmates.[59] After many years of discovery efforts, a trial finally began on October 2, 1978. At its conclusion, the court had heard 349 witnesses and had received 1,565 exhibits into evidence. The case involved issues of overcrowding, inmate security, and numerous prison services. Presiding over the case was federal judge William Wayne Justice.

In 1980, Judge Justice declared the Texas prison system to be unconstitutional. The court ordered the addition of new facilities to alleviate overcrowding; the abolition of arrangements that placed some prisoners in charge of others; the placement of any new prisons near urban areas of 200,000 population; changes in the staff-to-inmate ratio; the limiting of inmate populations; an adherence to the due process rights guaranteed by *Wolff;* and

Ruiz v. Estelle **was the Texas prison suit.**

The United States Constitution must be enforced within the confines of TDC prison walls, by court decree. **— Judge William Wayne Justice, 1980**

A shakedown in a Texas prison

improved medical, educational, occupational, and mental health services. As Judge Justice noted in the opinion in *Ruiz v. Estelle:*

> It is impossible for a written opinion to convey the pernicious conditions and the pain and degradation which ordinary inmates suffer within TDC prison walls — the gruesome experiences of youthful first offenders forcibly raped; the cruel and justifiable fears of inmates, wondering when they will be called upon to defend the next violent assault; the sheer misery, the discomfort, the wholesale loss of privacy for prisoners housed with one, two, or three others in a forty-five square foot cell or suffocatingly packed together in a crowded dormitory; the physical suffering and wretched psychological stress which must be endured by those sick or injured who cannot obtain adequate medical care; the sense of abject helplessness felt by inmates arbitrarily sent to solitary confinement or administrative segregation without proper opportunity to defend themselves or to argue their causes; the bitter frustration of inmates prevented from petitioning the courts and other governmental authorities for relief from perceived injustices.
>
> For those who are incarcerated within the parameters of TDC, these conditions and experiences form the content and essence of daily existence.

Despite the ruling in *Ruiz,* many Texas officials maintained that their prison system was the best in the nation, and the Texas Department of Corrections sought relief in the United States court of appeals on the argument that the reforms ordered by Judge Justice were beyond the jurisdiction of his court and should not be required. In 1982, the court of appeals upheld the lower court order,[60] but the reforms were not immediately forthcoming. By 1983, conditions in the Texas system had gotten worse, and there were allegations of corruption, graft, and mismanagement. Moreover, there were serious charges of brutality by prison officials. In fact, inmate Eroy Brown was acquitted of murdering his warden after he was able to convince a jury that he was being taken to a remote corner of the prison in Huntsville to be beaten to death.[61] In 1984, there was a new prison administration imposed in Texas, and a host of new reforms were set into action. It was quickly learned, however, that the attempts at reform not only exacerbated many of the old problems but also brought on a series of new ones (see Exhibit 16.4).

The New Mexico Inmate Massacre

The vilest deeds, like prison weeds
Bloom well in prison air.
It is only what is good in man
That wastes and withers there.
— Oscar Wilde

On February 1, 1980, New Mexico State Penitentiary distinguished itself for having the most gruesome prison riot in U.S. history. Nearly a thousand inmates seized the institution and took 15 guards as hostages. Prisoners threatened to kill all of the captives if state officials refused to meet their demands for improved conditions.[62]

The New Mexico institution, built in 1957 for 850 convicts, had been housing almost 1,200. A 1977 lawsuit by inmates described the prison as unsanitary and lacking medical facilities, and an investigation in 1979 found the facility to be dangerously understaffed and the guards poorly trained. When the riot broke out on February 1, only 18 guards were on duty. Inmates looted the prison hospital for drugs and set fires that gutted all five cell blocks. They had essentially two demands: relief of overcrowded conditions and an end to harassment by guards. The prison was quickly retaken by police and the National Guard, but not before many inmates had died from drug overdoses, burns, and smoke inhalation.

But the New Mexico incident was not just another prison riot. It was unmatched in savagery in terms of the nature of inmate violence. Investigators found that during the riot, there had been a seven-man inmate execution squad to exact revenge on convict informers. One prisoner was beheaded; another was found with a metal rod driven through his head; several had their arms and legs cut off or their eyes gouged out; and still others were charred by blowtorches or beaten beyond recognition.[63] In all, 33 fellow prisoners were brutally murdered.

In the wake of the New Mexico holocaust, numerous reforms were proposed, but one commentator reflected:

> Perhaps a disaster such as this can open the windows and allow fresh thinking to enter. But many are not optimistic. Little was learned from Attica. It is hoped more may be learned from Santa Fe.[64]

The aftermath of 36 hours of rioting at New Mexico State Penitentiary in 1980

Almost two years later, New Mexico State Penitentiary appeared to be no less a slaughterhouse. The trials of those charged with the killings inspired further bloodshed. As one prison official explained it: "Everybody is a potential witness against everybody else. No one knows who will testify against them, and that breeds tension."[65]

Attica and Beyond: The "Slow-motion" Prison Riots of the 1980s

Anytime they want you, they've got you.
— Custodial officer, Attica Correctional Facility, 1982

We can't do anything unless the inmates let us.
— Custodial officer, Attica Correctional Facility, 1985

Despite federal court intervention and concerted plans for change, conditions in many prisons across the nation in the 1980s remained unconstitutional and in a constant state of chaos. In the aftermath of the riot at Attica Correctional

---

EXHIBIT 16.4

Prison Conditions in Post-*Ruiz* Texas

In May, 1985, after thirteen years of bitter confrontation, *Ruiz* v. *Estelle* was finally settled — although with unsatisfactory results. Having made substantial gains, and while fearing the risk of pressing further for better living conditions for Texas prisoners in the face of an increasingly conservative federal judiciary, attorneys representing David Ruiz and his co-plaintiffs agreed to accept the state's plan to deal with the last remaining issue in the case, that of overcrowding.

In consideration of $7 million already awarded in legal fees and an estimated $1 *billion* necessary for eventual compliance with federal judge William Wayne Justice's reorganization orders, what changes are now visible in Texas prisons?

- *Staffing:* Prior to Judge Justice's 1980 decision, there existed only one guard for every 12 prisoners. Today there is one guard for every 5.4 prisoners.

- *Housing:* In 1979, there were over 3,000 prisoners sleeping on floors or crammed three to a cell. The final settlement calls for no triple-celling, no prisoners sleeping on floors, and about 6,000 of the system's 38,000 prisoners sleeping in single cells.

- *Inmate Guards:* As was typical in southern prisons, historically Texas has given authority to hand-picked prisoners for controlling their fellow inmates. One of the most critical and bitterly fought issues of the case, the corruption-riddled practice known as the "building tender" system, survived until at least 1983 but was finally dismantled.

- *Brutality:* Judge Justice ordered an end to physical abuse of prisoners by guards. Special Master Vincent Nathan, appointed by Judge Justice to oversee directed reforms, found that as of 1983 physical beatings were still the primary mechanism for controlling inmates. After 200 employees were disciplined for instances of brutality, reports of beatings finally tapered off.

- *Medical Care:* Judge Justice found intolerable the practice of untrained prisoners performing surgery on other prisoners. There have been dramatic improvements, including full-time physicians and dentists on every TDC unit as well as a new $40 million prison hospital in Galveston.

- *New Prisons:* TDC recently completed the last 4,000-man correctional institution to be built in the United States. The settlement calls for a maximum of 2,250 prisoners in any new unit.

Facility in 1971, a number of reforms were proposed and implemented. But as the years passed, conditions there began to deteriorate again. By the early 1980s, Attica had become overcrowded; it had absorbed inmates from two state hospitals for the criminally insane; most of the population were violent offenders; and the number of assaults on correction officers was steadily increasing. In September 1981, just a few days before the tenth anniversary of the riot, one officer who had been on duty during the 1971 rebellion commented that tensions at Attica once again were reaching the boiling point. "We have all the ingredients for a disaster here," he remarked. Another guard said, "This place could go right now."[66]

While Attica has not again exploded, it as well as correctional institutions across the nation are undergoing a series of what might be called "prison riots in slow-motion." In 1983, inmates at Attica took part in a general strike to protest prison conditions. At the peak of the protest, most of the institution's more than 2,100 prisoners refused to leave their cells for food, to participate in programs, or to work in the shops.[67] The following year, Attica came to the brink of explosion when a group of 182 inmates went on an

Now that the case is settled, however, the situation of prisoners is hardly satisfactory. The vacuum left by the removal of "building tenders" from the intricate prisoner-control network has given rise to a deadly situation, faced by prison administrators elsewhere but almost unheard of in Texas — prisoner gangs. Formed along racial and ethnic lines, prisoner gangs such as the Mexican Mafia, the Texas Syndicate, and the Aryan Brotherhood use methods ranging from simple extortion to contract murder in their struggle for control of prison rackets — drugs, alcohol, weapons, and prostitutes.

Partially as a result of *Ruiz*, massive mismanagement, corruption, lying, and incompetence on the part of prison managers are continually being uncovered. James Estelle, Director of the TDC throughout the *Ruiz* years, was removed amid accusations of incompetence, brutality, and lying. His replacement, Raymond Procunier, nationally recognized as a tough-minded prison administrator, lasted only one year before quitting the TDC in personal and professional frustration.

Along with losing control of inmates, and related to the collapse of the "building tender" system, the TDC seems to have lost control of lower-echelon guards. Instances of guards smuggling drugs into prisons, promoting prostitution within the prisons as well as outside, and sexual misconduct with inmates have plagued the TDC in its attempt to present itself as a system positively adapting to change.

Perhaps inevitably, blame for the conditions of pre- and post-*Ruiz* Texas prisons is being laid to the Texas legislature, the governor's office, and the prison board. Will Texas prisons eventually conform to "modern standards" of prison administration, at least as they are defined by the federal courts? It is hard to say. The more important questions remain, rarely asked and never answered. Did the unprecedented attack on Texas prisons by the federal government in *Ruiz* v. *Estelle* result in an increase or decrease in the quality of life for Texas prisoners? Did it improve or hurt the quality of the Texas criminal justice system, strengthen or weaken legitimacy of Texas prisons and, hence, prisons in America? For the first time since the start of *Ruiz* in 1972, no one is talking.

SOURCE: David B. Gulick, University of Delaware. Reprinted by permission of the author.

8-hour rampage in protest of the shooting of a fellow prisoner by guards.[68] Downstate from Attica at Sing Sing, on at least two occasions during 1983 there were protests over prison conditions.[69] In one incident, 17 correction officers were held hostage for 53 hours.

The "lockdown"

Then there was the "lockdown" at California's San Quentin Prison. Lockdown status means that inmates are confined to their cells around the clock — denied exercise, work, recreation, and visits. The measure was put in force during July 1984 at San Quentin as a result of a series of incidents that included the murdering of several guards and inmates by fellow prisoners. One purpose of the lockdown was to separate inmates from one another in an effort to prevent further violence. Another was to search cells for weapons, an endeavor that yielded homemade spears, knives, blowguns, and even bombs — composed of match heads, ground glass, and razor blades jammed into small containers that when exploded would have the effect of small fragmentation grenades.[70] A similar lockdown occurred in the federal penitentiary at Marion, Illinois, in 1985.[71]

In addition, during the first half of the 1980s there were many other recurring prison protests, uprisings, work stoppages, and lockdowns in Alabama, Michigan, Tennessee, Florida, and numerous other jurisdictions. The reasons for these "slow-motion riots" were twofold. As of 1985 prisons in 37 states had been found unfit by the federal courts. The deplorable conditions of confinement, combined with the very *fact* of confinement, produces anger, frustration, and emotions that are difficult to control. Moreover, penitentiaries are very dangerous places to live. Prisoners, many of whom have been incarcerated for violent crimes, assault and kill one another. There is sexual assault and racial unrest. The strong prey upon the weak and rivalries and jealousies are common. Seeking protection and status, many inmates join gangs. But the very presence of gangs within prison walls means additional violence, resulting from struggles over power, turf, and contraband (see Exhibit 16.5).

Cell blocks at San Quentin, where 900 inmates were held in lockdown in their 48-square-foot cells from June 1982 through the end of 1983.

Reform versus Law and Order

While the 1960s ushered in the era of prisoners' rights and the 1970s witnessed agitation for prison reform, calls for "law and order" in the 1980s brought into focus a dilemma for American corrections that had been evolving for decades. Initially, civil libertarians had agitated for the rights of prison inmates. The federal courts responded by casting aside the "hands-off" doctrine and strengthening mechanisms for inmates in their attempts to file suits against their keepers. Prisoners were no longer the complete slaves of the state, and they slowly won significant victories with respect to legal and medical services, religious expression, access to the media, and their general treatment inside penitentiary walls. Moreover, the courts began to take a more balanced look at the conditions of incarceration. The result was that correctional systems in most jurisdictions in the United States were declared unconstitutional and ordered to reform.

At the same time, however, a slow erosion of the rights of the accused, combined with calls for strict and certain punishment of criminal offenders in the 1980s, led to an unprecedented escalation in the size of prison populations. The ultimate consequence was an American corrections system that, while in the throes of reform, experienced deterioration at a more rapid rate.

Inside the Walls of Folsom Prison

Inside the Walls of Folsom Prison, a 1951 Warner Brothers film, was the first of several media events to focus on California's monument to an age of corrections that had long since passed. Sometime later the institution became further immortalized by Johnny Cash's *Folsom Prison Blues,* played in jukeboxes in thousands of honkytonks, road houses, and saloons across America. In 1985, Folsom Prison was again in the media, but on that occasion the portrayal was neither fictional nor lyrical.

Built in 1880 and located at the base of the Sierra foothills just northeast of Sacramento, because of its antiquated conditions Folsom had been a problem since its very beginning. In the last few years, however, it has become a caricature of everything that could possibly be wrong with prison life. Originally designed for some 1,700 inmates, by the mid-1980s the population had passed the 3,000 mark. In stock-pen conditions, prisoners were living two to a 6-foot by 8-foot cell. Most were violent offenders; and less than half the population was working or attending classes. The result was the turning of inmates' pent-up, nothing-to-lose ferocities upon one another. The outgrowth was the formation of gangs along racial lines.

By the close of 1985, the situation at Folsom Prison was out of control, with no immediate solution in sight. For the most part, the prison was being run by its three dominant gang syndicates — the Bloods, the Mexican Mafia, and the Aryan Brotherhood, all struggling for power in a situation fueled by racial animosities. What evolved was a vicious cycle of blood-feud vengeance. During 1985, inmate stabbings averaged almost one a day. As one Folsom inmate put it: "They stab someone, and we get 'em back."

Bob Englehart, *Hartford Courant*

"I sentence you to twenty years or until your prison becomes overcrowded."

Added to this state of affairs were indications that there was an emergent trend aimed at limiting the rights of prisoners. There was the ruling in ***Rhodes* v. *Chapman,***[72] decided by the U.S. Supreme Court in June 1981. The suit, filed in 1975, came from Kelly Chapman, an armed robber being held at the Southern Ohio Correctional Facility in Lucasville. Chapman argued that the one-man cell he shared with another prisoner gave him only 32 square feet of personal living space, an area about 4 feet wide and 8 feet long. That was less, he contended, than Ohio law required for five-week-old calves in feed lots. The district court agreed that the double-celling violated the Eighth Amendment and subsequently ordered Lucasville to reduce its inmate population. Governor James Rhodes of Ohio filed an appeal for the state, but the lower federal court's decision was affirmed by the U.S. court of appeals.

In an 8-to-1 decision, the Supreme Court reversed the lower court decision, holding that the double-celling was *not* unconstitutional at the Ohio

Rhodes v. *Chapman*

A dog in a California pound gets more running space than we do.
—California inmate, 1984

prison. The Court was not claiming that double-celling was itself constitutional, but rather, that given the nature of other services and conditions at the institution, the cell overcrowding was neither "cruel or unusual" nor the cause of physical or mental injury. Thus, as Justice Brennan pointed out, the Court had used the "totality of circumstances" test and found the double-celling to be constitutional. At this point, one can only speculate on the impact *Rhodes* v. *Chapman* will have on reform efforts to alter prison conditions.

Hudson v. Palmer

In *Hudson v. Palmer,*[73] decided by the Supreme Court in 1984, it was made clear that prison inmates had little, if any, privacy rights. On September 16, 1981, Ted S. Hudson, an officer at the Bland Correctional Center at Bland, Virginia, along with a fellow officer, conducted a shakedown search of inmate Russell Palmer's prison locker and cell. Looking for contraband, the officers discovered a ripped pillow case in a trash can near Palmer's cell bunk. Charges were instituted against Palmer for destroying state property, and he was ordered to reimburse the state for the material destroyed.

In petitioning the U.S. district court, Palmer asserted that Hudson had intentionally destroyed letters from his wife, pictures of his children, legal papers, and other noncontraband items. He also claimed that the search of his cell and the destruction of the noncontraband items were violations of his Fourth Amendment rights. The High Court ruled that a prisoner has no reasonable expectation of privacy in his prison cell entitling him to the protection of the Fourth Amendment against unreasonable searches. The Court noted that it would be impossible to accomplish the prison objectives of preventing the introduction of weapons, drugs, and other contraband into the premises if inmates retained a right of privacy in their cells. Imprisonment, the Court emphasized, carries with it the loss of many rights as necessary to accommodate the institutional needs and objectives of prison facilities, particularly internal security and safety. Moreover, the Court held that since the state of Virginia provided an adequate postdeprivation remedy by which Palmer could bring suit for any losses he suffered from the destruction of his personal property, he was not entitled to bring a civil rights suit against Hudson in federal court.

It would be difficult to predict how correctional systems will fully deal with prison overcrowding and the other problematic conditions of incarceration. Some jurisdictions have instituted procedures for early parole while others have placed a portion of their excess prisoners in local jails. But these are only temporary measures. Moreover, the early paroling of convicted offenders is unpopular with the public; the placement of prison inmates in local facilities further strains the already excessive jail populations; and neither approach addresses the basic need for better institutional conditions. A number of states and the federal system have allocated funds for new prison construction. But correctional facilities are costly to build, equip, and properly staff; the prison population continues to expand; and the funding for new institutions must come from increased taxation. Yet although citizens continue to ask for more swift and certain punishment for criminal offenders, they tend to be unwilling to bear the financial and social burden for new prison construction. As both taxpayers and the victims of crime, they feel that they would be paying twice for the misbehavior of lawbreakers. One new approach

The privatization of corrections

to the problem in the 1980s has been the **privatization of corrections** — the construction, staffing, and operation of prisons by private industry, *for profit.* Such an approach might be highly cost-effective, but there has been strong opposition to the privatization model (see Exhibit 16.6).

EXHIBIT 16.6

The Privatization of Corrections
One Commentator's View

A troubling industry is developing in response to the runaway demand for prison space. Private investors are eager to share in the $10 billion-a-year business of imprisoning the nation's almost 750,000 offenders. Like the military-industrial complex, this industry will capitalize on the public's fears to assure an ever-expanding system, while the basic insecurities remain.

Many citizens and elected officials see privatization as a way to make prisons more secure and efficient. I am skeptical, however, about many of the claims made by private prison operators.

Private operators claim that they can maintain better control of inmates than can public administrators. If the better wardens are hired away from the public sector and only compliant inmates are selected, private prisons may be more peaceful. Otherwise, the problem of misbehavior will remain the same.

Private operators claim they will avoid the lawsuits over prison conditions that have afflicted public institutions. This may be so, if they bring in more professional staff and quality leadership. But already a private operator in Texas is in court to defend his operation, after an inmate was killed by guards as he tried to escape from an overcrowded cell. And the State of Texas is a co-defendant.

Private operators claim they can build prisons faster. True.

Entrepreneurs can erect facilities without the encumbrance of plodding bureaucracies. They also avoid the lengthy process of going to the voters with a bond issue. Thus, the public is denied a voice in deciding whether new prisons are to be built.

Private operators claim they can build prisons more cheaply. While more efficient administration of construction may reduce costs, the savings are lost to the higher cost of private borrowing, as against public bonds. And, since prison construction is financed through tax shelters, the effect is to narrow the national tax base, shifting the burden of financing jails to our lower-income taxpayers.

What private operators don't mention is the possibility that, once entrenched, they will be able to raise prices with little restraint. Moreover, the cost rises as prison populations grow, since private operators charge a daily fee for each inmate. Public institutions are constrained by their budgets.

But this debate over particulars is secondary to the question of whether we need more jail space. The prison census continues to grow while crime declines. To some observers, the explanation is obvious — with more criminals out of circulation, there is less crime. Others say the drop in crime parallels a decline in the size of the crime-prone age groups. And now, they reason, because of toughened sentencing laws passed when crime was on the increase, imprisonment grows needlessly.

There is no clear relation between stiff sentences and a low crime rate. While Nevada incarcerates its offenders at the rate of 323 per 100,000 of its overall population, Minnesota locks them up at the rate of 52 per 100,000. Minnesota maintains a low level of serious crime while keeping its prisons within capacity by adjusting sentencing to the number of available beds. Nevada continues to record high crime rates.

The development of a private prison lobby is a further concern. Private operators whose growth depends upon an expanding prison population may push for ever harsher sentences. With the public's unabating fear of crime, and lawmakers shrinking from any move that appears to be soft on criminals, the developing private prison lobby will be hard to resist.

Private prison operators will work the crime trends both ways. Any drop in the crime rate will be attributed to long prison sentences. An increase will add weight to the call for more prisons. And the taxpayers will finance the profit-makers while double-locking their doors at night.

SOURCE: Kenneth F. Schoen, "Private Prison Operators," *New York Times,* March 28, 1985, p. A31. Reprinted by permission.

Summary

For the better part of U.S. history, prisoners were considered "slaves" of the state. Upon conviction, defendants experienced "civil death." The conditions in prison were generally brutal, and inmates had no recourse. The Supreme Court, furthermore, maintained a "hands-off" doctrine regarding correctional matters, refusing even to consider inmates' complaints.

The prisoners' rights movement began in 1961 when the High Court ruled in *Monroe* v. *Pape* that the long-dormant Section 1983 of the Civil Rights Act of 1871 was an appropriate mechanism for challenging the constitutionality of the conditions of prison life. Through a rush of petitions to the federal courts, convicts secured favorable decisions regarding legal services, the use of jailhouse lawyers, religious expression, media and mail services, medical programs, rehabilitative services, disciplinary proceedings, and the use of solitary confinement and corporal punishment.

During this period of prisoners' rights activity, however, many institutions across the nation continued to maintain archaic conditions. In the late 1960s, the Arkansas prison scandal erupted. It was the event upon which the 1980 film *Brubaker* was based, and it demonstrated that, as stated in a federal court's opinion in *Holt* v. *Sarver,* "a sentence to the Arkansas Penitentiary today amounts to a banishment from civilized society. . . ." In 1971, news from New York's Attica prison reached the press around the world. Attica's inmates revolted because of the conditions of incarceration, and the seige to recover the prison resulted in the deaths of scores of inmates and guards. In 1980, New Mexico State Prison distinguished itself for having the most gruesome riot in U.S. history. A year later, the entire Texas prison system was declared unconstitutional. The persistent problems across the nation continue to be overcrowding, poor programs, and a general lack of inmate safety. One solution that has been offered is the somewhat controversial privatization of corrections.

Key Terms

Arkansas prison scandal **(601)**
Attica **(586)**
"civil death" **(595)**
Estelle v. *Gamble* **(599)**
habeas corpus **(591)**
"hands-off" doctrine **(586)**
Holt v. *Sarver* **(601)**

Hudson v. *Palmer* **(618)**
Jackson v. *Bishop* **(603)**
Johnson v. *Avery* **(593)**
Meachum v. *Fano* **(606)**
Monroe v. *Pape* **(592)**
People v. *Lovercamp* **(608)**
privatization of corrections **(618)**

Procunier v. *Martinez* **(596)**
Rhodes v. *Chapman* **(617)**
Ruiz v. *Estelle* **(611)**
Section 1983 **(592)**
Wolff v. *McDonnell* **(606)**

Questions for Discussion

1. Why was the Supreme Court's decision in *Cruz* v. *Beto* based on Fourteenth Amendment rather than on First Amendment grounds?
2. How are inmates' rights to proper and adequate medical care protected by the Constitution?
3. By applying the criteria and reasoning of the court in *Jackson* v. *Bishop,* what other penal practices — in addition to whipping — could be considered cruel and unusual punishment? Why?
4. The decision in *Wolff* v. *McDonnell* was not retroactive to disciplinary proceedings that had failed

to follow the established due-process requirements. In this case, can the loss of "good time" credits through prior unconstitutional disciplinary hearings be reconciled? If *Wolff* were retroactive, how might prison authorities deal with sanctions already imposed?

5. What effects might *Rhodes* v. *Chapman* have on the direction of prison reform?

For Further Reading

Atkins, Burton M., and Henry R. Glick, eds. *Prisons, Protest, and Politics.* Englewood Cliffs, N.J.: Prentice-Hall, 1972.

Bowker, Lee H. *Prison Victimization.* New York: Elsevier, 1980.

Murton, Tom, and Joe Hyams. *Accomplices to Crime: The Arkansas Prison Scandal.* New York: Grove Press, 1969.

Wicker, Tom. *A Time to Die.* New York: Ballantine, 1975.

Notes

1. Ruffin v. Commonwealth, 62 Va. (21 Gratt.) 790, 796 (1871).
2. United States ex rel. Gereau v. Henderson, 526 F. 2d 889 (1976).
3. *Attica: The Official Report of the New York State Special Commission on Attica* (New York: Bantam, 1972), pp. 3–15.
4. See Tom Wicker, *A Time to Die* (New York: Ballantine, 1975).
5. National Advisory Commission on Criminal Justice Standards and Goals, *Corrections* (Washington, D.C.: U.S. Government Printing Office, 1973), p. 18.
6. David A. Jones, *The Law of Criminal Procedure* (Boston: Little, Brown, 1981), p. 574.
7. Coffin v. Reichard, 143 F. 2d 443 (1944).
8. Monroe v. Pape, 365 U.S. 167 (1961).
9. Preiser v. Rodriguez, 411 U.S. 475 (1973).
10. Ex parte Hull, 312 U.S. 546 (1941).
11. Johnson v. Avery, 393 U.S. 483 (1969).
12. Cited by John W. Palmer, *Constitutional Rights of Prisoners* (Cincinnati: Anderson, 1977), p. 88.
13. Younger v. Gilmore, 404 U.S. 15 (1971).
14. Wolff v. McDonnell, 418 U.S. 539 (1974).
15. Procunier v. Martinez, 416 U.S. 396 (1974).
16. Bounds v. Smith, 430 U.S. 817 (1977).
17. *National Law Journal,* December 24, 1984, p. 6
18. See Article I, Section 9.
19. Fulwood v. Clemmer, 206 F. Supp. 370 (D.C. Cir. 1962).
20. Howard v. Smyth, 365 F. 2d 28 (4th Cir. 1966); State v. Cubbage, 210 A. 2d 555 (Del. Super. Ct. 1965).
21. Jones v. Willingham, 248 F. Supp. 791 (D. Kan. 1965); Cooke v. Tramburg, 43 N.J. 514, 205 A. 2d 889 (1964).
22. Cruz v. Beto, 405 U.S. 319 (1972).
23. Childs v. Duckworth, CA 7, 33 CrL 2120 (1983).
24. Wolff v. McDonnell, 418 U.S. 539 (1974); Procunier v. Martinez, 416 U.S. 396 (1974).
25. Carothers v. Follette, 314 F. Supp. 1014 (S.D. N.Y. 1970).
26. Nolan v. Fitzpatrick, 451 F. 2d 545 (1st Cir. 1971).
27. Pell v. Procunier, 417 U.S. 817 (1974).
28. State of New York, *Correction Law,* Article 4, Section 70 (2).
29. O'Connor v. Donaldson, 422 U.S. 563 (1975).
30. Wilson v. Kelley, 294 F. Supp. 1005 (N.D. Ga. 1968).
31. Padgett v. Stein, 406 F. Supp. 287 (M.D. Pa. 1976).
32. William E. Cockerham, "Behavior Modification for Child Molesters," *Corrections* (January–February 1975): 77.
33. Knecht v. Gillman, 488 F. 2d 1136 (8th Cir. 1973).
34. Rutherford v. Hutto, 377 F. Supp. 268 (E.D. Ark. 1974); Jackson v. McLemore, 523 F. 2d 838 (8th Cir. 1975).
35. Estelle v. Gamble, 429 U.S. 97 (1976).
36. For example, see Gates v. Collier, 390 F. Supp. 482 (N.D. Miss. 1975).
37. Priest v. Cupp, 545 P. 2d 917 (Ore. Ct. App. 1976).
38. For further study of Devil's Island and the other French penal colonies, see George J. Seaton, *Isle of the Damned* (New York: Farrar, 1951); Aage Krarup-Nielson, *Hell Beyond the Seas* (New York: Dutton, 1940); Mrs. Blair Niles, *Condemned to Devil's Island* (London: Jonathan Cape, 1928).
39. Tom Murton, "Too Good for Arkansas," *The Nation,* January 12, 1970, pp. 12–17.
40. Tom Murton and Joe Hyams, *Accomplices to Crime: The Arkansas Prison Scandal* (New York: Grove Press, 1969), p. 7.
41. *Newsweek,* February 12, 1968, pp. 42–43.
42. Thomas O. Murton, *The Dilemma of Prison Reform* (New York: Holt, Rinehart and Winston, 1976), pp. 35–38
43. Holt v. Sarver, 309 F. Supp. 362 (E.D. Ark. 1970).
44. *Tennessee Code,* 41–707.
45. Sostre v. McGinnis, 442 F. 2d 178 (2d Cir. 1971).
46. Wilkerson v. Utah, 99 U.S. 130 (1878); Weems v. United States, 217 U.S. 349 (1910); Trop v. Dulles, 356 U.S. 86 (1958); Robinson v. California, 370 U.S. 660 (1962).
47. Jordan v. Fitzharris, 257 F. Supp. 674 (N.D. Cal. 1966).
48. Bauer v. Sielaff, 372 F. Supp. 1104 (E.D. Pa. 1974).
49. Landman v. Royster, 333 F. Supp. 621 (E.D. Va. 1971).
50. Novak v. Beto, 453 F. 2d 661 (5th Cir. 1972).
51. Jackson v. Bishop, 404 F. 2d 571 (8th Cir. 1968).
52. Landman v. Peyton, 370 F. 2d 135 (4th Cir. 1966).
53. Wolff v. McDonnell, 418 U.S. 539 (1974).
54. Meachum v. Fano, 427 U.S. 215 (1976); Montanye v. Haymes, 427 U.S. 236 (1976).
55. Costello v. Wainwright, 397 F. Supp. 20 (M.D. Fla. 1975).
56. People v. Lovercamp, 43 Cal. App. 3d 823, 118 Cal. Rptr. 110 (1974).
57. *New York Times,* December 13, 1981, p. 44.
58. Fred Cohen, "The Texas Prison Conditions Case: *Ruiz* v. *Estelle,*" *Criminal Law Bulletin* 17 (May–June 1981): 252–257.
59. Ruiz v. Estelle, 74–329 (E.D. Tex., Dec. 19, 1980).
60. *Ruiz* v. *Estelle,* F. 2d 115 (5th. Cir. 1982).
61. *New York Times,* July 8, 1984, p. E5.
62. *New York Times,* February 2, 1980, p. 1.
63. *U.S. News & World Report,* February 18, 1980, p. 68.
64. Kinesley Hammett, *Holocaust at New Mexico State Penitentiary* (Lubbock, TX.: C. F. Boone, 1980).
65. *Time,* October 26, 1981, p. 26.
66. *Newsweek,* September 7, 1981, p. 11.
67. *New York Times,* October 2, 1983, p. 48.
68. *New York Times,* July 22, 1984, p. 27.
69. *New York Times,* January 16, 1983, p. 1E; *Newsweek,* May 2, 1983, p. 13.
70. *Newsweek,* July 9, 1984, p. 62.
71. *New York Times,* June 19, 1985, p. A20.
72. Rhodes v. Chapman, 452 U.S. 337 (1981).
73. Hudson v. Palmer, U.S. Sup Ct (1984) 35 CrL 3230.

17

Probation, Parole, and Community-based Correction

Community-based corrections is the most promising means of accomplishing the changes in offender behavior that the public expects — and now demands — of corrections.

— National Advisory Commission on Criminal Justice
Standards and Goals, 1973

The public has assumed that the worst offenders — murderers, rapists, drug traffickers — serve substantial terms, but statistics show how easy it is for hardened criminals to get back on the streets.

— William French Smith, former U.S. attorney general,
commenting in 1984 on the need to abolish parole

The ostensibly self-defining principle of community-based correction rests on the fundamental dichotomy that offenders are either incarcerated or they are not. Logically, this suggests that the concept refers to all correctional strategies that take place within the community. Accordingly, there have been many types of court-determined sentences that could be viewed as community-based correction. Colonial sanctions of placement in the stocks and pillory, the ducking stool, the brank, and the wearing of the scarlet letter were certainly community-based. The same might be said of floggings in the public square and the more contemporary imposition of fines in lieu of imprisonment. But these are oversimplifications of the community-based correctional philosophy, for considerably more than the factors of sanction and location are involved. **Community-based correction** includes activities and programs within the community that have effective ties with the local environment. These activities and programs are generally of a rehabilitative rather than a punitive nature, and can include arrangements with employment, educational, social, and clinical service delivery sytems. Many also involve supervision by a community or governmental agency.

Within this context, the more typical forms of community-based correctional services include pretrial diversion projects; probation and parole; work and educational release activities; and furlough, restitution, and halfway house programs.

The reasons for community-based correctional strategies are numerous, encompassing a range of humanitarian, fiscal, and pragmatic motives. First, with the growth of the humanitarian movement in corrections, the notions of mercy and compassion combined with considerations of human dignity began to infiltrate sentencing practices and correctional decision making. For offenders who could not help themselves, and for others who represented diminished risks to society, it was felt that custodial coercion might be unnecessary. Second, for an untold number of lesser and situational offenders, many reformers held that the unfavorable consequences of imprisonment — the loss of liberty and self-esteem, the placement in physical jeopardy, and the fact that penitentiaries can be "schools of crime" — would impede successful rehabilitation and community reintegration. Third, from an economic point of view, it would cost far less to supervise criminals in the community than to maintain them in institutions. Furthermore, the families of those sent to prison often became financial burdens to the state. Fourth, many community-based correctional strategies were deemed to have the practical value of helping offenders to achieve positions in their neighborhoods and communities as opposed to the more negative implications of institutional banishment. Fifth, with the recent trends in prison overcrowding, reducing or

Community-based correction: Rehabilitative activities and programs within the community that have effective ties with the local government.

Situational offenders include essentially noncriminal types who feel that circumstances have forced them into illegal acts (such as an unemployed father who steals money to buy food or purchase Christmas gifts for his children).

altogether eliminating the offender's period of confinement has been viewed as a more pragmatic approach to the management and control of the less seriously involved criminal offenders. And sixth, since the onset of the 1960s, there seems to have developed a "last resort" philosophy in corrections which maintains that the traditional avenues of punishment and correction have not been working, and new, innovative approaches must be tested.

Criminal Justice Diversion

Criminal justice **diversion** refers to the removal of offenders from the application of the criminal law at any stage of the police and court processes.[1] It implies the formal halting or suspending of traditional criminal proceedings against persons who have violated criminal statutes, in favor of processing them through some noncriminal disposition or means. Thus, diversion occurs prior to adjudication; *it is a preadjudication disposition.*

The Development of Diversion

Diversion is not a new practice in the administration of justice. It has likely existed in an *informal* fashion for thousands of years, since the inception of organized law enforcement and social control. In ancient and modern societies, informal diversion has occurred in many ways: A police officer removes a public drunk from the street to a Salvation Army shelter; a prosecutor decides to *nolle pros.* a petty theft; a magistrate releases with a lecture an individual who assaulted a neighbor during the course of an argument. These are generally discretionary decisions, undertaken at random and off the record, and they tend to be personalized, standardless, and inconsistent. They are often problematic in that they may reflect individual, class, or social prejudices. Furthermore, they serve only to remove offenders from the application of criminal penalties with no attempt to provide appropriate jurisprudential alternatives.

Although these haphazard and unsystematic practices will continue, more formalized diversion activities impose social-therapeutic programs in lieu of conviction and punishment. These latter seem to have emerged within the juvenile justice system during the early part of this century. Among the first was the Chicago Boys' Court, founded in 1914 as an extralegal form of probation. As explained many years ago by Chicago municipal court judge Jacob Braude, the rationale of the Boys' Court was to process and treat young offenders without branding them as criminals:

The Chicago Boys' Court

> While the facility of probation is available to court, it is used at a minimum because before one can be admitted to probation he must first be found guilty. Having been found guilty, he is stamped with a criminal record and then telling him to go out and make good is more likely to be a handicap than an order.[2]

The Boys' Court system of supervision placed young defendants under the authority of one of four community agencies: the Holy Name Society, the Chicago Church Federation, the Jewish Social Service Bureau, and the Colored Big Brothers. After a time, the court requested a report of the defendant's activities and adjustment, and if they were favorable, he would be officially discharged from court having no criminal record.

Later developments in youthful diversionary programs included New York City's Youth Counsel Bureau. This agency was established during the early 1950s for handling juveniles alleged to be delinquent or criminal but not deemed sufficiently advanced in their misbehavior to be adjudicated and committed by the courts.[3] Referrals came from police, courts, schools, and other sources. The bureau provided counseling services and discharged those whose adjustment appeared promising. In many instances, the youthful defendants not only avoided criminal convictions, but arrest records as well. Alternative programs in the developing area of juvenile diversion included the District of Columbia's Project Crossroads, aimed at unemployed and underemployed first offenders ages 16 to 25 years who were charged with property offenses.[4] Upon agreement to enter the program, a youth's charge was suspended for 90 days, during which counseling, education, and employment services would be made available. At the end of the three-month period, project staff would recommend a *nolle pros.* of the charges, further treatment, or return to the court for resumption of prosecution.

Patterns of Diversion

As criminal justice diversion continued to evolve, the arguments in its favor increased. It was felt that its practice would reduce court backlog, provide early intervention before the development of full-fledged criminal careers, ensure some consistency in selective law enforcement, reduce the costs of criminal processing, and enhance an offender's chances for community reintegration. More importantly, however, it had been the conclusion of many social scientists and penal reformers that the criminal justice process, which was designed to protect society from criminals, often contributed to the very behavior it was trying to eliminate. This was typically accomplished by:

1. Forcing those convicted of criminal offenses to interact with other, perhaps more experienced criminals, thus, becoming socialized to a variety of criminal roles, learning the required skills and the criminal value system.
2. Denying convicted felons the opportunity to play legitimate roles.
3. Changing the individual's self-concept to that of a criminal. This occurs as a result of an individual being told by the courts that he or she is a criminal and being placed in an institution where inmates and guards define the individual as a criminal.[5]

Both the President's Commission on Law Enforcement and Administration of Justice in 1967 and the National Advisory Commission on Criminal Justice Standards and Goals in 1973 heavily endorsed the diversion concept, holding that it would not only offer a viable alternative to incarceration, but also minimize the potential criminal socialization and labeling of first offenders.

Primarily as a result of massive federal funding allocated by the Law Enforcement Assistance Administration for the prevention and reduction of crime, diversion programs of many types emerged and expanded throughout the nation during the 1970s. Most, however, were designed for youths, for minor crimes (such as assaults, simple thefts, and property damage resulting from neighborhood disputes), and for special offenders whose crimes were deemed to be related to problem drinking or narcotics use.

Youth Service Bureaus

Specifically recommended by the President's Commission and begun in California during 1971, youth service bureaus became common by the mid-1970s. They were similar in concept to New York's original Youth Council Bureau, but many operated as adjuncts to local police departments. They offered counseling, tutoring, crisis intervention, job assistance, and guidance with school and family problems for truants, runaways, and delinquent youths.

Public Inebriate Programs

In municipalities where public intoxication has remained a criminal offense, several diversionary alternatives to prosecution have been structured for public inebriates. Some are placed in alcohol detoxification centers rather than in jails. Others are referred before trial to community service agencies for more intensive treatment and care.

Civil Commitment

Based on a medical model of rehabilitation, civil commitment programs were founded on the notion that some types of criminality resulted from symptoms of illness rather than malicious intent. Such offenders as drug users, sexual deviants, and the mentally ill could be diverted either before or after trial to a residential setting for therapeutic treatment. Community protection was promised by the removal of offenders to a rehabilitation center, while those diverted received treatment instead of criminal sanctions and stigma. Civil commitment programs were most common in California, New York, and the federal system for the treatment of narcotics users.

Citizen Dispute Settlement

Citizen dispute settlement programs were designed to deflect from the criminal justice system complaints related to family and neighborhood quarrels and evolving from petty crimes, simple assaults, property damage, threats, and bad checks. Cases are diverted to mediation by a disinterested third party at the family or neighborhood level, and identified problem areas receive help through arbitration combined with help from local community service agencies.

Treatment Alternatives to Street Crime

During the 1970s, the Law Enforcement Assistance Administration funded many large-scale projects in major cities known as Treatment Alternatives to Street Crime, or TASC, which were designed to serve as a liaison between the criminal justice system and existing community treatment structures. TASC programs diverted drug-using arrestees into ongoing drug treatment facilities. The original criminal charge was held in abeyance until the treatment was completed. If treatment appeared successful, the charge was dropped by the courts.

The Impact of Diversion

It is difficult to assess the overall value and impact of the national diversion effort. Many programs have never been evaluated, and estimations of their effectiveness have been based on little more than clinical intuition and hunch. Among those that have undergone rigorous assessment, the findings have ranged from promising to bleak. Furthermore, several projects became steeped in controversy, resulting in some negative commentary on the entire trend of diversion.

On the more positive side, many programs seemed to be effecting measurable change with certain defendants. An example was the Manhattan Court Employment Project, operated by New York's Vera Institute of Justice from 1967 through 1970. Its focus was on male and female offenders charged with misdemeanors and minor felonies. Subjects were given job training and placement. Those who failed to show any progress were returned to the courts for prosecution. An evaluation in 1972 demonstrated that the recidivism rate among defendants whose charges were dropped was half that of the defendants returned for prosecution.[6] Conversely, the experience with the youth service bureaus was considerably less impressive. Although the bureaus were touted as models for diverting juveniles from the criminal justice system, a national assessment survey of the projects found that they contributed little to any community in helping solve the problem of youth crime.[7]

New York's highly controversial Narcotic Addiction Control Commission (NACC) also did little for the cause of criminal justice diversion. In 1966, NACC was established by statute as a comprehensive, statewide civil commitment program for the treatment of "narcotics addicts." In addition to arrestees, persons could come voluntarily to the courts to be "certified" for treatment. Upon certification, they were placed in residential treatment facilities. Curiously, however, a number of the NACC facilities had been purchased from the state's correctional system. They were staffed by prison guards (called "narcotic treatment officers" in NACC terminology) armed with clubs. The "patients" (referred to as "rehabilitants") were treated under conditions of tight security and often locked in cells at night — despite the fact that they had not been convicted of crimes, and that some were volunteers. The civil commitment program also included a period of community aftercare. Under conditions similar to parole, the patients could be returned to the treatment institution for violations of program rules, or returned to the courts for prosecution if the original commitment had been an outgrowth of an arrest or criminal complaint.[8]

By the mid-1970s, after tens of thousands of persons had been certified, diverted, processed, and treated, and after expenditures in excess of $1 billion, NACC was deemed a failure. The courts ultimately ruled that the confinement of voluntary cases was in violation of constitutional rights, and evaluation studies found the treatment to be no different or any more effective than that received in traditional correctional institutions.[9] As of 1980, NACC was neither certifying nor treating narcotics users; it had changed its name at least three times, and shifted into alternative roles in the management of drug abuse; and its rehabilitation facilities had once again become state prisons.

The numerous TASC programs funded by the Law Enforcement Assistance Administration have also done little for the image of pretrial diversion, for client outcome has been mixed. The requirements for entry into TASC diversion have not been particularly rigid. It is necessary for the offender to have used illicit drugs, to have been charged with anything but a serious violent crime, to have approval of the judge, and to agree to placement in a

New York's Narcotic Addiction Control Commission (NACC)

The effectiveness of TASC

local drug program. The result has been that many TASC participants have viewed the diversion program as an easy alternative to jail. Many show little motivation for treatment, and local drug program directors readily send them back to the courts for prosecution. [10]

The concept of pretrial diversion has been continued into the 1980s, but with somewhat less enthusiasm. Despite the problematic character of many of the programs, a few new and innovative operations have nevertheless emerged. A striking example is the Weekend Intervention Program (WIP) in Dayton, Ohio. Begun in 1978 and sponsored by the Wright State University School of Medicine, the WIP was structured in response to the growing concern over drunk drivers. First and second DWI (driving while intoxicated) offenders are given the option of conviction and sentence, or a three-day program of intensive therapy and alcohol education. Persons diverted to the WIP pay a fee for the services provided, making the operation self-supporting. A preliminary follow-up in late 1981 demonstrated that of those former patients contacted, some 90 percent were either drinking less or were totally abstinent, and only 9 percent had been rearrested for an alcohol offense. [11]

Weekend Intervention Program (WIP)

Probation

In the month of August, 1841, I was in court one morning, when the door communicating with the lock-room was opened and an officer entered, followed by a ragged and wretched looking man, who took his seat upon the bench allotted to prisoners. I imagined from the man's appearance, that his offense was that of yielding to his appetite for intoxicating drinks, and in a few moments I found that my suspicions were correct, for the clerk read the complaint, in which the man was charged with being a common drunkard. The case was clearly made out, but before sentence had been passed, I conversed with him for a few moments, and found that he was not yet past all hope of reformation. . . . He told me that if he could be saved from the House of Correction, he never again would taste intoxicating liquors; there was such an earnestness in that tone, and a look of firm resolve, that I determined to aid him; I bailed him, by permission of the Court. He was ordered to appear for sentence in three weeks from that time. He signed the pledge and became a sober man; at the expiration of this period of probation, I accompanied him into the court room. . . . The Judge expressed himself much pleased with the account we gave of the man, and instead of the usual penalty — imprisonment in the House of Corrections — he fined him one cent and costs, amounting in all to $3.76, which was immediately paid. The man continued industrious and sober, and without doubt has been by this treatment, saved from a drunkard's grave.

— John Augustus, 1852

This incident during the latter part of 1841 gave birth to the concept of probation in the United States. Augustus was a Boston shoemaker, and his method was to bail an offender after conviction, to provide him with friendship and support in family matters, as well as in job assistance. When the defendant was later brought to court for sentencing, Augustus would report on his progress toward reformation and request that the judge order a small fine and court costs in lieu of a jail sentence. [12] As such, John Augustus was the first probation officer. By 1858, he had bailed almost 2,000 defendants. His efforts led to the first probation statute, passed in Massachusetts in 1878. By 1900, four other states had enacted similar legislation, and probation became an established alternative to incarceration.

John Augustus, the father of probation

The Nature of Probation

Probation: A sentence not involving confinement that imposes conditions and retains authority in the sentencing court to modify the conditions of sentence or to resentence the offender if he or she violates the conditions.

Probation can be a rather confusing concept, for in the field of corrections the term has been used in a variety of ways. First of all, probation is a sentence. It is a sentence of conditional release to the community. More specifically, as defined by the American Bar Association, probation is a sentence not involving confinement that imposes conditions and retains authority in the sentencing court to modify the conditions of sentence or to resentence the offender if he or she violates the conditions.[13]

In addition to being a disposition, the word *probation* has also been used to refer to a status, a system, and a process.[14] As a status, probation reflects the unique character of the probationer: he or she is neither a free citizen nor a confined prisoner. As a system, probation is a component in the administration of justice, as embodied by the agency or organization that administers the probation process. As a process, probation refers to the set of functions, activities, and services that characterize the system's transactions with the courts, the offender, and the community. This process includes the preparation of reports for the courts, the supervision of probationers, and the obtaining and providing of services for them.

The Probation Philosophy

The premise behind the use of probation is that many offenders are not dangerous and represent little, if any, menace to society. It has been argued that when defendants are institutionalized, the prison community becomes their new reference point. They are forced into contact with hard-core criminals, the prison experience generates embitterment and hostility, and the "ex-con" label becomes a stigma that impedes social adjustment. Probation, on the other hand, provides a more therapeutic alternative. The term comes from the Latin *probare*, meaning to test or prove, and the probationer is given the opportunity to demonstrate that if given a second chance, more socially acceptable behavior patterns will result.

The probation philosophy also includes elements of community protection and offender rehabilitation. Probationers are supervised by agents of the court or probation agency. These are trained personnel with dual roles. They are present to ensure that the conditions of probation are fulfilled and to provide counseling and assistance in community reintegration. Furthermore, as with all types of community-based correction, it is generally agreed that the rehabilitation of offenders is more realistically possible in the natural environment of the free community than behind prison walls.

While these are the ideal philosophical underpinnings of probation, several more pragmatic issues have also entered into its use as an alternative to imprisonment. First, and as noted in the previous chapter, correctional institutions throughout the nation have become painfully overcrowded. With the almost prohibitive costs of new prison construction, probation is seen by many as a more economically viable correctional alternative. Second, and also as a matter of simple economics, the probation process is considerably cheaper than the prison process. The cost of maintaining an inmate in the Texas Department of Corrections, for example, was estimated in 1980 to be $7.50 per day, whereas the cost for supervising a probationer amounts to $0.65 per day.[15] In New York, where facilities are more numerous and prison industries are not structured to subsidize the costs of institutionalization, the expenditures for maintaining an inmate behind prison walls are even higher — approximately $46.50 per day or $17,000 per year. Third, within some sectors of the criminal justice community, imprisonment is being viewed more and more as cruel and unusual punishment. Prisons are dangerous places to live. Inmates are physically, sexually, and emotionally victimized on a regular basis. Probation, within this context, is considered to be the more humane avenue of correctional intervention.

Suspended Sentences and Conditional Release

There are a variety of terms that tend to be used interchangeably with probation, but which represent things that are quite different. The best known of these is the **suspended sentence,** a disposition that in and of itself implies supervision of the offender with a set of specified criteria and goals. The suspended sentence is a quasi-freedom that can be revoked at the pleasure of the court. Suspended sentences, furthermore, are of two types: *suspension of imposition* of sentence and *suspension of execution* of sentence. In the case of suspension of impositon, there may be verdict or plea, but no sentence is pronounced. Although uncommon, the presiding magistrate releases the defendant on the general condition that he or she stay out of trouble and make restitution for the crime. With the suspension of execution, the sentence is prescribed but is postponed or not carried out. In a number of jurisdictions, a sentence can be suspended, and this suspension is followed by an order for probation.

> **Suspended sentence:** A court disposition of a convicted person, pronouncing a penalty of a fine or commitment to confinement, but unconditionally discharging the defendant or holding execution of the penalty in abeyance upon good behavior.

Alternatively, the New York Penal Law, in addition to probation, provides for sentences of *conditional discharge* and *unconditional discharge.* The sentence of conditional discharge is similar to a suspended sentence:

> The court may impose a sentence of conditional discharge for an offense if the court, having regard to the nature and circumstances of the offense and to the history, character, and condition of the defendant, is of the opinion that neither the public interest nor the interests of justice would be served by a sentence of imprisonment and that probation supervision is not appropriate.[16]

Under the New York law, the period of conditional discharge is one year for a misdemeanor and three years for a felony, and the conditions generally involve making restitution or reparation for losses suffered by the victim. The sentence of unconditional discharge goes one step further, and the defendant is released without imprisonment, fine, probation, or any conditions whatsoever. Such a sentence is used when it is the opinion of the court that no proper purpose is served by the imposition of any conditions. For all purposes, such a discharge is a final judgment of conviction.[17]

The Presentence or Probation Investigation

Probation in the United States is administered by hundreds of independent government agencies, each jurisdiction operating under different laws and many with widely varying philosophies. In some jurisdictions, such as Hawaii, a single state authority provides services for all probationers. In other jurisdictions, probation descends from county or municipal authority, functioning under state laws, and guidelines, but is administered by the lower courts. In some areas, such as South Carolina, probation and parole are combined into a single state unit. In the federal system, probation is administered as an arm of the federal district courts.

Presentence investigation: An investigation undertaken by a probation agency or other designated authority at the request of a court into the past behavior, family circumstances, and personality of a person who has been convicted of a crime, in order to assist the court in determining the most appropriate sentence.

The presentence investigation is one of the basic services provided by the probation agency, and, as noted in Chapter 13, such reports are generally mandatory if probation appears to be a possible sentence. In their examination of the backgrounds and characteristics of defendants, these reports can vary widely in depth, content, and usefulness. In some regional offices in South Carolina, for example, selected presentence investigation reports are less than a single page in length, and contain only the basic facts of the defendant's criminal history and current offense, followed by a brief statement of the offender's prognosis and the probation agent's recommendation for sentencing. In contrast, some presentence investigations conducted in Kings County (Brooklyn), New York, have exceeded 30 single-spaced legal-sized pages, and recount numerous aspects of the defendant's life including whether he or she was the product of a normal birth delivery.[18] The norm, however, is somewhere between these two extremes, and includes the characteristics of the offender, the circumstances of the offense, an evaluative summary, and a recommendation. (See Exhibit 17.1.)

Studies have demonstrated that in most sentences involving probation, there is a high correlation between the presentence or probation officer's recommendation and the judge's sentencing decision.[19] This should not suggest, however, that judicial decision making is dictated by the content of a presentence report recommendation, or that judges and presentence investigators interpret defendants' life histories and background characteristics in remarkably the same way. Rather, there are a number of more logical factors at work. First, since probation is one of the most common sentences, the simple laws of chance are operative. Second, most criminal convictions occur as the result of guilty pleas. The details of the plea negotiation and the prosecutor's sentencing recommendation are generally known to the presentence investigator, and these typically influence his or her recommendation. Third, presentence or probation officers tend to be aware of the sentencing recommendations that will be acceptable to specific judges for given kinds of cases, and they often take the path of least resistance.[20]

The U.S. Supreme Court has upheld the validity of the presentence investigation as meeting the due-process requirements of the Constitution. In *Williams* v. *New York*,[21] decided in 1949, the Court held that, at sentencing, a convicted defendant does not have a Sixth Amendment right to cross-examine persons who have supplied information to a court (in a presentence report) regarding the sentencing. However, the Supreme Court has provided defendants with some safeguards in this matter. In the 1977 case of *Gardner* v. *Florida*,[22] for example, the Court ruled that a defendant is denied due process when a sentence is based, even in part, on confidential information contained in a presentence report that the defendant is not given the opportunity to deny or explain. Although both *Williams* and *Gardner* involved examinations of the nature of the presentence report in the context of capital cases, subsequent decisions in state courts of appeals served to apply the Court's rulings to noncapital cases as well.

Williams v. New York

Conditions of Probation

Most states have statutory restrictions on the granting of probation. In some jurisdictions, defendants convicted of such crimes as murder, kidnapping, and rape are ineligible for probation, as are second and third felony offenders. Others tend to be less specific, but structure their penal codes in such a manner as to preclude a sentence of probation for most serious offenders. In

Alabama, for example, persons convicted of crimes that typically call for sentences of death or imprisonment for ten years or more are ineligible for probation.[23] In North Carolina, "a person who has been convicted of any noncapital criminal offense not punishable by a minimum term of life imprisonment may be placed on probation. . . ."[24]

Thus, in most jurisdictions, probation is a statutory alternative to imprisonment for most felony convictions. Judges differ, however, in their approaches to granting it. As noted earlier, both plea bargaining and factors contained in the presentence report enter into the decision. In addition, there are such elements as the prosecutor's recommendation, anticipated community reaction, political considerations, court backlog, the availability of space in the prison system, and the judge's own feelings towards the particular offense or the offender. A Delaware judge commented, for example:

> Although the statutes permit it, I find sentences of imprisonment for convictions of marijuana possession to be unreasonable. . . . However, in *my* court, any person found guilty of a felony offense involving the exploitation of a child, sexually or otherwise, will receive the maximum term of imprisonment that the law allows.[25]

Upon the granting of probation and as part of their probation agreement, defendants are required to abide by a variety of regulations and conditions. These conditions are fairly standard from state to state. In New York, for example, which is typical of most jurisdictions, the conditions exhort the probationer to live a law-abiding and productive life, to work, to support his or her dependents, to maintain contact with the supervising probation officer, and to remain within the jurisdiction of the court (see Exhibit 17.2).

Special conditions of probation may also be imposed, by either the sentencing judge or the supervising probation agency. Many of these have been challenged by probationers as "improper," but most have been upheld by state appellate courts. Recent court decisions have affirmed the correctness of such special requirements as undergoing treatment for drug abuse,[26] abstaining from the use of alcohol,[27] serving a short jail sentence prior to release on probation with no credit for prior confinement,[28] refraining from operating a motor vehicle during the period of probation,[29] submitting to a search by the supervising probation officer,[30] and payment of restitution.[31] Some special conditions have been very specific yet at the same time trivial, but these too have been affirmed by the courts. In a 1980 New York case, for example, the court found proper a condition of probation that required a person convicted of embezzling from the bank account of a cemetery association to mow the lawn in the local cemetery during the grass-cutting season.[32]

Generally, conditions of probation are considered constitutional and proper unless they bear no reasonable relationship to the crime committed or the defendant's probationary status. Thus placement in a drug treatment program becomes an appropriate condition of probation only when the defendant's offense is considered to be a consequence of a drug-abuse problem. Conversely, abstinence from alcohol would be an improper condition for probationers who never had problems with drinking. Furthermore, while warrantless searches of probationers, their automobiles, and premises are permissible conditions if carried out by probation officers with just cause, the courts have ruled that such searches cannot be extended to all law enforcement officers.[33]

EXHIBIT 17.1

A Presentence Report

United States District Court Central District of New York

Name: John Jones

Address:
 1234 Astoria Blvd.
 New York City

Legal Residence:
 Same

Age: 33

Date of Birth: 2-8-40
 New York City

Sex: Male

Race: Caucasian

Citizenship: U.S. (birth)

Education: 10th grade

Marital Status: Married

Dependents: Three
 (wife and 2 children)

Soc. Sec. No.: 112-03-9559

FBI No.: 256 1126

Date: January 4, 1974

Docket No.: 74 – 103

Offense: Theft of mail by Postal
 Employee (18 U.S.C. Sec.
 1709) 2 cts.

Penalty: Ct. 2 – 5 years and/or
 $2,000 fine

Plea: Guilty on 12-16-73 to Ct. 2
 Ct. 1 pending

Verdict:

Custody: Released on own
 recognizance. No time in
 custody

Asst. U.S. Attorney:
 Samuel Hayman

Defense Counsel: Thomas Lincoln,
 Federal Public Defender

Drug/Alcohol Involvement:
 Attributes offense to need for
 drinking money

Detainers or Charges Pending:
 None

Codefendants (Disposition): None

Disposition:

Date:

Sentencing Judge:

Offense: Official Version. Official sources revealed that during the course of routine observations on December 4, 1973, within the Postal Office Center, Long Island, New York, postal inspectors observed the defendant paying particular attention to various packages. Since the defendant was seen to mishandle and tamper with several parcels, test parcels were prepared for his handling on December 5, 1973. The defendant was observed to mishandle one of the test parcels by tossing it to one side into a canvas tub. He then placed his jacket into the tube and leaned over the tub for a period of time. At this time the defendant left the area and went to the men's room. While he was gone the inspectors examined the mail tube and found that the test parcel had been rifled and that the contents, a watch, was missing.

The defendant returned to his work area and picked up his jacket. He then left the building. The defendant was stopped by the inspectors across the street from the post office. He was questioned about his activities and on his person he had the wristwatch from the test parcel. He was taken to the postal inspector's office, where he admitted the offense.

Defendant's Version of Offense. The defendant admits that he rifled the package in question and took the watch. He states that he intended to sell the watch at a later date. He admits that he has been drinking too much lately and needed extra cash for "drinking money." He exhibits remorse and is concerned about the possibility of incarceration and the effect that it would have on his family.

Prior Record			
Date	Offense	Place	Disposition
5-7-66 (age 26)	Possession of policy slips	Manhattan CR. CT. N.Y., N.Y.	$25.00 Fine 7-11-66
3-21-72 (age 32)	Intoxication	Manhattan CR. CT. N.Y., N.Y.	4-17-72 Nolle

Personal History. The defendant was born in New York City on February 8, 1940, the oldest of three children. He attended the public school, completed the 10th grade, and left school to go to work. He was rated as an average student and was active in sports, especially basketball and baseball.

The defendant's father, John, died of a heart attack in 1968, at the age of 53 years. He had an elementary school education and worked as a construction laborer most of his life.

The defendant's mother, Mary Smith Jones, is 55 years of age and is employed as a seamstress. She had an elementary school education and married defendant's father when she was 20 years of age. Three sons were issue of the marriage. She presently resides in New York City, and is in good health.

Defendant's brother, Paul, age 32 years, completed 2½ years of high school. He is employed as a bus driver and resides with his wife and two children in New York City.

Defendant's brother, Lawrence, age 30 years, completed three semesters of college. He is employed as a New York City firefighter. He resides with his wife and one child in Dutch Point, Long Island.

The defendant after leaving high school worked as a delivery boy for a retail supermarket chain then served 2 years in the U.S. Army as an infantryman (ASN 123 456 78). He received an honorable discharge and attained the rank of corporal serving from 2-10-58 to 2-1-60. After service he held a number of jobs of the laboring type.

The defendant was employed as a truck driver for the City of New York when he married Ann Sweeny on 6-15-63. Two children were issue of this marriage, John, age 8, and Mary, age 6. The family has resided at the same address (which is a four-room apartment) since their marriage.

The defendant has been in good health all of his life but he admits he has been drinking to excess the past 18 months, which has resulted in some domestic strife. The wife stated that she loved her husband and will stand by him. She is amenable to a referral for family counseling.

Defendant has worked for the Postal Service since 12-1-65 and resigned on 12-5-73 as a result of the present arrest. His work ratings by his supervisors were always "excellent."

Evaluative Summary. The defendant is a 33-year-old male who entered a plea of guilty to mail theft. While an employee of the U.S. Postal Service he rifled and stole a watch from a test package. He admitted that he planned on selling the watch to finance his drinking, which has become a problem, resulting in domestic strife.

Defendant is a married man with two children with no prior serious record. He completed 10 years of school, had an honorable military record, and has a good work history. He expresses remorse for his present offense and is concerned over the loss of his job and the shame to his family.

Recommendation. It is respectfully recommended that the defendant be admitted to probation. If placed on probation the defendant expresses willingness to seek counseling for his domestic problems. He will require increased motivation if there is to be a significant change in his drinking pattern.

Respectfully submitted,

Donald M. Fredericks
U.S. Probation Officer

SOURCE: Administrative Offices of the U.S. Courts, Division of Probation, "The Selective Presentence Investigation Report," *Federal Probation* 38 (December 1974): 53–54.

An illustration of how the appellate courts interpret the constitutional-ity of conditions of probation occurred in *Rodriguez* v. *State*,[34] decided by a Florida district court of appeals in 1979. After the appellant entered a plea of *nolo contendere* to the charge of aggravated child abuse, she was placed on probation for ten years, subject to the conditions that she (1) not have custody of her children, (2) not become pregnant, and (3) not marry without the consent of the court. Discussing the status of probation and the propriety of various conditions of probation, the court stated:

> We note initially that the constitutional rights of probationers are limited by conditions of probation which are desirable for the purposes of rehabilitation. The Fourth Amendment prohibitions of unreason-able searches and seizures and the Fifth Amendment privilege against self-incrimination are qualified by probationary status. Likewise, First Amendment rights of free speech and association may be limited by valid probationary conditions. We thus have no constitutional diffi-culty with the conditions imposed, if they are otherwise valid condi-tions of probation.
>
> The statutory authorization for imposition of probation merely provides that "[t]he court shall determine the terms and conditions of

---

EXHIBIT 17.2

Conditions of Probation

1. **Conditions relating to conduct and rehabilitation**

   (a) Avoid injurious or vicious habits;

   (b) Refrain from frequenting unlawful or disreputable places or consorting with disreputable persons;

   (c) Work faithfully at a suitable employment or faithfully pursue a course of study or of vocational training that will equip him for suitable employment;

   (d) Undergo available medical or psychiatric treatment and remain in a specified institution, when required for that purpose;

   (e) Support his dependents and meet other family responibilities;

   (f) Make restitution of the fruits of his offense or make reparation, in an amount he can afford to pay, for the loss or damage caused thereby. When restitution or reparation is a condition of the sentence, the court shall fix the amount thereof and the manner of performance;

   (g) Post a bond or other security for the performance of any or all conditions imposed;

   (h) Satisfy any other conditions reasonably related to his rehabilitation.

2. **Conditions relating to supervision.**

   (a) Report to a probation officer as directed by the court or the probation officer and permit the probation officer to visit him at his place of abode or elsewhere;

   (b) Remain within the jurisdiction of the court unless granted permission to leave by the court or the probation officer; and

   (c) Answer all reasonable inquiries by the probation officer and promptly notify the probation officer of any change in address or employment.

SOURCE: State of New York, *Penal Law*, 65.10.

probation. . . ." As previously noted, this court has held "overbroad" a condition of probation which prohibited the probationer from living with any female relative. One of our sister courts had held a condition of probation that the probationer marry to be "beyond the trial court's authority." The Florida Supreme Court has noted that a trial court may impose any valid condition of probation which serves a useful rehabilitative purpose. Trial courts have broad discretion to impose various conditions of probation, but a special condition of probation cannot be imposed if it is so punitive as to be unrelated to rehabilitation.

Applying these criteria to the instant case, we hold that the condition prohibiting custody of children has a clear relationship to the crime of child abuse and is therefore valid. The conditions relating to marriage and pregnancy have no relationship to the crime of child abuse, and relate to noncriminal conduct. Possibly these conditions could relate to future criminality, if the marriage or pregnancy resulted in custody of minor children who could be abused. But we hold that the conditions are not reasonably related to future criminality, since such custody of minor children is already prohibited by the valid condition directly addressed to custody. The conditions prohibiting marriage and pregnancy add nothing to decrease the possibility of further child abuse or other criminality.

Restitution Programs

Among the more widely endorsed conditions of probation in recent years is restitution: requiring offenders to compensate their victims for damages or stolen property (monetary restitution), or donate their time to community service (community service restitution).

The rationales for restitution are numerous. First, while fines imposed go directly into court or government treasuries, monetary restitution goes directly to the victims of crime, compensating them for injuries, time lost from work and other losses. Second, it forces the offender to take personal responsibility for his or her crime. Third, it has the potential for reconciling victims and offenders. Fourth, it can be incorporated into a probation program without the need for additional programs and expenditures. And fifth, it provides a vehicle for including the victim in the administration of justice.[35]

Despite these apparent virtues, restitution does have critics. It has been suggested that restitution can be a punitive sanction rather than a rehabilitative one, since it places an additional burden on offenders that they might not ordinarily have. Even more importantly, it carries the potential for nullifying any deterrent effects of punishment by allowing criminals to "write a check" and "pay a fee" for their offenses. Finally, it can be argued that restitution serves only the interests of those of reasonable financial ability, thus prohibiting such an option to the indigent. Although in many ways this latter argument is true, there are a number of alternatives that make restitution available to offenders at all levels of the socioeconomic ladder. There are, for example, community service restitution outlets through which juvenile vandals can work to repair the damage they caused, drunk drivers can work in alcohol detoxification centers, and other offenders can work in hospitals, nursing homes, or in juvenile counseling programs.[36]

Probation Services

At least in theory, probation service incorporates the casework approach. During the probationer's initial interview with his or her probation officer, an

Restitution requires offenders to compensate their victims for damages or to donate their time in service to the community.

evaluation is made to determine what type of treatment supervision is most appropriate. Based on information contained in the presentence investigation and on his or her skills in counseling and problem solving, the officer plans a treatment schedule designed to allow the probationer to make a reasonable community adjustment. This diagnostic aspect of probation intake examines the probationer's peer relationships, family problems, work skills and history, educational status, and involvement with drug or alcohol abuse. During the course of the probation period, the officer works with the offender in these designated areas as required. The treatment may be limited to one-to-one counseling, or it may involve referral to community service agencies for drug abuse treatment, vocational skill enhancement, or job assistance. Some probation agencies have special supervision units with officers specifically trained in these areas. Others provide psychiatric services or structured group counseling programs. Since probationers are convicted criminal offenders and one of the officer's roles involves community protection, a second function of the intake interview is to determine what level of community supervision appears necessary. Such supervision planning can involve regular visits to the probationer's home and place of employment, and can require the client to report to the probation office on a weekly, semimonthly, or monthly basis.

Although many probation agencies do operate in the manner outlined, in practice few probationers receive such individualized treatment and supervision, for many different reasons. First, the educational backgrounds, skills, and experiences of probation officers vary widely. A number of agencies require graduate education and related experience for a career in probation work, but others have no such prerequisites. This often results in the recruitment of inexperienced college graduates, and probation becomes an entry-level position for employment in the criminal justice field. Furthermore, in some states high school graduates with no training in counseling, psychology, social work, or any other behavioral field have managed to secure work in the probation area. Second, as with all occupations and professions, many probation officers have little dedication or interest in their work. This often results in apathy toward their clients' needs and problems, an avoidance of responsibility, and the "stealing of time" during business hours. As one probation supervisor in a southern state once illustrated the point:

> Our field office in ——— County gets first honors in truancy. It's staffed by only two people—the agent and a secretary, both of whom hate themselves and their jobs. . . . The clients know not to call in or show up for a report on Wednesday afternoons. It's well known throughout the county that ——— and ——— close up the office at noon and shack up for the rest of the day.[37]

A third problem is the low level of career mobility in probation work. Combined with moderate to low salaries in many jurisdictions are limited opportunities for advancement. This results in frustration, dissatisfaction, cynicism, and high staff turnover. Additionally, there is the issue of case-load size. Work loads range from a dozen probationers per officer in a few agencies to over 300 per officer in others. The treatment and supervision aspects of probation become even further diluted by the requirements to perform presentence investigations. In consequence, treatment becomes reduced to making a telephone call every other week to determine if a job is being maintained, and supervision amounts to as little as a mail contact each month to determine if the probationers are residing where they say they are.

Some jurisdictions have met this challenge by recruiting volunteers and paraprofessionals to assist in probation offices. In Travis County, Texas, for example, 160 volunteers assist 34 regular probation officers to manage the case load of 4,000 clients.[38] They include both men and women and some 25 percent are members of minority groups. Furthermore, almost 20 percent are law students from the University of Texas who assist in the preparation of presentence reports.

Finally, as is the case in police work, probation officers can differ dramatically in approaches to their work and attitudes toward their clients. There are probably many who can successfully mediate their dual roles as clinicians and supervisors. However, there are also many "social workers" and "rule enforcers" who operate only from these diverse ends of the spectrum. In addition, there are the "legalists," who stress the upholding of law for its own sake; there are "company agents," who focus almost exclusively on their upward mobility in the probation organization; and there are the stereotyped "civil service hacks," who seem to think of little else than the number of years left until retirement and in the meantime work hard at getting the lion's share of days off, sick pay, fringe benefits, lunch hours, and coffee breaks. Each of these types can negatively affect a probationer's potential for readjustment.

The working styles of probation officers

As a final note here, most clinicians will agree that even the most dedicated workers, including probation officers, often limit the impact of the assistance they provide by not giving sufficient help to those who could benefit most. Throughout the human service delivery network, including offender rehabilitation agencies, the nature and extent of client types vary widely. At one end of the spectrum, perhaps 5 to 25 percent, there are those with a minimum of problems. Many are highly motivated to fulfill the terms of their probation, and no matter what support and assistance is or is not provided, their chances for success are high. At the opposite end there is another 5 to 25 percent who are so dysfunctional and committed to an antisocial lifestyle that little can change them. With or without service and treatment, most of these typically fail. Those in the middle, the remaining 50 to 90 percent, can go either way, depending on the nature and intensity of the service and supervision provided. These are the persons who could benefit most from rehabilitation programs. Yet there seems to be a tendency within the helping professions — an inclination based on humanitarian concern — to focus the majority of energy and services on those who appear to need them most. As a result, within the probation system it is the most dysfunctional clients — those who will potentially profit the least — who receive most of the treatment and supervision available. In consequence, the middle group, that large percentage whose behavior is most receptive to change, tends to be neglected.

Shock Probation

In 1965, the Ohio state legislature passed the first **shock probation** law in the United States, allowing judges to incarcerate an offender for a brief part of the sentence, suspend the remainder, and place him or her on probation.[39] Under the Ohio statute, shock probation (also known as a *mixed* or *split* sentence) is not part of the original sentence. Rather, the defendant can file a petition requesting it between 30 to 60 days after sentencing, or the judge can order it in the absence of any petition. Its "shock" effect comes from the contention that the staggering effect of exposure to prison or jail can be a significant

Shock probation allows for brief incarceration followed by suspension of sentence and probation.

deterrent to crime. Eligibility for shock probation procedures follows the same statutory guidelines that govern the granting of probation in general.

Sentiments regarding the suitability of shock probation as a rehabilitative tool have been mixed. On the one hand, it represents a way for the courts to do the following:

- impress offenders with the seriousness of their actions without a long prison sentence
- release offenders found by the institutions to be more amenable to community-based treatment than was realized by the courts at the time of sentence
- arrive at a just compromise between punishment and leniency in appropriate cases
- provide community-based treatment for rehabilitable offenders, while still observing their responsibilities for imposing deterrent sentences where public policy demands it[40]

In addition, since imprisonment is only short-term, it inhibits absorption of the offender into the "hard rock" inmate culture. At the same time, the fiscal costs of shock probation are significantly lower than those of a full period of incarceration.

Opponents of shock probation argue vigorously that it is counterproductive as a rehabilitative tool. First, its deterrent effect is limited or totally negated by the job loss and broken community ties that occur with incarceration, however brief. Second, the purpose of probation is to *avoid* incarceration, not supplement it. Third, even a short period of incarceration has the potential for contaminating offenders through exposure to hardened criminals and the hostilities and resentment of prison life. Fourth, it stigmatizes offenders for having been in jail or prison and may add to their confusion of status and self-concept. Fifth, and perhaps most importantly, prison and probation are at opposite ends of the punishment and rehabilitation scale; they are mutually exclusive and therefore should not be mixed.[41] As one commentator expressed it:

> Once having determined that a person can be trusted in the community and can benefit most under community supervision, no appreciable benefits can be derived from committing [him or her] to a short period of incarceration.[42]

Although shock probation may be functional from the perspective of the criminal justice system in terms of the lower costs of probation versus imprisonment and the alleviation of prison overcrowding, there is no evidence yet that demonstrates that it reduces recidivism. Several empirical studies have examined the shock probation experience, but the findings remain inconclusive.[43]

Probation Violation and Revocation

Since probation is a conditional release, it does not guarantee absolute freedom. Arrests for new crimes or technical violations of the conditions of probation can result in **revocation** of probation and the imprisonment of the offender.

As noted earlier in this chapter, the conditions of probation are established by statute and special conditions can be applied by the sentencing court. There has been little argument as to whether a new arrest constitutes a violation of probation. Furthermore, the appellate courts have given the lower courts considerable latitude in imposing conditions of probation. Thus, such technical violations as nonpayment of a fine imposed as a condition of probation, failure to pay off civil judgments for fraud although able to pay, failure to make child support payments, failure to report to one's probation officer, and driving while intoxicated, to name only a few, have been grounds for violation and revocation. *Absconding* from probation supervision, that is, failing to report and concealing oneself from the probation authorities, represents a serious violation of probation. Finally, circumstantial evidence that a probationer engaged in illegal conduct can also be grounds for revocation. In one Texas case, evidence that demonstrated that before a burglary the probationer had been in contact with those who had committed the crime and later shared in the fruits of the offense was found to justify revocation.[44]

The issue of probation violation tends to underscore the tremendous discretionary authority that is at the disposal of the probation officer. Techni-

Revocation of probation

**East Gate at Folsom Prison is
part of the original building and
is still in use today.**

cal violations generally come to the attention of only the supervising officer. If
the defendant fails to report, reverts to the use of drugs, consorts with known
criminals, refuses to remain gainfully employed, or fails to live up to other
conditions of the probation contract, the officer has several options. He can
cite the probationer for violation, make continued and more intensive counseling and supervision efforts in order to bring about community adjustment,
or simply ''look the other way.'' Thus violation proceedings are initiated by
the probation officer, and these generally begin only when revocation is the
course decided upon. It should be emphasized, however, that although the
probation officer or department can recommend revocation, *only the court
has the authority to revoke probation.*

   In the event of a new arrest, a warrant may be lodged against the
probationer in order to prevent his or her release on bail. If the violation is only
technical, a warrant may also be issued and the violator taken into custody by
either the police or probation authorities. Some jurisdictions issue such detainers as a matter of course; others do so only when there is evidence to
believe that the probationer would abscond if left in the commuity pending a
revocation hearing.

   Once revocation is the direction decided on by the probation authorities,
the offender is given notice of such, the probation officer prepares a violation
report, and a formal court hearing is scheduled. Until only recently, revocation hearings reflected few procedural safeguards. In 1967, however, the U.S.

Mempa v. Rhay

Supreme Court held in ***Mempa v. Rhay*** that a probationer had a constitutional right to counsel at any revocation proceeding where the imposition of
sentence had been suspended but would be enjoined following revocation.[45]

Morrissey v. Brewer

In 1972, the Court ruled in ***Morrissey v. Brewer*** that when the potential for
parole revocation was at issue, an informal inquiry was required to determine
if there was probable cause to believe that the parolee had indeed violated the
conditions of parole.[46] The Court added the mandate of a formal revocation
hearing as well, with minimum due-process requirements. While *Morrissey*

was a parole case, its significance for probationers came the following year with ***Gagnon* v. *Scarpelli*.**[47] In *Gagnon,* the Court extended the holding in *Morrissey* to probationers, and also held that both probationers and parolees have a constitutionally limited right to counsel during revocation proceedings. (See Exhibit 17.3.)

Since *Mempa, Morrissey,* and *Gagnon,* both state and federal courts have made a number of significant decisions regarding revocation proceedings. In *United States* v. *Reed,* [48] while reversing a revocation order, a U.S. circuit court of appeals stressed the rehabilitative nature of probation and indicated that the accumulation of a few minor technical violations should not necessarily be grounds for revocation. In *United States* v. *Pattman,*[49] it was ruled that hearsay evidence that was "demonstrably reliable" need not be subject to confrontation and cross-examination in revocation proceedings. In other decisions, courts have held that revocation can be based on conduct occurring prior to the actual granting of probation,[50] that a probationer may not invoke the Fifth Amendment privilege against self-incrimination in revocation proceedings when asked to testify about technical violations of probation,[51] and that evidence to support a revocation of probation need not establish guilt "beyond a reasonable doubt."[52]

The Effectiveness of Probation

Probation is by far the most widely used criminal sanction. As of June 30, 1982, for example, of the more than 1.5 million persons in the American correctional population, some 63 percent were probationers. By contrast, 27 percent were in prisons and jails and only 10 percent were on parole.[53] There are many reasons for this, most of which evolve from the economic and humanitarian considerations that characterize the probation philosophy. In addition, some observers believe that probation is the most effective phase of the criminal justice process.[54] This notion, however, can be called into serious question. The vast majority of the studies of probation effectiveness are at least two decades old. Moreover, they may not be meaningful as indicators of the success of probation.[55] Further, more recent data even contradict the findings of the earlier research.

The most recent study of probation effectiveness found that most felony offenders placed on probation were still a considerable threat to the community. Commissioned by the National Institute of Justice and conducted by the Rand Corporation during the early 1980s, the study examined 1,672 felony cases from California's Los Angeles and Alameda counties. During the 40-month follow-up period of the study, 65 percent of those placed on probation were rearrested. Almost 80 percent of these, or 51 percent of the entire sample, were convicted of new crimes. Of the sample, 18 percent were reconvicted of serious violent crimes, and 34 percent were reincarcerated. Charges were filed against 53 percent of the felony probationers: 19 percent had only one charge, 12 percent had two charges, and 22 percent had three or more charges against them. As the figure in Exhibit 17.4 indicates, 32 percent of the entire study population experienced a filing for property crime, 22 percent for violent crime, and 12 percent for a drug law violation. (The percentages were based on 2,608 charges; some of the 1,672 cases had multiple charges.)[56] The Rand study, although descriptive of only one population, certainly suggests that probation may not be the most appropriate means for dealing with overflowing prison populations.

EXHIBIT 17.3

Due Process and Revocation Hearings

Mempa v. Rhay, 398 U.S. 128 (1967)

On June 17, 1959, 17-year-old Jerry Douglas Mempa was convicted in a Spokane, Washington, court of the offense of "joyriding" (riding in a stolen automobile). His conviction was based on a guilty plea entered with the advice of his court-appointed counsel. The court suspended the imposition of his sentence, and placed him on probation for a period of two years.

Several months later, the county prosecutor moved for the revocation of Mempa's probation on the allegation that he participated in a burglary on September 15, 1959. At the revocation hearing, he was not represented by counsel, nor was he asked if he wished counsel. Mempa admitted participation in the burglary, and the sole testimony connecting him with the crime came from a probation officer. There was no cross-examination of the officer's statements. Without asking Mempa if he had anything to say or any evidence to supply, the court revoked his probation and sentenced him to ten years in the state penitentiary.

In 1965, Mempa petitioned for a writ of *habeas corpus,* claiming he had been deprived of his right to counsel at the revocation proceeding at which the sentence was imposed. The Washington Supreme Court denied his petition, however. On appeal, the United States Supreme Court ruled in Mempa's favor. In its opinion, the Court did not question the authority of the state of Washington to provide for a deferred sentencing procedure coupled with its probation provisions. However, it emphasized that the "appointment of counsel for an indigent is required at every stage of a criminal proceeding where substantial rights of a criminal accused may be affected."

Mempa v. *Rhay* resulted in a variety of judicial interpretations. The Supreme Court's holding required that counsel be provided only at those revocation proceedings involving deferred sentencing, and did not apply to cases when the probationer was sentenced at the time of trial. Many lower courts treated the decision in exactly that way. However, other courts extended *Mempa* to all revocation proceedings, with the view that any revocation hearing was a "critical stage" that required due-process protection. Furthermore, although *Mempa* applied only to probation revocation hearings, a number of courts interpreted it to apply to parole as well.

Morrissey v. Brewer, 408 U.S. 471 (1972)

The decision in *Morrissey* v. *Brewer* related to parole revocation, but since parole and probation revocation are similar in nature, it had potential significance for both types of proceedings.

In 1967, John Morrissey was convicted in an Iowa court of falsely drawing checks, and he was sentenced to a maximum term of seven years' imprisonment. He was released on parole the following year, but within seven months, Morrissey was cited for violation of his parole. He was arrested, and admitted to purchasing an automobile without permission, obtaining credit under an assumed name, having become involved in an automobile accident, and failing to report these and other matters to his parole officer. He maintained that he had not contacted his parole officer due to sickness.

One week later, the parole violation report was reviewed, parole was revoked, and Morrissey was returned to prison. On a *habeas corpus* petition to the U.S. district court, Morrissey claimed that he had been denied due process under the Fourteenth Amendment in that his parole had been revoked without a hearing. The district court denied his petition, the U.S. court of appeals affirmed the lower court decision, and the U.S. Supreme Court granted *certiorari.*

The Court began its opinion stating that the revocation of parole is not part of a criminal prosecution and thus the full panoply of rights due a defendant in such a proceeding does not apply. However, the Court went on to state that parole revocation involves the potential termination of an individual's liberty, and therefore, certain due-process safeguards are necessary to ensure that the finding of a parole violation is based on verified facts to support the revocation.

In establishing procedural safeguards, the Court considered parole revocation to be a two-stage process: (1) the arrest of the parolee and a preliminary hearing, and (2) the revocation hearing. In designating a preliminary hearing for all parole violators. The Court held:

Such an inquiry should be seen in the nature of a preliminary hearing to determine whether there is probable cause or reasonable grounds to believe that the arrested parolee had committed acts which would constitute a violation of parole condition.

The Court also specified that at this preliminary review, the hearing officer should be someone not involved in the case, and that the parolee should be given notice of the hearing and the opportunity to be present during the questioning of persons providing adverse information regarding the alleged violation. Subsequently, a determination should be made to decide if the parolee's continued detention is warranted.

In reference to the revocation hearing, the Court held:

The parolee must have an opportunity to be heard and to show, if he can, that he did not violate the conditions or if he did, that circumstances in mitigation suggest the violation does not warrant revocation. The revocation hearing must be tendered within a reasonable time after the parolee is taken into custody. A lapse of two months as the state suggests occurs in some cases would not appear to be unreasonable.

And in terms of due process at revocation hearings:

Our task is limited to deciding the minimum requirements of due process. They include (a) written notice of the claimed violation of parole; (b) disclosure to the parolee of evidence against him; (c) opportunity to be heard in person and to present witnesses and documentary evidence; (d) the right to confront and cross-examine adverse witnesses (unless the hearing officer specifically finds good cause for not allowing confrontation); (e) a "neutral and detached" hearing body such as a traditional parole board, members of which need not be judicial officers or lawyers; and (f) a written statement by the fact finders as to the evidence relied on and reasons for revoking parole.

However, the Court left open the question of counsel: "We do not reach or decide the question whether the parolee is entitled to the assistance of retained or appointed counsel if he is indigent."

Gagnon v. Scarpelli, 411 U.S. 778 (1973)

During the year following *Morrissey*, the issue of right to counsel at revocation proceedings again came before the Court.

In July 1965, Gerald Scarpelli pleaded guilty in a Wisconsin court to a charge of armed robbery. He was sentenced to a term of 15 years of imprisonment, but the judge suspended his sentence and placed him on probation for a period of 7 years. The following month, he was arrested on a burglary charge, his probation was revoked without a hearing, and he was incarcerated in the Wisconsin State Reformatory to begin serving his original 15-year sentence.

Some three years later, Scarpelli applied for a writ of *habeas corpus*. After the petition had been filed, but before it had been acted upon, Scarpelli was released on parole. A U.S. district court judge ruled that the petition was not moot because of Scarpelli's parole status, because the original revocation carried "collateral consequences," namely, the restraints imposed by his parole. The district court then held that the revocation of probation without a hearing and counsel was a denial of due process. The court of appeals affirmed, and the state of Wisconsin appealed to the United States Supreme Court.

In its decision, the Court made two points:

Probation revocation, like parole revocation, is not a stage of a criminal prosecution, but does result in loss of liberty. Accordingly, we hold that a probationer, like a parolee, is entitled to a preliminary hearing and a final revocation hearing in the conditions specified in *Morrissey* v. *Brewer*.

Furthermore:

Counsel should be provided in cases where, after being informed of his right to request counsel the probationer or parolee makes such a request based on a timely or colorable claim:

1. that he has not committed the alleged violation of the conditions upon which he is at liberty; or

2. that, even if the violation is a matter of public record or is uncontested, there are substantial reasons which justified or mitigated the violation and made revocation inappropriate and that the reasons are complex or otherwise difficult to develop or present.

Parole

I believe there are many who might be so trained as to be left on their parole during the last period of their imprisonment with safety.

—Dr. Samuel G. Howe, 1846

The granting of parole is an act of grace, comparable to the pardoning power that was once the prerogative of the monarchy. As such, it is infected from the outset with the arbitrariness and unpredictability that is characteristic of penal institutions and other autocracies. — Jessica Mitford, 1974

Parole is release from incarceration on condition of good behavior.

Parole, from the French meaning "word of honor" and first used in 1846 by the Boston penal reformer Samuel G. Howe,[57] refers to the practice of allowing the final portion of a prison sentence to be served in the free community. Or more specifically, parole is:

> the status of being released from a penal or reformatory institution in which one has served a part of his maximum sentence, on the condition of maintaining good behavior and remaining in the custody and under the guidance of the institution or some other agency approved by the state until a final discharge is granted.[58]

Thus parole actually refers to two operations: (1) "parole release," the procedures used to establish the actual periods of confinement that prisoners serve, and (2) "parole supervision," the conditions and provisions that regulate parolees' postprison lives until the final discharge from their sentence.

The purposes of parole

For almost a century, parole has been an established part of American correctional theory and practice. It has had the ostensible purposes of ensuring that imprisonment is tailored to the needs of the inmate, ameliorating the harshness of long prison sentences, and hastening the offender's reintegration into the community when it appears that he or she is able to function as a law-abiding citizen. In addition, it has had the more subtle designs of alleviating the overcrowded conditions of correctional institutions, and assisting in maintaining prisons' social control through the threat of parole denial for instances of misbehavior.

The Origins of Parole

As a combination and extension of penal practices, parole has a long history. It seems to have first appeared in a most rudimentary form when the British economy declined during the latter part of the sixteenth century.[59] In its colonies, the need for cheap labor was critical. The British government began granting reprieves and stays of execution to felons physically able to work so they could be transported to the New World. The pardoned convicts became indentured servants, whose labor was sold to the highest bidder in the colonies. The newly arrived felons were required to work off their indenture, and the only other condition of their pardon was that they did not return to England.

Captain Alexander Maconochie of Norfolk Island, however, was the "father of parole" in its purest form. As noted in Chapter 14, Maconochie established a "mark system" whereby an inmate could earn early release by hard work and good behavior. Sir Walter Crofton's "Irish System" was a refinement of Maconochie's ideas, by which inmates could earn a conditional release through a "ticket-of-leave."

EXHIBIT 17.4

Charges Filed against Probationers: The Rand Study, 1985

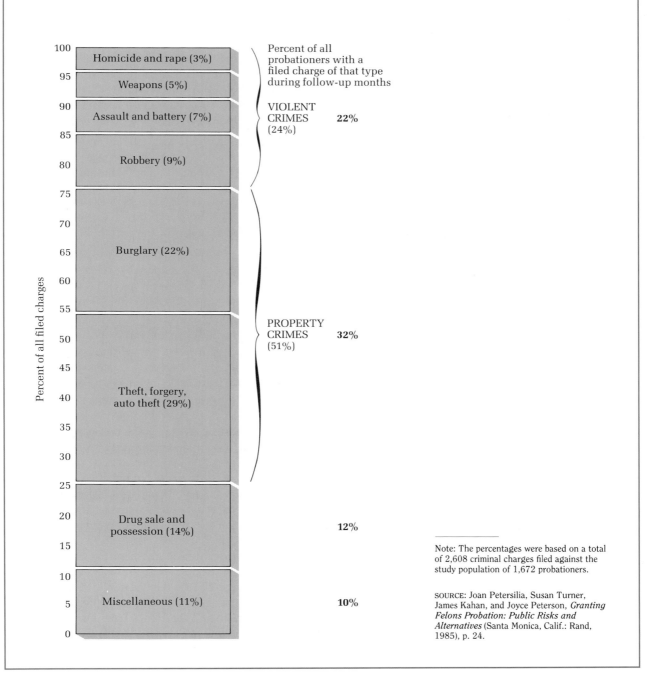

Percent of all filed charges

Homicide and rape (3%)	100
Weapons (5%)	95
Assault and battery (7%)	90
	85
Robbery (9%)	80
	75
Burglary (22%)	70 65 60 55
Theft, forgery, auto theft (29%)	50 45 40 35 30 25
Drug sale and possession (14%)	20 15
Miscellaneous (11%)	10 5 0

Percent of all probationers with a filed charge of that type during follow-up months

VIOLENT CRIMES (24%)   **22%**

PROPERTY CRIMES (51%)   **32%**

12%

10%

Note: The percentages were based on a total of 2,608 criminal charges filed against the study population of 1,672 probationers.

SOURCE: Joan Petersilia, Susan Turner, James Kahan, and Joyce Peterson, *Granting Felons Probation: Public Risks and Alternatives* (Santa Monica, Calif.: Rand, 1985), p. 24.

A Parole Agreement

STATE OF CONNECTICUT
BOARD OF PAROLE

PAROLE AGREEMENT

You have been granted a parole by the Board of Parole. It will be effective on the date indicated or as soon thereafter as your parole program is approved by the Division of Parole.

Parole gives you the opportunity to serve the remainder of your sentence outside of the institution. The Board of Parole may grant you a certificate of early discharge from your sentence at the recommendation of your parole officer after you have shown satisfactory progress while you are on parole. Until that time, or until the maximum expiration date of your sentence, you will remain in the legal custody of the Board of Parole and under the supervision of the Division of Parole of the Department of Correction.

A parole officer will be assigned to work with you and help you to adjust to life in the community. The parole officer will attempt to help you and will be available for counseling should any problems arise. You are urged to talk over any difficulties with the parole officer. The parole officer will also submit reports on your progress to the Commissioner of Correction, and, if requested, to the Board of Parole.

It is also the parole officer's duty to make sure that you abide by the conditions of parole found on the other side of this page. Those conditions have been carefully designed as guidelines for acceptable behaviour while you are on parole. If you should violate any of those conditions of parole, the officer has the authority from the Chairman of the Board of Parole and the Commissioner of Correction to return you to custody so that your parole status may be reviewed by the Board of Parole. By signing your name to the other side of this page you indicate your consent to abide by the standard and individual conditions of your parole listed there, as well as your awareness that failure to abide by those conditions will constitute a violation of parole and may result in your return to custody.

It is the hope of the Board of Parole in granting you this parole that you will accept it and its conditions as an opportunity to prove to yourself and to others that you are capable of living as a responsible, law-abiding citizen of society and of your community.

"Good time" laws

The concept of parole continued to evolve in the United States with the principles of **"good time"** laws and indeterminate sentencing. The notion underlying "good time" laws was modest. If, in the opinion of prison authorities, inmates maintained an institutional record of hard work and good conduct, they could be released after a shorter period than that imposed by the sentencing court. The purposes of the laws, however, were somewhat more complex. They were attempts to assist in the reformation of criminals, combined with endeavors to mitigate the severity of the penal codes; to solve the problems of prison discipline; and to get good work from inmates, thereby increasing the profits of the prison industries and contract labor.[60]

The first "good time" law was passed in New York in 1817. It provided that first-term prisoners on sentences of five years or less could reduce their

Parolee _____ No. _____ Release on or after _____

CONDITIONS OF PAROLE

1. Upon my release I will report to my parole officer as directed and follow the parole officer's instructions.

2. I will report to my parole officer in person and in writing whenever and wherever the parole officer directs.

3. I agree that the parole officer has the right to visit my residence or place of employment at any reasonable time.

4. I will maintain such gainful employment or other activity as approved by my parole officer.

5. I will notify my parole officer within 48 hours of any changes in my place of residence, in my place of employment, or of any change in my marital status.

6. I will notify my parole officer within 48 hours if at any time I am arrested for any offense.

7. I will not at any time have firearms, ammunition, or any other weapon in my possession or under my control.

8. I will not leave the State of Connecticut without prior permission of my parole officer.

9. I will obey all laws, and to the best of my ability fulfill all my legal obligations.

10. I will not at any time use, or have in my possession or control, any illegal drug or narcotic.

11. Your release on parole is based upon the conclusion of the Parole Panel that there is a reasonable probability that you will live and remain at liberty without violating the law and that your release is not incompatible with the welfare of society. In the event that you engage in conduct in the future which renders this conclusion no longer valid, then your parole will be revoked or modified accordingly.

12. I also agree to abide by the following INDIVIDUAL CONDITIONS:

Signed _____

Witness _____ Date _____

For the Board of Parole _____

Chairman   *Secretary*

sentences by one-fourth for good behavior. Although the New York statute was not immediately put into practice, shortly after midcentury more than half the states had provisions for time off for good behavior. Then, in 1869 Michigan adopted the first indeterminate sentencing law. In 1876, as a result of the efforts of Elmira Reformatory warden Zebulon Brockway, similar legislation was passed in New York. Under its provisions, an offender could be released at such time that his behavior demonstrated that he could be returned to society. Since the offender was being released prior to the expiration of sentence, special provisions were made for community supervision, and thus parole became a reality. By the second decade of the twentieth century, most states had indeterminate sentencing laws, and the nature of parole as it is understood today had become firmly established.[61]

Parole Administration

Parole versus probation

The terms *parole* and *probation* have often been mistakenly used interchangeably, but as is already apparent, there are many differences between the two. Probation involves a sentence by the court to community supervision in lieu of imprisonment; parole is a conditional release from a correction institution after a period of imprisonment has already been served. Beyond this preliminary distinction, there are numerous administrative differences. First, the authority to both grant and revoke probation falls within the realm of the lower courts. The authority to grant and revoke parole is held by an administrative board that can be (1) an independent state agency, (2) a unit within some larger state department, or (3) the same body that regulates the state's correctional institutions. Second, the supervision of probationers can be the function of a single court, a county agency, a state department or division, or some combination thereof in any given jurisdiction. Parole supervision services, however, are under the authority of a single state agency in all instances but are not necessarily under the leadership of the parole board.

The advantages and disadvantages of the various models of parole administration have been heavily debated. As to which model is actually followed, however, is generally a matter of state politics. In recent years, as both parole and correctional agencies have become more professionalized, the trend has been to combine administration of the two.

The Parole Board

The functions of parole boards are essentially fourfold: (1) to select and place prisoners on parole; (2) to provide continuing control over parolees in the

A parole board meeting at Sing Sing Prison, New York

community; (3) to discharge parolees from supervision when they complete their sentences; and (4) to review parole violations and determine whether revocation and return to prison is appropriate. Thus the overall task of the parole board is the implementation of indeterminate sentencing.

Since parole boards make decisions on parole release and revocation, as well as create policy regarding planning and supervision services, it seems logical that the efficiency and viability of the entire parole system depends on the qualifications, skill, and experiences of the members of the board. The American Correctional Association recommended that parole board members command respect and public confidence; be appointed without reference to creed, color, or political affiliation; possess academic training that would qualify them for their professional practice; and have intimate knowledge of the common situations and problems confronting offenders.[62] To these, the National Advisory Commission on Criminal Justice Standards and Goals added:

> No single professional group or discipline can be recommended as ideal for all parole board members. A variety of goals are to be served by parole board members, and a variety of skills are required. Knowledge of at least three basic fields should be represented on a parole board: the law, the behavioral sciences, and corrections. Furthermore, as a board assumes responsibility for policy articulation, monitoring and review, the tasks involved require persons who are able to use a wide range of decision-making tools, such as statistical materials, reports from professional personnel, and a variety of other technical information. In general, persons with sophisticated training and experience are required.[63]

However, surveys sponsored by the American Correctional Association and the National Council on Crime and Delinquency indicate that qualifications such as these are required by statute in only a minority of jurisdictions.[64] Independent observations have shown that in a number of states, some parole board members have had *no* exposure to the criminal justice system or offender problems prior to their appointments. This seemed to be especially the case in two selected jurisdictions where decision making was in the hands of part-time boards. Board membership included physicians, ministers, retail sales clerks, and small business operators — most of whom had an interest in correctional issues but few of whom had training or experience in law, social work, corrections, or related skills. This should not suggest, however, that all parole board members are ill-equipped for the responsibilities they share. Quite the contrary: there are many whose career experiences include law, probation, and parole, plus graduate degrees in one or more of the social or behavioral sciences.

Parole Officers

The characteristics of parole officers, or "agents" as they are referred to in some jurisdictions, vary as widely as those of board members. Some states require a graduate degree in an appropriate field; others expect only a high school diploma. Furthermore, what has already been stated regarding probation officers can be applied to parole officers, for in many ways the requirements and skills are similar. This is especially the case in such states as Florida and South Carolina, where both probationers and parolees are supervised by the same individuals and agency.

Eligibility for Parole

There are numerous statutory restrictions on the granting of parole. As a result, inmates are not automatically paroled as a matter of right. Parole eligibility, then, refers to the earliest date that an inmate can be considered for parole. However, due to the nature of their offenses and sentences, some prisoners can never be paroled.

A key factor in the determination of parole eligibility are the statutes regarding "good time." "Good time" refers to the number of days deducted from a sentence for good behavior, meritorious service, particular kinds of work, or other considerations. Some states have a fixed formula for allocating "good time," such as two or three days for each month served. In others, such as New York, it is left to the discretion of the prison authorities, but cannot "exceed in the aggregate one-third of the term imposed by the court."[65] "Good time," however, is not a matter of right; it must be earned, and as noted in the discussion of prison disciplinary proceedings, it can be forfeited for poor behavior.

Calculating parole eligibility

In calculating parole eligibility, there are almost as many statutory formulas as there are jurisdictions. For example, for any sentence less than life, eligibility begins:

- in four states, upon completion of one-third the maximum sentence, less "good time"
- in two states, upon completion of one-fouth the maximum sentence, less "good time"
- in ten states, upon completion of the minimum sentence, less "good time"[66]

Furthermore, in some states "good time" is not deducted, or there are special rules governing determinate sentences or first versus second and third felony offenders, or eligibility is left to the discretion of the parole board. For inmates serving life sentences, the rules governing eligibility are equally varied:

- in seven states, at "any time" (at the discretion of the parole board)
- in 34 states and the federal jurisdiction, after a specified number of years ranging from 5 in Nevada to 30 in Tennessee, with or without jail time
- in six states, variable depending on the offense or when the conviction occurred
- in ten states, *never,* unless the life sentence has been commuted or a conditional pardon has been granted[67]

The Parole Hearing

Parole hearings are generally private and are attended only by the inmate, the board, a representative of the institution in which the inmate is incarcerated, and a stenographer or stenotypist to record the proceedings. The board reviews the inmate's case as well as any institutional reports that may have been submitted; questions the inmate regarding his or her adjustment, plans if released, and perhaps the circumstances of the instant offense; and then offers the inmate an opportunity to make a statement on his or her own behalf. The inmate is then dismissed, and the board discusses the case and makes its decision.

The specific procedures used by different boards vary. In years past, one board member examined the institutional records and interviewed each inmate under consideration. He or she would then make a recommendation, and the entire board would either ratify or modify the recommendation in an executive session. Currently, several models exist. Some boards meet *en banc* for every case; others break up into groups to hold hearings in different parts of the jurisdiction. Since the mid-1970s, the U.S. Board of Parole and many of the larger states have been using hearing examiners, who make recommendations on which the board acts. Regardless of the particular procedure, parole authorities have been given wide discretion as to how hearings are actually conducted. This discretion, furthermore, has been uniformly supported by the courts. In *Menechino* v. *Oswald,*[68] decided by the U.S. court of appeals in 1970, the petitioner argued that his due-process rights had been violated by the general manner in which his parole hearing had been conducted. He claimed that the Constitution required that he be given:

1. notice
2. fair hearing with right to counsel, cross-examination, and presentation of witnesses
3. specification of the reasons used by the parole board in its determination

The court, however, ruled that the due-process clause did not apply to parole hearings since inmates, who are already imprisoned, do not have "present private interests" that require protection. The following year, though, the court did hold that written reasons for the denial of parole must be given to an inmate.[69] Finally, in 1979, the U.S. Supreme Court in *Greenholtz* v. *Inmates of Nebraska Penal and Correctional Complex* affirmed previous decisions that parole hearings need not have all the elements of due process that are required at criminal trials.[70]

Parole Selection

An overview of contemporary parole practice suggest that many release decisions often reflect variable, arbitrary, and sometimes whimsical standards. A variety of legislative mandates, for example, express the vague policy that a prisoner should be paroled only when such action is not incompatible with the welfare of the community.[71] More specific criteria have included such factors as the offender's prior criminal record, his personality and physical condition, social history, employment record, intelligence, family status, institutional conduct, parole plan, prior probation or parole history, and his stated intentions for the future, among others. Yet questions exist as to how these variables should be weighted in determining if or when a prisoner should be released. Factors that are deemed significant may be emphasized although they may indeed have no significance at all.

In a number of settings the decision to release falls within a political arena. The recommendations of a sentencing judge, a prosecuting attorney, or an active press can invariably affect the paroling process when such gestures have implications for the political power base held by a member of the parole board. Moreover, in Arizona, Arkansas, California, and the federal system, crime victims are permitted to testify at the release hearings of inmates convicted of victimizing them — a practice with a probable impact on parole decision making.[72]

Selection decisions that emerge from such a nexus of policy, autocracy, and whim typically fall within the spectrum of "intuitive prognosis," "common sense," expediency, and hunch. The members of a paroling board *guess,* or give their premonitory feeling on a minimum of information submitted to them; they may observe potential candidates and make predictions based on insight, intuition, and inductive assumption; or they may examine various types of more or less scientific data to arrive at a decision. Further confounding this process is the inclination to rest decisions on a majority rule or, in some jurisdictions, on unanimous verdict.

Finally, predictions of human behavior are especially problematic when the subjects under review have already demonstrated a reduced capacity to function in a socially approved manner. Selection decisions may totally bypass *all* those considered less likely to succeed. Indeed, conservative parole boards have been known to release only those prisoners who are seen to be good risks while denying parole to the remainder.[73]

Statistical Prediction Methods

Scientific **parole prediction** emerged as an attempt to inject some degree of precision into the selection of prospective parolees. The goal was to increase the number of conditional releases to those likely to succeed, and to reduce the numbers granted to those likely to fail.

Essentially, parole prediction refers to "the estimate of probability of violation or nonviolation of parole on the basis of experience tables, developed with regard to groups of offenders possessing similar characteristics."[74] An *experience table* summarizes the postinstitutional experience of a given release group. The table classifies offenders by their admission characteristics and uses only those characteristics that are the most differentiating as to postrelease response or adjustment in an aftercare setting. The experience table is similar to an actuarial table, which calculates or estimates insurance risks, but rather than indicating mortality or morbidity rates for each type of person, it points to violation or recidivism rates.[75]

However, *parole prediction tables do not predict,* and for a variety of reasons. First, they are often heavily based on factors present in the inmate's social situation prior to arrest, and thus generally do not include postsentence variables such as institutional behavior and relationships. Second, they cannot anticipate differences in parole officers' attitudes and willingness to revoke parole. Third, they are based on data from presentence reports, a portion of which is of questionable accuracy. Fourth, the solely empirical approach of prediction methods is weakened by the absence of any theoretical basis for selecting particular variables for their predictive accuracy. In the final analysis, then, statistical prediction methods seem to generate the same level of accuracy as the success rate in parole systems not using such methods.[76]

The Salient Factor Score Index

Somewhat related to statistical prediction methods is the Salient Factor Score Index used by the U.S. Board of Parole. The **salient factor score,** which ranges from 0 to 11, is based on a number of elements (education, employment history, marital status, prior convictions and commitments, plus a number of others) combined to suggest four categories of parole prognosis: very good, good, fair, or poor. The case is then given an offense severity rating, which is taken from a structured schedule that designates various crimes as having specific levels of severity. These are combined into a matrix that suggests how many months an inmate ought to remain incarcerated prior to being paroled. As indicated in Exhibit 17.6, an inmate incarcerated for motor vehicle theft

Parole prediction: "An estimate of probability of violation or nonviolation of parole on the bases of experience tables, developed with regard to groups of offenders possessing similar characteristics."

Parole prediction tables do not predict.

The salient factor score grades offenders into categories of parole prognosis.

EXHIBIT 17.6

Salient Factor Score Matrix
for Adult Inmates

		Parole Prognosis (Salient Factor Score)			
Severity of Offense	Examples of Offense	Very Good (9–11)	Good (6–8)	Fair (4–5)	Poor (0–3)
Low	Immigration law violations Minor theft (under $1,000)	6–10 months	8–12 months	10–14 months	12–16 months
Low Moderate	Alcohol law violations Marijuana possession (under $500) Forgery, fraud (under $1,000)	8–12 months	12–16 months	16–20 months	20–25 months
Moderate	Bribery of public official Possession of hard drugs by user (under $500) Possession of marijuana (over $500) Sale of marijuana (under $5,000) Receiving stolen property to resell (under $20,000) Motor vehicle theft	12–16 months	16–20 months	20–24 months	24–30 months
High	Burglary or larceny from bank or post office Sale of hard drugs to support habit Sale of marijuana (over $5,000) Possession of soft drugs (over $5,000) Embezzlement ($20,000–$100,000) Organized vehicle theft Receiving stolen property ($20,000–$100,000) Robbery (no weapon or injury) Theft, forgery, fraud ($20,000–$100,000)	16–20 months	20–26 months	26–32 months	32–38 months
Very High	Robbery (weapon) Sale of soft drugs (over $5,000) Extortion Sexual act (force)	26–36 months	36–45 months	45–55 months	55–65 months
Greatest	Aggravated felony (weapon fired or serious injury) Aircraft hijacking Kidnapping Willful homicide	Greater than above. However, specific ranges are not given due to the limited number of cases and the extreme variations in severity possible within the category.			

SOURCE: Abridged from the U.S. Board of Parole's Salient Factor Score Index. See Peter B. Hoffman and Lucille K. DeGosten, "Parole Decision-Making: Structuring Discretion," *Federal Probation* 38 (December 1974): 12.

(moderate severity) with a "very good" salient factor score (9–11 points) could conceivably be paroled after 12 to 16 months. However, a forcible sex offender (very high severity) with a "poor" salient factor score (0–3 points) might be held for 55 to 65 months. The index is a guide, furthermore, that can be overridden by the parole board's judgment.

The advantage of the Salient Factor Score Index is that it makes parole decision making more consistent by controlling discretion. It eliminates negative input from institutional treatment and custodial staff, and curbs the influences of board members' whims, prejudices, and hunches. On the other hand, it precludes the idea of individualized justice and makes potential parolees "prisoners" of their past mistakes.[77]

American Law Institute Guidelines

Given the lack of specific criteria for parole decision making in many jurisdictions, combined with the weakness in the various prediction methods, the American Law Institute in its *Model Penal Code* has suggested an alternative approach. Rather than determining who should be paroled, the emphasis should be on who ought *not* to be paroled, using the following primary reasons for denial:

1. There is a substanial risk that he will not conform to the conditions of parole.
2. His release at that time would depreciate the seriousness of his crime or promote disrespect for law.
3. His release would have substantially adverse effect on institution discipline.
4. His continued correctional treatment, medical care, or vocational or other training in the institution would substantially enhance his capacity to lead a law-abiding life when released at a later date.[78]

Even this, however, has problems, since it includes no criteria for determining when the inmate denied parole should ultimately be released.

Mandatory Release

One final matter here is the issue of repeated denials of parole in spite of an inmate's eligibility for conditional release. It is not uncommon, for example, for a parole board to request a recommendation from the district attorney or chief prosecutor from the county in which a defendant was convicted. Depending on the nature of the case, the prosecutor's parole recommendation can influence the board's decision. Similarly, there can be opposition to an inmate's parole by the police, the news media, the victims of the crime, and the public at large. Consider, for example, the case of Richard Speck, convicted and sentenced to a life term for the brutal murder of eight student nurses in Chicago in 1966. Given the sentiment of Illinois residents and the agitation of the victims' families, it is likely that Speck will never be paroled. In fact, in 1984, he was denied parole for the fifth time.[79]

In less notorious cases, where an inmate is serving an indeterminate sentence and parole is repeatedly denied, another factor comes into play: "good time" credits. In New York, for example, an inmate can potentially earn as many as 10 days of "good time" for each 30 days served. A felon given a sentence of 25 years for forcible rape in the the first degree could be released

Richard Speck has been repeatedly denied parole from his life sentence for the murder of eight student nurses in Chicago in 1966. In some states and cases, felons convicted of less vicious crimes and serving indeterminate sentences are allowed "good time" credits toward early mandatory release — even if parole has been denied several times.

long before serving 20 years, even if parole had been repeatedly denied. He becomes a **mandatory release** case—his release is a matter of law. In New York and Missouri, inmates who are mandatory releases are subject to the same conditions as parolees and are under the supervision of a parole officer. In all other states, however, their release is unconditional.*

Mandatory release: A release from prison required by statute when an inmate has been confined for a time period equal to his or her full sentence minus statutory "good time," if any.

Conditions of Parole

As with probationers, all individuals released on parole are released under a series of conditions, the violation of which can result in revocation and return to prison. These are the "dos and don'ts" of parole, and they originated under the ticket-of-leave system.

Parole conditions are fairly uniform from state to state and can be grouped into two general areas: *reform conditions,* which urge parolees toward a noncriminal way of life; and *control conditions,* which enable the parole agency to keep track of them. The most common conditions include the following:

Reform Conditions:

Comply with the laws.
Maintain employment and support dependents.
Refrain from use of drugs.

Control Conditions:

Report to parole officer upon release and periodically thereafter.
Cooperate with the parole officer.
Get permission (or notify) to change employment or residence.

In addition, as with probationers, there may be special conditions of parole geared to the particular treatment and control needs of a given person.

In many jurisdictions, the list of parole regulations tends to be extreme, designed to control almost every aspect of the parolee's life. Since 1970, however, a number of states, such as Alaska, Connecticut, Massachusetts, and Ohio, have abandoned a number of the restrictions, including regulations on marriage and divorce, association with undesirables, motor vehicle usage, and alcohol use. Until the late 1960s, the conditions of parole in New York included a prohibition against "having sexual relations with anyone other than your lawful spouse." This restriction allegedly crept into the New York rules as a result of the moralistic Irish Catholic influence that dominated that system during its early years. However, such a condition was considered unreasonable and unenforceable, and both parolees and parole officers alike tended to ignore it. On the other hand, some conditions have been abolished because they were violations of broad constitutional rights. In *Hyland* v. *Procunier,*[80] for example, a condition that required a parolee to secure permission before making a public speech was ruled invalid. Similarly, in *Sobell* v. *Reed,*[81] the court struck down a rule that denied a parolee the right to make an antiwar speech. In both cases, the courts held that conditions that impinged upon First Amendment rights of free speech were beyond the parole authority.

---

* In New York and perhaps other jurisdictions, when the maximum sentence is life, no "good time" credits can be earned. However, parole after completion of the minimum sentence is possible.

Parole Supervision and Services

Like probation officers, parole officers are responsible for supervising, aiding, and controlling the clients assigned to their case loads. As counselors, officers serve to ease parolees' reentry into society and to aide them in overcoming any obstacles to community adjustment. In addition to individual counseling, they may help in the development of employment plans and job readiness, work with families in the resolution of problems, and orchestrate referrals to community agencies for the handling of certain persistent difficulties. Some parole agencies have special units that focus on such areas as alcoholism, drug use, and unemployment, or on the more unique concerns presented in the supervision of mentally ill or retarded offenders.

Parole officers, on the other hand, also have conflicting roles. In addition to being counselors, they have the duty to police the behavior of those under their supervision. In New York and many other states, parole officers are armed peace officers, and as such, as one officer put it:

> It's a rather contradictory bag to be in. We're what you might call "gun-carrying social workers." Or better yet, how about if we refer to it as the discipline of "authoritarian casework"?[82]

Although quasi–law enforcement responsibilities are apparent in probation supervision, they are considerably more pronounced with respect to parole. Parolees tend to be the more dangerous and serious offenders. Many have been incarcerated for long periods of time, with intensive exposure to prison violence and the inmate culture. Furthermore, the stigma of the ex-con label and former inmate status lessen the potential for community adjustment. All of these combine to stress the law enforcement role of the parole officer and hinder the effective pursuit of rehabilitative goals.

Parole Violation and Revocation

The violation and revocation process in parole is very similar to that described for probation. After a new arrest or serious technical violation, a warrant is issued and the parolee is taken into custody. Pursuant to the Supreme Court decision in *Morrissey* v. *Brewer,* the delinquent parolee is given a measure of due process during his or her preliminary and revocation hearings, and the parole board can make one of two decisions: "restore to supervision" or "return to prison."

"Dead time"

Should parole be revoked, the next issue involves exactly how much time the parolee must serve in prison. This decision is made by the parole board either at the revocation hearing or during the next board meeting at the institution. A bitterly disputed matter in this regard is whether "street time" — the period spent under parole supervision prior to violation — should be credited against the remaining sentence. In some jurisdictions, the parole board establishes the violator's "date of delinquency" — the point at which the violation occurred. From that date on, any time served on the street is considered "dead time." Thus, if an inmate with a 15-year sentence is paroled after three years, serves two years in the community in good standing but is then declared delinquent. Five years of his sentence will be considered as having been completed. The parole board may put a three-year "hold" on him, meaning that he will be eligible for parole consideration in three years. However, in other jurisdictions, the time spent on the street in good standing is not credited in this manner.

This issue has also been addressed with respect to probation violation, and in regard to both probation and parole revocation, the denial of street-time credit represents a nonjudicial increase in sentence. This argument notwithstanding, the courts have consistently upheld the right of states to deny street-time credits. They have done so on the theory that since the probationer or parolee was not physically in custody, he was not "serving a sentence."[83]

Parole Discharge

Individuals can be discharged from parole in a number of ways. First, they can "max out." That is, they can reach their **maximum expiration date** — the date that their entire full sentence formally terminates. Second, in more than half the states and the federal system, parolees can be discharged by the parole board prior to their maximum expiration date. In this instance, however, a number of jurisdictions require that some minimum parole period must be served. In Ohio, for example, discharge can occur after one year of satisfactory supervision, and after five years in the case of a life sentence. Under New York's executive clemency statute, if the time remaining on the maximum sentence at the time of parole is more than five years, the board can issue a discharge after five consecutive years of satisfactory supervision. Third, discharge can occur through commutation of sentence or pardon by the governor. Pardon also represents the chief mechanism through which the civil rights lost upon conviction and imprisonment can be restored in about half the states. In the balance, they are automatically restored upon release from the penitentiary, discharge from parole, or at the final expiration of sentence. In Hawaii, Indiana, Massachusetts, Michigan, and New Hampshire, however, a defendant's civil rights are not lost upon conviction of a felony offense.[84]

The maximum expiration date is the date on which the full sentence ends.

Executive clemency

Trends in Community-based Correction

As of January 1, 1985, the prison population in the United States was almost 464,000. This represented an increase of 41 percent since 1980 and of 55 percent since 1977. At the beginning of the 1980s, there were some 225,000 parolees and mandatory releasees under the supervision of parole authorities, an additional 365,000 under the supervision of various community agencies, plus well over 1.4 million under court-ordered probation. Given the overcrowding in contemporary prisons and the pressures on state correctional systems to remedy the unconstitutional conditions of many of their facilities, combined with the trend toward mandatory prison sentences for violent offenders, it is likely that the character of inmate populations across America will undergo some change. Prisons and penitentiaries will more and more become places for holding the serious criminals, at least for a time, and there will be an increased use of community corrections for other types of offenders. Thus probation, court diversion, and other forms of community-based supervision and service will become even more significant in the overall correctional spectrum. The criminal justice system has long since begun its attempts to meet this challenge of community-based supervison. However, many issues and alternatives remain problematic, casting considerable doubt over the effectiveness and future use of community supervision.

Furlough and Temporary Release

Furlough: An authorized, unescorted absence from a correctional institution for a specified period of time.

As a generic concept, the **furlough** is an authorized, unescorted absence from a correctional institution for a specified period of time.[85] It is a temporary release from prison granted for the purpose of enabling inmates to reestablish community contacts and family ties on a gradual basis. It has emerged in a variety of forms, including the home furlough, work release, and educational release.

Home Furlough

A home furlough is a short leave of absence from the institution, often taken on weekends, and lasting anywhere from 24 hours to a week. As defined in the New York State Correction Law:

> "Furlough program" means a program under which eligible inmates may be granted the privilege of leaving the premises of an institution for a period not exceeding seven days for the purpose of seeking employment, maintaining family ties, solving family problems, seeking post-release housing, attending a short-term educational or vocational training course, or for any matter necessary to the furtherance of any such purposes.[86]

The furlough serves a number of rehabilitative, humanitarian, and pragmatic purposes. It is a mechanism of release transition whereby inmates can begin

An early depiction of how the prison system releases ex-offenders into a world hostile to their reputation and lack of job skills. Today work release, halfway houses, and prerelease centers can help guide the transition from prison to productive society.

THE IN AND OUT OF OUR PENAL SYSTEM.

The law against them.   The world against them.

the normalization of family relationships, reestablish contacts with the outside community, and prepare for eventual permanent release. In addition, prison administrators view the furlough as an avenue for better institutional management, feeling that the promise of a home visit for good behavior fosters better compliance with custodial regulations. In settings where conjugal visitation is either impractical or not permitted, the furlough also has the benefit of reducing sexual frustrations among segments of the inmate population.

Virtually unknown before the late 1960s, home furloughs have been adopted by most states as well as the federal system. Eligibility criteria vary, however, from one jurisdiction to the next. In New York, for example, it is a matter of legislative statute and applies only to inmates who are within one year of parole eligibility or conditional release, and who have not been convicted of any escape, absconding, or violent offenses.[87] In other jurisdictions, eligibility is a matter of legislative, judicial, or correctional policy, with the criteria ranging from highly specific to hopelessly vague.

Work Release

In many ways similar in concept and purpose to the home furlough, work release is an alternative to total incarceration whereby inmates are permitted to work for pay in the free community but must spend their nonworking hours back at the institution. Work release is not a recent correctional innovation; it was initiated under Wisconsin's Huber Law (introduced by Senator Huber for the temporary release of jailed misdemeanants) in 1913. However, the idea has been only slowly accepted, and it was not until the early 1970s that work release became a widespread correctional practice for felony offenders.[88] Eligibility criteria are similar to those adopted for home furloughs, restricting release to those nearing parole or conditional release who do not represent significant risk to the community.

"We'll continue this tomorrow. I'm on a work-release program and I have to be back in my cell by six o'clock."

In addition to the advantages of furloughs in general, work release offers the benefit of potentially reshaping an offender's self-image and promoting the process of decarceration. Furthermore, releasees can assume some financial responsibilities by paying their own transportation to and from the institution, contributing to their room and board, supplementing any welfare benefits that are being given to their families, and beginning payments on any court-ordered restitution. Thus work release can also serve in the interests of the taxpaying community.

However, work release has been faced with many obstacles to its effective implementation. It has been opposed on the grounds that prisoners take jobs away from law-abiding citizens; releasees have been exploited by some employers who feel that "cons" should not be paid at normal wage levels; and prison-based training has not always been usable in the modern employment market. The distance between many correctional institutions and active job centers has also restricted work release efforts. Most prisons are in isolated rural areas, and it is generally neither feasible nor cost-effective to transport inmates over long distances on a daily basis. This has been mitigated, to some extent, by the housing of inmates nightly in jails and detention centers located near their job sites. Some jurisdictions have provided for residential work release centers. These offer not only living facilities for working inmates, but counseling and supervised recreation during evening and weekend hours.

Study Release

As a natural extension of the work release principle, study release is offered to minimum security, parole-eligible inmates with the motivation for vocational or academic enrichment. Following the criteria and regulations of a state's work release project, study release provides opportunities for full-time, on-site participation in vocational school and college programs.

Experiences with Temporary Release

Home furloughs and work and study release programs have been widely utilized in most states and the federal systems. During 1977, for example, the Federal Bureau of Prisons granted more than 26,000 home and work furloughs (including multiple furloughs for some inmates); New York furloughed some 7,500 inmates during the same year; and New Jersey was approving various types of temporary release at the rate of 8,000 per month.[89] During the mid-1970s, furthermore, furloughs combined with work and study releases were occurring at a monthly rate of 30,000 nationally, with escapes ranging from 2 percent in California to 12 percent in Wisconsin.[90] In addition, a number of follow-up studies have demonstrated that selected temporary release programs and centers have fostered high levels of motivated participation and low rates of recidivism.[91]

However, temporary release programs also have their critics, and crimes committed by inmates on work release or home furlough are quickly made conspicuous. A work release center in New York City came to national attention during the mid-1970s when it was learned that almost half of its residents had either escaped or were returned to prison for disciplinary violations, and that 70 percent of the absconders were ultimately arrested for new crimes.[92] Similarly, the work release project at Chino prison in California was terminated when it was discovered that a number of the participating inmates were engaging in armed robberies instead of going to work, and that others not actually in the program had somehow obtained weeklong passes out of prison.[93] Perhaps the most notorious incident involved Calvin F. Smith, an inmate of the District of Columbia Correctional Facility at Lorton, Virginia, who had been convicted in 1973 of first-degree murder, burglary, and robbery and sentenced to 20 years to life. Just 20 months after his commitment, Smith was arrested in a railroad station with a sawed-off shotgun in his possession. It seems that he had been on furlough at the time, making unescorted trips as the prison's "entertainment coordinator." [94] Furlough and work release have been particularly controversial in Delaware, where, during the 1980s, a number of released inmates were quickly returned on new murder charges.[95]

In spite of such incidents of bad publicity, the concept of temporary release continues to hold promise as a form of partial incarceration, as a bridge between the prison and open society, and as another treatment mechanism in the spectrum of community-based correctional services. Perhaps many of the difficulties in existing programs might be eliminated, or at least minimized, with better screening of candidates and monitoring of releasees. However, the kind of public outrage that can be generated when even a few isolated violent crimes are committed by persons who are supposed to be behind bars provides little support for its use as an acceptable correctional tool. This, combined with many unresolved questions as to whether temporary release actually reduces recidivism, and the political realities associated with rehabilitative risk-taking at the potential expense of public safety, suggest only a guarded prognosis for the implementation of such programs on a continuing basis.

Perhaps more promising are the *halfway houses* and *prerelease centers* that have been developing since the 1960s. Designed for inmates who are just a few months away from their parole dates, these residential facilities in urban locations provide individual counseling, vocational guidance, and job placement. Residents are required to abide by minimum security regulations, attend counseling and therapy sessions, and actively seek employment when ready.

Whether halfway houses are effective mechanisms for community reintegration is open to question. As of 1976, there were some 400 halfway houses and prerelease centers housing 10,000 offenders. A national survey of their experience found significant levels of escape, recidivism, and returns to prison for disciplinary violations. But, since recidivism seemed to be no higher among prerelease center residents than among other newly released inmates, it was recommended that the halfway house concept be expanded.[96] There seems to be little likelihood that this will occur, however, not only because of the sensitive political nature of the concept, but also due to the opposition of many communities to "placing convicts in our backyards."

Partial incarceration, halfway houses, and prerelease centers

Abolish Parole?

In 1938, FBI Director J. Edgar Hoover commented that the biggest job of law enforcement was the chasing down of the "canny recidivists," "mad dogs," and "predatory animals" who have been "cloaked by the mantle of parole."[97] In response to Hoover and other critics of parole, the late Edwin H. Sutherland wrote in 1947:

> The antagonism toward parole is probably greater than toward any other penal policy. This is surprising, for there is no well-known student of penology who is not wholeheartedly in favor of the principle of parole, and who does not insist that parole in practice is better than

any available alternative in practice. These students insist, first, that parole should be evaluated not as an abstract principle but in comparison with the only available alternative, which is the determination in court at the time of the trial of the definite date of release, and the complete release at that time without subsequent supervision. They insist, second, that those who are released on parole serve at least as long inside prison walls for a specific type of crime as do those sentenced on definite terms, and in addition remain under supervision outside the prison for periods which generally range from one to three years, and that parole therefore is not leniency but on the contrary is more severe and is a better method of protecting society against crime than the alternative method. They insist, third, that persons released from prison on parole do not commit more crimes than persons released at the expiration of sentences without supervision, for the same offenses.[98]

Arguments about parole

Currently, arguments about parole still persist. In 1971, for example, as a conclusion to its study of criminal justice in America, the American Friends Service Commitee called for the abolition of parole.[99] Later in the 1970s, U.S. Bureau of Prisons Director Norman Carlson, Attorney General Griffin Bell, and Senator Edward M. Kennedy also argued for the abolition of parole.[100] The reasons for this antiparole position have generally been the same for all opponents:

1. The procedures of parole decision-making are unguided by explicit standards and by traditional elements of due process;
2. The tasks which parole is supposed to perform — the accurate prediction of the offender's likelihood of recidivism, and the monitoring of rehabilitative progress — are beyond our present capacities; and,
3. Aside from questions of effectiveness, it is unjust to base decisions about the severity of punishments on what the offender is expected to do in the future.[101]

Senator Kennedy has added that sentencing disparities are compounded by parole, since it encourages some judges to impose the kind of harsh sentences that the community expects. He suggested that if flat or determinate sentencing policies were adopted, parole would not be needed:

> Under this system of judicially fixed sentences, parole release would be abolished and whether or not a prisoner has been "rehabilitated" or has completed a certain prison curriculum would no longer have any bearing on his prison release date.[102]

The current system is actually a nonsystem. It defeats the reasonable expectation of the public that a realistic penalty will be imposed at the time of conviction, and that the sentence received will be the sentence served.
— Senator Edward Kennedy, 1984

From the perspective, too, of many inmates, parolees, civil libertarians, criminal justice reformers, and informed observers, parole is not without faults. The parolee has often been described as a "walking suspension of the Constitution,"[103] a status that seems to have evolved from the alternative theories upon which the concept of parole is based. First, there is the *grace theory,* which holds that parole is a privilege, a gift from the state and board of parole that must be returned if certain conditions are violated. Second, there is the *custody theory,* which states that parolees, although walking the streets in the free community, are legally in the custody of the parole board. As a result, they remain in a quasi-prisoner status, they are not fully at liberty, and their constitutional rights remain limited and abridged. And finally, there is the *contract theory,* which argues that since parolees are required to agree to certain terms and conditions in return for their conditional freedom, the violation of those conditions represents a "breach of contract," which can result in revocation of parole. As parole antagonist Jessica Mitford has put it, it is "a curious sort of 'contract,' in which one side has all the bargaining powers and in which the contracting parolee, if accused of breaking it, has no redress in the courts."[104]

With this context, one parolee has commented:

> They've set up the whole system to make you fail. I guess they have a business going in this state and once they get you hooked into the system they don't want to let you go. They want you to come back. They let you out of here on a yo-yo. You're out there a little while, then they pull the string, zap, you're back. They got a good thing going here, man, can't you see it. They don't want to lose you.[105]

Similarly, another parolee has said:

> If your parole officer, or the system, decides that they want you back inside, there's nothing you can do to prevent it. . . . My last time out I was doin' real good—a job, reporting, the whole thing. Then my PO gives me a toss and finds an ad for a toy gun in my pocket. With two

The revolving door

"priors" for armed robbery I didn't stand a chance. I was gonna get it for my nephew, but to the board, as they put it, I was "about to lapse into criminal ways and company."[106]

The movement to abolish parole earned renewed vigor in 1984 when the results of a 12-state study by the Bureau of Justice Statistics documented that the average prison stay for felony offenders was three years or less — with 3.3 to 6.5 years for murderers and 2.1 to 5.3 years for rapists (see Exhibit 17.7).[107] In reaction to the study, U.S. Attorney General William French Smith called for the abolition of parole nationwide, and further commented:

> The public has assumed that the worst offenders — murderers, rapists, drug traffickers — serve substantial terms. The study shows how easy it is for hardened criminals to get back in the streets.[108]

Added to this were the widely publicized statements of Washington Redskins placekicker Mark Moseley, whose only sister had been brutally raped and murdered in 1979 by a convicted rapist while on parole after having served less than half of his sentence.[109]

EXHIBIT 17.7

Average Time Served in Prison by Felony Offenders

State and Release Period	Number Released	Average Time Served, in Months		
		All Felonies	Serious Violent Crimes*	Serious Property Crimes†
Delaware, 1980–82	1,371	17.8	32.5	10.3
Illinois 1978–82	21,202	23.1	34.0	‡
Iowa, 1979–83	4,623	32.8	48.6	26.1
Maryland, 1982	3,649	29.5	50.5	21.7
Ohio, 1980–81	12,026	24.6	40.5	20.9
Oklahoma, 1982	2,232	15.4	28.3	13.5
Oregon, 1979–82	5,704	17.2	28.4	14.0
Pennsylvania, 1981–82	6,202	26.7	38.1	21.1
Washington, 7/81–6/82	1,325	26.9	41.3	21.0
Wisconsin, 1/80–5/83	6,679	29.2	39.7	25.2
Wyoming, 7/80–6/83	759	22.9	39.0	20.1

* Murder, nonnegligent manslaughter, rape, robbery, aggravated assault.
† Burglary, larceny, auto theft, arson.
‡ Data not available.

SOURCE: *Time Served in Prison.* Bureau of Justice Statistics Special Report, June 1984, p. 3.

On the other side of the issue are many who argue strongly to retain parole. In the words of Donald J. Newman, dean of the College of Criminal Justice at the State University of New York at Albany:

Parole was accepted because it was viewed as rehabilitative, for supervised reentry into the community is almost always safer and more effective than simply opening the gates. In general, giving due deference to critics of parole who see it as either too lenient or too harsh, years of experience have generally proved its efficiency and effectiveness.[110]

Elsewhere Newman stated:

We cannot cavalierly throw away a reform so hard won and so generally effective simply to satisfy the frustrations of the moment or to scapegoat our deeper failure to really address the crime problem.[111]

But is parole generally effective? Curiously, there have been few comprehensive studies of parole outcome. A review of 19 studies examining the effect of parole on recidivism, as reported in the highly controversial book, *The Effectiveness of Correctional Treatment,* concluded that

men released on parole are likely to return to prison at a lower rate while on parole than men discharged from prison without parole. However, *after release from parole the rate of return to prison is similar to that of dischargees.*[112]

Although this projects a rather negative picture of parole effectiveness, other data indicate somewhat the opposite. Daniel Glaser's study of more than 1,000 federal parolees relased from prison during 1957–1958 found that 65 percent made a satisfactory community adjustment.[113] More recently, the National Council on Crime and Delinquency conducted the most comprehensive study of parole effectiveness ever undertaken. Of 104,182 offenders released on parole between 1965 and 1970, 75 percent were found to have finished their paroles successfully. Success rates varied from 90.1 percent for persons convicted of homicide, to a low of 64.9 percent for car thieves.[114]

To many, these data clearly suggested that parole is considerably more effective than previously believed. But is it really? The answer should be an unqualified "probably not," for a variety of factors could force one to conclude that the overall failure rate of only 25 percent is a "tip of the iceberg" phenomenon. First of all, in studies of parole outcome, how are "success" and "failure" defined? Generally, a failure is anyone who was returned to prison for parole violation, was arrested and convicted for a new offense while under parole supervision, or was an absconder at the time of the follow-up. Thus recidivism subsequent to "maxing out" is generally not accounted for. Second, studies have shown that many parole violations that could conceivably result in revocation go undetected.[115] Third, and perhaps most importantly, it has been well documented that official criminal statistics are poor measures of the incidence and prevalence of offense behavior. As pointed out in Chapter 4, arrest rates reflect only a small portion of the crimes actually committed. If the sole measures of parole failure are technical violations, new arrests, and absconding, then little faith can be placed in available rates of parole success.

This argument would certainly serve in the interests of those who wish to abolish parole. Yet to abolish parole at this point would be premature.

There are too many unanswered questions. For example, can parole be justified on grounds other than rehabilitation? Are *all* of parole's functions without usefulness? Are there any viable alternatives to parole?

The movement toward parole abolition began during the late 1970s in Maine, and by the mid-1980s California, Colorado, Illinois, Minnesota, New Mexico, Connecticut, North Carolina, and Washington had either abolished parole or severely restricted its use. It is unlikely, however, that this trend will move with any due haste during the balance of the 1980s. Longer definite sentences are the suggested alternative. But prisons are already overcrowded, and the inescapable fact is that parole remains one of the few economically viable alternatives to long-term imprisonment.

Summary

Community-based correction involves programs and activities within the community that are generally of a rehabilitative, nonpunitive nature. Such correctional approaches include criminal justice diversion, probation and conditional release, restitution programs, and furlough and temporary release.

Criminal justice diversion refers to the removal of offenders from the application of the criminal law at any stage of the police or court processes. Diversion as such began with the Chicago Boy's Court in 1914. Today its use is widespread for both juvenile and adult offenders, but its impact is difficult to assess.

The concept of probation emerged in 1841 with the work of John Augustus. Today probation is a status, a system, and a process. As an alternative to imprisonment, it is the most widely used adjudication disposition, encompassing elements of both community protection and offender rehabilitation.

Parole, common in the United States for almost a century, refers to the practice of allowing the final portion of a prison sentence to be served in the community. In contrast to probation, which involves community supervision in lieu of imprisonment, parole occurs after some part of the prison term has been completed.

Both probation and parole are subject to conditions, the violation of which may result in incarceration. The United States Supreme Court, through a series of decisions during the 1970s, has established guidelines regarding the due-process requirements at probation and parole revocation proceedings.

Other forms of community-based corrections include furlough and temporary release programs, restitution, and the use of halfway houses.

Key Terms

community-based correction (624)
diversion (625)
furlough (660)
Gagnon v. *Scarpelli* (643)
"good time" (648)
mandatory release (657)

maximum expiration date (659)
Mempa v. *Rhay* (642)
Morrissey v. *Brewer* (642)
parole (646)
parole prediction (654)
probation (630)

restitution (637)
revocation (641)
salient factor score (654)
shock probation (639)
suspended sentence (631)
Williams v. *New York* (632)

Questions for Discussion

1. What are the differences between probation and parole in terms of organization and administration, eligibility and selection, supervision and services, and conditions and revocation?
2. In *Mempa* v. *Rhay,* why did the Court restrict its ruling on right to counsel to cases involving deferred sentencing?
3. Which would appear to be the more effective form of parole authority structure: an independent parole board or a board housed within the state correctional system? Why?
4. Should parole be abolished? Why?

For Further Reading

Hirsch, Andrew, and Kathleen J. Hanrahan. *Abolish Parole?* Washington, D.C.: U.S. Government Printing Office, 1978.

Inciardi, James A., and Duane C. McBride. "The Parole Prediction Myth." *International Journal of Criminology and Penology* 5 (August 1977): 235–244.

McCleary, Richard. *Dangerous Men: The Sociology of Parole.* Beverly Hills: Sage, 1978.

Nimmer, Raymond T. *Diversion: The Search for Alternative Forms of Prosecution.* Chicago: American Bar Foundation, 1974.

Notes

1. Duane C. McBride, "Criminal Justice Diversion," in *Crime and the Criminal Justice Process,* ed. James A. Inciardi and Kenneth C. Haas (Dubuque, Iowa: Kendall/Hunt, 1978), p.246.
2. Jacob M. Braude, "Boys' Court: Individualized Justice for the Youthful Offender," *Federal Probation* 12 (June 1948): 9–14.
3. Daniel Glaser, James A. Inciardi, and Dean V. Babst, "Later Heroin Use by Marijuana-Using, Heroin-Using, and Non-Drug-Using Adolescent Offenders in New York City," *The International Journal of the Addictions* 4 (June 1969): 145–155.
4. Leon G. Leiberg. *Project Crossroads: Final Report* (Washington, D.C.: National Committee for Children and Youth, 1971).
5. McBride, "Criminal Justice Diversion," p. 250.
6. *The Manhattan Court Employment Project: Final Report* (New York: Vera Institute of Justice, 1972).
7. Arnold Schechter and Kenneth Polk, *Youth Service Bureaus, National Evaluation Program, Phase I Assessment* (Washington, D.C.: U.S. Government Printing Office, 1977).
8. James W. Brown, Roger Mazze, and Daniel Glaser, *Narcotics Knowledge and Nonsense: Program Disaster Versus A Scientific Model* (Cambridge, Mass.: Ballinger, 1974); Nicholas Regush, *The Drug Addiction Business* (New York: Dial Press, 1971).
9. *New York Times,* the following issues: June 30, 1970, p. 35; August 31, 1970, p. 31; September 16, 1970, p. 35; September 18, 1970, p. 29; October 8, 1970, p. 45; October 10, 1970, p. 10.
10. See McBride, "Criminal Justice Diversion," p. 257.
11. Harvey A. Siegal, *The Weekend Intervention Program: Three Years of Success in Helping the Drinking Driver* (Dayton: Wright State University School of Medicine, 1981).
12. See John Augustus, *A Report of the Labors of John Augustus, for the Last Ten Years, in Aid of the Unfortunate* (Boston: Wright & Hasty, 1852); reprinted as *John Augustus, First Probation Officer* (New York: National Probation Association, 1939).
13. American Bar Association Project on Standards for Criminal Justice, *Standards Relating to Probation* (New York: Institute for Judicial Administration, 1970), p. 9.
14. National Advisory Commission on Crminal Justice Standards and Goals, *Corrections* (Washington, D.C.: U.S. Government Printing Office, 1973), p. 312.
15. Division of Information Services, *TACP Shock Probation Survey* (Austin: Texas Adult Probation Commission, 1980).
16. State of New York, *Penal Law,* 65.05
17. State of New York, *Penal Law,* 65.20.
18. These observations were made by the author.
19. James A. Inciardi, "The Impact of Presentence Investigations on Subsequent Sentencing Practices," Paper presented at the Annual Meeting of the American Sociological Association, August 1976, New York, N.Y.
20. Robert M. Carter and Leslie T. Wilkins, "Some Factors in Sentencing Policy," *Journal of Criminal Law, Criminology, and Police Science* 58 (December 1967): 503–514.
21. Williams v. New York, 347 U.S. 241 (1949).
22. Gardner v. Florida, 430 U.S. 349 (1977).
23. *Code of Alabama,* 15–22–50.
24. *General Statutes of North Carolina,* 15A–1341 (a).
25. Personal communication, October 1979.
26. Cox v. States, 283 S.E. 2d 716 (Ga Ct. App. 1981).
27. People v. Mitchell, 178 Cal. Rptr. 188 (Cal. Ct. App., 1981).
28. State v. Behrens, 285 N. W. 2d 513 (Neb. Sup. Ct., 1979).
29. State v. Wilson, 604 P. 2d 739 (Idaho Sup., 1980).
30. Wood v. State, 378 So. 2d 111 (Fla. Dist. Ct. App., 1980).
31. State v. Alexander, 267 S. E. 2d 397 (N.C. Ct. App., 1980).
32. People v. Sprague, 430 N.Y.S. 2d 260 (N.Y. Sup. Ct. App. Div., 1980).
33. See Barber v. State, 387 So. 2d 540 (Fla. Dist. Ct. App., 1980).

34. Rodriguez v. State, 378 So. 2d 7 (Fla. Dist. Ct. App., 1979).

35. See Gilbert Geis, "Restitution by Criminal Offenders: A Summary and Overview," in *Restitution in Criminal Justice,* ed. Joe Hudson and Burt Galaway (Lexington, Mass.: Lexington, 1977), pp. 246–264.

36. For a further discussion of restitution, see Larry Siegel, "Court Ordered Victim Restitution: An Overview of Theory and Action," *New England Journal of Prison Law* 5 (1979): 135–150.

37. Personal communication, April 1977.

38. E. Kim Nelson, Howard Ohmart, and Nora Harlow, *Promising Strategies in Probation and Parole* (Washington, D.C.: U.S. Government Printing Office, 1978), pp. 16–17.

39. *Ohio Revised Code,* 2947.06.1, July 1965.

40. Paul C. Friday and David M. Petersen, "Shock of Imprisonment: Comparative Analysis of Short-term Incarceration as a Treatment Technique," Paper presented at the InterAmerican Congress of the American Society of Criminology and the InterAmerican Association of Criminology, Caracas, Venezuela, November 1972.

41. Friday and Petersen, "Shock of Imprisonment"; Harry E. Allen and Clifford E. Simonsen, *Corrections in America* (New York: Macmillan, 1981), p. 161; Kenyon J. Skudder, "In Opposition to Probation with a Jail Sentence," *Federal Probation* 23 (June 1959): 12–17; National Advisory Commission, *Corrections,* p. 321.

42. Eugene N. Barkin, "Sentencing the Adult Offender," *Federal Probation* 26 (June 1962): 11–16.

43. See David M. Petersen and Paul C. Friday, "Early Release from Incarceration: Race as a factor in the Use of 'Shock Probation,'" *Journal of Criminal Law and Criminology* 66 (March 1975): 79–87; Joseph A. Waldron and Henry R. Angelino, "Shock Probation: A Natural Experiment on the Effect of a Short Period of Incarceration," *The Prison Journal* 57 (Spring–Summer 1977): 52.

44. Villarreal v. State, 166 Tex. Cr. R. 610, 217 S. W. 2d 207 (1958).

45. Mempa v. Rhay, 398 U.S. 128 (1967).

46. Morrissey v. Brewer, 408 U.S. 471 (1972).

47. Gagnon v. Scarpelli, 411 U.S. 778 (1973).

48. United States v. Reed, 573 F. 2d 1020 (8th Cir., 1978).

49. United States v. Pattman, 535 F. 2d 1062 (8th Cir., 1976).

50. United States v. Jurgens, 626 F. 2d 142 (9th Cir., 1980).

51. Watson v. State, 388 So. 2d 15 (Fla. Dist. Ct. App., 1980).

52. United States v. Lacey, 661 F. 2d 1021 (5th Cir., 1981).

53. *Probation and Parole 1983,* Bureau of Justice Statistics Bulletin, September 1984.

54. See, for example, Vernon Fox, *Introduction to Corrections* (Englewood Cliffs, N.J.: Prentice-Hall, 1985), p. 139.

55. For a discussion of probation effectiveness studies, see Harry E. Allen, Chris W. Eskridge, Edward J. Latessa, and Gennaro F. Vito, *Probation and Parole in America* (New York: Free Press, 1985), pp. 256–266.

56. Joan Petersilia, Susan Turner, James Kahan, and Joyce Peterson, *Granting Felons Probation: Public Risks and Alternatives* (Santa Monica, Calif.: Rand, 1985).

57. G. I. Giardini, *The Parole Process* (Springfield, Ill.: Thomas, 1959), p. 9.

58. Edwin H. Sutherland, *Principles of Criminology* (Philadelphia: J. P. Lippincott, 1947), p. 534.

59. Harry Elmer Barnes, *The Story of Punishment: A Record of Man's Inhumanity to Man* (Montclair, N.J.: Patterson Smith, 1972), pp. 68–80.

60. See E. C. Wines, "Commutation Laws in the United States," *Report of the Prison Association of New York,* 1868, pp. 154–170.

61. See David Dressler, *Practice and Theory of Probation and Parole* (New York: Columbia University Press, 1969), pp. 56–76; Marjorie Bell, ed., *Parole in Principle and Practice* (New York: National Probation and Parole Association, 1957).

62. National Advisory Commission, *Corrections,* p. 399.

63. National Advisory Commission, *Corrections,* p. 399.

64. William Parker, *Parole: Origins, Development, Current Practices and Statutes* (College Park, Md.: American Correctional Association, 1975); Vincent O'Leary and Kathleen J. Hanrahan, *Parole Systems in the United States* (Hackensack, N.J.: National Council on Crime and Delinquency, 1976).

65. State of New York, *Correction Law,* Section 803.

66. Parker, *Parole,* pp. 60–66.

67. Parker, *Parole,* pp. 60–66.

68. Menechino v. Oswald, 430 F. 2d 403 (2d Cir., 1970).

69. Johnson, U.S. ex. rel. v. Chairman, New York State Board of Parole, 363 F. Supp. 416, aff'd, 500 F. 2d 925 (2d Cir., 1971).

70. Greenholtz v. Inmates of Nebraska Penal and Correctional Complex, 422 U.S. 1 (1979).

71. See, for example, *Tennessee Code,* 40–3614.

72. Wilmington (Delaware) *News-Journal,* June 1, 1984, p. A5.

73. James A. Inciardi and Duane C. McBride, "The Parole Prediction Myth," *International Journal of Criminology and Penology* 5 (August 1977): 235–244.

74. Peter P. Lejins, "Parole Prediction—An Introductory Statement," *Crime and Delinquency* 8 (July 1962): 209–214.

75. James A. Inciardi and Dean V. Babst, "Predicting the Post-release Adjustment of Institutionalized Narcotic Addicts," *Bulletin on Narcotics* 23 (April–June 1971): 33–39.

76. Inciardi and McBride, "Parole Prediction Myth."

77. See William E. Amos and Charles L. Newman, eds., *Parole: Legal Issues/Decision-making/Research* (New York: Federal Legal Publications, 1975), pp. 169–210.

78. Don M. Gottfredson, Peter B. Hoffman, Maurice H. Sigler, and Leslie T. Wilkins, "Making Paroling Policy Explicit," *Crime and Delinquency* 21 (January 1975): 36.

79. *U.S. News & World Report,* September 17, 1984, p. 16.

80. Hyland v. Procunier, 311 F. Supp. 749 (N.D. Cal., 1970).

81. Sobell v. Reed, 327 F. Supp. 1294 (S.D. N.Y., 1971).

82. Personal communication, October 1981.

83. See Richard C. Hand and Richard G. Singer, *Sentencing Computation Laws* (Washington, D.C.: American Bar Association, 1974).

84. See O'Leary and Hanrahan, *Parole Systems.*

85. E. Eugene Miller, "Furloughs as a Technique of Reintegration," in *Corrections in the Community,* ed. E. Eugene Miller and M. Robert Montilla (Reston, Va.: Reston, 1977), p. 201.

86. State of New York, *Correction Law,* 26, 851–4.

87. State of New York, *Correction Law,* 26, 851–2.

88. Elmer H. Johnson and Kenneth E. Kotch, "Two Factors in Development of Work Release: Size and Location of Prisons," *Journal of Criminal Justice* 1 (March 1973): 44–45.

89. Louis P. Carney, *Corrections: Treatment and Philosophy* (Englewood Cliffs, N.J.: Prentice Hall, 1980), p. 221.

90. Carney, *Corrections.*

91. See Gordon Bird, "Community Centered Treatment of Offenders," in *Criminal Rehabilitation: Within and Without the Walls,* ed. Edward M. Scott and Kathryn L. Scott (Springfield, Ill.: Thomas, 1973), pp. 133–142; National Institute of Justice, *U.S. Department of Justice Exemplary Projects Program* (Washington, D.C.: U.S. Government Printing Office, 1979); *Criminal Justice Newsletter* 7 (December 6, 1976): 6.

92. *New York Times,* September 2, 1975, p. 23; *New York Times,* December 27, 1977, p. 24.

93. Michael S. Serrill, "California," *Corrections* (September 1974): 39–40.

94. *Corrections Magazine* 1 (March–April 1975): 53.

95. Wilmington (Delaware) *News-Journal,* March 26, 1984, p. A1.

96. Richard P. Seiter, *Halfway Houses: National Evaluation Program* (Washington, D.C.: U.S. Government Printing Office, 1977).

97. J. Edgar Hoover, *Persons in Hiding* (Boston: Little, Brown, 1938), pp. 189–190.

98. Sutherland, *Principles of Criminology,* p. 551.

99. American Friends Service Committee, *Struggle for Justice: A Report on Crime and Punishment in America* (New York: Hill & Wang, 1972).

100. Bob Wilson, "Parole Release: Devil or Savior?" *Corrections Magazine* 3 (September 1977): 48.

101. Andrew von Hirsch and Kathleen J. Hanrahan, *Abolish Parole?* (Washington, D.C.: U.S. Government Printing Office, 1978), p. 1.

102. Edward M. Kennedy, "Toward a New System of Criminal Sentencing: Law with Order," *The American Criminal Law Review* 16 (Spring 1979): 361.

103. Jessica Mitford, *Kind and Unusual Punishment: The Prison Business* (New York: Vintage, 1974), p. 238.

104. Mitford, *Kind and Unusual Punishment,* p. 239.

105. Mitford, *Kind and Unusual Punishment,* p. 237.

106. Personal communication, November 1979.

107. *Time Served in Prison,* Bureau of Justice Statistics Special Report, June 1984.

108. *USA Today,* June 25, 1984, 1A.

109. *USA Today,* February 24, 1984, p. 10A.

110. Donald J. Newman, *Introduction to Criminal Justice* (Philadelphia: J. P. Lippincott, 1978), p. 358.

111. Donald J. Newman, "No, Don't Abolish Parole," *New York Times,* February 10, 1981, p. A23.

112. Douglas Lipton, Robert Martinson, and Judith Wilks, *The Effectiveness of Correctional Treatment: A Survey of Treatment Evaluation Studies* (New York: Praeger, 1975), p. 150.

113. Daniel Glaser, *The Effectiveness of a Prison and Parole System* (Indianapolis: Bobbs-Merrill, 1964).

114. Don M. Gottfredson, M. G. Neithercutt, Joan Nuffield, and Vincent O'Leary, *Four Thousand Lifetimes: A Study of Time Served and Parole Outcome* (Hackensack, N.J.: National Council on Crime and Delinquency, 1973).

115. See, for example, James A. Inciardi, "The Use of Parole Prediction with Institutionalized Narcotic Addicts," *Journal of Research in Crime and Delinquency* 8 (January 1971): 65–73.

Part 5

Juvenile Justice

CHAPTER 18
The Juvenile Justice System

18

The Juvenile Justice System

The selectmen of every town are required to keep a vigilant eye on the inhabitants to the end that the fathers shall teach their children knowledge of the English tongue and of the capital laws, and knowledge of the catechism, and shall instruct them in some honest lawful calling, labor, or employment. If parents do not do this, the children shall be taken away and placed with masters who will so teach and instruct them.

— The Code of 1650, General Court of Connecticut

drunk or stoned and they didn't seem to be making any kind of trouble. I made them grind out their joint and pour out the rest of the wine and told them to sit in the patrol car. The complainant said he would be satisfied if the kids promised not to return, so I drove them around for fifteen minutes lecturing them on the virtues of neighborliness, good deeds, and wholesome all-American conduct. They said they'd behave themselves, so I let them go with just a warning.[15]

This discretionary power of the police is generally unreviewed. The style of the officer, the circumstances of the incident, and the policies of the department typically play a role in the decision to release or to detain juveniles. Studies have demonstrated, however, that numerous other factors can come into play: the attitude of the victim; the juvenile's prior record; the seriousness of the offense; the age, sex, race, and demeanor of the offender; the likelihood of adequate parental handling of the matter; the time and location of the incident; the availability of a service agency for referral; and the officer's perception of how the case will be handled by the court.[16] Consideration of these factors by a police officer, consciously or otherwise, is more likely to result in an "on the street disposition" or no action at all. Beyond these, there is the third option — taking the juvenile into custody.* Yet even in this event, the police still have alternatives. Some law enforcement agencies in large urban areas have their own diversion and delinquency prevention programs to which they may send a juvenile, while status offenders may be brought to social service agencies for counseling and treatment. With felony offenses, and particularly those involving violence, there is the fourth police option — referral to the juvenile court.

Petition and Intake

Petition: In juvenile proceedings, a document alleging that a youth is a delinquent, a status offender, or a dependent child and asking that the court assume jurisdiction over the juvenile.

Intake hearing

The mechanism for bringing juveniles to the attention of the courts is through a **petition**, as opposed to an arrest warrant. This can be filed by the police, a victim, parents, school officials, or a social worker. Like an arrest warrant, the petition specifies the alleged offense or delinquency, the name and address of the child, the names and residences of his or her parents, and a description of the circumstances of the offense. This petition initiates the formal judicial processing of a juvenile (see Exhibit 18.4).

After the petition is filed an **intake hearing** is held, conducted by the court as a preliminary examination into the facts of the case. However, it is not presided over by a judge nor does it occur in open court. Rather, the hearing officer is usually a referee with a background in social work or one of the behavioral sciences, an attorney, a probation officer, or someone else assigned by the juvenile court. The purpose of this hearing is to protect the interests of the child and to quickly dispose of cases that do not require the time and expense of formal court processing.

In effect, the intake officer makes a legal judgment of the probable cause of the petition, and this may be the only time that the sufficiency of the evidence is evaluated. The officer may also conduct a brief investigation into the background of the juvenile, have an informal hearing with the child and

---

* It might be noted here that there are 29 jurisdictions in the United States that avoid the term *arrest* with respect to juveniles, preferring the expression *taking into custody*. Moreover, in the juvenile codes of 10 of these jurisdictions, it is expressly stated that *taking into custody* is *not* arrest. Although for all practical purposes being taken into custody is the same as being arrested, the latter term is avoided to protect youths from a criminal record.

EXHIBIT 18.9

Waiver of Jurisdiction Statutes in Selected States

Alabama

Jurisdictional age: 18

Waiver age: 14; waiver permitted only where child charged with felony or is already under commitment as a delinquent.

California

Jurisdictional age: 18

Waiver age: 16

Colorado

Jurisdictional age: 18

Waiver age: 14; waiver permitted only where child charged with felony.

Delaware

Jurisdictional age: 18

Waiver age: 16; waiver also permitted where child is 14 or older and charged with commission of a felony.

District of Columbia

Jurisdictional age: 18

Waiver age: 15 where child is charged with felony; 16 where child is already under commitment as delinquent child, without regard to offense; and 18 where person is 18 or older and charged with any offense allegedly committed before reaching 18.

Florida

Jurisdictional age: 18

Waiver age: 14; waiver mandatory upon demand of child and parent or guardian.

Georgia

Jurisdictional age: 17 in case of delinquent or unruly child; 18 in case of deprived child.

Waiver age: 15 generally; in case of a child charged with offense punishable by death or life imprisonment, waiver age is 13.

Illinois

Jurisdictional age: 17 in case of child alleged to be delinquent; 18 in case of child alleged to be minor in need of supervision, neglected or abused minor, or dependent minor.

Waiver age: 13

Indiana

Jurisdictional age: 18

Waiver age: Waiver permitted where child is 14 or older and certain aggravating circumstances are present; in addition, unless specified mitigating circumstances are present, waiver is mandatory where child is 10 or older and charged with murder, or 16 or older and charged with a Class A or Class B felony, involuntary manslaughter as a Class C felony, or reckless homicide as a Class C felony, or where child of any age is charged with a felony and has been convicted previously of a felony or nontraffic misdemeanor.

Maryland

Jurisdictional age: 18

Waiver age: 15, except jurisdiction may be waived over any child charged with offense punishable by death or life imprisonment.

Mississippi

Jurisdictional age: 18

Waiver age: 13

Montana

Jurisdictional age: 18

Waiver age: 16; waiver permitted only in case of child charged with criminal homicide, arson, aggravated assault, robbery, burglary or aggravated burglary, sexual intercourse without consent, aggravated kidnapping, possession of explosives or criminal sale of dangerous drugs for profit.

New Hampshire

Jurisdictional age: 18

Waiver age: No age given (waiver permitted only where child charged with felony).

Oklahoma

Jurisdictional age: 18

Waiver age: No age given (waiver permitted only where child charged with felony).

Oregon

Jurisdictional age: 18

Waiver age: 16

Pennsylvania

Jurisdictional age: 18

Waiver age: Waiver permitted where child is 14 and charged with felony; waiver mandatory in case of child charged with murder, unless case has been transferred to juvenile court from criminal court.

Virginia

Jurisdictional age: 18

Waiver age: 15 (waiver permitted only where child charged with felony).

Wisconsin

Jurisdictional age: 18

Waiver age: 16

Wyoming

Jurisdictional age: 19

Waiver age: No age given

finally occurred in 1966 with ***Kent v. United States,*** the first Supreme Court evaluation of the constitutionality of juvenile court proceedings (see Exhibit 18.10). The ruling in *Kent* held that there must be waiver hearings, and although such hearings need not conform to all the requirements of a criminal trial, they must measure up to the essentials of due process and fair treatment.

Should *any* juvenile be dealt with in the criminal courts?

Although *Kent* accorded a measure of constitutional safeguards to waiver proceedings, the question remains as to whether *any* juvenile should be dealt with in the adult criminal courts. On the one hand, there is the pragmatic issue of community protection and the state's right to wage war against its enemies. On the other, there is the more abstract and philosophical consideration of confinement in a penitentiary as an appropriate treatment for what is defined under state statutes as delinquent behavior. Of even greater significance is the matter of juveniles and capital punishment. Thirty states currently permit the execution of criminals regardless of their age. Although the majority of nations around the world have set 18 as the minimum age for capital punishment, 288 juveniles have been executed in the United States

---

EXHIBIT 18.10

Kent v. United States

Morris A. Kent, Jr., had first come under the authority of the District of Columbia juvenile court in 1959. He was age 14 at the time and had been apprehended as a result of several housebreakings and an attempted purse snatching. He was placed on probation, in the custody of his mother, and from time to time he was contacted by the juvenile court officials.

Two years later, on September 2, 1961, an intruder broke into the home of a District of Columbia woman, took her wallet, and raped her. Fingerprints found in the apartment matched those of Kent, having been taken during his juvenile court contact in 1959. At this point 16 years of age and still on juvenile probation, Morris Kent was taken into custody by the police. After almost two days of interrogation, he admitted his involvement in these and several other housebreakings, robberies, and rapes.

Following Kent's apprehension, his mother obtained an attorney, who promptly conferred with the social service director of the juvenile court. In a brief meeting, they discussed the possibility that the court might waive its jurisdiction and transfer the case to the district court for trial — a waiver that the attorney indicated he would oppose. Meanwhile, Kent was being held in detention, during which time there was neither an arraignment nor a hearing by a judicial officer to determine probable cause for arrest. Kent's attorney, however, arranged for psychiatric examinations of his client, after which he filed two motions with the juvenile court. The first was for a hearing on the question of the waiver of juvenile court jurisdiction; accompanying it was a psychiatrist's affidavit certifying that Kent "is a victim of severe psychopathology" and

recommending hospitalization for psychiatric evaluation. The second motion, in behalf of effective assistance of counsel, was for access to the social service file that had been compiled by the staff of the juvenile court during Kent's probation period.

The juvenile court judge did not rule on these motions; he held no hearing; and he did not confer with Kent, his mother, or his attorney. Rather, the judge entered an order stating that after "full investigation, I do hereby waive" jurisdiction of Kent and directing that he be "held for trial for [the alleged] offenses under the regular procedure of the U.S. District Court for the District of Columbia." The judge made no findings; he did not recite any reason for the waiver; and he made no reference to the motions filed by Kent's attorney.

After the juvenile court waived its jurisdiction, Kent was

---

under laws that permit some young offenders to be tried as adults.[43] The last such execution was in 1964, when the state of Texas electrocuted James Andrew Echols, convicted of a rape — a crime that is no longer punishable by death as the result of *Coker* v. *Georgia* — committed at age 17.[44] The youngest person to be executed during the current century was a 13-year-old, electrocuted in Florida in 1927.[45]

During the early part of the 1980s, there were no less than 25 juveniles on death row in the United States. The youngest was Ronald Ward, convicted and sentenced to death at age 15 in 1985.[46] Opponents of the death penalty argue that the execution of any juvenile is "cruel and unusual punishment" in violation of the Eighth Amendment. Moreover, they hold, a child's behavior is different from that of an adult. On the other hand, supporters of the death penalty insist that youthful offenders should not be permitted to wrap themselves in the shield of age in order to escape responsibility for their crimes. Interestingly, the U.S. Supreme Court has not only remained silent on the matter of juveniles and the death penalty, but also bypassed an opportunity to

Children on death row

indicted by the grand jury and received a jury trial in the criminal court. On the rape, he was found not guilty by reason of insanity. Yet he was found guilty on six counts of housebreaking and robbery, for which he was sentenced to a term of 30 to 90 years. On appeal to the U.S. court of appeals, Kent's attorney argued that the detention, interrogation, and fingerprinting were unlawful. As to the proceedings by which the juvenile court waived its jurisdiction, he attacked them on statutory and constitutional grounds: " . . . no hearing occurred, no findings were made, no reasons were stated before the waiver, and counsel was denied access to the social service file." The court of appeals affirmed the lower court decision, and the United States Supreme Court granted *certiorari*.

By a 5-to-4 majority, the High Court nullified the juvenile court's waiver of jurisdiction, holding that such a waiver is a "critically important" stage in the juvenile process and must be attended by minimum requirements of due process and fair treatment as required by the Fourteenth Amendment. Specifically, the Court set forth four basic safeguards required by due process during waiver proceedings:

1. If the juvenile court is considering waiving jurisdiction, the juvenile is entitled to a hearing on the waiver.
2. The juvenile is entitled to representation by counsel at such hearing.
3. The juvenile's attorney must be given access to the juvenile's social records on request.
4. If jurisdiction is waived, the juvenile is entitled to a

statement of reasons in support of the waiver order.

The ruling in *Kent* was initially limited in scope, since it was seemingly based on an interpretation of the waiver requirements under District of Columbia statutes rather than on constitutional principles. However, following the many references to *Kent* in *In re Gault* and subsequent cases, the requirements stated in *Kent* have taken on constitutional dimension and are applicable to *all* juvenile court waiver decisions.

SOURCE: Kent v. United States, 383 U.S. 541 (1966).

evaluate the conflicting arguments on the matter. An appropriate time was 1982 in the case of *Eddings* v. *Oklahoma*.[47] At age 16, Monty Lee Eddings had murdered a police officer. He entered a *nolo contendere* plea at trial and was sentenced to death. Instead of ruling on the constitutionality of the death penalty for juveniles as most court observers had expected, the Supreme Court chose to set aside the death sentence and remand the case to the Oklahoma Court of Criminal Appeals for further consideration of the "mitigating factor" of Eddings's emotional disturbance. In 1985, after Oklahoma's highest court had resentenced Eddings to life imprisonment, the Supreme Court agreed to review Eddings's case for a second time. However, once again the appropriateness of the death penalty for juvenile offenders was not the argument at issue.[48] (On this occasion it was the state that filed the appeal, seeking a decision that would allow it to put Eddings to death.)

Juvenile Detention

The temporary detention of youths pending juvenile court action presents significant problems for both juvenile justice officials and those youths held in custody. As noted in the first section of this chapter, the Supreme Court's ruling in **Schall v. Martin** sanctioned the practice of preventive detention for certain juvenile arrestees. In that case, on December 13, 1977, 14-year-old Gregory Martin, along with two other youths, had been arrested on charges of robbery, assault, and weapons violations. For 15 days Martin had been held in detention, after which he was adjudicated a juvenile delinquent and placed on probation. While still in detention, however, Martin instituted a *habeas corpus* class-action suit on behalf of *all* youths being held in preventive detention pursuant to New York's Family Court Act. When the case reached the U.S. Supreme Court, it was held that preventive detention was permissible with respect to an accused juvenile delinquent when there was evidence that he or she presented a "serious risk" of committing a crime before adjudication of the case. The New York procedure was upheld because it served the legitimate purpose of community protection and because there were numerous procedural safeguards in the New York Juvenile Court Act intended to safeguard against erroneous deprivations of liberty.

Schall v. *Martin* is most significant to the issue of juvenile detention, not just because it validated the constitutionality of New York's statute, but because of the perspective on juvenile justice reflected in the High Court's opinion:

> Juveniles, unlike adults, are always in some form of custody. Children, by definition, are not assumed to have the capacity to take care of themselves. They are assumed to be subject to the control of their parents, and if parental control falters, the State must play its part as *parens patriae*. In this respect, the juvenile's liberty interest may, in appropriate circumstances, be subordinated to the State's *parens patriae* interest in preserving and promoting the welfare of the child.[49]

In addition to its contention that preventive detention acts in behalf of the welfare of a child, the Court also noted that such detention is for a limited period of time, as most youths are released after only a few days. And therein lies the dilemma for both youths "in trouble" and the juvenile justice system as a whole. Jails and detention centers, particularly those that mix juveniles with adults, can be depressing and exceedingly dangerous places. For example:

- In August 1984, a 15-year-old California girl arrested for assaulting a police officer hanged herself after four days of isolation in a local jail.
- In 1982, a 17-year-old boy was taken into custody and detained for owing $73 in unpaid traffic tickets, only to be tortured and beaten to death by his cellmates.
- In a West Virginia jail a truant was murdered by an adult inmate; in an Ohio jail a teenage girl was raped by a guard.
- In December 1982, 15-year-old Robbie Horn hanged himself in a Kentucky jail where he had been held for only 30 minutes. His offense: arguing with his mother.[50]

Although one might argue that these are just isolated cases, in fact no one really knows the full extent of the problem. As is the case with crime victims in the general population, victimizations within jails are reported only infrequently. What *is* known, however, is the relative extent to which youths find themselves in contact with jail populations—both juvenile and adult. During 1982, for example, the most recent year for which such data are available, there were 536,122 youths placed in juvenile detention and correctional facilities, with an average commitment period of 106 days.[51] The average *daily* census of youths in juvenile institutions was 48,701, and almost all of these were adjudicated delinquents committed for long periods (see Exhibit 18.11). However, when considering that some 27 percent of the daily population were detainees and more than 500,000 youths were admitted to juvenile institutions during the course of the year, simple extrapolation suggests that almost 150,000 nonadjudicated youths were detained in 1982. By the same reasoning, almost 38,000 status offenders and dependent, neglected, and abused children were detained in jails at some point during 1982.

These data refer only to juvenile institutions. Youths are also detained in local jails for *adults*. The National Jail Census conducted on June 30, 1983, found that during the 12-month period prior to that date, 105,366 juveniles had been admitted to adult jail facilities. The vast majority of these were detained while awaiting intake and adjudication hearings.[52] Moreover, this figure did not include juveniles in the states of Connecticut, Delaware, Hawaii, Rhode Island, and Vermont—jurisdictions that, having no local jails, maintain integrated jail-prison systems.

Juvenile Corrections

Although data periodically emerge as to the number of juveniles held in jails and correctional institutions, relatively little is known about the extent of juvenile delinquency and youth crime, the number of status offenders and the nature of their "misbehavior," the size and character of the juvenile justice population as a whole, the dispositions that result from both informal and formal juvenile hearings, and the recidivism rates of adjudicated youths. The reason is that in many jurisdictions juvenile laws require that records of youthful offenders be sealed or destroyed to protect minors from being labeled as criminals. In fact, findings from a U.S. Bureau of Justice Statistics survey conducted in 1984 indicated that 26 states do not retain police and court

EXHIBIT 18.11

Selected Characteristics of Youths in Juvenile Institutions, 1982

Characteristic	Number of Juveniles	Percent
	48,701	100
Sex		
Male	42,182	87
Female	6,519	13
Average age	15.4 years	
Custodial status		
Detained	13,156	27
Committed	35,178	72
Voluntary	367	1
Reason held		
Delinquency	45,351	93
Status Offense	2,390	5
Other*	960	2
Length of stay		
Detained	15 days	
Committed	163 days	

* This category includes youths held for dependency, neglect, abuse, emotional disturbances, mental retardation, and admissions by self or parent without adjudication.

SOURCE: Adapted from U.S. Department of Justice, Office of Juvenile Justice and Delinquency Prevention, *Children in Custody: Advance Report on the Census of Public Juvenile Facilities,* December 1983.

records pertaining to juveniles.[53] As a result, any conclusions as to the nature and effectiveness of juvenile corrections are at best tentative.

Diversion

The juvenile due-process requirements derived from *Kent, Gault,* and *Winship,* combined with rising costs of operating correctional institutions, have resulted in the wider use of community-based treatment for adjudicated juveniles. A recent trend has been the greater use of diversion programs, with many young offenders being placed in remedial education and drug abuse treatment programs, foster homes, and counseling facilities. The effectiveness of these programs has not been demonstrated. However, a recent examination of studies of juvenile diversion initiatives concluded:

> One common component to all rationales for diversion seem to be that *less* intervention is better than *more* intervention. Thus, whatever else

it involves, diversion necessarily implies an attempt to make the form of social control more limited in scope. Studies of diversion programs indicate that instead of limiting the scope of the system, diversion programs often broaden it. They do this by either intensifying services or by taking in more cases. The latter is referred to as a "widening of the net" effect.[54]

Probation

Probation is by far the primary form of community treatment in the juvenile justice system, and the probation process for youths is essentially the same as that for adults. At any given time as many as 500,000 youths are on probation in the United States. The tendency toward such widespread use of juvenile probation evolved from the same rationales as diversion, combined with the findings of studies conducted decades ago that found that most juvenile probationers had been discharged from supervision under favorable circumstances.[55] In other words, most had finished their probation time with no new arrests or technical violations, or at least none severe enough to warrant revocation of probation. However, "discharge under favorable circumstances" is hardly what one could call a forceful measure of probation effectiveness. As noted in the examination of self-reported criminal behavior in Chapter 4, relatively few criminal and delinquent acts ultimately result in arrest. Moreover, for most juveniles on probation, supervision is generally minimal. Therefore, violations of the conditions of probation rarely come to the attention of court officials.

Correctional Institutions

Finally, there are the juvenile correctional institutions, which are generally of two types. There are the *cottage systems* similar to many of the nation's facilities for women offenders. They are typically structured as campuslike environments with dormitory rooms rather than cells. For serious juvenile offenders there are secure *training* and *industrial schools,* which generally resemble medium-security penitentiaries for adults.

Nearly all juvenile correctional facilities have a variety of treatment programs — counseling on an individual or group basis, vocational and educational training, recreational and religious programs, and medical and dental facilities. A number of these institutions also provide legal services for juveniles, and a few have substance abuse treatment programs.

Regardless of the settings and available services, juvenile facilities are still places of confinement that militate against rehabilitation in the same ways as adult penitentiaries do. They have been described as "crime schools" offering only an "illusion of treatment" under conditions that represent "legalized child abuse."[56]

As to the effectiveness of juvenile corrections, and the juvenile justice process as a whole, the lack of comprehensive evaluative data leads only to speculation. However, data from the largest follow-up study of juveniles ever conducted provide at least a few insights. In 1985, researchers at the University of Pennsylvania's Center for Studies of Criminology and Criminal Law released a preliminary report on a study of 13,160 Philadelphia male youths born in 1958.[57] Data were gathered from schools, the police, and the juvenile court on each youth, and the findings, however tentative, were nevertheless significant because they were based on a generalizable urban population.

Of the 13,160 juveniles in the 1958 birth cohort, 4,315 — or some 33 percent — had at least one police contact prior to reaching age 18. Of these, 42 percent were one-time offenders, 35 percent were nonchronic recidivists, and the remaining 23 percent were chronic recidivists. The 4,315 offenders had committed a total of 15,248 delinquent acts and, significantly, the chronic recidivists were responsible for almost two-thirds of all the delinquencies. In other words, most of the offenses had been committed by the 992 chronic delinquents. An analysis of the juvenile court dispositions of all of the delinquent youths and their subsequent recidivism suggested that lenient treatment for serious crimes early on in delinquent careers tended only to exacerbate subsequent lawbreaking behavior. Based on these and other data, the researchers concluded:

> Juvenile courts should consider close probation supervision for perhaps first- and certainly second-time violent Index offenders [those committing FBI Index crimes]. When these offenses occur early in the life of delinquents (as they do for chronic offenders) there is a temptation to be lenient and give the delinquent the opportunity for self-induced change. Yet we know that the chronic offender is detached from the schools and other community-based socialization and control agents. Failure to impose sanctions, failure to impose necessary controls early can encourage further delinquency.

The study suggested that the majority of delinquents were one- or two-time offenders, that most of the serious delinquencies were perpetrated by a small group of hard-core offenders, and that the juvenile justice system in the United States might have had a greater effect on reducing subsequent delinquent behavior if it took somewhat stronger measures with young offenders when they *first* came to its attention.

Summary

The juvenile justice system in the United States was designed with the philosophy that, as minors, young offenders have a "special status" which requires that they be protected and corrected, and not necessarily punished. Given this special status, juveniles can come to the attention of the courts as delinquents, for having violated the criminal law; as status offenders, for having departed from the behavior expected of youths; and as dependent or neglected children, for having been the victims of abuse, neglect, or abandonment.

Juvenile justice processing is grounded in the notion of *parens patriae*, a position which holds that a child's natural protectors have been either unwilling or unable to provide the appropriate care. Thus, the state must take over the role of parent. As an outgrowth of *parens patriae*, juvenile offenders were rarely treated with the "due process of law" accorded to adults by the Bill of Rights.

Much of juvenile justice processing is informal, with a wide degree of discretion permitted at every stage. Police who take juveniles into custody have the options of releasing youths with a reprimand, referring them to police-based diversion programs, or detaining them for court processing. Similar discretionary alternatives are apparent in the juvenile courts. The actual court process is considered a civil matter. Moreover, it is not a trial, there is no jury, and the judge presides *in behalf of* the child.

It was not until 1966 that the United States Supreme Court first evaluated juvenile court proceedings and the constitutional rights of children. During that year, *Kent* v. *United States* brought the juvenile justice system within the framework of the Constitution and the Bill of Rights. Subsequently, *In re Gault* in 1967, *In re Winship* in 1970, and *Breed* v. *Jones* in 1975 extended basic due-process rights to juvenile court proceedings.

Although juvenile justice philosophy and procedure have attempted to provide fair and beneficial treatment for children, the system as a whole suffers from a number of serious difficulties. First, the persistence of status offender laws in many jurisdictions places nondelinquent youths in contact with criminals and reduces the ability of the juvenile courts to more effectively deal with youths involved in serious criminal conduct. Second, there are many questions as to the wisdom of transferring delinquents to the adult courts for formal criminal processing. Third, the widespread practice of confining juveniles in detention facilities has placed the health and welfare of many youths at high risk. Fourth, regardless of the disposition of juvenile delinquents and status offenders, little is known as to the effectiveness of juvenile correctional approaches.

Key Terms

adjudication (677)

adjudication hearing (692)

adjudication inquiry (692)

autonomous juvenile courts (683)

Breed v. *Jones* (693)

"child savers" (683)

Questions for Discussion

1. Given the *parens patriae* philosophy of the juvenile justice system in the United States, would delinquent youths be better off in the adult criminal courts with its strict guarantees of due process of law?
2. Do status offender laws serve any real purpose for today's youth? Should such laws be fully abolished? Why?
3. Should youthful murderers be given capital sentences, placed on death row, and executed?
4. How might contemporary juvenile correctional programs and procedures be best upgraded or reformed? What ought to be done with juvenile offenders?

For Further Reading

Finckenauer, James O. *Scared Straight! and the Panacea Phenomenon.* Englewood Cliffs, N.J.: Prentice-Hall, 1982.

Rubin, H. Ted. *Juvenile Justice: Policy, Practice, and Law.* Santa Monica: Goodyear, 1979.

Wooden, Kenneth. *Weeping in the Playtime of Others: America's Incarcerated Children.* New York: McGraw-Hill, 1976.

Notes

1. Wilmington (Delaware) *News-Journal,* August 7, 1985, p. A3.
2. *Philadelphia Inquirer,* December 11, 1983, p. 19-A.
3. *New York Times,* February 14, 1982, p. 39; *New York Times,* October 10, 1982, p. 24.
4. *USA Today,* October 11, 1985, p. 3A.
5. *Miami Herald,* March 27, 1982, p. 2.
6. *New York Times,* February 26, 1984, p. 24.
7. *New York Times,* January 8, 1984, p. 19.
8. Schall v. Martin, 35 CrL 3103 (1984).
9. President's Commission on Law Enforcement and Administration of Justice, *Task Force Report: Juvenile Delinquency and Youth Crime* (Washington, D.C.: U.S. Government Printing Office, 1967), pp. 2–3.
10. Evelina Beldon, "Courts in the United States Hearing Children's Cases," *Children's Bureau Publication* 65 (Washington, D.C.: U.S. Department of Labor, 1918), p. 8.
11. Illinois Juvenile Court Act, *Illinois Statutes,* 1899, Section 131.
12. President's Commission, p. 3.
13. U.S. Department of Justice, *A Comparative Analysis of Juvenile Codes* (Washington, D.C.: U.S. Government Printing Office, 1980), p. 7.
14. Norval Morris and Gordon Hawkins, *The Honest Politician's Guide to Crime Control* (Chicago: University of Chicago Press, 1969), p. 91.
15. Personal communication, October 15, 1982.
16. Irving Piliavin and Scott Briar, "Police Encounters with Juveniles," *American Journal of Sociology* 70 (September 1964), pp. 206–214.
17. H. Ted Rubin, "The Emerging Prosecutor Dominance of the Juvenile Court Intake Process," *Crime and Delinquency* 26 (July 1980), pp. 299–318.
18. See Charles E. Silberman, *Criminal Violence, Criminal Justice* (New York: Random House, 1978), pp. 309–370.
19. H. Ted Rubin, *Juvenile Justice: Policy, Practice, and Law* (Santa Monica, Ca.: Goodyear, 1979), pp. 86–108
20. U.S. Department of Justice, Office of Juvenile Justice and Delinquency Prevention, *Children in Custody: Advance Report on the Census of Public Juvenile Facilities,* December 1983; *The 1983 Jail Census,* Bureau of Justice Statistics Bulletin, November 1984.
21. H. Ted Rubin, *Juvenile Justice,* 86–108.
22. Kent v. United States, 383 U.S. 541 (1966).
23. In re Gault, 38 U.S. 1 (1967).
24. In re Winship, 397 U.S. 358 (1970).
25. Breed v. Jones, 421 U.S. 519 (1975).
26. McKeiver v. Pennsylvania, 403 U.S. 548 (1971).
27. Personal communication, December 2, 1985.
28. Miranda v. Arizona, 384 U.S. 436 (1966).

29. The Uniform Juvenile Court Act has been reprinted in its entirety in Samuel M. Davis, *Rights of Juveniles: The Juvenile Justice System* (New York: Clark Boardman, 1983), pp. A1–A53.

30. For example, see *Colorado Revised Statutes Annotated,* Section 19–2–102(3)(c)(i), 1978.

31. Fare v. Michael C., 442 U.S. 707 (1979).

32. West v. U.S., 399 F.2d 467 (5th Cir. 1968).

33. New Jersey v. T.L.O., 105 S.Ct. 733 (1985).

34. H. Ted Rubin, *Juvenile Justice,* p. 269.

35. H. Ted Rubin, *Juvenile Justice,* p. 270.

36. Herbert A. Bloch and Frank T. Flynn, *Delinquency: The Juvenile Offender in America Today* (New York: Random House, 1956) p. 471.

37. Bloch and Flynn, *Delinquency,* p. 471.

38. Personal communication, September 17, 1985.

39. Charles E. Silberman, *Criminal Violence, Criminal Justice,* pp. 309–370.

40. *Juvenile Justice and Delinquency Prevention Act of 1974* (P. L. 93–415).

41. Sophonisba P. Breckinridge and Helen R. Jeter, "Juvenile Court Legislation in the United States," *Children's Bureau Publication* 70 (Washington, D.C.: U.S. Department of Labor, 1919), p. 19.

42. Negley K. Teeters and John Otto Reinemann, *The Challenge of Delinquency* (Englewood Cliffs, N.J.: Prentice-Hall, 1950), pp. 290–313.

43. *National Law Journal,* August 8, 1983, p. 4.

44. Coker v. Georgia, 433 U.S. 583 (1977); Echols v. State, 370 S.W. 2d 892 (1963).

45. *National Law Journal,* August 8, 1983, p. 4.

46. *USA Today,* October 11, 1985, p. 3A.

47. Eddings v. Oklahoma, 455 U.S. 104 (1982).

48. Oklahoma v. Eddings, 36 CrL 4184 (1985).

49. Schall v. Martin, 35 CrL 3103 (1984).

50. *Newsweek,* May 27, 1985, pp. 87–89.

51. U.S. Department of Justice, *Children in Custody.*

52. *The 1983 Jail Census,* Bureau of Justice Statistics Bulletin, November 1984.

53. *New York Times,* October 21, 1985, p. A17.

54. Sharla Rausch and Charles Logan, "Diversion from Juvenile Court: Panacea or Pandora's Box?" Paper presented at the 33rd Annual Meeting of the American Society of Criminology, Toronto, November 6, 1982.

55. For example, see Frank Scarpitti and Richard Stephenson, "A Study of Probation Effectiveness," *Journal of Criminal Law, Criminology, and Police Science* 59 (1968), p. 361.

56. Kenneth Wooden, *Weeping in the Playtime of Others: America's Incarcerated Children* (New York: McGraw-Hill, 1976).

57. Paul E. Tracy, Marvin E. Wolfgang, and Robert M. Figlio, *Delinquency in Two Birth Cohorts: Executive Summary* (Philadelphia, Pa.: Center for Studies in Criminology and Criminal Law, The Wharton School, University of Pennsylvania, 1985). This effort was a replication of the original *Delinquency in a Birth Cohort* study which followed up more than 10,000 Philadelphia youths born in 1945. See Marvin E. Wolfgang, Robert M. Figlio, and Thorsten Sellin, *Delinquency in a Birth Cohort* (Chicago: University of Chicago Press, 1972).

Epilogue

The Changing Face of Criminal Justice in America

Our legal system has failed in the protection of the innocent and the punishment of the guilty. The rights of victims must come before the rights of the accused.

— President Ronald Reagan, 1981

A far greater factor is the deterrent effect of swift and certain consequences: swift arrest, prompt trial, certain penalty and — at some point — finality of judgment.

— Chief Justice Warren Burger, 1982

Many decades ago, a prominent American statesman described the administration of criminal justice in the United States as "a disgrace to our civilization."[1] He had little use for the privilege against self-incrimination and he would give police a freer hand to interrogate suspects. He referred to the protection against unreasonable search and seizure as "another constitutional restriction which has been used to save men from conviction." The rule that a defendant must be confronted by the witnesses who testify against him he considered to be "undue tenderness toward the defendant." In addition, criminal procedure had become "a mere game in which the defendant's counsel play with loaded dice"; the jury had become a "box of nondescripts of no character"; and the trial by jury had come to be regarded as a fetish to such an extent that "the verdict becomes rather the vote of the town meeting than the sharp, clear decision of the tribunal of justice." And finally, he lamented, if the guilty ever did manage to get convicted, the punishment was likely to be far too mild.

These observations on the nature of American constitutional-criminal procedure were not offhandedly disregarded as the impromptu remarks of a frustrated political conservative. Many found them to be both challenging and foreboding, for they had come from the only person in American history to occupy the two most exalted offices the nation had to offer. The remarks had been made by William Howard Taft, president of the United States from 1909 to 1913, and chief justice of the United States Supreme Court from 1921 to 1930.

Taft's harsh words had not been made without basis. They came at a time when the nation seemed to be overrun by a growing legion of criminals against which the courts appeared to be powerless. "Mafia" and "Black Hand" extortion threats were stealing front-page headlines, as syndicated writers warned of Italian conspiracies to export secret criminal societies across the ocean to America. Muckraking journalists spoke of the many "crooks," "vile sluts," and "shameless politicians" who had become millionaires while honest citizens faced rising prices and scarce jobs. In the East and Midwest, organized crime syndicates were becoming visible, prostitution and police corruption were widespread and working hand in hand, racketeering had become a scare word attached to labor organizations, and such names as Johnny Torrio and Al Capone were beginning to receive national recognition. And too, there was the Black Sox scandal of 1919, when gambler Arnold Rothstein fixed the World Series by bribing eight star players of the Chicago White Sox to suddenly "lose their talent." The police and courts were accomplishing so little against the march of crime that one *Washington Post* writer commented: "There is no time to waste on hairsplitting over the infringement of liberty."[2]

Upon reflection of Taft's opinions, it is curious how history seems so often to repeat itself, and how approaches to the problem of crime in America have cyclical paths. The sentiments about crime and justice expressed during the early 1980s by President Ronald Reagan and Chief Justice Warren Burger were not too far removed from those of their predecessor of half a century earlier. Recent history suggests some shifting back to the Taft philosophy.

The United States versus Crime in the Streets: Two Models of Criminal Justice

The Due-process Model

In the 1960s, the **Warren Court** — the Supreme Court under the leadership of Chief Justice Earl Warren — announced a large number of decisions that were in accord with what the late Herbert Packer called the **due-process model** of the criminal justice system.[3] This model stresses the possibility of error in the stages leading to trial and thus emphasizes the need for protecting procedural rights even if the implementation of these rights prevents the legal system from operating with maximum efficiency. Although no model can possibly describe reality in a completely satisfactory manner, the Warren Court's decisions in the area of criminal law extended a relatively strict version of the due-process model to cover the arrest-through-trial stages of the criminal process. This was accomplished as the Court incorporated one provision after another of the Bill of Rights into the due-process clause of the Fourteenth Amendment, thereby obligating the states to guarantee criminal defendants many of the constitutional safeguards that were already routinely accorded those accused of federal crimes. By 1969, nearly all of the Bill of Rights's provisions relating to criminal violations were binding upon the states as elements of Fourteenth Amendment due process. Among these were the Fifth Amendment right to be free from compulsory self-incrimination;[4] the Sixth Amendment rights to counsel,[5] speedy trial,[6] confrontation of hostile witnesses,[7] and compulsory processes for obtaining witnesses;[8] and the Eighth Amendment prohibition of cruel and unusual punishments.[9] The process of **nationalizing the Bill of Rights** reached its climax in two decisions announced shortly before the end of the Warren Court era. In 1968, the Court held that the Sixth Amendment's guarantee of trial by jury applies to state criminal trials involving serious or nonpetty offenses.[10] One year later, the Court finally ruled that the Fourteenth Amendment makes the Fifth Amendment's proscription of double jeopardy binding upon the states,[11] thus overruling the famous 1937 *Palko* decision, which had upheld the validity of a Connecticut statute permitting the state to bring criminal defendants to trial twice for the same offense upon a showing of legal error prejudicial to the state's case in the original trial.[12]

Of all of the Warren Court decisions forcing the states to institute procedural changes in their criminal justice processes, none was more controversial than *Mapp* v. *Ohio*,[13] which established the basic parameters of illegal search and seizure in state cases. Decided in 1961, *Mapp* is generally credited with being the "opening gun" of the constitutional criminal law revolution.

If *Mapp* can be termed the opening gun, then *Miranda* v. *Arizona* can be said to have constituted the most damaging direct hit — at least as far as law enforcement authorities and states' rights theorists of interposition were

Chief Justice Earl Warren

The nationalization of the Bill of Rights

The constitutional law revolution of the 1960s

Drawing by Lorenz. © 1964 The New Yorker Magazine, Inc. Used by permission.

concerned.[14] *Miranda* was actually the Warren Court's attempt to clarify its earlier holding in *Escobedo* v. *Illinois,*[15] that when a police inquiry into an unsolved crime shifts from the investigative to the accusatory stage, the police must warn the suspect of his right to remain silent and honor his request to consult with his attorney. Many state and lower federal court judges who disapproved of the thrust and spirit of *Escobedo* had interpreted the majority opinion as applying only in cases where the accused had requested counsel, thus rendering the decision inapplicable to the vast majority of confession cases. Consequently, the High Court expanded the doctrine further in the 1966 *Miranda* case. By a 5-to-4 majority, the Court established a series of procedural prerequisites that had to be met before a suspect could be subjected to a process of custodial interrogation.

Despite the claims of dismayed and disappointed law enforcement officials that *Miranda* was unwise and would unduly hamper legitimate police and prosecutorial practices, the Court displayed little hesitancy in applying the *Miranda* guidelines to the line-up stage of the criminal justice process. In 1967, another five-man majority, in *United States* v. *Wade,*[16] concluded that the Sixth and Fourteenth Amendments entitle suspects required to appear in a police line-up to have an attorney present to observe the fairness of the proceedings. Accordingly, Justice Brennan's majority opinion held that any in-court identification of a defendant by a prosecution witness would be inadmissible if it had been "tainted" by either a line-up conducted in the absence of counsel or by a line-up that the defendant's attorney had shown to be unfair. Once again, the Court provoked the anger of police officials and prosecutors, who complained that they were being forced to fight criminals while "handcuffed" and "with three strikes against them."[17]

The Crime Control Model

What has occurred in the past several years undoubtedly has brought great pleasure to those who were critical of the Court's prior judicial activism on behalf of defendants' rights. Whereas the Warren Court clearly was attuned to Herbert Packer's due-process model of criminal justice, the contemporary Court, until recently under the tutelage of Chief Justice Burger, can best be described as predisposed to support Packer's alternative model of the legal process — the **crime control model,** which emphasizes the virtues of managerial efficiency and is based upon the proposition that the repression of criminal conduct is the most important function of the criminal process, not the promulgation of procedural rules that may occasionally prevent the prosecution of an innocent man, but more frequently result in the release of the factually guilty. Proponents of this model, according to Professor Packer, put a premium on the values of speed and finality, prefer that truly guilty suspects be convinced of the rationality of entering a guilty plea, and cannot understand why obviously guilty defendants should go free simply because of errors on the part of police or court personnel.

The **Burger Court**'s greater sensitivity to the crime control model and the new majority's inclination to seriously limit the Warren Court's criminal procedure work first became clearly evident in the 1971 case of *Harris* v. *New York.*[18] At his trial for two counts of selling heroin, Harris, the petitioner, had taken the witness stand in his own defense to categorically deny the first alleged sale and to claim that the second sale actually involved only a small quantity of baking soda. In an effort to impeach the credibility of Harris's testimony, the prosecutor read a statement in which Harris had admitted both sales in response to police interrogation immediately after his arrest. How-

The crime control model of the legal process

The Burger Court

ever, no *Miranda* warnings had been given to Harris prior to his questioning by police. Thus, the question for the High Court to resolve was whether a statement obtained in violation of *Miranda* standards could be introduced into evidence for the limited purpose of cross-examining the defendant and discrediting his testimony. In a strongly worded opinion, Chief Justice Burger, speaking for the majority, argued that *Miranda* applies only to the prosecutor's presentation of the state's case; if the defendant voluntarily takes the witness stand, the prosecutor must be permitted to introduce statements ordinarily barred by *Miranda* because of the necessity of preventing perjury. Accordingly, Harris's conviction was affirmed, and the process of weakening or qualifying *Miranda* had begun.

Three years later, in *Michigan* v. *Tucker,*[19] the High Court further blunted *Miranda*'s applicability in cases involving evidence obtained as the result of an improper interrogation. While undergoing interrogation concerning a rape case, Tucker was advised of all of his rights except the right to have a court-appointed attorney if he were unable to afford counsel. In response to questions about his activities on the night of the crime, Tucker told the police of a friend who could corroborate his alibi. Unfortunately for Tucker, his "friend" offered testimony that was highly damaging to the defense's case and that was a major factor in Tucker's subsequent conviction. Thus the Court had to decide whether evidence that had been obtained as a result of an interrogation in which the defendant had not received the full *Miranda* warning nevertheless should be admissible in the courtroom. Speaking for the majority in a somewhat ambiguous opinion, Justice Rehnquist answered this question in a positive manner, a result that continued the trend toward the erosion of *Miranda*.

Paralleling the Burger Court's movement away from *Miranda* has been its undercutting of the *Wade* guarantee of an attorney's presence whenever a suspect is asked to participate in a police line-up. In *Kirby* v. *Illinois,*[20] a five-man majority held that the *Wade* ruling entitles only defendants who have been indicted or otherwise formally charged with a serious crime to have an attorney present to observe the line-up procedure. The majority relied upon the argument that the Sixth Amendment right to counsel does not become a constitutional necessity until the "critical stage" of the criminal justice process, which is marked by the onset of formal prosecutorial proceedings. Since the large majority of line-ups take place well before the accused is indicted, *Kirby* clearly constitutes an evisceration of the principles underlying the *Wade* decision. Indeed, one wonders why the majority did not simply overrule *Wade* rather than attempt to justify the highly debatable proposition that the dangers of unfairness and mistaken identity against which *Wade* had been directed were somehow more likely to be present after the indictment than in the time period immediately after arrest.

Due Process versus Crime Control

In retrospect, the 1960s and 1970s reflect a scenario of contradiction for criminal justice in America. With the advantage of hindsight, it is highly ironic that while the tumultuous and crime-ridden sixties provoked a call for "law and order" resulting in a "war on crime," the United States Supreme Court, much to the dismay of numerous observers, particularly law enforcement officials, announced a series of decisions that were regarded as anything but sympathetic to the mounting war on crime. Through *Mapp, Miranda, Wade,* and other opinions, the Warren Court affirmed and gave tangible substance to the due-process model of criminal justice. The legal rights of the accused were

Chief Justice Warren Burger

strengthened and constitutional guarantees were more fully solidified. Furthermore, the number of executions in America dramatically declined during the 1960s, in part because of widespread anticipation that, if given the opportunity, the Supreme Court would be inclined to declare the death penalty to be violative of the cruel and unusual punishment clause of the Eighth Amendment. The activities of the High Court had offered credibility to a concept of "justice" in America; but in so doing, the Court drew considerable criticism for "handcuffing" the police and prosecutors at a time when "crime in the streets" was perceived to be at epidemic levels.

Conversely, while crime and violence were less visible during the 1970s, Supreme Court decision making began to erode the foundation of criminal due process. Although the impact of the war on crime was seemingly apparent in the decreased visibility of street violence and a deceleration in the rates of many serious crimes, many of the High Court's key decisions diverted from a due-process model to a crime control model. In the *Harris, Tucker,* and *Kirby* decisions, for example, defendants' rights were narrowed considerably.

The Supreme Court and the 1980s War on Crime

As the United States moved into the 1980s, the rights of the accused achieved few gains. Moreover, limitations were placed on the police use of deadly force. More noticeable, however, was the fact that the crime control model of criminal justice was further strengthened by a broad-based assault on the exclusionary rule. Perhaps the most significant issue to face the Court in this behalf was the "good faith" exception. At its center was the argument that evidence obtained illegally by the police should be admissible in court if it had been gathered in a "good faith" effort to respect civil liberties. The Supreme Court's long-standing exclusionary rule barring tainted evidence was assailed on the ground that it helped criminals escape prosecution while failing to deter police misconduct. Civil libertarians maintained that the rule placed important limits on searches, thereby preserving the full integrity of the Fourth Amendment.

In 1981, a bill was sponsored by South Carolina Senator Strom Thurmond to eliminate the exclusionary rule entirely, replacing it with a civil remedy for defendants whose rights were violated. A second bill, introduced by Arizona Senator Dennis DeConcini, was designed to modify the rule, permitting judges wide discretion in deciding when to admit illegally seized evidence. Moreover, bills were introduced in several states to create the "good faith" exception.[21] But debate on these bills was postponed in anticipation of the High Court's ruling in several cases that were working their way up the judicial ladder.

The 1982–1983 Supreme Court term began with the expectation that the justices would resolve the controversy over the "good faith" exception. Pending in this behalf was *Illinois* v. *Gates,*[22] a case in which the "probable cause" for the issuance of a search warrant was called into question. There was the feeling, too, that the long-awaited exception would be established with *Gates,* for it appeared that even the High Court looked upon the exclusionary rule with some disfavor. As Chief Justice Burger had commented in an earlier case:

> I see no insurmountable obstacle to the elimination of the Suppression Doctrine if Congress would provide some meaningful and effective remedy against unlawful conduct by government officials.[23]

In *Gates,* however, the Court avoided the "good faith" issue, as a majority of the justices determined that it would be inappropriate to consider a matter which had not been addressed as the case had been moving through the state courts. The *Gates* decision was significant nevertheless, for it removed one of the cornerstones of the Fourth Amendment's suppression doctrine by overruling the *Aquilar – Spinelli* standards for testing the reliability and credibility of informants' information about suspects' criminal activities.[24] During the following term, however, in the companion cases of *U.S.* v. *Leon* and *Massachusetts* v. *Sheppard,*[25] a limited "good faith" exception was adopted. The High Court ruled that the Fourth Amendment rule should *not* be applied so as to bar the use of evidence obtained by officers acting in reasonable reliance on a search warrant issued by a detached and neutral magistrate but ultimately found to be invalid.

Beyond *Gates, Leon,* and *Sheppard,* the Supreme Court established further modifications of the exclusionary rule, particularly during its 1983 – 1984 term. In *Oliver* v. *U.S.* and *Maine* v. *Thornton,*[26] the Court reaffirmed the "open fields" exception to the Fourth Amendment's warrant requirement that it had recognized 60 years earlier.[27] The Court's explanation in these cases was that landowners had "no reasonable expectation of privacy" because "open fields do not provide the setting for those intimate activities that the amendment is intended to shelter from Government interference or surveillance."

Nix v. *Williams, New York* v. *Quarles,* and *Berkemer* v. *McCarty,*[28] all decided in 1984, represented further erosions of the holding set forth almost two decades earlier in *Miranda* v. *Arizona.*[29] *Nix* v. *Williams* established the "inevitable discovery" exception to the exclusionary rule. It was a follow-up to the case in which the "Christian burial speech" of an Iowa law enforcement agent had led to Robert Williams's confession of where he had hidden the body of 10-year-old Pamela Powers, whom he had raped and murdered on Christmas Eve in 1968. The finding of the body had led to Williams's conviction, but this was overturned by the High Court in *Brewer* v. *Williams*[30] in 1977. The reason the Court indicated was that the accused's attorney had not been present when the location of the body was pointed out. At Williams's second trial, evidence about the body was admitted, but not the accused's involvement in its discovery. The High Court held in its 1984 ruling that Pamela's body was admissible since under the circumstances of the search, it would have been "inevitably discovered" by lawful means.

In *Quarles,* the Court put forth a narrow "public safety" exception to *Miranda,* holding that police officers may "ask questions reasonably prompted by concern for the public safety." And finally, it was declared in *Berkemer* v. *McCarty* that although anyone in police custody and accused of a crime — no matter how minor the offense — must be formally advised of the right against self-incrimination prior to questioning, an ordinary traffic stop does not constitute custody. The police may question motorists without first warning them against self-incrimination.

The fact that a number of the High Court's recent decisions have served to modify both *Miranda* and the exclusionary rule has led some observers to label the Burger Court as conservative. Moreover, they predicted a trend aimed at unraveling the rights accorded to suspects during the era of the Warren Court. Without question, the Court under Chief Justice Burger has broken less ground in the area of civil liberties than it did under the 15-year tutelege of Chief Justice Earl Warren. At the same time, the Burger Court restricted some Warren Court decisions that afforded broad protections to the

The Burger Court is not as conservative as some liberals feared, and not as conservative as some conservatives hoped.
—Arthur J. Goldberg, former Supreme Court justice, 1985

accused in criminal proceedings. But to label the Burger Court as conservative would be an overstatement. On more than one occasion, "conservative" justices Rehnquist, Powell, and O'Connor came down hard in favor of civil liberties claims. Moreover, "liberal" justices Marshall and Brennan occasionally supported tighter constraints on the rights of the accused. If anything, the U.S. Supreme Court during the first half of the 1980s was a divided court, composed primarily of strong individualists who did not necessarily follow the lead of Chief Justice Burger.

Justice under Reagan

The first half of the 1980s have witnessed a significant political shift to the conservative right. This was certainly clear in the election of Ronald Reagan to his first term as president of the United States. Voters left no doubt as to what they wanted. The 1980 election represented the strongest shift in three decades, hinting at a conservative domination that might conceivably last for the balance of the twentieth century. Reagan carried the presidency with 43.3 million votes, and 489 of 538 electoral votes. Jimmy Carter, by contrast, drew only 42 percent of the popular vote and won only six states and the District of Columbia.[31] When Reagan was reelected in 1984, the outcome was even more dramatic. He carried 49 states and won 59 percent of the popular vote and 525 electoral votes. Walter Mondale, on the other hand, won only 41 percent of the popular vote and 13 electoral votes.[32]

A "conservative" is a liberal who was mugged last night.
—Frank Rizzo, 1978

EXHIBIT E.1

Selected Attitudes of the Classes of 1977, 1984, and 1987

	Percent		
Attitude	Class of 1977	Class of 1984	Class of 1987
Political Views:			
Far left	2.2	2.1	1.9
Liberal	32.6	19.6	19.2
Middle-of-the-road	50.7	60.0	60.3
Conservative	13.9	17.1	17.5
Far right	0.6	1.2	1.2
Proportions Who Agree That:			
Courts are too concerned with the rights of criminals	50.1	65.9	68.8
The death penalty should be abolished	43.3	34.5	28.9
Marijuana should be legalized	48.2	39.3	25.7

SOURCE: *The Chronicle of Higher Education*, February 11, 1974, p. 8; February 9, 1981, p. 8; February 1, 1984, p. 14.

Numerous indicators suggest that the conservative trend might endure. Seats in the House of Representatives, first of all, are controlled by population, and there has been a major shift in the population to the sunbelt region of the South and West. The new settlers in these areas include many older Americans whose values generally lean to the conservative side. Thus, the southern and western conservative states have gained more political power. Both House seats and electoral votes shifted to these geographical areas at the expense of the more liberal states in the East and Midwest. The 1980 census data indicated, for example, that the conservative block gained 17 seats and electoral votes, with an equal number lost in more liberal areas.[33]

Perhaps the most telling factor for both present and future, however, has been the shift back to "traditional" values by American youth, especially on college campuses. Each year, the University of California and the American Council on Education develop a national profile of college freshman characteristics and attitudes. Exhibit E.1, which highlights selected areas of student response from this profile, clearly suggests that liberalism may indeed be a thing of the past. Comparing the graduating classes of 1977, 1984, and 1987, the number of liberals declined while conservatives and middle-of-the-roaders increased. Perhaps most significant was the trend toward more conservative views with respect to the rights of the accused, the death penalty, and the legalization of marijuana.

These data, combined with the growing conservatism among older Americans, suggest that the trend toward strict and rigid punishments for criminal offenders and the erosion of defendants' rights are the result of political views that stress societal protection over due process. And this, furthermore, is clearly the position of the Reagan administration.

The vehicle for President Reagan's criminal justice agenda has been the federal courts. He is opposed to those judges who view courts as mechanisms for political action and social experimentation, while preferring those who exercise "judicial restraint." Perhaps the most potent weapon in Reagan's criminal justice reform campaign will be the crop of new judges he has named. Coinciding with his two terms as president, there has been a rapid expansion within the federal judiciary, which permitted Reagan, through the end of 1985, to nominate more than 200 to the bench — mostly conservative white

The Reagan administration is the strongest and most supportive we have seen in as long as I can remember.
— **Jerald Vaughn, International Association of Chiefs of Police, 1985**

This is the first administration in years that has come into office with an agenda to set back civil liberties. — **Alan Dershowitz, 1985**

Reagan's justices are more conservative and tough-minded, something that will influence the collective body of thought in the judiciary over time. — **William Webster, FBI Director, 1985**

"This here court finds you guilty as charged, which you no doubt, indeed, probably are, or you wouldn't be hanging around like that."

AFTER YOU... RETIREMENT BURGER

MARSHALL BRENNAN

males.[34] By the time he leaves office in 1988, it is likely that he will have named more than half of the 761-member federal judiciary.

At the helm of Reagan's reform movement has been U.S. Attorney General Edwin Meese, an arch-conservative who has many liberal and moderate court observers worried. Meese's plan has been to do more than just convict and incarcerate a greater number of serious criminal offenders. His aim has been to fashion basic changes in the justice system that would tip the balance away from suspects toward victims and the state. It has been the position of both Meese and Reagan that during the 1960s and 1970s the judiciary became too lenient toward the accused and helped to accelerate a surge in crime.

The Reagan justice agenda, and particularly the role of Attorney General Meese, brought on controversy. In an interview published in *U.S. News & World Report* during the latter part of 1985, when asked if suspects should have the rights accorded by the *Miranda* decision, Meese responded:

> Suspects who are innocent of a crime should. But thing is, you don't have many suspects who are innocent of a crime. That's contradictory. If a person is innocent of a crime, then he is not a suspect.
>
> The Miranda decision was wrong. We managed very well in this country for 175 years without it. Its practical effect is to prevent the police from talking to the person who knows the most about the crime—namely, the perpetrator. As it stands now under *Miranda*, if the police obtain a statement from that person in the course of the initial interrogation, the statement may be thrown out at the trial. Therefore, *Miranda* only helps guilty defendants. Most innocent people are glad to talk to the police. They want to establish their innocence so that they're no longer a suspect.[35]

This comment, particularly the statement that "if a person is innocent of a crime, then he is not a suspect," was especially worrisome to both liberals and conservatives. By linking suspicion with guilt, Meese seemed to be undercutting the fundamental presumption of innocence. Senator Joseph Biden of Delaware hastened to point out that Meese himself had been the subject of an intensive criminal investigation. "The attorney general's statement," remarked Biden, "was overwhelming proof of why we need *Miranda*."[36]

Other comments by Meese evoked the ire of members of the Supreme Court. On another occasion, the attorney general stated that the "theory of incorporation," that is, the nationalization of the Bill of Rights, was on intellectually shaky ground and a questionable legal doctrine.[37] This drew rebuttal from Justices Brennan, Stevens, and Rehnquist, precipitating a debate that was unprecedented in recent history between the Supreme Court and the White House.[38]

In the final analysis, the changing character of American justice is not wholly the result of increasing rates in crime, nor is it exclusively a consequence of the influences of conservative political administrations. Marxist theorists would argue that criminal law and social policy are instruments of the state and the dominant ruling classes, structured only to serve their own interests and to perpetuate the existing social and economic order.[39] When considering how the federal judiciary is being restructured, one might find some support for the Marxist view. For after all, a great number of the new federal judges have been chosen in the Reagan-Meese mold. Furthermore, with the retirement of Warren Burger in 1986, and four of the remaining

If a person is innocent of a crime, then he is not a suspect.
—Edwin Meese, 1985

You don't have many suspects who are innocent of a crime.
—Edwin Meese, 1985

The Constitution not only is, but ought to be, what the judges say it is. — Charles Evans Hughes, 1937

The constitutional views endorsed [by Mr. Meese] are little more than arrogance cloaked as humility. —Justice William Brennan, 1985

justices well past retirement age, Reagan clearly has the potential for restruc-turing the Supreme Court prior to the end of his second term. Yet in counter-point to the Marxist position, it must be remembered that the "state" — the political guardians at both the national and local levels — obtain and maintain their positions at the pleasure of the electorate. It was the American voters who propelled Ronald Reagan into the presidency, and they did so overwhelmingly — *twice*. Moreover, while court observers and constitutional scholars debated the White House plans for restructuring justice in the United States in 1985, polls by the National Opinion Research Center found that nearly 80 percent of the American public favored the death penalty and 78 percent felt that the courts should deal more harshly with criminals.[40] It would appear that Ronald Reagan, Edwin Meese, and most federal justices are no more than reflections of the growing conservatism in the United States.

The mood is different now. The public wants criminals clobbered, and that is what we are doing. **—Stephen Trott, U.S. Department of Justice, 1985**

autrefois convict   A plea of "formerly convicted" in not guilty proceedings on double jeopardy grounds.

auxiliary police   Trained and uniformed (but unarmed) volunteer civilians who work with local police.

bail   1. To effect the release of an accused person from custody in return for a promise that he or she will appear at a place and time specified and submit to the jurisdiction and judgment of the court, guaranteed by a pledge to pay to the court a specified sum of money or property if the person does not appear. 2. The money or property pledged to the court or actually deposited with it to effect the release of a person from legal custody.

bailiff   A court officer whose duties are to announce the arrival and departure of the judge and to maintain order in the courtroom.

battery   The nonlethal culmination of an assault.

bench trial   A trial in which the judge, rather than a jury, determines innocence or guilt.

bench warrant   A document issued by a court directing that a law enforcement officer arrest and bring the person named therein before the court (usually) one who has failed to obey a court order or a notice to appear.

bifurcated trial   In criminal proceedings, a special two-part trial proceeding in which the issue of guilt is tried in the first step and, if a conviction results, the appropriate sentence or applicable sentencing statute is determined in the second step.

bigamy   The act of marrying while a former marriage is still legally in force.

bill of particulars   A written statement that specifies additional facts about a charge.

bind over   Based on the decision by a court of limited jurisdiction, to require that a person charged with a felony appear for trial on that charge in a court of general jurisdiction, as the result of a finding of probable cause at a preliminary hearing held in the limited jurisdiction court.

blackmail   The taking of money or property through threats of accusation or exposure.

booking   The administrative record of an arrest.

breach of the peace   The breaking of the public peace by any riotous, forcible, or unlawful proceeding.

breaking and entering   The unlawful entry into a building or structure with the intent to commit a crime therein.

brief   A document prepared by counsel to serve as the basis for an argument in court, setting out the facts of and the legal arguments in support of the case.

burglary   *See* breaking and entering.

capacity   In criminal usage, the legal ability of a person to commit a criminal act; the mental and physical ability to act with purpose and to be aware of the certain, probable results of one's conduct.

capias   A bench warrant.

capital offense   1. A criminal offense punishable by death. 2. In some penal codes, an offense that may be punishable by death or by imprisonment for life.

carnal knowledge   The act of having sexual bodily connection.

case law   Law that results from court interpretations of statutory law or from court decisions where rules have not been fully codified or have been found to be vague or in error.

case load   1. In corrections, the total number of clients registered with a correctional agency or agent on a given date or during a specified time period, often divided into active supervisory cases and inactive cases, thus distinguishing between clients with whom contact is regular, and those with whom it is not. 2. In the courts, the number of cases requiring judicial action at a certain time, or the number of cases acted upon in a given court during a given time period.

certiorari, writ of   A writ issued from the U.S. Supreme Court, at its discretion, to order a lower court to prepare the record of a case and send it to the Court for review.

challenge for cause   A challenge to remove a potential juror on the basis of a sound legal reason to do so.

change of venue   The movement of a case from the jurisdiction of one court to that of another which has the same subject matter jurisdictional authority but is in a different geographic location.

charging document   A formal written accusation submitted to a court, alleging that a specified person(s) has committed a specific offense(s).

charging the jury   The instructions to the jury by the presiding judge as to the rules of law in the case, the possible verdicts, and the ordering of jurors to retire to the jury room, consider the facts and testimony, and to return a just verdict.

child molesting   The handling, fondling, or other contacts of a sexual nature with a child.

civil commitment   A nonpenal commitment to a treatment facility resulting from findings made during criminal proceedings, either before or after a judgment.

civil law   The body of codes that regulate the rights between individuals or organizations.

classification   The process through which the educational, vocational, treatment, and custodial needs of an offender are determined.

clearance rate   The proportion of crimes that result in arrest or that the police claim to have solved.

commitment   The action of a judicial officer ordering that a person subject to judicial proceedings be placed in a particular kind of confinement or residential facility, for a specified reason authorized by law; also, the result of the action, the admission to the facility.

common law   Customs, traditions, judicial decisions, and other materials that guide courts in decision making, but that have not been enacted by the legislatures into statutes or embodied in the U.S. Constitution.

community-based correction   Rehabilitative activities and programs within the community that have effective ties with the local government.

commutation   The reduction of a sentence to a less severe one.

complaint   Any accusation that a person(s) has committed an offense(s), received by or originating from a law enforcement or prosecutorial agency, or received by a court.

conditional release   The release by executive decision from a federal or state correctional facility of a prisoner who has not served his or her full sentence and whose freedom is contingent upon obeying specified rules of behavior.

confidence games   The obtaining of money or property by means of deception through the confidence a victim places in the offender.

consent of the victim   Any voluntary yielding of the will of the victim, accompanied by his or her deliberation, agreeing to the act of the offending party.

conspiracy   Concert in criminal purpose; the combining of two or more persons to accomplish either an unlawful purpose or a lawful purpose by some unlawful means.

constitutional law   The legal rules and principles that define the nature and limits of governmental power, and the duties and rights of individuals in relation to the state.

contempt of court   Intentional obstruction of a court in the administration of justice, or an act calculated to lessen its authority or dignity, or failure to obey its lawful orders.

conviction   The judgment of a court, based on the verdict of a jury or judicial officer, or on the guilty or *nolo contendere* plea of the defendant, that the defendant is guilty of the offense(s) with which he or she has been charged.

corrections   A generic term that includes all government agencies, facilities, programs, procedures, personnel, and techniques concerned with the intake, custody, confinement, supervision, or treatment, or presentencing or predisposition investigation of alleged or adjudicated offenders.

counterfeiting   The making of imitation money and obligations of the government or a corporate body.

court   An agency or unit of the judicial branch of government, authorized or established by statute or constitution, and consisting of one or more judicial officers, which has the authority to decide upon cases, controversies in law, and disputed matters of fact brought before it.

court calendar   The court schedule; the list of events comprising the daily or weekly work of a court, including the assignment of the time and place for each hearing or other item of business, or the list of matters that will be taken up in a given court term.

court clerk   An elected or appointed court officer responsible for maintaining the written records of the court and for supervising or performing the clerical tasks necessary for conducting judicial business; also, any employee of a court whose principal duties are to assist the court clerk.

court of record   A court in which a complete and permanent record of all proceedings or specified types of proceedings is kept.

court reporter   A person present during judicial proceedings who records all testimony and other oral statements made during the proceedings.

crime   -An intentional act or omission in violation of criminal law (statutory and case law), committed without defense or justification, and sanctioned by the state as a felony or misdemeanor.

crime clock   A display used by the FBI in its *Uniform Crime Reports* to illustrate the annual ratio of crime to fixed time intervals.

Crime Index   In *Uniform Crime Reports* terminology, a set of numbers indicating the volume, fluctuation, and distribution of crimes reported to local law enforcement agencies, for the United States as a whole and for its geographical subdivisions, based on counts of reported occurrences of *UCR* Index crimes.

crime rate   The number of criminal offenses per 100,000 population.

criminal bankruptcy   The fraudulent declaration of excessive indebtedness or insolvency in an effort to avoid partial or full payment of one's debts.

criminal justice   The structure, functions, and decision processes of those agencies that deal with the management and control of crime and criminal offenders: the police, the courts, and corrections departments.

criminal law   The branch of jurisprudence that deals with offenses committed against the safety and order of the state.

criminal nuisance   Any conduct that is unreasonable and endangers the health and safety of others.

criminal proceedings   The regular and orderly steps, as directed or authorized by statute, of a court of law, taken to determine whether a person accused of a crime is guilty or not guilty.

criminal trespass   Crimes that are generally misdemeanors or violations, and are differentiated from burglary when breaking with criminal intent is absent or when the trespass involves property that has been fenced in a manner designed to exclude intruders.

critical stage   Any decision or processing point made by criminal justice agencies or personnel that is so important that the U.S. Supreme

Court has attached to it specific due-process rights.

culpability Blameworthiness; responsibility in some sense for an event or situation deserving of moral blame.

custody Legal or physical control of a person or thing; legal, supervisory, or physical responsibility for a person or thing.

de facto In fact, in reality.

defendant A person formally accused of an offense(s) by the filing in court of a charging document.

defense A broad term that can refer to any number of causes and rights of action that would serve to mitigate or excuse an individual's guilt in a criminal offense.

definite sentence A sentence of incarceration having a fixed period of time with no reduction by parole.

deliberation A full and conscious knowledge of the purpose to kill.

delinquency Criminal law violations that would be crimes if committed by an adult.

delinquent A juvenile offender who has been adjudicated by an officer of a juvenile court.

desecration The defacing, damaging, or mistreatment of a public structure, monument, or place of worship or burial.

detainee Usually, a person held in local, very short term confinement while awaiting consideration for pretrial release or first appearance for arraignment.

detention The legally authorized confinement of a person subject to criminal or juvenile court proceedings, until the point of commitment to a correctional facility or until release.

determinate sentence A sentence of incarceration for a fixed period of time.

deviance Conduct which the people of a group consider so dangerous,

embarrassing, or irritating that they bring special sanctions to bear against the persons who exhibit it.

directed verdict A judge's order to a jury to acquit the accused.

discretion The authority to choose between alternative actions.

dismissal The decision by a court to terminate adjudication of all outstanding charges in a criminal case, or all outstanding charges against a given defendant in a criminal case, thus terminating court action in the case and permanently or provisionally terminating court jurisdiction over the defendant in relation to those charges.

disorderly conduct Any act that tends to disturb the public peace, scandalize the community, or shock the public sense of morality.

disturbing the peace Any interruption of the peace, quiet, and good order of a neighborhood or community.

diversion The removal of offenders from the application of the criminal law at any stage of the police or court processes.

double jeopardy A constitutional safeguard that protects citizens from being tried more than once for the same offense.

driving while intoxicated (DWI) *or* **driving under the influence (DUI)** The operation of a motor vehicle while under the influence of alcohol or narcotics.

drunkenness The condition of being under the influence of alcohol to the extent that it renders one helpless.

due process of law A concept that asserts fundamental principles of justice and implies the administration of laws that do not violate the sacredness of private rights.

duress and consent Any unlawful constraints exercised upon an individual forcing him or her to do some act that would not have been done otherwise.

embezzlement The fraudulent appropriation or conversion of money or property by an employee, trustee, or other agent to whom the possession of such money or property was entrusted.

en banc "In bank," or on the bench; the court with all its qualified judges presiding in a case.

entrapment The inducement of an individual to commit a crime not contemplated by him or her, undertaken for the sole purpose of instituting a criminal prosecution against the offender.

evidence Any species of proof, through the medium of witnesses, records, documents, concrete objects, and circumstances.

evidence in chief The first or direct examination of a witness.

ex post facto After the fact.

exclusionary rule The constitutional guarantee that prohibits, in court, the use of illegally obtained evidence.

excusable homicide Deaths from accidents or misfortunes that may occur during some lawful act.

extradition The surrender by one state to another of an individual accused or convicted of an offense in the second state.

felony A crime punishable by death or by imprisonment in a state or federal penitentiary, usually for one year or more.

felony-murder doctrine The rule that provides that if a death occurs during the commission of a felony, any person involved in the commission of that felony can also be charged with first-degree murder.

fine The penalty imposed upon a convicted person by a court, requiring that he or she pay a specified sum of money to the court.

forcible rape Having sexual intercourse with a female against her will and through the use of threat of force or fear.

forgery   The making or altering of any document or instrument with the intent to defraud.

fornication   Sexual intercourse between unmarried persons.

fraud   Theft by false pretenses; the appropriation of money or property by trick or misrepresentation, or by creating or reinforcing a false impression as to some present or past fact that would adversely affect the victim's judgment of a transaction.

frisk   A pat-down search of a suspect's outer clothing.

furlough   An authorized, unescorted absence from prison for work or study, visiting one's family, or for some other reason deemed rehabilitative by correctional authorities, for a specified period of time.

gambling   The playing or operation of any game of chance that involves money or property of any value that is prohibited by the criminal code.

"good time"   The amount of time deducted from time to be served in prison on a given sentence(s) and/or under correctional agency jurisdiction, at some point after a prisoner's admission to prison, contingent upon good behavior and/or awarded automatically by application of a statute or regulation.

grand jury   A body of persons who have been selected according to law and sworn to hear the evidence against accused persons and determine whether there is sufficient evidence to bring them to trial, to investigate criminal activity generally, and to investigate the conduct of public agencies and officials.

habeas corpus, writ of   The writ that directs the person detaining a prisoner to bring him or her before a judicial officer to determine the lawfulness of the imprisonment.

habitual offender   A person sentenced under the provisions of a statute declaring that persons convicted of a given offense, and shown to have previously been convicted of another specified offense(s), shall receive a more severe penalty than that for the current offense alone.

harassment   Any act that annoys or alarms another person.

hearing   A proceeding in which arguments, witnesses, or evidence are heard by a judicial officer or administrative body.

homicide   The killing of one human being by another.

hung jury   A jury that after long deliberation is so irreconcilably divided in opinion that it is unable to reach any verdict.

in loco parentis   A position in reference to a child of that of lawful parent or guardian.

in re   In the affair of; concerning.

incest   Sexual intercourse between parent and child, any sibling pair, or between close blood relatives.

indecent exposure (exhibitionism)   Exposure of the sexual organs in a public place.

indeterminate sentence   A sentence of incarceration having a fixed minimum and a fixed maximum term of confinement.

indictment   A formal charging document returned by a grand jury based on evidence and testimony presented to it by the prosecutor.

inferior courts   The lower courts, or courts of limited jurisdiction.

information   A formal charging document drafted by a prosecutor and tested before a magistrate.

initial appearance   The first court processing stage after arrest, in which the accused is taken before a magistrate, given formal notice of the charge, and notified of his or her legal rights.

insanity   Any unsoundness of mind, madness, mental alienation, or want of reason, memory, and intelligence that prevents an individual from comprehending the nature and consequences of his or her acts or from distinguishing between right and wrong conduct.

intent   The state of mind or attitude with which an act is carried out; the design, resolve, or determination with which a person acts to achieve a certain result.

intermittent sentence   A sentence to confinement interrupted by periods of freedom.

jail   A confinement facility administered by an agency of local government, typically a law enforcement agency, intended for adults but sometimes also containing juveniles, that holds persons detained pending adjudication and/or persons committed after adjudication, usually those committed on sentences of a year or less.

judgment   Any decision or determination of a court.

jurisdiction   The territory, subject matter, or persons over which lawful authority may be exercised by a court or other justice agency, as determined by statute or constitution.

jury nullification   The refusal or marked reluctance on the part of a jury to convict, because of the severe nature of the sentence involved.

jury panel   The group of persons summoned to appear in court as potential jurors for a particular trial, or the persons selected from the group of potential jurors to sit in the jury box, from which second group those acceptable to the prosecution and the defense are finally chosen as the jury.

jury poll   A poll conducted by a judicial officer or by the clerk of the court after a jury has stated its verdict but before that verdict has been entered into the record of the court, asking each juror individually whether the stated verdict is his or her own verdict.

"just deserts"   The philosophy that the punishment should fit the crime; that punishment should be the prime consideration in sentencing.

justifiable homicide Those instances of death that result from legal demands.

justification Any just cause or excuse for the commission of an act that would otherwise be a crime.

larceny The taking and carrying away the personal property of another with the intent to deprive permanently.

lewdness Degenerate conduct in sexual behavior that is so well known that it may result in the corruption of public decency.

loitering Idling or lounging upon a street or other public way in a manner that serves to interfere with or annoy passersby.

mala in se crimes Criminal acts, such as murder and rape, that are considered to be in and of themselves, or inherently and essentially, evil.

mala prohibita crimes Criminal acts that are not necessarily evil in and of themselves, but that are wrong because they have been prohibited by the state.

malice aforethought The intent to cause death or serious harm, or to commit any felony whatsoever.

mandamus, writ of A writ, with the meaning "we command," issued from a superior court directing a lower court or other authority to perform a particular act.

mandatory release A release from prison required by statute when an inmate has been confined for a time period equal to his or her full sentence minus statutory "good time," if any.

mandatory sentence A statutory requirement that a certain penalty shall be set and carried out in all cases upon conviction for a specified offense or series of offenses.

manslaughter The unlawful killing of another, without malice.

mens rea "Guilty mind" or criminal intent; the capability of an individual to distinguish between right and wrong.

misdemeanor A crime generally punishable by no more than a $1,000 fine and/or one year of imprisonment, typically in a local institution.

misprision of felony The offense of concealing a felony committed by another.

mistake of law Any want of knowledge or acquaintance with the laws of the land insofar as they apply to the act, relation, duty, or matter under consideration.

mistrial A trial that has been terminated without a verdict and declared invalid by the court because of some circumstance that creates a substantial and uncorrectable prejudice to the conduct of a fair trial, or that makes it impossible to continue the trial in accordance with prescribed procedures.

moral turpitude Depravity or baseness of conduct.

motion An oral or written request made to a court at any time before, during, or after court proceedings, asking the court to make a specified finding, decision, or order.

murder The felonious killing of another human being with malice aforethought.

mutual agreement program A program providing for a form of contract between a prisoner and state prison and parole officials wherein the prisoner undertakes to complete specified self-improvement programs in order to receive a definite parole date, and the agency promises to provide the necessary educational and social services.

nationalization of the Bill of Rights The extension of the constitutional protections guaranteed by the Bill of Rights to defendants in state criminal trials.

natural law A body of principles and rules, imposed upon individuals by some power higher than man-made law, that are considered to be uniquely fitting for and binding on any community of rational beings.

negligence In legal usage, generally, a state of mind accompanying a person's conduct such that he or she is not aware, though a reasonable person should be aware, that there is a risk that the conduct might cause a particular harmful result.

no bill A grand jury's refusal to indict an accused.

nolle prosequi The terminating of adjudication of a criminal charge by the prosecutor's decision not to pursue the case, in some jurisdictions requiring the approval of the court.

nolo contendere A plea of "no contest" or "I do not wish to contest," with the same implication as the guilty plea.

obscenity That which is offensive to morality or chastity and is calculated to corrupt the mind and morals of those exposed to it.

occasional property crime Those types and instances of burglary, larceny, forgery, and other thefts undertaken infrequently or irregularly, and often quite crudely.

official criminal statistics The enumerations of crimes that come to the attention of law enforcement agencies; arrest compilations; and characteristics of offenders and crimes based on arrest, judicial, and prison records.

opinion The official announcement of a decision of a court together with the reasons for that decision.

organized crime Business activities directed toward economic gain through unlawful means.

pardon A "forgiveness" for the crime committed that bars any further criminal justice processing.

parens patriae A philosophy under which the state takes over the role of the parent.

parole The status of being released from a correctional institution after a portion of the sentence has been served, on the condition of maintaining good behavior and remaining in the custody and under the guidance of the institution or some other agency approved by the state until a final discharge is granted.

parole revocation The administrative action of a paroling authority removing a person from parole status in response to a violation of lawfully required conditions of parole including the prohibition against commission of a new offense, and usually resulting in a return to prison.

parole supervision Guidance, treatment or regulation of the behavior of a convicted adult who is obliged to fulfill conditions of parole or other conditional release, authorized and required by statute, performed by a parole agency, and occurring after a period of prison confinement.

parole violation An act or a failure to act by a parolee that does not conform to the conditions of parole.

parolee A person who has been conditionally released by a paroling authority from a prison prior to the expiration of his or her sentence, and placed under the supervision of a parole agency, and who is required to observe conditions of parole.

parties to offenses All persons culpably concerned in the commission of a crime, whether they directly commit the act constituting the offense, or facilitate, solicit, encourage, aid or attempt to aid, or abet its commission; also, in some penal codes, persons who assist one who has committed a crime to avoid arrest, trial, conviction, or punishment.

per curium An unsigned opinion of the court.

per se By itself; alone.

peremptory challenge A challenge to remove a potential juror on the basis of any reason or no reason at all.

perjury The intentional making of a false statement as part of testimony by a sworn witness in a judicial proceeding on a matter material to the inquiry.

perpetrator The chief actor in the commission of a crime, that is, the person who directly commits the criminal act.

petit jury A trial jury (as opposed to a grand jury).

petition 1. A written request made to a court asking for the exercise of its judicial powers, or asking for permission to perform some act where the authorization of a court is required. 2. In juvenile proceedings, a document alleging that a youth is a delinquent, a status offender, or a dependent child and asking that the court assume jurisdiction over the juvenile.

pickpocketing The theft of money or articles directly from the garments of the victim.

plagiarism The copying or adopting of the literary, musical, or artistic work of another and publishing or producing it as one's own original work.

plaintiff The customary name for the person who initiates a civil action. In some states the prosecution in a criminal case (that is, "the people," as represented by government) is called the "plaintiff." "Complaint," "complaining party," and "complaining witness" are also used to mean the plaintiff.

plea A defendant's formal answer in court to the charge contained in a complaint, information, or indictment, that he or she is guilty or not guilty of the offense charged, or does not contest the charge.

political crime Illegal activity considered by offenders to be essential and appropriate in achieving necessary changes in society, including treason, sedition, espionage, sabotage, war collaboration, and radicalism and protest.

polygamy The practice of having several spouses.

pornography Literature, art, film, pictures, or other articles of a sexual nature that are considered obscene by a community's moral standards.

posse comitatus The body of persons that a sheriff or county authority may summon to assist him or her in law enforcement.

postconviction remedy The procedure or set of procedures by which a person who has been convicted of a crime can challenge in court the lawfulness of a judgment of conviction or penalty or of a correctional agency action, and thus obtain relief in situations where this cannot be done by a direct appeal.

prejudicial error In criminal proceedings, an error of such substance that it serves to compromise the rights of the accused.

preliminary hearing A hearing before the court designed to protect defendants from unwarranted prosecutions.

premeditation A design or conscious decision to do something before it is actually done.

presentence investigation An investigation undertaken by a probation agency or other designated authority at the request of a court into the past behavior, family circumstances, and personality of a person who has been convicted of a crime, in order to assist the court in determining the most appropriate sentence.

presentment A written notice of accusation issued by a grand jury, based on its own knowledge and observation rather than on testimony and evidence presented by the prosecution.

presiding judge The title of the judicial officer formally designated for some period as the chief judicial officer of a court.

presumptive fixed sentence A fixed determinate sentence within a limited range established by statute.

pretrial conference A meeting of the opposing parties in a case with the judicial officer prior to trial, for the purposes of stipulating those things that are agreed upon and thus narrowing the trial to the things that are in dispute, disclosing the required information about witnesses and evidence, making motions, and generally organizing the presentation of motions, witnesses, and evidence.

pretrial detention   Any period of confinement occurring between arrest or other holding to answer a charge, and the conclusion of prosecution.

pretrial discovery   Disclosure by the prosecution or the defense prior to trial of evidence or other information that is intended to be used in the trial.

pretrial release   The release of an accused person from custody, for all or part of the time before or during prosecution, upon his or her promise to appear in court when required.

prima facie **case**   Meaning "at first sight," it refers to a fact or other evidence presumably sufficient to establish a defense or a claim unless otherwise contradicted.

prison   A state or federal confinement facility having custodial authority over adults sentenced to confinement.

prisonization   The socializing process by which the inmate learns the rules and regulations of the institution and the informal rules, values, customs, and general culture of the penitentiary.

proactive patrol   A police patrol model characterized by active search for criminal activity or suspicious behavior.

probable cause   A set of facts and circumstances that would induce a reasonably intelligent and prudent person to believe that a particular person has committed a specific crime; reasonable grounds to make or believe an accusation.

probation   A sentence not involving confinement that imposes conditions and retains authority in the sentencing court to modify the conditions of sentence or to resentence the offender if he or she violates the conditions.

probation revocation   A court order in response to a violation of conditions of probation, taking away a person's probationary status, and usually

withdrawing the conditional freedom associated with the status.

probation termination   The ending of the probation status of a given person by routine expiration of probationary period, by special early termination by court, or by revocation of probation.

probation violation   An act or failure to act by a probationer that does not conform to the conditions of his probation.

probationer   A person who is placed on probation status and required by a court or probation agency to meet certain conditions of behavior, who may or may not be placed under the supervision of a probation agency.

professional theft   Nonviolent forms of criminal occupation pursued with a high degree of skill to maximize financial gain and minimize the risks of apprehension.

prosecutor   An attorney who is the elected or appointed chief of a prosecution agency, and whose official duty is to conduct criminal proceedings on behalf of the people against persons accused of committing criminal offenses.

prostitution   The offering of sexual relations for monetary or other gain.

public intoxication   The condition of being severely under the influence of alcohol or drugs in a public place to the degree that one may endanger persons or property.

public order crime   Crimes against public order and safety, mostly misdemeanors, that account for a considerable portion of criminal justice activity.

ransom   The demanding of money for the redemption of captured persons or property.

rape   The unlawful carnal knowledge of a female against her will.

reactive patrol   A police patrol model whereby the police respond only when there is a call for assistance.

reception center   A central receiving institution where all felony offenders

of a given jurisdiction sentenced to a term of imprisonment are committed for orientation and classification.

recidivism   The repetition of criminal behavior.

recidivist   A person who has been convicted of one or more crimes, and who is alleged or found to have subsequently committed another crime or series of crimes.

reformatory   A prison model generally for youthful or young adult offenders.

release on recognizance (ROR)   The release of an accused from jail on his or her own obligation rather than on a monetary bond.

removal of landmarks   The relocation of monuments or other markings that designate property lines or boundaries for the purpose of fraudulently reducing the owner's interest or holdings in lands and estates.

reparole   A release to parole occurring after a return to prison from an earlier release to parole, on the same sentence to confinement.

reprieve   The postponement of the execution of a sentence for a definite period of time.

respondeat superior   The doctrine under which liability is imposed upon an employer for the acts of his employees that are committed in the course and scope of their employment.

respondent   The person who formally answers the allegations stated in a petition that has been filed in a court; in criminal proceedings, the one who contends against an appeal.

restitution   A court requirement that an alleged or convicted offender pay money or provide services to the victim of the crime or provide services to the community.

robbery   The felonious taking of the money or goods of another, from his person or in his presence and against his will, through the use or threat of force and violence.

search warrant   A written order, issued by a magistrate and directed to a law enforcement officer, commanding a search of a specified premises.

seduction   The act of enticing or luring a woman of chaste character to engage in sexual intercourse by fraudulently promising to marry her or by some other false promise.

sentence review   The reconsideration of a sentence imposed on a person convicted of a crime, either by the same court that imposed the sentence or by a higher court.

sequestration   The removal of the jurors (and alternates, if any) from all possible outside influences.

severance   In criminal proceedings the separation, for purposes of pleading and/or trial, of multiple defendants named in a single charging document, or of multiple charges against a particular defendant listed in a single charging document.

sexual assault   Any sexual contact with another person (other than a spouse) that occurs without the consent of the victim or is offensive to the victim.

sheriff   The elected chief officer of a county law enforcement agency, usually responsible for law enforcement in unincorporated areas and for the operation of the county jail.

shock probation   A type of probation that allows for brief incarceration followed by suspension of sentence and probation.

shoplifting   The theft of goods, wares, or merchandise from a store or shop.

sodomy   Certain acts of sexual relationship including fellatio (oral intercourse with the male sex organ), cunnilingus (oral intercourse with the female sex organ), buggery (penetration of the anus), homosexuality (sexual relations between members of the same sex), bestiality (sexual intercourse with an animal), pederasty (unnatural intercourse between a man and a boy), and necrophilia (sexual intercourse with a corpse).

split sentence   A sentence explicitly requiring the convicted person to serve a period of confinement in a local, state, or federal facility followed by a period of probation.

status offense   An act declared by statute to be a crime because it violates the standards of behavior expected of children.

statute   A written law enacted by legislation.

statutory law   Law created by statute, handed down from legislatures.

statutory rape   Having sexual intercourse with a female under a stated age (usually 16 or 18, but sometimes 14), with or without her consent.

stay of execution   The stopping by a court of the carrying out or implementation of a judgment, that is, of a court order previously issued.

stop and frisk   The detaining of a person by a law enforcement officer for the purpose of investigation, accompanied by a superficial examination by the officer of the person's body surface or clothing to discover weapons, contraband, or other objects relating to criminal activity.

street crime   A class of offenses, sometimes defined with some degree of formality as those that occur in public locations, that are visible and assaultive, and that thus constitute a group of crimes which are a special risk to the public and a special target of law enforcement preventive efforts and prosecutorial attention.

subpoena   A written order issued by a judicial officer, prosecutor, defense attorney, or grand jury, requiring a specified person to appear in a designated court at a specified time in order to testify in a case under the jurisdiction of that court, or to bring material to be used as evidence to that court.

superior courts   The courts of record or trial courts.

suppression hearing   A hearing to determine whether or not the court

will prohibit specified statements, documents, or objects from being introduced into evidence in a trial.

surety   A third party who posts bond.

suspect   A person considered by a criminal justice agency to be one who may have committed a specific criminal offense, but who has not been arrested or charged.

suspended sentence   A court disposition of a convicted person, pronouncing a penalty of a fine or commitment to confinement, but unconditionally discharging the defendant or holding execution of the penalty in abeyance upon good behavior.

theft   The unlawful taking, possession, or use of another's property, without the use of threat of force, and with the intent to deprive permanently.

tort   A civil wrong for which the law gives redress.

transactional immunity   In grand jury proceedings, the immunity against prosecution given to a witness in return for testifying.

trial   The examination in a court of the issues of fact and law in a case, for the purpose of reaching a judgment.

trial *de novo*   A new trial, conducted in a court of record as an appeal of the result of a trial in a lower court (not of record).

true bill   A grand jury's endorsement of the charge or charges specified in the prosecutor's bill.

Uniform Crime Reports   A nationwide compilation of crime statistics published annually by the FBI, based on information supplied by local law enforcement agencies.

use immunity   In grand jury proceedings, a limited immunity that prohibits the government only from using a witness's compelled testimony in a subsequent criminal proceeding.

usury   The taking of or contracting to take interest on a loan at a rate that exceeds the level established by law.

vacated sentence   A sentence that has been declared nullified by action of a court.

vagrancy   The condition of being idle and having no visible means of support.

venire   A writ that summons jurors.

verdict   The decision of the jury in a jury trial or of a judicial officer in a nonjury trial, that the defendant is guilty or not guilty of the offense for which he or she has been tried.

violation   Offense defined in criminal codes to be less serious than a misdemeanor (also called "infraction" in some jurisdictions).

violation of privacy   Any unlawful trespass, interception, observation, eavesdropping, or other surveillance that serves to infringe on the private rights of another.

violent personal crime   Criminal acts resulting from differences in personal relations in which death or physical injury is inflicted.

voir dire   An oath sworn to by a prospective juror regarding his or her qualifications as a juror.

voyeurism (peeping)   The surreptitious observance of an exposed body or sexual act.

waiver of jurisdiction   The process by which the juvenile court relinquishes its jurisdiction over a child and transfers the case to a court of criminal jurisdiction for prosecution as an adult.

warrant   Any of a number of writs issued by a judicial officer that direct a law enforcement officer to perform a specified act and afford him protection from damage if he performs it.

white-collar crime   Those offenses committed by persons acting in their legitimate occupational roles.

writ   A formal written order issued by a court commanding specified individuals to do (or abstain from doing) some specified act.

Copyrights and Acknowledgments and Illustration Credits

Chapter 5
130 © Robert Burroughs;
134 Bettmann Archive; 143 © David
R. Frazier

Part 2
152–153 Culver Pictures

Chapter 6
154 Peter Southwick/Stock, Boston;
159 Library of Congress; 160 Library
of Congress; 161 Western History
Collections, University of Oklahoma
Library; 163 Courtesy of Bell
Helicopters; 164 Library of Congress;
167 Wide World Photos; 172 Okamoto/
Rapho/Photo Researchers; 173 ©
George Gardner; 176 Courtesy of
Pinkerton's, Inc.; 177 Courtesy of
Pinkerton's, Inc.; 178 Jim Anderson/
Woodfin Camp; 179 Library of
Congress; 180 Eve Arnold/Magnum;
181 New York Post Photo by John
Waldvogel; 182 Wide World Photos

Chapter 7
186 James Holland/Stock, Boston; 189
Sepp Seitz/Woodfin Camp; 190 © Jill
Freedman; 191 Bob Pacheco/EKM
Nepenthe; 194 © 1983 Jaydie
Putterman; 198 Charles Gatewood/
Stock, Boston; 201 Maje Waldo/Stock,
Boston; 202 © Jill Freedman; 205 ©
Jill Freedman; 208 Wide World Photos;
212 Stock, Boston; 213 © Charles
Gatewood; 215 Daniel S. Brody/Stock,
Boston; 216 © Bill Beall

Chapter 8
220 Chauvel/Sygma; 222 Glenn
Shirley Western Collection, Stillwater,
Oklahoma; 224 © Robert Burroughs;
226 © Jill Freedman; 227 Wide World
Photos; 231 Wide World Photos;
233 Martin J. Dain/Magnum;
240 Wide World Photos; 243 Daniel
S. Brody/Stock, Boston; 254 Wide
World Photos; 258 © Jill Freedman;
263 Wide World Photos

Chapter 9
266 © George Gardner; 271 Library of
Congress; 275 Wide World Photos;
282 Wide World Photos; 284 Charles
Gatewood/Image Works; 285 Danny
Lyon/Magnum; 288 © 1977, The
Courier-Journal and Louisville Times
Co. Reprinted with permission. Photo
by Bob Steinau; 289 Wide World
Photos; 292 UPI/Bettmann; 296 Stock,
Boston; 300 James A. Inciardi

Part 3
304–305 Erich Salomon/Magnum

Chapter 10
306 Library of Congress; 308 Missouri
Historical Society, #485a; 309 Allen
Hess/Library of Congress; 317 Western
History Collections, University of
Oklahoma Library; 331 top: James A.
Inciardi; 331 bottom: HBJ Collection;
333 top left: Library of Congress; 333
bottom left: Supreme Court Historical
Society; 333 center: Supreme Court
Historical Society; 333 top right: Wide
World Photos; 333 bottom right: Wide
World Photos; 339 Wide World Photos

Chapter 11
342 Frank Siteman/Stock, Boston; 347
Louis Kostiner/Library of Congress;
360 Western History Collections,
University of Oklahoma Library; 361
Stock, Boston; 363 UPI/Bettmann; 364
Yvonne Freund/Photo Researchers;
372 Brown Brothers; 377 Flip
Schulke, Life Magazine © 1964 Time
Inc.; 378 Daniel S. Brody/Stock,
Boston; 382 Wide World Photos

Chapter 12
390 Brown Brothers; 397 James A.
Inciardi; 399 James A. Inciardi; 401
Michael O'Brien/Archive Pictures; 402
H. Armstrong Roberts; 404 © 1983
Jaydie Putterman; 421 Robert Mills,
Library of Congress; 428 © Michael
Grecco; 435 Library of Congress

Chapter 13
446 Kent Kirkley/Texas Monthly; 449
Culver Pictures; 453 Keystone-Mast
Collection, California Museum of
Photography, University of California,
Riverside; 458 David Burnett/Woodfin
Camp; 470 Danny Lyon/Magnum; 472
Granger Collection; 477 Wide World
Photos; 479 David Burnett/Woodfin
Camp; 483 Wide World Photos; 484
Owen Frank/Stock, Boston; 486 Eddie
Adams/Time Magazine; 487 Chris
Troyano/Huntsville Item; 489 top:
Charles Gupton/Sygma; 489 bottom:
Yvonne Hemsey/Gamma-Liaison; 492
UPI/Bettmann; 495 Wide World Photos

Part 4
502–503 Neil Leifer/Time Magazine

Chapter 14
504 © Paul Conklin; 506 public
domain; 507 public domain; 508
public domain; 509 Robert Mercer/
Time Magazine; 514 H. Armstrong
Roberts; 517 top: U.S. Bureau of
Prisons; 517 bottom: Courtesy of the
American Correctional Association;
518 Courtesy of the American
Correctional Association; 519 Library
of Congress; 523 Courtesy of the
American Correctional Association;
527 Courtesy of the American
Correctional Association; 529 James A.
Inciardi; 530 © Jill Freedman; 532
Brooklyn Historical Society; 534 H.
Armstrong Roberts; 537 Courtesy of J.
Robert Lilly

Chapter 15
540 David Burnett/Woodfin Camp;
543 Danny Lyon/Magnum; 546 Culver
Pictures; 549 Charles Harbutt/Archive
Pictures; 550 UPI/Bettmann; 551
Steve Hanson/Stock, Boston; 555
Courtesy of the American Correctional
Association; 560 Michael Douglas/
Image Works; 562 Eric Kroll/Taurus;
568 Pamela Price/Picture Cube; 569
Arthur Grace/Stock, Boston; 573
Courtesy of the American Correctional
Association; 579 Eric Kroll/Taurus;
580 George L. Walker/Black Star

Case Index

Pages on which cases or terms are introduced are set in italics. Page numbers followed by "n" indicate that the case or term appears in a note.

Name Index

Blackmun, Henry Andrew, 243, 244, 339, 383, 478
Blackstock, Nelson, 171
Bloch, Herbert A., 715n
Block, Eugene B., 185n
Blumberg, Abraham S., 265n, 365–67, 389n
Bogdanoff, Alex, 491
Bonaparte, Charles J., 170
Bonnie, Richard J., 32n
Bosket, Willie, Jr., 676
Boudreau, John F., 102n
Bowers, William J., 471, 491, 501n
Bowker, Lee H., 621
Brace, Charles Loring, 684
Brandeis, Louis Dembits, 333
Brando, Marlon, 11
Brant, Irving, 151n
Braswell, Michael, 583n
Braude, Jacob, 625, 669n
Breckinridge, Sophonisba, 715n
Brennan, William Joseph, 244, 333, 339, 478, 482, 486, 618, 720, 724, 726
Brenner, Robert N., 303n
Brewster, Benjamin H., 366
Briar, Scott, 210–11, 219n, 714n
Bridenbaugh, Carl, 184n
Bristow, Allen P., 218
Britt, David, 303n
Brockway, Zebulon, 521–22, 539n, 649
Broderick, John J., 21n
Broeder, D. W., 445n
Brokow, Tom, 181
Brooks, Charles, Jr., 486
Brooks, Chet, 608
Brown, Eroy, 612
Brown, James W., 669n
Brown, John, 604
Brown, Richard Maxwell, 179, 185n, 501n
Brown, Roscoe, 463
Browning, Frank, 728n
Brownmiller, Susan, 91, 567–68, 583n
Broyles, J. Allen, 32n
Buck, Carrie, 138–39
Budd, Grace, 19
Buffum, Peter C., 583n
Bugliosi, Vincent, 32n
Bullard, Charles, 176–77
Bunker, Archie, 432
Burch, Nancy Jo, 676, 704
Burger, Warren Earl, 243, 244, 257–58, 259, 263, 329, 338, 339, 386, 478, 486, 561, 717, 719, 720–21, 722, 724

Burgess, Anthony, 598
Burkhart, Kathryn W., 583n
Burnham, David, 270
Burr, Raymond, 187
Burrows, Jim, 176
Burrows, Rube, 176
Bush, George R., 63n
Bye, Raymond, 491

C

Calandra, John, 412
Caldwell, Robert G., 539n, 550, 582n, 605
Calvert, Roy E., 488, 501n
Cameron, Mary Owen, 103n
Canon, Bradley C., 341n
Capone, Al "Scarface," 38, 39, 69, 99, 527, 718
Cardozo, Benjamin, 238, 333
Carey, Hugh, 262
Carlson, Norman, 664
Carney, Louis P., 583n, 670n
Carpenter, John, 604
Carr, Walter S., 500n
Carroll, George, 228–30
Carroll, Leo, 568, 583n
Carter, Dan T., 389n
Carter, Jimmy, 171, 724
Carter, Robert M., 669n
Cash, Johnny, 617
Cassidy, Butch, 176
Caute, David, 32n
Chambers, Carl D., 32n, 33n, 265n
Chamelin, Neil C., 82, 103n
Champagne, Anthony, 341n
Chaney, James, 13
Channing, Henry, 679n
Chapman, Kelly, 617
Chapman, Mark David, 415
Chappell, Duncan, 103n
Charrière, Henri, 599
Chessman, Caryl, 382, 383, 487, 490
Chevigny, Paul, 303n
Chew, George Wing, 491
Chilton, Robert, 228
Chimel, Ted Steven, 242–43
Christie, N., 129n
Christman, Henry M., 151n
Churchill, Winston, 12, 505
Cirofici, Frank, 490
Clark, Charles L., 539n
Clark, Henry, 10
Clark, Tom, 241
Clay, Henry, 221
Cleaver, Eldridge, 549, 582n
Clements, William, 610

Clemmer, Donald, 572, 582, 582n, 583n
Clinnard, Marshall B., 103n
Cloward, Richard A., 583n
Cockerham, William E., 621n
Cohen, Fred, 621n
Cole, George F., 354, 389n
Colquhoun, Patrick, 156, 159, 184n
Conner, John, 604
Connolly, Charles P., 219n
Conrad, Earl, 103n
Conrad, John P., 500
Cook, David J., 177, 185n
Cook, Fred, Jr., 171n
Coolidge, Calvin, 171
Coolidge, Edward, 244–47
Cooper, D. B., 93, 96
Coppola, Frank J., 357
Cormier, Bruno M., 583n
Cornell, David C., 250
Corson, William R., 33n, 185n
Costello, A. E., 302n
Costello, Frank, 8, 411–12
Couzens, M., 129n
Cox, Archibald, 728n
Craig, Jonathan, 12n
Crawford, William, 539n
Creamer, J. Shane, 242, 264, 264n, 265n
Creighton, Frances, 491
Cressey, Donald R., 32n, 129n, 359, 389n, 583n
Crofton, Walter, 520, *521*, 646
Cronin, Tania Z., 728
Cronin, Thomas E., 728
Crowe, Dorothy, 214
Cruse, John, 676
Cumming, Elaine, 214
Cumming, Ian, 214
Cummings, Homer S., 526
Curran, William J., 389n
Curtis, Joseph, 680
Cushman, Robert F., 265n

D

Daley, Richard, 14, 162, 277
Daley, Robert, 219n, 275
Dalsheim, Stephen, 549
Darrow, Clarence, 430
Datesman, Susan K., 583n
Davis, Kenneth Culp, 219n, 389n
Davis, Roger Trenton, 461
Davis, Samuel M., 715n
Day, William R., 238
Dean, James, 7, 11, 38, 39
Dean, John, 33n, 171

de Beaumont, Gustave, 515, 539n, 583n
DeConcini, Dennis, 722
Dederick, Charles, 563
De Frances, Vincent, 103n
DeGosten, Lucille K., 655
de la Vega, Arturo, 282, 283
Denault, Genevieve C., 102n
Derias, Joseph, 604
Dershowitz, Alan M., 52, 462–63
de Tocqueville, Alexis, 515, 539n, 583n
Dewer, Leroy, 588
Dickens, Charles, 366
Diderot, Denis, 510
Diem, Ngo Dink, 13
Dill, Forrest, 444n
Dillinger, John, 6, 171, 464, 526
Dillingham, Steven, 583n
Dodd, David J., 129n
Doig, Jameson W., 685
Douglas, William O., 55, 224, 241, 244, 265n, 375–76, 378, 402, 478, 594
Downing, Rondal G., 388, 389n
Doyle, Popeye, 274
Dressler, David, 670n
Duncan, Gary, 426–27
Dunn, Marvin, 302
Dunne, Finley Peter, 495
Duval, Claude, 157
Dwight, Lewis, 516

E
Earle, Alice Morse, 539n
Earp, Wyatt, 162
Eastman, George D., 303n
Echols, James Andrew, 207
Eddinger, Monty Lee, 708
Edell, Laura, 214
Edge, L. L., 31n, 464, 527
Edward the Confessor, 59–60
Edwards, Loren E., 103n
Egan, Eddie, 274–75
Ehrlichman, John, 28
Ehrmann, Sara, 491
Einstadter, Werner J., 103n
Ellis, Edward Robb, 302n
Epstein, Edward Jay, 30, 33n, 185n
Erikson, Kai T., 43, 62, 63n
Ervin, Sam J., 424
Escobedo, Danny, 254–55, 262
Eskridge, Chris W., 670n
Estelle, James, 615
Estrada, Armando, 282, 283
Eubank, Earle Edward, 539n
Evans, Kenneth R., 82, 103n
Evers, Medgar, 13

F
Faragher, William E., 102n
Faretta, Anthony, 383
Fargo, William G., 178
Fahey, Richard P., 302n
Faison, Adrienne, 302n
Farmer, J. S., 206
Farmer, James, 12
Feeley, Malcolm M., 341, 341n, 389n
Feinman, Clarice, 582n
Ferguson, R. Fred, 219n
Field, Stephan J., 473
Fielding, Henry, 156, *158*, 175
Fielding, John, 156, 158–59, 175
Figlio, Robert M., 715n
Finch, Stanley W., 170
Finckenauer, James O., 685, 714
Fischetti, Charlie, 8
Fish, Albert, 19
Fisher, Irving, 6
Fishman, Joseph F., 525, 539n, 583n
Fitzpatrick, Linda Rae, 16
Floyd, Charles "Pretty Boy," 6, 526
Flynn, Frank T., 539n, 715n
Flynn, William J., 170
Fogelson, Robert M., 303n
Folks, Homer, 681
Fonda, Henry, 377
Fooner, Michael, 185n
Foote, Caleb B., 444n
Ford, Gerald R., 18, 349
Fortas, Abe, 333, 375
Foster, E., 476
Fox, Vernon, 582n, 670n
Francis, Willie, 476–77
Frankel, Marvin E., 444, 445n, 466, 498, 500n, 501n
Frankfurter, Felix, 239, 252, 318, 333, 366
Franks, Robert, 47–48
Freed, Daniel, 444n
Friday, Paul C., 670n
Friedman, Lawrence M., 62, 63n
Friedman, Leon, 341n
Friloux, Anthony C., 364, 389n
Fromme, Lynette, 18
Fugate, Caril Ann, 38
Fulsher, Fred, 24
Furman, William, 478
Furnas, J. C., 63n

G
Gacy, John Wayne, 19
Gagnon, John H., 582n, 583n
Galati, Raymond A., 95, 98
Galaway, Burt, 670n
Garabedian, Peter G., 575

Garcia, Armando, 282, 283
Gardner, Roy, 527
Gardner, Cleamtree, 290–92
Gardner, Edward, 290
Garofolo, James, 129n
Gault, Gerald Francis, 694–95
Gaye, Marvin, 91
Gaye, Marvin, Sr., 91
Geis, Gilbert, 103n, 670n
Geis, Robley, 103n
Geiser, Robert L., 91, 102, 103n
Gelles, Richard J., 91
Genn, Hazel G., 129n
Genovese, Kitty, 114–16
Genovese, Vito, 411
Gentry, Curt, 32n
George the Third, 528
Gerassi, John, 728n
Gerth, Jeff, 32n
Giallombardo, Rose, 103n, 582, 582n, 583n
Giardini, G. I., 670n
Gibbons, Don C., 582n
Gideon, Clarence Earl, 373–75, 377
Gilmore, Gary Mark, 482–83, 487
Gillers, Stephens, 33n
Ginger, Ann Fagan, 264, 445n
Giraudoux, Jean, 366
Glaser, Daniel, 129n, 667, 669n, 671n
Glick, Henry R., 621
Godwin, John, 102n
Goetz, Bernhard Hugo, 181
Goffman, Erving, 582, 582n
Goldberg, Arthur J., Jr., 255, 333, 475
Goldfarb, Ronald, 444, 444n, 538, 539n
Goldman, Eric F., 31n, 32n
Goldstein, Herman, 204–205, 212, 218, 218n, 219n, 302, 302n
Goldwater, Barry, 17, 20–21
Gonzales, Jose Manuel Miguel Xavier, 472
Good, Sandra, 18
Goodman, Andrew, 13
Goodman, Paul, 10–11, 32n
Gottfredson, Don M., 670n, 671n
Graham, Fred P., 728n
Graham, Hugh David, 32n, 185n, 501n
Graham, Jack Gilbert, 47
Gray, Horace, 394
Greenberg, Steven M., 236, 265n
Greene, Jack R., 219n
Greenstein, Theodore, 219n
Grezschowiak, Stephen, 491
Griswold, Ervin N., 241, 338
Gross, Harry, 9
Grossman, Brian A., 219n

Moseley, Mark, 666
Moss, Frank, 281
Mueller, G. O. W., 63n
Murphy, A. J., 556
Murphy, Patrick V., 199, 218n, 256, 275
Murton, Thomas O., 600–601, 621, 621n
Musto, David F., 103n
Myers, Daisy, 10
Myers, William, 10
Myles, Elvin, 386–87

N

Naftalis, Gary P., 444, 445n
Nagel, Stuart S., 444n
Nash, Jay Robert, 464
Nathan, Vincent, 614
Nation, Carry, 44
Neary, Beth Lynch, 389n
Neithercutt, M. G., 671n
Nelson, E. Kim, 670n
Nelson, George "Baby Face," 6, 526
Nelson, Knox, 600
Ness, Eliot, 39
Neubauer, David W., 341n
Newman, Charles L., 670n
Newman, Donald J., 667, 671n
Newman, Paul, 316
Nichols, F. L., 103n
Niederhoffer, Arthur, 215, 218n, 219n, 265n
Niles, Blair, 621n
Nimmer, Raymond T., 669
Nixon, Richard M., 28–30, 167, 257–58, 478
Norris, Clarence, 376–77
Nowak, Marion, 32n
Nuffield, Joan, 671n

O

O'Bryan, Ronald, 69–70, 96
O'Bryan, Tim, 69
O'Connor, Sandra Day, 333, 339, 350, 724
Ohmart, Howard, 670n
O'Leary, Vincent, 670n, 671n
O'Neil, Jack, 490
Orland, Leonard, 582, 583n
Orwell, George, 537, 598
Osborne, Thomas Mott, 491
Osmond, Humphrey, 32n
Oswald, Lee Harvey, 13, 38
Oswald, Russell, 590–91
Owensby, Earle, 549

P

Packer, Herbert, 720, 728n
Palko, Frank U., 418
Palmer, Deborah J., 302n
Palmer, John W., 621n
Palmer, Russell, 618
Palmer, Ted, 583n
Pappas, Nick, 583n
Pare, Richard, 341n
Parker, Bonnie, 6, 171, 526
Parker, Isaac C., 327
Parker, Robert Leroy, 176
Parker, William, 670n
Partridge, Eric, 206
Patterson, Haywood, 103n, 376
Paulsen, Monrad G., 500n
Peel, Robert, 51, 156, 159, 510
Penn, William, 512–13
Peoples, Kenneth D., 151n, 501n
Perez, Leander H., 426
Petersen, David M., 103n, 670n
Petersilia, Joan, 647, 670n
Peterson, Joyce, 647, 670n
Petty, Charles S., 389n
Phillips, Steven, 351, 394, 430, 444, 445n
Pickett, Robert S., 681
Pierce, B. K., 681
Pierce, Chester M., 501n
Pierce, Glenn L., 501n
Pike, Luke Owen, 151n, 184n, 444n, 539n
Piliavin, Irving, 210–11, 219n, 714n
Pinkerton, Allan, *176*–77
Pisciotta, Alexander W., 685
Pittman, David J., 103n
Place, Etta, 176
Plate, Thomas, 218n, 275
Polansky, Roman, 17
Polk, Kenneth, 669n
Pollock, Frederick, 59, 63n
Poole, Eric D., 389n
Pope, Noah, 525, 531
Porter, Bruce, 302
Posner, Richard, 129n, 341, 341n
Pound, Roscoe, 59, 318
Powell, J. C., 539n
Powell, John Janus, 66–67, 102n
Powell, Lewis F., Jr., 258, 339, 478, 724
Powell, Ozie, 376
Powers, Edwin, 583n
Powers, Pamela, 259, 263, 723
Prassel, Frank R., 184n
Presley, Elvis, 7
Price, Victoria, 371, 376
Pringle, Patrick, 184, 184n

Prior, David, 294
Procunier, Raymond, 615
Prouse, William J., 231
Prynne, Hester, 508
Puttkamer, Ernst W., 444n, 501n
Puzo, Mario, 39
Pyle, C. Victor, 462–63

Q

Quay, Matthew, 280
Quarles, Benjamin, 260
Quinn, Jane Bryant, 366
Quinn, William, 591
Quinney, Richard, 103n, 729n

R

Radzinowicz, Leon, 539n, 583n
Rankin, Anne, 444n
Rankin, Hugh F., 63n
Rather, Dan, 181
Rausch, Sharla, 715n
Raymond, Allen, 728n
Reagan, Nancy, 181
Reagan, Ronald, 52, 53, 162, 333, 348, 350, 403, 416, 719, 724–27
Reckless, Walter C., 31n
Redford, Robert, 600
Reed, Stanley F., 395, 477
Regoli, Robert H., 389n
Regush, Nicholas, 669n
Rehnquist, William H., 258, 329, 339, 340, 350, 440, 478, 494, 724, 726
Reid, Sue Titus, 501n, 582n, 583n
Reilley, James W., 444n
Reilly, J. Tim, 445n
Reinemann, John Otto, 681, 715n
Reinhardt, James M., 63n
Reiss, Albert J., Jr., 191, 218n, 302n
Rembar, Charles, 134, 151, 151n, 393, 444n
Reno, John, 176
Reno, Semeon, 176
Reppetto, Thomas A., 184, 184n, 303n
Retsky, Harold G., 582n
Rexroth, Kenneth, 10, 32n
Reynolds, Quentin, 103n
Rhodes, James, 617
Rhodes, Robert P., 444n
Rice, Robert, 41
Richardson, James F., 184n, 302n, 430
Richardson, Richard J., 388n
Riedel, Marc, 501n
Riis, Jacob, 106–107
Rivkin, Stan, 400, 401
Roberson, Willie, 376
Robin, Gerald D., 302n
Robinson, Louis Newton, 126, 129n
Robison, James, 578, 583n

Rockefeller, John D., 600
Rockefeller, Nelson, 591
Rockefeller, Winthrop, 600–601
Rockwell, George Lincoln, 13
Rodriguez, Roman, 282, 283
Roebuck, Julian, 302n
Rogers, Will, 366
Romilly, Samuel, 510, 512
Roosevelt, Franklin D., 523
Roosevelt, Theodore, 106, 107, 118,
  170, 270
Rosenberg, Louis, 490
Rosenthal, Herman, 490
Rosenwaike, Ira, 184n
Rosett, Arthur, 359, 389n
Ross, J. G., 583n
Roszak, Theodore, 32n
Rothman, David J., 681
Rothstein, Arnold, 718
Roy, C., 103n
Royko, Mike, 32n, 276–77, 302n
Rubin, H. Ted, 312, 318, 341n, 698,
  714, 714n, 715n
Rubinstein, Jonathan, 199–200, 218,
  218n, 302n
Ruiz, David, 614
Rusche, George, 539n
Rutledge, John, 331
Rutledge, Wiley B., 349
Rybarczyk, Max, 491

S

Sacco, Nicola, 490
Sadler, Lloyd, 600
Safire, William, 280, 302n
Sagarin, Edward, 219n
Sanders, Ed, 15–16, 32n
Sarat, Austin, 501n
Sarrel, Philip M., 82
Scarpelli, Gerald, 645
Scarpitti, Frank R., 583n, 715n
Schechter, Arnold, 669n
Scheider, Roy, 274
Schmidhauser, John R., 388, 389n
Schoen, Kenneth F., 619
Schuessler, Karl F., 501n
Schwartz, Bernard, 728
Schwartz, Murray A., 389n
Schweitzer, Louis, 405
Schwerner, Michael, 13
Scott, Edward M., 670n
Scott, George Ryley, 501n
Scott, Kathryn L., 670n
Seale, Bobby, 432
Seaton, George J., 621n
Seidenschmer, Jacob, 490

Seiter, Richard P., 671n
Seidman, D., 129n
Sellin, Thorstein, 129n, 501n, 715n
Serpico, Frank, 278, 300
Serrill, Michael S., 670n
Sevick, J. R., 583n
Shaffer, Ron, 219n
Shard, Willie, 260–61
Shearer, John D., 539n
Sheehan, Susan, 582n
Sheppard, Jack, 157
Sheridan, Walter, 32n
Sherman, Lawrence W., 218n, 298,
  302, 302n
Sherman, Michael, 582
Shinburn, Maximilian, 176
Shulman, Harry Manuel, 129n
Siegal, Ben, 8
Siegal, Harvey A., 669n
Siegal, Larry J., 219n, 670n
Siegler, Harry, 356–57, 360
Sigler, Maurice H., 670n
Silberman, Charles E., 392–93, 444n,
  714n, 715n
Sills, David L., 63n
Silverstein, Lee, 389n
Simon, William, 582n, 583n
Simonsen, Clifford E., 539n, 565,
  582n, 583n
Singer, Neil M., 582n
Singer, Richard G., 670n
Singleton, Edgar, 464
Skinner, Arthur, 139
Skirbekk, S., 129n
Skolnick, Jerome H., 213, 219n
Skudder, Kenyon J., 670n
Slater, Dan, 53
Sliwa, Curtis, 180
Sloman, L., 32n
Smith, Bruce, 184n, 185n, 219n
Smith, Calvin F., 663
Smith, Gerald, 578
Smith, John, 604
Smith, Patterson, 539n
Smith, Samuel W., 483
Smith, Tyce, 444n
Smith, William French, 666
Smyth, Frank, 389n
Solomon, David, 32n
Sondern, Frederic, 32n
Sonnichsen, C. L., 317
"Son of Sam," 206
Sparks, Richard F., 129n
Spear, C., 501n
Speck, Richard, 656
Spencer, Herbert, 195
Stanford, John, 680

Starkweather, Charles Raymond, 38,
  39
Statman, Alan J., 264, 265n
Stedman, Murray S., 341n
Steffens, Lincoln, 105, 106–107, 118,
  129n, 269, 302n
Steinmetz, Suzanne K., 91
Stephen, James Fitzjames, 59, 63n
Stephenson, Richard, 715n
Stevens, John Paul, 339, 349, 469, 726
Stewart, Potter, 241, 244–47, 333,
  383, 478
Stone, Harlan Fiske, 171
Stout, Jared, 583n
Strauss, Murray A., 91
Strauss, Leo, 63n
Strauss, William A., 32n
Strick, Anne, 414, 445n
Strumpf, Harry P., 389n
Stuardo, José, 409
Stuckey, Gilbert B., 445n
Sturtz, Herbert, 444n
Suffet, Frederick, 444n
Sullivan, Dennis, 219n
Sullivan, Jack, 492
Sundance Kid, 176
Sutherland, Arthur, 133
Sutherland, Edwin H., 23, 32n, 46,
  63n, 100, 102, 102n, 103n, 663–64,
  670n, 671n
Sutherland, George, 371–72
Sutton, Willie, 94, 96–97, 103n
Swiggert, Howard, 185n
Sykes, Greshamn M., 575n, 582n,
  583n
Sylvester, Sawyer F., 219n

T

Tafoya, William L., 219n
Taft, William Howard, 229, 718–19
Takagi, Paul, 289, 303n
Taney, Roger Brooke, 333
Tappan, Paul W., 46, 63n, 500n, 539n,
  566, 582n, 583n
Tates, James, 297
Tate, Sharon, 17, 18–19
Teeters, Negley K., 471, 501n, 539n,
  681, 715n
Terry, John, 228–29
Thayer, Paul, 98
Thomas, Andrew, 476
Thomas, Charles C., 302n
Thompson, Craig, 728n
Thurmond, Strom, 722
Till, Emmett, 10
Toch, Hans, 583n
Toland, John, 464

Torrio, Johnny, 718
Tracy, Paul E., 715n
Trojanowicz, Robert C., 203
Trotter, Robert J., 103n
Truzzi, Marcello, 103n
Turner, Susan, 647, 670n
Turpin, Dick, 157
Tweed, William Marcy, 280
Twining, Albert C., 250

U

Ungar, Sanford, J., 129n, 171

V

Valtierra, Manuel, 254
van den Haag, Ernest, 492, 500, 505
Van Houten, Leslie, 18–19
Van Vechten, C. C., 129n
Vanzetti, Bartolomeo, 490
Verri, Alessandro, 511
Vidmar, Neil, 501n
Vines, Kenneth N., 388n
Vinson, Fred M., 395
Viorst, Milton, 31
Vito, Gennaro F., 670n
Vold, George B., 539n
Voltaire, François, 510
von Hirsch, Andrew, 500n, 671n

W

Wald, Patricia M., 444n
Waldron, Joseph A., 670n
Walker, Nigel D., 32n, 500n
Walker, Samuel, 297n
Wallace, George, 21, 377
Wallace, Michael, 32n
Wallace, Mike, 181
Wallace, S. Sayre, 388n
Wallerstein, James S., 129n
Ward, David A., 103n, 583n
Ward, Ronald, 676, 707
Warren, Charles, 341n

Warren, Earl, 135, 229, 253, 257, 281,
    423, 719, 723
Wasby, Stephen L., 341n
Washington, George, 330, 333
Waskow, Arthur I., 293, 303n
Watkins, Donald, 377
Watson, Charles, 18
Watson, Richard W., 388, 389n
Watters, Pat, 33n
Webb, Walter Prescott, 184n
Webster, Daniel, 138, 366
Webster, William H., 171, 282
Wecter, Dixon, 31n
Weems, Charlie, 376
Welch, Robert, 17
Welch, Saunders, 158
Wells, Henry, 178
Wells, Kenneth M., 80, 102n
Wells, Warren, 430
Werner, M. R., 302n
West, D. J., 103n
West, Dorothy, 103n
Westley, William A., 214n, 283, 302n
Weston, Paul B., 80, 102n
Whisenand, Paul M., 129n
White, Byron Raymond, 232, 243, 244,
    248–49, 339, 426, 440, 478, 606
White, Theodore H., 32n, 577n
Whitebread, Charles H., II, 32n
Whited, Charles, 219n
Whitehead, Don, 171
Whitten, R. H., 185n
Wice, Paul W., 389n, 444, 444n
Wicker, Tom, 583n, 621, 621n
Wickersham, George W., 238
Wigmore, John H., 63n
Wilde, Oscar, 566, 612
Wildhorn, Sorrel, 185n
Wilkins, Leslie T., 669n, 670n
Wilks, Judith, 583n, 671n
Williams, Alexander S. "Clubber," 267,
    268–70
Williams, Diana, 680
Williams, Edward Bennett, 365

Williams, Robert, 259, 263, 723
Willoughby, E. I., 129n
Wilson, Bob, 671n
Wilson, James Q., 23, 31, 32n, 191,
    217, 218n, 286, 302n, 578–79,
    583n
Wilson, Margaret, 539n
Wilson, Orlando W., 218n, 219n
Wilson, Scott, 604
Wilson, Woodrow, 333
Wines, E. C., 670n
Wise, David, 33n, 185n
Witherel, George, 179
Witmer, Helen, 583n
Witt, Elder, 265n
Wittrock, Frederick J., 176–77
Wolfgang, Marvin E., 103n, 473, 501n,
    583n, 715n
Wood, Natalie, 11
Wooden, Kenneth, 714, 715n
Woodward, Bob, 33n, 265n
Woods, Arthur, 299
Worton, William A., 299
Wright, Andrew, 376
Wright, Benjamin Fletcher, 63n
Wright, Leslie, 290
Wright, Roy, 376
Wyle, Clement J., 129n

Y

Yablonsky, Lewis, 582n
York, Duke of, 60–61
Younger, Cole, 176

Z

Zalman, Marvin, 500n
Zeisel, Hans, 444, 445n
Zerman, Melvyn Bernard, 441, 444,
    445n, 454, 500n
Zibulka, Charles J., 471, 501n
Zimmerman, Isidore, 489, 501n
Zimring, Franklin E., 488, 500, 500n,
    501n
Zumwalt, William, 500n

Subject Index

Lower courts, 310, *312–20*
LSD (D-lysergic acid diethylamide), 25, 84

M

Maccabees, 182
McCarthy-Army hearings, 7
Magistrates, 157
Magistrate's Act of 1968, 326–27
Magna Carta, 137–38, 426
Mala in se, 57–58
Mala prohibita, 57–58
Malice aforethought, *68–69*
Malpractice suits (police), 294–95
Mandamus, writ of, *332*
Mandatory release, *657*
Mandatory sentence, *459*
Manhattan Bail Project, 405, 406
Manhattan Court Employment Project, 628
Mann Act of 1910, 82, 170, 525
Manslaughter, *70–72*
March on Washington for Jobs and Freedom, 12
Marihuana Tax Act of 1937, 83–84
Marijuana, 24–25, 56, 84, 292
Mark system, *520–21*
Marital violence. *See* Family violence
Martinson report, 578–79
Mass murder, 18–19
Maximum expiration date, *659*
Maximum-security prisons, *542–44*
Mayhem, 73
Meat and Poultry Inspection Acts, 327
Medical examiner, *370*
Medium-security prisons, *544*
Menacing, 73
Mens rea, *48–49*
"Merit selection," 348
Mescaline, 25, 84
Methamphetamine, 84
Methadone, 84
"Mexican Mafia," 617
"Miami Vice," 83
Militarization of law enforcement, 162–63
Minimum-security prisons, *545–46*
Minor courts. *See* Lower courts
Minutemen, 17
Miranda warning rules, 256–58, 260, 262
Miscegenation, 57
Misdemeanor courts. *See* Lower courts
Misdemeanors, *58*
Misprision of felony, *48*

Missouri Plan, *348–49*
Mistake of fact, *51–52*
Mistake of law, *53*
Mistrial, *434*
M'Naghten Rule, *51*
Mob violence, 10
Model Penal Code, 176
Molly Maguires, 176
Moll-buzzing, 66
Money laundering, 142–43
Morphine, 84
Motions, *418*
    for directed verdict, 437
    posttrial, 148, 442
    pretrial, 147, 418–21, 442
Motor vehicle theft, 110
Motorized patrols, 202
Muckraking, 106
Multiple-clearance method, 206–207
Municipal courts, 318–20
Municipal law enforcement, 174–75
Murder, 44
    consent and, 54
    degrees of, 68–70
    legal aspects of, 98–99
Mutual pledge, *156*

N

NAACP. *See* National Association for the Advancement of Colored People
NAACP Legal Defense and Education Fund, 475
Narcotic Addiction Control Commission (NACC), 628
Narcotics paraphernalia, 85
Narcotics use. *See* Drug use
National Advisory Commission on Civil Disorders, 281, 282
National Advisory Commission on Criminal Justice Standards and Goals, 30, 126, 297, 314, 323–24, 414, 454, 554, 651
National Association for the Advancement of Colored People (NAACP), 10, 293, 296–97
National Commission on Law Observance and Enforcement, 5, 6, 126, 398
National Commission on the Causes and Prevention of Violence, 90
National Crime Survey (NCS), 120–22
National Institute of Law Enforcement and Criminal Justice, 27
Nationalizing the Bill of Rights, 17, *719*, 726

National Legal Aid and Defender Association, 386, 387
National Motor Vehicles Theft Act of 1919, 525
National Opinion Research Center (NORC), 117, 119–20, 121
National Security Agency (NSA), 169
Natural crimes, 42–43
Natural law, *41–43*
NCS. *See* National Crime Survey
Necessity defense, 56–57
Necrophilia, 81
Negligent homicide, 71
Neighborhood Foot Patrol Program (Flint), 203
New Mexico inmate massacre, 612–14
New York City Criminal Court Act of 1962, 349–50
New York City police system, 162–65
New York (state), court system, 310
Night watch, *156*
1984 (Orwell), 537, 598
"Nixon Court," the, 258
"No-bail presumption," 403
No bill, *146*, 411
Nolle prosequi (nol. pros.), 355, 420
Nolo contendere, 147, 358, *415*
NORC. *See* National Opinion Research Center
North Ward Citizens' Committee, 182
Not-guilty plea, 147, 414, 416
NSA. *See* National Security Agency
Nuisance, criminal, 86
Nullum crimen sine poena, 57

O

Objections, 436–37
Obscenity, 81
Occasional property crime, *92–93*
OCR. *See* Organized Crime and Racketeering Section
Office of Drug Abuse Law Enforcement (ODALE), 30, 167
Office of Economic Opportunity (OEO), 379
Office of Law Enforcement Assistance (OLEA), 26–27
Office of National Narcotics Intelligence (ONNI), 167
Office of Vital Statistics, 113
Ohio, courts of common pleas, 309
Oklahoma, courts in, 310
Omnibus Crime Control and Safe Streets Act of 1968, *26*, 253
ONNI. *See* Office of National Narcotics Intelligence

Presentment, *408*

President's Commission on Law Enforcement and Administration of Justice (President's Crime Commission), *21–24,* 119, 126, 149–50, 297, 313, 314, 326, 398, 472

Presumptive fixed sentence, *466–67*

Pretrial detention, *400–402*

Pretrial motions, 147–48, 363–65, 418–21

Pretrial service representatives, 370

Preventive control (of police), 297–98

Preventive detention, *402–405*

Prima facie case, 437

Prison argot, 575

Prison community, *571*

Prison contraband, 565

Prison guards, 549, 574

Prison industries, 518–20

Prison inmates
 classification of, 552–56
 code of, *572–74*
 prisonization of, *571–72*
 rights of, 591–92
 sex among, 566–70
 social system of, 570–74
 women, 574–76

Prisonization, *571–72*

Prisons, *525*
 administration of, 547–49
 clinical treatment programs in, 561–63
 coeducational, 569–70, 576
 conditions in, 607–16
 disciplinary proceedings in, 603–607
 discipline in, 564–66, 599–607
 education programs in, 559–60
 effectiveness of, 576–80
 facilities in, 551–52
 federal, 524–25
 health and medical services in, 557
 history of, 512–24
 industrial, 522–24
 labor and industry in, 518–20, 560–61
 legal services for, 593–94
 overcrowding in, 606, 611, 612, 614, 617–18, 624
 personnel of, 548, 549–50
 reform, 616–18
 rehabilitative services in, 556–63, 597–99
 religion in, 557–58, 595–96

routine in, 550–51
 sex in, 566–70
 social system in, 570–74
 types of, 542–47
 vocational training in, 547, 559–60
 See also Attica Prison

Privacy, violation of, 86, 618

"Private eye," 177

Privatization of corrections, *618–19*

Probable cause, *223–24*

Probation, *630*
 conditions of, 632–33, 636–37
 effectiveness of, 643
 juvenile, 711
 nature of, 630
 origin of, 629
 versus parole, 650
 philosophy of, 630
 presentence investigation, 631–32, 634–35
 restitution and, 637
 revocation of, *641*
 services for, 637–39
 shock, 639–41
 violation of, 641–43

Probation officers, 637–39, 641–42

Procedural due process, *139–41*

Procuring, 82

Professional Thief, The (Sutherland), 100

Professional theft, *100–101*

Prohibition, 43–44

Prompt arraignment rule, *252–53*

Property offenses, 77–80, 112
 occasional, *92–93*

Prosecutors, *351–62*
 decision to prosecute, 353–55
 plea negotiation and, 355–62
 presentation of state's case by, 434
 roles and responsibilities of, 351–52

Prostitution, 81
 legalization of, 81–82, 292
 as Part II offense, 111

Protective sweep doctrine, *236*

Psilocybin, 84

Psychedelic drugs, 24–25

Public defender, 367, 378, 384–85

Public inebriate programs, 627

Public order crime, 85–87, 101

Public trial, *424–25*

Punishment
 banishment, 506–507
 colonial, 507–508
 corporal, *506–508,* 517
 ideology, 509
 versus reformation, 508–509

solitary confinement, 513–15, 516, 602
 See also Death penalty; Prisons, discipline in

Punitive control (of police), 298–99

Pure Food and Drug Act of 1906, 49, 83

Purse-snatching, 119

R

Racism
 capital punishment and, 472–73, 474
 Freedom Riders and, 12
 Jim Crow laws and, 10
 in prisons, 588, 601, 617
 violence and, 10, 13, 289

Rack, 506–507

Rand Study, 643, 647

Ransom, 78

Rape, *82*
 definitions of, 110, 456
 forcible, 81, *82,* 110
 marital, 90
 as Part I offense, 110
 patterns in, 89–90, 92
 prison, 567–68
 punishments for, 462–63
 statutory, 52, 54, 81

Raymond Street Jail, 532–33

Reasonable certainty, 143

Reasonable doubt, 147, 433

Rebel Without a Cause, 11, 39

Rebuttal, 147, 438

Reception center, *554*

Reclassification, 207, 555

Recorder's court. *See* State courts

Recross-examination, 436

"Red Hannah," 604–605

Redirect examination, 436

Reformatory era, *520–22*

Rehabilitation, as goal of sentencing, *452–53*

Rehabilitation services, in prison, 524

Release on recognizance (ROR), 145, *405–407*

Reliability, *124–25*

Religion, in prison, 557–58, 595–96

Religious practice, as criminal justification, 56

"Rent-a-cops" (private police), 178–79

Reprieve, *148*

Respondeat superior, 49–50, 57

Restitution, *637*

Retained counsel, 365–67

Retribution, *449–50*

Revocation
    of parole, 258–59
    of probation, *641*–43, 644–45
Right to counsel, 370–71
Rikers Island Penitentiary, 534–35
Riots, 13, 612–14
    See also Attica Prison
Roadblock inspections, 232
Robbery, *73–75*
    organized, 93–94
    as Part I offense, 110
Rocky Mountain Detective Association,
    177
ROR. *See* Release on recognizance
Rule of Four, *336*
Rules of evidence, 434–36
Runaways, 111

S

Sabotage, 101
St. Valentine's Day Massacre, 39, 69
Salient factor score, *654*–56
San Francisco Bail Project, 407
San Quentin Prison, 616
Scarlet letter, 508
Scarlet Letter, The (Hawthorne), 508
"Scavenger's Daughter," 506
Scottsboro Boys, 376–77
Search and seizure, *223*
Searches
    abandoned property, 235
    automobile, 228–30
    border, 234
    consent, 231–34
    electronic eavesdropping, 234–35
    fresh pursuit, *231*
    incident to arrest, 224–27
    "open fields" exception, 235
    "plain view" doctrine and, *236*
    spot checks, 230–31, 232
    stop and frisk, 227–28
    warrantless, 224–27, 231–36
    See also Exclusionary rule
Search warrants, 222, *223*–24
    search without, 224–27, 231–36
SEC. *See* Securities and Exchange
    Commission
Secret Service, 167, 169, 170
Section 1983, *592*
Securities and Exchange Acts, 327
Securities and Exchange Commission
    (SEC), 167
Sedition, 101
Sedition Act of 1798, 137
Seduction, 81–82
Segregation
    civil rights movement and, 12–13

Jim Crow laws on, 10
    Supreme Court on, 12
Self-defense, 56
Self-incrimination. *See* Amendments,
    Fifth
Self-reported crime, *123–26*
Sentences
    concurrent, 469
    consecutive, 469
    definite, *458*–59
    determinate, *457*–58
    intermittent, *459*
    mandatory, *459*
    mixed, 639–41
    presumptive fixed, *466*–67
    split, 639–41
    suspended, *631*
Sentencing, 148, 448–69
    alternatives in, 454–60, 456
    disparities in, 460–61, 462–66
    objectives of, 449–53
    process of, 467–69
    reform of, 466–67
    statutory, 453–*54*
Sentencing councils, 467
Sentencing guidelines, 467
Sentencing institutes, 467
Separate system, 514–16, *515*
Sequestration, *432*–33, 439
Severance of charges or defendants,
    motion for, 420
Sex offenses, 80–83, 86n, 111
Sexual assault, 81
    See also Rape
Shakedowns, 276–77, 544
Sheriffs, *156*, 160–61
    county, 174–75
    in courtroom, 368
    weaknesses of, 172–73
Shock probation, *639–41*
"Shoo-fly" cops (internal
    investigations), 298–99
Shoplifting, 77, 87, 93, 100
Show-up, 260–61
"Silent majority," 17–18
Silent system, *516*–17, 518
"Silver platter" doctrine, 239–40
Sing Sing Prison, 518, 519, 520n
Situation offenders, 624
"Skip tracers" (bounty hunters), 399,
    400–401
Skyjacking, 96
Slavery, white, 170
Smith Act, 395
"Smuggler's Alley," 162–63
Sobriety test, 86
Sodomy, 81, 82

Soledad Brother (Jackson), 549
Solitary confinement, 513–15, 516,
    602
Soul on Ice (Cleaver), 549
*Sourcebook of Criminal Justice
    Statistics*, 128
South Carolina Moderators, 179
Sovereign immunity, *294*
Special Committee to Investigate
    Crime in Interstate Commerce,
    8
Special Weapons and Tactics (SWAT)
    teams, 208
Special intent, 49
Speedy trial, *421*–24
Speedy Trial Act of 1974, *424*
Spirit of the Laws, The (Montesquieu),
    510
Spot checks, 230–31, 232
Spouse abuse, 90
Standing mute, 147, 414
Star Chamber, 424, 424n
State account system, *519*
State courts, 309–24
    appellate, 311
    case loads in, 314, 315, 318, 324
    diagrams of, 311, 312, 313
    felony, 320
    lower, 310, 312–20
    trial, 309, 310
    unification of, 323–34
State of Prisons (Howard), 510
State planning agencies (SPAs), 27
State police agencies, 172–74
State's case, 147, 434–36
State use system, *519*
Status offense, *678*, *699–702*
Statutes of limitation, 416–17
Statutory law, *50*, 61
Statutory rape, 52, 54, 81
Statutory sentencing, 453–*54*
Sterilization, 139
Sting operations, 208
Stocks and pillory, 507
Stolen goods, buying, receiving, or
    possession of, 78, 111
Stop and frisk, *227–28*
Straight sentence, 457–58
Street crime, 15, 40
"Strip cells," 602
Students for a Democratic Society
    (SDS), 14
Study release, 662
Substantive due process, *138–39*
Summation, 438
"Summer of Love," 15–16, 25
Superior courts, 309, 310, 311

C 8
D 9
E 0
F 1
G 2
H 3
I 4
J 5